ESSENTIALS OF

BUSINESS MANAGEMENT

ESSENTIALS OF
BUSINESS MANAGEMENT

P. L. Mehta MCom, ACA, AICWA, MBA (USA)
Ex-Lecturer in Management, St. Xavier's College, Kolkata

New Central Book Agency (P) Ltd
LONDON
HYDERABAD ERNAKULAM BHUBANESWAR
NEW DELHI KOLKATA PUNE GUWAHATI

NCBA

REGD OFFICE

8/1 Chintamoni Das Lane, Kolkata 700 009, India
email: ncbapvtltd@eth.net

OVERSEAS

NCBA (UK) Ltd, 149 Park Avenue North, Northampton, NN3 2HY, UK
email: ncbauk@yahoo.com

EXPORT

NCBA Exports Pvt. Ltd, 212 Shahpur Jat, New Delhi 110 049
email: ncbaexports@ncbapvtltd.com

BRANCHES

212 Shahpur Jat
New Delhi 110 049
email: ncbadel@ncbapvtltd.com

Shop Nos. 3 & 4, Vinayak Towers
681/B Budhwar Peth, Appa Balwant Chowk
Pune 411 002
email: ncbapune@ncbapvtltd.com

Shop No. 15, Bharati Towers, Ground Floor
Forest Park, **Bhubaneswar** 751 001
email: ncbabub@ncbapvtltd.com

House No. 3-1-315, 1st Floor
Nimboliadda, Kachiguda, **Hyderabad** 500 027
email: ncbahydb@ncbapvtltd.com

GSS Shopping Complex, 1st Floor
Opposite College Post Office, Convent Road
Ernakulam 682 035
email: ncbaernk@ncbapvtltd.com

Radhamayee Complex (Second Floor)
Opp. SBI, Panbazar, Jaswanta Road
Guwahati 781 001
email: ncbaguwahati@ncbapvtltd.com

ESSENTIALS OF BUSINESS MANAGEMENT • P. L. Mehta

First Published: 1999
With Additions: 2000
Reprinted: 2014

PUBLISHER
New Central Book Agency (P) Ltd
8/1 Chintamoni Das Lane, Kolkata 700 009

TYPESETTER
Logs Computer Services (P) Ltd, Kolkata

PRINTER
New Central Book Agency (P) Ltd
Web-Offset Division, Dhulagarh, Sankrail, Howrah

COVER PRINTER
Biswanath Studio, Kolkata 700 006

ISBN 978 81 7381 362 7

Price: ₹ 395.00

PREFACE

In Chapter 1 we have discussed some principles of management. Many managers, particularly senior executives, are certainly concerned with these areas exclusively. Their working days are devoted to planning their organisation's future, setting objectives and generally concentrating on survival and progress. When they are members of the board of directors or other governing body they are responsible for formulating policy and making the final decisions on corporate planning and corporate strategy. Yet all the planning and strategy is of no use without the work of the functional departments of the organisation. These are the sections of the undertaking which actually make it work on a practical basis. In chapters 2-5, we discuss from areas of management called functional areas, viz., marketing, financial, personnel and materials.

It is at the functional level that management expertise has to be married to technical expertise, and where functional technical knowledge is as important as managerial skill.

The need for managerial expertise

Although the operation of functional departments requires function knowledge and expertise it does not follow that a person highly qualified in the technical sense will necessarily turn out to be a good functional manager. An efficient factory superintendent, highly effective in the mechanics of running a factory, may not prove a success as a production manager where much more managerial skill is needed. A competent sales representative may prove quite unsuccessful if promoted to the position of area sales manager. In fact, it is the transition from the purely technical level to one where a certain amount of true managerial skill is needed that is frequently the most difficult.

Here the term "technical" is used in its widest sense and includes such areas as accounting, marketing, personnel and purchasing. Once any sort of supevisory of managerial element is present in a job then the occupant of that post must start to practise management skills in addition to technical skills.

A functional department will not be most efficiently managed unless the manager has technical knowledge of a high order. This is for two reasons. Subordinate staff have more respect for a manager who is fully competent in the technical aspects of their department, and a properly qualified manager is able to solve technical problems with authority and confidence.

It is a fact that practically all functions are now served by professional bodies who lay down minimum standards of knowledge and experience. They also require a minimum standards of ethical conduct in order to maintain public confidence in the work of their members. In the U.K. and the U.S.A. some professional bodies have gained statutory recognition while others are so highly regarded that senior posts in most organisations are reserved for members of those bodies. Among the functions so circumscribed are financial, purchasing, marketing and personnel.

In countries where independent professional bodies have not gained the same kind of recognition it is usual to find that statutory qualifications are required of people aspiring to certain functional management positions.

The role of the functional expert has become increasingly important as new techniques and new concepts have been introduced, and to which management must pay attention to remain successful in the long-run. Even top management, where the requirement of technical expertise is at its lowest, must be aware of technical problems and understand what they are about.

The manager in charge of a functional department, for example, purchasing, should have total control of his function and be responsible for all aspects of its operation in respect of its technical performance. However, the department must be operated within the framework of the organisation as a whole and thus the functional manager is subject to the constraints set for the general running of the undertaking.

Examples are working within the requirements of the corporate plan, adhering to budgets, co-ordinating the department's operations with the needs of other functions, and working with the advice of staff officers such as the personnel department when recruiting staff.

P. L. Mehta

Acknowledgements

1. Amitabha Sen
2. Prof. M. M. Rahman
3. S. Rangarajan
4. Dr. Md. Hanif
5. Dr. Amitabha Mukherjee
6. Prof. Swapan Sengupta
7. Dr. Madhusree Mukherjee
8. Prof. Rajib Dasgupta
9. Malay Kumar Bal (Jaico Book Distributors)
10. Prof. Paramita Goswami
11. Prof. Sandip Paul
12. Prof. Tridip Sengupta
13. Principal Pranab Sarkar
14. Dipak Dasgupta (Indian Book Distributing)
15. Prem Prakash (Modern Book Depot)
16. Subhajit Basu

CONTENTS

1

Introduction

1.1 DEFINITION AND MEANING OF MANAGEMENT

There are various definitions of management. As early as in 1903 Frederick W. Taylor defined management as "knowing exactly what you want people to do, and then seeing that thay do it in the best and cheapest way." Henri Fayol, in the early 20th century, defined it as the "process of forecasting, planning, organising, commanding, coordinating and controlling". E. F. L. Brech called it : "the social process of planning, coordination, control and motivation." Writing in the 1980s Tom Peters defined it as "organisational direction based on sound common sense, pride in the organisation and enthusiasm for its works". It is clear that management is partly the process of getting things done through people and partly the creative and energetic combination of scarce resources into effective and profitable activities and the combination of the skill and talents of the individuals concerned.

In short, management is a social process entailing responsibility for the effect and economical planning and regulation of the operations of an enterprise, in fulfilment of a given purpose or task. Such responsibility involves:

(a) Judgment and decision in determining plans and in using data to control performance and performance against plans;

(b) The guidance, integration, motivation and supervision of the personnel comprising the enterprise, and carrying out its operations.

Simply put, Management is the art of getting things done through and with people in formally organised groups.

While Brech's definition seems to imply that management is a skill, Harold Koontz specifically states that it is an art. We could, therefore, take the essence of these two statements and define management as the art or skill of directing human activities and physical resources in the attainment of predetermined goals. Inherent in these definitions is the implication that management is about making decisions and this view is universally accepeted.

Difference with administration

Much greater difficulty arises when we attempt to define 'administration'. There appears to be little common ground among the various authorities and writers on this activity and even Henri Fayol, one of the fathers of the study of management, fails to make clear the distinction between the two. The problem is that the word 'administration' is used both to describe the activity of implementing policy decisions and also to describe the narrower activity of regulating the day-to-day operations of a section of an organisation such as the office. In addition, we often use the word to describe the very top functions in public service, the most notable being that of the adminstration of an Indian Prime Minister.

It can safely be said that administration is part of management and is rarely taken to be involved in policy-making decisions. It will certainly be very much concerned with the implementing of policy, but its freedom of action will be limited by the decisions of those charged with the laying down and planning of general objectives.

Synopsis for Learning

Q. 1. **What is management ?**

Ans. Management is largely involved in policy-making decisions. It is the art or skill of directing human activities and physical resources in the attainment of predetermined goals.

Q.2. **What is administration?**

Ans. Administration is concerned with policy implementation.

1.2 IMPORTANCE OF MANAGEMENT

The purpose of management is to ensure that an organisation's goals are attained in an efficient and effective manner. By efficient we mean doing things in a systematic way without unecessary waste. For example, a firm which produces quality products at the lowest possible cost and distributes them with minimal transportation charges is efficient. By effective we mean doing the right things. A firm may produce a commodity that nobody wants to buy. So, even if it is efficient, it may not succeed. In general, successful management involves being both *efficient* and *effective*.

A manager is someone whose primary activities are a part of the management process. In particular, a manager is person who plans and makes decisions, organises, leads (directs) and controls human, financial, physical and information resources.

The way organisations are managed is changing by necessity. Globalisation is now an accepted fact of everyday life. The United States, Germany, and Japan — the three dominant world economies — have slower growth than the developing giants in China, India, and Indonesia. To remain or become competitive, managers in the developed countries have to restructure and rethink how people are managed.

In the new global economy that is slowly emerging human resources, information technology, speedy decision making, strategic alliances, use of the skills of a diverse workforce, and knowledge of how to combine individualism and teamwork can provide competitive edge opportunities for small entrepreneurs, mid-sized companies, or large conglomerate multinational firms.

As we close the 20th century and enter the new millennium, managers are going to have to use new, as well as proven, methods and tools to manage human resources. The history of management suggests that managers are intelligent and can learn new methods. The wake-up call has been sounded and, as this book will indicate, changes in how management is practiced will be the rule in organisations around the world.

To live well, a nation must produce well. Organisations certainly need to produce well, but, to do this, they must be managed effectively.

Participative management. Quality assurance. Customer service programmes. New technology implementation. Employee stock-purchase programmes. Just-in-time production systems. Managing diverse work teams. Making ethical decisions. Leading employees. Reward programmes. Entrepreneur programmes. Organisational change techniques. All of these management approaches have one thing in common — they must be managed.

Management has assumed greater significance due to the increase in international competitiveness. Competitiveness refers to the relative position of a person, unit, firm, or nation in comparison to other individuals, units, firms, and nations. And traditional management approaches that worked yesterday or that have not been modified to fit the current situation are proving inadequate.

Management is the process undertaken by one or more individuals to coordinate the activities of others to achieve results not achieveable by one individual acting alone. Peter Drucker believes that the work of management is to make people productive. To regain our competitive edge in the international areana, society must have managerial competence. Drucker states: "Management, its competence, its integrity, and its performance will be decisive both to the United States and to the free world in the decades ahead."

Another view of management is presented in the popular best-seller, *In Search of Excellence*, where Peters and Waterman state:

There is good news from America. Good management practice today is not resident only in Japan. But, more important, the goods news comes from treating people decently and asking them to share, and from producing things that work .... Even management's job becomes more fun. Instead of brain games in the sterile ivory tower it's shaping values and reinforcing through coaching and evangelism in the field — with workers and in support of the cherished product.

Drucker's view emphasises performance, quality, and service. On the other hand, Peters and Waterman emphasise mentorship, a love for managing and working with people; communicating with them and getting the job done.

Effective managers intend to make their employees productive, and they also have the ability to inspire people. Also, improving the industrial and service performance of any nation will require managers to be in the forefront, applying the best techniques, knowledge and understanding every single day. How the techniques and knowledge are applied will vary across groups, countries, and situations.

1.3 WHY STUDY MANAGEMENT ?

Learning about management is important for two reasons. First, our society depends on specialised institutions and organisations to provide the goods and services we desire. These organisations are guided and directed by the decisions of one or more individuals designated as "managers." In capitalistic countries, it is managers who allocate society's resources to various — and often competing — ends. Managers have the authority and responsibility to build safe or unsafe products, seek war or peace, build or destroy cities, or clean up or pollute the environment. Managers establish the conditions under which we are provided jobs, incomes, lifestyles, products, services, protection, health care, and knowledge. It would be very difficult to find anyone who is neither a manager nor affected by the decisions of a manager.

Second, individuals not trained as managers often find themselves in managerial positions. Many individuals presently being trained to be teachers, accountants, musicians, salespersons, artists, physicians, or lawyers will one day earn their livings as managers. They will manage schools, accounting firms, orchestras, sales organisations, museums, hospitals, and government agencies. The world offers many opportunities to managers and entrepreneurs who are creative, knowledgeable, and tuned in to what people need and what they can afford.

The future success of the United States, Canada, Japan, France, Germany, or any industrialised nation in the global village lies in managing productivity, being able to cope with environmental changes, and properly managing the workforce. These challenges will require well-educated, knowledgeable, and hard-working individuals deciding that a management career is of value to them personally. Managing is one of the most stimulating and rewarding careers one can seek and choose.

1.4 MANAGEMENT : SCIENCE OR ART?

Management, like all other practices — whether medicine, engineering or accountancy — is an art. It is know-how. It is doing things in the light of the realities of a situation. Yet managers can perform better by using the organised knowledge about management. It is this knowledge that constitutes a science which essentially provides a framework of analysis. Thus, the truth is that management is both an art and a science. The practice of management is an art but the organised knowledge underlying the practice is to be treated as a science. In this context science and art are not mutually exclusive; they are complementary. So management is partly an art and partly a science.

As science improves, so should art. In truth, the science underlying managing is fairly crude and inexact. This is so because the many variables with which managers deal are extremely complex. Nevertheless, such management knowledge can certainly improve managerial practice.

Executives who attempt to manage without management science have to rely on luck, intuition, or past experience. As Harold Koontz has opined: "In managing, as in any other field, unless practitioners are to learn by trial and error there is no place they can turn to for meaningful guidance other than the accumulated knowledge underlying their practice."

The Elements of Science

Science is organised knowledge and its most important feature is "the application of the scientific method to the development of knowledge. Thus, any science comprises clear concepts, theory, and other accumulated knowledge developed from hypotheses (assumptions that something is true), experimentation and analysis."

The Scientific Approach

The scientific approach, illustrated in Figure 1.1, first requires clear concepts — mental images of anything formed by generalisation from particulars. These words and terms should be exact, relevant to the things being analysed, and informative to both the scientist and the practitioner. From this base, the scientific method involves the determination of facts through observation. After classifying and

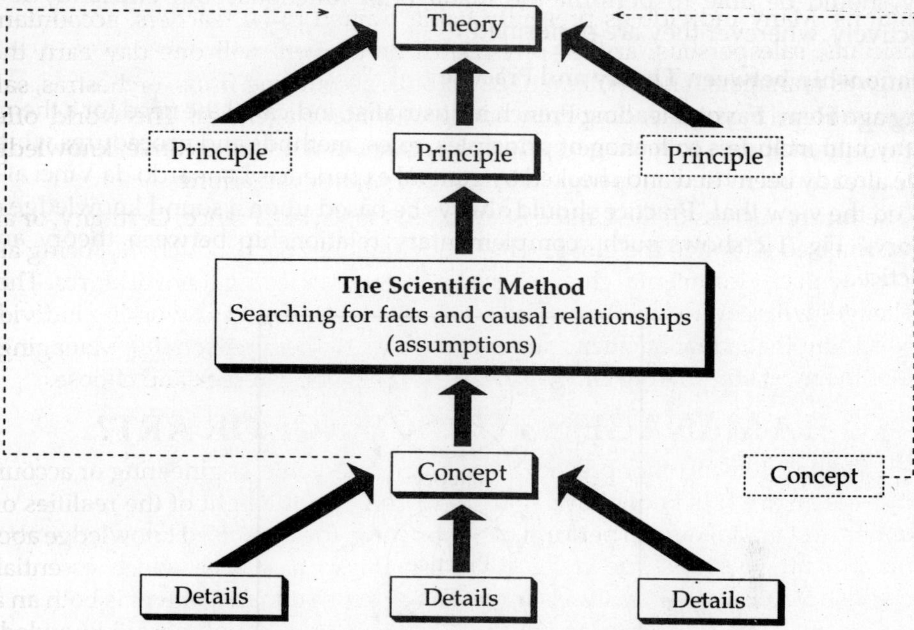

Fig. 1 : Scientific Aspects of Management

analysing these facts, scientists look for causal relationships. When these generalisations or hypotheses are tested for accuracy and appear to be true, that is, to reflect or explain reality, they are called "principles." They have value in predicting what will happen in similar circumstances. Principles are not always true, but they are considered valid enough to be used for prediction.

Role of Management Theory

In the area of management, the primary role of theory is, as Koontz comments, "to provide a means of classifying significant and pertinent management knowledge. In the area of assigning an effective organisation structure, for example, there are a number of principles that are interrelated and that have a predictive value for management. Some principles give guidelines for delegating authority; these include the principles of delegating by results expected, the principle of equality of authority and responsibility, and the principle of unity of command."

Managers who apply theory to managing usually mixes scientific principles with realities. As Koontz has noted: "A manager may find that the advantages of giving a controller authority to prescribe accounting procedures throughout an organisation outweigh the possible costs of multiple authority. But if they know theory, these managers will know that such costs as conflicting instructions and confusion may exist, and they will take steps (such as making the controller's special authority clear to everyone involved) to minimise disadvantages."

It is now widely assumed by writers on managements that there is a systematic body of knowledge constituting a core of principles of management that tend to be true in most managerial situations. It is additionally assumed that if managers understand this body of knowledge and know how to apply it to given situations they should be able to perform the managerial functions both efficiently and effectively, wherever they are performed.

Relationship between Theory and Practice

Long ago Henri Fayol, a leading French industrialist, indicated the need for a theory that would include a collection of principles, roles, methods and procedures which have already been tried and checked by general experience. Leonardo da Vinci also voiced the view that "Practice should always be based upon a sound knowledge of theory." Fig. 1.2 shows such complementary relationship between theory and practice.

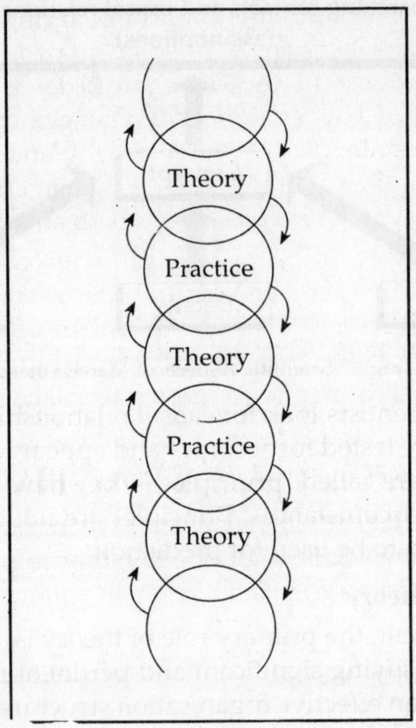

Fig. 1.2 : Management Theory and Practice are dependent on each other

In short, a theory cannot be developed in isolation (or in vacuum). Instead, it must be based on the practical experience and observation of practitioners. The theorists, in their turn, develop the theory which seeks to explain the cause-and-effect relationships involved in a set of phenomena. From the theory certain principles are derived. These principles must be tested by the practitioner. If they are verified in all possible situations, they become laws and govern future actions. If they are falsified, the theorists must again attempt to develop a new theory or enunciate new principles. Thus, the relationship goes like this:

a theory ⟶ results in principles ⟶ which become laws ⟶ which result in practice ⟶ which leads to theory ⟶ and so on.

Thus, the conclusion is that management theory, well understood, is the basis for improving the management action of all practising managers.

F. W. Taylor, 'father of scientific management', assumed that management is the mechanical application of certain principles. This is an unproved and probably a false belief. Instead, there is some element of truth in the belief of Oliver Sheldon, the renowned British management philosopher and practitioner, that "undoubtedly, there is a science of management, but it is so be sharply distinguished from the art which employs that science."

In actuality, management is neither an art nor a science, but it is a combination of both (as shown in Fig. 1.2). It requires both to be successful. However, this combination is not a fixed proportion but is found in varying proportions in differing situations. In fact, the manager needs to understand people, read situations, reflect on and use applicable past experience. These are all descriptions of management as an art. The application of Fayol's scientific management principles, the use of modern high speed computers for decision-making and statistical analysis — all these are examples of management as a science. Managers work in both areas on a daily basis, demonstrating that management is both an art and a science.

In general, efficient managers use the scientific approach in arriving at decisions. In various aspects of planning, leading, communicating and dealing with the human element, however, managers must also use the artistic approach. In short, management is not an exact science like chemistry or physics but rather a social science like sociology or psychology. It is mainly concerned with analysisng human behaviour in organisations.

1.5 MANAGEMENT ACTIVITIES

The term 'management' refers to management of an organisation. An organisation is a group of two or more people working together in predetermined fashion to attain a set of goals, such as profit maximisation or community welfare. See Fig.1.3.

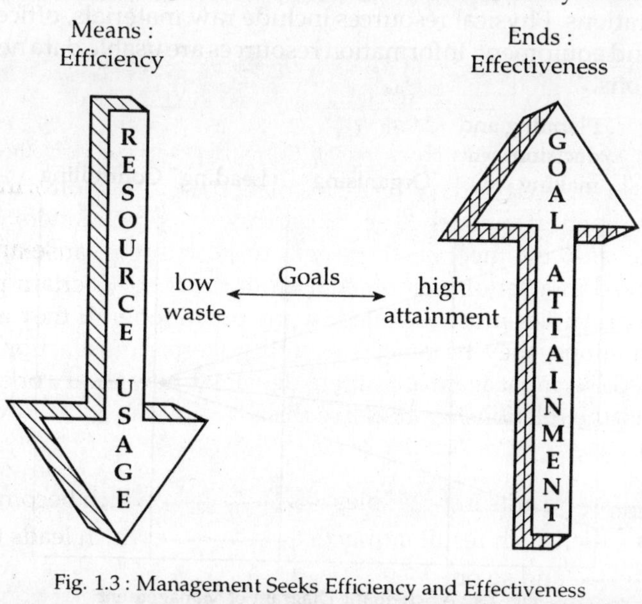

Fig. 1.3 : Management Seeks Efficiency and Effectiveness

Management is, therefore, concerned not only with getting activities completed (effectiveness), but also with doing so as efficiently as possible.

Can organisations be efficient and yet not be effective? Yes, by doing the wrong things well! A number of business schools have become highly efficient in processing students. Through the use of computer-assisted learning, large classes, and heavy reliance on part-time faculty, the administrators have significantly cut the cost of educating each student. Yet some of these colleges have been criticised by students, alumni, and government departments for failing to educate their students properly. Of course, high efficiency is associated more typically with high effectiveness. And poor management is most often due to both inefficiency and ineffectiveness or to effectiveness achieved through inefficiency.

However, management is actually a very complex process. Thus we need to develop a definition of management that better captures the true nature of the process. Basically, management is marshalling both human and material resources towards common organisational goals. Traditionally, this process has been divided into several broad activities. The more technical or analytical side of management involves goal-setting for the organisation, and planning the internal activities so that the end results are the desired ones. Each of these, in its turn, involves technical knowledge and many specific skills. Some managers specialise in one or other of these functions. The other basic aspect of management involves dealing with people — the human side of an enterprise.

Systems Theory

Management is perhaps best understood from the point of view of systems theory. Systems theory suggests that organisations utilise four basic kinds of inputs, or resources, from their environments: human, monetary, physical and information. Human resources include managerial talent, labour and so forth. Monetary resources are the financial capital the organisation uses to finance both on-going and long-term operations. Physical resources include raw materials, office and production facilities, and equipment. Information resources are usable data needed to make effective decisions.

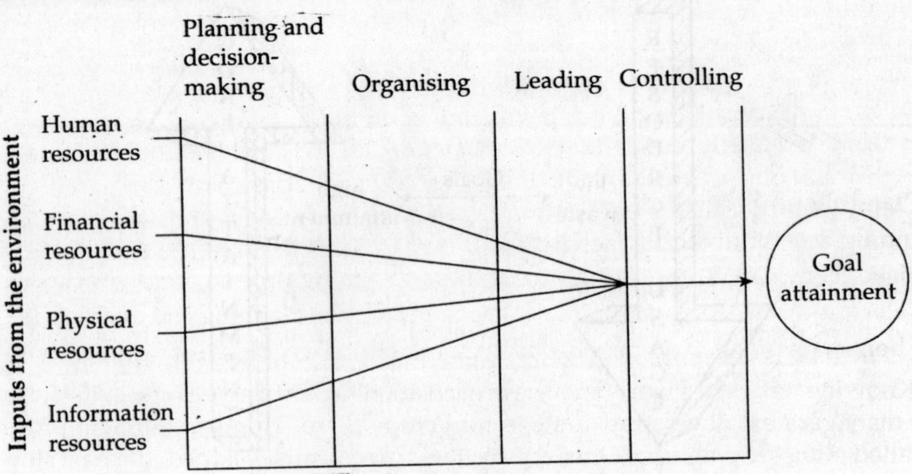

Fig. 1.4 : A Schematic Diagram of Management

Optimum Utilisation of Resources

The manager's job involves combining and coordinating these various resources to achieve the organisation's goals. Management, as illustrated in Fig. 1.4, can be defined as follows:

Management is the process of planning and decision-making, organising, leading (directing) and controlling an organisation's human, financial, physical and information resources to achieve organisational goals in an efficient and effective manner.

Management is the process by which human efforts are coordinated and combined with other resources to accomplish organisational goals and objectives. Management has been defined as "the art of getting things done through people" (Mary Parker Follett). Management requires an understanding of the economic principle of division of labour, which breaks tasks down into subtasks, and the coordination of effort, which reorganises the subtasks in an efficient and effective whole.

Five Functions

Managers perform five basic functions: decision-making, planning, organising, directing (leading) and controlling as Fig. 1.5 shows.

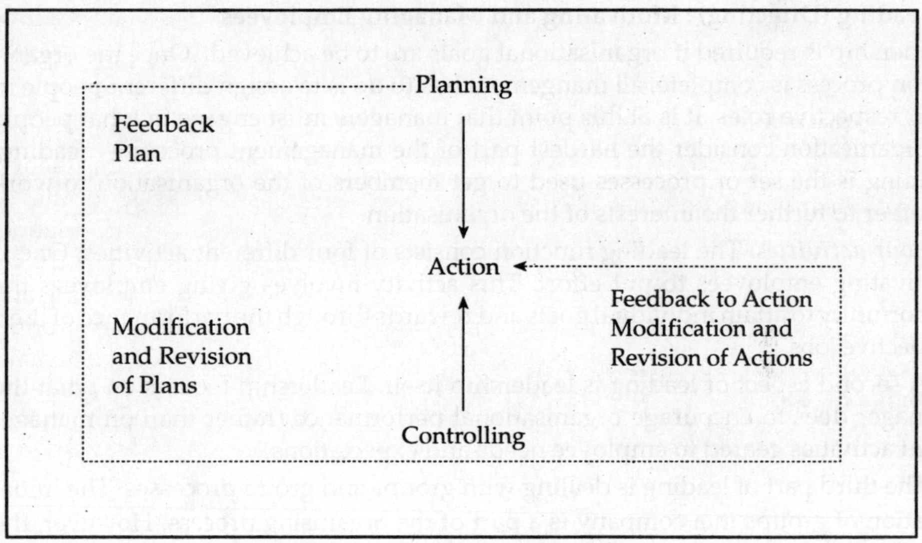

Fig. 1.5 : The Management Process

1. Planning : A Programme of Action

Planning means determining an organisation's goals and deciding how best to achieve them. Decision making, a part of the planning process, involves choosing or selecting a course of action from a set of alternatives. Planning and decision-making help maintain managerial effectiveness by serving as guides for future activities.

Knowing where he (she) wants the organisation to be at a given time in the future, the manager next develops a strategy for getting there. This development process is called strategic planning. Once the strategic plans are developed, the next step is to implement them — to put the plans into effect. Specifying where the organisation is to go and how it is to get there involves making many decisions, and many more will have to be made along the way.

2. Decision-making : Determining Courses of Action

Decision-making is choosing from alternative courses of action. Planning is the means of converting an idea into a reality, that is, determining the goals and objectives of the organisation and the means of attaining them. Planning involves making decision about a course of action and establishing priorities relating to the action.

3. Organising : Co-ordinating Activites and Resources

Organising and directing an enterprise require that managers establish patterns of relationships (structures, hierarchies) among people and other resources that work to produce an output or accomplish a common goal or objective. Organising and directing relate to the flow of work through the organisation under someone's guidance.

Once a manager has developed a workable plan, the next phase of management process is to organise the people and other resources necessary to carry out the plan. Organising is concerned with co-ordinating various activities and resources at the disposal of management.

4. Leading (Directing) : Motivating and Managing Employees

Leadership is required if organisational goals are to be achieved. Once the organisation process is complete, all mangement has to do is to assign different people in their respective roles. It is at this point that managers must engage in what people in organisation consider the hardest part of the management process — leading. Leading is the set of processes used to get members of the organisation to work together to further the interests of the organisation.

Four activities: The leading function consists of four different activities. One is motivating employees to put effort. This activity involves giving employees the opportunity to attain individual goals and rewards through the performance of their respective jobs.

A second aspect of leading is leadership itself. Leadership focuses on what the manager does to encourage organisational performance (rather than on management activities geared to employee needs and expectations).

The third part of leading is dealing with groups and group processes. The initial creation of groups in a company is a part of the organising process. However, the manager must then deal with group members and activities, on an ongoing basis, from an interpersonal perspective.

The fourth component of leading is communication. This is a basic aspect of a firm's promotional strategy.

Importance. Leadership influences persons to act for a common end or purpose. A skillful leader knows the personality, character, wants, behaviour patterns, and organisational requirements of subordinates.

5. Controlling : Correcting Deviations from the Plan

The final phase of management process is controlling. As the organisation moves toward its (established or pre-determined) goals, management must maintain its progress. It must make sure what the organistion is performing in such a way as to arrive at its 'destination' at the specified time. Monitoring a firm's operations and correcting deviations from established goals constitute the controlling function. Controlling involves taking appropriate actions to ensure that organisational goals and objectives are planned and carried out, i.e., the firm achieves maximum effectiveness. In short, controlling helps ensure the effectiveness and efficiency needed for successful management.

Management by objectives (MBO) is a relatively recent innovation in management that often improves performance and morale. MBO involves the joint establishment of objectives and performance review procedures in an effort to improve productivity. This principle is based on the theory that people find satisfaction in their work and accept responsibility for their performance. To be effective, MBO should have the approval and commitment of top management and provide a means for participation by subordinates in the setting of objectives, a degree of self-determination in implementing plans, and a periodic review of performance.

Synopsis for Learning

Q.1. What is management?

Ans. Management is partly a process of getting things done through people and partly the creative and energetic combination of scarce resources into certain activities to achieve organisational goals.

Q.2. What is the basic goal of management?

Ans. Optimum utilisation of scarce resources.

FUNCTIONS

Since managers bring together the money, manpower, materials, and machinery to operate a business, they must plan for the future, organise the enterprise, direct the activities of employees, and control the whole business.

In truth, managers are people who make decisions. When several persons get together in an organisation, one of them has to act as a leader to manage and handle the business affairs in an orderly and efficient manner. Management is the process of getting work done through other persons. Managers do not produce a finished product, nor do they directly sell a product to a customer. Instead they direct others to do these things. Figure 1.6 shows the 5 Ms of management. What specifically do managers do? The process of (management) includes planning and decision-making, organising, directing, and controlling the activities of an enterprise to achieve specific objectives. Managers perform these functions in varying degrees at different organisational levels. These are the basic managerial tasks.

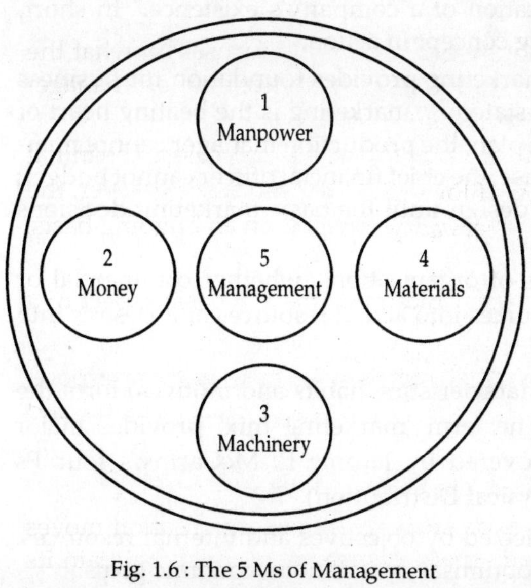

Fig. 1.6 : The 5 Ms of Management

1.6 FUNCTIONAL (AREA) MANAGEMENT

Managers at different levels may work in various areas within the same organisation. In any given firm there may be marketing, personnel, financial and materials management at all levels.

(a) Marketing Managers

Marketing managers are those people whose primary duties are related to the marketing function — getting whatever the organisation produces (be it Hindustan Motor's Ambassador cars, *The Business India* news magazine, or any food products into the hands of consumers and clients). The marketing function includes several specific activities: pricing, product development, promotion, distribution and the study of consumer psychology.

The marketing function is of vital importance to many organisations. Indeed, in recent years, many successful firms (such as Reliance and Tata Chemicals) have adopted what is termed the marketing concept. This approach to management is based on the promise that everything the organisation does should be geared toward enhancing customer satisfaction. As Peter Drucker has put it : "Business has only two functions — marketing and innovation."

'Marketing' is different from 'selling'. Selling refers to the flow of goods and services from seller to the buyer. While marketing focusses on the needs of the buyer, selling on the needs of the seller. Thus, selling is only a component of marketing, which is a broad sense.

Marketing is identifying, anticipating, stimulating and satisfying customer wants and needs. According to Professor Hansen: "Marketing is the process of discovering and translating consumer needs and wants into product and service specifications, creating demand for these products and services, and then in turn expanding this demand." The centre of all marketing activities is the customer. W. J. Stanton defines marketing as: "a business philosophy which states that the customers want satisfaction is the economic and social justification of a company's existence." In short, marketing management is the marketing concept in action.

P. F. Drucker has pointed out that marketing provides foundation for business planning and decision-making. He has stated: "...marketing is the beating heart of many operations...The President cannot plan; the production manager cannot manage; the purchasing agent cannot purchase; the chief financial officer cannot budget; and the engineer and designer cannot design until the basic marketing decisions have been made."

Marketing is important for all types of organisations, whether commercial or non-commercial. It converts latent resources into actual resources and desires into accomplishment.

The customer, *i.e.*, his personality (characteristics, habits and motives) form the base of all the marketing activities. The term 'marketing mix' provides major marketing stimuli and is very well covered by Jarome E. McCarthy's four Ps (Product, Price, Promotion, Place or Physical Distribution).

The marketing mix is, in its turn, affected by objectives and internal resources. The objectives are: target return, profit optimisation and non-economic goals.

In turn, the objectives and resources, the marketing mix and the consumer are affected by various external forces such as social, ethical, legal, competitive, political, technological, macro-economic, cultural and international.

Now most marketing problems are solved by using a scientific method, called marketing research. Its general procedure includes various steps such as the situation analysis, the informal investigation, the formal or final investigation (it includes formation of hypothesis, determination of the types and sources of data, preparation of questionnaries, sample survey and conducting the test investigation), collection of data, tabulation, analysis and interpretation, preparation of the report and application or follow-up.

(b) Financial Managers

Financial managers deal primarily with an organisation's financial resources. Their areas of concern include accounting, financial planning and investment.

Finance is the life-blood of any type of business. It helps in procuring all the factors of production. It acts as a motivator to the active, *i.e.*, human resource. In short, finance makes the business run.

Ellis writes: "Financial Management is the operational activity of a business that is responsible for obtaining and effectively utilising the funds necessary for efficient operations." He further writes: "The financial manager sits on the horns of a dilemma. He is charged with the responsibility of having money ready to spend for current and investment purposes and at the same time must get and keep sufficient money on hand to enable the business to achieve its profit objective. A workable balance between cash inflow and cash outflow must be constantly maintained. This calls for continuous planning, controlling, organising and maintaining relationships with the source of current and capital funds. A sound business rests on a sound financial foundation, the construction of which is the foremost responsibility of the financial manager."

The first major task of the finance department is financial forecasting and planning. It involves forecasting for short-term and long-term funds, on the basis of fund-flow analysis. Another important function is of evaluation of investment alternatives by using the pay-back method, present-value method or discounted cash flow (DCF) method.

A third function of the finance department is to formulate policies and take decisions relating to block capital, depreciation of fixed assets and distribution of profits. The finance manager has to take decision regarding acquisition of the risk and capital funds on the basis of such considerations as suitability, volume and stability of income; control, flexibility; nature of the eonomy, industry and organization and also social responsibilities.

The finance department also exercises controls through financial analysis, involving various ratios such as liquidity, leverage, activities, and profitability. Accouring to Brech, the main responsibilities of the finance controller or director are the following:

(1) To report in financial terms the results for the last year.

(2) To report on the relationship between the various kinds of funds obtained by the business and the way in which these funds have been used.

(3) To provide quantitative and/or financial data to management to facilitate planning, decision-making and control.

(4) To draw the attention of the Board of Directors to problem areas.

(5) To advise management on all matters in the financial field.

(6) To assist the management in policy decisions regarding distribution or retention of profits.

(c) Personnel (human resource) managers

Personnel managers are concerned with hiring, maintaining, and discharging employees. They are typically involved in human resource (manpower) planning, employment (recruitment, selection and placement), training (and development), designing, compensation and benefit systems, formulating performance appraisal systems, job evaluation and discharging low-performing (inefficient) and problem employees (the troublemakers).

Effective utilisation of an organisation's physical and material resources depends upon the skill and dexterity of human resources. As Peter Drucker has observed: "...The resources capable of enlargement can only be human resources...They (all other resources) can be better utilised or worst utilised but they can never have an output greater than the sum of the inputs. Of all the resources of an organisation, the human factor can grow and develop. When we speak of growth and development we imply that the human being himself determines what he contributes." So, it is of paramount importance for management to handle the complex set of relationships among the individuals at work so as to get the work done efficiently. Personnel management or modern human-resource management consists essentially of "maintaining these relations on a basis which enables all those engaged in the undertaking to make their best personal contribution to the effective working of the undertaking." Edwin B. Flippo defines personnel management as under:

"Personnel management is the planning, organising, directing, and controlling of the procurement, development, compensation, integration, and maintenance of people for the purpose of contributing to organisational goals."

Personnel management is vital for all managers. Strauss and Sayles aptly comment that "although personnel work is a separate speciality, it is also at the heart of every manager's job." Every manager who plans, staffs, organises, directs, and controls necessarily accomplishes these functions and applies them to people in organisations. His responsibilities include manpower planning; staffing; directing; motivating and imposing discipline on people. Modern writers have suggested that 'personnel management' should be replaced by 'human resource management' to signify the importance of employees as organisational instruments which require careful planning, organisation, development and control.

The personnel department of the organisation is concerned with various policies concerning personnel such as recruitment and selection, placement, training, promotion, transfer, discipline, compensation, labour and welfare, job-evaluation, trade unions and collective bargaining and merit-rating.

The personnel problem also involves "consideration of labour-management relations, industrial disputes and the legislative framework, employee communication and personnel record and audit. Firing (dismissal, discharge, etc.) is also crucial problem for the personnel manager. The personnel manager has also to handle the problems of building of morale, and solving the grievances."

(d) Materials Managers

Finally, managers of materials deal with procurement and purchase of inputs for various departments and divisions within the organisation. They are also concerned with inventory control, materials requirements, planning and importing.

Materials management is a broad term, embracing such functions as the coordination of planning, sourcing, purchasing, moving, storing and controlling materials in an optimum manner so as to provide a useful service to the customer at the minimum possible cost.

Material management consists of the following three functions :

1. **Material Planning and Control**. This function, which is performed on the basis of sales forecast and production plans, involves estimating the individual requirements of parts, preparing materials budget, forecasting the levels of inventories, scheduling the orders and monitoring the performance in relation to production and sales.

2. **Purchasing.** This function includes selection of sources of supply, negotiating and finalisation of terms of purchase, placement of purchase orders, follow-up, maintenance of smooth relations with suppliers, approval of payments to suppliers, evaluating and rating suppliers.

3. **Stores and Inventory Control.** This function involves physical control of materials, preservation of stores, minimisation of obsolescence and damage through timely disposal and efficient handling of materials, maintenance of stores records, proper location of bought-in materials and stocking. The stores department is also responsible for the physical verification of stocks and recording them with book figures. Inventory control covers aspects such as setting optional inventory levels, ABC analysis, and just-in-time manufacturing.

Advantages of Integrated Materials Management

Organisations adopting an integrated materials management programme enjoy the following advantages :

1. **Clearer Accountability.** Through centralisation of authority and responsibility for all aspects of materials function, a clear-cut accountability is established. Various user departments can direct their problems in respect of materials to one central point so that necessary action can be taken at all times. This very fact helps in evaluating the performance of the materials management department in an objective manner.

2. **Better Coordination.** When a central materials manager is responsible for all functions, the departments under the materials manager achieving a common identity. This results in better support and co-operation for performing various materials management functions. The user departments also find that they have to approach one department for discussing and solving their materials problems. This creates an atmosphere of trust and confidence. As a result, better relations between the user departments and the materials management department are established.

3. **Improved Performance.** As all the inter-related functions are integrated organisationally, greater speed and improved accuracy result in much better communication. The need for materials is quickly brought to notice by materials planning. Purchase department is informed about stock levels and order status by stores and inventory control departments. All these call for rational decisions leading to lower costs, better inventory turnover, reduced stock-outs and a general reduction in paper work.

4. **Adaptability to EDP.** The centralisation of the materials function in recent years has made it possible to design data processing systems. All information with regard to materials function is centralised under the integrated materials management function. This very fact can facilitate the collection and analysis of data, leading to correct decisions.

5. **Other Advantages.** Furthermore, under a central materials manager, a team spirit is developed. This results in better morale and co-operation. Such an integrated set-up gives enormous scope for growth and development. An individual under such a set-up does not remain confined to only one function, and he gets, over a period, exposed to broader aspects of the materials management function.

Synopsis for Learning

Q.1. What are the three major areas of management?

Ans. Marketing, personnel, and financial. Of these, the first one seems to be of strategic importance to a firm.

Q.2. What is the fourth area of management ?

Ans. The fourth area relates to management of materials and involves purchase and procurement decisions.

1.7 SCHOOLS OF MANAGEMENT THOUGHT

Scientific Management School

Classical management theory includes two different approaches to management; scientific management and classical organisation theory. Here we are concerned with the former.

Scientific management, which is concerned with the management of work and workers, grew from the pioneering research of five people: Frederick W. Taylor (1859-1915), Frank Gilbreth (1861-1924), Lillian Gilbreth (1878-1972), Henry Gantt (1861-1914), and Harrington Emerson (1853-1931). Taylor played the dominant role and is considered as the 'father of scientific management'.

F. W. Taylor

The concept of Scientific Management (hecenforth Scientific Management), that is, the taking of a precise approach to the problems of work and work organisation, was pioneered by F. W. Taylor. At the beginning of the 20th century, there was considerable concern about labour productivity in the U.S.A. Business was expanding and capital was readily available, but labour was in short supply. Hence a primary goal of management was to use existing labour more efficiently. Taylor was primarily concerned with developing solutions to the problems of labour efficiency.

Taylor's main hypothesis was that the proper organisation of the work force and work methods would improve efficiency. It was based on his own work experience in the American steel industry. He brought about a mental revolution on the part of both managers and workers. Work should be a co-operative effort between managers and workers. Work organisation should be such that it removed all responsibility from the workers, leaving them only with their particular task. By specialising and training in this task, the individual worker would gradually achieve perfection in his job performance; work could be organised into production lines and items could be produced efficiently and the same standard could be maintained. Actual performance standards would be determined by job observation and analysis and this would become the normal way of working.

Four Main Principles

Taylor summarised the essence of Scientific Management in the following four steps:

Firstly, managers develop a science for each element of a man's work, which replaces the old rule-of-thumb method.

Secondly, the managers scientifically select and then train, teach and develop the workers, whereas in the past the workers chose their own work and trained themselves as best as they could.

Thirdly, the managers co-operate with workers in the best possible way. This will ensure that all of the work is done in accordance with the principles of the science which have been developed.

Fourthly, there is an almost equal division of work and responsibility between the management and the workers. The managers take responsibility of all the work for which they are better fitted than the workers, while in the past almost all of the work and the greater part of the responsibility were thrown upon the workers.

The adoption of these four principles would benefit everyone in the organisation. The organisation would gain by cutting all wasteful and inefficient use of resources. Managers would gain because they had a known standard of work to set and observe. Workers would also gain because they would always do the job the same way. Everyone would also benefit financially from the increase in output, sales and profits and the reflection of this is high wage and salary levels.

Impact

The work of Taylor had significant impact. By applying his principles to job specialisation, manufacturing organisations came to rely heavily on mass-production techniques.

Criticisms

However, Taylor's principles were soon criticised. Workers felt that Scientific Management was just a way of getting (i) more work from each employee and to reduce the total number of workers a firm thus needed. (ii) Secondly, Taylor completely ignored the human side of enterprise.

Critics have pointed out that it is not possible to achieve a continuous increase in labour productivity without motivating the workers. Workers are to be treated as human beings, not as machines. This was the essence of behavioural management theory.

Conclusion

Thus, the works of Taylor and those following the scientific management school led the standardisation of work and put the concepts of productivity and efficiency into practice. Labour productivity, no doubt, increased but scientific management also helped to create boredom, dissatisfaction and alienation of the workers.

Synopsis for Learning

Q. What are the four main principles of scientific management ?

Ans. Scientific management focused on employees within organisations and on ways to improve their productivity. Four major principles of scientific management advocated by Taylor are the following :

1. All managers must be trained to use scientific principles, replacing the old rule-of-thumb methods for solving problems.
2. Managers should select and train their workers rather than let them choose their own work habits and procedures.
3. Managers should divide work responsibility as evenly as possible between themselves and their workers.
4. Managers should co-operate with workers to ensure that all work is done in accordance with scientific principles.

The Management Function School

Whereas scientific management deals with the jobs of individual employees, the 'father of modern operational management theory' is the French industrialist Henri Fayol. His main observations on the principles of general management first appeared in 1916 in French.

A popular concept that describes what managers do in their daily managerial activities was offered by Henri Fayol. He stated that managers perform five functions or processes: planning organising, commanding, coordinating, and controlling. These managerial process have been widely used to describe the managerial job.

In fact, Fayol was the first to identify firm specific managerial functions. He felt that these functions accurately reflect the core of the management process. Most practicing managers even today are familiar with this description of their jobs.

Industrial Activities

Fayol found that activities of an industrial undertaking could be divided into six groups as shown in Fig. 1.7: (i) technical (production), (ii) commercial (buying, selling and exchanging), (iii) financial (search for, and optimum use of, capital), (iv) security (protection of property and persons), (v) accounting (including statistics), and (vi) managerial (planning, organization, command, coordination, and control).

Pointing out that these activities exist in business of every size, Fayol observed that the first five were well known, and consequently he devoted most of his book to an analysis of the sixth.

General Principles of Management

Realising that principles of management are flexible, not absolute, and must be usable regardless of changing and special conditions, Fayol listed fourteen, based on his experience. They are summarised in Fig. 1.7.

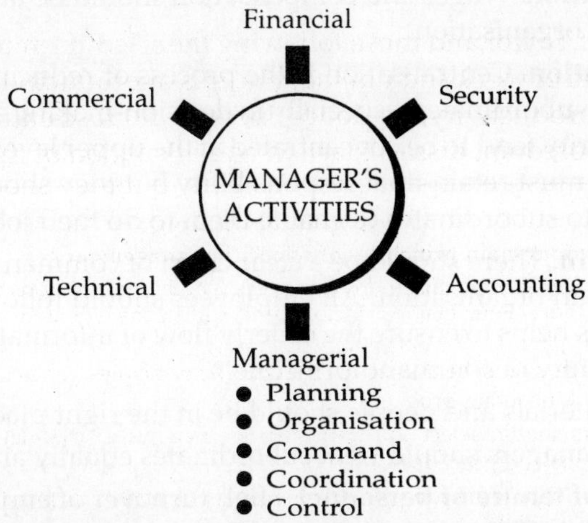

Fig. 1.7 : Fayol's Activities in Industrial Undertaking

Fayol's 14 Principles of Management

In addition to the five managerial functions, Fayol also described 14 principles of management for more efficient managerial behaviour and more effective organisations.

These 14 principles are summarised as follows:

1. **Division of labour.** The more people specialize, the more efficiently they can perform their work. Fayol described work specialisation as the best way to use the human resources in an organisation. Division of labour increases total production by simplifying the tasks required of each worker. The assembly line, which permits mass production to flourish, is a good example.
2. **Authority and responsibility.** Authority was defined by Fayol as "the right to give orders and the power to exact obedience." Responsibility means being accountable and goes hand in hand with authority in organisations. A superior can delegate authority to his juniors, but he cannot delegate (and thus avoid) responsibility.
3. **Discipline.** Discipline implies that members follow the rules and regulations that govern the organisation. Discipline results from good leadership at all levels in the organisation. In includes fairness, rewarding superior performance, and willingness to penalise employees promptly for breaking the rules.
4. **Unity of command.** Each organisational member receives orders from only one superior. If an employee reported to more than one boss, there would be confusion.
5. **Unity of direction.** In order to avoid having different policies and procedures, those activities within the organisation which have the same common objective should be directed by only one manager using one plan.
6. **Subordination of individual interest to the common good.** The interest of one employee or group of employees should not prevail over that of the organisation as a whole.

7. **Remuneration.** Wages and compensation should be fair both to employees and to the organisation.
8. **Centralisation.** Centralisation is the process of reducing the importance of the role of subordinates, especially in decision-making and planning. Power and authority tend to be concentrated at the upper levels in an organisation. Managers must retain final responsibility but they should delegate enough authority to subordinates to enable them to do their jobs.
9. **Scalar chain.** There should be a clear chain of command from the top to the bottom of an organisation. All employees should follow this chain of command. This helps to ensure the orderly flow of information and is consistent with the unity of command principle.
10. **Order.** Materials and people should be in the right place at the right time.
11. **Equity.** Managers should treat subordinates equally and fairly.
12. **Stability of tenure of personnel.** High turnover of employees, which is not good for the efficient functioning of the organisation, should be avoided.
13. **Initiative.** Managers should give subordinates the freedom to formulate and implement plans after the plans have been finalised by management.
14. **Esprit de corps.** Management should encourage harmony, team spirit, and togetherness, thereby helping to give the organisation a sense of unity.

Conclusion

There are certain common elements in Weber's concept of bureaucracy, Taylor's ideas of scientific management, and Fayol's principles of management. Some of Fayol's principles are practiced even today. Others are in disfavour as they do not address today's challenges associated with intense international competition, rapidly changing technology, and customer demands for quality.

Fayol regarded the elements of management as its functions — planning, organising, commanding, coordinating, and controlling. A major portion of his treatise is given over to an examination of these functions, and his observations are, on the whole, still valid after even decades of study by and experience of others in the field. Throughout Fayol's treatise there exits an understanding of the general applicability of principles. He pointed out that these principles apply not only to business but also to political, religious, philanthropic, military, and other undertakings. Since all enterprises require managing, it follows that the formulation of a theory of management is necessary for achieving both effectiveness and efficiency.

Synopsis for Learning

Q. **What is Henri Fayol's contribution to management?**

Ans. Henri Fayol (1841-1945), manager of a French coal mine, also studied management in search of techniques that would improve the production of coal. Fayol suggested that management involved planning, organising, commnading, coordinating, and controlling. He is generally credited with providing Taylor encouragement to search for more scientific methods.

Behavioural School of Management

The classical management theory viewed organisations and jobs from a mechanistic point of view. That is, organisations were throught of as machines and workers as cogs within those machines. No doubt most classical management theorists recognised the role of individuals. But they focused on controlling and standardising the behaviour of these individuals. By contrast, Behavioural Management Theory (henceforth BMT) placed much more emphasis on individual attitudes and behaviours and on group processes.

The Essence of BMT

Behavioural Management Theory (BMT) also applied psychological concepts to industrial settings. Hugo Munsterberg (1863-1916), a member of the behavioural school, suggested that psychologists could make (empirically) valuable contributions to management in the areas of selection and motivation. (Industrial psychology is still a major part of any management course).

It was Mary Parker Follet who first appreciated the need to understand the role of behaviour in organisations. In particular, she was interested in adult education and vocational guidance, and she felt that organisations should become more democratic in accommodating employees and managers.

The Hawthorne Studies

Elton Mayo (1880-1949) was another member of the behavioural school. The first experiment that he carried out is known as the Hawthorne Studies. These studies were carried out over the period 1929-1936. It involved manipulating illumination for one group of workers and comparing subsequent productivity to that group whose illumination was not changed. Surprisingly, when illumination was increased for the experimental group, productivity went up in both groups. In fact, productivity continued to increase in both groups, even when the lighting for the experimental group was decreased. It was not until the lighting was reduced considerably (to that of moonlight) that productivity began to decline.

Incentive Plan

Another experiment established a piece work incentive plan for a work group. According to classical management theory, each man should try to maximise his pay by producing as many units as possible. Mayo and his associates found otherwise. They discovered that the social group informally established an acceptable level of output for its members.

Workers who overproduced were branded as 'rate busters' and under-producers were labeled 'chiselers'. To be accepted by the group, workers had to produce at the accepted level. As they approached this level, workers slowed down to avoid overproducing.

Human Element

Other studies led Mayo and his associates to conclude that the human element was much more improtant in the work place than previous theorists had realised. In the lighting experiment, for example, the peculiar results were attributed to both groups of participants receiving special attention and sympathetic supervision. The incentive pay plans did not work because wage incentives were less important than social acceptance in determining output. In short, individual and social processes played a major role in shaping worker attitudes and behaviour.

The Human Relations Movement (HRM)

The HRM grew from the Hawthorne studies and was popular approach to management for many years. Classical management theory in general and scientific management in particular assumed a simple stimulus-response relationship in the workplace. If jobs were properly designed and appropriate incentives established, predictable results would follow. Workers would perform their jobs as they were told and would maximise output to increase their pay.

Human relations theory, however, suggested a more complex process. (See Fig.1.8). It proposed that workers respond primarily to the social context including social conditioning, sentiments, and interpersonal situations and relations at work. An underlying assumption of HRM was that management concern for the worker would lead to increased satisfaction which would, in its turn, result in better performance. Two writers who helped advance the HRM were Abraham Maslow and Douglas McGregor.

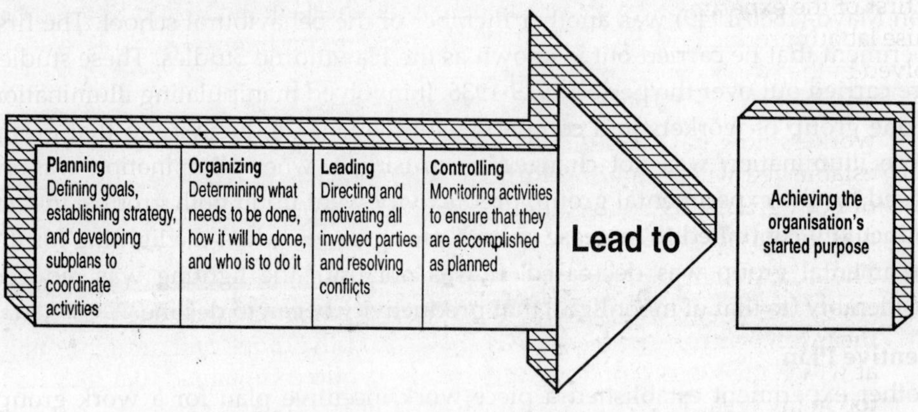

Fig. 1.8 : Scientific Management v. Human Relations

To sum up, the three main principles of the human relations school are the following:

1. Individuals need to be given importance in their own right and must also be seen as superior team members.
2. The need to belong at the workplace is of fundamental importance, as critical in its own way as both pay and rewards and working conditions.
3. There is both a formal and informal organisation, with formal and informal groups; the informal group exerts a strong influence over the formal.

Conclusion

In short, however, what started out of the survey of the working environment thus finished as the first major piece of research on the attitudes and the values prevalent among those drawn together into working situations. The Hawthorne Studies gave rise to concepts of social man and human relations at the work place. They were the first to place importance on them and to set concepts of groups, behaviour, personnel relations and worker identity in individual and commercial situations.

Motivation and Work Behaviour

Perhaps the most famous and pioneering work carried out by the human relations school of management was the Hawthorne Studies at the Western Electric Company in Chicago during the period 1924-1933.

This was an early series of experiments on motivation and work behaviour. Its main findings, which broke new ground at the time, led to an entirely new outlook on motivation psychology and resulted in a changed approach — both in research and in practice. The experiment was originally designed to discuss the relation between the working environment and work output. But it ultimately finished as major studies of work groups, social factors and employee attitudes and values, and the effect of these at the place of work.

The Hawthorne Works employed about 30,000 people during that period. It used to make telephone equipment. Elton Mayo was appointed adviser to the company because there was both poor productivity and a high level of employee dissatisfaction.

Four Stages

The first of the experiments was based on the hypothesis that it would be possible to raise labour productivity just by improving working conditions. Four stages were involved in the whole experiment:

(i) The first stage was the improvement of the lighting for the group of female workers; to give a measure of validity to the results, a control group was established whose lighting was to remain consistent. However, the output of both groups improved and continued to improve whether the lighting was increased or decreased.

(ii) The second stage extended the experiments to include rest pauses, variations in starting and finishing times, and variation in the timing and length of the the lunch break. At each stage the output of both groups rose until the point at which the women in the experimental group complained that they had too many breaks and that their work rhythm was being disrupted.

(iii) The third stage was a major attitude survey over 20,000 of the company's employees. This was conducted over the period 1928-1930.

(iv) The fourth and final stage consisted of observation in depth of both the informal and formal working groups in 1932. The final stage (1936) drew all threads together and resulted in the commencement of personnel counselling schemes and other staff-related activities based on the overall conclusions drawn by Mayo and his co-workers as also the company's own researchers.

The Main Findings

The main findings were :

(a) Social factors are of great importance at work. Both the behaviour and motivation of individual workers are affected by group relationships.

(b) It was discovered that an informal organisation of work-groups exists alongside the formal organisation and that these informal group patterns contribute as much to work satisfaction and worker motivation as does the physical environment; more so in some cases.

(c) Job satisfaction and social satisfaction are important to the worker.

(d) Work-groups are inclined to set their own standards of behaviour and their own levels of output, often in disregard of organisational requirements. Any member of a work-group who fails to conform is subject to social pressure applied by the group.

(e) The need for adequate communication between workers and management was established as was the need for satisfactory social relations.

Perhaps the greatest contribution that the Hawthorne experiment made to industrial psychology and the study of motivation was the realisation of the need for full understanding of the human factor in industrial relations and work, and the significant part work-group behaviour has on individual worker performance.

Conclusion

The conclusion here is that the problem of motivation is a strictly human problem. It is very complex and the results of positive attempts to motivate are rarely predictable. What motivates one worker may have no effect at all on another, or may even cause antagonism. Workers in a group will react differently from the individual worker to any particular stimulus. Furthermore, the group is less likely to be reasonable and may be more intransigent that the individudal. It is also true that what motivates positively on one occasion may fail entirely on another, even with the same worker or group of workers.

Synopsis for Learning

Q. **What is the main finding of the Hawthorne Studies?**

Ans. Changing illumination for the test group, modifying rest periods, shortening workdays, and varying incentive pay systems had no effect on productivity. Other factors — especially social factors such as morale, satisfactory interrelations among members of a work group (a sense of involvement and belonging) and effective management — a kind of managing that stressed human behaviour, especially group behaviour, as also interpersonnel skills as motivating, controlling, leading and communicating — would lead to an improvement in productivity. This phenomenon, drawing basically from people being 'noticed' and 'recognised', is known as the Hawthorne Effect.

1.8 MODERN VIEW OF MANAGEMENT

The modern view of management is that it is the creation and continuous improvement of organisational systems that — when used by organisational members — lead to increased value for the customers of its products or services. Continuous improvement is required in an internationally competitive world characterised by rapidly changing technology and customer demand for higher levels of value. Continuous improvement refers to the constant refinement and improvement of products, services, and organisational systems to yield improved value to customers. The term continuous improvement is derived from the Japanese term Kaizen, meaning small but continuous improvement.

The modern view of management is that management does not refer to the behaviour of a manager whose primary role is to maintain the *status quo*. Nor does it refer to managerial behaviour that is focused primarily on planning, on organising, on commanding, or on controlling the behaviour of others. Such a traditional definition tells us what managers do without telling us for what purpose they engage in such activities. To be sure, managers do serve such functions. However, this classic definition misses the purpose of management in the 21st century, which is to provide increased value to customers. The new definition is a pronounced shift away from the old "command and control" connotation of the "M" word (management).

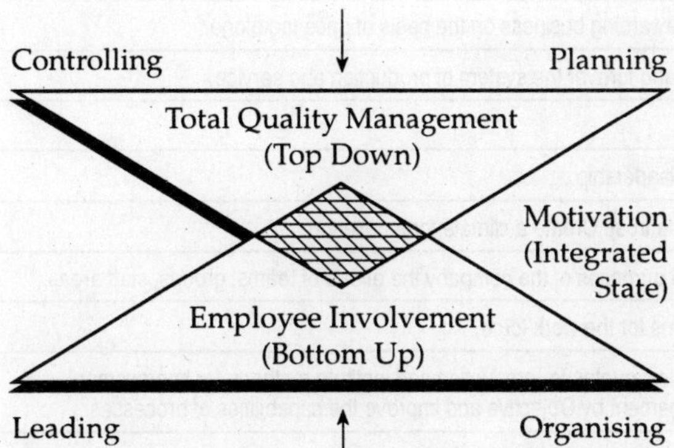

Fig. 1.9 : Integrating Total Quality Management and Employee Involvement

Modern writers seek to integrate Total Quality Management (TQL) with the traditional functional approach to describing management needs to be explored. Figure 1.9 helps us to visualise the merger of two approaches to the study of management by combining the ideas of TQM with the ideas of employee involvement. Employee involvement refers to the participation and involvement of employees in their jobs in order to increase the value provided to customers. The figure shows how the classic managerial functions of planning, organising, leading, and controlling are now shared with nonsupervisory employees in a TQM organisation. Classical models of management segregated the four functions as strictly the purview of managers.

In Fig. 1.9 TQM is a model for deciding what is important to work on (customer value and system process improvement), while employee involvement is a model for deciding how to go about working on these objectives.

Managers in the most admired firms of the world understand the importance of the quality of products and services and how to deliver quality to customers. These managers also understand that they are operating in a globally competitive marketplace and that they must compete globally in order to prosper.

Deming's 14 Points of Management

One way to understand the changes required of modern managers is to review the prescriptions of W. Edwards Deming, an influential American who is credited with remaking Japanese industry after World War II. Deming's 14 ponts (Table 1.1) are widely viewed as directives for a new way to manage. Deming described his 14 points as no less than a complete agenda for managerial action. The 14 points are the basis for transformation of American industry. It will not suffice merely to solve problems, big or little. Adoption and action on the 14 points are a signal that the management intends to stay in business and aims to protect investors and jobs.

Table 1.1 : Deming's Revised 14 Points of Management	
1.	Management must demonstrate constantly their commitment to a widely published statement of the purposes of the company.
2.	Learn the new philosophy, top management and everybody.
3.	Understand the purpose of inspection, for improvement of processes and reduction of cost.
4.	End the practice of awarding business on the basis of price tag alone.
5.	Improve constantly and forever the system of production and service.
6.	Institute training.
7.	Teach and institute leadership.
8.	Drive out fear. Create trust. Create a climate for innovation.
9.	Optimise toward the purposes of the company the efforts of teams, groups, staff areas.
10.	Eliminate exhortations for the work force.
11.	(a) Eliminate numerical quotas for production and institute methods for improvement. (b) Eliminate Management by Objective and improve the capabilities of processes.
12.	Remove barriers that rob people of pride of workmanship.
13.	Encourage education and self-improvement for everyone.
14.	Take action to accomplish the transformation.

Deming's prescriptions are anything but business as usual. He stresses themes of quality, leadership, horizontal management, continuous improvement, employee involvement, and training. His model is substantially different from the old bureaucratic model of inward-looking administrators whose primary interest is in directing and controlling the behaviour of others.

Deming's themes influence managerial activities throughout the world. The Japanese instituted a Deming Prize shortly after World War II to recognise substantial advancements in quality.

Deming was not the only pioneer in Total Quality. In some areas others made even greater contributions to the advancement of quality in organisations. They helped managers to realise that the practice of management had evolved in the twilight of the twentieth century.

Other Pioneers in Total Quality

Joseph Juran viewed quality as a cross-functional integration issue. His work began after World War II and has continued to today. Juran was concerned with processes that spanned at least two of the functions of design, production, marketing, or finance. His ideas have influenced the way managers structure organisations and terms today.

Kaoru Ishikawa, working through the 1950s and 1960s, was concerned with the prevention of defects before they occurred. From 1970 to present day, Philip Crosby is noted for his ideas relating to the cost of quality. The cost of quality is the cost incurred as a result of producing poor-quality products and services. Crosby helped U.S. managers understand that improved quality can lead to lower costs if the product or service and the process that generated it are designed correctly.

1.9 THE NEED OF MANAGERS IN ORGANISATIONS

Managers of an organisation must be prepared to anticipate and adapt to change by keeping in touch with the external environment and the organisation's customers. For the firm to prosper and grow in a changing environment, managers must articulate a vision, as well as goals and objectives for the future.

1. Keeping in Touch with the Environment

A key function of managers is keeping the organisation in touch with the external environment. By maintaining close contact, managers are prepared to structure the organisation and its activities to capitalise on opportunities that the environment offers and to avoid threats inherent in that environment. Effective managers relate the organisation to its environment and then guide internal activities to maximise the external opportunities and minimise the external threats. Managers need to be externally focused in spite of the temptation to act solely in terms of the firm's internal organisational activities.

Change tends to be a natural part of organisational life, for both external organisational environments and customers change. Moreover, in the internationally competitive environment of today, change is virtually assured. It takes exceptional management to anticipate and to profit from change.

2. Keeping in Touch with Customers

Increasingly today the essence of management is being defined in terms of service to the customer. One of the most popular management books published recently has been Peters and Waterman's book, *In Search of Excellence*. The authors define excellent companies in terms of several characteristics, including being "close to the customer". Excellent companies learn from the people they serve. They provide unparalleled quality, service, and reliability — things that work and last. They succeed in differentiating the most commodity-like products. Consumers' needs are addressed as quality becomes a fundamental way of managing a company.

3. Establishing Vision, Goals, and Objectives

Nearly all management scholars agree on the need for managers at all levels to envision and describe the future for the organisation; the only difference of opinion may be in the length of the time horizon. As entire managerial levels disappear in many organisations, and as organisations become flatter and flatter, the remaining managers have become more involved with visions, goals, and objectives for the future.

An increasing number of firms understand that a dramatic commitment to their customers through Total Quality is a necessary part of survival in these internationally competitive times. This commitment to quality starts with managerial leaders.

One characteristic common to a number of TQ companies is strong leadership — a chief executive who leads the charge with a strong belief in quality. Leadership is the most improtant ingredient for launching and sustaining a quality-improvement process. Leaders of TQ companies establish clear, results-oriented goals for continuous improvement, and communicate their expectations.

Peter Drucker, one of the most noted of all management theorists, summed it up rather succinctly: "The foundation of effective leadership is thinking through the organisation's mission, defining it and establishing it, clearly and visibly. The leader sets the goals, sets the priorities, and sets and maintains the standards."

4. Ensuring Performance to Realise the Vision

Once the vision has been established, managers take the lead to ensure that the vision is achieved. They do this by steering performance to make it consistent with the vision. Many refer to this managerial behaviour as controlling.

1.10 IS MANAGEMENT A PROFESSION ?

Various efforts have been made to classify management as a profession. If it is, it has to satisfy the following criteria of profession :

1. A codified body of knowledge.
2. A long period of formal education and training, controlled by the profession.
3. Controlled entry, usually by means of a formal examination.
4. An enforced code of ethics, with discipline imposed on those who break it.

A study of the world of business indicates that there is at present a relatively uniform body of management knowledge. Moreover, most managers in the middle and upper levels of management have had long years of formal education and training.

There is hardly any effort to control entry into management. Additionally, many professional organisations, companies and managers are striving for greater social responsibility and more ethical behaviour.

Edgar Schein has defined the characteristics of professionals and has evaluated managers against two other characteristics. Professionals, Schein asserts, do the following :

1. They make decisions based on general principles.
2. They attain their status by achieving certain objective standards of performance.

Management meets these crietria in some areas and not in others. Management makes use of proven knowledge contributed by practicing managers, social scientists, and other professionals. And the existence of management training at educational institutions and inside organisations (such as various management development programmes) indicates that there are generally accepted principles of management to study. But management does not have a uniformly accepted set of objective performance standards by which to evaluate it, nor is there a common code of conduct to govern the practices of its members.

The professions of law, medicine, and accountancy are licensed, and serious infractions of the professional codes may result in disbarment from practice in a given profession. 'Management' does not have any such professional monitoring body or agency and, therefore, cannot be classified as a profession in the strictest sense of the word. It can, however, be considered as a profession in the same general sense that allows engineers, teachers, writers, and other educated and devoted (dedicated) people to be treated as professionals.

For our purpose it matters little whether or not managers can be certified as professionals at this time. What matters is the general direction management is taking. We need to recognise that, as a field of study, management is growing. More people in the ranks of management today have been exposed to formal training in graduate and postgraduate courses than in the past. Modern management as a separate field of study began in the 1950s. The progress in that short period of time is an indicator of the long-range growth of management.

Synopsis for Learning

Q.1. Is management an art ?

Ans. Yet it is.

Q.2. **Is management a science ?**

Ans. It is a science, too.

Q.3. **Is management a profession ?**

Ans. Management is undoubtdly a profession. In India also, management has been recognised as a profession.

APPENDIX : Detailed Analysis of Each Function of Management

Management has also been called the art of decision-making, since managers have to devote a lot of time choosing among alternative solutions to business problems.

Management serves an organisation by performing certain functions. These four key functions are planning, organising, directing, and controlling. Figure 1.10 identifies these functions and indicates their relationships to one another. It is these tasks that managers should be skilled in performing if they are to succeed in their work. These functions might be performed in any sequence dictated by the situation. These functions are different but interdependent, and it is the manager's role to co-ordinate them. These functions are performed at all levels of the management pyramid in varying degrees. We may now analyse each function separately.

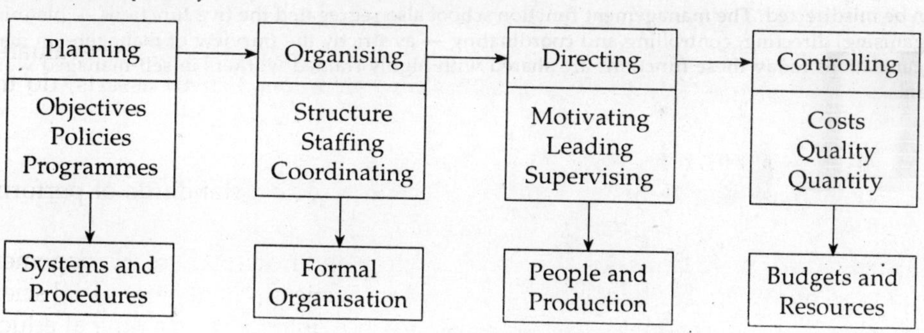

Fig. 1.10 : Analysis of Management Functions

Logically, planning seems to be the first function, which is followed by the other three. Some people also regard decision-making and policy-making as functions. In practice, however, these two activities more often get mixed with one or more management functions.

Planning

Planning is deciding in advance what the organisation's objective ought to be and what its members ought to do to attain these objectives. As such, planning is future-oriented. To reach the future goals, managers must attend to three important issues:

- *Where is the organisation now?* Managers must be aware of the strengths and weaknesses of the organisation. They need to understand how these strengths and weaknesses position the firm relative to customers' demands and to competitors' positions.
- *Where does the organisation want to go?* With knowledge of where the organisation is now, managers need to decide the appropriate future goals for the organisation. They also need to determine factors that could hinder attainment of these goals, in order to anticipate and work around those factors.

- *How will the organisation reach the goals*? Strategies, policies, and procedures that will enable the organisation to reach its goals need to be developed in detail.

Recognising that the future is uncertain, managers must be ready to change plans to reflect changes in the external environment of the firm. For example, the Persian Gulf War in 1991 caused firms to revise their plans and objectives for sales in that year.

Organising

Organising involves structuring work relationships. People, resources and tasks need to be structured and grouped for efficient performance of the organisation's goals.

Directing

Directing, motivating, or leading refers to managerial behaviour aimed at causing employers to accomplish the tasks assigned to them. Attempts at motivation have ranged from the use of threats and whips in ancient times to the use of money and perks in more recent times. Today many managers recognise that motivation is a complex individual and group process. An important motivational task for today's managers is to determine the needs of individuals and groups, and to design ways to satisfy their needs through effective job performance.

Controlling

Controlling means ensuring that the organisation is actually achieving its planned objectives. Some discuss planning and control together and describe "planning and control systems" because controlling involves comparing actual performance with planned performance. An example of control activity is measuring production output for the day, comparing the output to the objective, and then if the output falls short, assigning more people or authorizing overtime to increase the output to match the objective.

Coordinating

Coordinating is the process of integrating the activities of individuals and units so as to provide unity of action in the pursuit of the organisation's goals. Many view coordinating as the very essence of management. Thus it is an activity that should underlie all managerial activities, rather than be described as a separate managerial function.

A drawback of the management function school is that it does not describe why managers perform the functions. Is it to improve internal efficiency, or to increase profits, or to serve customers or for personal gains — monetary, perks, reputation ? With no indication of purpose, managerial activity can be misdirected. The management function school also segregated the five functions — planning, organising, directing, controlling and coordinating — as strictly the purview of managers. In many organisations today these functions are shared with highly trained workers in self-managed works teams.

GLOSSARY

Art Practice; skill acquired by experience.

Business An organised profit-seeking approach to providing people with the goods and services they want.

Controlling The managerial function of measuring and correcting individual and organisational performance to ensure that events conform to plans. It involves measuring performance against goals and helping to correct them. In short, comparing actual performance against expected performance.

Coordination Achieving harmony of individual and groups efforts toward the accomplishment of group purposes and objectives.

Decision making The selection of a course of action from among alternatives, a rational selection of a course of action.

Effectiveness The achievement of objectives; the achievement of desired effects.

Efficiency Achievement of the ends with the least cost or other unsought consequences.

Human relations A management approach that brings employees and the organisation together to achieve the objectives of both.

Hawthorne Studies Research carried out by Elton Mayo and others at Hawthorne, Chicago, plant of Western Electric Company from 1924 to 1933. The research findings emphasise the organisation as social unit and members of organisations as social beings with social needs to be satisfied. In short, pioneering research on worker behaviour and motivation.

Managers Those who undertake the task and functions of managing, at any level in any kind of enterprise.

Manager, functions of Planning, organising, staffing, leading (directing) and controlling.

Managers, goal of To so establish and maintain an environment for performance that an individual will contribute to group objectives with least cost — in money, time, effort, materials discomfort, or dissatisfaction to create a surplus value and profit.

Objectives, or goals The ends toward which activity is aimed — the end points of planning.

Organisation A concept used in a variety of ways such as (i) a system or pattern of any set of relationships in any kind of undertaking, (2) enterprise itself, (3) cooperation of two or more persons, (4) the intentional structure of roles in a formally organised enterprise.

Organising Establishing an intentional structure of roles for people to fill in an organisation and effectively bringing together human and material resources to attain objectives.

Planning Setting objective, and formulating the steps to attain them. Selecting missions and objectives — and the strategies, policies, programmes, and procedures for achieveing them; decision-making; the selection of a course of action among alternatives.

Profession Any occupation, especially learned or scientific or artistic.

Science Organised knowledge of pertinence to an area, usually an area of practice.

Scientific management An approach started around 1900 that used engineering techniques such as time and motion analysis to increase plant efficiency, by establishing the one best method for each task. A term originally used as denoting the work and approach of F. W. Taylor and his co-workers and associates in analysing management. It implies that the methods of scientific inquiry, analysis and summary can be applied to the activities of managers. It later implied time study and similar methods used by Taylor and his followers to analyse activities of people in organisations. Basically, it sought to develop (1) ways of increasing productivity by making work easier to perform and (2) methods for motivating people to take advantage of labour-saving techniques it developed.

For the sake of analysis the whole scheme can be divided into five different but interrelated aspects : (1) replacing rules-of-thumb with rules-of-scheme, (2) obtaining harmony, rather individualism, and (3) developing workers to the fullest extent possible.

Essentially, the technique attempted to develop (1) ways of increasing productivity by making work easier to perform and, (2) methods for motivating people to take advantage of labour-saving techniques it developed.

2

Marketing Management

Business has only two functions — innovation and marketing.

Peter Drucker, 1970

[Syllabus

- **Nature, scope and importance**
- **Basic marketing functions**
- **Features of marketing in India**
- **Modern concept of marketing**
- **Difference between marketing and selling**
- **Marketing mix (*i.e.,* product, price, promotion and place)**
- **Product life cycle**
- **Packaging and branding**
- **Pricing policies and strategies**
- **Sales organisation — Sales manager's functions and responsibilities**
- **Promotional strategies and techniques**
- **Respective rules of private distribution system and public distribution system in India.]**

SUBJECT MATTER OF MARKETING MANAGEMENT

This chapter begins by defining marketing and discussing the marketing concept, the foundation of contemporary marketing management.

After defining marketing we will define a related but different term — the modern marketing concept. Next, we provide an overview of effective marketing management, which includes market research and developing marketing strategies.

Marketing today is widely used by both profit and non-profit organisations to attain their objectives. Whether what is being marketed is fast food or industrial toxic gas detectors in India, marketing is, basically, the same. This chapter shows how to carry out marketing activities and how to understand and relate to those activities.

Then the reader will be introduced to the concepts and tools needed to design, implement and control effective marketing programmes. This chapter has two goals.

First, we introduce the concept of marketing by focusing on its centrality to the firm. **Two guiding principles** behind marketing are: **customer analysis** and **competitor analysis**. The idea is that successful marketing begins with the needs of customers and provides a better offering than the competition.

Of course, these objectives must be accomplished subject to the service and financial goals of the organisation.

Finally, the chapter closes with an overview of marketing implementation. The heart of any implementation resides in planning the marketing efforts and in product, communication, pricing and distribution decisions.

2.1 NATURE, SCOPE AND IMPORTANCE

What is marketing ?

Marketing links two basic functions in the community — production and consumption. Marketing is an activity which seeks to satisfy the needs and wants of customers through marketing exchange. On a marketing transaction, the buyer purchases a product and pays the supplier an agreed price for his wares.

Marketing occurs at many levels all over the world. Marketing is obviously a part of small business. The shopkeeper must know what customers want and must make goods or buy them from suppliers at a cost that will be both affordable and attractive to customers, yet provide a profit to the shopkeeper.

Marketing also occurs at the national level. Government planners and regulators have a profound effect on the vitality of an economy, and the economy, in turn, affects the lives of every person or institution in the country. Indeed, the health of the market within a country has spillover effects on surrounding countries and even on the world economy at large.

According to Philip Kotler: "Marketing is a social and managerial process by which individuals and groups obtain what they need and want through creating, offering and exchanging products of value with others."

Marketing is seen as being the primary management function that coordinates the activities involved in developing and manufacturing suitable products for specified markets, converting consumer purchasing power into effective demand, and in moving the products to the user in order to attain company objectives. The strategic role of marketing manager is concerned with profitability (preferably expressed as a return on investment) and, hence, with profits.

According to the American Marketing Association : Marketing management is the process of planning and executing the conception, pricing, promotion and distribution of goods, services, and ideas to create exchanges with target groups that satisfy customer and organisational objectives.

Two definitions of marketing

The definition given above is that :

Marketing is an activity directed at satisfying customer needs and wants through exchange transactions in the marketplace.

Another definition goes as follows :

Marketing is the management process responsible for identifying, anticipating and satisfying customer requirements profitably.

What does marketing actually do ?

The management and staff of a company's department would be responsible for a number of inter-related activities. Let us assume for a moment that the company manufactures and sells a range of consumer durable products, such as televisions, radios and Hi-Fis. The marketing department might be responsible for :

(a) ***identifying market opportunites*** : It should research the needs and wants of the different types of customer to be found in the market. This is called 'market research'. At the same time it needs to be aware of technological developments taking place outside the company, and of new product development activities being undertaken within the enterprise.

From its market research and its study of technological developments, the marketing people identify (or forecast) :

1 trends in the demand pattern for existing products;

1 marketing opportunities for new products;

1 detailed needs for the further new product development that the company should undertake.

(b) ***managing products*** : The marketing function should be responsible for forecasting and managing the rate of supply and distribution of the company's existing products. Equally important will be its prime role in determining what new products should be developed by the company and launched into its various markets. These new products should be designed in such a way as to meet the differing requirements of differing sections or 'segments' of the total market.

(c) ***choosing and motivating the channels of distribution*** : Since a manufacturer cannot supply all of its customers directly, it must use distributors to stock and sell its products on its behalf. It must select those wholesalers and retailers who will best look after its interests, and who will put most effort into selling its products to these customers.

Since wholesalers and retailers are an important 'channel of distribution' their efforts must be encouraged and supported by that manufacturer. After all, the final sale of the company's products to the customer is not (in this particular case) in the hands or control of the manufacturer, but in those of the wholesalers and/or retailer.

(d) ***advertising and promoting products and services*** : The marketing function will be responsible for communicating to target customers the existence of its products and the benefits to be obtained from purchasing them. The advertising and promotional process is aimed at the target customer group so that it:

- communicates to the customer
- encourages the customer to consider the product or service and understand its benefits
- persuades the customer
- supports the wholesaler and retailer in selling the product to the customer
- reassures the customer that he or she has made the correct purchase decision
- encourages the customer to make further purchases of the company's products or services.

Advertising and promotional effort aim to stimulate the potential buyer into becoming interested in purchasing — which it will be the retail salesperson's job to change into a decision to purchase — so that the sale is made.

(e) ***setting prices*** : The marketing activity will be closely involved in agreeing and setting market prices, terms of supply and payment conditions. Other functional activities, such as finance and credit control, will also be involved in this important business area. For it is essential to the achievement of successful and profitable trading that :

- such prices are quoted both to the distributor and to the final customer that encourage them to buy the company's products, yet allow the company to make a reasonable amount of profit.

Marketing management thus involves several activities. This chapter is devoted to discussing these subjects, shown in Fig. 2.1, which presents an overview of the basic

Fig. 2.1 : Marketing Management in Action

components of marketing management and their interrelationships. Understanding the changing marketing environment and the organisation's markets, in turn, provides a basis for developing effective marketing strategies. Then various marketing programme decisions are made (prices, advertising, distribution, etc.). Together, these activities make up a marketing strategy which is then implemented and controlled.

Universality of the Concept

Let us look at this definition in greater detail. We begin with what is marketed. Marketing can be applied to ideas, goods, and services. We normally think of marketing in terms of selling of such physical products as clothing, food, automobiles, and electronic wares. Indeed, marketing is an essential activity for all who sell such goods. At the same time, marketing can be applied to the promotion of ideas. Heads of religious bodies or political parties and educators are all engaged in the marketing of ideas. Finally, marketing is a central perhaps **the central**, activity for services. Whether one sells soaps, clothing, motor cars or banking services, marketing is likely to be a key part of the business.

This definition of marketing emphasises one compound goal or objective for marketing : the creation of exchanges that satisfy needs. The notion of exchange might even be called the *sine qua non* of marketing. By exchange, we mean the transfer of things of value between two or more parties. The parties are the buyer and the seller. Furthermore, marketing exchanges entail more than economic arrangements. The aims of both parties in an exchange often entail lasting relationships of mutual benefit.

But what constitutes a successful marketing exchange? The compound goal of marketing is to create exchanges that satisfy needs. But whose needs are to be served by the creation of exchanges? In general, a successful exchange is one in which all parties to the exchange achieve mutual satisfaction.

The final component of marketing concerns the "how" of marketing. Need-satisfying exchanges are created by identifying unfulfilled needs, designing products and services to meet these needs, pricing the offerings in an optimal way, communicating the terms of trade, and getting the offerings to customers when and where they need them. All this must be done in a way that not only meets customer needs, but also fulfills firm objectives and beats the competition.

In its true sense, marketing management is a process involving analysis, planning, implementation, and control; it covers goods, services, and ideas; it rests on the notion of exchange; and its goal is to give satisfaction.

It may apparently seem that the marketing manager is a person whose primary task is to stimulate the demand for the company's product. However, in practice, the marketing manager performs various other tasks, such as influencing the level, timing and composition of demand in a way that will help the organisation achieve its objectives. **Marketing management is essentially management of demand** (while sales management is management of supply).

IMPORTANCE

Marketing is perhaps the most important of all managerial functions. If this function is not properly performed, the overall managerial effectiveness will be lost as all other functions will be useless. In fact, marketing is a method of managing a business so that each critical business decision — whether by the Sales Department, the Purchase Department, the Production Department or the Finance Department — is made with the full and prior knowledge of the impact of that decision on the customer.

Marketing managers are those people whose primary duties are related to the marketing function — getting whatever the organisation produces into the hands of customers and clients. The marketing function includes several specific activities: pricing, product development, promotion, distribution and the study of consumer psychology.

The marketing function is of vital importance to many organisations. Indeed, in recent years, many successful firms (such as Procter & Gamble and Colgate-Palmolive) have adopted what is termed the 'marketing concept'. This approach to management is based on the promise that everything the organisation does should be geared toward enhancing customer satisfaction.

Marketing is the function of a profit-making enterprise that is vital to its success and long-term survival. Without effective marketing the enterprise will cease to exist.

This chapter begins by defining marketing and discussing the marketing concept, the foundation of contemporary marketing management. After defining marketing, we will define a related but different term — the marketing concept. Next, it provides an overview of effective marketing management, which includes market result and developing marketing strategies.

Marketing today is widely used by both profit and non-profit organisations to attain their objectives. Whether what is being marketed is hamburgers or industrial toxic gas detectors in India, marketing is basically the same. This chapters shows how to carry out marketing activities and how to understand and relate to those activities.

Salient Features

Marketing can be described as the function that identifies the needs of the buying public, assesses the extent of these needs and to satisfy them in the most effective and profitable way. It is sometimes argued that marketing creates needs, but this is disputed by most authorities on marketing. According to these authorities the marketing function merely draws attention to unsatisfied needs but cannot create new needs.

As Peter Drucker puts it: "Marketing is so basic that it cannot be considered a separate function. It is the whole business seen from the point of view of its final result, that is, from the customers' point of view. Business success is not determined by the producer but by the consumer."

The task of demand management is performed by marketing managers who carry out marketing research, planning, implementation and control. And as Philip Kotler has pointed out: "within marketing planning, marketers must make decisions on target markets, market positioning, product development, pricing, distribution channels, physical distribution, communication, and promotion."

The key components of this definite are the following :

1. Meeting customer needs profitably because the marketer's job is to convert customers' needs into profitable opportunities.
2. Identifying new needs and wants and satisfying them (*i.e.*, buyer-orientation).
3. Developing a favourable attitude to the customer, not the product.
4. To do everything to provide the customer sufficient value, quantity and satisfaction for his money.

Scope

Marketing management is now a subject of growing interest in all types of organisations — profit-seeeking and non-profit-seeking, commodity producing, service-generating, small or large, domestic or international.

All organisations — commercial and non-commercial — face market-like tasks because they have 'customers' and 'products'. Their functions include the task of managing exchange process and they are all engaged in promoting customer interest. In this context, Kotler has used the term 'meta-marketing' to describe the processes involved in attempting to develop and maintain exchange relationship for products, services, institutions, places or causes.

In recent years, service industries such as banking, insurance, transport and communication and tourism have all adopted the marketing approach. Of late, professional service providers — such as accountants, business consultants, physicians and architects have taken a keen interest in marketing. They are now doing a lot of publicity to promote their services.

Non-profit organisations such as hospitals, universities, charitable trusts, co-operative societies are launching **social marketing** campaigns to discourage cigarette smoking, excessive drinking, hard drug usage, and so on. International firms are investing heavily to improve their global marketing skills. Today, even public-sector enterprises like Coal India Ltd. or Steel Authority of India Ltd. (SAIL) are undertaking market research and advertising.

Marketing activity shape the decisions and, ultimately, the financial position of an organisation. For example market research may have a major impact on the decision to introduce a new product. This decision may affect all functional areas of the firm — production, finance and personnel.

Moreover, the efficiency and effectiveness with which a new product is introduced may affect the market standing of a firm for many years. Indeed, the long-term survival of an organisation depends on the effectiveness of marketing activities.

The marketing function is the primary mechanism for linking the organisation with its environment. The marketing function is, therefore, central to the firm.

MARKETING CONCEPT

The foundation for contemporary marketing management is the marketing concept, which provides an orientation for conducting business, a way of thinking, and a basic approach to business problems.

Marketing itself is, of course, a specific function in the enterprise. But the marketing concept is fundamental to the overall rationale and conduct of the enterprise.

Marketing requires spearate work and a distinct group of activities. But it is, first the central dimension of the entire business. It is the whole business seen from the point of view of its final result, that is, from the customer's point of view.

The marketing concept may be defined thus :

The most important managerial task within the organisation is that of understanding the needs and wants of customers in the market, and of adapting the operations of the organisation to deliver the right goods and services more effectively and efficiently than its competitors.

This means that management in the enterprise has two main areas of reasponsibility :

(i) ***remaining sensitive to market needs*** : the management of the enterprise must be aware of the nature of market demand, and of changes that occur in it. The nature of market demand, and the need to supply it effectively — yet profitably — should be the driving force behind the decisions of all the company's managers, not just its marketing function.

(ii) ***market-oriented operations management*** : the whole enterprise should be run so that (a) marketing objectives may be achieved; and (b) the enterprise trades in a competitive and profitable manner.

For instance, the dominance in world market share enjoyed by Japanese car manufacturers shows the effectiveness of the marketing concept when applied throughout the operations of the business. Manufacturers like Nissan, Toyota and Honda

- design, builld and supply the type of cars people want to buy;
- manufacture the cars to a consistent, high quality;
- produce large volume, so that the cost per unit is reduced;
- price and sell the cars so that the business runs at a profit.

The marketing concept is illustrated in Fig. 2.2. Making sure that the decisions

Fig. 2.2 : The Marketing Concept

and operations of any organisation (whether in the profit or not for profit sector) are market sensitive is simple common sense. If the business does not provide the would-be customer with :

- the right information about the product, and
- the right product, accessible and availability to the customer : at the right time; at the right price; and with the right guarantees, after-sales service (etc.)

then in a competitive market, the customer will not buy the product. He (or she) will take their custom elsewhere.

As Figure 2.2 shows, the marketing concept is made up of three components. Starting with customer needs and wants, a firm must develop an organisationally integrated marketing strategy and thereby accomplish its organisational goals. Let us look now at each of the three components.

Customer Orientation

The principal task of of the marketing function in a management concept is not so much to be skillful in making the customer do what suits the interests of the business as to be skillful in conceiving and then making the business do what suits the interests of the customer.

As Peter Drucker has put it: "A business is defined by the company's name, statute or articles of incorporation. It is defined by the customer satisfaction when he buys a product or service. To satisfy the customer is the mission and purpose of every business. The question, "What is our business?" can, therefore, be answered only by looking at the business from the outside, from the point of view of customer and market.

Since no business has the skills and resources to be all things to all people, management must identify which customer preferences can and should be met. Deciding which preferences and potential customers to serve is crucial, given any firm's limited resources and competitive strengths. Selectively choosing target markets is an integral part of the philosophy suggested by the marketing concept. The alternative is to try to serve all potential customers in a mediocre fashion and thus to fall short in providing customer satisfaction and achieving organisational goals.

Organisational Integration

The marketing concept offers key guidelines for planning, organising, integrating and managing the entire enterprise — not just marketing. Its philosophy should span the entire organisation because marketing and nonmarketing functions in a company together determine whether the company as a whole is customer oriented.

Although marketing by definition links the firm and its customers, most departments and employees in a company affect how customers perceive the firm. Only through leadership at the top, with related organisational structures, policies, and procedures, can the marketing concept be integrated throughout the firm.

This requires that executives answer the question "What business are we in?" with the answer "that of deciding which customers to serve and then satisfying them." The marketing concept is not marketing as a business function but marketing as a philosophy for doing business. It applies to accounting, finance, personnel, production, and all other business functions. Without satisfied customers who return again and again, all of these functions cease to exist!

Goal achievement

In most companies, the marketing function was once viewed as responsible for achieving only sales objectives, not broader organisational goals. The marketing concept was "obtaining profitable sales," not just high-volume sales.

Although organisations vary in what they want to accomplish, they are all concerned with more than meeting sales goals. Not-for-profit organisations — such as India's Post and Telegraph Department — are concerned with costs as well as revenues.

Over time, there is need to reorganise the role of marketing in achieving non-profit goals, such as altering a firm's image or increasing its market share. Non-profit organisations have a number of goals.

No doubt, the underlying goal of all marketing activity is customer satisfaction. Variations exist in the extent to which organisations have adopted the marketing concept. Such variations have been related to firm size, channel level (manufacturers, middlemen, retailers), and type of customer (consumer or industrial).

Consumer goods firms have implemented the marketing concept more extensively than industrial producers, and most larger firms tend to adopt and implement the concept more extensively than small and medium-sized firms. But the differences are diminishing.

Is the Marketing Concept Adequate?

In reality, however, the marketing concept simply tries to prove the fact that few businesses survive over the long term if they taken an "us versus them" approach. For a profit or nonprofit organisation to remain viable, its marketing exchanges must be perceived as mutually beneficial.

It has been said, however, that the perception of mutual benefit is not enough. The marketing concept is losing its relevance in today's environment because, most organisations are not sufficiently responsive to society. This would require company management to include the consideration of social implications in their decision processes and their management control procedures.

Marketing is the management function which organises and directs all those business activities involved in assessing and converting customer purchasing power into effective demand for a specific product (or service) and in moving the same to the final consumer (or user) so as to achieve the profit target or other objectives set by a company. The marketer's job is to convert needs into profitable opportunities.

2.2 BASIC MARKETING FUNCTIONS

Marketing involves more than just selling. The marketing process involves eight basic functions: **buying, selling, transporting, storing, standardising and grading, financing, risk taking, and obtaining marketing information**. Figure 2.3 illustrates these marketing functions. Some firms use all of them, but most carry out only some.

Fig. 2.3 : The Marketing Functions

1. Buying

When applied to marketing, the purchasing function is called buying and involves deciding the type and amount of goods to be purchased. Managers typically base such decisions on a forecast of consumer demand. In the case of large retailers, buying involves thousands of merchandise orders that vary in quality and quantity. In the case of a small boutique in a small town, the decision is much more limited and is likely to involve purchases that are but a fraction of those made by a large retailer.

2. Selling

The selling function is probably most closely associated with marketing and really is its central activity. Selling includes identifying buyers, developing a promotional campaign to attract their business, and concluding the sale. The process involves much more than simply handing over the merchandise and raising the volume of sale. In truth, marketing people usually spend more time and effort identifying potential buyers and encouraging (inducing) them to buy by attracting them to the company's goods and services than just by selling what the company has produced, and tendering the sale. Selling can occur through the written media. Advertisements in magazines and newspapers are part of selling, as are catalogues.

3. Transporting

For selling to take place, the company must also engage in transporting — the process of moving goods from where they were manufacured or purchased to where they are needed. In many instances, the manufacturer performs this function by shipping the goods to wholesalers. The wholesaler, in turn, breaks up the shipment into smaller lots and transports them to retailers. Customers then visit the retail store to purchase the goods.

Although the manufacturer-wholesaler-retailer sequence is the most common, it is not the only way to carry out the transportation function. For example, some wholesalers buy in large quantities from the manufacturer and then sell directly to customers, while some manufacturers ship directly to retailers. In some cases, the manufacturer also owns and operates a direct retail outlet. Some companies transport goods directly to the customers. However the business does it, transportation is an important marketing function because it gets the goods or services to a location where customers buy them.

4. Storing

Following transporting comes the process of storing, or warehousing, goods. Few firms operate hand to mouth; instead, most firms store goods until they are demanded. Even small retail stores have godowns or back rooms where they keep some stock. If they need more room or space they take it on rent from others. Large firms typically have their own warehouses, although they also rent or purchase storage space if they run out of room. Companies selling services also keep inventories by hiring more workers to be utilised during busy periods.

However, storing goods is expensive. So managers have to weigh the benefits of having the goods on hand against the expense.

5. Standardising and Grading

When one goes to a electronic goods store to buy 100-watt light bulbs, one does not want to be bothered with testing each bulb until one finds enough 100-watt bulbs. Likewise, if one needs a shirt, one does not want to try on every shirt in the store looking for the one that fits. Companies meet this need by standardising. Standardising is establishing specifications or categories for products. For example, when General Electric makes a light bulb, the company makes it to certain specifications, such as 100-watts. Clothing manufacturers make shirts to certain size specifications. The company then labels the product with this information. Standardisation is important in helping customers identify the specific characteristics they are looking for — such as size, weight, height, texture, ingredients, or colour.

Closely related to standardising is grading, which involves sorting goods into classes on the basis of quality. For example, eggs and dairy products are graded. Meat, fruit, and farm produce are also sorted by quality. Grading goods make it much easier for the consumer to decide what to buy.

6. Financing

As a marketing function, financing is paying for merchandise to sell and arranging for credit to buyers. There are various aspects of financing in the area of marketing. Applied to marketing, this process has two major parts : financing the purchase of the goods and financing the sale of the goods.

In the first case many marketers pay for their merchandise at the end of the month. When this time rolls around, they issue a cheque to the seller. If the marketers cannot afford to pay for the goods out of current revenues, they will typically arrange for a short-term loan with the local bank and draw on these funds. When marketers sell goods, they sometimes offer financing terms to buyers. For example, large U.S. firms like General Motors, Ford Motor, General Electric, and Sears all offer their customers financing arrangements.

If consumers buy a General Motors automobile, they can arrange financing for it through General Motors Acceptance Corporation (GMAC). The buyer can pay the bill in monthly instalments. In recent years, this has been an important marketing approach for the automobile industry. The auto dealer can offer loans at interest rates that are usually below what local lending institutions would charge. The object is to make it easier to buy a new car. The buyer need not come with ready cash.

Many manufacturers and wholesalers also provide financing arrangements to the business that purchase their merchandise. This ranges from giving the buyer 30 days to pay for the merchandise (in essence, a month of free credit) to allowing the buyer to pay for it over a long period of time. A good example of the latter occurs when the manufacturer has a great deal of inventory and is willing to ship it to the seller under an arrangement whereby the customer pays for it as it is sold. This arrangement permits both sides to come out ahead.

7. Risk Taking

As a marketing function, risk taking is the process of assuming potential liability. When marketers take possession of merchandise, they run the risk that the goods will be destroyed by fire, be stolen, or (perhaps worst of all) have no market demand and not sold. Some marketers reduce this risk by purchasing insurance against such calamities as fire and theft. Others limit their risk by assuming ownership of no more merchandise than they believe they can sell over the next 30 days. Still others, like brokers, never take possession of goods. They simply try to identify buyers and sellers, and then bring the two groups together. In this case, the risk is that of losing a lot of time trying to put together a deal that eventually falls through. For virtually all business, risk taking is an inherent part of the marketing function.

8. Obtaining Market Information

Market information helps business identify and address consumer needs. Businesses need answers to many types of questions, from how consumers behave to what the most effective advertising is, to where to sell the merchandise. Large companies spend crores of rupees each year obtaining market information. A T & T wants to know how well it is providing telephone service and what additional services customers would like. Tandoor wants to knows if there is a growing number of vegetarians, so it can develop new frozen dinners. Citi Bank wants to know what new financial services they can offer their customers. To a large degree, then, marketing effectiveness is based on accurate information.

MODERN MARKETING CONCEPT

Kotler's View

The modern concept of marketing, as suggested by Philip Kotler, holds "the key to achieving the needs and wants of target markets and delivering the desired satisfactions more effectively and efficiently."

Four Components of Modern Marketing

Four components (or building blocks) of the modern marketing concept are the following :

1. Target Market

It is not possible for a company to operate in every market and statisfy every need of the customer. It is also not possible to do a good job within one broad market. As Kotler has rightly put it: "Companies do best when they define their target market(s) carefully and prepare a tailored marketing programme."

2. Needs of Customers

Defining a target market does not necessarity mean that a company can fully understand the needs of (all) customers. According to Kotler: "A customer-oriented company would trace its customer-satisfaction level at each period and set improvement goals. Customer satisfaction is the best indication of the company's future profits."

3. Co-ordinated Marketing

It is a pity that most employees in any organisation are not trained and motivated to work for the customer. This is why there is almost always need for co-ordinated marketing. Such marketing means two things :

Firstly, the various marketing functions — sales promotion advertising, product management, pricing market research, and so on — must be co-ordinated among themselves, keeping in view the needs of customers.

Secondly, marketing must be well co-ordinated with the other company departments. Marketing works only when all employees appreciate the impact they have on customer satisfaction.

4. Profitability

The ultimate purpose of the whole marketing concept is to help organisations achieve their goals. So it is absolutely essential for marketers to be involved in analysing the profit potential of different marketing opportunities.

2.3 SALIENT FEATURES OF MARKETING IN INDIA

The relative emphasis of business functions ebbs and flows with changes in the business cycle and economic development. In less developed economies like India, fiscal policy and employement take center stage, and marketing receives relatively less attention. Nevertheless, issues related to the distribution of goods and services, a sub-area of marketing, are very important in such economies. As economies mature, marketing becomes indispensable. Yet economic conditions shape the relative importance of marketing and all business functions. In this context, we may refer to seven features of marketing in India. These are :

1. Large size and vast potentiality

The size of the market in India is very large. It has a vast potentiality on the simple ground that it is the second most populous country in the world. India's population in 1997-98 was 952 million. By 2001, it will be 1 billion !

Interestingly enough, the biggest consumption boom is taking place in rural areas. Furthermore, even low and middle-income households are significant purchasers of manufactured goods. India now has a consuming class of 540 million — two-thirds of all households. That should make the marketing men of the world feels excited. Nowadays villagers are willing to pay a premium for packaged and branded goods, because they promise better quality. And the rural rich increaseingly buy cars and VCRs. Some 10% of rural households (having on an average five members) are potential buyers of reasonably sophisticated manufactured goods. So the potential market size is very large. And as India's economic reforms bear fruit the market potential should be converted into reality in the 21st century.

As India's rural development speeds up, the market for sophisticated consumer goods will be wider. It is interesting to note that agricultural growth accelerated in the 1990s, helping start new businesses in transport and construction as well as manufacturing. The spread of electricity has raised productivity in the countryside, as well as increasing rural demand for electrically driven gadgets. As electricity spread, television has presented India's villagers with the joy of the consuming life.

The recessionary phase observed in some of India's industries is almost over. The industrial sector is now in much better shape. So the underlying trend is much stronger than that indicated by official statistics.

It appears that economic reforms will continue raising GDP growth to an unprecendented 6-8% a year by the year 2000, with industrial output rising by 11% and services by 8.9% annually. There will be a highly Westernised elite keen to exhibit its wealth by spending its money on the most expensive global brands and large enough to justify local production of luxuries.

2. Predominance of the urban sector

No doubt 70% of Indian people live in rural areas. But the market for most consumer goods and virtually all industrial products is predominantly urban. However, India's rural market has grown rapidly in recent years due to increase in income of the farmers, largely due to the Green Revolution. Moreover, agricultural prices have also risen due to general inflationary trends in the economy. But that has created additional purchasing power in rural areas and this, in its turn, has created demand for manufactured goods.

3. Near-monopoly situation

On the supply side of the market, for most mass consumption goods there prevail in India near-monopolistic conditions. This is largely due to fact that industries have been unduly protected for a long period of time (through high tariffs). This has made them less and less competitive in the domestic market. Monopoly has arisen in Indian industries due to the limited size of the domestic market for industrial goods and the general scarcity of industrial enterprise.

4. Sellers' market

For most goods and services India's vast market is largely, if not entirely, a sellers' market. This is due to very large demand and restricted supplies. Virtually what is produced is sold out easily and quickly. Almost every commodity has a ready market. This is more so in case of mass consumption goods. In other words, almost any product, so long as there is need for it, is sold with little or virtually no effort. There is not much promotional activity in case of most goods.

5. Large Number of Intermediaries

There are numerous channels of distribution in private trade — sole selling agents, distributors, wholesalers, stockists, semi-wholesalers, retailers and so on. Due to such a large chain of intermediaries the consumer has to pay high prices unnecessarily.

6. Poor Quality of Products

There is hardly any guarantee of the quality of products sold by different retail outlets. We often read newspaper reports on adulterated food articles and even life-saving drugs (medicines).

7. Dual System

There is some sort of dichotomy in India as is exemplified by rural and urban marketing. But this is not the whole truth. There is a dual system of marketing. The foreign firms operating in India, called the multinational corporations, have progressive outlook and they follow consumer-oriented policies. They engage in marketing research, product planning and development. Although they operate in a narrow urban market they charge reasonable prices for their products to be able to remain competitive in the long run. They also try their best to maintain quality of their products. Their basic objective is to provide maximum consumer satisfaction with reasonable amount of profit. These firms also advertise their products regularly and have succeeded in building over the years a brand name or company image like the Philips India Ltd. or Reckitt & Colman India Ltd. In contrast, most domestic firms, which include numerous small businesses, are virtually indifferent to consumer interest. They do not care much for the scientific process of marketing and their objective is not profit-seeking, but profiteering.

Conclusion

In this context the following quote from Peter Drucker is highly relevant: "Marketing is generally the most neglected area in the economic life of the developing countries. It is the most backward part of the economic system. In the underdeveloped countries of the world, the most glamorous fields such as manufacturing or construction are generally highlighted while marketing is treated with neglect, if not with contempt."

2.4 APPLICATION OF MODERN MARKETING IN INDIA

It is of considerable importance to apply these concepts in the Indian business environment to achieve what may be called 'excellence in marketing.' By learning the modern marketing concept and adopting this in practice, Indian companies can avoid the following adverse developments :

a. Sales decline

Sales decline can be prevented by properly applying the modern marketing concept. Suppose a newspaper publishing company is experiencing falling sales. To reverse the trend it has to undertake consumer research and attempt to redesign its newspaper properly to meet the needs. So it has to publish sufficient information on those subjects which are highly relevant and quite interesting to readers.

b. Slow growth

Slow growth of sales will force companies to tap new markets. Indian companies need marketing know-how if they are to identify and select new opportunities.

c. Changing Buying Patterns

In a dynamic world characterised by constant and rapid changes in the taste and preference of buyers, companies have to acquire more marketing know-how if they are to continue producing value for buyers.

d. Growing Competition

In a world characterised by growing intensity of competition there is hardly any scope for complacency. Complacent companies may suddenly be attacked by powerful rivals and forced to learn new marketing techniques to be able to meet the challenge and survive in the long run. Since offense is the best form of defence, most organisations should adopt offensive marketing strategy. Maruti Udyog, for instance, had to introduce new models to be able to compete closely with Hindustan Motors and the Tatas.

e. Increasing Marketing Expenditures

In the real commercial world, most companies find their expenditures for advertising, sales promotion, marketing research, and customer service getting out of hand. This very fact gives signal to management that it is time to undertake corrective actions and improve marketing policy and strategy. In fact, in the area of marketing, everything can be improved upon. True marketing starts where the buyers say 'no'.

MARKET RESEARCH AND MARKETING RESEARCH

Considerable confusion exists in relation to the two terms 'market research' and 'marketing research'. They are often used interchangeably. But they are not the same. The term 'marketing' covers activities associated with sales and distribution of product(s). Broadly speaking, it covers such activities as sales promotion, advertising and market research, all activities which promote and organise the sales of product to the purchaser.

A. Market Research

Before launching a new product or improving an existing one it is necessary to discover its potential sales volume in order that the resources to be devoted to it may not go waste in an attempt to find a fairly large market. The activity used to try to establish whether the potential customers are likely to buy, and to discover the best form the product should take, is known as market research.

By various means the market researcher attempts to establish what is likely to attract buyers in a particular product line in sufficient numbers in regard to design, size, price and other relevant features that influence a customer's buying decision. For instance, if it is decided by a radio manufacturer to launch a new portable radio on to the popular market, it will be necessary for him to know as accurately as possible what physical size the equipment should be, its frequency range, its sound level and quality and so on. If the received is to replace a existing model, it will also be useful to know what the public's opinion is of the present sets and what improvements should be made, and what features should be retained. By researching these matters the chances of a successful product launch are better than if no such research is carried out.

Similarly, in retail trade, the opening of a new store will be contemplated only after research into the population of the selected area, the proportion of those likely to become active customers, the average income of the area, the normal buying habits of the potential customers, their particular tastes and so on. Only if this research shows enough customers are likely to patronise the potential store, and that its revenue will thus be sufficient to justify the required capital expenditure, will the retail store be opened.

Desk Research

Desk research seeks to examine the broad determinants of potential demand by using (i) published material, *e.g.*, government statistics, and (ii) the firm's own sales records. These determinants are price and the various conditions of demand. More specialist facts used may be obtained from relevant periodicals and trade journals.

More precise information on potential sales necessitates a planned, consumer-oriented market research programme in potential markets. This would cover many aspects of market behaviour, particularly consumer reaction to the product — especially with regard to its quality, packaging, delivery dates and after-sales service and to price cuts.

Desk research involves researching past records, both internal and external, on matters relating to the proposed project. Past sales and other records, past reports from sales representatives and other data are used to form an estimate of possible sales based on past sales volume, customer complaints and suggestions gathered by sales representatives during their calls. Information can be gathered from external sources such as government publications, trade journals as also the sales literature of competitors to give indications of market trends, technical innovations and what competitors have to offer.

Field Research

This involves active fieldwork in interviewing potential customers, preparing questionnaires and having them completed by the public at large or by selected sections of the public offering samples, or having selected categories of potential customers carry out tests by using the product or prototypes of the product and reporting on questionnaire form specially prepared for the purpose.

How the active or field research is done will depend almost entirely on what type of product is to be launched. The distribution of free samples is common in research on foodstuff (new breakfast cereals like cornflakes, instant tea and the like) and cleaning materials such as washing powders, whereas high cost capital equipment requires research through personal contact with potential buyers, the preparation of detailed specifications and analysis of the reactions of the potential buyers.

Test Marketing

Before a national major sales campaign is undertaken some form of test marketing would probably be carried out so that modification could be made to correct any deficiencies. For instance, such a test might reveal that certain features of the product were unnecessary, thus permitting greater standardisation. Moreover, not all potential customers have identical preferences. The firm would therefore consider (i) a 'market mix' — producing different models at different prices — and (ii) varying sales methods and channels of distribution.

B. Marketing Research

Marketing research helps to implement a communications model by measuring how many people from target markets are in each stage — how many are unaware of the product, how many are aware of it without knowing what it has to offer, and so forth. This enables managers to evaluate the worth of influencing customers to move from one stage to the next, closer to purchase.

Market research is concerned with the assessment of the market for a completely new or well-established product or service and confines itself strictly to this. Market research, on the other hand, takes a much broader view. It refers to the systematic collection, assimilation and analysis of facts and opinions to assist managerial decision-making in identifying market opportunities for a firm's existing or potential goods and/or services. Marketing research is concerned with all the factors bearing on marketing policy and plans. These factors include research and evaluation of marketing opportunities, investigating media and their effectiveness, research on a broad scale into customers' desires and needs, consideration of different methods of distribution and the organisation's public image compared to its competitors' and other factors bearing on the general marketing problems of the organisation. Market research is part of marketing research, but the latter has much wider implications. Marketing research is also related to test market, a market comprising a fairly large group of consumers within a limited geographical area, which firms use to market new products as a means of testing consumer response before starting large-scale production and mass national marketing of those products throughout the country.

Difference between market research and marketing research

Market research relates to data gathering about the market itself. Marketing research relates to the gathering, recording and analysing of data about matters relating to the marketing of goods and services. In other words, the former seeks to research markets, their structure and the people in them. The latter attempts to study the most effective way of reaching such markets and to provide them with maximum satisfaction.

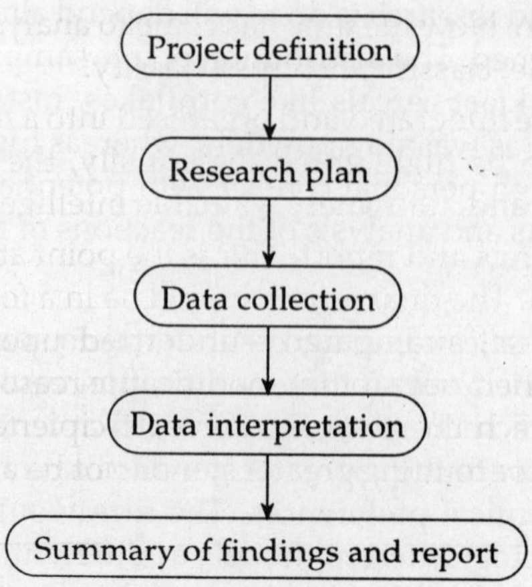

Fig. 2.4 : The Marketing Research Process

The process is described in Fig. 2.4. It consists of five main phases :

(1) **Project definition**. The purpose of the project must be defined (and redefined) with a view to establishing the underlying thinking and the relevance to the marketing task. At this stage it is useful to explore the following :

- Whether published material exists which may remove the need to undertake such a project.
- The cost-benefit justification for the expense which may be incurred.

A number of pitfalls should be avoided :

- Using vague terms of reference
- Stating the wrong problem
- Undertaking projects with a hidden or undisclosed purpose.

(2) **Research plan**. The plan must list the following :

Its objectives

- Tasks involved (to include those that can be undertaken with internal resources as well as those that call for outside help).
- The most appropriate methodology to be used.
- Detailed plan and review procedures.

(3) **Data collection.** This is an important stage in the implementation programme of work. Sources of information must be identified and, if found to be useful, acquired. Internal sources should also be located and collated. More specifically, the following steps need to be pursued in a systematic way :

- The identification of sources of information — both external and internal. This step calls for a thorough analysis of published data, of which huge quantities exist in libraries and other reference establishments.
- If the research involves interviewing of individuals, a sample interview/questionnaire filling exercise needs to be carried out.
- Responses to be analysed and errors, ambiguities or inconsistencies identified and corrected.
- Data collected and collated.

(4) **Data interpretation**. Now the time has come to analyse the data collected, find out its essentials, tabulate, classify and cross-classify.

Relevant data are to be integrated and organised into a manageable form. Important relationships are to be highlighted. Essentially, the data is gradually being turned into information and, ultimately, valuable intelligence.

(5) **Summary of findings and report**. This is the point at which effective communication is put to the test. The final report should be in a format which can be easily decoded by its 'audience', and, if necessary, acted upon. Quite often excellent research projects fail in their aims for the very simple reason that they are presented in a manner or style which the most significant recipients cannot relate to. Obviously, if they cannot relate to the report, they will not be able to act upon it either.

Synopsis for Learning

Q.1. What is marketing?

Ans. Marketing is a total system of business activities designed to plan, price, promote, and distribute want-satisfying products to target markets in order to achieve organisational objectives. This definition has two significant implications:

(i) The entire system of business activities should be customer-oriented. Customers' wants must be recognised and satisfied.

(ii) Marketing should start with an idea about a want-satisfying product and should not end until the customers' wants are completely satisfied.

Q.2. What is modern marketing concept?

Ans. The marketing concept acknowledges that a business geared to serve the needs and requirements of customers will achieve better results over a longer period of time than a company whose executives are not so motivated. The key point here is that the company is marketing-oriented. It has placed its customers and their needs or wants at the very centre of its business decisions. The company strives always to identify these needs as accurately as possible so that it can match them more precisely with the products or services it is offering within its resources and capabilities.

2.5 DIFFERENCE BETWEEN SELLING AND MARKETING

It may apparently seem that marketing and selling are the same thing. But a close look reveals that there are differences between the two concepts.

In the language of Philip Kotler: "The selling concept holds that consumers, if left alone, will ordinarily not buy enough of the organisation's product. The organisation must therefore undertake an aggressive selling and promotion effort." Salesmanship consists of transferring a conviction by a buyer to a seller.

Kotler's concept of selling assumes that consumers normally show buying inertia or resistance and they may be induced to buy a commodity by attracting them to a product. It also assumes that the company is having a wide range of tools and techniques of effective selling and promotion. These tools can be used to stimulate more (and effective) buying.

In practice, we observe that the selling concept is applied most aggressively with 'unsought goods', *i.e.*, those goods which people normally do not think of buying, such as insurance, costly reference books and non-life insurance policies. The industries producing such goods or rendering such services have been constrained to develop various sales promotion techniques with perfection in order to locate prospects and hard-sell them on the product benefits. Even in case of sought goods like motor cars or refrigerators such hard selling occurs.

The selling concept is also used in practice by non-profit organisations such as fund raisers, college admission offices, and various political parties (both at the time of election as also at normal times).

In general, firms practise the selling concept when they have excess capacity due to low demand. Their basic aim is to sell what they make rather than make what the market wants. In most industrially advanced countries, a huge production capacity is often created at a high cost without carrying out proper market survey or undertaking marketing research. As a result, the point has been reached where most markets are buyer markets (*i.e.*, the buyers are dominant) and sellers have to struggle hard to find customers. As Kotler has put it : "Prospects are brightened by television commercials, newspaper advertisements, direct mail, and sales calls. At every turn, someone is trying to sell something. As a result, the public identifies marketing with hard selling and advertising."

However, the truth is that the most important part of marketing is not selling. Selling is a specific term. Marketing is a very broad term. Selling is only one aspect of marketing. As Peter Drucker puts it : "There will always be need for some selling. But the aim of marketing is to make the selling superfluous. The aim of marketing is to know and understand the customer well so that the product or service fits him and sells itself. Ideally, marketing should result in a customer who is ready to buy. All that should be needed then is to make the product or service available".

This view makes it quite clear that selling, to be effective, must be preceded by various important marketing activities such as assessment of consumer needs, marketing research, product development, pricing, and physical distribution. If the marketing people can perform the tasks well, they will be able to sell their products easily and quickly. In other words, if a marketer can effectively do the job of identification of consumer needs, development of appropriate products (which can satisfy the needs) and pricing, distributing and promoting these identified goods, these products will sell well (*i.e.*, without much consumer resistance). When National designed its Walkman, when Sony designed a video game, and when Eureka Forbes introduced its vacuum cleaners, these manufacturers were flooded with orders because they had designed the 'right' product based on careful marketing research and appropriate groundwork.

The marketing concept is much broader (and wider) than the selling concept. It holds that the key to achieving the goals of a modern organisation consists in determining what customers need or what target markets want and delivering the desired satisfactions more effectively and efficiently than competitive sellers.

The contrast between selling and marketing should be made clear by now. As T.Levitt has put it: "Selling focuses on the needs of the seller; marketing one the needs of the buyer. Selling is preoccupied with the seller's need to convert his product into cash; marketing with the idea of satisfying the needs of the customer by means of the product and the whole set of things associated with creating, delivering and finally consuming it."

The four main building blocks of the modern marketing concept are : target market, customer needs, coordinated marketing, and profitability. These are shown in Fig.2.5, which clearly shows the difference between marketing and selling concepts.

According to Kotler : "the selling concept takes an inside-out perspective." It starts with the production unit — be it a farm or factory, focuses on the company's existing products, and calls for aggressive sales promotion to generate as much profit as possible from increased volume of sales. By contrast, the marketing concept takes an outside-in perspective. It starts from a well-defined market, focuses on the needs of customers (actual and potential), and seeks to coordinate all the activities that will affect customers, and generates profits by creating customer satisfaction.

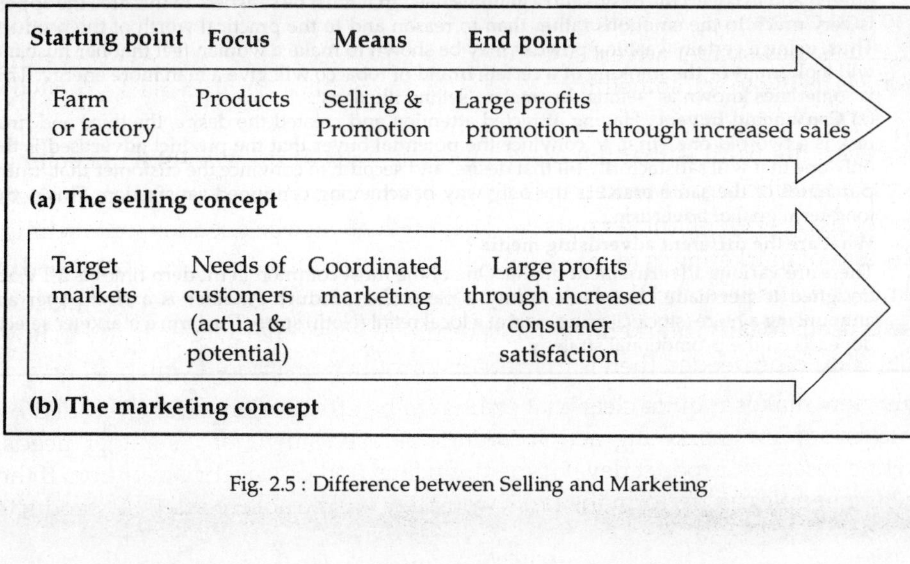

Fig. 2.5 : Difference between Selling and Marketing

Strategy v. Tactics

Another writer observes that the distinction between marketing and selling is highlighted by the difference between strategy and tactics — marketing is basically a study of strategy, whereas selling is essentially a tactical operation.

Production orientation v. User orientation

Finally, while marketing has user orientation, selling has production orientation. To quote P.F. Drucker: "Actually, marketing is so basic that it is enough to have a strong sales-force and to entrust marketing to it. Marketing is not only much broader than selling, it is not a specialised activity at all. It is the whole business seen from the point of view of its final result, that is, from the customer's point of view."

Synopsis for Learning

Q.1. What is marketing ?

Ans. Marketing is a broad term and embraces every activity required to find customers for introducing, informing about, creating a desire for and actually supplying the goods or services an organisation provides. Thus, it is involved in market research to determine the probable extent of market, advertising to introduce and inform about its goods and services, public relations to promote a persuasive image and selling to ensure the satisfaction of the demands created by its other activities.

Q.2. What is selling ?

Ans. Selling is this only one aspect of marketing — the part of marketing that actually places the goods or services in the hands of the customer. Selling involves the effort of finding the actual customers and then persuading them actually to buy.

Q.3. What is the difference between selling and marketing ?

Ans. While selling is a supply-oriented activity, marketing is a demand-oriented activity.

Q.4. What are the functions of advertising ?

Ans. Advertising is concerned with selling an organisation's goods or services. It performs the following three main functions :

(a) **Providing Information** : The primary task of advertising is to make the public aware of an organisation's products or services. On the launching of a new product the company will introduce the product to the potential market and will give all the information considered necessary to generate the interest of potential buyers.

(b) **Persuasion** : The second task of advertising is to generate a desire for the product being offered and to covert the desire into a genuine need that must be satisfied. In this area the appeal is very much to the emotions rather than to reason and to the practical worth of the product. Thus, using a certain washing powder may be shown to make a woman feel that her husband will look smart or the smoking of a certain brand of tobacco will give a man more energy. This is sometimes known as 'selling dreams' or 'selling illusions'.

(c) **Convincing buyers** : Having attracted attention and created the desire, the third and final task is a twofold one : first, to convince the potential buyer that the product advertised is the only one that will satisfactorily fill that desire, and second, to convince the customer that future purchases of the same brand is the only way of achieving continued satisfaction. This is the long-term goal of advertising.

Q.5. What are the different advertising media ?

Ans. There are various advertisement media. One of the most common in modern times is a TV ad, designed to persuade customers to buy a particular product. Another is a newspaper ad, announcing a huge (stock clearing) sale at a local retail (cloth) store. The form a marketer selects depends on the promotional strategy.

2.6 THE MARKETING MIX

Introduction

This section defines and describes the marketing mix. It then places this concept within the wider context of the marketing management process. The marketing mix is one of the most fundamental concepts associated with the marketing process. It is well understood by most modern marketers and is systematically applied in many industries, especially those that deal with physical products.

The marketing mix represents an assemblage of tasks and subtasks which ultimately will help to satisfy the customer's requirements in such a way as to enable the firm to attain its objectives in an optimum fashion.

Effective marketing consists of a consumer-oriented mix of business activities planned and implemented by a marketer to facilitate the exchange or transfer of goods, services or ideas so that both buyers and sellers gain in some way. Marketing is essentially a mix of various business activities intended ultimately to result in an exchange of useful goods and services.

The various elements of marketing need to be carefully employed in order to achieve the maximum success and it is necessary to combine them in the most effective way, given the circumstances at any particular time. The combination of these elements is known as the marketing mix.

Definition

According to Kotler, the marketing mix refers to the set of controllable variables and their levels that the firm uses to influence the target market. Marketing mix refers to the range of competitive dimensions along which firms promote their products to customers and potential customers including the styling, quality etc. of the goods and services themselves, their prices, their advertising, and promotion, their packaging, their distribution, and their selling and servicing. While any variable controlled by the firm's decision-makers could be included as part of the marketing mix, E. Jerome McCarthy (Basic Marketing: A Managerial Approach, 6th edn. 1978, p.39) has populariesed a four-factor classification called the four **Ps: product, price, promotion and place**.

The term marketing mix describes the result of management's efforts to creatively combine interrelated and interdependent marketing activities. In the language of Philip Kotler : "Marketing mix is the set of marketing tools that the firm has to pursue in the target market to fulfill its marketing objectives." Faced with a wide choice of media, messages, prices, distribution methods and other marketing variables, the marketing manager must select and combine the 'ingredients' of the organisations.

To achieve organisational objectives, the marketing executives must constantly try to fashion a mix of marketing procedures and policies. This mix must be altered as new problems develop and environmental changes occur.

Four Elements

Since every possible activity can be placed in one of the categories. McCarthy's 4Ps constitute a framework that may be utilised to develop a simple marketing plan. Preparation of a marketing strategy would rquire consideration of each major mix area, and may involve the development of sub-strategies within each category.

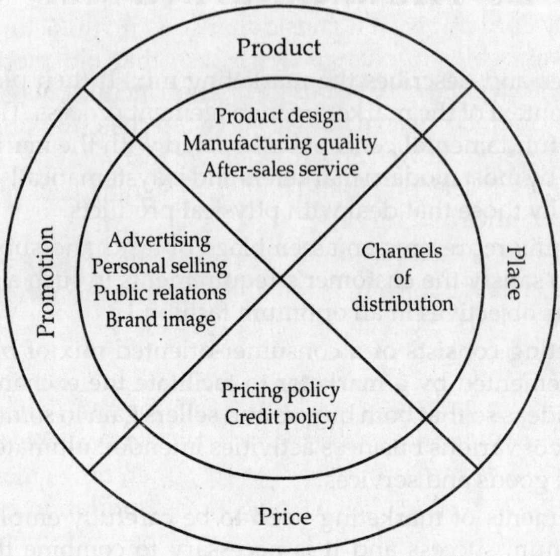

Fig. 2.6 : The Four Ps of Marketing

Because these marketing mix variables may be influenced by managers they are also called controllable variables. These are the variables which management can manipulate and effort is wasted if any one aspect of the mix is emphasised in isolation. See Fig. 2.6 which shows the particular marketing variables under each head. For the mix to be effective each aspect must be planned and developed to constitute one aspect of the total marketing effort.

The First Element: Product

The most basic marketing mix tool is the product, which stands for "the firm's tangible offer to the market, including product quality, design, features, branding, and packaging". The product or service offered constitutes the link between company and consumer. A. M. Ferguson has put it "The first mark of a good business is the ability to deliver — to deliver its product or service on time and in the condition which the client was led to expect." In conditions of rapid technological change, product competition is dynamic. Companies offering superior, differentiated products will increase their sales at the expense of rivals. Although rivals may respond and offset the initiator's advantage this response will take time.

The term product refers to what the organisation offers to its prospective customers or client without regard to whether the offering is a tangible good like a car, or a service such as an airline trip.

Because customers often expect more from an organisation than a simple, tangible product, the task of marketing management is to provide a complete offering — a total product — that includes the 'extras' that go with it (such as prompt after-sales service, consumer credit, free delivery to customers, and the opportunity to exchange an unsuitable product).

The product the customer receives in the exchange process is the result of a number of product strategy decisions. Product development and product planning involve making sure that the goods and services offered have the attributes customers desire. As Henry Ford put it: "It is considered good manufacturing practice, and not bad ethics, occasionally to change designs so that old models will become obsolete and new ones will have to be bought. Our principle of business is precisely to the contrary. We cannot concieve how to serve the customer unless we make for him something that, as far as we can provide, will last forever." Product strategy includes such activities as selecting brand names, designing packages, and developing appropriate warranties and service plans.

Product strategies must take the other three elements of the marketing mix into consideration. Price, distribution and promotion enhance the attraction of a marketable product.

The Second Element : Place

Place, the second key marketing mix tool, stand for the various activities the company undertakes to make the product accessible and available to target customers. Determination of how goods move to the customer, how quickly, and in what condition, involves place or distribution strategy. Transportation, storage, materials handling and the like are physical distribution activities. Selection of wholesalers, retailers, or other types of distributors is also a place problem because these intermediaries comprise channels of distribution.

Every organisation, however, does not have the resources or ability to manage all the activities required in the distribution process. Thus organisations may concentrate on activities where they have a unique advantage. Wholesalers, retailers, and various other specialists, such as airlines, have developed to allow for specialisation and to make the distribution process more efficient. For example, the Pepsi Cola Corporation, which specialises in the production and promotion of soft drinks, finds it efficient to utilise independent bottlers and retailers to distribute its products to the ultimate consumer.

Channel of distribution. In this context, we may refer to a key concept, *viz.*, channel of distribution. A channel of distribution is a complete sequence of marketing organisation involved in bringing a product from the producer to the ultimate consumer. Its ultimate purpose is to make possible transfer of ownership and/or possession of the product. This concept will be discussed in detail later in this chapter.

The Third Element : Price

A critical marketing mix tool is price. The amount of money, or sometimes goods or services, given in exchange for something is its price. In other words, price is the amount of money customers have to pay for the product. Just as the customer buys a product with cash, so a manufacturer buys the customers' cash with the product.

Prices are always on trial. Pricing strategies and decisions require establishing appropriate prices and careful monitoring of the competitive market environment. Prices are subject to rapid chane, partly because — unlike the other three elements of the marketing mix — price is relatively easy to change. Of course, changes that are poorly thoughtout can lead to disaster. Companies adopt different pricing policies and strategies. These are largely governed by the pricing objectives of business firms. Pricing may be an important marketing feature where quality is not of paramount importance. As a general rule, desirous customers equate low prices with low quality and are likely to question the quality of a product selling for substantially less than that of its competitors. If a top-quality product is offered at a very low price suspicion is aroused as to whether a new and improved model is about to be introduced. Often a manufacturer or supplier may price a product or range of products at substantially reduced price(s) simply because of a fall in cash intake and this is the only way to generate revenue quickly.

The Fourth Element : Promotion

Promotion, the fourth market mix tool, stand for the various activities the company undertakes to communicate with it customers and to promotion its products to the target market. The basic aim of all promotion or selling efforts is to increase sales of the product and thus improve the product's market share. Promotional efforts may take a variety of forms. Perhaps the most important of these is advertising. In addition to advertising, many other promotional devices are available to companies to bring their products to the attention of the public: for example, price-reduction offers, free samples, gifts, discount coupons, attractive prizes and so on.

The essence of promotion is communication. Advertising, personal selling, publicity, and sales promotion are all forms of communication that (i) inform, (ii) remind, or (iii) persuade. The firm's promotion mix is its particular combination of these communication tools. Some firms may emphasise advertising, while others hardly advertise at all. An IBM sales representative explains how a computer will help an organisation. A departmental store employee offers a free sample of coffee. Promotion provides information that encourages consumers to respond. Obviously, what is to be communicated is persuasive information about the other elements of the marketing mix such as the uses for the product or the new low price being offered during a particular period when demand is low (or stock-level is high).

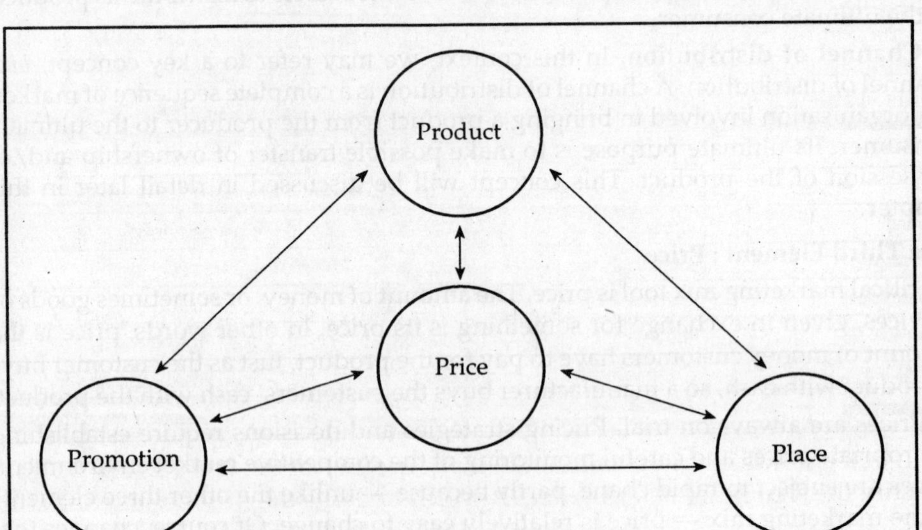

Fig. 2.7 : Interaction among Marketing Tools

Conclusion : The Art of Blending the Elements

In short, a marketing manager uses four marketing tools — decision areas — that ineract with one another. These are product, promotion, distribution and price. Their interaction is illustrated in Fig.2.7.

The blending of these four tools is referred to as the marketing mix. A manager's selection of an marketing mix is very important. Different combinations of ingredients may be used. In marketing, there is no standard formula for a successful combination of marketing elements. Marketing mixes will vary from company to company, depending upon the kinds of markets they serve. For example, a company concerned primarily with marketing consumer goods might emphasise such factors as packaging, promotion and advertising, while companies marketing industrial goods might stress technical features of the product, prices, personal selling and after-sales service. Marketing mixes also vary from situation to situation. The blending of the various elements of the marketing mix is no doubt a creative activity.

The market has at his (or her) disposal a number of components. The ability to mix them in response to an identified set of requirements, coupled with a number of other objectives, is one of the major requirements of effective marketing.

Practical Relevance of the Concept

The 'four Ps model' of the marketing mix has probably gained acceptance because of its elegance rather than its validity in all situations. Regrettably, what has been gained in simplicity has been sacrificed in universal appropriateness. It is easy to find examples of marketing programmes which do not fit into the four Ps model. It is, therefore, important to emphasise at the outset that this model is not of universal validity.

The theory underlying the Four Ps concept is that, if one manages to achieve the right product at the right price with the appropriate promotion and in the right place, the marketing programme will be effective and successful. However, one must bear in mind that each of the four Ps can be broken down into a number of sub-components. Table 2.4 lists some of these.

Table 2.4 : The subcomponents of the four Ps

Product	Price	Place	Promotion
Brand	Credit terms	Channels	Advertising
Packaging	Payment period	Locations	Sales promotion
Warranties	Discounts	Transport	Publicity
Service	Instalments	Delivery	Personal Selling
Features	Commissions	Stocks	Public Relations
Guarantees	General cost/benefit in use	Customs clearance	Creation of brand image

In other words, it is not sufficient to think in terms of the four Ps. One needs to identify the significant subcomponents which underlie the firm's marketing strategy.

Management can manipulate all these varibles and if the mix is to be effective each dimension must be developed as one aspect of the total marketing effort. No one dimension should be emphasised in isolation. Otherwise, the whole marketing effort will go waste. For example, pricing decisions should not be separated from consideration of product and promotion policies. McCarthy emphasises that pricing decisions do not take place in isolation from the decisions made with respect to the product being produced or sold, to the promotion and advertising decisions being made, and to the location or place decisions. It hardly makes any sense, for example, to reduce price in the hope of stimulating sales unless one has an advertising programme to inform potential consumers of the price change and the locations at which the product can be found.

The particular marketing mix used at any one time will depend upon many circumstances such as the economic climate, the strength of the competition and sometimes on the need for an improved inflow of revenue. Different organisations, even in the same industry, often use different mixes successfully because their particular circumstances demand a particular mix.

MARKETING STRATEGY

Marketing cannot fulfill its managerial (or societal) role unless customer needs and wants are understood and satisfied. The development of an overall marketing strategy helps ensure that mutually beneficial exchange occur. It is oriented toward the long run, comprised of fundamental decisions (not day-to-day adjustments), and developed with an eye to competition as well as markets. Developing marketing strategy includes deciding which customers to target and how to position products (and the organisation) relative to competitors in the minds of existing and potential customers.

Developing marketing programmes involves identifying alternative combinations of marketing variables (for example, higher-quality, higher-priced pizza or pastry and then judging how well these combinations match the market opportunity. The core of such matching is forecasting potential customer response to the mix of marketing variables. Then, the programme with the greatest potential is implemented.

Let us consider the luxury car market. The guidelines and policies that constitute a strategy for the luxury car market must be oriented toward creating the highest quality image possible.

They include:

- A high, narrow pricing range that conveys an image of price exclusiveness.
- New models that offer high technical quality, few repairs, and excellent warranty coverage.
- Advertising media and messages that impart an exclusive, high-quality image.

These illustrative guidelines and policies (marketing strategy) narrow the range of marketing actions that are appropriate given the overall marketing objectives (*e.g.*, quality image). Basically, a marketing strategy outlines how marketing objectives will be achieved.

1. Target Market Selection

A target market may consist of all end users or one or more subgroups in a product-market. Making decisions about target markets is one of management's most important tasks.

Strategic decisions involving target markets include:

- *Deciding whether to go after an entire product-market by using a mass-marketing approach or to concentrate marketing strategy on only a portion of the market.*
- *Determining when to modify an existing target market strategy.*
- *Deciding to stop serving a particular target market.* Increasingly, managements face the question of whether to withdraw from a market. Maturing products, slow growth rates, competition, and environmental changes gradually alter the attractives of target markets.

Target market selection is guided by an organisation's mission and objectives. So target market decisions must be properly positioned within this larger context. Moreover, their strategic implications are to be assessed. Once selected, the target market provides the focus for setting marketing objectives and designing the marketing program.

2. Marketing Objectives

Marketing objectives should be consistent with corporate objectives and should be stated for each target market in terms of sales, market share, profit contribution, and other qualitative aims, such as improving a brand image. Objectives are sometimes divided into two groups: *market performance objectives* and *market support objectives*. The former are specific outcomes such as sales and profits. The latter relate to tasks that precede the final performance outcome and may include building customer awareness, engaging in educational efforts, and creating a brand image.

Objectives help shape the marketing mix for each target market. A firm seeking to increase sales in a target market by 6% for the coming year would probably make only limited changes in the existing marketing programme. Alternatively, striving for a substantial sales increase, say 20%, could require major changes in the composition of the marketing programme, including increases in the marketing budget for elements of the programme (*e.g.*, size of the sales force).

Objectives must, at least to some extent, be measurable. Otherwise, it will not be possible to identify progress toward their achievement. In marketing, measurability is not easy. A support objective could include changing a brand image in the minds of potential customers and progress toward that objective could be measured by making a survey of customers' intentions and feelings. This is often done. Objectives should be stated very carefully, for developing measurable and attainable standards.

3. Marketing Programme

A firm's marketing must consist of an integrated strategy aimed at providing customer satisfaction. To develop such a strategy, a firm uses demand-influencing variables that together constitute the marketing mix. The marketing mix has various parts (or components) that must be properly combined for a successful end result — Table 2.5. It includes the product (or service) offered by the firm, the marketing channels it uses (wholesalers, distributors, retailers) to make the product available to customers, the price it charges for the product, and promotion (advertising, personal selling, sales promotion and publicity). Other terms often used to describe the components of the marketing mix are the marketing programme, the marketing offer, and the 4-Ps (product, place, price, and, promotion). These variables must be consistent with one another, and ideally, they complement one another for a synergistic result. Building a quality, prestige product and combining it with inconsistent mix ingredients such as heavy price discounting would yield a poorly integrated, internally inconsistent marketing programme. The mix ingredients would conflict with one another in the minds of customers.

Table 2.5 : Marketing Mix Variables

Product	Place (Distribution)	Price	Promotion
Features Quality Packaging Branding Services Guarantees Assortment	Types of channels / middlemen Store/distributor location Storage Transportation and logistics Service levels	Last price Credit terms Discounts Allowances Flexibility	Promotion blend Advertising Media Copy Timing Personal selling Selection and training Motivation Allocation Sales promotion Publicity

The creative role that management must play in moving from knowledge of the market to the formulation of marketing programmes is both a major challenge and an opportunity. But in a dynamic world, those who take up the challenge stand to gain much.

Building a marketing programme for a target market consists of determining how large the marketing budget should be, allocating the budget to the marketing mix variables of the firm, and determining the best use of the resources for each marketing mix variable. Over time, organisations make many important decisions about the marketing mix, including:

1. The development of new products or services, the improvement of product, and the elimination of products.
2. The choice of channel intermediaries (agents, brokers, wholesalers, distributors, and retailers) or the use of direct distribution for reaching target markets.
3. The setting of pricing objectives and strategies that are consistent with the target markets and with the other elements of the marketing program.
4. The development of advertising, sales promotion, and publicity programs to accomplish the communication objectives assigned to the promotion function.
5. The formulation of personal selling goals; the determination of the type number, and location of sales-people; and the adoption of policies for managing sales-people (such as compensation policies).

Given various possible marketing programmes that could be developed and the difficulty of estimating the likely revenue and cost results of each alternative program, these are complex decisions. Management must determine the level and combination of marketing variables that will yield the most favourable profit contribution, net of marketing costs. *Estimating the responsibilities of target markets to alternative marketing mixes is perhaps the key uncertainty in all of marketing management.*

Finally, the terms *strategy* and *tactics* are often used in marketing management discussions. Strategy (or strategic) decisions provide a broad, long-term framework (a year or usually more) for marketing action. They are fundamental decisions that guide day-to-day actions. Tactical decisions determine how marketing strategies are to be carried out on a day-to-day basis. The strategy of a company is implemented by day-to-day tactical decisions, such as setting the exact prices, deciding whether or not to include prices in advertising copy, deciding how frequently to offer sale prices and on which items, and opening new locations.

It is important to realise that marketing management usually involves this sequential process. Implementation occurs only after programming decisions are made; programming decisions are based on target market decisions and realistic objectives; target market decisions and realistic objectives hinge on in-depth market opportunity analyses; all of these stages benefit from keeping a keen eye on the shifting environment; and, together, these stages make a major contribution toward achieving the corporate mission.

Synopsis for Learning

Q.1. What is marketing mix?

Ans. Marketing mix refers to the whole set of marketing tools that the firm uses to pursue its marketing objective in the target market.

Q.2. What are four marketing Ps?

Ans. There is no universal list of the particular aspects of the marketing function that go into the marketing mix, but they fall under four main headings with subdivisions providing an analysis of the mix. The main headings are :

1. **Product** — This includes product design, the quality of manufacture and, of course, after-sales service.
2. **Price** — This must relate to product quality and the particular market aimed at. The policy of giving consumer credit also falls under this heading.
3. **Place** — This involves the channels of distribution to be used, *e.g.*, sales through agents, wholesalers, direct, and so on. In countries like India distinction is often drawn between private distribution and public distribution.
4. **Promotion** — This includes advertising, selling, public relations and the creation of a brand name where this is advantageous. Promotional activities go by the name 'marketing communications' — products to the target markets. Thus, a company has to hire, train, motivate sales people in order to set up communication and promotion programmes consisting of advertising, publicity and direct marketing, sales promotion and public relations.

2.7 THE PRODUCT LIFE CYCLE

The Product

The product or service is the heart of the marketing mix. Without a product there is no chance of satisfying the customer's needs. At the same time it is essential to note that what the company considers as its product is not necessarily what the custmer buys. Peter Drucker summarized this simple notion many years ago by saying: 'Until the customer has derived final utility, there is really no "product"; there are only "raw materials".

The product or service offered constitutes the link between company and consumer. In conditions of rapid technological change product competition is dynamic. Companies offering superior, differentiated products will increase their sales at the expense of rivals. Although rivals may also respond to the initiator's advantage this response will take time to make its effect felt. So for some time at least the initiator enjoys the advantage of a partial monopoly situation.

Innovation resulting from a company's research and development efforts can result in the emergence of new products, new production technologies, or new material which give the innovating company a decisive cost or distinct quality advantage. Such fundamental changes limit the lives of products and we may talk in terms of a typical life cycle, followed by products introduced to the market. The product life cycle is an indipensable tool for product planners and for marketers in general. Simply put, the product life cycle (PLC in short) is a graphic depiction of a product's sales history from its marketing inception to its withdrawal from the market. Product life cycles are, in fact, sales volume curves. Products begin their lives with the first sale of the product, rise to some peak, and then decline until their

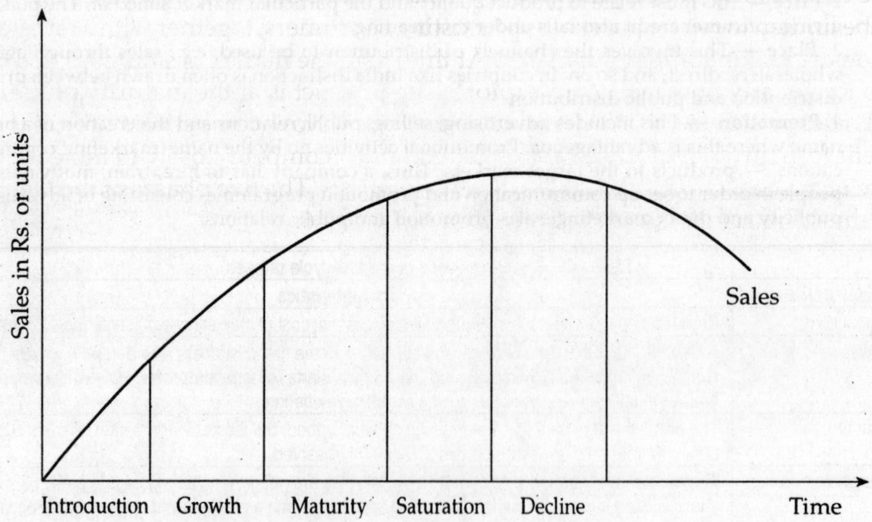

Fig. 2.8 : Difference between Selling Orientation and Marketing Orientation

contributions to profits are insufficient to justify their presence in the market. While this pattern is common, it varies from product to product. Dettol has been used for many years. Personal computers and cellular phones are comparatively new products. Some products such as Standard 2000 or Dolphin cars failed at the very start of their lives. Fig.2.8 shows a typical life cycle for a product, A, and this can be divided into five phases:

1. Product Launch

This follows the successful development of a new product, and is normally preceded by consumer-testing of product prototypes and possibly test-marketing of the product in a limited geographical area. Once the product has proved itself viable through this initial screening then a nation-wide product launch can be implemented. When the product is first put on the market there are two main tasks to be achieved. Firstly, potential consumers must be made aware of the availability of the product. Secondly, consumer resistance must be overcome and people convinced of their need to make the purchase. While this is being done, often through extensive promotion and advertising, sales volume will not be high. At this stage only those with more adventurous buying habits (usually young high-income consumers) will purchase the product.

2. Growth Phase

Once the product begins to gain market-acceptance, with 'average' consumers beginning to buy it, then rapid sales-growth is experienced. At this stage the product reaches the mass market, and during this growth-phase competitors may well begin to enter the field with rival products. So the distinctiveness of the original product gradually fades in the face of imitations, and its market share declines.

3. Product Maturity

Once the majority of potential customers have made their first purchases then sales will be limited to repeat purchases by existing consumers, together with a few slower customers making initial purchases. At this stage the market is saturated, for there is no longer any new market to explore. The product is at the maturity phase, and total sales will remain at a fairly constant level. Now competitors are unable to benefit from growth of the total market and must compete closely to increase their share of the constant market at the expense of rivals. The five phases of the life-cycle and their characteristics are summarised in Table 2.6.

Table 2.6 : Characteristics of the life-cycle phases

Phases of life-cycle	Characteristics
Introduction	Product is new; awareness in the marketplace is low; cost of marketing is quite high; profits are low.
Growth	Assuming that the product has given satisfaction to the first customers who bought it, others follow suit. Sales increase fairly rapidly and the product starts to generate profits. However, competitors notice the success and start planning a competitive offering.
Maturity	The product is reaching the maturity and sales are good, but the battle for market share is about to begin. First signs of pressure on margins can be observed.
Saturation	The market has reached a point at which total sales are not growing any more, the battle for market share is intense and, unless the product is associated with a strong brand loyalty, price becomes a major factor in buying patterns.
Decline	Sales and profits are starting to fall and the future of the product does not look healthy. At this stage, remedial strategy (*e.g.*, modifying the product, repositioning, or even deleting the product from the range) is needed.

4. Saturation

The market for certain products reaches a saturation point after the initial high demand is fully satisfied. This usually happens in case of durable goods which offer their services over a long period of time. For example, there is hardly any demand for black and white TV sets due to change in trade and preference of buyers. Sometimes, market saturation is reached due to technological progress which makes an existing product obsolete. An example is manual typewriter. Its demand has reached the saturation point due to the introduction of computers.

5. Decline

By extensive promotional activity during the period of maturity and by minor restyling of products it may be possible to maintain (prolong) the current level of sales. However, sooner or later, sales will begin to decline as consumer tastes change and as superior products are launched. If left to follow the downward trend the product will eventually disappear as sales fall to low levels. Long before this happens, however, management may decide to drop the product once it ceases to contribute a reasonable amount toward company overheads and profits.

Product-range Strategy

Most companies market a number of different products and must formulate a product range strategy, providing for a regulated form of new product launches, with new products growing as old products reach maturity, so as to maintain an appropriate product mix of newly launched products, growth products and mature products.

Concluding Comments

Traditionally, the PLC has been thought of as reflecting the life of a product class or product category as a whole. The life cycle of black and white television sets as a group, without regard to model or brand, would clearly illustrate the concept. However, marketing managers also use PLC ideas in evaluating specific brands of products because most brands, as well as most products, have limited market lives.

The PLC, while useful to find at the stages of market acceptance, has its greatest practical use as planning tool. Furthermore, there have been a number of attempts to formulate marketing strategies that can be grouped as 'appropriate' to one stage or another of the PLC. For example, once a product entrers the declining stage, the appropriate steps to take are to cut back on promotion and other marketing activities.

The true value of the PLC should flow from an understanding of the changes in competitive conditions that occur at each stage and a clear idea of why they occur. The PLC also highlights the fact that conditions will change and that the PLC encourages the marketing planner to develop product improvements, or even totally new products to protect the organisation against the almost inevitable demise of their market offering.

Marketers can use the PLC as a basis for developing market strategies. Various marketing mix aspects are likely to be adjusted as a product moves through the life cycle stages. Marketing strategy formulation should always take the PLC into consideration. The PLC alone cannot tell the strategist what to do, but it is too powerful a concept to be ignored.

In general, marketing managers attempt to move their products successfully into the maturity phase of the PLC and then keep them there for considerable periods of time. However, certain products like toys, snack foods, cereals etc. are expected to have short lives. Marketers must be aware of this so that they can develop strategies appropriate to different phases of PLCs.

Managing the Product through Its Life Cycle

All products pass through life cycle. An ideal sequence of sales might be represented as follows:

product introduction → rapid growth → slow growth → leveling off → decline

Of course, some products never move beyond the introductory phase, others skip a stage or two, and still others continue on idenfinitely as if renewed from time to time. Whatever the pattern of sales, management must apply proper marketing tactics throughout the life cycle of a product. In this sense, the product life cycle is at least partially controllable by management. Each stage in the life cycle of a product will require a different balance among marketing strategies. Resources must be allocated to advertising, promotions, personal selling, distribution, and pricing in a way that meets the goals of the firm. During the product introduction phase, profits do not exist and the objective typically is to increase consumers' product awareness and trial purchases (and stimulate a healthy repurchase rate in the case of frequently purchased products). Advertising will be heavy to inform people. Promotions will be used to motivate dealers and consumers. The sales force will concentrate its efforts on building distribution. The price may be set low to prevent competition. Or it may be set high to reap early rewards.

During periods of rapid growth, necessary adjustments must be made. These should, in turn, be guided by market research, including so-called extensive studies of awareness, attitudes, intentions, trial purchase rates, and repeat purchase rates.

Advertising will shift from informative presentations to persuasion and may be reduced somewhat from initially high introductory levels. Promotion, too, will be reduced and shifted from trial-inducing tactics, such as sampling, to repeat purchase teasers, such as discount coupons. The sales force will work to strengthen dealer relationships and ensure that deliveries, product quality, and so forth will be fulfilled. Prices may be lowered somewhat to meet the competition.

Slow growth and leveling off periods demand still other responses. Advertising and promotion may have to be changed again to combat wear-out (*i.e.*, a decline in ad effectiveness over time) or meet the competition. Prices may have to be lowered still further. Market segmentation taskes on a special urgency as a means of survival and furthering of the goals of the firm.

As the *decline* phase approaches, the firm faces difficult decisions and market share must be weighed against goals and capabilities of the firm and the nature of the market and competition.

A final set of product decisions concern product-line planning. The firm must decide whether to have a product line and, if so, what its composition should be. The role of the product line also changes over time, with the leveling-off phase of the product life cycle revealing the product line's maximum contribution. Given the decision to employ product lines, the marketer's task must be viewed as allocating marketing expenditures to the support of policies that will best meet the firm's goals for profitability, market share, and growth. Enhancing brand equity and capitalising on it through line extensions demands special attention.

The product life-cycle concept is no doubt a fascinating concept, alluring in its simplicity, but a difficult one to apply in practice. The main difficulty is that it is very difficult to anticipate the life-cycle of a product in advance. Very few product managers can diagnose with clarity the precise phase of the life-cycle in which their respective products lie. Through statistical evidence one can assume that the product is moving from 'growth' to 'maturity'. If, for instance, one notices that a competitor is increasing its advertising budget and/or offering special discounts, one can assume that the growth phase is about to end. These are all of very little, if any, scientific value.

To the extent that one needs to understand where products are in their life-cycle for planning purposes, the concept has limited practical value. On the other hand, there are a few general principles associated with the concept which are of much practical importance.

All the evidence seems to suggest that product life-cycles are becoming shorter and shorter. This is particularly true in the field of domestic appliances and high-technology products, such as computers and cameras.

Synopsis for Learning

Q.1. What is product life cycle ?

Ans. The product life cycle refers to the typical sales pattern followed by a product over time as changing consumer tastes and technological innovation cause new products to emerge which supersede existing products.

Q.2. What are the phases of product's life cycle ?

Ans. The life cycle of a product has four phases : (a) product launch; (b) product growth phase; (c) product maturity; and (d) product decline.

2.8 PACKAGING AND BRANDING

Even after a product is developed and branded, it is important to adopt strategies for other product-related aspects of the marketing mix. One such product feature — and a strategic one for some products is packaging, which consists of all the activities of designing and producing the container or wrapper for a product. A package is the actual container or wrapper. Thus packaging is a business function and a package is an item.

A package is basically an extension of the product offered for sale. In many situations the packaging may be more important than the product it contains.

Packaging involves decisions about labels, inserts, instructions for product use, graphic design, as well as decisions about the sizes and types of physical containers for individual product items with the outer package.

Objectives

Three main objectives of packaging are :

1. **Protection**. The basic objective of packaging for industrial goods such as components and machinery is to protect the product while in transit. But packaging for consumer goods has a broader aim.

2. **Cognizability**. It is not enough for packaging to protect the product. Since the product is meant for sale in final form to the ultimate customers, it must also make the particular brand recognisable and appealing to buyers. This is very important in the case of packaged foodstuffs and other frequently purchased items from supermarkets and self-service stores. Here several brands of a product are displayed next to one another on the shelves, and it is important that the colour and design of a package attract the attention of the customers and thus play a major part in promotional strategy. The packaging lends charm to the product and reinforces the brand name. If the packaging does not induce the consumer to pick the commodity's brand in this situation, then all previous promotional efforts to differentiate these brands are wasted. Thus, **packaging is an aid to advertising**.

3. **Shortage and usage**. Packaging also facilitates the storage and use of products. Thus packages may be so designed as to conduce to the ease of handling by consumers and by members of the channel of distribution.

Functions. A package design is supposed to attract attention and convey an easily identifiable image. It must tell consumers what the product is and why they should buy it. In short, packaging provides :

(i) A containment function
(ii) A protection-in-transit function
(iii) A storage function
(iv) A usage facilitation function
(v) A promotion function.

Firstly, packaging protects the product on its way to the consumer. A package protects a product during shipment. Furthermore, it can prevent tampering with products — notably medications and food products — in the warehouse or the retail store.

Secondly, it provides protection after the product is purchased. Compared with bulk (that is, unpackaged) items, packaged goods generally are more convenient, cleaner, and less susceptible to losses from evaporation, spilling, and spoilage.

Thirdly, it becomes a part of company's trade, marketing, wholesaling and retailing programme. A product must be packaged to meet the needs of wholesaling and retailing middlemen.

Fourthly, it becomes a part of a company's consumer marketing programme. Packaging helps identify a product and thus may prevent substitution of competitive products.

All these suggest that developing and designing a package is not unlike designing the product itself. The package designer must be as buyer-oriented as the product designer.

Advantages

Ultimately, a package may become a product's differential advantage or at least a significant part of it. Today, with its marketing significance fully recognised, packaging is a major factor in the competition for customers. Therefore, full responsibility and authority for packaging should be with a firm's marketing department.

Recent developments have prompted even greater attention to packaging. Due to shortage of shelf space, it is not easy for manufacturers to get their products displayed in a retail outlet. If other marketing-mix elements are comparable, retailers are likely to purchase and display products having attractive functional packaging.

Furthermore, the widespread use of self-service selling means that the package must do the selling job at the point of purchase. In addition, the public's growing concerns about safeguarding products until they are purchased must be considered in packaging. Once the product is purchased, the package may still play a role. Many food products are now packaged so that they can go straight from the shelf or freezer into an oven.

Continuing developments call for management's scrutiny. We see new packaging materials replacing traditional ones — uncommon shapes, attractive look and other new features. All are intended to provide benefits to retailers and/or consumers and, as a result, selling points for marketers.

Disadvantages

However, packaging creates the following problems:

1. Packaging exhausts natural resources.
2. Packaging is too expensive.
3. Some forms of plastic packaging are health hazards.
4. Packaging is deceptive.
5. Used and discarded packaging contributes significantly to the consumer protection problem.

Conclusion

Marketing executives face a challange to solve these problems. At the same time, they must retain or even enhance the positive features of packaging, such as product protection, consumer convenience, and marketing support.

BRANDING OF PRODUCTS

The word brand is comprehensive. A brand is a name and/or mark intended to identify the product of one seller or group of sellers and differentiate the product from competing products. Branding helps buyers to determine which manufacturers' products are to be avoided and which are to be bought.

Branding serves both the buyer and the seller. Without branding, a buyer would find it difficult to recognise products that had proved satisfactory in the past.

Branding also helps seller to attract and build cadres of loyal customers and to show that that the firm stands behind what it offers. A brand that has achieved a quality reputation over time may make introducing new products very difficult. Part of the attraction of Clinic special shampoo is in connection with the original Clinic, a branded product with a long record of public acceptance.

Role of the brand

A 'brand' is an identity given by a supplier to its products or services. This identity comprises a number of values.

The brand might be given the supplier's own name, such as Heinz or Philips. It might be given a trademark such as Golden Wonder of Horlicks which is unconnected with the supplier's name. Or it might be based on the name of a retailer, such as Marks and Spencer or C&A modes.

The potential influence a brand identity can have is enormous. Brands must be well supported by advertising and promotion to enable companies to act as market leaders. Brands are used to differentiate products from their competitors. Brand identity is also used to facilitate recognition by buyers. This is because customer recognition and perception of different products is affected by their response to brand identity. Different brand identities will cause customers to see broadly similar products or services in different ways. They will seek them out and pay more for them.

Brand identities are important to consumer behaviour because they 'speed' the potential customer through the buying process described in an earlier chapter. Customers seeing a favoured brand (to which they may exhibit brand loyal behaviour), may cut short the analysis of alternatives prior to the purchase decision and proceed more rapidly towards the actual purchase. Brand loyal behaviour may therefore lessen the perceived difficulty or confusion associated wth making choices within the purchase process.

At the same time, the build up of brand loyal behaviour may decrease customer sensitivity to price. A strong brand image may well be linked to a higher price within the marketing mix.

The use and promotional support of brand identity is also a major factor in sustaining manufacturer capacity to market branded goods in the face of retailer preference for own brands. Therefore, suppliers may make strenuous efforts to build up and maintain a strong base of brand loyalty — a customer behaviour.

Brand Names and Trade Marks

A brand is any name, term, symbol, sign, design, or a unifying combination of these that identifies and distinguishes one product from another competitive product. A brand name is the verbal part of the brand. It consists of words, letters, and/or numbers that can be vocalised : Colgate, Cinthol and Gillette are all brand names. A brand mark is the part of the brand that appears in the form of a symbol, design, or distinctive colour or lettering. A brand mark is recognised by sight but cannot be expressed when a person pronounces the brand name.

Many branded products rely heavily upon some symbol for identification. Such unique symbols are referred to as brand names. When a brand name or company name is written in a distinctive way, this is called a logo.

A trademark is a legally protected brand name or brand mark. The owners of trademarks have exclusive rights to their use. Thus, the word 'trademark' is a legally defined term. A brand name is either a registered trademark or it is not.

A trademark is a brand that has been adopted by a seller and given legal protection. A trademark includes not just the brandmark, as most people think, but the brand name as well.

A brand name suggests what the product is supposed to do. It associates the product with an image that is meaningful to customers.

Brand names are often used in reinforcing an overall product concept. Good brands like Tata Tea, or Nescafe may communicate product attributes far better than any other variable in the marketing mix. Brand names and symbols say something about the product. But the brand name goes one step ahead of this. It says something about the buyers for whom the product is intended.

A good brand name is something that makes a product distinctive and easily remembered. It has something that sticks in the buyers' minds. To achieve this quality, most brand names are short, easy to pronounce, and unique.

CLASSIFICATION

One method of classifying brands is on the basis of ownership. The usual distinction is between '**producers**' (manufacturers) brands and '**distributors**' brands, the latter being owned by retailers or wholesalers.

Most of the brand names we are familiar with are owned and advertised by the firms that actually manufacture these products. These brands are called manufacturer brands (or national brands). But we frequently encounter products whose names are owned by retailers. Such brands are called distributor brands (or private brands). Brands owned and used by wholesalers are also called distributor brands.

Generic Brands

Some products carry neither a manufacturer's nor a distributor's brand. These are called generic brands and have certain consumer features such as a plain package.

Brand extension

The strategy of planning an 'old' name in use in 'new' areas is called brand extension. The objective of brand extension is to increase a company's market share or at least to prevent a fall in revenue in the face of falling demand.

Family brand

One form of brand extension is family branding. This practice involves using a single brand over a whole line of fairly closely related items. The basic objective of such branding is to take advantage of a brand's reputation and the goodwill associated with the name.

Individual brand

A product that proves dangerous or is of poor quality can destroy an organisation's overall image. A company's one brand may suffer greatly because of quality problems with other brands of the same name. This explains why some firms use individual brand names rather than family brand names.

Brand image

The symbolic value associated with the brand is referred to as brand image. This is why people say or think that 'this is my kind of product' or 'this is my brand.'

Changing a Brand Name

A change in the market environment or an initial 'mistake' in brand name selection may mean that a name or a symbol has to be changed. The original product name may have been a bad choice that was made worse over time. Or, the symbol served long and well, but it became inappropriate as times changed. This is why the name of Binaca has been changed and made Sibaca.

Reasons for Branding

For consumers, brands make it easy to identify goods or services. They help shoppers in moving quickly through a supermarket, departmental store, or any retail store and in making decisions regarding purchase. Brands also help assure consumers that they will get consistent quality when they reorder.

For sellers, brands can be promoted. They are easily recognised when displayed in a store or included in advertising. Branding reduces price comparisons, because brands are an important factor that needs to be considered in comparing different products. Finally, branding can add prestige to otherwise ordinary commodities (*e.g.,* Titan Watch, Kwality Icecream etc.).

However, all brands are not widely and favourably recognised by their target markets. And among those that are so recognised, many are unable to maintain a position of prominence. However, as a result of such activities as aggressive promotion and careful quality control, a few brands retain their leadership positions over a long time (*e.g.,* Dettol or Boroline). Consequently, huge amounts of money are spent to acquire companies that have dominant brands.

Reasons for Not Branding

Two responsibilities come with brand ownership :

(1) promoting the brand
(2) maintaining a consistent quality of output. Many firms do not brand their products because they are either unable or unwilling to assume these responsibilities.

Some items are not branded because they cannot be physically differentiated from other firms' products. Coal, cotton, wheat, etc. are examples of products for which product differentiation, including branding, is generally unknown. The perishable nature of products such as fresh fruits and vegetables too discourage branding.

Selecting a Good Brand Name

Some brand names are so good that they contribute to the success of products (*e.g.*, Philips radio); others are so poor that they are a factor in product failures (*e.g.*, Standard 2000 cars). Occasionally, products achieve success despite poor brand names. Brands can trasform ordinary commodities into preferred products!

Synopsis for Learning

Q.1. What is packaging ?

Ans. Packaging involves decisions about labels, inserts, instructions for use and graphic design.

Q.2. What is labelling ?

Ans. Labelling refers to informing about the product.

Q.3. What is the basic objective of packaging ?

Ans. The basic objective of packaging for industrial goods is to protect the product while in transit. In case of consumer goods, packaging must also make the particular brand (of the product) recognisable and appealing to buyers.

Q.4. What is a brand ?

Ans. A name, term, symbol or combination of these to identify a firm's products and differentiate them from competing products.

Q.5. What is the importance of branding ?

Ans. Brands can transform an ordinary commodity to a preferred product. Most brands are favourably recognised by their target markets. Moreover, branding can add prestige to otherwise ordinary commodities.

2.9 PRICING POLICIES AND STRATEGIES

Goal and Constraints in Pricing

Long gone are the days when prices were set haphazardly as an automatic and more or less fixed markup over costs. Today, price is viewed in an active and not merely reactive sense as one way to stimulate demand, compete effectively, or both. As a marketing tool, price offers a number of benefits to the firm. Firstly, unlike most communication, product, or distribution strategies that entail up-front costs as well as involved plans and procedures for their implementation, price changes do not require costly expenditures and can be made very easily and quickly. Secondly, consumers find appeals based on price easier to understand and respond to than the more indirect and abstract effects of advertising, product attribute, and distribution-based (*e.g.*, location) appeals. Finally, even when other marketing techniques such as personal selling or image advertising are the primary concern, price can give some extra support to the firm to make the other marketing tools more effective. On the other hand, price cutting can be taken as a threat by competitors and lead to price wars, in which all companies suffer. Also, price cuts can lead to negative inferences about product quality.

Significance of Pricing

Price has a special significance in that it ultimately 'pays' for all of the firm's activities. The price of a product is the major determinant of a firm's sales revenue.

Thus, proper pricing of a product or service is expected to increase demand. Price is perhaps the most flexible element of the marketing mix because it can be changed rapidly in response to changes in the business environment.

A price serves as a marketing tool by adding symbolic value to a good or service. A high price may suggest a status good, a low price may suggest a bargain and a discount coupon or rebate may be used to encourage purchase by people who would otherwise not buy the product offered.

Price is also related to other marketing variables such as product, place and promotion. Pricing strategies support the firm's other marketing strategies and must themselves be supported by these other strategies. In other words, all four aspects of the marketing mix must fit together to stimulate demand. Pricing must be coordinated with other aspects of marketing strategies. Prices bear a special relationship to promotion. One job of promotion is to show the potential buyer that an item is worth the price charged.

Price and marketing effectiveness

The ability to obtain a relatively high price for a brand indicates that the marketing plan behind the item is competitively sound and well-conceived. Price is often indicative of overall market effectiveness. The ability to maintain prices and volumes in the face of relatively stiff competition certainly indicates an excellent marketing organisation. Non-price competition allows the marketer to emphasise other marketing mix elements rather than relying solely on a lower price to gain customers.

Proper pricing facilitates all marketing activities. The marketing manager should realise that if products are too high other marketing variables will be adversely affected. Promotional efforts may not be as effective, for example, or it may be more difficult to obtain and utilise the desired channels of distribution. On the other hand, properly priced goods make the promotional programme far more effective than it used to be otherwise, and members of channels of distribution are usually more willing to handle items that represent good competitive values.

In short, price decisions can enhance or impede the marketing strategy or programme. Marketers seek to develop an integrated, internally consistent, and realistic combination of marketing mix elements. Prices should fit into a firm's marketing strategy, increasing the appeal of the marketing programme to the target market. **Pricing** begins with an understanding of the corporate mission, target markets, and marketing objectives. Then, pricing objectives (such as increasing market share) are developed. Next, management must estimate how much flexibility it has in establishing prices. Here, costs are studied to determine the lowest price level necessary to meet profit and other organisational objectives. Demand and competition determine the other end of the pricing strategy — the highest possible prices, or "what the market will bear." Prices are set between these extremes by deciding on price strategies that are consistent with pricing objectives. Specific methods are then used to set prices. Finally,.managerial skill is employed in pricing implementation and control, which includes effective monitoring to obtain feedback on the response of customers and competitors.

Role of Price in Marketing Strategy

Price is often used to enhance the image of a product, to increase sales through discount pricing, or — in combination with promotion, to build future sales. At times, however, price is an inactive element of the marketing mix, with firms using traditional markups over cost or following industry leaders.The use of price as a competitive tool may be avoided to fear of retaliation and price wars. But whether pricing is an active or inactive element, it is an integral part of the overall marketing programme. Determining the role that prices should play relative to other marketing mix variables establishes important boundaries and guidelines for pricing decisions.

Management faces two types of pricing decisions. New products must be priced, and the prices of existing products must be adjusted in the face of changing competitive, cost, and market conditions. Pricing strategies, particularly for new products, are a high- level responsibility shared by marketing and other executives. Pricing usually involves more executives from marketing and sales than other corporate areas, but these executives share the responsibility for pricing with other high-level executives. Lower-level executives are usually given a narrow range of discretion on specific items.

Price is used in different ways by different companies, depending on the role it plays in the overall marketing programme. Both the manufacturer's and the dealers' margins make possible a variety of customer services and help support various promotional efforts.

The role assigned to price in the marketing programme should be consistent with decisions about other marketing mix variables. Decisions to set a price on an item should consider the impact that the price might have on other items in the *product line*. Many firms carry substitute products (Procter & Gamble's Tide and All detergents) or complementary products (cricket balls and bats). In pricing one product, the impact on related products must be considered.

Pricing decisions are intertwined with *promotional decisions*. A price change may bring changes in labeling, advertising copy, or advertising messages. The costs associated with such changes may be greater than the additional revenue generated by the price change. On the other hand, promotional expenditures, by increasing sales, may result in production and marketing economies of scale, thus reducing unit costs and allowing greater flexibility in setting prices. Price levels must be appropriate to the promotional image that is projected. *Pricing decisions must also be made in light of channel/distributor interests.*

The pricing process begins with the goals of the firm and the objectives for the brand in question. Common options are to view price as a means to achieve or maintain market share, stimulate primary and secondary demand, increase short- or long-run profitability, signal competitors that one will respond aggressively to threats or alternatively wishes to avoid a price war, discourage new entrants, strengthen and reward intermediaries (*e.g.*, by providing them with healthy margins), communicate value to consumers, stay within the law, or simply act in a socially responsible way. Most of these ends require that the firm conduct research to determine the relationship between price and sales.

With rare exceptions, prices are constrained to fall within a relatively narrow range. At the bottom end, costs provide a floor below which the firm cannot survive for long. At the top end, prices are constrained by competitive undercutting or by a ceiling on what consumers can afford or what they feel gives them value. In between lie the degrees of freedom open to a firm.

The determinants of costs must also be found out. Fixed costs that are large relative to variable costs often dictate low pricing in order to increase capacity utilisation. On the other hand, large variable costs relative to fixed costs sometimes force the price up. In either case, however, efforts will be made to drive down both fixed and variable costs. Economies of scale, and product line considerations play roles here. Moreover, overall strategic goals must be taken into account. An overall cost leadership orientation will results in lower prices than will a product differentiation approach, for example.

Pricing must be coordinated with all the tactics used in implementing the marketing mix. This is not only because the various tactics interact and can thwart or augment each other but also because profits and other goals are proportional to the magnitude of marketing mix expenditures that stimulate demand. Therefore, the effects or demand of all of the marketing tactics including price must be ascertained when determining price.

Pricing Policies and Practices of Modern Firms

Pricing come in various forms, they are not limited to a single "purchase price." Quantity discounts, "2 for 1" deals, promotion allowances, coupons, and other sales promotion techniques widen the scope of pricing tactics. Let us explore the options open to a marketer.

For a new product, either a price skimming or penetration pricing tactic is warranted. With *price skimming*, a high price is set. The hope is that there are enough customers who will be willing to pay a premium for the brand. As this market dries up, price will be reduced gradually to draw in other customers. Price skimming is used when one wants to create an image of high product quality, when rivals will be slow to enter the market and when buyers value the product highly.

Penetration pricing is the tactic of introducing a product at a low price, perhaps in anticipation of future cost declines and a fast growing market. Over time, the price may be raised, but not necessarily. Penetration pricing is frequently employed as part of a market share strategy, as well as a means to generate primary demand. Unlike skimming, penetration pricing tends to discourage new entrants in that it signals strong price competition and relatively low profits. Penetration pricing works best when production and distribution channels are in place, consumers are price sensitive, and the product is a frequently purchased good, and sufficient economies of scale are enjoyed by the firm. We will speak more about these two pricing strategies later in this chapter.

The prices of industrial goods are strongly influenced by costs and competition. Indeed, many such goods are sold through competitive bidding arrangements.

By contrast, pricing of consumer goods necessarily is done much more on the basis of company needs and before presentation to the consumer. Although market research is performed, so many buyers are involved, with different tastes and resources, that an "average" price must be set. In addition, the manufacturer must often take wholesalers and retailers into account when setting price. Intermediaries require incentive and compensation (reward) for their efforts. This complicates the price-setting task.

Pricing decisions must be made throughout the life cycle of a product. Increases in competition throughout the product life cycle drive prices downward. At the same time, variations in growth, market share, and profitability across brands in a product line interact with price decisions in a complex way and has to be watched carefully.

Pricing Objectives

Many firms fail to establish specific objectives for their pricing programmes. Pricing objectives should be clear, concise, and understood by all involved in making pricing decisions. Furthermore, these objectives should be so stated as to enable those charged with pricing responsibility to compare performance with them.

A study of pricing in corporations highlight the diversity of pricing objectives in some of the largest companies. Very few firms state their pricing objectives in terms of maximising profits. Rather, most try to attain a satisfactory or target level of profits or return on investment (ROI).

Studies have indicated that most important corporate pricing objectives are the following:

- To meet the prices of competitors.
- To follow the price of the most important marketer in each area.
- To maintain existing market share.

Even companies whose primary pricing objectives were stated in terms of profit margin or return on investment had collateral pricing objectives:

- To promote new products.
- To stabilise industry prices.
- To maintain a full line of consumer goods including products and novelties.

Specific pricing objectives used by firms are shown in Table 2.7. Organisations usually have a set of objectives — some primary, others collateral; some short run, others long run. Whatever their type, objectives should be specific, written, and operational.

Table 2.7 : Pricing Objectives

Growth	***Cash flow***
Sales or profit growth	Rapidly recover new product development costs.
Market share growth	***Enhancement of other strategy elements***
Profit	Provide a promotional theme.
Maximise return on investment	Make a product "visible" and create interest.
Maximise (or satisfice) short- and long-run profits	Fill out the firm's product line.
Competitive	Contribute to the image of the product and the firm.
Discourage entrants, and speed exit of marginal firms.	Build traffic.
Maintain price leadership.	Be regarded as "fair" by middlemen and customers.
Discourage price-cutting and stabilise market prices.	
Rapidly establish market position.	

Establishing Prices

Setting pricing objectives, determining the extent of pricing flexibility, and selecting price strategies provide considerable direction to management for setting specific prices. But how are prices for specific products actually set? A sound approach to pricing must incorporate cost, competition, and demand factors. More than one price-setting method is typically used, and all three factors should be considered.

Cost-Oriented Approaches

Because costs establish the floor for a possible price range, two commonly used cost-oriented approaches show how cost is actually used to set prices.

Cost-Plus / Markup Pricing. Cost-plus pricing simply involves adding a percentage of the cost to set the price. Markup pricing is a variation of cost-plus pricing in that markups are calculated as a percentage of the selling price rather than as a percentage of the cost. But since only the cost and the desired percentage markup on selling price are known to the manager, a formula may be used to determine the price :

$$\text{Selling price} = \frac{\text{Average unit cost}}{1 - \text{Desired markup percentage}}$$

If an item costs Rs 7 and the markup is 30%, then the price is set at Rs 10 [Rs 7 ÷ (1 – 0.3)].

Manufacturers usually add an allowance for fixed overhead costs to unit variable costs and then add a percentage markup (on price) to cover selling, administrative, and general expenses as well as a desired profit percentage.

Wholesalers and retailers typically mark up each class of products by a different fixed percentage over the prices they pay. Unlike manufacturers, trading organisations seldom attempt to allocate fixed and operating expenses to each product. Instead, percentage markups for each product category are most frequently determined by industry tradition, company strategy (*e.g.*, price-level strategy), individual operating expenses (rent, insurance, pilferage, etc.) expected turnover, and various other factors.

Successful new ventures are sometimes founded on innovative, low margin pricing, in the hope of high volume to provide a good return.

Break-Even and Target Return Pricing

Another cost-oriented method — break-even pricing — determines the level of sales needed to cover all of the relevant fixed and variable costs.

Target return pricing. Popular among manufacturers, is based on break-even analysis. The total costs of producing and offering goods for sale are determined, and a target percentage return is then added to those costs at the standard output level. The sum of the total costs and the target return is the total revenue that must be generated. The selling price is determined by dividing the target total revenue level by the standard output level. Suppose that a firm has a standard output level of 80,000 units and that management wishes to achieve a 20% return on the total costs at that level of output (Rs. 2,60,000). Then Rs 52,000 (20% x Rs 2,60,000) is added to Rs 2,60,000 to obtain a target total revenue of Rs 3,12,000 and the price must be set at Rs. 3.90 (Rs 3,12,000 / 80,000) to achieve that revenue.

The obvious weakness of this and other cost-oriented pricing methods is that prices determined according to these methods are derived from costs without regard to market demand. The actual quantity sold at the determined price could easily be greater or less than the quantity required. Yet this method helps ensure that prices exceed all costs and, therefore, contribute to profit. It is also essential to incorporate inflation factors into price-setting methods and to install systems that provide timely information on increasing costs.

Competition-Oriented Approaches

Many firms set prices largely in relation to the prices of competitors. Although management in such a firm cannot totally disregard cost and demand factors, it gives primary attention to positioning its firm's prices relative to the prices of competing firms.

Going-Rate Pricing. One method is **going-rate pricing** — setting prices equal to or a certain percentage above or below competitors' prices. Whether or not this method is appropriate depends on the firm's pricing objectives; the structure of the industry (*e.g.*, oligopoly); whether there is excess capacity; the relative production, selling, and administrative costs of competitors; and customers' perceptions of the firms' products compared to those of competitors. Furthermore, managers often use competitive pricing when :

(i) They believe that larger competitors are better able to select appropriate prices, so they "follow the leader."

(ii) Retaliatory price changes are likely beyond a given range, and price changes by competitors have a substantial effect on company sales.

(iii) Costs, demand, and other factors that affect sales and profits are stable enough to make it possible to rely on following general industry pricing trends.

Many retailers employ competition-oriented pricing methods in conjunction with the cost markup method. Retailers hire comparison shoppers who survey competitors' prices on selected items, and individual store managers are given the authority to adjust prices.

Perceived Value Pricing. The task of determining prices for industrial products is basically the same as the task of determining prices for consumer products. Yet the price of an industrial product is probably determined somewhat more by the exact potential benefit that the product offers the buyers. This is especially true when an industrial product faces little direct competition.

Perceived value pricing is also applicable to consumer products, for which it is often based on a psychological pricing strategy. This pricing method is, of course, based on price elasticity. The willingness of customers to pay a higher price depends on their perception of the fairness of the price — of the quality they get for the price they pay.

Perceptions sometimes differ from reality, and conducting market research on perceptions as they affect demand elasticity is often very useful.

Once prices have been established, plans to implement and control pricing decisions must be executed. Company sales-people, channel resellers, and ultimate consumers or users are most immediately affected by price decisions. The responses of customers to price decisions are often anticipated through marketing research. But the reactions of sales-people and distributors should also be sought, because these two groups are usually responsible for implementing price decisions.

PRICING TECHNIQUES AND METHODS

A wide range of pricing strategies are available to marketing managers. See Table 2.8. And managers may use several strategies to arrive at a price that reflects market realities, costs, consumer perception and other considerations. Pricing strategies may be broadly categorised under five headings as shown in this Table.

Table 2.8 : Basic Pricing Strategies

1. Differential pricing strategies (i) One-price policy (ii) Variable pricing (iii) Second market discounting (iv) Skimming **2. Competitive pricing strategies** (i) Customary pricing (ii) Charm pricing (iii) Penetration pricing (iv) Predatory pricing (v) Inflationary pricing	**3. Product line pricing strategies** (i) Loss leaders pricing (ii) Captive pricing (iii) Price lining **4. Psychological and image pricing strategies** (i) Odd price vs. even price strategy (ii) Prestige pricing / price signalling **5. Distribution-based strategies** (i) F.O.B. (ii) Delivered prices (iii) Basing-point pricing

Differential Pricing

(i) One price

A basic pricing decision is whether to maintain a fixed price regardless of who the customer is or to vary the price from buyer to buyer. Organisations that sell the same product at different prices to different buyers have a differential pricing strategy. Charging the same price from all buyers is termed a one-price strategy (or one-price policy).

A one-price policy provides the advantage of simplicity of administration that leads, in turn, to lower personnel expense. Thus, a departmental store's one-price policy allows it to employ less experienced, lower paid clerks. The television dealer, however, must hire active sales people — and pay them comparatively high commissions — to administer its variable price policy.

(ii) Variable price

However, some strong companies, even at the retail level, charge different prices from different customers. This is known as variable pricing. Such pricing practice is observable in electronic goods and real estate. There are many situations where seller and buyer engage in a bit of give and take. The variable pricing policy allows for this.

(iii) Second market discounting

Second market discounting is a differential pricing strategy designed to sell the brand at one price in the core target market and at a reduced price in a second market segment. For example, cinemas, airlines and electric supply corporations vary their prices among buyers. The cinema's noon price is usually less than the evening price. The price differences to different market segments are usually treated as 'discounts' rather than price variants.

New Product Prices. Determining the prices of new products is basically similar to determining the prices for any other products. Pricing objectives for new products consider the role that these products (and their prices) will play in the organisation's overall marketing strategy. Typically, the pricing objectives for new products have more latitude than those for existing products.

Pricing flexibility is also greater for new products. For products in the growth, maturity, or decline stages of the product life cycle, there is usually growing competition and a smaller number of acceptable prices. The prices of such products often have to be reduced. New products with some degree of competition usually offer the option of a skimming or penetration strategy. We have already discussed these two strategies earlier in this chapter. So here we make a brief review of the two concepts.

(iv) Skimming and price reduction strategies

A skimming price is a high price intended to 'skim the cream of the market'. It is best employed at the start of a product's life (cycle) when the product is novel and consumers are uncertain about its value. For example, pocket calculators first sold at prices of around Rs 800. They can be now purchased for as little as Rs 150.

This pattern of changing a high price and systematically reducing price over time allows companies to generate sufficient revenue initially that covers the cost of product development but also the initial high costs of bringing the product to target market. A skimming strategy assumes a relatively strong (inelastic) demand for the product, often because the product has status value or because it is a truly new, breakthrough item. Price is used as a means to segment the market on the basis of buyers' income or degree of need for the product. As prices are reduced in response to competitive pressures, new market segments become key targets.

Thus, a skimming pricing strategy sets introductory prices at high levels relative to costs so as to "skim the cream" off the market. In the absence of immediate competition and price-inelastic customers, firms often consider it safe to set initial new product prices high relative to costs and to lower the prices gradually as market conditions change. Skimming profits allows sellers to recover their investment rapidly, though the high margins tend to attract competition. Makers of personal computers charged high prices at the outset, but there has been competitive price warfare in recent years.

(v) Penetration pricing

We have already discussed in detail this pricing strategy. We know that a penetration pricing strategy sets new product prices low relative to costs. This strategy is usually employed to rapidly acquire a large share of a potential market.

2. Competitive Pricing

Competitive pricing strategies are used by organisations that have competitive pricing objectives. Dominant firms exploit their positions. Weak firms may opt for the role of a follower. Organisations concerned with meeting competition quite naturally set prices at levels equal to those of competitors. This is known as going rate pricing. This strategy is adopted to avoid price war.

Price leadership strategies are generally implemented by organisations that have large shares of the market. Such an organisation has adequate market-information and enough control over its distribution system to determine a price level that others will follow. The price leader typically is able to make price adjustments without starting a price war and can make its announced price stick. Some organisations, especially those in weak competitive positions, adopt a follow-the-leader strategy, simply by pricing as the market leader does.

(i) Customary Pricing

Customary pricing is the practice of using a simple, well-known price for an extended period of time. Thus, for as long as possible, newspaper publishers have tried to maintain the price of a daily paper at Rs 1.50, theatres have attempted to keep the price of movie tickets at about Rs 15. The logic of customary pricing seems to be that consumers get used to paying a certain amount over time and, especially for frequently purchased products, might come to resent a price change. In fact, frequent changes in price cause confusion and consumer irritation (if not complete resistance).

(ii) Charm Pricing

Sellers often set prices on the basis of the presumed psychological meaning of the numbers used to express the prices — a method called charm pricing. A high price is set with the hope that buyers will consider the product as unique, consisting of special features. A high price might even be sought by some potential purchasers as part of their need to express a particular lifestyle or demonstrate their wealth and tastes. Prices of goods and services in boutiques, specially shops, and exclusive restaurants often arise from a conspicuous consumption pricing policy.

Another form of charm pricing is called *odd-or-even pricing*. A common belief among some retailers is that a price should end only in an odd number (usually a 5, 7 or 9) or only in an even number (typically an 8). Furthermore, whenever possible, it is recommend that the odd or even number be part of an overall price set just below a round number.

Still another variant of charm pricing is what one might call *representational pricing*. Here, the seller selects a price for a product on the basis of the symbolic meaning of the number as reflected in another object, event, or behaviour associated with that number. The practitioners of representational pricing hope that the effect or feelings connected with a number will transfer to their products and perhaps be remembered more readily.

Relatively low margins discourage the entry of competitors and often allow the entering firm to establish itself with a large market share. However, if a market is large enough, even low prices may attract competitors. The appropriateness of a penetration strategy depends on the firm's ability to retain its desired market share once competition develops.

Thus, a penetration price is a low introductory price. It may even result in a loss. A penetration pricing strategy is implemented when a competitive situation is well established (or soon will be) and a low price in the introduction stage of the product life cycle will be necessary to break into the market. It is an alternative to skimming. Its objective is to enable the product to become established and survive in the long run. This method has two advantages :

1. Firstly, penetration price reduces the threat of competitive imitation because the small profit margin discourages low-cost imitators from entering the market.
2. Secondly, by increasing the size of the total market and / or market share, the marketer establishes a strong brand loyalty and increases the brand's dominance in consumers' minds. To restrict competition, a monopolist might employ the practice of pricing low to eliminate competition, and then pricing high. This is known as predatory pricing strategy. (In some countries this pricing practice is unlawful.)

If the odds are against retaining an initial foothold, it may be better to skim and profit more heavily for a short time. The uncertainty that accompanies new products cannot be totally eliminated. Monitoring new product prices is therefore very difficult. Although well-developed strategies should not be abandoned lightly, management must be prepared to make ongoing adjustments to better match prices with distributor and customer requirements.

3. Product Line Pricing

Many pricing strategies consider the product line as the appropriate unit of analysis rather than individual product items. The objecctive is to maximise profits for the total product line rather than to obtain the maximum profits for any individual item in the product line. A camera manufacturer may set low prices for camera in the hope of making significant profits on films. This is known as *captive pricing strategy*.

(i) Leader pricing and Balt pricing

A common pricing policy that sacrifices profit on a particular item for total profit is loss **leader pricing**. **Balt pricing** is used to attract customers by advertising low-priced models of, say, televisions.

(ii) Price Lining Policies

In some marketing situations, there appear to be prices that are often attractive. Dress manufacturers often charge Rs 299 for a shirt, Rs 275 for another, Rs 225 still another. These prices are greatly attractive to buyers. The practice of charging different prices for almost similar varieties of dresses is called *price lining*.

(iii) Price Lining

Price lining is the strategy of offering a number of variations of a type of product with each variation priced at a different level. Generally, three different versions of a product will be displayed at three different prices. The three product versions are known as a "price line". The practice is nearly universal in the retail trade: fast-food chains offer three sizes of hamburgers (papa, mama and teen burgers); appliance stores sell inexpensive, medium-priced and high-priced brands of radios and televisions; and supermarkets provide inexpensive dealer brands and moderate and high priced national brands of the same products.

In addition, the ability to offer a price line gives merchants considerable leverage to entire buyers to seek products just above their normal price and quality level. This practice is termed *trading up* and is, of course, practised by the automobile sellers.

One danger with price lining is that it may be confusing and makes producers' tasks more difficult. Too many alternatives and options may be costly to produce, stock and maintain as well. Then too, if some consumers originally willing to pay a higher price find that the lower priced model is "satisfactory", sellers may even earn less revenue.

(iii) Psychological and Image Pricing

Some companies charge old prices like Rs 19.90 or Rs 4.98 or Rs 90.99. Such prices have a favourable psychological effect on consumers. However, such prices may result in more sales, especially if the market is dealing in relatively cheap items.

Status goods like Adidas T-shirts are often priced high. These are called prestige price, which are charged to portray a quality image for a brand.

5. Distribution-based Pricing

Many prices are based on geographical distances separating the buyer from the point of sale or point of production. The prices are not always higher as the buyer moves away from the seller. However, in most cases, geographic pricing policies reflect management's attempts to recover some or all of the costs involved in shipping products over distances.

(i) F.O.B.

A common form of geographic pricing is F.O.B. which may be read 'freight on board' or 'free on board'. The letters are followed by a specific place such as F.O.B. Calcutta or F.O.B. factory.

(ii) Delivered price

When a departmental store advertises that the price of a sofa is Rs 5,000 delivered in an area, the delivery charges are included in the price paid by the consumer.

A variation of this is ***zone pricing***, where geographic zones are delineated and prices increase as the number of zone lines crossed in completion of the transaction accumulate. The parcel post system employs zone pricing, charging a customer on basis of the weight of the parcel and the number of zones it will travel before arriving at its destination.

A company that views the whole country as its delivery zone and charges the same price in every location is practicing a special form of delivered pricing called uniform delivered pricing. Such prices are called postage stamp prices and are attractive to marketers in that they simplify pricing and nationwide advertising.

(iii)Basing-point pricing

This pricing system involves the selection of one or more locations to serve as basing points. Customers are charged prices and shipping fees as if their orders were shipped from these points regardless of where the commodities actually originated.

6. Establishing the Exact (Administered) Price

Many marketers, especially retailers and wholesalers, rely on a simple method for determining their resale price. The cost of the product is noted and a simple percentage markup is added to arrive at the selling price. For example, cost of Re 1 and a markup on selling price of 33.3% yields a selling price of Rs 1.50. The 50-paise markup is expressed as 33.3% because 50 paise is one-third of the selling price of Rs 1.50. The term markup on selling price is then used. Certain industries have established traditional markups for the various channel members.

Keystoring is the term for the retailer's policy of doubling the wholesale price of an item and making this the regular price. During puja season, many stores will price their merchandise at keystore plus another 15%. Thus, when the product goes on sale, the price is only marked down to the traditional keystone price. For example, an item bought for Rs 20 that is marked up to sell for Rs 46 is then put 'on sale' for Rs 40. However, consumers have realised that the real price is Rs 40 and they are now waiting for the product to go on sale below the Rs 40 level before purchasing.

(i) Cost-plus Pricing

Manufacturers often choose to use a pricing method similar to mark-up in that they determine what costs were involved in producing an item and then add an amount to the cost total to arrive at a price.

Like mark-up cost-plus is easy to use once an appropriate addition to the cost has been determined.

Much government contracing is done on this basis, with the supplier of a product or service submitting the cost figures associated with a particular assignment and adding a reasonable profit margin to yield a total price for the project.

Average-cost method

If a marketer identifies all the costs associated with the manufacturing and marketing of a product or provision of service, it will be possible to determine what the average cost of a single unit of the product or service might be.

$$\frac{\text{All costs (Rs 80,000)}}{\text{No. of units produced (100)}} = \text{Average cost of a single unit} = \text{Rs } 800$$

To do this, however, it is necessary to know how much of the product will be demanded and produced.

If a margin for profit was added to the total cost figures, a likely price for a unit of the goods could be calculated. Thus, with a profit margin of Rs 20,000 we have

All costs (Rs 80,000) + Profit (Rs 20,000) = Rs 1,00,000.

$\frac{\text{Rs } 1,00,000}{100 \text{ units}}$ = Average cost of a single unit including profit margin = Rs 1,000

Because the total cost figure of Rs 1,00,000 now includes a margin for profit, the price of a single unit of the product will be Rs 1,000.

(ii) Target Return Pricing

A marketing manager using target return pricing first calculates a total fixed cost figure. A target return, usually expressed as a percentage of investment (or net capital employed), is added to total cost to arrive at a figure representing total fixed costs and target return.

RESALE PRICE MAINTENANCE

One important aspect of pricing practice is that, particularly in the case of consumer goods, the firm producing a product is concerned with a channel of distribution and must give some consideration to intermediate prices, for example those of wholesalers and retailers. Under resale price maintenance the producer controls prices all the way to the final consumer. Resale price maintenance is an example of a restrictive pricing practice normally followed by monopolists or oligopolists. It refers to agreements whereby manufacturers independently or jointly set minimum prices at which their products could be sold by wholesales and retailers. It is a practice whereby a supplier prescribes price at which all retailers are to sell the product to final buyers. The main objective of resale price maintenance centres on the fact that it restricts or eliminates retail price competition and, by prescribing uniform retail margins, it serves to protect inefficient retailers.

The practice of resale price maintenance is illegal in some countries such as the U.K. This has led to the rapid expansion of mass retailers such as supermarket chains. One important aspect of pricing in practice is that, particularly in the case of consumer goods, the firm producing a product is concerned with a channel of distribution and must give some consideration to intermediate prices, for example, those of wholesalers and retailers. Under resale price maintenance the producer controls prices all the way to the final buyer.

Now, the practice is largely illegal in most countries. Still, prices may be recommended by the manufacturer. But under the law, each distributor must have complete freedom to accept or ignore the recommendation.

Resale price maintenance in the Indian context refers to agreements between suppliers collectively to withold goods from a retailer who fails to charge the maintained price. As per the Monopolies and Restrictive Trade Practices Act of 1969 (amended in 1984) if retail price maintenance is in the public interest then this can be done under the following situations : that, in the absence of retail price maintenance,

(i) the quality and variety of goods available for sale would be substantially reduced;

(ii) the number of establishments in which the goods are sold would be substantially reduced;

(iii) retail prices would increase;

(iv) goods would be sold by retail under conditions likely to endanger health, in consequence of their misuse by the public; and

(v) any necessary services actually provided in connection with — or after the sale of — the goods by retail would cease to be provided or would be substantially reduced.

CHANGING PRICES

Nonprice competition is often stressed in marketing strategies, in part because price changes are easy for competitiors to counter. It is far more difficult to directly counter a strong brand image with unique product features than with a price change. Marketing strategies consist of a large number of marketing variables, of which the price variable is sometimes considered the best.

CONCLUSION

No doubt, price is an important part of a company's marketing strategy. However, price is only one factor which the modern company has to consider in planning its marketing effort. If a company is to succeed in sustaining its growth and profitability over time then it needs to maintain a constant stream of products which are acceptable to consumers (which often involve market research to determine what consumers want and how these wants are changing over time). It must also differentiate these products in the eyes of consumers from similar products offered by competitors, by means of styling differences, distinctive packaging and professional efforts geared to bring the company's products to the attention of consumers.

Synopsis for Learning

Q.1. What is resale price maintenance ?

Ans. In short, resale price maintenance refers to the pricing technique under which the supplier forces the dealer to sell his (her) product on a minimum price. In other words, resale price maintenance refers to fixing by manufacturers of minimum prices at which their products may be resold by distributors. Prices must be stated as recommended prices in advertisements and dealers can sell above or below that price. This practice is followed in oligopoly.

Q.2. What is the consequence of resale price maintenance ?

Ans. Resale price maintenance often leads to formation of price-fixing cartels of producers. In many countries, this practice has been stopped by passing laws. Manufacturers can still recommend retail price but cannot legally enforce it.

2.10 SALES MANAGEMENT

Effective sales executives insist upon sound organisation. They recognise that the sales organisation must achieve both qualitative and quantitative personal-selling objectives.

Importance of the Sales Function to Organisations

In marketing, the sales function is most typically considered part of promotion. It is one of the ways in which information about products and services is presented to customers, and it plays an important role in promoting practically all products. For complex and expensive products, personal selling is very important, because it requires persuasive and informative promotional efforts that can only be delivered personally. But even in marketing consumer packaged goods, such as paper towels and cookies, the sales function is important to secure retailer cooperation. Convincing a retailer to allocate shelf space to new consumer products, or to not take away shelf space from existing products in favour of a competitor's new products, often requires the same persuasive and informative promotional effort as selling new computers. It seems clear, therefore, that sales can seldom be overlooked in a company's overall marketing strategy.

Functions of Sales-people

For many companies, sales-people show a company's marketing orientation: people committed to understanding and serving customers as much as possible while maintaining their company's profitability and reputation. A well-trained and motivated sales-force can be the focal point where all aspects of a company's marketing strategy come together — the means by which that strategy is communicated to customers. At the same time, sales-people can contribute substantially to develop and enhance the company's overall marketing efforts. There is a mutual influence between a company's marketing orientation and its sales-people's behaviour. Companies that show a marketing orientation through other aspects of their marketing mix (*e.g.*, products, advertising, pricing, distribution) hire better performing sales-people, which, in turn, increases the company's reputation and marketing effectiveness. For many companies, the sales-force is the primary point of contact with customers and the market environment.

In addition to being responsive to customer needs, sales-people must also respond to requests from other areas of their own organisations. For example, management may ask sales representatives to provide new product ideas or to evaluate proposed advertising, sales promotions and after-sales service. Salesperson inputs is important because local markets can vary substantially from national trends. Sales-people also identify opportunities for new business for other areas of their company and coordinate their activities with other marketing efforts, such as sales promotions and advertising.

Sales-people demonstrate a marketing orientation via their close association with the company's image. For many customers, the salesperson "is" the company, and buyers equate continuity in the sales-force with supplier continuity in all other areas. This often translates into customers wanting to deal with the same person on a repeated basis. Although sales-people can sometimes transfer an account relationship to other personnel, over time they can expect to accumulate a number of personal customer relationships that they must maintain.

Overall, it is easy to see that sales-people do not find the sales stereotypes of yesterday. Although their primary responsibilities are to respond to the demands of actual and potential customers and to present their companies' products in the best possible manner, sales-people contribute significantly to a company's overall marketing efforts. Their jobs often require understanding and coordinating virtually all areas of the business, and their efforts influence many other aspects of the marketing mix.

Selling is a part of a company's promotional effort. However, the conduct of the selling function is based on the existence of a sales organisation. The sales organisation is the medium through which personal-selling strategy is implemented. A well-designated sales organisation performs the selling function effectively and efficiently.

2.11 SALES ORGANISATION

A sales organisation serves two main purposes. It is both an orienting point for cooperative endeavour and a structure of human relationships. It is a group of individuals trying jointly to reach certain important objectives, and bearing informal and formal relations to one another. The whole concept of a sales organisation is based on the implicit notion that individual members cooperate to attain corporate goals.

Some companies' structures allow sales managers to supervise many sales-people. For example, a company with a relatively simple product line and homogeneous customer base may have 20 to 30 sales-people under a single manager, with sales-people operating effectively with little supervision. A sales-force organisation with 20 sales-people and a span of control of 10 is illustrated in Fig.2.9. For companies with complex product lines or customer relationships, it may be impractical for a sales manager to have more than five or six sales-people to supervise. Moreover, as the total number of sales-people needed to serve the market increases, so does the number of managers required to maintain the same span of control.

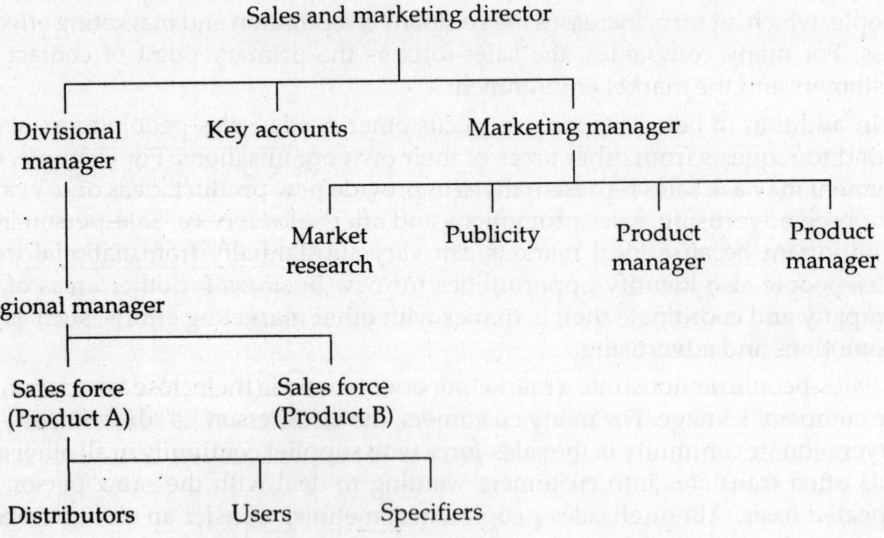

Fig. 2.9 : Sales organisation with span of control at 10

Fig. 2.10 illustrates a company that also has 20 sales-people, but with a span of control of 5. The narrower span of control adds a layer of management.

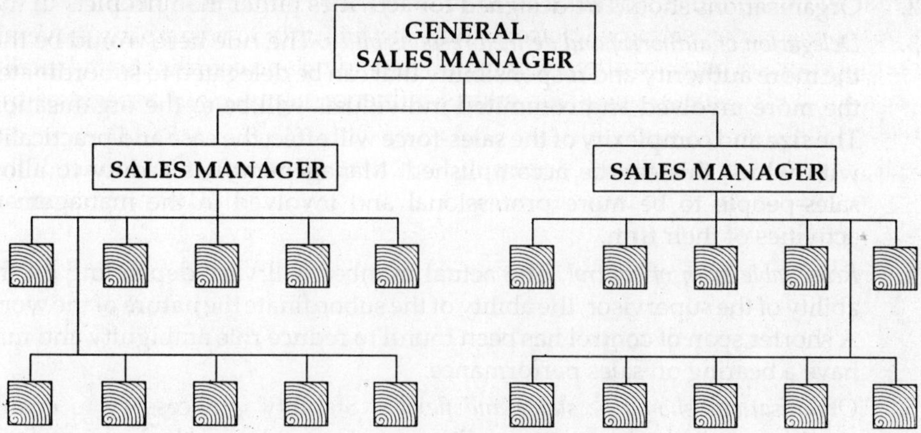

Fig. 2.10 : Sales organisation with span of control at 5

CHOICES IN SALESFORCE ORGANISATION

In addition to establishing corporate and marketing strategy and formulating sales-force objectives, one of the important tasks of management is organising selling effort. Decisions have to be taken on various dimensions of the organisational problem, such as the type of organisational structure, the degree of specialisation and the size of the sales-force.

PRINCIPLES OF ORGANISATION

P. F.Drucker suggests that good organiation structure does not by itself produce good performance but a poor organisation structure makes good performance impossible. Fig. 2.11 shows the sales organisation of a large firm.

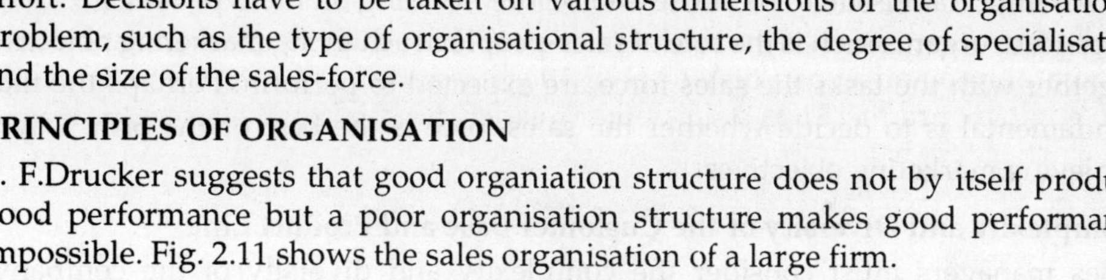

Fig. 2.11 : Sales organisation of a large firm

The following six points may be noted in this context:

1. Organisational structure should be marketing-oriented.
2. Organisations should be designed for activities rather than people.
3. *Delegation of authority and defined responsibility.* The rule here would be that the more authority and responsibility that can be delegated to subordinates, the more involved and commited individuals will be to the organisation. The size and complexity of the sales-force will affect the ease and practicality with which this can be accomplished. Management has a duty to allow sales-people to be more professional and involved in the management activities of their firm.
4. *Reasonable span of control.* The actual number will vary depending on the ability of the supervisor, the ability of the subordinate the nature of the work. A shorter span of control has been found to reduce role ambiguity and may have a bearing on sales performance.
5. *Organisations should be stable and flexible.* Stability is necessary to ensure continuing viable operating conditions and procedures which are efficient, together with flexibility to enable the enterprise to adjust to dynamic market conditions or particular customer or competitive circumstances.
6. *Organisations should be balanced and coordinated in the activities to be performed.* So sufficent care has to be taken to recruit, train and motivate employees.

An important issue to be addressed before deciding on the type and size of the sales-force organisation is the role of sales-people in achieving marketing objectives together with the tasks the sales force are expected to perform. Perhaps the most fundamental is to decide whether the sales-force is the best or the only way of achieving marketing objectives.

Complexity and Diversity of the Customer Base and Product Line

Sales managers must consider the complexity and diversity of the company's customers and products when structuring sales-forces. Sales managers can deploy sales-people on the basis of geography, product, account size, or combinations of these variables in order to better respond to market conditions.

Geographic Structure

Geographic structure is one of the most commonly used and easiest to administer methods for deploying the sales-force. In a typical design, managers divide the company's total market (state, multistate, national or global) into regions and subregions with roughly equal sales potential. Each region is a single salesperson's exclusive responsibility and is designed to provide adequate challenge and compensation. Because markets differ in physical proximity, regions can vary substantially in terms of the geographic area they cover.

Geographic structures hold several advantages. Sales-people have well-defined territories over which they can take ownership, which, in turn, often motivates sales-people toward greater commitment to their customers and to closer relationships. When rewards are linked directly to performance, geographic territories also improve the sales-people's performance and control. In addition, geographically based sales territories make travel expenses easier to manage.

Managers may choose geographic districts based on their market potential vis-a-vis whatever criteria make the most strategic sense for goal setting and performance evaluation (*e.g.*, sales volume, profitability, number of potential accounts). Districts may also vary in terms of sales challenge or customer sophistication, and, in this way, managers can use them to differentiate sales-people. Inexperienced sales-people are often assigned less challenging areas with lower sales potentials and later promoted to more challenging and rewarding areas. Given the challenges involved in selling a diverse or complex product line, some companies organise their sales-forces by *product category*. A shortcoming of the product structure approach is that companies will sometimes have several sales-people visit the same customer, with each one selling something different. This can result in higher travel expense and unnecessary duplication of effort. Multiple sales calls can also dilute the seller's bargaining power. Dilution of bargaining power has been a serious concern to consumer products firms, as large retailers with centralised purchasing dominate the retail market.

Account size provides another basis for structuring the sales-force, with customer size normally measured in terms of sales volume or the diversity of the products purchased. Relationships with customers who buy large quantities or large classes of products often require special handling. Large customers may have their own product specifications, materials management demands or special pricing requirements. Some even require special promotional programmes from producers to help achieve their own marketing objectives.

Differences among customers' demands can be substantial and make it impractical to have the same sales-force call on customers of different sizes within the same area. This has led some firms to organise their sales-force by account size, where some sales-people specialise on a few large accounts and others service many smaller accounts.

Providing Market Intelligence and Influencing the Marketing Mix

A typical sales organisation performs many of the functions and tasks that sales-people may take on, which appear in Table 2.9.

Table 2.9 : Functions and Related Tasks Performed by Sales-people

Functions and Tasks	Affected Areas of the Marketing Mix
Selling Function 1. Plan 2. Develop leads 3. Identify decision-makers 4. Make sales calls 5. Respond to current accounts 6. Negotiations	Promotion, Pricing
Working with Others 1. Expedite orders 2. Handle shipping arrangements 3. Assist service personnel	Product, Distribution
Servicing the Product 1. Learn and test equipment 2. Supervise installation 3. Train customers 4. Supervise and perform repairs	Product, Distribution

Managing Information 1. Provide technical information to customers 2. Manage customer feedback 3. Summarise information on customer needs 4. Perform competitive assessments	Product, Promotion
Servicing Accounts 1. Set up displays and shelves 2. Take inventory for customers 3. Handle local advertising	Promotion, Distribution
Attending Meetings 1. Attend sales conferences and meetings 2. Attend client and customer conferences 3. Attend product exhibitions	Distribution, Promotion
Timing and Recruiting Train and recruit new sales representatives	Promotion, Distribution
Distribution 1. Maintain relations with distributors 2. Sell to distributors 3. Handle terms of repayment and credit	Distribution, Pricing
Entertaining 1. Entertain clients (*e.g.*, dinners, lunches) 2. Host parties for clients	Promotion Distribution
Travelling	

Some experts argue that in fact the sales function bridges the gap between consumers and products, and that it significantly influences all areas of the business. Table 2.11 lists important areas for both buyers and sellers, touching on all the four areas of the marketing mix: product, price, promotion and distribution.

Sales as a Shared Function

Although companies need sales professionals to promote products and services, contact between buying and selling organisations occurs at many other functional levels and every encounter brings with it the potential for enhancing the business relationship. For example, complex installations such as specialised manufacturing machinery and large-sale computer systems often require substantial effort to meet customer needs and extensive training of servicer personnel. In these situations, the sales process involves technicians, trainers and sales professionals who must act as a team in their commitment to customer satisfaction and to sustaining a marketing orientation.

Even if companies are not in highly competitive situations, it is important that employees other than sales personnel see themselves as potential sales-people. Employees should see that at different times they can fulfill different sales roles and that encounters with their customers can often involve tasks such as needs assessments, presentations and closings.

THE ROLE OF SALES MANAGEMENT IN MARKETING MIX

Marketing programmes revolve around four major components of the marketing mix : products to be sold, pricing, promotion and distribution channels (Fig.2.14). The promotion component, in turn, includes advertising, personal selling, sales promotion (point-of-purchase displays, coupons and bargain counters, for example) and public relations. Fig.2.12 indicates the role of sales management in the marketing mix.

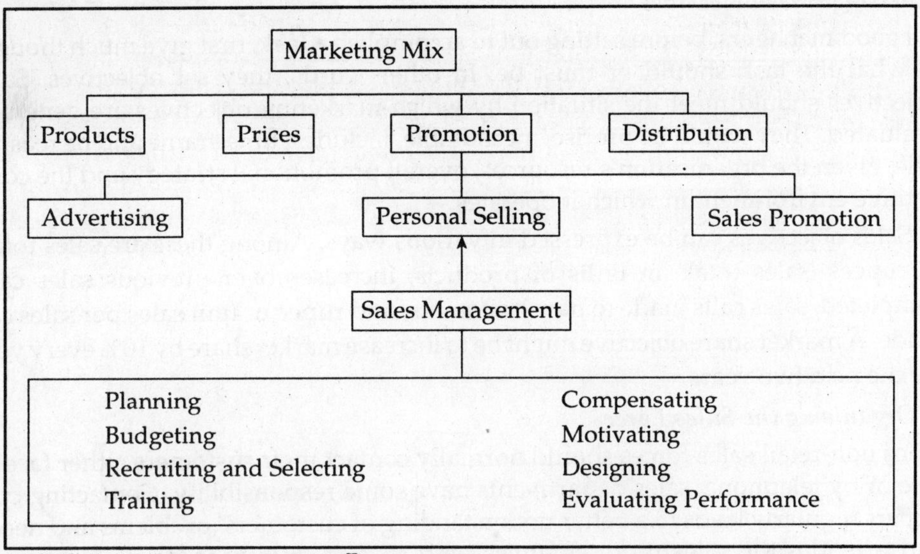

Fig. 2.12 : Position of Sales Management in the Marketing Mix

In a broad sense, sales management refers to management of all marketing activities, including advertising, sales promotion, marketing research, physical distribution, pricing and product selling. The American Marketing Association has defined it as "the planning, direction and control of personal selling, including recruiting, selecting, assigning, supervising, paying and motivating as these tasks apply to the personal sales-force."

Most modern sales managers have certain broad responsiblities. They are in charge of personal-selling activity, and their primary assignment is management of the personal sales force.

Sales personnel, like most employees, require some degree of supervision and management. However, most sales people, outside retail stores, work on their own most of the time. They work away from the presence of their direct supervisors. This is the main reason why the task of the sales manager differs significantly from that of other managers. Indeed, a large part of the sales manager's job is to attempt to create a situation in which the sales persons can be placed and then supervised and monitored from time to time.

Definition

The sales manager is the marketing manager actively dealing with planning, organising, directing and controlling the pesonal selling effort. Sales managers are responsible for a number of administrative tasks. These include planning and organising the efforts of the sales force, recruiting and maintaining a well-trained sales force, supervising and motivating the sales force and evaluating and controlling the sales force[1].

In fact, the task of managing a sales force involves a number of specific activities. The major activities involved in operating a a sales force are the following :

1. Thus, while sales managers are primarily responsible for planning, organising, directing and controlling sales force, they have ample opportunities to engage in the personal selling process.

1. Setting sales objectives

All good managers, before setting out to accomplish a task, first give much thought to what the task should or must be. In other words, they set objectives. Sales objectives should meet the situation by which marketing objectives are generally evaluated. They would be precise, measurable, include a time-frame and be reasonable, given the organisation's resources, overall promotional strategy and the competitive environment in which it operates.

Sales objectives can be expressed in various ways. Among these are sales totals in rupees, sales totals in units of products, increases over previous sales calls completed, sales calls made to new customers, and rupee or unit sales per sales call made. A market share objective might be to increase market share by 10% every year for the next five years.

2. Organising the Sales Force

Since non-retail sales forces should normally contact their customers either face to face or by telephone, sales departments have some responsibility. Contacting customers regularly leads to a better understanding of customers' problems and needs and provides the sales representatives with an opportunity to develop personal relationship with the client. However, for this some form of organisation is required to avoid the practice of several company representatives calling on the same customers where this is unnecessary. Duplication of calls is a waste of resources and can annoy the clients.

3. Recruiting and Selecting the Sales Force

The third important function of the sales manager is the personnel one. It starts with finding and hiring individuals in sales department of an organisation. Finding the person who is both interested in a sales job and qualified to fill it requires that the sales position be systematically evaluated so as to determine what it requires. No one is a 'born salesperson'. Sales-people, no matter what their qualifications, are not universally acceptable in all selling situations. Thus, the sales manager must decide what characteristics a given sales position requires. The job requirements for an order-taker may be quite different than those of an order-getter. These requirements must be carefully thought out and matched with job candidates, not only for the sake of the sales organisation but also for the sake of the individuals hired. Clearly, the task is to get the right persons for the job. Some traits and accomplishments commonly considered when recruiting sales personnel are educational background, intelligence, self-confidence, problem-solving ability, speaking ability, appearance, achievement orientation, friendliness, empathy and involvement in community organisations.

4. Training the Sales Force

After sales personnel have been recruited and selected, they must be trained. Training programmes vary from company to company. Some companies use an apprentice-type system by sending the newcomer into the field with an experienced sales person to 'learn the art of selling'. Others put the recruit through an intensive training programme at headquarters or at a regional office before actually putting him (or her) out in the field. A few organisations believe in a 'sink or swim' method whereby new people are sent out on their own to succeed or fail.

A typical sales training programme is likely to cover the following areas :

(1) Company policies and practices;

(2) Industry and competitor's background;

(3) Product knowledge and selling techniques.

In many successful sales organisations, training to develop the skills of experienced sales personnel is an on-going process. Most sales representatives can benefit from a refresher course, a few days' learning about new products, or just a break from their regular schedules. Thus, continuing learning is often carried out at the home office, at sales conventions, or then at a local hotel or conference centre.

5. Compensating the Sales Force

Sales work is generally visible. It involves the attempt to achieve clearly measurable results. For this reason, most sales managers feel that sales people who achieve the highest performance, in terms of some specific measure, should receive the highest compensation. Financial incentives are not the only motivations of a sales person, but they are important and deserve the sales manager's close attention. The ideal compensation plan for sales people should be simple so that disagreements over the size of pay and bonuses might be avoided.

6. Motivating the Sales Force

For some people, selling itself is highly motivating. Yet most sales people need occasional support from management. Sales contests, bonus plans, prizes and trips to be made and sales conferences in exciting cities, like New York, Paris, Tokyo and London can all be of great help to the sales manager who is seeking to keep sales force motivation high. Periodic sales meetings are also useful, both for creating a feeling of group support and mutual interest as well as for providing a time for training and for spreading information.

7. Evaluating and Controlling the Sales Force

An organisation's overall marketing plan must be translated into a series of area sales plans or sales plans that specify regional, district, or other territorial goals. Evaluation of a sales manager's or a sales representative's performance is based on whether he (she) meets the prescribed goal or objective.

8. Managing Sales Agents

Many marketing organisations have no sales force of their own because they use selling agents or manufacturers' agents. In these organisations sales managers face the problem of managing sales people who are not under their direct control. Dealing with agents may require special care and skill but good sales managers can prove their worth by handling these relationships fairly and smoothly. See Fig. 2.13.

Conclusion

Good sales managers must be good leaders. The effective leader has to coordinate the activities of subordinates and settle internal disputes, when necessary. Since a leader represents his employees in dealing with higher management, he often must assume responsibility for the group's failures. The effective leader should provide a model of behaviour for employees to follow, often developing strong mutual trust and good rapport with subordinates.

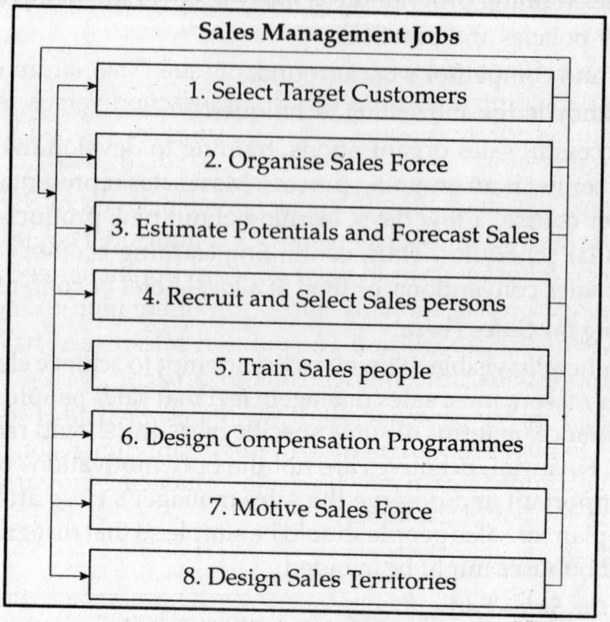

Fig. 2.13 : Sales Management Functions

Good managers must be efficient in performing the following functions — organising and motivating employees, setting goals, enforcing rules and defining expectations. Effective leadership in a sales organisation is necessary, so that the sales-persons should respect the manager's leadership ability and be willing to follow directions. This respect is often built on a proven record of sales by the manager, as well as his willingness to help sales people perform to the best of their abilities. Sales managers should operate in given positions with direct responsibility for helping achieve the sales and profit objectives of the firm.

RELATIONSHIP MARKETING

An important factor contributing to the changing nature of sales is the growing importance of relationship marketing. Sales-people are typically a company's primary contact with its customer base. Relationship marketing is also important in selling consumer products, particularly consumer durable goods such as automobiles, personal computers and electronic home entertainment equipment like video games. It is easier and less costly to get repeat business from existing customers than to create new business from noncustomers. It makes good financial sense, therefore, for sales-people to establish good relationships with customers and preserve long-term repeat business.

CHARACTERISTICES OF SALESPEOPLE

Introduction

Many sales management problems could be eliminated — or at least minimisted — if a successfull sales type could be found. This would imply that successful sales-people are born, or have acquired the necessary skills or possibly have been self-taught by experience. The sales manager's task is to find such people.

The Salesperson

No doubt, sales situations are in some ways unique. The nature of the job (new business versus providing after-sales service; transaction versus relationship selling) may mean that entirely different characteristics are needed to be effective in different situations.

Sales managers, like marketing managers must, respond to changes in supply, demand or the framework in which business is conducted. People operating at the boundary between different units in a dynamic environment need a wide range of skills, from strategic problem-solving and profit-orientation to highly developed communication skills or capabilities. The modern salesperson has had to acquire more qualities, more skills and a more flexible approach.

In a marketing context, personal selling facilitates the mathching of product or service offerings to buyer requirements. An important dimension of selling ability is the individual's competence in matching and influencing the variety of needs and behavioural complexities of the buyer.

Attributes of Sales-people

So, to perform his job efficiently, the salesperson must have certain inherent and certain acquired qualities. The common qualities or attributes of sales people are the following:

(1) Personality and physical characteristics

In case of direct selling, a good salesperson must have two basic qualities. The first one is empathy, which may be defined as the important central ability to feel as the other fellow does in order to be able to sell a product or service. The second is the ego drive, which can be described as the need to conquer: a desire to want and need to make a sale. In many sales situations, life is tough against aggressive competition. Sales-people must be motivated by failure, not shattered by it. The ideal is the person who has lots of empthy and drive. Super sales-people have both the qualities. Someone who has lots of empthy but is low on drive may lack the killer touch by being unable to close a sale. Someone with lots of drive but who is low on empathy is probably the salesperson. Someone with little empthy and low drive is in the wrong job.

Certain factors which are very important in most selling jobs are : the direct selling abilities, the territory management skills, the customer service level and the product and application knowledge of an individual. On the basis of these factors, we may refer to the following desirable attributes of a salesperson:

- personal engry and initiative
- the ability to organise and plan (+ flexibility)
- a moderate level of educational attainment
- the ability to adapt to a variety of personalities and behaviours
- concern with personal and professional development
- a desire and need for recognition.

A successful salesperson should have the following characteristics :

- He should be tall, physically impressive and energetic.
- He should develop good work habits and perseverance, and be willing to work long hours and enjoy solving problems.

- He must seek and enjoy recognition from others for selling accomplishments.
- He must have a broad range of interests but should not be extensively involved in civic and professional organisations.
- He should not be highly educated in a formal manner but must be intellectually capable.
- He may be emotional and somewhat disorganised but adaptable and flexible in his work habit.
- He should not be very much sensitive to the reactions and feelings of others.
- He should view selling as a professional career and should not have much interest in achieving status beyond the selling position.

However, the link between personal factors and performance depends on a number of factors such as the type of product, the market, the buyer or buying organisation, the characteristics of the firm, its culture and ethos, the type of manager and management style and the type of sales-person.

2. *Enthusiasm*

Sales-people must be enthusiastic about their job, their product, their company and themselves. This is the major characteristic which often turns failure into success in selling. Job involvement can be related to enthusiasm. However, in reality, people who work long hours show perseverance and determination and enthusiasm and are more likely to be successful sales-people.

3. *Confidence*

Those people who possess higher levels of self-confidence are more likely to be successful. No doubt belief in one's own ability and belief in the product and the company are conveyed to buyers with positive effect. However, sales-people will have to adjust their proposal or presentation and be able to make quick, important decisions. A lack of confidence can lead to loss of opportunities and, ultimately, sales.

4. *Intelligence*

Higher levels of intelligence do not always lead to higher levels of sales performance. Sales-people who overanalyse or criticise may lack conviction. In selling, mental and verbal agility, for example, often seems to be preferable to written or analytical skills.

5. *Self-worth*

The ability and desire to be motivated by non-monetary incentives such as status, self-esteem and sociability seem to play a part in effective selling. The most important motivating factor is the satisfaction obtained by doing a good job.

6. *Knowledge*

A salesperson should have adequate knowledge of the product, company, customers, competitors, markets and territories. Product knowledge is rated by sales managers to be the most highly rated feature in successful sales-people.

7. *Product knowledge*

Knowledge of the product, its benefits and how it is used together affect sales performance. Detailed product knowledge by itself is not sufficient but is a necessary pre-condition and a major factor in effective selling.

8. *Competitors*

Along with product knowledge the salesperson must have a detailed knowledge of competitors' products. In addition, sales-people must know and understand their competitors' sales policies, organisation pricing and promotion strategies. Such knowledge is very important. In fact, the golden rule of selling is 'never knock competitors'. Success comes from strengths rather than from negative criticisms. A knowledge of competitors will enable positive benefits for a product to be identified and more closely matched with customers' needs and wants.

9. *Market knowledge*

It is the responsibility of the marketing manager to decide marketing strategy and policies and give proper weightage to the four Ps of the marketing mix but the individual salesperson should have the ability to understand and translate the application of marketing effort to individual customers and circumstances. An essential component of the selling job is to provide management with information on competitors, market conditions and trends. Sales-people may have a narrow outlook but intelligently collected information from various sales areas can be used to win competition and promote sales.

10. *Customer knowledge*

Equally vital for the salesperson is the ability to develop and maintain ongoing customer relationships. The specific tasks include providing technical information, handling complaints and providing other aspects of customer service as appropriate. Effective selling can be demonstrated as the ability to meet a buyer's needs and wants in preference to any competitor product. Customer knowledge means being able to distinguish the buyer's preference correctly identified between two or more products and, therefore, the salesperson stressing the 'right' things in influencing a customer's choice.

11. *Territory knowledge*

Good territory knowledge is also important in effective selling. This requires management skills by the individual in the efficient allocation of time between customers, prospects and travelling. Good skills in planning routes and sales calls, together with an appropriate but not excessive time on non-selling activities, are all important determinants of sales-force productivity.While some flexibility in the use of time will always be required, the ability to plan and manage a territory are also important determinants in effective sales performance.

12. *Company*

Sales-people should have an adequate knowledge of their own company, including its history, ownership, direction and aspirations of the owners. This means knowledge of the organisation, its structure, personalities, rules, procedures and disciplines.

13. *Skills*

Skills are a combination of factors (personality and knowledge contribute to these) which can be used to practise the job more effectively. Skills are of three types — communication skills, matching skills and persuasive skills.

(i) ***Communication skills***. Personal selling combines with advertising and promotion to from a communication link among sellers, intermediaries and buyers (final users). The more complex the distribution channel and the larger the number of intermediaries, the higher will be the cost of achieving communication objectives. No one single communication technique can be effective to all participants. Often, it is the combination of personal selling with other forms of promotion which is most effective. No doubt the effectiveness of personal selling can be increased and the

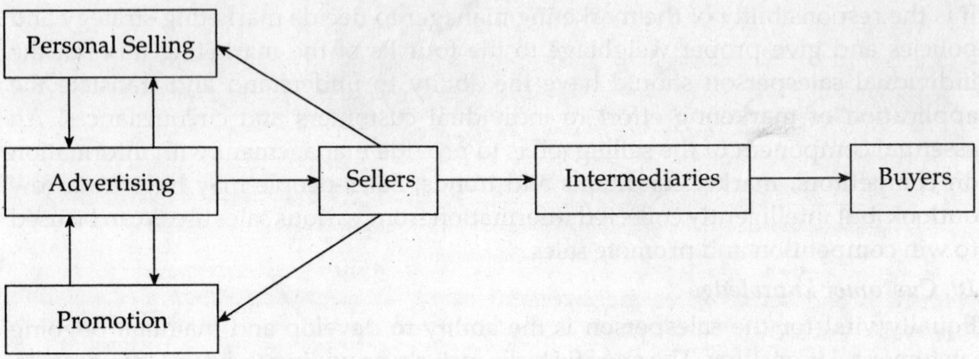

Fig. 2.14 : A marketing communications model

cost reduced by support from other promotional expenditure. Figure 2.14 presents a framework which shows how communications may work in the sales area.

(a) The communicator is the source or sender of the message represented by the salesperson, by the firm and by other forms of contact with the public.

(b) The sales message content and the way it is presented should integrate with other forms of communicaion. Promotional objectives will attempt to achieve the following:

1. Create or increase awareness of the company or product.
2. Alter perceptions held by exisiting or potential buyers about the product or the company and create or build a favourable image and comparative advantage over competitors.
3. Encourage a purchase decision.
4. Aid conviction about the purchase decision and reassure buyers.
5. Provide the necessary follow-up and after-sales service.

(c) The means by which the communication is conveyed is usually via a salesperson at the client's premises although it may sometimes be at trade shows, exhibitions, social event, factory visits or other locations. Sales-people are the most expensive but also the most effective means of communication.

(d) The audiénce, as represented by buyers and prospects, will be important to successful outcomes in the sales process. Partcularly in industrial companies and intermediaries, the complexities of organisational buyer must be understood and evaluated by sales-people.

(e) Communication is a two-way process and personal selling should be adaptive, flexible and direct.

15. Marketing skills

The characteristics and skills required will be those which best match the role to be performed and the tasks which must be undertaken. Where this matching can be extended to the similarity between buyers and sellers, sales performance can be further improved.

Effective selling also requires a selling style appropriate to the prospect. There is need to match seller with buyer.

16. Persuasive skills

Understanding the communication process and the ability to appreciate the importance of matching the benefits of sellers to the needs of buyers are necessary but not sufficient conditions to complete the sales process.

A third dimension of skill — persuasive abilities — needs to be added. No matter how well the company has conducted and managed the marketing process, the customer will still face a variety of options from competing suppliers.

A key aspect of a company's performance is its ability to generate and close sales. Most often, this is done in person by the sales-force. An essential part of this process is not only information about products, service or the company but the ability to persuade buyers against equally able competitors.

The correct interpretation of buyers' needs and the application of selling effort is vitally important. The ability of the salesperson to make effective presentation in line with buyer's needs makes the difference between success and failure in selling.

Experience is important in assessing what has previously worked— or, in most cases, failed to work — with prospects. Training, education and basic ability all contribute to what constitutes persuasive abilities, as does effectiveness in the selling process itself.

These, in their own turn, constitutes the following stages:

(i) finding prospects (customers);

(ii) making contact;

(iii) defining prospects needs/problems;

(iv) stimulating a desire for the firm's offering;

(v) closing the sale; and

(vi) retaining the sale and customer.

The relevance of these stages to the communication process is important. No doubt careful use of stylised approaches to selling is required. Sales- and product-oriented approaches which fail to assess and measure the true nature of buyers needs and problems will be ineffective no matter how well presented or how persuasive sales-people make their case.

Selling today requires an approach based on insight response or customer problem-solving rather than selling the available product.

Synopsis for Learning

Q.1. What are the primary responsibilities of sales managers ?

Ans. Sales managers are responsible for organising the sales effort, both within and outside their companies. Within the company the sales manager builds formal and informal organisational structures that ensure effective communication not only inside the sales department but in its relations with other organisational units. Outside the company, the sales manager serves as a key contact person with customers and the public at large and is responsible for building and maintaining an effective distribution network.

Q.2. What are the secondary roles of sales managers ?

Ans. Sales managers have other responsibilities as well. They are responsible for participating in the preparation of information critical to the making of key marketing decisions, such as those on budgeting, quotas and territories. They participate — to a greater or lesser extent — in decisions on products, marketing channels and distribution policies, advertising and other promotional activities, and pricing. Thus, the sales manager is both an administrator in charge of personal-selling activity and a member of the executive group that makes marketing decisions of all types.

Q.3. What are the basic responsibilities of sales-persons ?

Ans. The basic responsibilities of sales managers (of consumer and industrial products) are to direct and control the sales people that report to them. Specifically, sales managers must set objectives, develop plans, execute programmes and evaluate performance. A basic understanding of the factors that influence the market for the firm's products and a knowledge of buyers' decision processes and their reactions to different sales approaches increase the sales manager's effectiveness.

Q.4. What are the most difficult tasks of the sales managers ?

Ans. Perhaps the most difficult tasks of the sales manager are organising personnel into territories, scheduling appropriate training and sales meetings, making sure that sales reports are submitted on time and evaluating the performance of the sales force on a periodic (regular) basis. These tasks must be carried out with little contact with sales-people who are continually on the road.

Q.5. What are the administrative duties of sales managers ?

Ans. Sales managers also perform certain administrative duties. The primary task in this area is the effective management of the field sales office, which involves organising and training the office personnel to ensure a smoothly running operation. Communicating with others is an essential part of a sales manager's job, and the the successful manager is one who is efficient at both verbal and written communication.

Q.6. What is the finance function of the sales manager ?

Ans. A sales manager also devotes some time to perform financial planning and control activities, the most common task being the analysis of selling expense data. But, to simply minimise selling expenses is not the objective. One of the tasks of the sales manager is to eliminate waste in sales expense, while trying to maximise the revenue-generating ability of these expenditures.

2.12 PROMOTIONAL STRATEGIES AND TECHNIQUES

Promotions are incentives directed at consumers or dealers to get them to buy a specific brand. Whereas advertising is most often designed to induce a psychological response prior to action or reinforce a previous exposure to an ad or previous purchase, promotions are attempts to stimulate actions directly. The most common consumer promotions are free samples, price cuts and discounts, contests, games and prizes. **Speciality advertising** is really a type of promotion whereby free gifts in the form of a pen, calendar, coffee mug or other items are given to a consumer. The gift serves as a reward for performing the desired action (patronising dry cleaner *X*, buying magazine *Y*) and usually bears the name and telephone number of the sponsor as a constant reminder. Typical dealer promotions include point-of-purchase displays, cash allowances, credits, gifts, bonuses, '2 for 1' deals, contests, prizes and free advice or information.

An important point to stress is that the communication mix strategies are interdependent and, sometimes, mutually reinforcing. This is nowhere more evident than with advertising and promotion. In other words, **advertising and sales promotion are complimentary**.

Personal selling is the direct presentation of a product to a prospective customer by a representative of the organisation selling it. Personal selling takes place face to face or over the phone, and it may be directed to a middleman or a final consumer.

Advertising is impersonal mass communication that the sponsor has paid for and in which the sponsor is clearly identified. The most familiar forms of ads are found in the broadcast (TV and radio) and print (newspapers and magazines) media.

Sales promotion is demand granting activity designed to supplement advertising and facilitate personal selling. It is paid for by the sponsor and frequently involves a temporary incentive to encourage a purchase. Many sales promotions are directed at consumers. The majority, however, are designed to encourage the company's sales force or other members of its distribution channel to sell its products more aggressively. This latter category is called trade promotion. Included in sales promotion are a wide spectrum of activities, such as contests, trade shows, in-store displays, rebates, samples, premiums, discounts and coupons.

Public relations encompasses a wide variety of communication efforts to contribute to generally favourable attitudes and opinions towards an organisation and its products. Unlike most advertising and personal selling, its does not include a specific sales message. The targets may be customers, stockholders, a government agency, or a special-interest group. Public relations can take many forms, including newsletters, annual reports, lobbying and sponsorship of charitable or civic events.

Publicity is a special form of public relations that involves news stories about an organisation or its products. Like advertising, it involves an impersonal message that reaches a mass audience through the media. But several things distinguish publicity from advertising : It is not paid for, the organisation that is the subject of the publicity has no control over it, and it appears as news and, therefore, has greater credibility than advertising.

Importance of Promotion

Some form of promotion is necessary to make consumers — and the people with which an organisation interacts — aware of existence of a product. It is not enough to have a good product. People must be familiar with the product's benefits. The attributes and qualities of a product must be made known to the actual and potential buyers. Promotion is applied communication used by marketing people to exchange persuasive messages and information between buyers and sellers. Personal selling, advertising, publicity, public relations and sales promotions are promotional methods that may be used to communicate a message.

Communication with a purpose

The job of marketing is to identify consumer wants and to try to fill those wants by developing appropriate products — priced right, packaged for convenience, and properly distributed. The role of promotion in the marketing function is to convey news, to tell consumers about the benefits of the product. This communication — often termed 'selling the product'—is an inseparable part of the marketing functions.

Three purposes

Promotion serves the following three purposes :

1. Promotion informs. 2. Promotion persuades. 3. Promotion reminds.

These three aspects of promotion may now be briefly described :

1. *Information.* The essence of promotion is communication. If the management of Ariel is planning a sales, communicating price savings to potential customers must be a part of the plan. A price cut will not be beneficial to anyone unless promotion communicates to consumers the fact that a sale is underway. A company's promotions provide other information as well, such as trading hours, whether or not returns or exchange of goods sold will be allowed, and whether purchase can be made with credit cards. Thus, the broad goal of promotion is to inform potential buyers.

2. *Persuasion.* Plain communication of information is not enough for effective promotion. With less time for comparative shopping, consumers turn to advertising for product information. However, providing information is not the only purpose of marketing communication. Marketing managers exist in a competitive environment and as competitiors they want consumers to buy their brands. Thus, persuasion is a primary goal of promotion. In fact, the classical definition of promotion is persuasive communication.

3. *Reminder.* In a modern market-based economy, competitors are free to 'tempt' loyal customers with their own informative and persuasive managers. Thus, reminding customers, in addition to informing and persuading them, may be a promotional objective. The major goal of promotion is to sustain customers preference(s) for different products. A secondary promotional goal is attracting new customer.

In short, the three basic purpose of promotion are to inform, persuade and remind.

Five Elements of Promotion

Five main elements of promotion are personal selling, advertising, publicity, public relations, sales promotion and public relations. These promotional efforts are of two general types. They involve either direct communication, usually on a face-to-face basis, or indirect communication *via* some medium, such as TV (see Fig. 2.15).

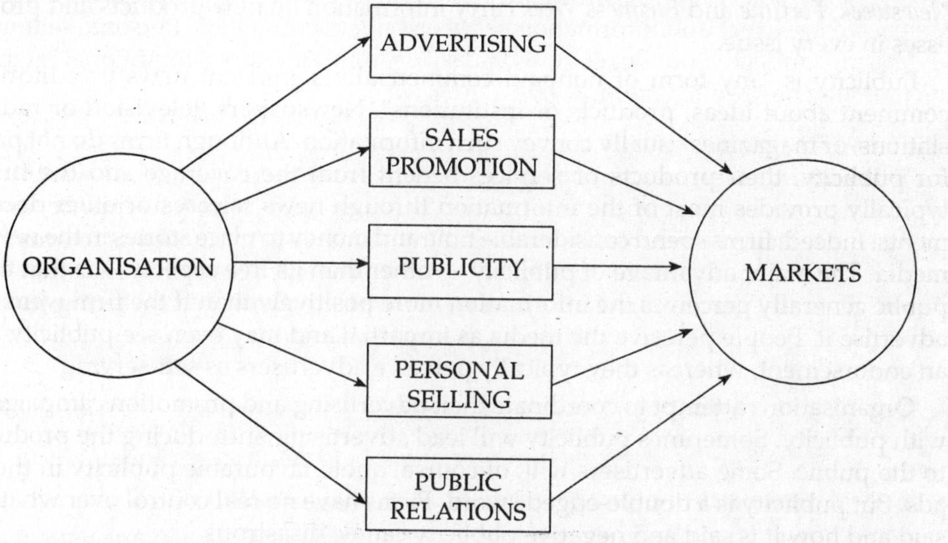

Fig. 2.15 : The communication mix : the organisation's link to its markets

1. Personal selling

Personal selling is a person-to-person dialogue between buyer and seller where the purpose of the interaction, whether face-to-face or over the phone, is to persuade the buyer to accept a point of view or to convince the buyer to take a specific course of action. However, in some situations, this method is quite expensive to employ.

2. Advertising

Advertising is basically an action by a firm to promote sales of its products, the basic aim being to increase the number of customers who prefer its products to those of its competitors. This can be achieved in two ways. Firstly, advertising can be used to inform consumers of the existence and location of the product(s) to which it is directed. Secondly, advertising can influence the nature of consumers' preference to the benefit of the firm's products. Advertising is essentially a source of information on prices and product attributes available to potential buyers. In this way, advertising enhances information flows among traders (retailers) and buyers. Advertising includes any informative or persuasive message carried by a mass medium and paid for by a sponsor who signs the message. It consists of paid messages by identified sponsors through nonpersonal channels (media). Advertisement bears a signature, in the form of a company or brand name. Any medium other than a live salesperson may be used. While most advertising is carried by common media like radio and television, effective marketers have developed some very clever and innovative media for delivering their messages, *e.g.*, huge balloons high in the air in a prominent place bearing company's and/or product's name such as Boroline.

3. Publicity

Advertising is a paid form of message delivery. Publicity is similar to advertising except that it involves an unpaid and unsigned message, even though it may use the same mass media as advertising does. When information about a product is considered newsworthy, mass media tend to communicate such information free of cost. Thus, the organisation being publicised neither signs nor pays for the message. *Newsweek*, *Fortune* and *Business Week* carry information on new products and processes in every issue.

Publicity is "any form of nonpaid commercially significant news or editorial comment about ideas, products or institutions". Newspapers, television or radio stations, or magazines usually convey such information. Although firms do not pay for publicity, their products or services benefit from the coverage and the firm typically provides most of the information through news releases or other documents. Indeed, firms spend considerable time and money to place stories in the news media. The major advantage of publicity — other than its free aspects — is that the public generally perceives the information more positively than if the firm were to advertise it. People perceive the media as impartial and may even see publicity as an endorsement, whereas they typically perceive advertisers as self-serving.

Organisations attempt to coordinate their advertising and promotion campaigns with publicity. Sometimes publicity will lead advertising, introducing the product to the public. Some advertisers will, of course, quote favourable publicity in their ads. But publicity is a double-edged sword. Firms have no real control over what is said and how it is said and negative publicity can be disastrous.

Third Party

An important distinguishing characteristic of publicity is that it always involves a third party, such as a newspaper reporter or an editor, who has the ultimate power to determine the nature of the message. Because of the credibility associated with the third party and because the information is generally factual rather than persuasive, publicity scores high in believability. In other words, people are more convinced by publicity than by advertisement.

Positive and Negative Publicity

Publicity can be both positive and negative. In fact, because the message is in the hands of the media and not in the hands of the business or organisation providing the product, publicity can be both helpful and harmful.

Publicity is no doubt 'free' in the sense that mass media are not paid to communicate the message. But the truth is that publicity should be properly managed. Marketers may take considerable time and effort in getting news releases and interviews through company spokespersons, interacting with newspapers and on broadcasts so that a favourable corporate organisational image is built up. When an organisation systematically plans and distributes information to manage the nature of the publicity it receives it is engaged in public relations. No doubt, all forms of promotion may influence an organisation's relationship with the general public. This is why public relations has traditionally concentrated on the management of publicity.

When a company introdcues a new product it issues a news release, or a short statement describing the product. Photographs, films and video tapes are distributed to the media to accompany the news release. Of course, it is necessary for the public relations department to coordinate its efforts with other promotional departments.

The Press Conference

The press conference is another form of publicity that can create goodwill and positive relations between the organisation and the public. But this is a costly method of publicity.

4. Sales Promotion

Sales promotion is defined as those promotional activities other than personal selling, advertising and publicity that are intended to stimulate customer purchase or dealer effectiveness in a specific time period. Thus special offers of free goods, discount coupons, display items for household use, training programmes, in-store demonstrations and trips to attractive vacation spots for top sales people are examples of sales promotion. Such special promotions are different from advertising as they are temporary offers of a material reward to customers, sales people or sales prospects (or potential buyers).

The intent of sales promotion programmes is to amplify or bolster the advertising and personal selling messages offered by the organisation. Usually the effects are felt at the point of purchase. The main purpose of sales promotion is to achieve short-term objectives. Free samples or discount coupons encourage a first-time trial of product. The use of a premium offer or special discount may stimulate interest in a product and thus encourage off-season sales. Whether the sales promotion takes the form of a trade show, a consumer rebate, a point-of-purchase display for retailers, or free gifts (such as pens and calendars for wholesalers to give away) the best sales promotion support is to be co-ordinated with other promotional activities.

5. Public Relations

Fostering good public relations now plays a very important role in sales promotion. It has been described by the Institute of Public Relations, U.K., as the deliberate, planned and sustained effort to establish and maintain mutual understanding between an organisation and its public.

Goodwill and a good reputation cannot easily be acquired; they take a long time and a lot of trouble to build up. Conversely they are destroyed fairly easily and quickly and once gone they take a much longer time to rebuild. Confidence, once lost, is not easily regained. Even relatively minor incidents, such as an impolite representative or an unhelpful telephone operator, can destroy the organisation's public image. The need for special attention to public relations is, therefore, obvious.

Conclusion

The effective marketer must seek to integrate all the four elements of personal selling— advertisement, sales promotion, publicity and public relations. This integration is termed a **promotional mix** or a **promotion mix**. Such a programme ideally would be planned to meet the information requirements of all target customers.

PROMOTIONAL STRATEGIES

The number of promotional strategies available to an organisation is limited by the creativity of the individuals responsible for developing them. However, some common and quite basic strategies are widely used (or practised). These are the following :

Pull and push strategies

The primary target of a promotional strategy may be either the ultimate consumer or a member of the distribution channel. Using this as a basis for classification, the basic strategies of push (pushing) and pull (pulling) have been developed. A push strategy is one that emphasises personal selling, advertisement and other promotional efforts aimed at members of the channel of distribution. Thus, the manufacturer of a product heavily promotes that product to wholesalers and other dealers. The wholesalers then promote the product heavily to retailers who, in turn, direct their selling efforts to customers. Frequently the wholesalers and retailers are offered strong price incentives or discounts as part of this process. The term 'push' comes from the fact that the manufacturer, with the help of other channel members, pushes the product through the channel of distribution. The push strategy may be thought of as a step-by-step approach to promotion, with each channel member organising the promotional efforts necessary to reach the channel member next in the line. See Fig.2.16.

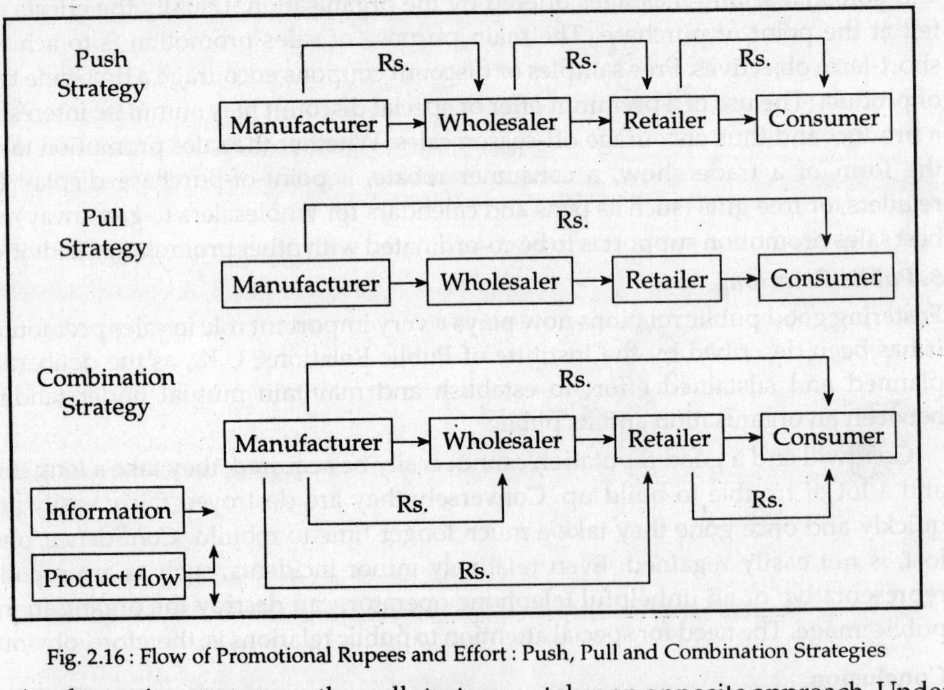

Fig. 2.16 : Flow of Promotional Rupees and Effort : Push, Pull and Combination Strategies

An alternative strategy — the pull strategy — takes an opposite approach. Under the pull strategy, the manufacturer attempts to stimulate demand for the product by promotional efforts aimed at the ultimate consumer or industrial buyer located at the other end of the channel of distribution. The goal is to generate demand at the retail level in the belief that such demand will encourage retailers and wholesalers to stock the product. Each channel member will 'pass back' the demand. In other words, the demand at the buyer end of the channel pulls the product through the channel of distribution.

Most products are sold to us by the push approach. The push strategy suggests a step-by-step promotional effort. The pull strategy attempts to develop ultimate buyer demand and a smooth flow of products from the manufacturer to the buyer *via* cooperative middlemen.

Producers aim their promotional mix at both middlemen and users. Thus, a promotion programme aimed primarily at middlemen is called a push strategy and a promotion programme directed primarily at end users is called a pull strategy. Fig. 2.17 contrasts these two strategies.

Using a push strategy means a channel member directs its promotion primarily to middlemen that are the next link forward in the distribution channel. The product is "pushed" through the channel. The producer will promote heavily to wholesalers, who then also use a push strategy to retailers. In turn, the retailers promote to consumers. A push strategy usually involves a lot of personal selling and sales promotion, including contests for sales people and displays at trade shows. This promotional strategy is appropriate for many manufacturers of industrial products, as well as for various consumer goods.

With a pull strategy, promotion is directed to end users — usually ultimate consumers. The objective is to motivate them to ask retailers for the product. The retailers, in their turn, will request the product from wholesalers and wholesalers will order it from the producer. In effect, promotion to consumers is designed to "pull" the product through the channel. This strategy relies on heavy advertising and various forms of sales promotion such as discount for bulk purchase, free samples, or in-store demonstrations.

There is little incentive for retailers to provide shelf space for minor variations of existing brands unless they are confident that they will sell. So manufacturers of consumer packaged goods often use a pull strategy to get in large quantities new products stocked in supermarkets.

Combination Strategies

Clearly, a marketing organisation would not limit itself to using only a push or only a pull strategy. Effective marketing plans generally make use of both push and pull strategies.

Hard and Soft Strategies

Some marketers may think of the *hard sell* and *soft sell* as sales techniques rather than strategies. However, they can be termed promotional strategies because some companies employ them on a long-term or continuing basis.

Supporters of the *hard sell* believe that aggressive persuasion of individuals is the best way for consumers to learn the true benefits of the product. Sales people believe that the repetitive promotional efforts emphasising the same benefits over and over again will ultimately be effective. They attempt to prove to prospective buyers that they need the product offered. Sales personnel do not accept 'No' for an answer under a hard sell strategy. Insurance people and those who sell water purifier or vacuum clearner, or even used cars are frequently seen as proponents of the hard sell.

The hard sell promotional strategy, whether adopted by a TV advertiser or a sales person, in essence makes 'No' an unacceptable answer. Comments like 'buy now', 'you can't afford to pass this up', 'you will need this eventually', and 'pay me now or pay me later' are typical of this never-say-no promotional strategy.

Actually few marketers can totally avoid the hard sell strategy. Makers of extremely popular products holding large shares of markets may be able to advertise their products to consumers simply by showing happy people using the items. Let us take the case of washing machines or refrigerators. Even these products, however, are also promoted more aggressively by sales people calling on retailers, displays in supermarkets, price concessions or discount coupons for bulk purchase and sometimes attractive gifts during a particular part of the year. The growing intensity of competition makes a total reliance on soft sell approaches almost impossible.

Comparing the Two Strategies

Explaining soft sells is more difficult for two reasons : (1) the communications and sales messages are more subtle and (2) the soft sell takes many forms. The soft sell is not as blatant or conspicuous in the direct asking for the order. While repetition may be utilised, there are subtle variations in the way things are communicated. It is not possible in practice to draw a clear line between the two — the hard sell and the soft sell. The difference is in the eye of the customer. Determining whether a promotional strategy is a hard or soft sell one is largely a matter of perception and judgement.

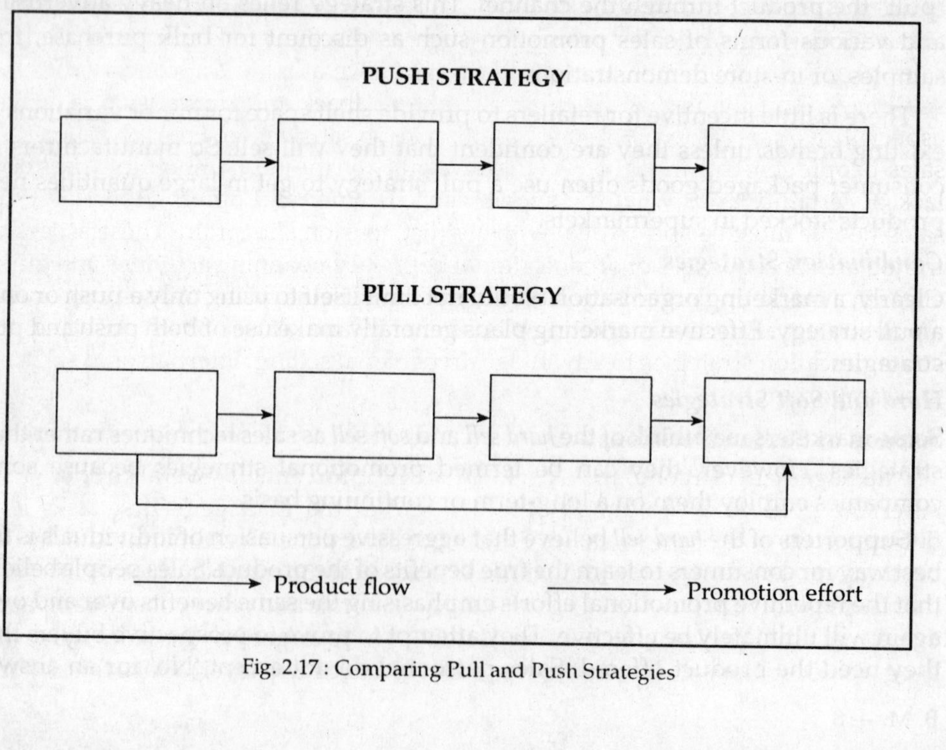

Fig. 2.17 : Comparing Pull and Push Strategies

PERSONAL SELLING

Face-to-face communication, although expensive, is the most compelling medium available to most sellers, especially for industrial products. Personal contact permits a dynamic adjustment of needs and offerings on the part of both buyer and seller, and it facilitates the gaining of a commitment. Moreover, sales-people sort out problems subsequent to the sale (*e.g.*, late delivery), provide feedback about the market, and generate new business. In an age where everything and everyone seems to get lost in the crowd, personal selling lets the firm tailor its offerings, reach the right customer, communicate complex benefits and terms and push control deeper into the channel of distribution. Although more expensive on a per customer basis than advertising, personal selling frequently costs less in absolute terms when the number of customers is small, the items are high-priced, or both.

For decades, researchers and practitioners have searched in vain for the magical profile of the "ideal" salesperson. At one time or another, sales-people were thought to need money more than achievement, to have high ego strength, empathy, verbal skills, aggressiveness, an aloof attitude, unusual levels of drive, or to be loved and so on. Eventually, the ideal salesperson could be described by any and all attributes, and no one — or everyone — could be suitable for the purpose.

The Ideal Salesperson

There is no such thing as the ideal salesperson. But there are a few fundamental attributes or abilities common to most successful outside sales-people. First and foremost, they must be motivated. Sales-people must value the intrinsic and extrinsic rewards associated with selling and believe that working hard will earn them these rewards. Secondly, leading sales-people tend to have high levels of self-confidence and self-esteem, especially in relation to the specific job at hand. To the extent that attaining high levels of sales is consistent with their task-specific self-image, sales-people are motivated to work hard to achieve at a level in concert with that self-image. Thirdly, the ability to learn from feedback and supervision is crucial, especially as it serves to promote and reinforce job satisfaction. Fourthly, successful sales-people generally cope better with ambiguity on the job. (Ambiguity arises from lack of certainty as to what the supervisor, customer and others expect). Fifthly, sales-people must be able to deal with conflict, tension and strain. These aspects of the job are consequences of organisational boundary-spanning activities and differences in interests, points of view, and job pressures. Finally, effective selling requires an ability to analyse customer needs and plan and adjust one's activities and communication strategies to advantage. In personal selling, interpersonal skills are most important.

Aspects of Selling Decisions

The management of a company's personal selling effort entails several key decisions. After the goals and profitability are set, one of the manager's first tasks is to determine the size of the sales force. This might be done by estimating the desired productivity of sales-people and taking into account the number of total customers (actual plus potential) as well as geographic, economic and other considerations. At the same time, the manager must decide how to organise the sales force (by geographic territory, customer type, product brand or whatever). Once this is done, the manager can determine the size of each territory or the number of accounts and/or products that each salesperson will have. These decisions should, if possible, be based at least partly on target sales or profit figures. A recruitment, selection and training programme must be designed as well. Finally, supervision, compensation, work standards (*e.g.*, call norms), and general planning, management, and control mechanisms must be set in place. Many of these issues can be approached through various normative models that have been proposed by marketers to aid in planning and decision-making. Job design, leadership, and career development principles are important, too.

Just as advertising and promotion are mutually reinforcing activities, so too may personal selling interact with other modes in the communication mix to more effectively generate sales. A key decision is whether to pursue a push, a pull or a combination strategy. That is, should the firm place major emphasis on selling to intermediaries (the push strategy), to final customers (the pull strategy), or both? The push strategy requires a vigorous sales force, dealer promotions and relatively high margin pricing. The pull strategy rests largely on advertising with perhaps some consumer promotions. Most firms use a combination-pull strategy; industrial goods sellers rely relatively more on a push strategy, whereas the strategies of consumer goods sellers are more balanced or lean toward a pull strategy. The choice of balance between push and pull depends on how and where consumers make decisions, the size of the market, what consumer media habits are, the nature and complexity of the product, the competition, market growth, market share and so forth.

In spite of the growing importance of promotion and advertising in selling products, personal selling still occupies an important place in marketing strategy. The reason is simple. Although advertisement can make consumers familiar with a product, the final persuasion to buy is often achieved through personal selling. For many companies sales-force costs are the largest single item in the marketing budget. It is, therefore, important that appropriate people are recruited and trained as members of sales-force. Furthermore, sales-force is to be correctly organised and employed to achieve the best possible result.

Personal selling is the most widely used means by which organisations communicate with their customers. There are many companies who have achieved considerable success even without advertising. It is the most commonly used promotional tool. Money spent on personal selling far exceeds money spent on advertising. This becomes clear when one considers the numbers of people engaged in selling and the cost of training, compensation and incidental expenses account associated with selling.

The importance of personal selling varies considerably across organisations. Some organisations may rely almost entirely on their sales forces to generate sales while others use them to support a putting strategy based on advertising. Some organisations employ sales people who do little professional selling, while others employ engineers and scientists as technical sales representatives. After all, the marketing manager must decide which selling skills and job descriptions are appropriate to the sales objectives to be achieved.

Three types of selling positions

There are three basic categories of selling positions. These are commonly referred to as order-taking, order-getting and sales-support positions. These people, who do very little creative selling, are called order-takers. They write up orders, check invoices for accuracy and ensure timely order processing. By contrast, order-getters must seek out customers, analyse their problems, discover how the product for sale might solve those problems, and then bring these solutions to the attention of the customer.

After-sales-service

After-sales-service is a necessary part of selling any piece of complex machinery or electrical equipment to final consumers or industrial buyers. Good after-sales-service can give a company a competitive edge over equivalent alternative products and so help to maintain and increase company sales. Furthermore, good servicing will help maintain product performance, enhancing quality reputation and increasing the chance that consumers will buy the same product again and again. However, such services are expensive to provide. So companies providing them must ensure providing sufficient service to ensure customer-satisfaction without over-staffing.

Creative-selling

Creative selling is the ability to explain the product and its inherent qualities (or special attributes) in terms of benefits and advantages to the prospective buyer and to persuade and motivate the prospect to purchase the right quality and volume of product or service. Whereas the order-taker's job is to keep the sales, the order-getter's job is to make the sale. In other words, the primary function of the creative sales person is to generate a sale that might not occur without his (her) efforts. The salesperson, in this case, is virtually required to interpret the prospect's need and to convince the prospect of the benefits the new product being offered can provide.

Sales support

Some sales people are involved in special selling situations. A salesperson of this sort is the so-called 'missionary'. Missionary sales personnel in fact readily take or actively seek orders; their primary responsibility is to build goodwill by distributing information to customers and prospective customers and by checking it, to be sure that buyers are being satisfactorily serviced by company representatives and pan necessary orders to channel members such as wholesalers. They are employed by the manufacturer to perform a kind of public relations function.

Pharmaceutical companies employ missionaries, called 'detailers', to call on doctors and provide them with information on the latest prescription and non-prescription products. Detailers do not take orders; sales occur only when the doctor prescribes medication for patients.

In many organisations, the sales-person in contact with customer is supported by a sales team. If a creative sales person successfully closes a deal, he (she) has perhaps called upon a technical specialist or master salesperson for help (assistance). Sometimes, the customers may be provided with the name and phone number of a sales correspondent, someone at company headquarters who can answer questions about delivery, after-sales service, installation and repair parts when the salesperson is away from the home office.

The effective sales team is a good representation of the marketing concept in action. It reflects an effort to satisfy customers, not just to sell products.

The creative selling process includes the following steps : (1) locating and qualifying the prospects (prospecting means identifying likely buyers from lists of previous customers, referrals, trade lists, advertising inquiries), (2) approaching the prospect (making an initial contact and establishing rapport with the prospect); (5) closing the sale; and (6) following up.

ADVERTISING

The basic aim of all promotion or selling efforts is to increase the sales of the product and possibly improving the product's market-share. Promotional efforts can take a variety of forms, but perhaps the most important of these is advertising. Promotion, including advertisement, is basically and essentially a form of communication.

To be effective, advertising aimed at supporting the marketing strategy for a company's products (services) must ultimately influence buyer purchase decisions (sales). However, the relationship between advertising and sales is difficult to sort out. Advertising combines with a host of other influences to determine buyers' purchase decisions. The problem is to figure out what contribution advertising made to those decisions.

This dilemma causes marketing managers to disagree about the objectives for advertising. Some managers believe that advertising should achieve communication objectives, while others argue for setting sales objectives.

Communication Objective

Supporters of communication objectives feel that advertising should contribute to the entire company sales effort but should not be expected to achieve any given level of sales. They argue that it is not fair to expect advertising to do the whole job of meeting a company's sales objectives. Instead, advertising objectives should state expected performance in terms of what audiences should think and feel — developing awareness of product benefits, generating positive attitudes and emotions toward the product, or creating a strong intention to buy as and when the need arise.

The primary purpose of advertising is to convey to audiences information about a company and its products. On the basis of this information, customers form beliefs, likes and dislikes, predispositions and intentions that later influence purchase decisions. In this way, advertising contributes to the total selling effort of a marketing strategy but does not carry the entire burden of generating sales.

Communication objectives should be derived from studying people in target groups. The fundamentals of buyer behaviour offer guidelines on what to study.

Sales Objectives

Proponents of sales-related objectives hold that advertising should achieve such performance as growth in sales, market share, or even profits.

Advocates of sales-related objectives argue that such objectives tie advertising directly to the same kinds of performance objectives that are expected from the overall marketing strategy. Further, they point out that the relationship between achieving communication objectives and generating sales is not clear. In fact, the controversy would not exist if effective communication always led to higher sales, market share and profits. However, being aware of a product and knowing certain benefits may not be enough to influence consumers to purchase, particularly if these benefits are not important to them.

There is probably a middle ground. Sales objectives provide little guidance to those who must design advertising campaigns and sales as a measure of advertising effectiveness do not explain why an advertising campaign was (or was not) successful. Communication objectives are more useful than sales objectives for determining what to say to audiences. Furthermore, measures to determine how well communication objectives have been achieved are widely available. For these reasons, communication objectives should play at least a part in determining the mission of advertising. At the same time, managers should be concerned about the extent to which achieving communication objectives contributes to sales-related measures of performance.

Three Major Concerns

Three special concerns of advertising include repetition, message execution and operations management.

Repetition. One operational objective of advertising might be to produce as many repetitions as are needed for as many people in a target groups as is possible. Still another strategy is to introduce new product attributes not advertised earlier.

Message execution. How should one design and implement an advertisement? At least three issues must be addressed here. One is *media involvement*. Different media create different problems and offer different opportunities.

A related issue is *product involvement*. Just as consumers are involved to different degrees with different media, so too do they find products to be important in varying degrees. *Brand involvement* can be a factor. People are attached to or identify with brands to different degrees.

Finally, message execution should take into account how consumers will react to a message and the processes they will go through as they react. Marketing people have found that the following sequences occur most frequently in real-world decision making :

1. learn → feel → do
2. feel → learn → do
3. do → learn → feel
4. do → feel → learn

By 'learn' we mean the comprehension, information integration and decision-making activities. 'Feel' refers to needs, motives, affective responses, attitudes and preference formation. 'Do' stands for actual trial or repeat buying activities or other behaviours: shopping, examination of independent consumer reports, talking to a salesperson, making a purchase and so on.

If advertisers have detailed and correct information about how consumers react to messages and the processes they go through in decision-making, they can create more effective ads. After all, advertising is largely based on information about buyers.

These considerations are, of course, only rough guidelines. In the final analysis, any ad will reflect the particular philosophy, history and style of the ad agency that creates it. Thus marketers must not only know their own products, customers and competitors well but must also carefully evaluate alternative agencies and ad executions to arrive at a proper fit. These are largely subjective decisions.

Two Types of Advertising

Advertisement is of two types, *viz.*, product advertising and institutional advertising.

Product Advertising

Advertising for Babul Gum, Maggie noodles, and many other brands are clearly intended to suggest purchasing a particular product. When Godrej announces a special price on refrigerators, the message is that the refrigerators must be bought now if the low price is desired. This type of advertising is called product advertising because it features a special product. Because the Godrej refrigerator advertisement suggests an immediate purchase, it is also a direct-action advertisement. Many advertisements seen on television and many direct mail advertisements are of this type. Direct action advertisements, in general, utilise discount coupons to encourage people to buy now. Much retail advertising emphasises direct action. Less aggressive advertisements, designed to sell products as well as to build brand image rather than to sell merchandise right now, are also forms of product advertising. This type of advertisement calls for indirect action. The indirect action advertisement makes use of a soft-sell approach directed to stimulate sales over the longer run.

In this context we draw a distinction between the following two types of advertising :

(i) ***Primary-Demand Advertising.*** Sometimes advertising is designed to increase the total demand for a good (such as woollen clothing) or service, rather than a particular brand. This is called primary demand advertising.

(ii) ***Selective Advertising.*** More typically, advertisements are designed to increase the demand for a particular brand of product. Advertising with this objective is called selective advertising. When Pepsi-Cola calls itselfs "the right choice" it is implying that other soft drinks might not be much of a good choice.

Institutional Advertising

Institutional advertisements aim to promote a corporate image, to stimulate generic demand for a product or to build goodwill for an industry. Such advertisement is likely to have long-term effects.

General Objectives

The basic objective of advertisement is to sell the product. Since advertisement is only one element of the marketing mix, effective advertisement campaigns are developed as part of an overall marketing strategy and are tightly coordinated with the other facts of the promotional mix.

In general, advertisers expect to accomplish four broad communication goals:

(i) to generate attention;

(ii) to be understood;

(iii) to be believed; and

(iv) to be remembered.

These goals relate to sales, but they are primarily matters of communication. If these broad objectives are not considered and met, the more specific objectives will not be met either. If attention is not paid to an advertisement, the more specific objective — such as enhancing a brand image — cannot be achieved. Likewise, an advertisement must be understood and believed if it is to reinforce or change perceptions about a brand's characteristics. If it is not remembered, it will have little effect on buyer behaviour. Although these broad objectives permeate most of advertising, the development of advertisement campaigns requires that objectives must be more specific.

Specific Objectives

Encouraging increased consumption of a product by current users, generating more sales levels, increasing brand awareness, increasing repeat purchases and supporting the personal selling effort are typical objectives for specific advertisements. Opportunities in the marketplace, competitive advertising c ampaigns, stage in the product life cycle and prior marketing strategy decisions, such as selection of a target market segment — all influence the development of specific advertising objectives.

Regardless of the form advertising takes or advertising media used, its ultimate objective is to sell more goods and services. To this end, advertisement may introduce a new product or encourage people to buy the good or service more often. Sometimes, companies use ads that attempt to create a positive image of the firm, in the hope that customers will be more induced to buy from a company they admire.

THREE FUNCTIONS

Advertising performs the following three functions :

1. Provision of information

Firstly, advertising communicates information about changes in a product or in the price of the product to a large numbers of potential customers in an efficient and relatively cheap manner. So they are relieved of the burden of having to collect this information at a cost.

In fact, a good deal of price and product information is provided by advertisement. New product often offer a challenging marketing problem. Because consumers have little or no experience with the product, the advertisement decision is complicated by the firm's lack of experience on the effectiveness of advertisement for that particular product. In the absence of any information, the manager must use his own judgement on advertising effectiveness and choose some level of advertising. Advertisement is usually more beneficial for new products, because consumers have no information about such products. This is why a singificant amount of advertising is devoted to new products. For instance, extensive advertising campaigns accompanied the introduction of processed food, video recorders and instant coffee makers to the consumer market. The cost of informing consumers about new products makes their introduction more difficult.

False Advertisement. False advertisement is the provision of incorrect information. Typically, a product's qualities are exaggerated in order to increase sales. This distorts consumer choice and this is why advertisement is treated as a technique of demand manipulation (rather than genuine demand creation).

2. *Persuasion*

Perhaps more important than its informative role is persuasive function of advertising. Advertisement helps to overcome consumer resistance to new products, and it is an important factor in competition since it aims to persuade customers to buy one company's product or brand in preference to alternatives offered by competitors.

3. *Product Differentiation*

Advertisement plays an important part in differentiating products in the eyes of consumers. Although differentiation may well be based initially upon differences in the charactersitics of competing products — differences in design, quality, performance, colour, patented features, trade marks, packaging and so on — it is advertising which stresses these differences and brings consumers to regard one brand of a product as being different from another. Often the actual physical differences between competing products is small. In such cases advertisement assumes even greater importance. It emphasises the psychological satisfactions to be derived from one brand as opposed to alternatives. It also highlights the appropriateness of this brand to particular groups of consumers.

The marketing of a new product is affected by the ease with which the consumer can ascertain the characteristics of the product. For example, if a shopper considers buying a package of forzen beans, he can find out important characteristics like appearance, smell and taste only after the beans have been bought, cooked and eaten. When a new product is introduced, the major promotional problems is not only making consumers aware of its existence but also of its physical characteristics. Advertising is well suited to this effort.

The Advertising Mix

Advertising is a paid, nonpersonal presentation of offerings (ideas, goods or services) by an identified sponsor. It can be defined as a form of promotion in which a firm attempts to persuade someone to a particular point of view. Of all of the marketing mix components, advertising is the most intuitively relevant one for communicating the product concept. Advertising also reduces important perceptual and value barriers between customers and the firm. Through advertising, customers come to know about the existence of a new product. They can also gain information such as where they can buy it, at what price, and when it will be available. In addition, advertising can reduce value barriers by demonstrating the product's worth and hence the reason why it is priced at the selected level. By reducing value barriers, the feeling of risk associated with a purchase is lowered.

Advertising is intended to create brand loyalty. Loyal customers are likely to buy the same brand all the time even if competitors offer nearly identical products.

Operations aspects

Finally, the advertising effort must be well managed. Two critical concerns here are advertising media, copy testing and advertising budgeting. The company must also decide which advertising media to use — television, radio, cinema, newspapers, magazines, specialised journals, direct-mailing and so on. This will depend largely on the products being advertised and the target population to be reached.

Copy testing refers to measurement of the effectivenesss of advertising. Although statistical and mathematical modelling can be used to establish the relationship between advertising expenditures and sales (or market share), more frequently the effects of ads are determined by gauging their impact on intermediate variables, such as consumers' awareness, knowledge, recall or recognition of the ad; their beliefs about the product's attributes; their interest in the product, and their intentions to buy or not to buy. Such indirect measurement is employed because it is easier, cheaper, and yet thought to be reasonably valid.

Since no company has unlimited resources for promoting products it is important that a company has a promotion policy and decides how much to spend on advertising, and which advertising media to use, so as to achieve a desired level of product-sales in the cheapest way. How much money a company spends in total on advertisement will depend to a large extent upon its level of sales, the amount that competitors are spending and the return which the company expects on its investment in advertising.

Advertising budgets are set in a variety of ways. Sometimess, a budget is made on the basis of subjective judgements by executives. A second method is simply to fix the budget to that of the competitor's: to meet the competitor's budget, exceed it, or fall below it by some percentage. Usually, however, budgets are set as a percentage of sales (*e.g.*, last quarter's or this quarter's expectations). A better way is to set ad budgets at levels needed to achieve some desired goal. The *objective and task method* attempts to do just this. The organisation first defines a specific goal to be achieved — say, "60% awareness of our new brand in market *Y* by next year". Next, the tasks — number of repetitions, media selection, spokesperson, and so forth — are designed to reach the goal. The budget is then set on the basis of the tasks needed to reach the goal.

CREATION OF ADVERTISING CAMPAIGN

Perhaps the most creative part of advertising is planning an *advertising campaign*. The campaign determines what to say to target audiences and how to say it so that people will listen to and understand the messages and remember them when buying decisions are made. Fig. 2.18 shows (next page) the steps that creative specialists follow to design a campaign.

Marketing Position Statement

A marketing plan should provide a position statement explaining how a company's product (or service) is to be differentiated from those of key competitors. This statement is derived from an analysis of market opportunities. The most important assessments are those of customers' market requirements and competitors' strengths and weaknesses. The advertiser's own strengths and weaknesses must also be considered.

Complimentary Role of Advertising and Salesmanship

The role of personal selling varies considerably across firms. In a typical industrial organisation, personal selling dominates the marketing programme — almost to the exclusion of other forms of promotion. At the other extreme, mail order firms (like the *Reader's Digest*) rely entirely on advertising and employ no field sales-people at all.

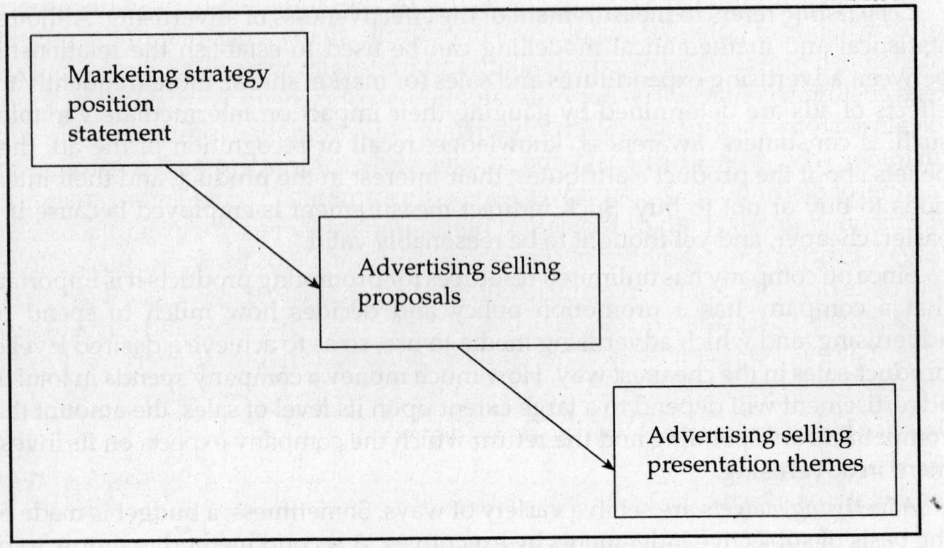

Fig. 2.18 : Advertising Creative Strategy Decisions

Promotion involves a communication process in which prospective customers are made aware of the existence and relatively desirability of a firm's products and services. The promotional mix is a combination of the promotional tools — personal selling, advertising, publicity, sales promotion and public relations designed to sell goods and services. Each element of the promotional mix has a part to play in the marketing programme. For most companies, the focus of the promotional effort is on advertising. Advertising is designed to build awareness of the product class and to inform the customer about product features (such as durability, safety, fuel efficiency, etc., as in case of cars). Sales promotion techniques, such as discount coupons as in the case of light consumer goods, are used to get buyers to take immediate action to choose and pick up items in retail stores. Personal selling helps answer customer questions and provides an opportunity to persuade buyers to sign purchase orders.

Although personal selling or salesmanship is crucial in developing and maintaining distribution of consumer goods, communication to the mass market can be accomplished more efficiently through advertising.

Advertising is a direct effort to create sales and makes use of many media. Advertising is often used by a firm to "open the door" for its sales-people, especially in the industrial market. That is, for the salesperson to be effective, the firm and products that the salesperson represents should already be familiar to the potential buyer. In this case, advertising complements and enhances the direct selling effort. Yet direct contact is usually essential for obtaining an order.

The primary decision in the design of the promotional mix usually is whether to put the major emphasis on personal selling or on advertising. Sales promotion is typically viewed as supplementary.

Push versus Pull

The personal selling technique is often used when an organisation believes that a product needs to be pushed through channels of distribution. Sales force push means that represntatives talk to prospective buyers and literally push the product into the hands of potential customers. For example, many small manufacturers rely on the push provided by personal selling and trade fairs and exhibitions to gain and keep customer contacts. The opposite situation occurs when advertising pull is used to gain customer acceptance. With advertising pull, promotion is directed at the final customer who, in his turn, asks the retailer of the product to pull it through the channel of distribution. Heavy advertising is the common practice among marketers of consumer goods (both durables and non-durables). Let us, for example, take the case of Procter and Gamble. But there are exceptions. For example, the Cadbury chocolate bar does not receive much advertising support. Yet it is a leading seller in India. Its success is directly related to the push provided by a large and efficient sales force that has been able to get this convenience good in almost every part of the country.

Balance between Personal Selling and Advertising

For many products, a given sales level can often be reached by using various combinations of advertising and personal selling, as is indicated in Fig. 2.19.

Fig. 2.19 : Balancing Personal Selling and Advertising Expenditures

Fig. 2.19 shows that Rs 1 crore in sales can be achieved through high expenditures on personal selling, high levels of advertising, or some combination between these extremes. This point is illustrated by the promotional strategies of two hypothetical firms, which we call *X* Co. and *Y* Co. *X* Co. employs a huge sales force who sell door-to-door to their neighbours, whereas advertising plays a relatively minor role in its marketing strategy. In fact, *X* Co. spends a small percent of sales on this promotional activity, and the primary purpose of much of its advertising seems to be to recruit additional sales-people, whereas specific products are rarely routed. *Y* Co., in contrast, has relied on large advertising expenditure to make customers aware of its products and to draw them into its numerous retail stores spread all over the country that handle its cosmetics. Although *Y* Co. employs sales-people to call on retailers and to help close the sale of its products at cosmetic counters, its high sales level and extensive distribution could not be maintained without heavy and aggressive advertising. The proper balance between personal selling and advertising must be determined for each organisation. These two promotional tools complement each other and each has its rightful place in any marketing programme.

Advantages of Personal Selling over Advertising

In contrast to advertising, personal selling establishes a two-way communication between the salesperson and buyer that allows the sales message to be adopted to the special circumstances of the customer. Personal selling is especially important when there is need for a detailed explanation or demonstration of the product. A salesperson is free to vary the message according to the motivations and interests of each prospective buyer. Moreover, when objections are raised, the salesperson is there to put forward tailor-made counter-arguments and suggest explanations. Advertising can only respond to objections that are important to customers. Furthermore, personal selling can be specifically directed to knowledgeable and genuine customers, whereas a great deal of advertising is wasted because many people in the audience have no use of the product. Personal selling is more flexible in that the sales force can vary in size from one person to thousands. By contrast, advertising must be purchased as a campaign in fairly large blocks. Perhaps the most important advantage of personal selling is that it is considerably more effective than advertising in closing the sale.

Conclusion

Synchronising personal selling with advertising is particularly important. Advertising may prove uneconomic unless the sales force capitalises upon the interest created. Personal selling effort is wasted in explaining details that might be explained by advertising. But when sales personnel and the advertising use the same appeals — if both tell the same story — the promotional impact becomes stronger. The timing and sequence with which different phases of the personal selling and advertising efforts are executed affect the firm's chances for marketing success. An advertising effort should be implemented within the context of the larger marketing effort. The same is true also of personal selling effort.

2.13 CHANNEL OF DISTRIBUTION

The marketing system is made up of a large number of organisations and individuals, linked together by flows of information, products, negotiations, risks, money and people. Specific firms together form a channel of distribution that connects products with people and organisations that consume the products. Each channel in the marketing system seeks to satisfy the needs and wants of targeted end users, and also to meet the objectives of the channel's participants (Fig. 2.20).

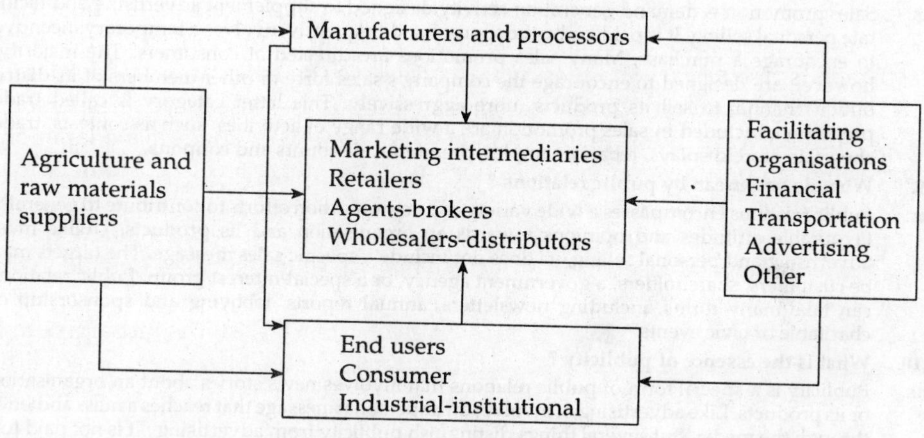

Fig. 2.20 : The Marketing System

Each organisation in the distribution channel performs particular activities in connecting end users with desired goods and services. This point may now be explained and illustrated.

Synopsis for Learning

Q.1. What is the nature of promotion ?

Ans. Promotion is a demand-stimulating activity.

Q.2. What are the determinants of a company's promotional mix ?

Ans. Four factors influence a company's promotional mix, *viz.*, (1) the target market, (2) the nature of the product, (3) the stage of the product's life cycle and (4) the promotional budget, *i.e.*, the amount of money available for promotion.

Q.3. How does a firm communicate with its potential customers ?

Ans. Three marketing mix activities of product planning, pricing and distribution are performed mainly within a business or between a business and the members of its distribution channels. However, through its promotional activities, a firm communicates directly with potential customers. And it is a complex process.

Q.4. What is the basic objective of promotional methods ?

Ans. The basic objective of promotional methods is to influence. More specifically, promotion is the element in an orgaisation's marketing mix that serves to inform, persuade and remind the market of a product and/or the organisation selling it, for influencing the recipients' feelings, beliefs, or buying behaviour.

Q.5. What are the five different forms of promotion ?

Ans. There are five forms of promotion : personal selling, advertising, sales promotion, public relations and publicity. Each has distinct features that determine in what situations it will be most effective.

Synopsis for Learning (contd...)

Q.6. What is personal selling ?

Ans. Personal selling is the direct presentation of a product to a prospective customer by a representative of the organisation selling it. Personal selling takes place face to face or over the phone, and it may be directed to a middleman or a final consumer.

Q.7. What is advertising ?

Ans. Advertising is impersonal mass communication that the sponsor has paid for and in which the sponsor is clearly identified. The most familiar forms of ads are found in the broadcast (TV and radio) and print media (newspapers and magazines).

Q.8. What is sales promotion ?

Ans. Sales promotion is demand generation activity designed to supplement advertising and facilitate personal selling. It is paid for by the sponsor and frequently involves a temporary incentive to encourage a purchase. Many sales promotions are directed at consumers. The majority, however, are designed to encourage the company's sales force or other members of its distribution channel to sell its products more aggressively. This latter category is called trade promotion. Included in sales promotion are a wide range of activities, such as contests, trade shows, in-store displays, rebates, samples, premiums, discounts and coupons.

Q.9. What do you mean by public relations ?

Ans. Public relations encompasses a wide variety of communication efforts to contribute to generally favourable attitudes and opinions towards an organisation and its products. Unlike most advertising and personal selling, its does not include a specific sales message. The targets may be customers, shareholders, a government agency, or a special-interest group. Public relations can take many forms, including newsletters, annual reports, lobbying and sponsorship of charitable or civic events.

Q.10. What is the essence of publicity ?

Ans. Publicity is a special form of public relations that involves news stories about an organisation or its products. Like advertising, it involves an impersonal message that reaches a mass audience through the media. But several things distinguish publicity from advertising : It is not paid for, the organisation that is the subject of the publicity has no control over it, and it appears as news and, therefore, has greater credibility than advertising.

Q.11. What is the difference between advertising and salesmanship ?

Ans. Communication to the mass marketing can be accomplished most effectively through advertising. But salesmanship is still crucial in developing and maintaining distribution of various consumer goods.

Q.12. What is the relation between advertising and salesmanship?

Ans. In case of most consumer goods and few industrial goods advertising complements and enhances salesmanship (*i.e.*, the direct selling effort). So salesmanship and advertising are to be viewed as complementary. One complements the other.

2.14 RESPECTIVE RULES OF PRIVATE DISTRIBUTION SYSTEM AND PUBLIC DISTRIBUTION SYSTEM IN INDIA

A distribution system can be defined as the set of people, organisations and equipment involved in the satisfactory flow of goods or services from the producer to the customer, and it is designed to help achieve the manufacturer's goals and objectives. The design of the distribution system and how it affects customer satisfaction and the achievement of company goals and objectives depend on various factors.

One of these factors is the product or service being marketed. The choice of a distribution system needs to be an integral part of the overall marketing strategy.

Another factor affecting the design of distribution systems is the company's brand objectives. Some companies seek widespread recognition for their products and want them to be available wherever and whenever the customer needs it. If many retail establishments are available, the company may use a distribution approach that maximises the number of stores that carry the brand and use mass advertising to create recognition. In fact, a company's distribution system can affect all other areas of the marketing mix.

Marketing Intermediaries

Most of the goods and services available in a modern economy are produced at relatively few locations to obtain the cost advantages of large-scale production. This creates a need for a distribution function — a way of connecting suppliers with consumers. Three options exist :

- Each producer can go directly to consumers of its products or services.
- Each consumer can go to the producers.
- Intermediaries can help perform the activities necessary to link suppliers with customers.

The marketing system contains examples of all three approaches. For many goods and services, due to the costs involved and the types services desired by consumers, the direct producer-consumer exchange is simply not feasible. Marketing intermediaries form distribution channels to fill this gap between producers and end-users. Intermediaries drastically reduce the number of buyer-seller transactions. The size and complexity of the modern market-based economy like that of India in advanced societies make the transactional function provided by intermediaries essential.

By taking advantage of the economies obtainable through large-scale purchases and specialisation and by greatly reducing the number of transactions needed to bring end-users and producers together, middlemen perform functions that are often not posible for manufacturers or end-users.

Companies in the distribution channel perform various functions — procurement, storage, packaging, financing, transportation and counselling. A substantial portion of the price paid by customers for products and services is frequently accounted for by activities performed by these companies.

The term 'channel of distribution' suggests a path that goods take as they flow from producers to consumers. In this sense, the channel of distribution is defined by the organisation(s) or individual(s) along the route from producer to consumer. Because the beginning and ending points of the route must be included, both producer and consumer are always members of the channel of distribution. However, there may be intermediate steps along the way. Several marketing institutions have been developed to facilitate the flow of the physical product, or title to the product, from the producer to the consumer. Organisations that serve as marketing intermediaries (middlemen) specialising in distribution rather than production are external to the producing organisation. When these intermediaries join with a manufacturer in a loose coalition to engage in exploiting joint opportunities, a channel of distribution is formed.

Any discussion of distribution channels concerns a product that has taken on its final form. The channel of distribution for an automobile, for example, begins after the product becomes a finished automobile. It does not include the paths new materials (such as steel) or component parts (such as tyres) take to the automobile manufacturer who is an industrial user in these other channels.

Two Tasks

The channel must accomplish two major tasks : (1) transferring the title to the product and (2) facilitating the physical movement of the goods to their ultimate destrination (which is a simple matter of transportation).

What a Channel Involves

All but the shortest of channels (such as from producer direct to consumer channels) include one or more channel members who perform activities between the producer and the final user. These intermediaries are individuals or organisations specialising in distribution rather than production. They are of two broad categories, *viz.*, merchant intermediaries who take title to the product and agent intermediaries who never own the goods. But they perform a number of marketing functions, such as selling, that facilitate faster transaction in the exchange process.

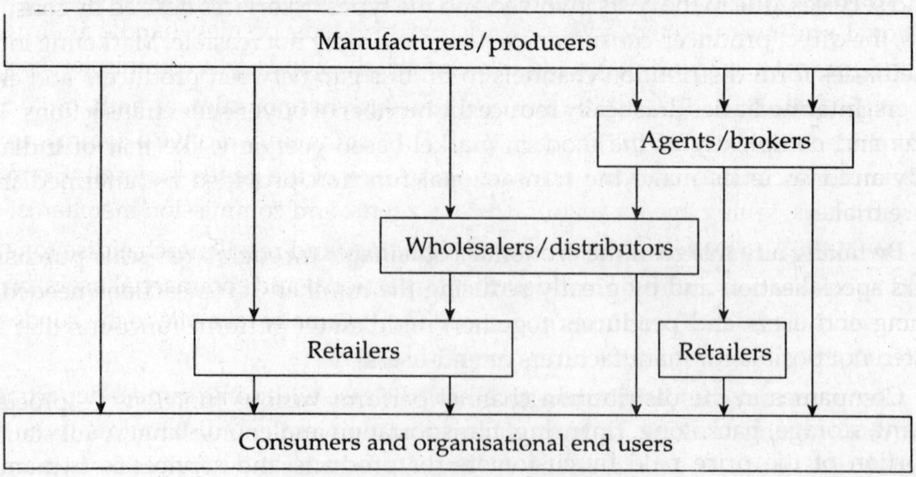

Fig. 2.21 : Alternative Marketing Channels

In most cases, intermediaries are independent organisations tied to the producers who deal only by mutual agreements. They are not owned by the producers. Other intermediaries are owned by produers, such as the company-owned sales branches and sales offices.

In service marketing, there appears to be hardly any channel of distribution. When a beauty parlour delivers a product, such as a haircut or make-up advice, it deals directly with the customers. The shortest of distribution channels is found in these cases.

Two Types of Channel of Distribution

For the sake of analysis, we may draw a distinction between two types of channel of distribution, *viz.*, the conventional channel and vertical marketing systems. The former is characterised by loosely aligned, relatively autonomous marketing organisations that have developed a system to carry out a trade relationship. By contrast, vertical marketing systems are far more formally organised systems because channel members are either owned by a manufacturer or a distributor, linked by strong contracts or agreements, or managed and coordinated as an integrated system.

Transportation companies, financial institutions or other functional specialists who sell a service that helps the flow of goods and services are not included in the channel of distribution. They are merely facilitators, playing only a minor role by providing a limited service that is useful to the channel member.

Over time, inefficient intermediaries are eliminated from the marketing system. The competitive marketplace generates new distribution alternatives when entrepreneurs see better ways to provide cost-effective services to buyers and when buyers are willing to consider different levels of customer service. Currently, one of the most rapidly expanding distribution concepts is nonstore marketing via such means as mail, telephone, vending machines, and door-to-door selling.

Classification of Intermediaries

Marketing intermediaries can be classified by ownership of goods :

Retailers. Businesses that buy and resell merchandise to consumer and organisational end-users. Retailers may take title to goods or may handle them on a consignment basis without taking title and sell the goods on a commission basis.

Agents/Brokers. Businesses that negotiate purchase or sales, or both, but do not take title to the goods in which they deal. They commonly receive a commission or fee and may or may not take physical possession of the goods they sell. Examples are brokers, selling agents, manufacturer's agents and commission merchants.

Wholesalers/Distributors. Businesses that buy and resell merchandise to retailers and other merchants or to industrial, institutional and commercial users, but do not sell in significant amount to end-users. They normally take title to the goods they sell.

Retailers may also lease store space, as is the case with some camera departments in retail establishments. Unlike retailers and wholesalers/distributors (who take title to the goods they handle), agents/brokers, because they do not take title are not required to take market risk (the risk of price fluctuations).

Middlemen may also be classified by their level in the channel of distribution. Alternative marketing channels are shown in Fig. 2.21. Closest to consumers and organisational end users are retailers. Manufacturers may employ salespersons for contacting wholesalers and distributors and sometimes own their sales offices and branches. If sales personnel cannot be economically justified by the sales volume and the profits from their activities (due perhaps to a limited product line), manufacturers may use agents or brokers on a commission basis.

There are important relationships between marketers at a given level of distribution. Marketers may join together for mutual advantage in voluntary groups and retailer cooperatives. Pooled buying groups include, for example, independent grocers who work cooperatively to lower the costs of goods purchased from wholesalers. Pooling of orders has allowed independent grocers to receive better prices from wholesalers and to compete with chain stores. Shopping centres also illustrate horizontal channel relationships, with the combination of stores creating a greater customer-attracting force than would the stores as separate and dispersed establishments.

Wholesaling versus Retailing

The two principal distribution sectors are wholesalers and retailers. The retail sector includes such establishments as food stores, automotive dealers, general merchandise stores, restaurants and speciality stores.

Merchant wholesalers purchase, sort, assemble, grade and store goods in large quantities and sell this merchandise to retailers and to institutional, agriculture, government, professional and industrial users. These wholesalers also extend credit and a variety of services both to customers and suppliers, many of whom are small businesses. For their customers, they provide delivery service and sales promotion suggestions. To their suppliers, they pass on marketing information about changes in consumer behaviour and purchasing habits.

Types of Channels

A channel of distribution exists because its participants, through specialisation of functions and transactional efficiencies, can perform the marketing function better with intermediaries than without them. Arrangements in a channel are continually modified to improve efficiency and to strengthen advantages over competing channels.

The channel of distribution is the system of institutions used to deliver goods to the final consumer. The intermediaries who make up a given channel might include brokers, manufacturers' representatives, distributors, wholesalers and retailers. Some or all might be wholly owned by the manufaturer or even by one of the intermediaries. Alternatively, the system might consist of independent businesses that buy and sell the goods of producers or act as the producers' agents through contractual agreements. Still another possibility is that a manufacturer might sell directly to its customers without going through intermediaries. For instance, direct mail, a sales force coupled with delivery through common carriers, or mobile company stores might be used. With greater sophistication in communication, market research, operations and delivery firms are frequently turning to **direct marketing** to reach customers. No matter what system is employed to bring the goods to market, certain functions must be fulfilled: transportation, storage, transfer of title, provision of credit or other special services, assortments, selling, delivery, receipt of funds and so on.

Channel decisions must be considered carefully for three main reasons. First and most obvious, the channel of distribution is an essential link, a gatekeeper to the market. Shelf space in the supermarket or an account with an aggressive distribution is not only a necessity but tends to function as a self-fulfilling prophecy. That is, the channel stimulates demand, just as advertising, product design and price cuts do. Secondly, it is very expensive and time-consuming to set up and maintain a distribution channel. The commitment risks are great and there is little room for error. Moreover, it is difficult to make changes in a channel once the channel has been set in place. Thirdly, the channel of distribution may provide the competitive edge over rivals. This edge may be a unique location, efficient delivery and inventory practices, special selling skills, market monitoring services or some other advantage.

Most consumer goods manufacturers find that it is easier and cheaper to go through independent wholesalers or distributors than it is to sell to retailers. Industrial goods firms sometimes sell through distributors, yet in many cases they find direct selling possible.

If management decides to sell through intermediaries, then it must choose the breadth of coverage needed to reach consumers. Three possibilities exist. One is an intensive distribution system, in which the producer seeks as many outlets for its products as possible in a market area. This option is most appropriate for selling to the mass market, particularly by producers of convenience consumer goods (*e.g.*, breakfast cereal or paper napkins) or undifferentiated industrial goods (*e.g.*, nuts and bolts). Buyers of these goods do little shopping around, purchase with a minimal amount of deliberation, and value convenience more than anything else. Intensive distribution also lends itself to products whose costs per unit to store, display, or sell are low.

A second breadth of coverage option is exclusive distribution. This is the polar opposite of intensive distribution in that only a single outlet per market area is utilised. The producer hopes to create a unique image for its product, to obtain more vigorous selling efforts and to extend its control over certain practices of the distributor or retailer (for instance in pricing, quality control, or market monitoring). In exchange, the intermediary receives the right to be the sole seller for the producer's area. Most automotive companies, some manufacturers of expensive musical instruments and certain applicance-makers use exclusive distribution arrangements.

Selective distribution is the third option for achieving breadth of coverage. Here, the firm seeks more than one, but considerably fewer than all outlets in a market in the hope of obtaining many of the advantages of exclusive distribution while at the same time reaching further into the market. However, being a compromise tactic, it shares one disadvatnage of both polar extremes. Selective distribution is especially appropriate for medium to moderately high priced shopping, speciality or industrial goods where personal selling is required.

Vertical marketing system is so designated because the channel operates as a cohesive, integrated network of organisations and is managed by one of the channel members. In the conventional channel, the participants function on an independent basis, there is a lack of overall channel coordination, and the arrangement is usually less than optimal.

Management must decide on the type of channel to be utilised. Vertical marketing system is the predominant form for consumer products, while direct distribution is often used by industrial firms. Many types of conventional channels of distribution also function within the marketing system. The selection of a channel strategy provides a basis for identifying suitable channel types for a given firm.

In addition to choosing a breadth of coverage option, the user of intermediaries also must decide upon the vertical *length of the channel system*. Here, too, at least three possibilities exist : corporate, contractual, or independent (also termed conventional or administered) systems.

The **corporate marketing channel** is one in which all stages from manufacture to distribution come under single ownership.

The advantages of a corporate system include lower costs (through standardization and other economies of scale) and greater control than with the other options. In particular, a firm can achieve more influence over hiring, pricing, promotion and selling, provision of service, and even product quality with a corporate system than it can with a contractual or an independent system. On the other hand, corporate systems require very large capital investments, are risky both financially and legally (*i.e.*, they may invite anti-trust actions), and tend to be less adaptive to changing market and competitive conditions. It should be noted that some firms employ a modified corporate channel system by vertically integrating partway into distribution.

Contractual channel system consists of collections of more or less independent companies bound by legal agreements akin to exclusive distribution, yet going even further. The most common contractual systems are franchises, but retail cooperatives and voluntary chains organised by wholesalers are also examples.

Under franchising, the franchisor provides the franchisee with materials, a product, financial knowhow, and other services. An exclusive right to sell the franchisor's product or service in a market area is also provided. The franchisee, in turn, agrees to abide by certain requirements and procedures dealing with selling, product or service quality, and other marketing functions, and perhaps also to pay a fee and/or percentage of revenues.

Independent channel system — the third vertical option — consists of loose associations of separate private enterprises that cooperate with each other for mutual gain. Typically, an independent wholesaler or distributor handles the goods for many producers and manufacturers. The services that independent intermediaries provide include such functions as storage and inventory control, delivery to retailers, provision of credit to buyers, a sales force, transfer of title and information gathering on the marketplace. The intermediary usually buys goods from a manufacturer at a discount and resells them to retailers at a profit.

In an exclusive distribution arrangement, the wholesaler, distributor or retailer does not market competing brands. Instead, the brand is carried by only one firm in a trading area. With selective distribution, a product is available in more than a single outlet or chain, but not everywhere that such a product might be carried. In addition to type of product, a strong brand image that attracts sufficient customers, adequate margins to support the necessary services and availability of qualified intermediaries are factors that suggest the choice of selective approaches. Over time, companies may change distribution intensity as the needs of target markets change or as marketing strategy is modified. Intensive distribution involves a broad network (departmental stores, discounters, speciality stores and other appropriate outlets). In this context, we may cite the example of Kodak film which is distributed through an intensive retail network.

IMPORTANCE OF DISTRIBUTION CHANNEL

A company's distribution or channel systems gives the company greater control of the flow of goods from the manufacturing site to the final customer. It also allows it to stabilise production schedules, which, in turn, contributes to efficient operations and better employee relations. Members of distribution system are marketing entities in their own right and share many of the same marketing challenges faced by producers.

The distribution centres are involved in marketing their services to many customers that would not be approached by the manufacturing divisions, as well as to some shared customers. A company's distribution centres are concerned with what services to offer, how to price those services, what type of sales-force to hire, and where to locate service facilities to reduce transportation costs. Examples of how marketing mix elements are manifest in the case of distribution-focused companies are illustrated in Table 2.10.

Table 2.10 : Marketing Mix Concerns of Distribution Focussed Companies

Company	Industry	Product	Price	Promotion	Distribution
TISCO	Steel distribution	Grades of steel in stock; customer services	Standard pricing for services; repeat business discounts	Direct sales; order-taking function	Location of distribution centres; relationships with transportation providers
McDonalds	Food retailer	Product assortment; national and private labels	Pricing for profitability by line; promotional discounting	Advertising	Location of stores based on population and shopping habits
McKesson	Drug wholesale	Product assortment and depth	Quantity discounts	Direct sales; order-taking function	Warehouse location; relationships with transportation providers

Synopsis for Learning

Q.1. What is channel of distribution ?

Ans. A channel of distribution refers to the set of people organisation and equipment involved in the satisfactory flow of goods or services from the producer to the consumer (final buyer).

Q.2. What are the features of private distribution system in India ?

Ans. There is no clear-cut rule or method relating to the distribution of goods in India through private channels. Various methods of distribution are adopted in India. Sometimes sales are through retailers. At times, selling agents are appointed. Agency sales are assuming more and more importance in India in recent years.

As a company achieves its goal of having the distribution system contribute as much as the company's revenue and profits as its manufacturing operations, the marketing concerns of the service centres will become increasingly important. In fact, the distribution side can become more important to success than the manufacturing side, particularly in the marketing of commodity products for which availability influences purchasers' decisions. Many steel products are difficult to differentiate as to manufacturer and are sold as commodities. This means that products are interchangeable between manufacturers and when one manufacturer does not have the product, customers will contact other manufacturers until they find the desired product. By having a variety of products available at a distribution centre, a company meets a greater proportion of customer requests than other manufacturers.

Managing Channel Relationships

Distribution decisions do not end with the design and establishment of the channel. Rather, choices must be made continuously with regard to channel modifications and ongoing management. Consumer tastes and purchase habits change, competitors invent new products and ways of marketing and intermediaries' loyalties and levels of performance shift over time. The firm must evaluate the effectiveness of its current channel relations and alter them as necessary. This might mean adding or eliminating wholesalers or retailers to change the breadth of coverage. More fundamentally, it might even mean introducing or bypassing a level in the length of the channel or exploring entirely new ways of bringing goods to the market. Which of these options is chosen will depend on the discovery of new markets or evolutions in old ones, competitive moves by rivals, or inadequacies in the existing arrangements.

Direct Marketing

Direct marketing is another marketing tactic that closely resembles promotion, although there are key differences. Direct marketing tactics allow firms to communicate directly to potential customers (usually through multiple media). Consumers, in turn, but directly from the firm. No intermediaries such as wholesalers or retailers are used. The most widely used means of direct marketing communication is through mail catalogues. However, direct marketing by telephone and television companies are also common. Typical examples of direct marketing include catalogue companies, publishing houses and book and record clubs. Financial service organisations such as credit card divisions now increasingly use direct marketing as well. Direct marketing works especially well with consumers who do not have the time, ability, or inclination to travel to stores. Of course, so many companies use it that it may have lost its edge.

PUBLIC DISTRIBUTION

Over the years, Indian public distribution system has come to be accepted as an effective instrument of controlling the prices of essential commodities. When the supplies of essential consumer goods do not increase in proportion to the rise in demand, it becomes essential for the State to accept the responsibility of providing these items at fair prices through the PDS.

Meaning

Public distribution system refers to the distribution of essential commodities through fair-price shops at controlled price, *i.e.*, prices fixed by the government from time to time. The public distribution system has been introduced due to the compelled necessity to maintain stable prices through efficient supply management. Various unfair trade practices such as creating artificial scarcity of goods with a view to earning excessive profit have called for the elimination of the middlemen from the channel of distribution of essential commodities. Herein lies the need for and importance of the public distribution system. Both foodgrains and industrial raw materials are released to the market just after the harvest when prices are generally low. In such a situation, the government has considered it necessary to set up various agencies to buy these products at support prices to ensure a certain minimum profit to the producers. The FCI is one such institution. These goods, purchased by the government agencies, are channelised through the public distribution system to the ultimate consumers. This is to ensure supplies of essential commodities even in the off-season at fair and stable prices. Due to public distribution system in India, we find the dual pricing system in case of most essential commodities.

Objectives

The principal objective of the PDS is to ensure adequate supplies of essential consumer goods to weaker sections of the population at stable prices in order to protect them from inflationary pressures. Since the demand for such commodities is inelastic, even the slightest fall in their output and availability leads to a sharp increase in prices. Moreover, as most of these commodities are agriculture-based, their prices are subject to large seasonal variations. The PDS, therefore, seeks to control prices, reduce fluctuations in them and achieve an equitable distribution of certain essential consumer goods.

Fair price shops

The number of fair shops has increased from 2.39 lakhs in March 1979 to 4.10 lakhs in March 1995. Nearly 80% of these fair price shops are located in rural areas.

State Agencies

Public agencies procure a certain proportion of the output of essential commodities and distribute them to weaker and vulnerable sections of society. The producers are allowed to sell the balance in the free market at higher prices and recover the loss made on sales to the government agencies.

Both Central and State Governments distribute essential commodities. FCI distributes foodgrains and sugar in some States. Co-operative societies also distribute sugar in some States. The STC distributes edible oils. The Department of Coal and Coal India Ltd. distribute soft coke, IOC, Hindustan Petroleum, Bharat Petroleum etc. distribute kerosene. The National Consumers' Co-operative Federation distributes controlled cloth and tea and the Coffee Board distributes coffee.

The responsibility for procuring and supplying seven essential commodities, namely, wheat, rice, sugar, imported edible oil, kerosene oil, soft coke and controlled cloth to the States is with the Central Government agencies, such as the FCI, State Trading Corporation of India, National Cooperative Consumers' Federation and

Coal India Ltd. Moreover, various public sector oil companies are entrusted with the task of supplying these commodities at prices which are determined by the Central Government from time to time. The State Governments are authorised to add to these prices incidental changes like handling, transportation etc., while fixing the retail prices.

At the State level, Food and Civil Supplies Department, Civil Supplies Corporation, Essential Commodities Corporations, apex consumer co-operative federations and fair price shops are all responsible for supplying essential commodities.

Criticisms of the PDS

However, the working of PDS has been criticised on several grounds :

1. **Dislocation**. Firstly, it is wrong to believe that once a fair price shop is set up, the common man's requirements of consumer goods are met at reasonable prices. The fair price shops do not often lift the sanctioned quotas due to one reason or the other, causing dislocation in the smooth flow of commodities from producing centres to numerous (and often distant) consuming areas.

2. **Poor Quality**. Secondly, the poor quality of commodities supplied seems to be the proximate cause of poor offtake of commodities like wheat and rice in urban areas. Easy availability in the open market also tends to reduce the quantity of purchase from the PDS.

Experience has shown that when the supply of a commodity covered under the PDS is abundant, consumers turn away from the fair price shops and buy their requirements as far as possible from the open market. This happened in case of sugar in 1976, when the free market price dropped below the official fair price. This implies that wherever alternative sources of supplies are operating and are easily accessible to consumers, the fair price shops lose importance. Thus the PDS is effective mainly in times of shortages and rising prices.

3. **Poor image**. Moreover, the image of fair price shops, as a distributor of quality goods, is poor. The general impression of the people is that sub-standard goods are being sold through fair price shops.

4. **Lack of integrated approach**. An efficient PDS requires strong link among production, procurement, transportation, storage and distribution of the selected commodities. In the past, responsibilities for these have been divided among many people and, thus, there has been a lack of an integrated system or an integrated approach which alone could ensure an efficient PDS.

5. **Lack of demand-supply balance**. Continuous increase in production in response to rising demand is absolutely essential to ensure price stability. There are few problem areas of continued demand-supply imbalance in essential commodities like pulses, edible oils, sugar, etc. It has not been possible to achieve technological breakthrough in the production of pulses and oilseed while sugarcane production has been marked by cyclical fluctuations.

The problem posed by the stagnation in the production of pulses is compounded by the fact that the supply of pulses cannot be increased significantly through imports. In case of edible oils and sugar — which are highly prone to speculation— the strategy has been, in addition to the thrust on production, to import edible oils on a regular basis and to import sugar as and when required. A reasonable level of stocks tends to reduce the scope of speculation in these sensitive items and provides a powerful weapon to the Government to influence their prices through regulated releases.

6. **Lack of profit margin**. Low profit margin turned out to be the major complaint of fair price shopowners. Most of the shopkeepers have to go to warehouses more than once to take delivery of their allotted quotas.

7. **Partial success**. The role of PDS in controlling prices has been partly effective as in the case of foodgrains and to some extent in edible oils. While procurement of cereals has been rising in recent years, the offtake has fallen sharply. The existence of a buffer stock is acting as a cushion against any attempt by traders to raise prices artificially in times of shortages.

8. **Leakages**. The strengthening of the PDS has almost put an end to black marketing of foodgrains in the country. However, in the case of edible oils, despite massive imports year after year, strict control on their prices could not be enforced largely due to leakages from the PDS. There are instances of imported oil being sold in the open market at higher prices.

9. **Urban bias**. A close look at the geographical distribution of fair price shops reveals that administrative convenience — rather than the essential objectives of the PDS — had determined its expansion. It has an urban bias, with most of the shops being located in cities and towns. As a consequence the benefits of PDS are available to the urban rich and not to the rural poor.

10. **Public procurement**. Finally, it may also be emphasised that the operation of price control and rationing has to be supplemented by public procurement. The government's procurement drive has not been very effective over the years.

In truth, the public distribution system is yet to render services to inaccessible areas and to the poorer sections of the community. The Civil Supplies Corporations, consumers' co-operative societies and marketing societies may be utilised so as to expand the system and make it more effective.

Conclusion

In India, the majority of the people still live in the rural areas. These under-privileged and weaker sections of the community should be adequately covered by the PDS. The basic needs of their daily life must be met by governments and, finally, the commodities that raise the standard of living and bring some comforts to the level of living should also be made available to them. An effective and widespread action-oriented public distribution system is essential to enliven our developing economy. It is to be noted that the Seventh Plan (1985-90) strategy recognised the public distribution system as a permanent feature of the economy. The revised 20-point programme needs to expand public distribution system through more fair price shops including mobile shops in far-flung areas in order to cater to industrial workers, student hostels and make available to students textbooks and exercise books on a priority basis as also to give sufficient consumer protection.

A recent trend in PDS is to rely on selling through Panchayats. In the rural areas, agricultural inputs like seeds, fertilisers, etc. are being distributed by the PDS through Panchayats.

In a mixed economy like our own, both private and public distribution systems should be geared up to cater to the needs of the vast population so that the poor people can enjoy an improved standard of living in near future.

Public distribution system has assumed more importance after the new economic policy was announced by the Government in July 1991. Now, essential commodities such as kerosene, cooking gas, etc. are being distributed both through private and public agencies.

Synopsis for Learning

Q.1. What is public of distribution ?

Ans. Public distribution refers to allocation of essential commodities through fair price shops at government controlled prices.

Q.2. What are the basic objectives of India's public distribution system ?

Ans. Three basic objectives are (i) to control prices, (ii) reduce fluctuations in prices and (iii) achieve an equitable distribution of essential commodities at fair prices.

Q.3. What is the utility of public distribution ?

Ans. Public distribution system has been created by the need to maintain stable prices of essential commodities through supply management.

When a firm is trying to explore a new market which is different from that for existing products, it has to fall back on some form of market research.

Initially a firm may be producing similar goods and some indications of potential demand may come from wholesalers, retailers or even customers in conversation with the firm's representatives. Such suggestions can be checked with those of other distributors.

When the reaction is generally favourable, more thorough market research can be carried out, probably through a specialist market research organisation. Market research can cover desk research, field studies and test marketing.

GLOSSARY

Advertising Any persuasive message carried by a paid medium or a sponsor of the message.

Agent Channel intermediary responsible for bringing buyers and sellers together, so as to complete a transaction. Agents never take title to the goods, but they sometimes take possession of those goods.

Basing point pricing Changing customers prices and shipping fees as if their orders had been shipped from a particular location. The actual place of shipment is not necessarily used to determine the prices and shipping charges.

Brand A name, term symbol, sign, design, or unifying combination of these that identifies and distinguishes one product from a competing one.

Brand name The verble portion of brand.

Channel of distribution The complete sequence of marketing organisation involved in bringing a product from the producer to the ultimate consumer or business user.

Delivered pricing Setting a price that includes payment for delivering the product to the customer. Also called freight allowed pricing.

Four P's of Marketing Product, price, place and promotion.

Freight on board (FOB) A term that identifies the point at which title passes from seller to buyer. At this point the buyer bears shipping expenses and assumes all other responsibility.

Generic brand The same as generic products.

Generic products Products that carry neither a manufacturer's nor a distributor's brand. These goods are plainly packaged with stark black lettering that simply lists the contents.

Logistics The activities concerned with achieving a smoothly controlled flow of goods through an organisation and its channels of distribution.

Loss leader A product, typically a familiar and commonly purchased one, sold at a loss in an effort to attract buyers who may purchase the items that are profitable for the seller.

Marketing The activities involved in developing product, price, distribution, and promotional mixes that meet and satisfy the needs of customers.

Marketing concept The management philosophy that stresses consumer orientation, long-range profitability and the integration of marketing and other organisational functions.

Marketing management A special application of general management techniques to the firm's marketing operations.

Marketing mix The specific combination of interrelated and interdependent marketing activities engaged in by an organisation. The basic element of the marketing mix are product, price, distribution and production. These elements are also referred to as marketing's controllable variables.

Marketing myopia The failure of a firm to broadly define its purpose on the basis of a consumer orientaion.

Marketing research The systematic and the objective process of gathering, recording, and analysing data for marketing decision making.

Marketing strategy It includes the identification and evaluation of opportunities, analysis of market segments, selection of (a) target markets and (b) planning an appropriate marketing mix. Marketing strategy is the effort and marketing mix is the result.

Odd prices A price that is few paise less than the nearest round rupee price. The objective is to psychologically "lower" the price of the item.

Packaging The making of decisions about labels, inserts, instructions, graphic design, shipping cartons, and sizes and types of containers.

Penetration price A price that is set at a low level fo that a product might quickly establish itself in the market. Most often employed when a product faces an established competitive market.

Price lining The setting of prices by a seller in accordance with certain "price points" believed to be attractive to buyers.

Product A good or service, tangible or intangible, offers a bundle of satisfaction to customers.

Product life cycle A marketing management concept providing a graphic description of a product's sales history. It is depicated as having five stages: introduction, growth, maturity stagnation and decline.

Product line Within a firm's assortment, any group of products that are fairly closely related.

Product mix The total product offering of a marketing firm. All products, regardless of type, are included in the product mix.

Product strategy Planning and developing the mix of primary and auxiliary demensions of a product's attributes.

Promotion The marketing communication process utilising personal or non-personal means to remind, inform, and persuade buyers or potential buyers of the organisation's product. One of the 4Ps of the marketing mix.

Promotion mix The totality of an organisation's promotional effort, including advertising, personal selling, sales promotion and publicity.

Publicity Messages that are unsigned and unpaid though they reach the public *via* mass media. Publicity always involves a third party, such as a newspaper or television reporter, who holds the power to determine the nature of the message.

Publicity relations The activities involved in actively seeking to manage the nature of the publicity an organisation receives.

Pull strategy A marketing strategy that utilises promotion to stimulate ultimate consumers to demand a product, thereby "pulling" that product through the channel of distribution.

Push strategy A marketing strategy whereby a supplier promotes a product to the other channel members rather than to the ultimate buyers.

Resale price maintenance One important aspect of pricing, particularly in the case of consumer goods, is that the firm producing a product is concerned with a channel of distribution and must give some consideration to intermediate prices, for example, those of wholesalers and retailers. Under resale price maintenance, the producer controls prices all the way to the final consumer.

Return on investment price A price that has been set fo that a desired return on investment is earned if the product is sold at that prices.

Sales management The marketing management activity that deals with planning, direction, and control of the sales force or personal selling effort.

Sales promotion Those promotional activities — other than advertising, personal selling, and publicity — that stimulate consumer-purchaser-dealer effectiveness. Typically, a temporary offer of a reward to customers or dealers is made.

Skimming price A relatively high price intended to "skim the cream" off the market that is gradually lowered. Typically such a price is charged at the start of a product's life cycle and assumes that demand is strong enough to support higher price levels.

Target return pricing The determination of a price level intended to yield a particular level of profit to the organisation.

Uniform delivered pricing A pricing strategy whereby an organisation charges the same price for a given product in all locations. Also called postage stamp pricing.

3

Financial Management

The major aim of any business is to employ its capital in such a way as to provide the most profit. However, this must not be achieved at the expense of safety. In its efforts to make profits a company can 'over-reach' itself so that everyuthing ends in disaster.

R. R. Pitfild

[Syllabus

- **Objectives and scope**
- **Estimation of financial requirements of a firm**
- **Features of sound capital plan**
- **Financial policies regarding fixed capital and working capital structure and its determinants**
- **Characteristics of a sound capital structure**
- **Retained earnings and dividend policy**
- **Organisation of finance department**
- **Financial control — its nature and importance**
- **Roles of banking and non-banking special institutions in providing short-term, medium-term and long-term finance to business firm]**

SUBJECT MATTER OF FINANCIAL MANAGEMENT

The survival or failure of an enterprise in the private sector sooner or later rests on how successful it has been financially, and it is increasingly the case that finance and its implications enter into the management of public bodies and corporations as well. The influence of the finance function is, therefore, all-pervading. Whoever exercises financial control of an organisation, therefore — whether called the chief accountant, financial director, treasurer or some other title — bears considerable responsibility and wields considerable power.

The primary occupation of the financial function is to ensure that adequate funds are available for such capital expenditure as new plant and equipment and for working capital to meet revenue expenses such as wages and salaries, materials and all the inevitable administration expenses.

The need for capital expenditure will be ascertained from the long-range plans of the organisation which will have set out the objectives and targets to be achieved and the strategies and tactics required for success. It is the responsibility of the finance functions to prepare regular capital budgets to ensure that funds are available for such expenditure and to advise on suitable sources of funds if these cannot be generated from within the concern. Similarly, the finance function is very concerned with a continuing flow of working capital to meet the revenue and running expenses of the organisation, and so must prepare cash flow forecasts and cash budgets to ensure the availability of liquid funds for working capital purposes. Both capial ital and cash budgets must be subject to budgetary control.

There are financial implications in virtually all business decisions. Finance managers make decisions regarding which assets their firms should acquire, how those assets should be financed and how the firm should manage its existing resources. If these responsibilities are discharged properly, financial managers will help to maximise the values of their firms.

3.1 MEANING, SCOPE AND OBJECTIVES

IMPORTANCE OF FINANCE

Finance is the oil of wheel and spirit of trade, commerce and industry. It is the life-blood of any business. No business activity can be carried out without adequate finance. For starting and running any type of business — large, medium or small — there is need to obtain money and capital (finance). Finance is needed for various purposes: for acquiring land, construction buildings, installing plant and machinery, for paying wages and salaries as also for covering various other types of business expenses such as payment of insurance, taxes and bills. The importance of finance has increased much in recent years for three main reasons : (i) adoption of capital-intensive techniques of production, (ii) mass production and (iii) difficulties of raising sufficient finance.

DEFINITIONS OF BUSINESS FINANCE

Finance may be defined as that administrative area or set of administrative functions in an organisation which relate with the arrangement of cash and credit so that organisation may have the means to carry out its objectives as satisfactorily as possible.

In a modern money-using economy, finance may be defined as the provision of money at the time it is wanted.

Business finance may also be defined as that business activity which is concerned with the acquisition and conservation of capital funds in meeting the financial needs and overall objectives of business enterprise.

In short, business finance can be broadly defined as the activity concerned with the planning, raising, controlling and administering of the funds used in the business.

From the above definitions, it is clear that finance deals with the arrangement of sufficient amount of capital to achieve the objectives of the enterprise. Only procurement of capital is not enough, it is equally vital to use it in the best possible manner. Financial management is a broad term and includes financing planning, raising the needed funds, financial analysis and control.

Financial Management deals with all the financial problems of corporate enterprises. These problems include the financial aspects of the promotion of new enterprises and their administration during early development, the accounting problems connected with the distinction between capital and income, the administrative problems created by growth and expansion, and finally, the financial adjustments required for reviving up or rehabilitating of a corporation which has come into financial difficulties.

THE FINANCE FUNCTION

There are three ways of defining the finance function. Firstly, the finance function can simply be taken as the task of providing funds needed by an enterprise on favourable terms, keeping in view the objectives of the firm. This means that the finance function is solely concerned with the acquisition (or procurement) of short-term and long-term funds. However, in recent years, the coverage of the term 'finance function' has been widened to include the instruments, institutions and practices through which funds are obtained. So, the finance function covers the legal and accounting relationship between a company and its source and uses of funds. For example, in financial management, we discuss debt-equity ratio (determined by the government), as also various accounting and legal aspects of dividend policy. No doubt, the basic function of the finance manager is one of determining how funds can best be raised (*i.e.*, at the minimum possible cost). In other words, the essence of finance function is keeping the business supplied with enough funds to fulfil its objectives. But such a definition is too narrow and is not of much practical use. No doubt, the finance function is much broader than mere procurement of short-term and long-term funds so that a firm's working capital and fixed capital needs can be met.

Another extreme view is that finance is concerned with cash. This definition is much too broad and thus is not really meaningful.

The third view — based on a compromise between the two — is more useful for practical purposes. This definition treats the finance function as the procurement of funds and their effective utilisation in business. The finance manager takes all decisions that relate to funds which can be obtained as also the best way of financing an investment such as the installation of a new machinery inside the factory or office building. The cost of the machinery may be financed by making a public issue of 8% cumulative preference shares. At the same time, he has to consider whether the additional return (cash flow) expected from the new machinery is sufficient to cover the cost of capital in terms of interest to be paid over a period of time. In this case, the finance decision is based on an analysis of the alternative sources and uses of funds. To start with the finance manager has to draw a plan outlining the company's need for funds. Such financial plan is based on forecasts of financial needs of the company. Such forecasts are based on sales forecasts.

In the next step, the finance manager has to raise necessary funds to meet the company's need for fixed and working capital. Then, in the third step, he has to put the acquired funds into effective uses. The sequence of the three-step process is presented below:

1. Drawing a financial plan and forecasting financial needs

↓

2. Raising necessary funds

↓

3. Putting funds into proper use.

In a broad sense, the finance function covers the following six major activities :

1. financial planning;
2. forecasting cash inflows and outflows;
3. raising funds;
4. allocation of funds;
5. effective use of funds; and
6. financial control (budgetary and non-budgetary).

The last function is very important. Through financial control the finance manager tries to bring performance closer to the targets.

SCOPE OF FINANCE FUNCTION

No doubt, the scope of finance function is wide because this function affects almost all the aspects of a firm's operations. The finance function includes judgments about whether a company should make more investment in fixed assets or not. It is largely concerned with the allocation of a firm's capital expenditure over time as also related decisions such as financing investment and dividend distribution. Most of these decisions taken by the finance department affect the size and timing of future cash flow or flow of funds.

CLASSIFICATION OF FINANCE FUNCTION

Finance function can be classified into two broad categories, *viz.*, (i) executive finance function and (ii) incidental finance function. While the former requires administration skill in planning and execution, the latter largely covers works of a routine nature, which are necessary to implement financial decisions at the executive level.

Six Executive Functions

Six basic executive finance functions are the following :

1. Determining asset-management policies

All finance functions are concerned with the control of both cash flows and non-cash assets. The reason is easy to find out. The finance managers must know how much cash will be 'tied up' in various kinds of non-cash (or non-liquid) assets. Without the information, it is not possible to estimate and arrange for necessary cash requirements. In fact, the formulation of sound and consistent asset management policies is an indispensable pre-requisite to successful financial management.

2. Determining the allocation of net profits

This relates to retained earnings (corporate savings) and dividend policy. Most companies have to achieve balance between two alternatives, *i.e.*, payment of dividends and the retention of earnings for acquiring additional assets.

3. Estimating cash flow requirements and control of such flows

An important responsibility of the finance manager is to ensure an adequate flow of cash as and when it is needed. Otherwise, the smooth operation of a company may not be possible. Since cash flow originates from sales and cash requirements are closely related to sales volume, adequate cash can be provided at the proper time only after forecasting cash needs.

4. Taking decision on needs and sources of new external finance

On the basis of sales forecasts, the financial managers will have to draw a plan to borrow funds from external sources. Such debt capital will add to the firm's own cash resources and thus improve its financial position. External capital may be obtained by borrowing funds from commercial banks. The finance manager must be competent enough to determine exactly when additional funds from external sources will be needed. He (she) has also to judge how long they will be needed, how economically they can be raised (*i.e.*, at the lowest possible cost) and from which sources will they be repaid.

5. Carrying on negotiations with outside financiers

The finance manager has also to carry on negotiations with outsiders to be able to arrange for necessary external financing in required amount and on time. For obtaining working capital, a line of credit has to be established with commercial banks. Again sufficient time has to be devoted for completing arrangements for long-term financing. Long-term financing requires more skillful negotiations than short-term financing.

6. Checking upon financial performance

It is also necessary for the finance manager to evaluate the wisdom and efficiency of financial planning. Such evaluation is to be based on past performance of the company. This will enable the finance manager to improve the standards, techniques and procedures of financial planning and control which are important aspects of the finance function.

Interrelationship. It may be noted that all the six functions are interrelated. This means that a change in decision with respect to any one of the functions will call for a change in decision relating to some or all other functions.

Incidental function. The incidental finance functions include supervision of cash inflows and outflows and maintaining cash balances and record keeping. These functions are so simple that these need not be explained in detail.

GOALS OF FINANCIAL MANAGEMENT

The primary objective of a company is to maximise its market value, or its value to its shareholders. A company's market value is represented by the market price of its ordinary shares over a long period of time. The market price of shares is a reflection of the company's investment and financing decisions. A simple example will make the point clear. A company may cut its research and development expenditures and thus raise the market value of its shares rather artificially. But this action will have an adverse effect on the firm's share prices in the long run. It is because without sufficient expenditure on R&D a firm cannot reduce cost or develop new products which can be sold profitably. If profits fall, dividends will also fall. The end result will be a fall in the market price of its shares in the long run.

PROFIT MAXIMISATION V. WEALTH MAXIMISATION

Often maximisation of profit is treated as the sole objective of a business firm. But this creates a number of problems. This objective ignores the timing of cash flows (*i.e.*, expected returns). However, it is essential in any financial planning to take into consideration the time pattern of cash flows from a project. Secondly, the profit maximisation goal does not take into account the risk or uncertainty associated with expected cash flows from an asset (such as a new machine). In fact, some investment projects are much more risky than others. This means that the expected flow of cash would be more uncertain if risky projects were undertaken. Moreover, the profit maximisation hypothesis does not take into consideration the effect of dividend policy on the market price of a company's shares. If the objective of a company were to maximise earnings per share, it would not pay any dividend. The value of a share depends largely on the amount of dividend paid. This is one main reason for paying dividends. So maximisation of earnings per share cannot be a realistic objective. For all these reasons, the objective of maximising earnings per share is different from maximising market price per share.

The market price of a company's share is the crucial variable in any financial decision. It takes into account present and prospective earnings per share, the timing and risk of such earnings, the company's dividend policy and various other factors that may affect the market price of the share — directly or indirectly. Thus, the market price acts an indicator of the company's performance and progress. It indicates whether management is operating efficiently or not. So there is continuous appraisal of management performance.

In recent years the profit maximisation as the goal of the business enterprise has been criticised on various grounds. It is now widely agreed that the proper goal of financial management is wealth maximisation. It is because on the basis of this objective than financial decisions can and should be evaluated. In fact, the central issue of financial management and policy is the rational use of funds. This can be achieved by comparing advantages of potential uses of funds with the cost of alternative (potential) sources so as to accomplish the broad financial goals of an enterprise. Furthermore, finance managers are involved in evaluation of investment projects (or choices relating to allocation of financial resources). This aspect of financial management is also related to wealth maximisation (or maximisation of the market value of the firm) than profit maximisation.

RESPONSIBILITIES OF FINANCIAL MANAGERS

Financial management is important in all types of businesses, including banks and other financial institutions, as well as industrial and service firms. Financial management is also important in governmental operations, from schools to hospitals to highway departments. The task of financial managers range from making decisions regarding plant expansions to choosing what types of securities to issue to finance expansion. Financial managers also have the responsibility for deciding the credit terms under which customers may buy, how much inventory the firm should carry, how much cash to keep on hand, whether to acquire other firm (merger analysis), and how much of the firm's earnings to plough back into the business versus pay out as dividends.

It is also becoming increasingly important for people in marketing, accounting, production, personnel and other areas to understand finance in order to do a good job in their own fields. Marketing people, for instance, must understand how marketing decisions affect and are affected by funds availability, by inventory levels, by excess plant capacity, and so on. Similarly, accountants must understand how accounting data are used in corporate planning and are viewed by investors.

Thus, there are financial implications in virtually all business decisions, and non-financial executives simply must know enough finance to work these implications into their own specialised analyses. Because of this, every student of business, regardless of his or her major should be concerned with financial management.

The financial manager's task is to acquire and use funds so as to maximise the value of the firm. Here are some specific activities :

1. **Forecasting and planning**. The financial manager must interact with other executives as they look ahead and lay the plans which will shape the firm's future.

2. **Major investment and financing decisions**. A successful firm usually has rapid growth in sales, which requires investments in plant, equipment and inventory. It is the taskof the financial manager to help determine the optimal sales growth rate, and he (she) must help decide what specific assets to acquire and the best way to

finance those assets. For example, should the firm finance with debt, equity, or some combination of the two, and if debt is used, how much should be long term and how much should be short term ?

3. **Coordination and control**. The financial manager must interact with other executives to ensure that the firm is operated as efficiently as possible. All business decisions have financial implications, and all managers — financial and otherwise — need to take this into account. For example, marketing decisions affect sales growth, which, in turn, influences investment requirements. Thus, marketing decision makers must take account of how their actions affect (and are affected by) such factors as the availability of funds, inventory policies and plant capacity utilisation.

4. **Dealing with the financial markets**. The financial manager must deal with the money and capital markets. Each firm affects and is affected by the general financial markets where funds are raised, where the firm's shares and debentures are traded, and where its investors either make or lose money.

5. **Risk management**. All business face risks, including natural disasters such as fires and floods, uncertainties in commodity and share prices, changing interest rates, and fluctuating foreign exchange rates. However, many of these risks can be reduced by purchasing insurance or by hedging. The financial manager is usually responsible for the firm's overall risk management programmes, including identifying the risks that should be hedged and then hedging them in the most efficient manner.

In short, financial managers make decisions regarding which assets their firms should acquire, how those assets should be financed, and how the firm should manage its existing resources. If these responsibilities are performed optimally, financial managers will help to maximise the values of their firms, and this will also maximise the long-run welfare of consumers and employees.

FINANCIAL DECISION MAKING

The three main components of the finance function are : (1) investment decisions, (2) finance decision and (3) dividend payment decisions. These three components (aspects) of the finance function interact among themselves, through a common thread, *viz.*, the cost of capital in order to enable the firm to maximise wealth — the main objective of financial management.

OBJECTIVES

A company is a body corporate having perpetual existence. For ensuring that this perpetual existence is on acceptable lines and a company does not have to go out of business, it has to earn profit or generate surplus from its operations. It is the primary task of financial managers to ensure this. This means that a company's financial management function should focus on the fact that generation of surplus forms the basis of a company's short-term operational and long-term viability.

Management of capital is a task usually assigned to a financial officer — the treasurer or controller. The financial manager has the responsibility for achieving the following objectives:

1. Evaluate sources of funds and their costs.
2. Decide upon fund sources to be used.

3. Determine how the funds are to be effectively used.

Generation of surplus from its operations is precondition for a company's success. This largely ensures its smooth functioning, healthy growth and long-term viability. Efficient financial management requires rational decision-making and forecasting.

Since corporate decision-making is essentially group decision-making, it is essential that risk and return are matched over a period of time.

The long-term survival of an enterprise in the private sector largely depends on its financial performance and results. Financial management is also of considerable importance to public bodies and corporations. The influence of the finance function is, therefore, all-pervasive. Whoever exercises financial control of an organisation, therefore, whether the chief accountant, director of finance or treasurer or financial controller bears considerable responsibility.

Financial management provides a broad analytical and conceptual framework for all types of financial decision-making. The primary goal of the finance function is to ensure that adequate funds are available for such capital expenditure as new plant and equipment and for working capital to meet current expenses such as wages and salaries, materials and all administrative expenses.

Financial management is concerned with both acquisition of funds and their allocation. Thus it is primarily concerned with issues related to the acquisition of external funds. But it is mainly concerned with the efficient and rational allocation of funds among alternative uses.

Synopsis for Learning

Q.1. What is financial management ?

Ans. Financial management is the operational activity of a business that is responsible for obtaining and effectively utilising the funds necessary for efficient operations.

Q.2. What is the objective of financial management ?

Ans. The objective of financial management is to see that adequate cash is on hand to meet required current and capital expenditures and otherwise to assist in maximising profits.

Q.3. What is financial planning ?

Ans. The financial planning function involves "long-range plans for plant expansion, replacement of machinery and equipment, and a miscellany of expenditures, causing large cash drains. The finance manager assists in the analysis of cash flows over the planning period."

Q.4. What do financing forecasting and planning involve ?

Ans. Financial forecasting and planning involve three (main) functions : (1) financial analysis ascertaining the capabilities and needs of the organisation; (2) prediction of the needs for funds over the short-run operating period, including cash flow, cash budgets, and sources of current capital; (3) prediction of the need for funds over a long-run period including investment fund flow, capital budgets, alternative capital expenditure proposals, cost of capital and conditions of the capital market.

3.2 ASPECTS OF FINANCIAL OPERATIONS

Financial management is concerned with three different aspects relating to the financial operations of a firm, *viz.*, investment decision, financing decision and dividend policy decision. These three aspects of financial management may now be briefly discussed.

1. Investment Decision

The investment decision is a long-term decision and is related to the selection of durable goods or real assets in which funds will be invested by the firm. The assets which can be acquired are usually divided into two broad categories: (1) long-term (or fixed) assets (like plant, equipment and machinery) which will yield a return over a long period of time, (2) short-term (or current) assets which can easily be converted into cash within a year's time. Thus a firm's asset selection decision falls into two parts: (1) capital budgeting which involves the first category of assets and (2) working capital management which is related to decision-making related to short-term (current) assets.

2. Financing Decision

While investment decision is largely concerned with choosing an optimum mix of assets or with the composition of the fixed asets of the firm, the second decision, *viz.*, financing decision, relates to the financing-mix or capital structure or leverage. The term 'capital structure' is used to refer to the proportion of debt (fixed-interest securities or outsiders' capital) and equity capital (variable-dividend securities or owners' capital).

The average enterprise uses two categories of debt financing; short-term and long-term obligations. Short-term financing represents debts having a maturity of less than one year. In long-term financing the debt obligations are of one year or longer. The financing decision is broadly concerned with the choice of the proportion of these sources to finance the investment requirements. A capital structure with a judicious mix of debt and equity capital is called a company's optimal capital structure. Thus one important dimension of the financing decision is ascertaining whether a firm's capital structure is optimal or not.

There is another aspect of financial decision, *viz.*, the determination of an appropriate capital structure, under existing conditions (in the context of the present financial environment of the company). Thus the financing decision covers two different, but interrelated aspects, *viz.*, (a) capital structure theory and (b) capital structure decision.

3. Dividend Policy Decision

All decisions relating to the dividend policy constitute the third dimension of modern financial management. This decision is not a separate decision. It has to be analysed in relation to the second decision, *viz.*, the financing decision. Firms have to make two decisions as far as distribution of net profit after tax is concerned: (1) distributing it to the shareholders in the form of dividend and/or (2) retaining it in the business. It is not that easy to say which course of action should be followed — dividend or retention. One strategic element of the dividend decision is, therefore, the dividend pay-out ratio which shows what proportion of net profits should be distributed among the shareholders in the form of dividends. The decision depends on two factors, *viz.*, the preferences of the shareholders and investment opportunities available within the firm. There is another, equally important, aspect of dividend policy. It relates to the various legal and other factors determining dividend policy of a firm in practice.

Synopsis for Learning

Q.1. What are the functions of finance department ?

Ans. The functions of finance department involve three major decisions the firm must make : (i) the investment decision, (ii) the financing decision, and (iii) the dividend payment decision.

Q.2. How are these functions related to one another ?

Ans. Each of the above three functions must be considered in relation to the objectives of the firm; an optimal combination of the three will maximise the value of the firm to its shareholders.

Q.3. What are the goals of financial management ?

Ans. Five important goals of the firm include (1) stockholder wealth maximisation, (2) profit maximisation, (3) managerial reward maximisation, (4) behavioural goals, and (5) social responsibility. Modern managerial finance theory operates on the assumption that the primary goal of the firm is to maximise the wealth of its shareholders, which translates into maximising the price of the firm's stocks and shares. Other goals also influence a firm's policy but are less important than share price maximisation.

3.3 ORGANISATION OF THE FINANCE DEPARTMENT

The basic duties and responsibilities for financial management are diverse and thus spread throughout the organisation. Since finance is the lifeblood of business, financial management is an integral part of the job of managers involved in planning and allocation of financial resources and control. No doubt, various area managers also influence the financial decisions of an organisation. For example, the production manager (industrial engineer) shapes the investment policy (by accepting necessary proposals of a new plant or factory), the marketing manager provides inputs through market survey and research in forecasting and planning; the purchase manager largely influences the level of investment in inventories; and the sales manager influences the determination of receivables policy. In spite of all these, financial management is highly specialised in nature and is to be handled by specialists. Financial decisions are of crucial importance for the survival and growth of an organisation. It is, therefore, essential to set up an efficient organisation for effectively performing the financial management functions.

Since the finance function is a major and strategic functional area of modern business, the ultimate responsibility for carrying out the financial management functions is entrusted with the top management: Board of Directors/Managing Director/Chief Executive. However, the exact nature of the organisation of financial management function differs from firm to firm depending upon the following factors : (1) the size of the firm, (2) the nature or area of its business, (3) the type of financing operations, (4) the ability, efficiency and competence of financial officers and (5) the financial philosophy of management. Similarly, the designation of the Chief Executive of the finance department also differs widely from firm to firm. In some companies they are known as Finance Managers while in others as Vice-President (Finance), or Director (Finance) or even Financial Controller. He reports directly to the top management. Various sections within the financial management area are headed by managers such as the controller and the treasurer.

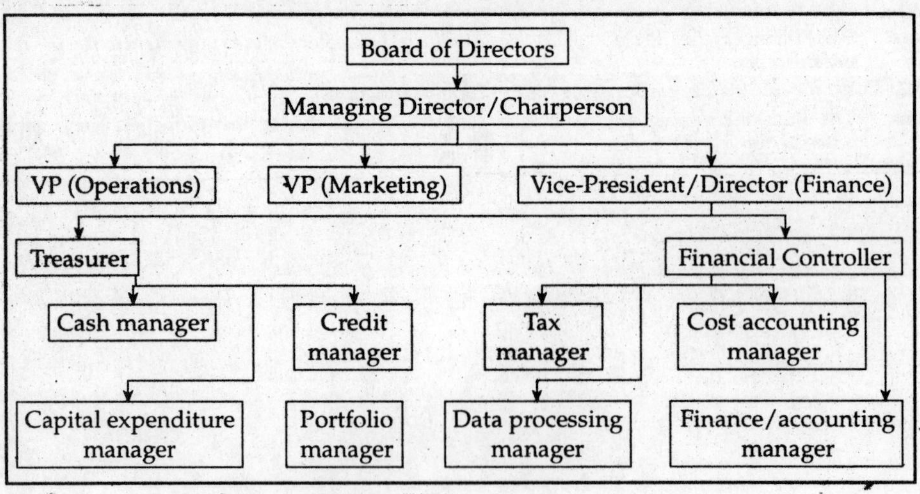

Fig. 3.1 : Organisation of Financial Management Function in a Firm

Fig. 3.1 depicts the organisation of the financial management function in a large modern firm.

The task and responsibility of the chief financial executive no doubt starts with the routine aspects of finance and accounting. But this does not end there. As a member of the top management he is closely associated with the formulation of policies as well as decision-making. He acts as a controller and treasurer, although he may have different designations in different firms and organisations. In different organisations the tasks of financial management and allied areas like accounting are distributed between these two key financial officers in different proportions. Their functions are mentioned below.

The most important concern of the treasurer is with the financing activities of the firm. He performs a wide range of functions such as (i) obtaining finance, (ii) developing good relationship with bankers for obtaining sufficient working capital as and when required, (iii) developing investor relationship so as to be able to acquire the much needed fixed capital, (iv) short-term financing, (v) cash management, (vi) credit administration, (vii) investments and (viii) insurance.

The functions of the financial controller are related mainly to two areas: accounting and control. The general functions commonly performed by him include: (1) financial accounting; (2) internal audit, (3) taxation, (4) management accounting and control, (5) budgeting, planning and control, (6) economic appraisal of projects and activities, (7) feasibility studies, and so on.

Another important point to note here is that the term objective provides a normative framework. This means that in financial management the focus is on what a firm should seek to achieve and on policies that should be followed if the firm is to reach certain goals. In other words, the framework is used to ascertain what a firm should seek to achieve with its three financial management decisions, viz., investment, financing, and dividend policy decisions.

Synopsis for Learning

Q.1. Why is financial management so important to an organisation?

Ans. Since finance is the life blood of business, financial management is so important to the overall organisation.

Q.2. Who is ultimately responsible for the finance function?

Ans. The ultimate responsibility for carrying out the financial management function is entrusted with the top management.

3.4 FINANCIAL MANAGEMENT PROCESS

Financial management is concerned with decision making in regard to the size and composition of assets and the level and structure of corporate financing. There are certain objectives of financial management which provide a basic framework for optimal financial decision-making. Such objectives are concerned with a method of choosing profitable investment projects and financing of such projects.

In the context of financial management the term 'objective' is used in the sense of a goal or decision criterion for the above three financial management decisions. The implication here is that what is relevant is not the overall objective or goal of a modern firm (or corporation) but an operationally useful criterion by which to make an overall assessment of a specific set of three interrelated financial management decisions.

The primary purpose of all businesses is to earn a profit by producing and distributing goods and services. The achievement of this goal requires a continuous supply of capital to operate the business. (Capital includes both money and credit). It is the flow of these capital funds within the firm with which financial management is primarily and essentially concerned. If the amount of funds available for running a business is not adequate, the amount of profit or even the firm's survival will be threatened.

The most important objective of financial management is to maximise the wealth of the owners (shareholders in the case of corporations). To achieve this objective, financial mangers must make sure that the company obtains, at the least possible cost, the funds it needs to meet its objective. (The cost of funds is measured in terms of interest rates). Therefore, the finance manager's job starts and ends with the company's objectives. Fig. 3.2 shows how the process of financial management works.

In most large and medium-sized firms, the person charged with the management of finances is the finance manager or the financial controller. He is responsible for

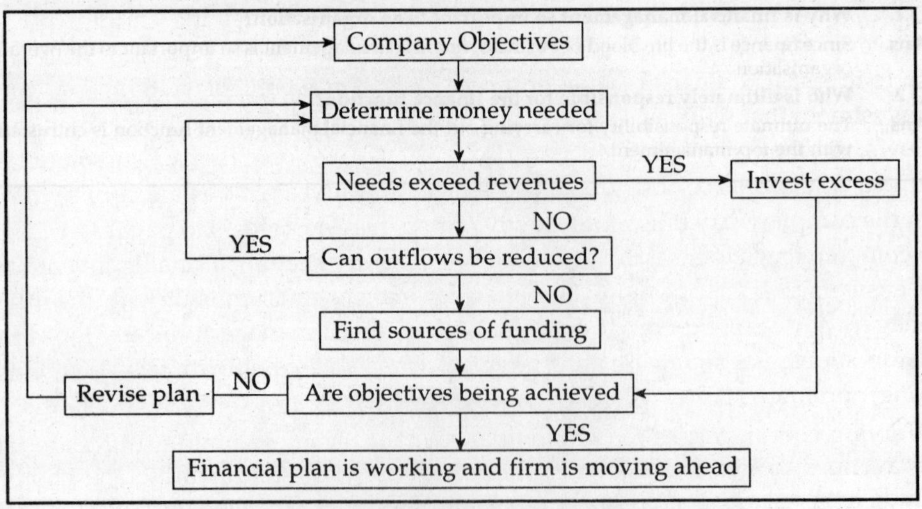

Fig. 3.2 : The Process of Financial Management

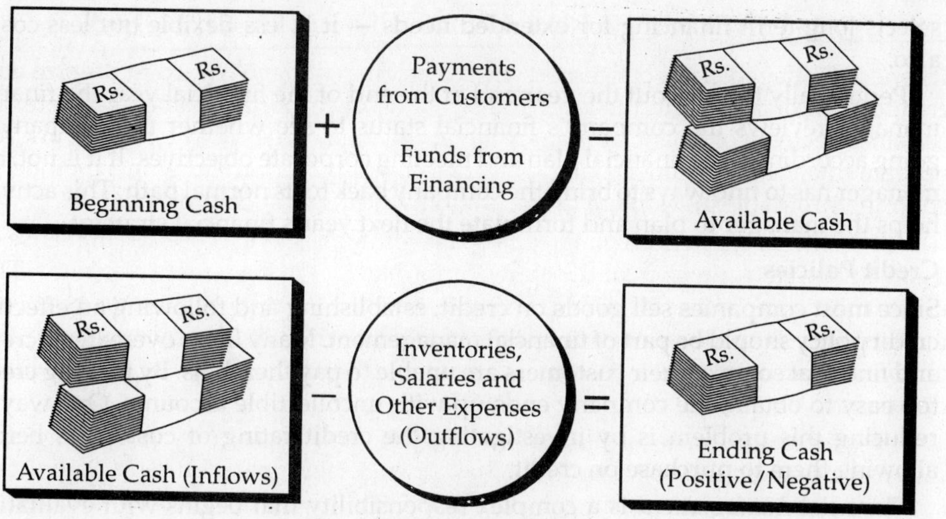

Fig. 3.3 : Simplified Cash Flow

developing, implementing, and controlling the financial plan of the company. This manager, in large organisations, heads a team of financial experts.

The finance manager begins by reviewing corporate objectives to determine the funds the company needs. Usually, the finance manager participates with the other managers (such as those in personnel, operations, and marketing) in planning these objectives. The objectives should be familiar and financially achievable. The basic task of the finance manager is to compare the expenses involved to the expected revenues. This information enabales the finance manager to predict cash flow and the movement of funds illustrated in Fig. 3.3.

The available cash at any given time consists of beginning cash *plus* customer payments and funds from financing. This is the money available to the company for adding to its inventory and covering current expenses.

The finance manager plans a strategy based on whether the ending cash is positive or negative. If cash inflows exceed cash outflows the company will have cash to invest. The finance manager's job is to find out a reliable and flexible form of investment that will pay a satisfactory rate of return. If cash outflows exceed cash inflows, the company will eventually run out of cash for operations. One solution is to find a way to reduce outflows. The Manager may investigate a variety of options. Can the company pay bills more slowly or persuade customers to pay faster ? Can the company cut expenses in some areas, perhaps by keeping a smaller inventory? For answers to such questions, the financial manger must consult with the other managers and staff experts. In addition, the financial manager typically looks for outside sources of financing that offer an acceptable combination of flexibility, timing, and interest rate.

Varying circumstances guide the finance manager in examining sources to tap and avenues to use for acquiring short-term and long-term funds. The choices include long-term and short-term financing techniques. The manager selects short-term techniques when flexibility is important or needs are limited. The manager selects long-term financing for extended needs — it is less flexible but less costly also.

Periodically throughout the year and at the end of the financial year the finance manager reviews the company's financial status to see whether the company is going according to its financial plan and meeting corporate objectives. If it is not, the manager has to find ways to bring the company back to its normal path. This activity helps the manager to plan and formulate the next year's financial strategy.

Credit Policies

Since most companies sell goods on credit, establishing and following an effective credit policy should be part of financial management. Many firms overextend credit and find that some of their customers are unable to pay their bills. By making credit too easy to obtain, the company ends up with uncollectible accounts. One way of reducing this problem is by investigating the credit rating of customers before allowing them to purchase on credit.

Financial management is a complex responsibility that begins with evaluating how funding will help the company achieve its objectives. The financial manager must ensure that the company has money for its short-term and long-term needs and that it makes proper use of the money at its disposal. Finance may come from trade credit, the sale of shares, the acquisition of debt, or the sale of stocks. A well-designed financial plan is often necessary not only for profit and growth, but also for the firm's long-term survival.

Every business unit — irrespective of its size, structure, goal and objectives — may be viewed as a financial entity. Management of an organisation, particularly a profit-seeking business firm, is confronted with issues and decisions like :

(i) What kind of plant and machinery should the firm buy ?

(ii) How should it raise financial resources ?

(iii) How should it assess its financial performance at periodic intervals ?

The most important tasks of financial management are the following :

a. Investing

(i) Working capital management, management of current assets like cash, marketable securities, receivables, and inventories.

(ii) Allocation of fixed capital over time (called capital budgeting).

b. Financing

(i) Identification of sources of finance and determining the optimum mix of debt capital and equity capital.

(ii) Studying and monitoring sources of funds and raising funds on the basis of such exercises.

c. Dividend Distribution

(i) The amount of dividend to be paid (and earnings retained).

(ii) The stability of dividend.

Financial management consists of creating a financial plan, carrying out the plan, monitoring the flow of funds, and making adjustments as needed. The financial plan identifies the timing, amount, and sources of funds needed to achieve company objectives. In a large company, the person charged with these responsibilities is the financial manager, who may head a team of financial experts.

Scope

Financial management is broadly concerned with the acquisition and use of funds by a business firm. Its scope may be defined in terms of the following four questions:

(i) How large should the firm be ana how fast should it grow?

(ii) What should be the composition of the firm's assets?

(iii) What should be the mix of the firm's financing?

(iv) How should the firm analyse, plan, and control its financial affairs?

The last question is quite relevant due to the fact that, in modern complex organisations, financial managers are assuming new and complex responsibilities with the passage of time.

Importance

An essential financial function is to ensure that funds are available when required by the company to expand operations, and that funds generated by the firm's business are invested profitably. The finance manager evaluates the financial performance of the various divisions and operating units of the company. He builds and maintains important relationships for the company with members of the financial community such as commercial banks, investment bankers, insurance companies, brokerage firms, stock exchanges, government regulators, bond and credit rating agencies, and the financial press.

The chief finance manager plays a dynamic role in a modern industrial organisation and affects its future development. With growing influence that—now extends far beyond records, reports, the firm's cash position, paying bills, and acquiring funds — the financial manager is concerned with:

(1) investing funds in real assets;

(2) determining the best mix of financing and dividends in relation to a company's overall objective.

Investment of funds in assets determines the size of the enterprise, its operating profits and its business risk as also its liquidity position. Obtaining the best mix of financing and dividends determines the firm's financial charges and its financial risk.

Synopsis for Learning

Q.1. What are the most important tasks of financial management?

Ans. The three important tasks of financial management are : (i) investing; (ii) financing and (iii) dividend distribution.

Q.2. What is the main concern of financial management?

Ans. Financial management is mainly concerned with the acquisition and use of funds by a business firm.

3.5 NATURE AND PURPOSE OF FINANCIAL PLANNING

In the past, financial management was rarely a major concern for a business. Today most firms have their own financial people who work with the bank, negotiating terms, comparing rates among competing financial institutions, and matching resources to the company's needs as determined by its strategic plan.

Efficient financial management is critical to the survival of a company and effective financial management can contribute greatly to its profits. Financial management begins with creation of a financial plan, which identifies the timing and amount of funds needed and as also the source of those funds. It also includes carrying out all the plans, monitoring the flow of funds to ensure that it is adequate, and adjusting the company's financial strategy as necessary. Successful financial management ensures that a company has adequate financial resources to meet objectives for the current operations and long-term growth.

A firm's profitability is largely determined by the way it manages its capital fund. Therefore the first essential step in any sort of financing planning is to (1) determine the amount and kind of capital needed and (2) plan its use to meet the needs.

Types of Capital

The capital requirements of a modern firm can be divided into two broad categories: working capital and fixed capital. The use of this capital is reflected by the assets listed on the firm's balance sheet. Assets are items of monetary value owned by a business.

The business-person often refers to the sum-total of current assets as the working capital of the firm. These typically consist of cash, inventories, and accounts and notes receivable. Accountants define working capital as the excess of current assets over current liabilities. This is sometimes called net working capital. For purposes of financial analysis, working capital is the value of the assets that can readily be turned into cash for current use in operating the firm — the excess of current assets over current liabilities.

Working capital circulates within the firm by revolving from one form to another, as illustraed in Fig. 3.4. This emphasises its constant change from cash to inventories

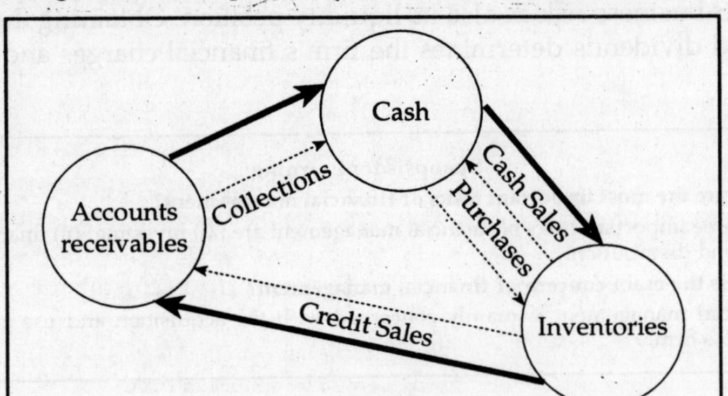

Fig. 3.4 : The circular flow of working capital and the firm's operating cycle

to accounts receivable and finally to cash. The main purpose served by working capital is to provide funds to pay current bills. The task of financial management is to ensure there is neither too much nor too little working capital on hand. Fig.3.5 shows the kinds of current assets used as working capital.

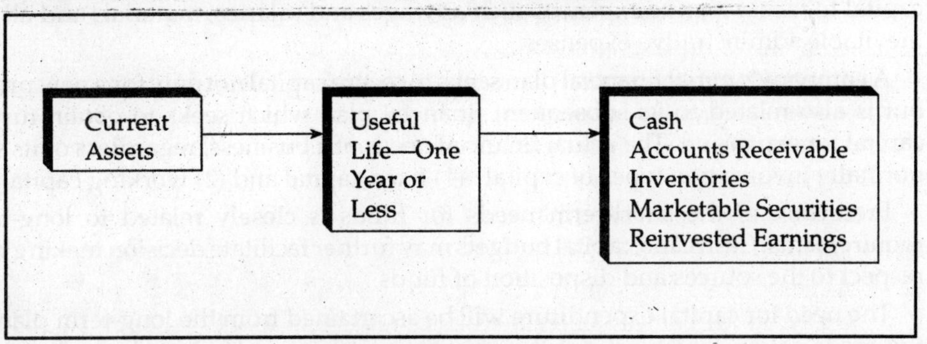

Fig. 3.5 : Working Capital Assets

Acquiring fixed capital involves a different kind of financial planning than for working capital. Fixed capital is used to purchase assets needed over a long period of time. Examples are buildings and land. Fixed capital is money invested in fixed assets to be used over a long period of time. Since fixed assets are essentially of a permanent nature, they become part of a company's permanent capital structure. Fig. 3.6 illustrates the various kinds of fixed assets used in a business.

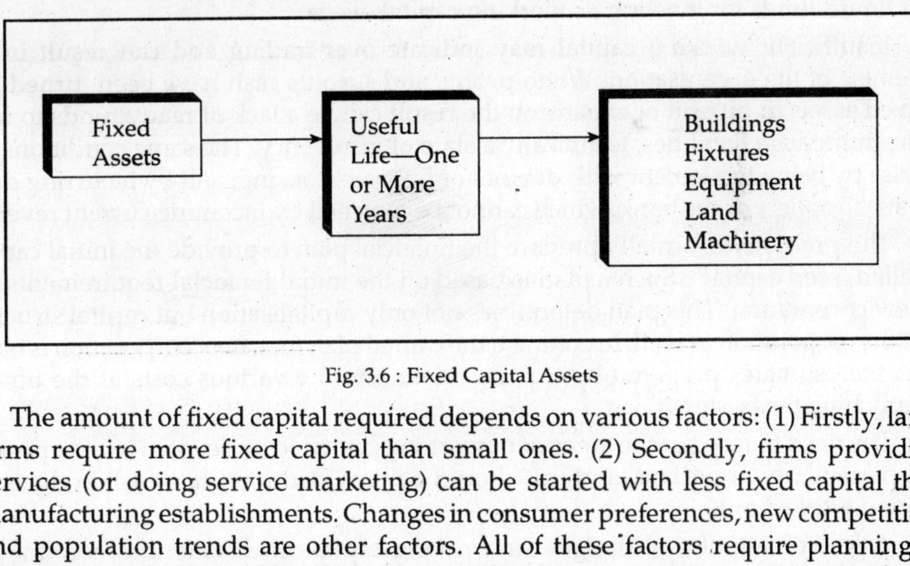

Fig. 3.6 : Fixed Capital Assets

The amount of fixed capital required depends on various factors: (1) Firstly, large firms require more fixed capital than small ones. (2) Secondly, firms providing services (or doing service marketing) can be started with less fixed capital than manufacturing establishments. Changes in consumer preferences, new competition, and population trends are other factors. All of these factors require planning in advance in order to avoid making errors in fixed asset acquisitions. For most firms, fixed capital assets constitute the bulk of investment in the business.

Synopsis for Learning

Q.1. What are the main types of capital needed by a modern firm?

Ans. Most modern firms need two types of capital— working capital and fixed capital. However, the amount of fixed capital required depends on various factors.

3.6 FORECASTING THE FINANCIAL NEEDS

The primary occupation of the finance manager is to ensure that adequate funds are available for such capital expenditure as new plant and equipment and for working capital to meet revenue expenses such as wages and salaries, materials and all the inevitable adminstrative expenses.

A company's initial financial plan seeks to secure capital not only for a new project but is also related to its subsequent financial plan which seeks to obtain further capital for expansion. The actual financial needs of a business, regardless of its size, normally involve two types of capital : (1) fixed capital and (2) working capital.

Prediction of the short-term needs for funds is closely related to long-term requirements. Cash cand capital budgets may further facilitate decision making with respect to the sources and disposition of funds.

The need for capital expenditure will be ascertained from the long-term plans of the organisation which set out the objectives and targets to be achieved and the strategies and tactics required for success. It is the responsibility of the finance department to prepare regular capital budgets to ensure that funds are available for such expenditure and to advise on suitable sources of funds if these cannot be generated from within the concern (*i.e.,* retained earnings). Similarly, the finance function of an organisation is very much concerned with a continuing flow of working capital to meet the revenue and running expenses of the organisation, and so must prepare the cash flow forecasts and cash budgets to ensure the availability of liquid funds for meeting its working capital needs.

Insufficient working capital may indicate over-trading and can result in the demise of the organisation. When profits and surplus cash have been turned into fixed assets in pursuit of expansion the result can be a lack of ready funds to meet the immediate liabilities, technically a state of insolvency. The same conditions can arise by being too lenient with debtors or by over-stocking, and by incurring debts with suppliers or the bank, which cannot be matched by incoming current revenue.

The promoters normally prepare the financial plan to provide the initial capital, called 'seed capital' . Such a plan is based on the initial financial requirements of a new corporation. This plan determines not only capitalisation but capital structure of the corporation as well. In contrast, the capital plan for a new corporation is based on the estimates prepared by experts relating to the various costs at the time of launching the business.

The need to forecast the amount of working capital to be devoted to new projects is particularly important, and this should be provided for when cash budgets are being worked out.

Any estimate of and budget for working capital must take into account two important factors : (1) the current and expected future rates of interest and (2) the expected rates of inflation. Both of these factors are beyond the control of the finance department, but must be included in the calculations of future working capital needs.

Borrowing also must be strictly regulated, especially in times of high interest rates Working capital is the basis for forecasting financial requirements. Financial ratios are often used to forecast financial requirements or capital needs.

Table 3.1 : Hypothetical Data for Financial Forecasting			
Liabilities and Owners' Equity	(Rs.)	Assets	(Rs.)
Creditors	50,000	Cash	10,000
Notes payable	150,000	Debtors	30,000
Ordinary shares	100,000	Inventory	60,000
Retained earnings	200,000	Plant and Equipment	400,000
Total	500,000	Total assets	500,000
		Additional data	
		Sales	500,000
		Net income	50,000
		Profit margin on sales	10%
		Plant capacity utilised	100%
Dividend payout rate — 25% of net income (earnings retention rate is 75%)			

To illustrate let us assume that the financial statement data are given in Table 3.1. The company wants to know what amount of additional financing is required if sales are expected to reach the Rs.600,000 level (a 20% increase). The percentage of sales approach is usually to the answer the questions.

Step 1. What balance sheet items vary directly with sales ?

Assume that the assets and accounts payable vary directly with sales.

Step 2. Express the balance sheet items that vary directly with sales as a percentage of sales (Rs 5,00,000).

Liabilities and Owners' Equity	Rs	Assets	Rs
Accounts payable	10.0	Cash	2.0
		Receivables	6.0
		Inventory	12.0
		Plant and Equipment	80.0
Total	10.0	**Total**	100.0
	100.0	Assets as a percent of sales	
	10.0	*Less*: Available credit from suppliers	
	90.0	Percentage of additional sales rupee to be financed	

For each Re 1.00 of sales, assets will increase Re 1.00. This increase must be financed. Accounts payable are assumed to be financed by suppliers who make credit available and so provide 10% of new funds. The firm must find additional financing from internal or external sources for 90% of each sales rupee. If sales are to increase from Rs 500,000 to Rs 600,000 then Rs 90,000 (= Rs 100,000 increase in sales × 90%) in new funds are required.

Step 3. How much of the financing required (Rs 90,000) can be financed internally from operations?

Since the sales revenue will be Rs 600,000 and the profit margin is 10%, profit will be Rs 60,000. Of this amount, Rs 15,000 is required for dividends (Rs 60,000 **x** 25% dividend payout). This leaves Rs 45,000 of net income available to finance some of the additional sales.

Step 4. How much of the financing requirement must be financed externally ?

If Rs 45,000 of the Rs 90,000 total requirement is provided internally then Rs 45,000 must be obtained from external sources.

The relationships reflected in this illustration can be expressed by the following formula :

External funds needed = $(A/TR)\ (S) - (B/TR)\ (S) - bm(Q)$

where

A/TR = assets that increase spontaneously with total revenue or sales as a percentage of total revenue or sales

B/TR = those liabilities that increase spontaneously with total revenues or sales as a percentage of total revenue or sales

S = change in total revenue or sales; m = profit margin sales

b = earnings retention ratio ; Q = total revenues projected for the year

External funds required = (Rs. 500,000) (– Rs. 100,000) (– Rs. 500,000)

$$\left[\frac{\text{Rs } 50{,}000}{\text{Rs } 500{,}000}\right] - (-\text{Rs } 100{,}000)$$

$$-(75\%)(10\%)\ (\text{Rs } 600{,}000)$$

= Rs 45,000 (the same as computed above)

To summarise, the relationship between sales and assets is the key question in forecasting financing requirements. The formula used in this illustration can be used in different ways by changing the assumptions.

Synopsis for Learning

Q.1. What does a companys initial financial plan seek to achieve?

Ans. A companys initial financial plan seeks to secure capital not only for a new project but is also related to its subsequent financial plan which seeks to obtain futher capital for expansion.

Q.2. Which factors are likely to affect working capital needs of a company?

Ans. Any estimate of working capital must take into account two important factors : (1) the current and expected rates of interest and (2) the expected rates of inflation.

3.7 BUSINESS FINANCE

A modern firm requires two types of finance — short-term funds to meet working capital needs and long-term funds to purchase fixed assets like plant, equipment, machinery, etc. The sources of finance available to a company may be divided into two parts, *viz.*, internal and external.

Short-term (Working) Capital

Banks are the providers of relatively short-term loans. A typical bank loan is often described as a 'self-liquidating' loan, because it finances the purchase of raw materials which are transformed into saleable products within a few weeks or months. Banks also provide 'bridge finance', finance required to wipe out temporary deficits which arise during periods when expenditures exceed receipts.

Nowadays commercial banks are much flexible in the length and purpose of their lending. Medium and longer-term loans are supplied to industry and commerce. The banks also provide finance for industry indirectly, through their ownership of finance companies and other financial institutions.

Working capital is the financial lifeblood of an enterprise and insufficient working capital is a frequent cause of failure. Maintenance of an adequate flow of working capital is, therefore, a first duty of the finance function to ensure funds for continued operation.

The definition usually applied to working capital is that it is the excess of current assets over current liabilities. In other words, it is the total of assets, liquid — or easily made liquid — such as cash, trade debtors, finished stocks of raw materials and semi-finished goods, over liabilities that have to be met at short notice or in the normal course of business (certainly within one year) such as trade creditors, rent, rates and similar commitments. Insufficient working capital may indicate over-trading and can result in the demise of the organisation. When profits and surplus cash have been turned into fixed assets in pursuit of expansion the result can be a lack of ready funds to meet immediate liabilities, technically a state of insolvency. The same conditions can arise by being too lenient with debtors or by over-stocking, and by incurring debts with suppliers or the banks which cannot be matched by incoming current revenue.

The need to forecast the amount of working capital to be devoted to new project is particularly important, and this should be provided for when cash budgets are being worked out. Failure to make adequate provision restricts the amount of research and development that can be financed and thus is detrimental to the continued success of the enterprise. Very often the development of a new product requires the design and development of special tools, jigs and ancillary equipment and the necessary expenditure on these aspects of a new project must be accepted as a charge on working capital rather than as a charge against capital expenditure. There are two reasons for this. The first is that the control of revenue expenditure is more easily delegated to a department than capital expenditure and second, that development costs usually arise piecemeal as their need becomes apparent, and repeated applications for capital sums is an inconvenience administratively.

Any estimates and budgets for working capital must take into account two important factors: the current and probable future rates of interest and the probable trends in inflation. Both of these factors are beyond the control of the finance function, but must be included in the calculations of future working capital needs. Inflation erodes the buying value of working capital and this reduction in purchasing power must be countered as far as possible by an adequate product pricing policy, the establishment of cost-reducing practices throughout the organisation, a strict control on credit and the wise investment of surplus funds. Borowing also must be strictly regulated, especially in times of high interest rates.

Long-term (Fixed) Capital

Fixed capital is normally provided by the stockholders and bondholders, while working capital required for investment in current assets may be supplied, at least partly, by banks or by the market for commercial (short-term) papers. Fixed capital is regarded as tied up and consequently must be furnished permanently or for a long period of time. It is for this reason that stockholders and bondholders contribute fixed capital to a business.

However, there are some disadvantage of fixed capital. The debt must be repaid with interest. And the fixed interest charges may become a financial burden during periods of little or no earnings. The best way to obtain fixed capital is from funds provided by owners or creditors who will not be repaid for several years.

Regardless of the form of business organisation and ownership, the following are the important sources of business capital :

1. Owner's equity capital (proprietorships and partnerships)
2. Sales of securities (stocks and bonds)
3. Retained earnings (reinvestment of profits)
4. Lease financing (lease contracts).

Funds originally contributed by the owners as partners or shareholders are classified as net worth and make up the equity capital.

Retained Profits

By far the most important source of company finance is internal. A major portion of the capital funds of large quoted companies (*i.e.*, companies whose shares are dealt in on the stock exchange) derives from retained profits. Even in the case of a smaller company most of the capital requirements are generated within the company. A prudent policy of retaining a proportion of the profits within the organisation instead of distributing them entirely as dividend or other earnings to owner can build up funds for working capital or short-term capital projects. These retained profits can be invested for a return until they are needed.

In fact, not all profits are distributed among the shareholders. In addition to providing for depreciation and for a contingency fund profits will be regarded by a successful company as its major source of capital for future expansion.

External Capital

When a large amount of capital is required, the first step is usually to form a public company. But it is the second step which is really important — getting its share quoted on the Stock Exchange. In fact, as for a larger organisation (or a firm) a major source of capital is the new issue market. Large sums of money can be raised by selling shares and debentures to the public. The most important source of long-term capital, if the amount is a large one, is a share issue, either in the market and offered to investors generally or offered specifically to existing shareholders often in proportion to their existing holdings. The last method is called a 'rights issue'. Such finance is, of course, permanent in that once issued shares cannot be bought back by the issuing company. Small firms are limited in the amount of funds they can raise. Therefore long-term financing for these firms is usually from fixed asset mortgages and other forms of debt capital. Beginning a business on a limited budget is risky due to limited availability of funds to operate the business.

Big corporations have a distinct advantage, since they are able to sell securities through the capital market (by making public issues). Another alternative for larger business is to issue long-term credit instruments such as bonds and debentures. Fig.3.7 shows various sources of long-term funds and their advantages, for which these funds are used.

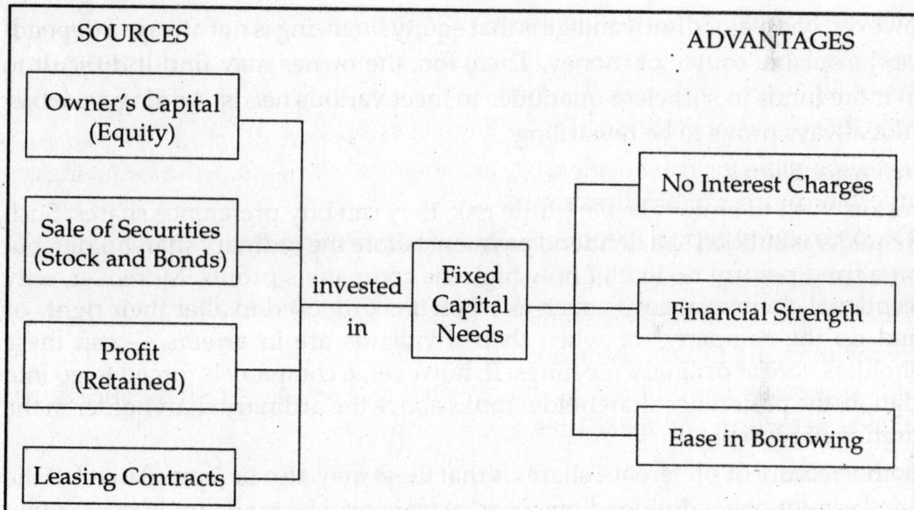

Fig. 3.7 : Long-term Capital Financing Sources

Equity Financing

Equity is the ownership claim to the resources of the firm. Ownership can be either (1) the initial funds or services contributed by the owner, (2) the additional money contributed later, or (3) the reinvested profits earned by the business.

1. SHARES

A share is exactly what the name implies — a participation in the provision of the capital of a company. It is of two types : ordinary shares and preference shares.

(i) Ordinary Shares

The dividend paid to the ordinary shareholder depends mainly on the prosperity of the company. If profits are high, the dividend is usually correspondingly high. If there are no profits, then there may be no dividend. Moreover, the payment of a dividend to an ordinary shareholder ranks last in the order of priority. Furthermore, if the company goes into liquidation the ordinary shareholder is repaid only after other creditors have been paid in full. Thus the 'ordinary share' is termed 'risk capital' (and often referred to as 'equity'). In return for bearing the risks of the business venture each ordinary shareholder has a say in the running of the company, voting according to the number of shares held. Thus, it is the ordinary shareholders who take the major risks and decisions regarding the policy of the company. So they are the real entrepreneurs. Moreover, unless a company is very large, the directors are often in a strong position in that they may hold or control a large proportion of the ordinary shares.

The use of equity financing offers the following advantages :

1. There are no interest charges to be paid to the owner.
2. A firm financed by equity capital is financially stronger and better able to withstand a business recession than one that uses debt.
3. Assuming the firm is well financed in the beginning, the owner's ability to obtain borrowed capital is improved.

However, one major disadvantage is that equity financing is not always a dependable and available source of money. Then, too, the owner may find it difficult to obtain more funds in sufficient quantities to meet various needs. Adding a partner does not always prove to be rewarding.

(ii) Preference Shares

If investors wish to undertake very little risk, they can buy preference shares. Such a shareholder is entitled to a dividend payment before the ordinary shareholder, but only at a fixed percent no matter how high the company's profits. Moreover, only in exceptional circumstances — such as when it is proposed to alter their rights or to wind up the company or when their dividends are in arrears — can these shareholders vote at ordinary meetings. If, however, a company is forced to go into liquidation, the preference shareholder ranks above the ordinary shareholder in the redemption of capital.

Another feature of preference shares is that these may also be 'cumulative'. If the company cannot pay a dividend one year, arrears may be made up in succeeding years before the ordinary shareholders receive any dividend. In recent years, preference shares have lost popularity due to their unfavourable tax treatment.

Other forms of long-term finance, which will require repayment at some future date, are the following :

2. Borrowing

(i) Debentures

Long term loans are usually obtained by issuing 'debentures'. These bear a fixed rate of interest irrespective of the profit made by the company. These are really redeemable long-term loans at fixed interest and secured on the assets of the company. Since this interest payment is a first charge on the income of the company, the risk to the investor's income is not so high. Moreover, in case of company failure, debenture-holders are paid out first. Debenture-holders secure certain rights over the borrowing firm which, in some, cases involve the right to sell off assets to secure repayment in the event of failure to meet interest payment as and when due. In fact, 'mortgage debentures' are secured on definite assets of the company. Another advantage of debentures is that they are redeemable after a specified period. If the company is unable to meet its interest charges or to redeem the loan when due, the debenture-holder can force it into liquidation.

Where profits are expected to rise in the future, therefore, a company may prefer to raise capital for expansion by issuing debentures. But it is the present-day corporation tax which is the main impulse in this direction. Debenture interest is included in the costs of a company for the purpose of calculating tax. Thus it reduces taxable profits. On the other hand, if finance is raised by shares, there is no prior interest charge and profits (which are subject to tax) will be that amount higher. This tax situation has, due to the introduction of corporation tax, led companies to finance capital expansion as far as possible by fixed-interest loans rather than by the sale of shares.

(ii) Bonds

The traditional method of sale of bonds is widely used by corporations to obtain long-term financing. A bond is a certificate of indebtedness indicating debt that is owed the bondholder by the corporation. It is a corporation debt that matures at a stated future date on which interest is paid annually or semi-annually.

Bonds may be at fixed or variable rates of interest and are repayable at a specific date. They are normally secured either on some asset or assets, or on a personal guarantee of someone of substance. Such loans do not as a rule attract any rights to the lender as do debentures. Bond financing generally attracts more capital than can be obtained by other forms of ownership. Corporations can issue more than one kind of bond to satisfy investors. Some investors choose to invest in bonds rather than in equities. Financing by bonds offers several advantages :

1. The sale of bonds does not affect management control. Unlike shareholders, bondholders have no voting rights.
2. Bond interest is a deductible expense for tax purposes.
3. Borrowing does not dilute the shareholders' equity because no additional shares are issued.

There are some disadvantages of bond financing as well. The debt must be repaid with interest. And the fixed interest charges may become a financial burden during periods of little or no earnings.

Synopsis for Learning

Q.1. What are the two main types of business capital ?

Ans. Capital for industrial and commercial enterprises are usually divided into two broad categories, *viz.*, debt (loan) capital and equity (risk) capital. Loan capital consists of those funds advanced (by creditors) at fixed or variable rates of interest which may or may not be secured by some mortgage on the assets of the company. Risk capital is that part of the capital stock which is raised by floating shares. The interest and dividends payable on these shares are not treated as costs of production for taxation purposes and they must be paid out of profits after paying taxes.

Q.2. How would a firm choose between loan capital and debt capital ?

Ans. Loan capital is more appropriate to firms operating in stable markets and which have a large part of their assets in the form of land and buildings which can be mortgaged for obtaining loans. Another feature of the loan capital is that borrowing money in this form does not affect the pattern of ownership of the business.

3.8 FINANCIAL PLANNING (OR A SOUND CAPITAL PLAN)

Capital plan is a part of the overall financial plan of a company — not only for a new project but also for future expansion of the firm. The forecast of a company's future capital needs is made on the basis of such a plan. A firm's financial need involves two types of capital, *viz.*, (1) fixed capital and (2) working capital. The features of a sound capital plan of a company are the following :

1. Estimation of financial needs

Firstly, it is necessary for promoters to make an accurate estimate of financial needs of various components of the capital plan as also an estimate of capital expenditure for launching an enterprise. A sound capital plan is one which provides adequate fixed capital as well as working capital.

2. Flexibility

Secondly, a capital plan must be sufficiently flexible. Promoters must make provision for adequate amount of finance to meet contigencies or to overcome unforeseen situations and circumstances. A firm should make a separate provision for contingencies in its initial capital plan.

Likewise, in the capital plan for expansion, the firm has to make sufficient provision for depreciation, earnings ploughback, secret reserves, conservative dividend policy and so on. In an inflationary environment, it is also necessary to take into consideration the rising costs and make necessary provision for such unforeseen additional costs.

3. Optimum use of available funds

Thirdly, the finance manager should take necessary steps to secure intensive and optimum utilisation of available financial resources and he should make efficient use of both fixed capital and working capital. Rational financial management is likely to ensure profitable operation. In the capital plan of corporation, proper balance has to be maintained between fixed capital and working capital as well as between owners' (equity) capital and borrowed (debt) capital. In most normal situations owned capital should be in the range of 50 to 60% of the total capital requirements as indicated by the capital plan.

4. Liquidity

It is also necessary for the capital plan of a corporation to make provision for necessary financial liquidity. And this is possible only when a company is having sufficient net working capital which has three broad components, *viz.*, share capital, reserves, and long-term loans. Since the most liquid of all assets (cash) is the least profitable of all, a firm must make a pragmatic compromise beteen the two conflicting considerations, *viz.*, liquidity and profitability.

It is not judicious on the part of the firm to sacrifice liquidity for the sake of profitability. A sound capital plan also requires that capital is obtained as cheaply as possible, while at the same time maintaining safety of the organisation. This is indeed one of the major principles of successful financial planning.

5. Method of Finance

The capital plan of a company determines not only its total requirements of fixed and working capital, but also the pattern of its capital structure. It is the task of promoters to take decisions in this matter. A company can issue only one class of securities such as equity shares or two classes of securities such as equity shares and preference shares. A company will usually also have a combination of share capital and loan capital in its capital structure.

In normal circumstances the usual proportion for a new company in the initial capital plans is : equity (share) capital 60%, preference share capital 20% and loan (debt) capital 20%. For a well-established company the normal proportion, while preparing capital plan for growth and expansion, is : equity (share) capital 30%, free reserves 10%, preference share capital 30%, bonds and loans 30%.

The usual practice for an established concern is to have 50% risk capital and 50% rentier capital for which a fixed payment has to be made in the form of fixed interest or fixed dividend.

6. Simplicity

A sound capital should not be unnecessarily complicated. This means that financial managers should try to evolve a simple capital structure which is quite easy to manage. This is possible only when there are no unnecessary varieties in the types of securities issued.

7. Clear Thinking and Foresight

It is also of paramount importance for management to demonstrate clear vision and foresight regarding the scope and scale of operations of a company. In a like manner, the finance manager (controller) should have the capacity to forecast various contingecies. He should also ensure that there is sufficient liquidity in the company's capital structure which is reflected in the current ratio, *i.e.*, ratio between current assets and current liabilities. In most normal situations the ratio is 2 : 1.

8. External Constraints

A firm's capital structure is influenced not only by internal (controllable) factors, but external factors as well. This simply means that due weightage has to be given to external influences while preparing the capital plan either for a new corporation or for an established concern in case of expansion and diversification. Environmental (exogenous) factors are those which are external to and beyond the control of a firm or its management. These external influences are so many in number that we cannot list them all. However, the most important of these are the following :

(a) ***Money market conditions.*** These largely determine the type of securties chosen, their initial issue price, as also the timing of public issue of capital.

(b) ***The state of the economy.*** Whether there is economic expansion and prosperity or there is depression and low return on capital the capital structure of a company will be affected.

(c) ***The attitude of investors.*** At times, investors prefer fixed interest debentures. At other times they prefer equity and preference shares for obvious reasons.

(d) ***The general level of interest rates.*** At a time when all types of interest rates are rising, it is not desirable to rely much on loan capital because it will raise the fixed cost of doing business. In other words, in times of rising interest rates, loan capital will impose heavy burden on the company and distort its capital structure. In the initial capital plan, maximum stress is given on owners' (equity) capital, while in the subsequent capital plan greater emphasis has to be laid on debt (borrowed) capital. The reason is easy to find out. A well-established company having steady earnings and assured profits can obtain loan at a concessional rate of interest. It can also take resort to trading on equity as much as possible. But a new corporation, due to lack of creditworthiness, cannot rely much on debt (loan) capital.

Fixed capital is acquired to be retained in business on a long-term basis to produce goods and services and is not for resale. A company's fixed capital need depends on its existing capital expenditure as also its future expansion and diversification plans. The need for fixed capital can be determined from the capital expenditure budget, which concentrates on major assets such as a new plant, machinery or land. Companies often acquire such resources by borrowing significant amounts (through long-term loans or bonds).

Synopsis for Learning

Q.1. What is capital plan?

Ans. Capital plan is a part of the overall financial plan of a company.

Q.2. What does a firms financial need involve?

Ans. A firms financial need involves fixed capital and working capital.

Q.3. What are the features of a sound capital plan?

Ans. The features of a companys sound capital plan are adequacy, flexibility, liquidity and simplicity.

3.9 CAPITAL STRUCTURE AND ITS DETERMINANTS

A firm's decision regarding financing of investment is concerned with choosing an optimum mix of debt and equity capital. A capital structure with a proper mix of both is termed 'the optimum (optimal) capital structure'. A reasonable proportion of both affects not only the cost of capital to a firm (which is its true opportunity cost) but also the total value of the firm in the market place.

Definition

To be more accurate, the term 'capital structure', or financial structure, or financial plan of a company refers to the composition of the long-term sources of funds. The term 'leverage' is also used to refer to the proportion of different long-term sources of funds to the total capitalisation of the firm. A firm's capital structure is said to be optimal or sound when the marginal or extra cost of each source of long term financing is the same. See the example below :

Example

A company is very eager to determine its optimal capital structure. From the following information, determine the optimal capital structure of the company :

Situations	Debt capital (Rs)	Equity capital (Rs)	After tax cost of debt	Cost of equity
1	4,00,000	1,00,000	9	12
2	2,50,000	2,50,000	6	10
3	1,00,000	4,00,000	5	15

Solution

Situations	Percentage of		Cost of		Average Total Cost (in %)
	Debt	Equity	Debt	Equity	
1	80	20	9	12	7.20 + 2.40 = 9.60
2	50	50	6	10	3.00 + 5.00 = 8.00
3	20	80	5	15	1.00 + 12.00 = 13.00

N.B. : If tax on debenture interest is taken into consideration, the cost of debt will be halved (aassuming 50% income tax). It is a deductable expense for tax purposes. See under 'Trading on Equity'.

So the optimal capital structure for the company is in Situation 2, where it uses 50% debt and 50% equity. At this level its combined average cost of capital is the minimum.

The Key Determinants

There are numerous factors, both qualitative and quantitative, including the subjective judgment of financial managers which conjointly determine a firm's capital structure. We may now briefly discuss the key factors governing a firm's capital structure decisions. The main factors are the following :

1. Profitability

The key word in capital structure is leverage. It can be defined as the employment of an asset or sources of funds for which the firm has to incur a fixed cost or pay a fixed sum (as the return per period).

Operating v. Financial

Leverage is of two types — 'operating' and 'financial'. The leverage associated with investment (or acquisition of assets) activities is referred to as operating leverage, while leverage associated with financing activities is called financial leverage. In general, the higher the level of (EBIT) and the lower the chance of downward fluctuation, the larger the amount of debt that can be employed.

2. Liquidity

The analysis of the cash flow ability of the firm to service fixed charges is of considerable importance to carry out capital structure planning.

The Coverage Ratio. In assessing the liquidity position of a firm in terms of its cash flow analysis, we use a ratio called the coverage ratio. It is the ratio of fixed charges to net cash inflows. It measures the coverage of fixed financial charges (interest plus repayment of principal, if any) to net cash inflows. In other words, it indicates the number of times the fixed financial requirements are covered by the net cash inflows. The higher the coverage ratio the larger the amount of debt (and other sources of funds carrying a fixed rate of interest) that a firm can use.

3. Control

Another consideration in planning the types of funds to use is the attitude of existing management towards control. Lenders have no direct voice in the management of a company. In most cases, the power to choose the management team rests with the equityholders. Accordingly, if the main objective of management is to maintain control, they may like to have a greater weightage for debt and preference share in additional capital requirements. This is so because by obtaining funds through them the management sacrifices little or no control.

4. Competitive parity

Another factor determining a company's optimal capital structure is the debt-equity ratios of other companies belonging to the same industry and facing a similar business risk. The rationale here is that the debt-equity ratios appropriate for other firms in a similar line of business should be appropriate for the company (under consideration) as well. The use of industry standards provides a benchmark. If a firm is deviating from its optimal capital structure, the market will give a red signal to the management that there is something wrong in the company's debt-equity mix. If the firm is out of line, it should identify the causes of such deviation and be satisfied that the reasons are genuine.

5. The nature of industry

The fifth determinant of a firm's optimal capital structure is the nature of the industry to which it belongs. The nature of industry largely determines the degree of financial leverage the firm can carry safely without any risk of bankruptcy. If an industry's sales are subject to periodic fluctuations, the firm should have a low degree of financial leverage. Such firms will always have high operating leverage.

6. Timing of issue

The question of timing of issue is also of considerable importance in determining a company's capital structure. It is often possible to make substantial savings through proper timing of security issues. It is in the rightness of things to make public offering at a time when the state of the economy as well as the capital market is ideal for providing the required funds. However, timing should not be the only consideration.

Timing analysis, for example, may suggest use of debt. But the company cannot go in for debt if its existing capital structure is already overloaded with debt.

7. Characteristics of the company

The nature and characteristics of the company in terms of its size, capital structure and goodwill (credit-standing) also play a very important role in determining the share of old securities and equity in its capital structure.

In general, firms enjoying a higher credit-standing among investors and lenders in the capital market are in a better position to get funds from their choicest sources. If the credit-standing is poor, the firm has limited choice regarding acquisition of funds.

Conclusion

Finance theory has been developed to the point where an ideal capital structure cannot be developed easily. Consequently, human judgment must be used to resolve the various conflicting forces in laying plans for types of funds sought.

Synopsis for Learning

Q.1. What is meant by a company's capital structure ?

Ans. The theory of capital structure is an important aspect of financial management. Capital structure is the mix of various long-term sources of funds used by the firm. The primary objective of all capital structure decisions is to maximise the market value of the firm by minimising the firm's overall cost of capital.

Q.2. What are the factors determining capital structure ?

Ans. There are various determinants of a company's optimal capital structure. The following factors seem to be the most important :
(i) Growth rate of future sales; (ii) Stability of future sales; (iii) Competitive structures in the industry; (iv) Asset composition of the individual firm; (v) Attitude of owners and management towards risk; (vi) Controlling power(s) of owners and management; and, (vii) Lenders' attitude toward the industry and a particular firm.

Q.3. What do you mean by 'gearing of the capital structure' ?

Ans. The ratio of loan capital to risk capital is of considerable practical significance inasmuch as it exerts much influence on the variability of the returns from investment. The ratio of a company's ordinary share capital to that part of capital which carries a fixed rate of interest (preference shares and debentures) is known as the gearing of the capital structure. The larger the proportion of ordinary to other capital, the lower the gearing of the capital structure. Thus, if profits are rising, the dividends on the ordinary shares will rise very much faster in those companies with high gearing than in those with low gearing. The opposite thing will happen when profits are falling. If the profits remain unchanged but the proportions between the ordinary shares and fixed interest securities are varied it will be found that the dividends on ordinary shares are much more variable when the gearing is greater. There are various ways of calculating gearing ratios.

Q.4. When is a company's capital structure said to be highly geared ?

Ans. A company's capital structure is said to be highly geared when the fixed charges claim an above-average proportion of either capital or income.

Q.5. What is the effect of gearing ?

Ans. The effect of gearing is to increase or decrease, more than proportionately, the return to the ordinary shareholder resulting from an increase or decrease in earnings before interest payment.

3.10 CAPITAL GEARING

Capital structure or financial structure or capital plan of a company is the make-up or composition of capitalisation, *i.e.*, the types of securities to be issued, as also the relative proportion of each type of securities in the total capitalisation.

The ratio between the various types of securities to total capitalisation goes by the name capital gearing. In other words, it is the ratio of fixed interest securities (debenture loans and preference shares) to the total capital.

High capital gearing means that the proportion of non-equity capital is relatively high. Low capital-gearing implies that the ratio of non-equity capital to equity is relatively low.

There is a relatively larger proportion of equity capital in total capital under low gearing (or financial leverage). By contrast, a relatively high proportion of fixed-interest securities in total capital implies high gearing. The following example will make the distinction clear. The figures (in Rs. '000) are all hypothetical.

Table 3.3 : High and Low Capital Gearing

Source of Finance	X Ltd. — Low gear	Y Ltd. — High gear
1. Equity share capital	700	400
2. Preference share capital	100	200
3. Debenture capital	200	400
Total	1,000	1,000

The ratio of loan debt capital to risk equity capital is of some significance because it has considerable influence on the variability of the returns from investment. The ratio of a company's ordinary share capital to that part of the capital which carries a fixed rate of interest (preference shares and debentures) is known as the gearing of the capital structure. The larger the proportion of ordinary to other capital, the lower the structure. In fact, the relationship between equity funds (net worth) and fixed-income bearing funds (debentures, preference shares and other borrowed funds) is called the capital gearing ratio. It is a usuful ratio because it shows the effect of the use of fixed-interest/dividend source of funds on the earnings available to the equity shareholders. Thus, if profits are rising, the dividends on ordinary shares will rise very much faster in those companies wiith high gearing than falling. If the profits are unchanged, but proportions between the ordinary shares and the fixed interest securities are varied it will be found that dividends on ordinary shares are much more variable when the gearing is greater.

Three factors

In case of capital gearing, three factors are to be taken into consideration in evolving a sound capital structure, *i.e.*, in assigning the relative importance to owners' capital and debt capital. The three factors are the following :

1. The volume of expected earnings
2. The stability of earnings
3. The predictability of earnings.

1. Preference for loan (debenture) capital

Those companies whose anticipated earnings are well above interest and sinking fund needs, the earnings are not volatile (or are fairly stable), certain and regular and whose success is more or less assured can rely more on loan capital or on bond finance. For a well-established company these conditions are normally specified in advance. Hence in case of such a company there may be quite a high proportion of borrowed capital to owners' (equity share) capital. By constrast, a new enterprise should not rely much on loan capital not only due to irregularity or uncertainty of earnings, but also due to lack of goodwill. Too much reliance on borrowing (*i.e.*, on bond or debenture capital) may impose considerable financial burden on such companies.

2. Importance of preference share capital

If the success of a company is quite assured but the company is not quite certain about its earnings, it can rely on preference share capital. Preference shares are suitable when the earnings are irregular but on an average there is a fair margin over the preference dividends.

3. Desirability of equity share capital

Equity share capital is always desirable under adverse conditions, *i.e.*, when earnings of a corporation are not only unpredictable and irregular, but uncertain and fluctuating as well. A speculative business, for example, not only runs the risk of considerable profit fluctuation, its immediate prospect of profitability is also bleak. So such a company can only raise equity share capital.

Conclusion

In the ultimate analysis, it appears that the determinants of a sound capital structure of a company in case of gearing depends largely, if not entirely, upon its financial position and earning power. Conservative investors have usually a special liking for bonds and preference shares. Institutional investors also show a similar preference due to legal restrictions on their approaching the capital market for equity shares. Bonds and preference shares also have a special appeal during recession and depression. The proportion of these two types of capital in the total capital of a company depends upon *three* factors : the company's financial position, its earning power and the security that can be offered by the company. The proportion of preference shares depends on the first two factors. If investors are guided by safety, regularity and security of income and capital, bonds and preference shares seem to be most suitable in a company's capital structure.

There is demand for equity capital in periods of business prosperity which are also characterised by inflation. In such periods both dividends and market value of shares rise. It is the task of management to evolve a proper mix of variable income securities (equity shares) and fixed income securities (debentures and preference shares) on the basis of these criteria. Usually, for a new company, at least 70% of total capital should consist of equity capital and the balance (30%) preference share capital and loan capital. In case of an established and at the same time a growing company (requiring more and more capital for expansion and diversification) there should be an equal proportion of both. An optimal capital structure refers to an optimum combination of share capital and loan capital.

3.11 CAPITALISATION

A company's financial plan seeks to answer two different but interrelated questions:

1. What amount of securities to be issued? To answer this question we have to refer to what is called 'capitalisation of a corporation.'
2. What kind of securities to be issued? This question is answered by making reference to the capital structure of a company. A company's capital structure indicates two things:
   (i) the form and proportion of different types of company securities to be issued and
   (ii) the different sources of raising finance.

Meaning

Capitalisation refers to a company's capital stock and debt. Capitalisation includes two things, *viz.*, (i) owners' (equity) capital and (ii) borrowed capital (represented by long-term indebtedness). And surplus in the business (*i.e.*, retained earning or undistributed profit) in the form of free reserve is also considered as an integral part of capitalisation.

Three Aspects

There are three different, but interrelated, aspects of capitalisation:

1. The market value of all kinds of shares,
2. The market value of all outstanding bonds, and,
3. The market value of undistributed profit (or retained earning which is also known as surplus capital or free reserve or corporate saving).

While formulating a sound financial plan of a company, the most important decision the finance manager has to make relates to the total amount of securities to be issued. Since capitalisation indicates the total par value of the outstanding amount of securities in the form of share capital, debenture capital and the face value of other long-term obligations it usually excludes short-term (temporary) bank loans. In short :

Capitalisation = Owners' (equity) capital + long term external (loan) capital.
= Equity share capital + retained earnings + debenture capital
+ bond capital (long-term loans).

The value of a business is determined by its ability to earn a reasonable return on net capital employed. The higher the rate of earnings and the greater the regularity of its earnings, the higher the value of the business and the larger the amount of financial capital (money) which can be safely invested in it. In other words, a business is worth that amount upon which a reasonable rate of return can be realised per annum on a regular basis. When a company is unable to earn the prevailing rate of return on its outstanding securities for a few year consecutively (while other companies belonging to the same industry and subject to the same degree of risk of business are earning the existing rate of return regularly and consistently), the company is said to be ***over-capitalised***.

By contrast, when a company's actual capitalisation (*i.e.*, total long-term resources) is lower than optimum as warranted by its (long-term) earnings capacity, the company is said to be ***under-capitalised***.

A company is said to have over-capitalisation when one of the following two things happens : (i) financiers overestimate its earnings, or (ii) promoters of the company underrate the rate of capitalisation or return on investment.

In each case two adverse consequences will follow : (1) falling dividends and (2) falling market value of shares. Each of the trends is discouraging from the point of view of the company's long-term survival and growth. A company is said to be under-capitalised if the following two discouraging trends are observed :

(i) Earnings are under-estimated.

(ii) Company promoters overrate the rate of capitalisation or return on investment. In this case also two disquieting trends will be observed, *viz.*, (i) rising dividends, and (ii) rising market value of shares.

Causes of Over-capitalisation

Over- or under-capitalisation implies unbalanced capital structure of a company. There are at least *seven* causes of over-capitalisation. These are listed below :

1. *Inflated assets*. The main cause seems to be company promotion with inflated assets. When this method is adopted we observe that the book value of a company far exceeds its real value.
2. *High cost of promotion*. The second cause is high cost incurred while promoting a company and high price paid for patents, trademarks, copyrights or even goodwill. High cost is normally incurred when promotional expenses are excessive and huge remuneration is paid to promoters.
3. *Inflation*. The third reason is company flotation in an inflationary environment when share prices are higher than normal. However, as the prosperity period is followed by recession and the boom conditions disappear, earnings gradually tend to fall. The end result is over-capitalisation.
4. *Shortage of equity capital*. The fourth cause is shortage of owners' capital due to wrong financial planning which leads to excessive borrowings (and too much dependence on debt capital). All these lead to some undesirable consequences such as continuous fall in dividends and the consequent drop in the market value of shares of the company. So shareholders suffer in two ways: (i) fall in dividend income and (ii) fall in the market value of the shares (which leads to capital loss if shares are sold).
5. *Depreciation policy*. Another cause of over-capitalisation is wrong depreciation policy which has an adverse effect on a company's operational efficiency. Such a policy adversely affects a company's operational results, *i.e.*, it leads to low profits (due to depreciated assets and the consequent capital erosion).
6. *Manipulation*. Over-capitalisation also occurs when, in an attempt to raise a huge amount of capital, a company takes the easy route of manipulating profits and paying dividends at a high rate, so as to be able to raise its share prices artificially. In such a situation the company will be able to retain hardly any profit for expansion and diversification.

7. *Government policy*. Finally, over-capitalisation may also occur due to external (environmental) factors such as government policy relating to taxes. Excessive corporation taxation may and often do create the problem of over-capitalisation.

Effects of Over-capitalisation

Over-capitalisation is likely to affect not only the company and its shareholders, but the society at large. The following points may be noted in this context :

A. On the Company

Over-capitalisation is likely to have *four* different effects on the company :

(1) low rate of dividend, (2) low market prices of shares and the consequent loss of confidence of investors, (3) manipulation of accounts to show artificial prosperity and (4) inadequate provision for depreciation, replacement and reserves.

B. On the Shareholders

Over-capitalisation has the following effects on the shareholders:

(1) fall in the value of shares,
(2) low, uncertain and fluctuating income,
(3) lower loan value of shares (*i.e.*, low value of shares when pledged for loans),
(4) destabilising speculation and exploitation of genuine investors, and, finally,
(5) erosion of company's real (not nominal) capital stock and shifting the burden of adjustment on to the shareholders.

C. On Society

Over-capitalisation has the following effects on the society:

(1) First, over-capitalisation leads to consumer exploitation through price increase and lowering of quality of products. In fact, when a company is over-capitalised it is forced to lower quality and raise price. However, this policy will be to be self-defeating in the long run. By raising price and lowering quality a company will lose its goodwill sooner or later. Its market share and sales revenue will fall and it will ultimately go out of business.
(2) Secondly, There will be panic among the people about such an over-capitalised company. And the majority of the owners of the company who belong to the middle-income group will suffer in two ways: fall in the rate of dividends and fall in share prices. The bond holders and other creditors will be adversely affected.
(3) Moreover, workers will also lose their jobs in such a declining organisation. An over-capitalised company will have a depressing effect on the whole economy. There will be misuse of society's scarce financial resources.

Remedies for over-capitalisation. The cure of over-capitalisation, as Sharlekar and Sharlekar have rightly put it, lies in "reorganisation of capital structure, if necessary, with reduction of share capital. Otherwise, sooner or later the corporation may have to face insolvency and liquidation." In this context they have suggested the following four remedies for over-capitalisation :

(1) Redemption of debentures or repayment of loans;
(2) reduction in the rates of interest on debentures or loans;

(3) reduction in the rates of dividend on preference shares; and

(4) reduction of issued or paid-up share capital.

All these measures are to be adopted simultaneously, as part of the company's capital reorganisation plan, to achieve the maximum possible effectiveness.

Causes of under-capitalisation. There are at least five causes of under-capitalisation:

1. *Accident*. Under-estimation of future earnings due to some accidental (chance) occurrence.
2. *Business cycles*. Unexpected increase in earnings during prosperity in case of companies floated in recession. This means that the business cycle movements can cause under-capitalisation.
3. *Assets appreciation*. Appreciation of assets seems to be the third cause of under-capitalisation. This is attributable to conservative dividend policy adopted by management which makes not only liberal depreciation provision but retains a huge protion of profit (without distributing it among shareholders) and lays stress on self-financing of growth (i.e., ploughing back of profits).
4. *Excess reserves*. Build-up of excess (huge) reserves also accounts for under-capitalisation.
5. *Modernisation*. Lastly, the adoption of latest production processes and techniques such as rationalisation, scientific management, financing investing from past savings as also increase in profits due to productivity rise and improvement in operational efficiency conjointly contribute to under-capitalisation.

Effects of under-capitalisation

1. Higher dividends on shares, not related to corporate growth.
2. Rise in share prices.
3. Growing intensity of competition due to the emergence of new rivals.
4. Liberal provision for depreciation.
5. Worker demand for higher wages and compensation (either directly or through their organisations).
6. Consumer demand for lower prices.

Remedies of under-capitalisation

To remedy the evils of under-capitalisation, the Indian Companies Act, 1956 has imposed an important restriction. It has stipulated that no allotment of shares can be done unless the minimum subscription has been obtained. We may also suggest four other remedies of under-capitalisation. These are the following :

1. ***Splitting up of shares***. The easiest remedy is for the directors to split up the shares in order to reduce earnings per share. This corrective measure does not affect the total capitalisation of a company because only the par value of share is reduced.
2. ***Increase in par value of shares***. The second remedy of under-capitalisation is to increase the par value of equity shares by revising upwards the value of assets. This will lead to a fall in earnings per share. Additionally, the company may offer the existing shareholders a share split-up and an increase in par value.

3. ***Issue of bonus shares***. Perhaps the most effective remedy for under-capitalisation is the conversion of reserves into shares. This will serve two purposes — reducing both dividend per share and the overall rate of earnings. This is why this method is most widely used.
4. ***Issue of shares and debentures***. Finally, where under-capitalisation is due to shortage of capital, a company may issue more shares and debentures to the public as per the guidelines of SEBI.

Conclusion

On balance it seems that under-capitalisation is the lesser evil because it can be easily rectified, particularly when earnings are abnormally high, as compared to the average earnings of the industry. By contrast, the remedies for over-capitalisation are not easy to find out. It can be remedied if and only if the existing shareholders and the creditors of the company give the permission to reorganise its financial (capital) structure by sacrificing a portion of their dividends and interests respectively. Thus, over-capitalisation can prove to be more damaging to the shareholders' interest, the company and the society. So the conclusion is that every modern organisation should try to achieve proper capitalisation. It is because over-capitalisation may lkead to over-spending and wasteful investment which may result in low earnings. Likewise, under-capitalisation may lead to closer of business altogether due to the inability of the organisation to meet its obligations (both to the shareholders and the outsiders) on time.

Synopsis for Learning

Q.1. What is capitalisation ?

Ans. The term 'capitalisation' refers to the composition of a company's long-term sources of funds, *i.e.*, its capital structure or the aggregate of the authorised par value of the stocks and bonds of a corporation.

Q.2. What is over-capitalisation ?

Ans. Over-capitalisation refers to possessing more capital than is necessary for the scale of operations being undertaken.

Q.3. What is under-capitalisation ?

Ans. Under-capitalisation often arises when business expands too quickly, making profits but being unable to turn them into cash sufficiently to pay debts.

3.12 TRADING ON EQUITY

The use of debt capital rather than equity capital is one way that financial management can increase the return on equity capital. A corporation may choose to borrow when debt financing appears to be the most cost-effective method of obtaining needed funds. At other times a corporation may find that the retention of earnings is a better way to obtain funds. As a general rule it is considered wise to borrow if more can be earned on borrowed funds than the funds cost.

For example, to borrow at 10% and earn 15% is profitable financing for anyone, incorporated or not. This principle is known as ***trading on the equity***, or ***leverage***.

Trading on the equity may also work in reverse. If business conditions worsen and earnings on total capital fall below 10%, the leverage factor is no longer favourable. The inability of a company to earn enough to pay the interest charges on its debt financing often leads to bankruptcy.

Meaning

Trading on equity refers to the practice of using borrowed money at fixed interest rates or issuing preference shares with constant dividend rates in the hope of obtaining a higher rate of return on the money used than the interest or preferred dividends paid.

Trading on equity means taking advantages of ownership. Here ownership means equity (capital) and trading means taking advantage of. A company is mainly interested in two aspects of its capital, *viz.*, (1) the funds invested by (equity) shareholders, *i.e.*, equity share capital, and (2) free reserve (set aside mainly for reinvestment purposes).

Determinants

In every country there are statutory rules relating to a company's composition of capital. The debt-equity ratio of a company is determined by the government through suitable Acts, such as the Companies Act passed by the Government of India in 1956. In order to be able to raise financial resources by selling bonds or debentures, a company will have to have a minimum amount of owners' (equity) capital. In other words, only on the strength of its equity (or ownership) capital, a company can raise finance from outsiders.

External capital usually takes the following three forms : (1) loans — short term, or long-term or even public deposits, (2) debentures and (3) preference shares.

These three sources of external capital go by the name *'rentier capital'* on which the company is required to pay rent or fixed interest either in the form of fixed dividends or fixed interest. Financing a company's business (investment activities) through such rentier capital is technically called 'trading on the equity'.

The term is used to mean that a company has financed the purchase (acquisition) of its fixed (as opposed to current) assets through the sale or issue of limited fixed interest (dividend) bearing assets. In short, when a company (corporation) uses loan capital as well as owned capital in the regular conduct of the business, it is said to be trading on the equity.

Let us consider the example of Table 3.4.

Table 3.4 : Trading on the Equity : A Hypothetical Example

A Co. Ltd.	No Trading on equity (Rs. Lakhs)	B Co. Ltd.	Trading on Equity (Rs. Lakhs)
Equity (Share) Capital	200	Equity Share Capital	200
Add: Rights Issue	200	Rights Debenture Issue	200
Profits before Tax	120	15% Interes on Debentures	30
Profits after Tax (50%)	60	Profits after Interest	90
Dividend on Equity Shares of 400	15%	Profits after Interest & Corporate Tax (50%)	45
		Dividend on Equity Share of 200	22.5%

In this example *A* Co. did not rely on trading on the equity method. And it was in a position to declare 15% dividend on Rs 400 lakhs of equity capital. By contrast, *B* Co. did take resort to trading on the equity by issue of 15% interest bearing rights issue of debenture capital worth Rs 200 lakhs. Therefore, the company was in a position to declare 22.5% dividend on its equity (share) capital worth Rs 200 lakhs[1].

It is quite clear that when the corporate tax rate is 50% of profits, *A* Co. had to make 30% profits in order to pay dividend at the rate of 15% on shares. Instead the company could sell debentures or attract public deposits of the same amount and still pay 15% interest without any tax. It is so because interest paid on bonds and debentures is a deductible expense for tax purposes.[2].

This simple example makes one thing clear at least. The fiscal system makes bond financing cheaper than equity financing. In other words, the cost of debt (loan) capital to a company is low due to favourable tax treatment (due to the fact that interest on debt is a deductible expense for tax purposes) whereas the cost of equity (risk) capital is disproportionately high (*i.e.*, due to the fact that corporate dividend is subject to corporate income tax[3].

In our illustration, since the tax rate is 50%, corporate tax saving on Rs 30 lakhs interest is Rs 15 lakhs. This tax relief gives a profit figure of Rs 45 lakhs (compared to Rs 60 lakhs in case of *A* Co.). This raises the equity dividend from 15% to 22.5%. This very fact provides the real justification of trading on equity, *i.e.*, to attract public deposits or to take loans from the public, make tax saving and thus, ultimately, push up the dividend rate.

Limitations

Just as a company's gain can be magnified when trading on equity so can its losses. It is also known as leverage. It refers to the advantage (or disadvantage) obtained by the use of borrowed funds; the effect of trading on equity is the use of senior capital in capitalisation (*i.e.*, a security that has a prior claim on assets and/or income in the form of borrowed funds, bonds, or preference shares, ranking ahead of junior equity, operating leverage being provided by having relatively fixed operating

1. If 50% of corporate profit is taxed there is a net profit of 22.5% on Rs 200 which can be declared as dividend.

2. Differently put, if the corporate tax rate is 50%, 15% of interest will be borne by the government. The government could obtain 7.5% corporate income as tax revenue if equity shares were issued and 15% dividend was paid.

3. In fact, there is double taxation of dividends in most cases. The same income is taxed twice — at the corporate level as also at the individual level.

expenses, relating to expanding or contracting sales or revenues, or by invested assets and earnings assets or deposits being made available relative to shareholders' equity or book value. There are several limitations on trading on equity. The following points may be noted in this context :

1. Fixed obligations

Firstly, in order to be able to pay handsome dividends and attract share capital, a company must earn more than what it has to pay as interest on bonds (debentures) or fixed dividend on preference shares. In our example, if profit is Rs 30 lakhs instead of Rs 120 lakhs, *i.e.*, a modest 7% return on net investment, hardly anything will be left over for distribution among shareholders as dividends. In this context, the entire profit of Rs 30 lakhs will have to be utilised for interest payment.

2. Earning fluctuations

Secondly, trading on equity carries good sense only when proper allowance is made for fluctuations in earnings. If a company is to make any real gain from trading on equity its ratio of net income to fixed charges has to be greater than 2 : 1 ratio. Since during a deep depression or a prolonged recession a company is likely to face considerable financial difficulties, it is in the rightness of things to maintain a safe ratio. In the financial literature this is called the safety factor, which ensures the payment of fixed charges, *i.e.*, interest on debentures and dividend on preference shares even though profits have dropped down by 50% (*i.e.*, profits have been halved). In our example, since the ratio of net profit to fixed charges is 3 : 2, the company is in a position to pay interest even though profit falls from Rs 60 lakhs to Rs 30 lakhs. It should not be missed that both profits and losses get inflated due to trading on equity.

3. Liquidity position

Thirdly, trading on equity is profitable only under the following circumstances : (i) when a company is a well-established one, (ii) when a company is engaged in non-speculative business and (iii) when sales volume and earnings (profits) of a company are more or less stable, regular and fairly certain. In reality, we observe that when a company is well-established, as is the case with public utility concerns, trading on equity is found to be profitable. Since such companies have maximum liquidity, they can undertake the risk of borrowing on a large scale and paying a huge sum in the form of interest and fixed dividends. Such companies may have equity capital of about 40% and debt capital of 60% in their capital structure.

However, in most manufacturing enterprises and commercial concerns we find modest trading on equity. In such companies borrowed funds may constitute even less than 40% due to lack of sufficient liquidity which is attributable to fluctuating sales, changing profits and, above all, narrow profit margins.

4. Diminishing returns

Trading on equity also suffers from diminishing returns. In fact, any increase in borrowing will raise the rate of interest in an imperfectly competitive capital market. This means that further borrowing will be more and more costly.

5. Huge fixed asset investment

To adopt this practice an enterprise will have to make a huge investment in fixed assets just to make its creditors (the lenders of funds) feel safe and secure.

Conclusion

The finance manager has to make a realistic compromise between liquidity and profitability while devising an optimal capital structure (which refers to a optimal mix of debt and equity).

Synopsis for Learning

Q.1. What is trading on equity?

Ans. Trading on equity refers to using fixed interest source of capital to boost the rate of return on the equity. It is also known as leverage or gearing which shows the relationship, measured in terms of either capital or income, between the funds provided to a company by its ordinary shareholders and long-term sources of funds carrying a fixed interest charge or dividend (*e.g.*, unsecured loans, debentures, and preference shares.)

Q.2. What is its importance ?

Ans. By doing trading on equity, a company can increase the market value of its share. This helps in raising more capital

3.13 RETAINED EARNINGS (RESERVES AND SURPLUS)

Whereas large and medium-size firms have a wide variety of sources of external finance available to them, internally generated funds and bank overdrafts tend to be the principal sources of finance for small firms. Usually we find that small and medium-size companies rely heavily on ploughing back of profits or on self-financing of business. For small companies the most important source of capital is internal, *i.e.*, for such companies most of the capital requirements are generated within the company.

Profit retained in the business is an important source of business financing. Retained earnings are profits of the firm that have not been paid as dividends to stockholders. As such, retained earnings are the major source of money for future growth. A typical American corporation retains between 35 and 60% of its earnings and pays the rest as dividends on equity shares each year. Usually a corporation's financial management will try to maintain a balance between retaining earnings and declaring sufficient dividends to satisfy the stockholders. Occasionally corporations retain all earnings and declare zero dividends. These dividends are not taxable to the shareholders until the shares are sold.

Advantages

In India and other developing countries it is a widely held view that smaller firms are at a disadvantage compared with large firms when seeking finance from external sources. Three major disadvantages of external financing are the following :

1. Some facilities are only available to the large firm (*e.g.*, the new issue market and some financial institutions do not deal with small loans).
2. Small firms have to pay more for their loan money than large firms; this is due to the greater element of risk and the fact that administrative costs of small loans are proportionately higher than those for large loans.
3. The unwillingness of some family-owned firms to share control of the business.

In India, there are certain other reasons which explain why small companies rely so much on corporate savings (retained earnings). Commercial banks and other banking and non-banking financial institutions do not provide adequate finance to small businesses because they have hardly any collateral security to offer. There has not been much change in the scene even after the nationalisation of banks in 1969 and in 1980. In some areas, loan is available from the unauthorised credit market. But interest charged on such loans is very high (and often exorbitant). So the major reliance is on ploughing back of profits or on retained earnings. However, in practice, due to high tax rates on companies and individuals most companies are not in a position to plough back profits considerably. There are a few advantages of relying on retained earnings.

1. Zero cost

First of all, if a firm uses undistributed profit (or retained earning) as a source of capital, there is no cost of capital to a firm. There is neither fixed cost (in the form of interest payment obligation) nor variable cost (in the form of dividend payment liability). Furthermore, if this method of raising capital is used there is no fall of earnings per share.

2. Permanence

Secondly, this source of finance is permanent in nature. By retaining earnings a company can make perpetual use of funds. It is just like floating capital or a revolving fund.

3. No change in managerial control

Thirdly, by using this method a company can exclude outsiders from exercising control over its day-to-day operations as also in its policy-making. If this method is used there is no change in control because the company is not required to increase its equity capital and there is no issue of any additional share or debenture.

4. No mortgage

Fourthly, when this method is used there is no need to mortgage a company's immovable properties like land or factory (office) building or even machinery and equipment.

5. No time lag

If this method is used no time is wasted in obtaining capital. By contrast, if a company makes a public issue, a lot of time is to be devoted to plan the sale of securities. Similarly, when a company applies for a bank loan various legal formalities are to be completed. All these take time and the investor often becomes impatient and drops a project even after completing its feasibility study. An issue of debentures through the money market also takes a lot of time. For all these reasons prudent management usually follows the practice of setting aside a substantial portion of earnings to be ploughed back into the business (rather than distributing the whole net profit after tax as dividends among shareholders). This very practice also serves another useful purpose: its strengthens the financial position of the company and makes its capital base sound.

6. Credit crunch

In the Indian context we find an extra advantage of this method of financing investment. When R.B.I. imposes credit squeeze on banks as part of its anti-inflationary programme bank credit becomes more costly and less readily available. In such a situation a company is forced to plough back a substantial portion of its profit not only for meeting its working capital needs but also for satisfying its requirement of fixed capital which is so much important for expansion and diversification.

7. Stability of dividend

One of the features of a company's sound dividend policy is stability of dividends. In a year of recession when profit is falling, such stability can be maintained only by accumulating large profits.

8. Creditworthiness

Large accumulated profits also enhance a company's credit standing. As Sarlekar and Sarlekar have put it : "Assured credit position helps the company to get easy and cheaper working capital from the money market and stable dividends make the market for share capital broad and active and thus attract a large body of investors and reduce the evils of speculation in the shares."

9. Social advantage

Nowadays companies are supposed to discharge their social obligations (or responsibilities). They are expected to add to society's stock of capital which is so important for creating jobs in the short run and accelerating the rate of growth of the economy in the long run. The easiest way to generate capital is to retain profits. So, the practice of self-financing of growth and expansion is considered to be socially desirable. The economic history of industrially advanced countries lends considerable support to.

Dangers (Disadvantages)

However, the practice of self-financing of investment is not an unmixed blessing. There are certain disadvantages of this method of financing growth and expansion. The main disadvantages are the following :

1. Monopoly formation

Excessive reliance on this method may lead to over-investment and monopoly formation through the amalgamation of a number of small and medium-sized firms. This method also induces firms to join hands with others, *i.e.*, collude and thus form oligopolies.

2. Misuse

Secondly, there is a strong chance of misuse of funds if this method is carried too far. Since it is virtually a costless method of financing investment, management may not be very careful about the use of internal funds which it succeeds in generating.

3. Manipulation of share prices

Thirdly, if this method is used, management will have an extra temptation to manipulate share prices. By declaring a high dividend even in a year of bad business a company can maintain stability of share prices and thus prevent shareholders from trasferring their capital elsewhere.

4. Over-capitalisation

Agains, there is the danger of over-capitalisation inasmuch as undue reliance on this method will induce firms to make frequent and excessive use of bonus shares. This method thus makes it difficult for a firm to evolve an optimal capital structure.

5. Displeasure of Shareholders

Again, if this method is adopted there will be frequent changes in shareholders. Those who are not interested in company growth and diversification (and higher potential dividend in the long run) will not like this practice of ploughing back of profits. The reason is simple: they get small dividend initially.

6. Social Waste

Finally, this method will lead to social waste. This is so because by using this method companies can by-pass the test of efficiency if they are constrained to approach the capital market for funds (which is so important for expansion). In other words, company savings may not necessarily be diverted in the most desirable direction (*i.e.*, the most profitable channels of investment). Hence this method will not enable a company to ensure an optimum utilisation of savings for the purpose of productive investment.

Corporate profits distributed to shareholders are called dividends. In India dividends are paid in cash every year. Sometimes interim dividend is also paid. In the USA, dividends are also paid in shares and stocks. Dividends may be paid only out of retained earnings and current profits and not from investment capital such as fixed assets or even inventories. In general, the more stable a company's earnings the more regular its payment of dividends.

Synopsis for Learning

Q.1. Why do companies retain earnings?

Ans. Companies retain earnings for various reasons : to obtain finance at zero cost, to maintain stability in dividend rate even in the face of fluctuating earnings and to reduce dependence on external finance.

Q.2. What are the dangers of self-financing of investment?

Ans. Six main disadvantages are : monopoly formation, misuse of funds, manipulation of share prices, over-capitalisation, displeasure of shareholders and social waste.

3.14 DIVIDEND POLICY

Importance

Dividend decisions are of crucial importance to a firm because investors prefer them over retained earnings. Perhaps the most important aspect of the dividend policy of a firm is its dividend payout (*D / P*) ratio, *i.e.*, the percentage share of the net earnings distributed as dividends among the shareholders. The most important point to note here is that dividend policy involves the decision to pay out earnings (net profits after tax) or to retain them for reinvestment in the firm. The retained earnings constitute the most important internal source of financing investment.

No doubt, the payment of dividends results in the reduction of cash and, therefore, in total financial assets of the firm. Thus, in order to maintain the existing level of asset, as also to finance new investments projects, the firm will have to obtain fund by making additional public issue of equity or debt. If the firm is unable to raise external resources, its long-run growth would be threatened. Thus, payment of dividends implies outflow of financial capital and a slowing down of the rate of future growth. Differently put, the dividend policy of a company affects not only the shareholders' wealth but long-term growth of the firm as well. So the optional dividend policy of a firm has to strike a balance between two conflicting considerations — current dividends and future growth which maximises the market price of a firm's shares and the value of the firm. The truth is that the *D/P* ratio of a firm will have to be determined with reference to two fundamental objectives — maximising the wealth of the firm's owners (the shareholders) and generating sufficient cash to provide funds for future growth. No doubt these two objectives are interrelated, but they are not mutually exclusive.

The modern view is that a firm's dividend policy should be such as to maximise the wealth of the owners in the long run. It is quite judicious on the part of the shareholders to take into consideration the long-term effects of a *D/P* ratio, *i.e.*, if the firm is paying dividends at a low rate and having high retentions, the firm is enabled to achieve faster growth in its level of future earnings. However, a close look reveals that shareholders have a clear-out preference for current dividends because of expectional uncertainty and imperfection of capital markets (due to a rise in the market rate of interest which reduces the value of the firm or the wealth of its owners). Moreover, the payment of dividends is likely to affect the price of shares : a low *D/P* ratio may lead to a fall in share price while a high ratio may lead to a rise in the market price of its shares.

The second important objective of dividend policy is to make sufficient provision for financing growth. It is not possible for a firm to achieve the objective of wealth-maximisation without acquiring (generating) adequate funds to implement acceptable projects. It is of strategic importance for a firm to make a financial forecast, *i.e.*, to forecast its future cash requirements. It should also take into consideration the external availability of funds as also certain market considerations. On the basis of these it will be in a position to determine both the amount of retained earnings needed and the amount of retained earnings available after the maximum dividends have been paid out. Thus, the conclusion that emerges from our above discussion is that payment of dividends should not be viewed as a residual, but rather a required outlay after which any remaining funds can be reinvested within the firm for expansion and diversification.

Modigliani and Miller have shown that in some circumstances, the shareholders' interests are unaffected by the decision between ploughback and the issue of new shares in the current period as the means to finance a given investment project. But Baumol has argued that none of the company's future plans and, in particular, investment decisions will in any way be affected by the decision for choosing among methods of financing. Ploughback or added stocks or added bonds are all equally happy decisions from the view point of the current shareholder.

To be most specific, company's dividend policy is important for the following reasons:

1. Firstly, it has a direct bearing upon investor attitudes. For example, a cutback in dividends is not treated with favour by the shareholders. This is normally associated with corporate financial problems. Furthermore, in setting a dividend policy, management must ascertain and fulfil the objectives of its owners. Otherwise, the shareholders may sell their shares, which, in turn, may bring down their market price. Shareholder dissatisfaction raises the possibility that control of the company may be seized by an outside group.
2. Secondly, dividend policy has an impact on the financing programme and capital budget of the firm.
3. Thirdly, it affects a company's cash flow position. A company suffering from liquidity crisis may be forced to restrict its dividend payments.
4. Finally, it lowers shareholders' equity, since dividends are paid from retained earnings, and so results in a higher debt- equity ratio.

If a company's cash flows and investment requirements are volatile, it will not be possible for the company to adopt a stable dividend policy and pay dividend regularly. It would be better to establish a low regular dividend rate that can be maintained even in years of bad business and low turnover (and profit).

Different Types of Dividend Policies

The basic objective of a company's dividend policy as pursued by its finance manager is to maximise owners' or shareholders' wealth (*i.e.*, the market value of the firm) while at the same time making adequate provision for financing the company. So, the first aspect of dividend policy is to decide how much dividend to pay and how much of total earning to retain. When a company's earnings increase, management does not automatically raise the dividend rate.

As a general rule, there is a time lag between increased earnings and the payment of higher dividend. Only when management is confident that the increased earnings can be maintained in the long run will they increase the dividend rate. Once dividends are increased, they are to be paid continuously at the higher rate.

The second aspect of the dividend policy relates to stability. The investors prefer a stable dividend rather than a fluctuating dividend. Stability here refers to consistency or lack of variability in the flow of dividends over time. To be more specific, in order to ensure stability of dividends a certain minimum amount has to be paid out on a periodic basis.

There are three variants of a constant dividend policy : (a) constant dividend per share, (b) constant D/P ratio, and (c) constant dividend per share plus extra (interim) dividend. The various types of dividend policies are the following :

1. Stable dividend-per-share policy

Many companies use a stable dividend per share policy since it is treated favourable by investors. Stability of dividend implies a low-risk company. Even in a year in which the company shows a loss rather than profit the dividend should be maintained to keep the confidence of investors — current and prospective — alive. By continuing to pay the dividend, the shareholders can be made to feel that the loss is temporary. Some shareholders rely on the receipt of stable dividend because it is a source of income with which they carry on their maintenance expenditure.

A stable dividend policy is also necessary for a company to be placed on a list of securities in which public financial institutions (mutual funds, insurance companies or even term-lending institutions like the Industrial Finance Corporation of India or the Industrial Development Bank of India) invest. Being on such a list makes a company's shares highly marketable.

2. Constant dividend-payout-ratio (dividend per share – earnings per share) policy

Under this policy a constant percentage of earnings is distributed as dividends every year. Because net profit after tax varies, dividends paid will also vary under this policy. The problem with this policy is that if a company's earnings fall drastically or there is a loss the dividends paid will be sharply curtailed or skipped altogether. This policy will not maximise market price per share since most shareholders do not want variability in their dividend receipts.

Influencing Factors

A company's dividend policy is influenced by a number of factors. The following factors the most important :

1. Fund needs of the firm

Perhaps the most important factor seems to be the fund needs of the firm. In order to estimate the fund needs the firm has to determine the likely cash flows and cash position of the company necessary for management to analyse the ability of the firm to sustain a dividend keeping in view to the possible future cash flows and cash position. Only by making such an analysis, a company can determine its likely future residual funds.

2. Liquidity position

In many dividend decisions the liquidity of a company seems to be a primary consideration. Since dividends represent a cash outflow, the greater the cash position and overall liquidity of a firm, the greater is its ability to pay a dividend. As James C. Van Horne has commented : "A company that is growing and profitable may not be liquid, for its funds may go into fixed assets and permanent current assets. Because the management of such a company usually desires to maintain some liquidity cash to give it flexibility and a protection against uncertainty, it may be reluctant to destroy this position in order to pay a large dividend." The important point to note is that a company's liquidity is largely influenced by its investment and financial decisions. While its investment decision determines the rate of asset expansion and its need for funds, the financing decision determines the way in which this need will be financed.

3. *Capacity to borrow*

The third factor determining dividend is the firm's ability to borrow. If a firm can borrow required sums easily and quickly, it may remain flexible. A large and established company has a strong access to capital markets. It can easily go ahead with a new issue. In truth, the greater the ability of the firm to borrow, the greater its flexibility and the greater its ability to pay a cash dividend. With ready access to external funds, management is not much concerned with the effect that a cash dividend has on its liquidity.

4. *Availability and assessment of information*

Most companies look at the dividend-payment ratios of other companies in the industry to maintain competitive parity. If a company is out of line with other companies having similar growth, it will want to justify its position and take necessary corrective action by collecting necessary information from security analysts and market reports.

5. *Control*

If a company pays substantial dividends, it will be required to raise capital at some future date through the sale of stock. This is likely to have an adverse consequence. The controlling interest of the company may get diluted if controlling shareholders do not (or cannot) subscribe the additional shares. These shareholders may prefer a low dividend payment and the financing of investment needs with retained earnings.

6. *Nature of shareholders*

In case of a closely-held company (whose shares are purchased by a limited number of persons and not by the public at large) management usually knows the dividend desires of its shareholders and may act accordingly. If most shareholders are in high income brackets and prefer capital gains to current income, the firm can follow the policy of paying a low dividend (which may be a blessing in disguise for its shareholders). However, as Van Horne has commented: "The low payment, of course, would be predicated upon having profitable investment opportunities for the retained earnings. The corporation with a large number of stockholders can judge their desires for dividends only in a market context."

7. *Restrictions imposed by loan agreements*

The restrictions imposed by loan agreements introduce rigidity in a firm's dividend-payment policy. Loan agreements often impose a restriction on payment of dividends. The restriction is imposed by the lenders to preserve the company's ability to service debt. Usually, it is expressed as a maximum percentage of cumulative earnings. When such a restriction is in force, it naturally influences the dividend policy of the firm. Sometimes dividend restriction is welcomed by management because in that case it does not have to justify to shareholders the retention of earnings.

LEGAL ASPECTS OF DIVIDEND PAYMENT

Dividend means "the sum paid and received as the quotient forming the share of the divisible sum payable to the recipient", or more simply, dividends are the profits of trading divided among the members in proportion to their shares. The mode of payment by a Company is determined by the articles. The directors are required by

Sec. 217 of the Companies Act (1956) to make a recommendation in the balance sheet regarding the rate of dividend which may be declared in the annual general meeting. But the rate cannot, in any case, exceed the one recommended in the annual report of the company.

The articles may provide for the payment of *interim dividend.* Such dividend may be declared at any time between two annual general meetings. Until a dividend is declared, it is not possible for the shareholder to force the company to pay it. But once it is declared, it becomes a debt due from the company to each shareholder, for the recovery of which he (she) can sue the company.

Any interim dividend is not to be treated as debt. So, the directors can skip it by passing a resolution. Section 93 empowers a company to pay, if authorised by its articles, dividends in proportion to the amount paid on each share where a larger amount is paid up on some shares than on others.

Section 205 imposes an obligation on managements to make provision for depreciation before declaring dividends as also to pay dividends only in cash. The section provides that no dividend can be declared or paid by a company except out of profits of the company calculating after providing for depreciation as laid down in Section 350.

Sub-section 2A to Section 205 further provides for the transfer of such percentage of its profits for the year, not exceeding 10%, as may be prescribed, before declaring or paying dividend out of the profits of the current financial year.

In case of inadequacy or lack of profits in any year, the company may declare dividend out of previous years profits and transferred to reserves in accordance with rule to be framed by the Central Government. Section 205A requires the transfer of unpaid or unclaimed dividends within 7 days of the expiry of 42 days from the date of the "Unpaid Dividend Account of . . . Co. Ltd./Co. Private Ltd." If the amount of the unpaid dividends is not transferred to such account, then the Company is bound to pay interest at the rate of 12% per annum.

A company may also pay dividend out of moneys provided by the Central or State Government for the purpose in pursuance of a guarantee given by such Government. Although a dividend is payable only in cash, capitalisation of profits or reserves for the purpose of issuing fully paid-up bonus shares or paying up any amount (for the time being) unpaid on any shares held by the members of the company is permissible under the Companies Act.

Dividend must be paid only to the registered shareholder to his order or to his bankers, or to the producers of coupons in respect of share warrants (Section 206). Any dividend declared by the company must be paid (or dividend warrant must be posted) within 42 days from the declaration of the dividend, to any shareholder entitled to payment of the dividend.

The only exceptions to this are :

(i) where dividend could not be paid by reason of some law;

(ii) where the instructions of the shareholder for payment of dividend cannot be complied with;

(iii) where there is a dispute as to the right to the dividend;

(iv) where the dividend has been adjusted against a claim of the company; or

(v) where the company's failure to pay the dividend or post the dividend warrant was involuntary, *i.e.*, not due to any fault on its part (Section 207).

Sub-section 2B to Section 205 imposes an additional restriction. It provides that a company which fails to redeem the redeemable preference shares as required by the new Section 80, inserted by the 1988 Amendment Act, must not declare any dividend on its equity shares.

Synopsis for Learning

Q.1. What do you mean by dividends ?

Ans. Corporate profits distributed to shareholders are called dividends.

Q.2. What are the major determinants of a firm's dividend policy?

Ans. A firm's dividend policy is a function of various factors. The most important factors influencing dividend policy are the following :

(i) **Company growth rate.** A company that is rapidly growing, even if profitable, may have to restrict its dividend payments in order to set aside needed funds within the company for expansion and diversification.

(ii) **Restrictive credit agreement.** Sometimes there is a restriction in a credit agreement that will set a limit to the amount of dividends that may be distributed.

(iii) Profitability. Dividend distribution is crucially dependent upon the profitability of the company.

(iv) **Earnings stability**. A company with stable earnings is more likely to distribute a higher percentage of its earnings than one with fluctuating earnings.

(v) **Maintenance of control.** Sometimes management of a company is reluctant to issue additional ordinary shares because it does not wish to dilute its control. So as a matter of policy it will retain a high percentage of its earnings. Internal financing enables a company to maintain greater internal control of the firm.

(vi) **Degree of financial leverage**. A company with a high debt-to-equity ratio stands a greater chance to retain earnings so that it can have the needed funds to meet interest payments and debts at maturity.

(vii) **Access to external finance.** A company that is capable of entering the capital markets easily and quickly can afford to have a higher dividend payment ratio. When there is a limitation to external sources of funds, more earnings will be retained to meet planned financial needs (*i.e.*, to pay dividends as also to grow).

(viii) **Uncertainty**. Payment of dividends reduces the degree of uncertainty in shareholders' minds about the company's current financial position and future prospects.

(x) **Tax penalties**. Finally, the apprehension of the possibility of penal taxation for excess accumulation of retained earnings may result in payment of high dividend.

3.15 FINANCIAL CONTROL

To make rational decisions in keeping with the objectives of the firm, the financial manager must have certain analytical tools. The company itself and outside suppliers — creditors and investors — all undertake financial analysis. The company's basic purpose is internal control. In particular, it is concerned with the profitability on investment in the various assets of the company and in the efficiency of asset management. But another equally important purpose is better understanding of what capital suppliers seek in financial capital and performance from it. Financial statement analysis is part of a larger information processing system on which informed decisions can be made.

As part of the planning process, organisations allocate financial resources to various organisational units such as divisions and departments. The basic question here is : how are the financial resources controlled? Generally, the organisation uses a specific control technique called budget. However, budgets are just one of several control techniques. See Fig. 3.8.

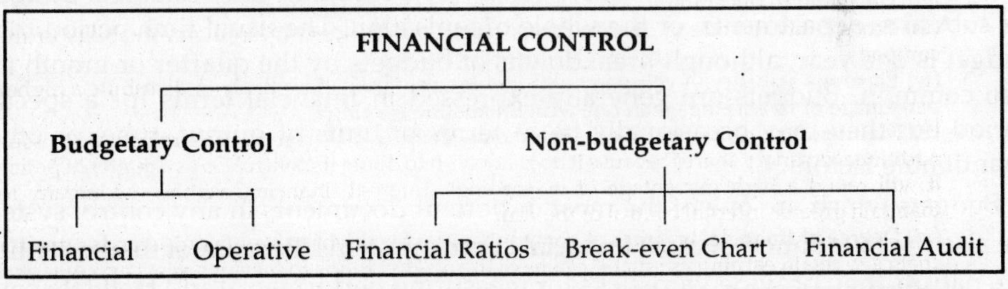

Fig. 3.8 : Types of Financial Control

A. Budgetary Control

Budgeting is a major tool for planning, motivating, and controlling business operations. The budgeting process requires management to determine its goals and objectives and to develop a co-ordinated plan for achieving those ends.

Budgetary control results from establishing department, center, or unit budgets that relate managerial responsibilities to the requirements of organisational goals and objectives and the continuous comparison of actual results with budgeted proposals to provide a basis for appropriate action. See Fig. 3.9.

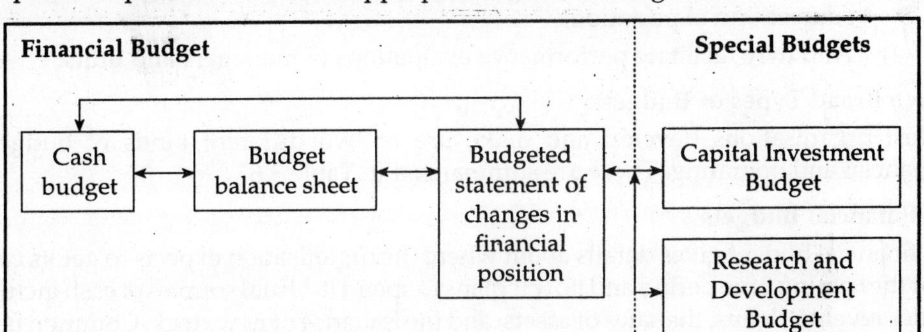

Fig. 3.9 : A Typical Finance Budget

The wealth (or comprehensive) budget is a relatively complete blueprint of the firm's future operations. It is usually prepared in terms of (1) an operating budget and (2) a financial budget. While the former produces an income statement and supporting schedules, the latter consists of a budgeted balance sheet indicating how the budget will affect the company's resources and obligations, including supporting schedules showing cash flow, capital expenditures and similar items affecting the balance sheet.

The budgetary control process involves monitoring operation so that opearting plans and targets can be attained. Budgetary control relies primarily on the analysis of differences (1) between actual costs and standard costs. Aspects of the control process involve (2) establishing lines of responsibility for performance, (3) communicating plans to those assigned performance responsibilities, (4) evaluating variances between actual results and budgeted estimates, and (5) taking appropriate action.

Budgeting involves expressing a set of planned activities for the coming time period in rupee or other quantitative terms. Organisations may establish budgets for subunits, departments, or the whole organisation. The usual time period for a budget is one year, although breakdowns of budgets by the quarter or month are also common. Budgets are generally expressed in financial terms for a specific period but they may occasionally be in terms of units of output, time, or other quantifiable factors.

Budgets which are one of the most important documents in any control system are also the foundation of most financial control systems. Because of their quantitative nature, they provide yardsticks for measuring performance and facilitate comparisons across departments, between levels in the organisations, and from one time period to another.

Four Purposes

In particular, budgets serve four primary purposes:

(1) They help managers co-ordinate resources and projects. (This becomes possible due to the use of a common denominator, usually rupees).

(2) They help define the standards needed in all control systems.

(3) They provide clear unambiguous guidelines about the organisation's resources and expectations.

(4) And they facilitate performance evaluations of managers and units.

Two Broad Types of Budgets

Most organisations develop and make use of two different kinds of budgets: financial and operating. These are summarised in Table 3.6.

1. Financial Budgets

A financial budget gives details about where the organisation expects to get its cash for the coming time period and how it plans to spend it. Usual sources of cash include sales revenue, loans, the sales of assets, and the issuance of new stock. Common uses of cash are to cover current expenses, repay debt, purchase new assets and pay dividends to shareholders.

Table 3.6 : Types of Budgets

Financial budget	Focuses on incoming and outgoing cash	(i) **Cash flow budget** : Focuses on short-run and current financial obligations. (ii) **Capital expenditures budget** : Focuses on major assets such as plant, equipment and property. (iii) **Balance sheet budget** : Focuses on what the organisation's balance sheet will look like if all other budgets are met.
Operating budget	Expresses planned operations in financial terms	(i) **Sales or revenue budget** : Focuses on anticipated income from normal operations. (ii) **Expense budget** : Focuses on anticipated expenses. (ii) **Profit budget** : Focuses on projected difference between sales or revenues and expenses.
Non-monetary budget	Expressed in terms that are not financial	

(i) Cash flow budget

One type of financial budget, the cash-flow budget, is a prediction of all sources of cash income or expenditures in monthly, weekly, or even daily periods so that the organisation can make sure that it has sufficient cash to meet its current obligations.

(ii) Capital expenditure budget

Another type of financial budget, the capital expenditure budget, concentrates on major assets such as a new plant, machinery or land. Companies often acquire such resources by borrowing large amounts (through long-term loans or bonds). So the capital expenditure budget is quite important. All organisations pay close attention to these budgets because of the large investments usually associated with capital expenditures. A capital budget is a plan for acquiring and maintaining long-term assets. The capital budget is also a technique of providing the means of financing these activities. A capital budget typically includes one or more of the following :

1. New facilities and major additions.
2. Major renovations and repairs to existing facilities.

A capital expenditure budget seeks to estimate the future cash inflows and outflows from each alternative project under consideration.

(iii) Balance Sheet Budget

The balance sheet budget forecasts the organisation's assets and liabilities in the where all other budgets are met. Hence it serves as an overall control framework to ensure that other budgets get mixed properly and yield results that are in the best interests of the organisation.

2. Operating Budgets

An operating budget is an expression of the organisation's planned operations in financial terms. This means that an operating budget outlines what quantity the organisation will produce, and what it will have to consume to achieve the production quota. Operating budgets are of the following three types :

(i) A sales (or revenue) budget

A sales (or revenue) budget focuses on the income the organisation expects to receive from normal operations. Firstly, sales are estimated for the period. Then the price of each item is calculated. These two are combined to create the revenue budget. Sales (or revenue) budgets are vitally important because they help the manager understand the future financial position of the organisation.

(ii) An expense budget

It outlines the anticipated expenses of the organisation in the coming (next) period. It also points out upcoming expenses so that the manager can better prepare for them.

(iii) A profit budget

If focuses on anticipated differences between sales or revenues and expenses. If budgeted sales and expenses are too close together, the profit budget may not be acceptable because the resultant profit is too small. In this case, steps may be needed to increase the sales budget (such as cutting or raising sales quotas) or to cut the expense budget (such as reducing inventory costs or improving scrappage rates).

B. NON-BUDGETARY CONTROL

There are three other tools of financial control, *viz.*, financial ratios, break-even analysis and financial audit.

(a) FINANCIAL RATIOS

The most commonly used ratios used for financial control are the following :

(i) Liquidity Ratios

Several liquidity ratios are used to learn how liquid (easily converted into cash) an organisation's assets are. The most common of these, the current ratio, is current assets divided by current liabilities. It indicates how many rupees of liquid assets are available for each rupee of the current liability. Creditors consider the current ratio a good index of an organisation's ablity to pay its dues on time.

Liquidity ratio, also known as acid test ratio measures the vulnerability of an organisation to pressure by creditors and others for immediate payment of liabilities. This is very significant in labour-intensive operations where a high proportion of outgoings are in cash for wages. The ratio takes into account only current assets that can be turned into cash immediately (sometimes referred to as 'quick assets') and so ignores stock and work-in-progress, which may take time to realise. The formula is:

$$\frac{\text{Cash + Debtors + Readily Realisable Securities}}{\text{Current Liabilities}}$$

or,

$$\frac{\text{Current Assets} - (\text{Stock + Work-in-progress})}{\text{Current Liabilities}}$$

$$= \text{Acid Test Ratio}$$

Ideally the minimum ratio should be 1 : 1. This means that all liabilities can be met in full immediately. Although in many spheres of activity less than this can be considered acceptable, nevertheless, in the event of failure of some debtors, for example, the organisation would be extremely vulnerable in the case of pressure by creditors. Conversely, if the ratio is much more than 1 : 1 the wisdom of holding what amounts to surplus funds could be questioned, as these could possibly be profitably used outside the organisation.

(ii) Debt Ratios

Debt ratios reflect ability to meet long-term financial obligations. The most commonly used debt ratio is total liabilities divided by total assets. The smaller this ratio, lesser is the risk of lending to the organisation. If management were to apply for a loan of Rs 30,000, for example, the bank would recognise that, even if the company were to go out of business, there would still be enough money left to repay the loan after all other debts were paid.

(iii) Return on Assets

A third important ratio is return on assets (*ROA*). The *ROA* is the percentage return to investors on each rupee of assets that they own. It serves as a yardstick for investors and managers to assess which of several investment opportunities is most profitable.

The common formula for *ROA* is $\frac{\text{Net income}}{\text{Total assets}} = \text{RAO}$

A variant of this is return on capital employed ratio. The formula employed to show the result as a percentage is

$$\frac{Profits}{Capital\ employed} \times 100 = ROCE\%$$

(iv) Other Ratios

Another frequently used ratio is return on investment (*ROI*). *ROI* is determined by dividing owners' equity by net income. This ratio represents the return to the investor from each rupee of equity.

Working capital ratio. The ratio employed here is how many times current liabilities are covered by current assets, expressed as follows :

$$\frac{Current\ assets}{Current\ liabilities} = Working\ capital\ ratio$$

The very minimum ratio is accepted as 1 : 1, in other words, the current liabilities can just be paid out of current assets. As some assets, such as stock or work in progress may take longer to convert into cash than the creditors will allow, a ratio of 2 : 1 or more is considered to be desirable, with 2 : 1 as normal.

Coverage ratios help in estimating the organisation's ability to cover interest expenses on borrowed capital. Operating ratios focus on functional areas rather than the total organisation. For example, inventory turnover (cost of goods sold divided by average daily inventory) reflects how efficiently the organisation is forecasting sales and ordering saleable goods.

Profitability ratios reflect the relative effectiveness of an organisation. For example, profits of Rs 5 lakhs are quite good on sales of Rs 20 lakhs (0.25) but are poor if sales were Rs 100 lakhs (0.05).

(b) BREAK-EVEN ANALYSIS (*BEA*)

An important form of financial analysis is break-even analysis (BBA). It is the technique of finding the point at which a project will cover its costs, or break-even. The break-even point is that point at which income of a firm equals costs and expenses. The value to management of determining a break-even point is not only to avoid loss, but to achieve as much volume as possible above it. The higher the rate of operation above the break-even point, the larger will be the net profit margin on sales, as fixed expenses will not, by definition, rise with larger volume.

BEA is essentially a technique for financial planning. We can define BEA as a procedure for identifying that point at which revenues and costs are equal and the project being examined is yielding neither profit nor loss. It might be used, then, to analyse the effects on profits of different price and output combinations or various levels of output.

Fig. 3.10 shows three cost curves relevant for BEA, *viz.*, fixed costs, variable costs and total costs.

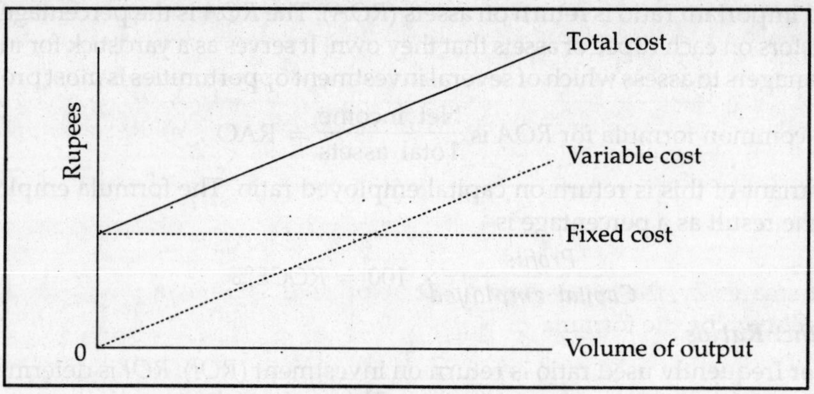

Fig. 3.10 : Three Cost Curves

Assumptions

The major assumptions underlying BEA are the following :

1. All costs can be separated reliably into their variable and fixed components within a relevant range of activity. (This is an aspect of what is nowadays called activity costing).
2. Fixed costs remain constant in total amount throughout a relevant volume range.
3. Variable costs do not change per unit and fluctuate in total in direct proportion to volume.
4. Selling prices remain constant at any relevant volume.
5. Production and sales volume will be equal.

Other important factors in BEA are revenue and profit. Revenue — the total rupee amount of sales — is calculated by multiplying the number of units sold by the sales price of each. Profit is then determined by subtracting total costs from total revenues. When revenues and total costs are plotted on the same axes, the break-even chart (graph) shown in Fig. 3.11 emerges. The point at which the lines representing total costs and total revenues cross is the break-even point. In Fig. 3.11, if this company sells more units than are represented by point *B*, it will realise a profit; selling below that level will result in a loss.

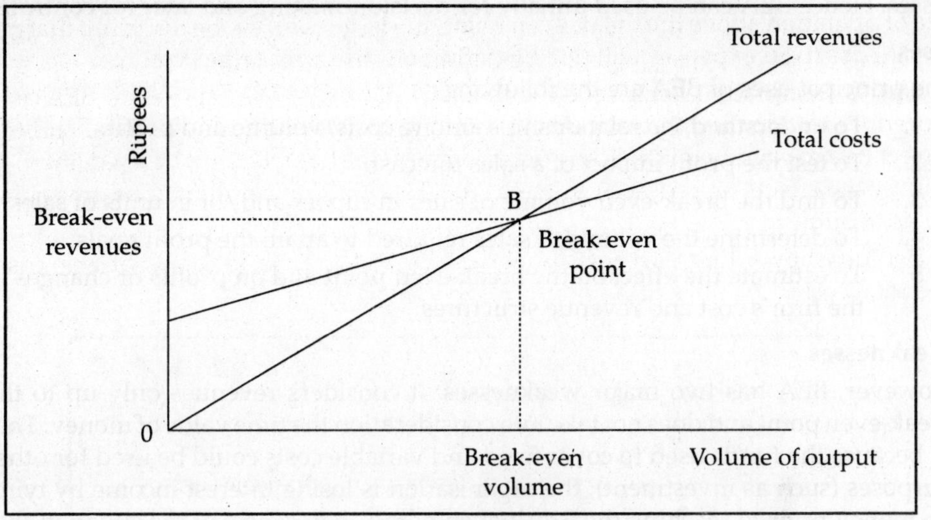

Fig. 3.11 : A Linear Break-even Chart

Mathematically, the break-even point (expressed as units of production or volume) is shown by the formula

$$BP = \frac{TFC}{P - AVC}$$

where

BP = break-even point

TFC = total fixed costs

P = price per unit and *AVC* = Variable cost per unit.

Assume Mr. X. is considering the production of a new fountain pen. He has determined that an acceptable selling price will be Rs 20. He has also determined that the average variable costs per pen will be Rs 15 and he has fixed costs of Rs 400,000 per year. The question is how many units he should sell each year to break even. Using the above formula, we find that

$$BP = 400{,}000 / (20\text{-}15) = 80{,}000 \text{ units}$$

Mr. X must sell at least 80,000 pens to break-even (*i.e.*, cover all costs and make neither profit nor loss). Further analysis would show that if he raised his price to Rs 25 per pen, he would need to sell 40,000 units to break-even, and so on.

Uses and Abuses

BEA is an extremely popular planning technique. It is often used to make an initial decision on whether to proceed with a project. BEA is also pertinent to control, because further analyses may be necessary as conditions change. For example, an initial BEA might have identified that sales of 80,000 units would be needed for a division to break-even. Midway through the project, however, material costs could rise, anticipated demand could change or price of the product could fall. All these, in turn, would signal to the organisation that it might wish to cancel the project to minimise losses. Hence BEA can be used initially for decision-making and later for control.

Uses

The principal uses of BEA are the following :

1. To understand the relationships among costs, volume and profit.
2. To test the profit impact of a sales forecast.
3. To find the break-even volume of sales in rupees and/or in units of sales.
4. To determine the volume of sales required to attain the profit goals.
5. To estimate the effect on the break-even point and on profits or changes in the firm's cost and revenue structures.

Weaknesses

However, BEA has two major weaknesses. It considers revenues only up to the break-even point and does not take into consideration the time value of money. That is, because the funds used to cover fixed and variable costs could be used for other purposes (such as investment), the organisation is losing interest income by tying up money prior to reaching the Break-even point — an aspect of the situation that BEA does not account for. Most situations in the real commercial world require that, after the preliminary BEA has been completed, more sophisticated techniques (such as rate-of-return analysis or discounted cash flow analysis) have to be used for the purpose of financial control. These techniques can help the manager decide whether to proceed or to divert resources into other areas.

(c) FINANCIAL AUDITS

Whereas most control techniques serve various other purposes, audits are used almost exclusively for control. Audits are independent appraisals of an organisation's accounting, financial, and operational systems. The two major types of fiinancial audit are the external audit and the internal audit.

(i) External Audits

These are financial audits conducted by experts who are outsiders. External audits are typically concerned with the extent to which the organisation's accounting procedures and financial statements are compiled in an objective and verifiable fashion.

(ii) Internal Audits

An internal audit is handled by employees of the organisation. Its primary objective is the same as that of external audit. Internal audit also focus on the efficiency and appropriateness of the financial and accounting procedures.

Synopsis for Learning

Q.1. What is financial control ?

Ans. Financial control refers to controlling the financial resources of a company.

Q.2. What are the different techniques of such control ?

Ans. Financial controls are of two broad categories, viz., budgetary control and non-budgetary control. Again, each can be divided into several sub-categories.

Q.3. Why is ratio analysis employed ?

Ans. To gain insight into the financial character of a firm.

3.16 ROLE OF COMMERCIAL BANKS

The financial system of a country consists of specialised and non-specialised financial institutions of both organised and unorganised financial markets. Fig. 3.12 shows a typical structure of financial market in a modern economy.

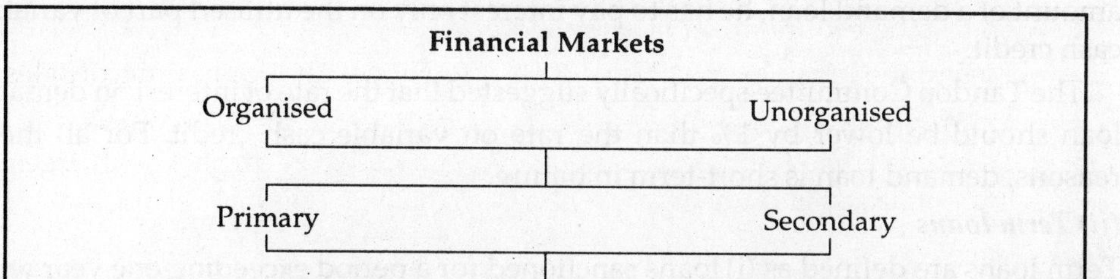

Fig. 3.12 : The Structure of Financial Market in a Modern Economy

Commercial banks are the fastest growing financial institutions in India. They are basically financial intermediaries — dealers in loans and dealers in debt.

BANK CREDIT

Commercial banks provide short-term credit to trade and industry. The volume of such credit extended by commercial banks in India increased from Rs 727 crores in 1951 to Rs 1,63,622 crores in 1994. In recent years commercial banks have introduced new methods of credit disbursement such as equity fund for small units or even venture capital for large undertakings.

Types of Credit

Commercial banks in India mainly provide short-term credit for meeting working capital needs of industry and commerce. The various types of finance provided by India's commercial banks are : (1) short-term loans and advances, (2) cash credit and (3) demand loans, (4) term loans, (5) purchase and discounting of commercial bills, (6) instalment (or hire-purchase) credit.

1. Loan

In the Indian context loans refer to advances repayable on demand or in instalments. Since such loans are necessarily made in lumpsums, fixed interest is payable on the entire amount. The borrower cannot draw funds beyond the sanctioned amount.

(i) Demand loans

Loans are usually of two types : demand loans and term loans. In India, demand loans refer to loans which have to be repaid as and when demanded by the creditor. So such loans are essentially short-term in character. But demand loans also refer to another type of financial accommodation — accommodation granted by the State

Bank of India to other commercial and co-operative banks. Demand loans are just one of the components of credit. The other component of credit is variable cash credit. In 1975 the Tandon Committee divided credit into these two categories. In a broad sense, demand loan refers to the minimum level of borrowing the debtor is expected to use throughout the year and, therefore, it is also regarded as a core portion of cash credit. While the borrower is supposed to pay interest on the entire amount of a demand loan, he has to pay interest only on the utilised part of variable cash credit.

The Tandon Committee specifically suggested that the rate of interest on demand loan should be lower by 1% than the rate on variable cash credit. For all these reasons, demand loan is short-term in nature.

(ii) Term loans

Term loans are defined as (i) loans sanctioned for a period exceeding one year with specific schedule of payment, (ii) interim cash credits/bridge loans pending disbursement of sanctioned term loans, and (iii) instalment credit where repayment is spread over more than one year. Such loans are made for purchasing fixed capital (*i.e.*, the capital cost of old and new projects).

Before independence the commercial banks have not been much helpful in providing long-term finance. Much of the commercial bank credits went for short-term loans against self-liquidating liquid assets. But over the entire Plan Period commercial banks have expanded their term loans. In the 1950s and 1960s such loans were quite small. However, commercial banks have expanded their term loans business during the last four decades. The bulk of loans is provided to industry.

2. Cash Credit and Overdrafts

These constitute running accounts from which the borrower can withdraw funds, as and when necessary, subject to the credit limits set by the banker. Cash credit is normally given against the security of physical stocks (*i.e.*, stocks of commodities). But overdrafts are allowed on personal or joint current accounts. Interest is payable not on the credit limits sanctioned but on the outstanding amount borrowed. These schemes are largely secured and of a self-liquidating nature. But banks provide them on 'clean basis' in some cases. In theory, these advances are of a short-term nature and are repayable on demand. But in practice these advances are rolled over from time to time. This very fact makes cash credits virtually long-term advances in a number of cases. So these are not highly liquid assets — even the most solvent borrower (who is making more and more profit) would hardly be in a position to repay such loans on demand.

3. Purchase and discounting of commercial bills

This is another method of advancing credit by banks. Such bills are of two types — internal and foreign. This method is adopted mainly to finance trade transactions and the movement of goods. As a general rule, bill finance is either repayable on demand or after a period not exceeding 90 days. In most cases we finds that bills traded in India are fake bills created out of book debts of industrial and business units.

4. Instalment or hire-purchase credit

Commercial banks also provide instalment or hire-purchase credit. Those who buy commercial vehicles like taxis or minibuses can obtain loans from commercial banks. Such loans are payable in 36 equal monthly instalments. During the period of the loan the vehicle has to be hypothecated to the lending bank. Nowadays, consumers also borrow money to purchase durable goods like cars, refrigerators, washing machines or even televisions. Such loans (along with interest) are payable in several instalments.

Conclusion

Among these six different systems of bank credit, cash credit/overdraft system remains the most important one. Latest data show that the share of cash credit and overdrafts in the total bank credit has declined over the years. However, there has not been much increase in the use of commercial bills as a method of obtaining credit from banks. The fact is that the major part of bill finance is in respect of internal bills rather than foreign (trade) bills. The ratio of outstanding credit to credit limits sanctioned — *i.e.*, the credit utilisation ratio — has improved significantly over the years. Borrowers are now utilising about 75 to 80% and credit limits. Now credit limits never exceed bank deposits.

So it is clear that commercial banks in India have been diversifying their operations very rapidly by granting not only loans and advances of different types but by providing various financial services through the setting up of subsidiaries/mutual funds for contributing to the equity of companies. It appears that in the coming years the banks will float many more subsidiaries to take up new lines of activity and diversify their functions and provide into a large number of financial services.

Synopsis for Learning

Q.1. What is a commercial bank?

Ans. A commercial bank is a financial intermediary—a dealer in loans and a dealer in debt. The term 'commercial' significs that it is a profit-seeking institution.

Q.2. What is the role of commercial banks in a modern economy?

Ans. Commercial banks provide the much needed working capital to trade and industry.

3.17 ROLE OF NON-BANKING SPECIAL FINANCIAL INSTITUTIONS

A strong and healthy corporate economy depends heavily on efficient channelisation of funds from savers to businesses, who need capital. Most transfers occur through specialised financial institutions which serve as intermediaries between suppliers and users of funds.

It is in the financial markets that demanders of funds, mainly companies, are brought together with those having surplus financial resources. Financial markets provide a mechanism through which the finance manager may obtain funds from various sources, including financial institutions. The financial markets are composed of money markets and capital markets. Fig. 3.13 depicts the general flow of funds among financial institutions and markets in a modern economy.

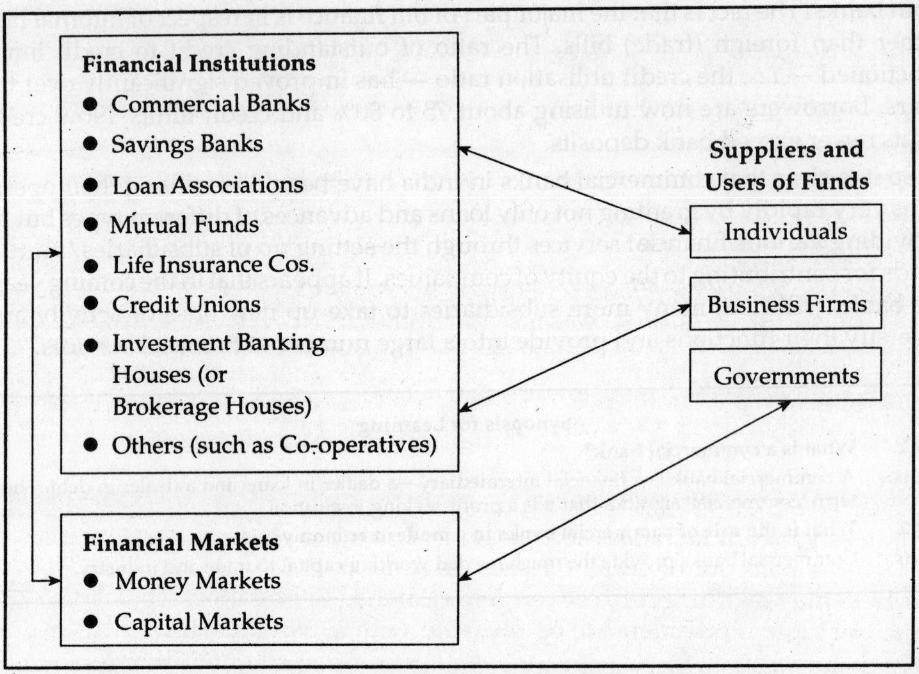

Fig. 3.13 : General Flow of Funds among Financial Institutions and Financial Markets

An important group of institutions called non-banking special financial organisations were set up in India after Independence. These are not banks but public financial institutions. They are not financial intermediaries because they do not generally mobilise savings from the public at large. Instead, they obtain their financial resources primarily from the Government or the RBI, but some of them sometimes may mobilise public savings, directly or indirectly. These term-lending institutions have mostly been set up statutorily by the Government, but some private sector participation in the ownership and funding of some of them may also exist. They are usually special (or specialised) institutions but some of them may have a much general functional coverage.

1. Industrial Finance Corporation of India (IFCI)

The IFCI is the pioneer among India's financial institutions. It was set-up on July 1, 1948.

Types of Assistance

The functions of the IFCI are: (a) guaranteeing loans raised by industrial concerns which are repayable within a period not exceeding 25 years and are floated in public interest; underwriting the issue of stocks, shares, bonds of debentures by guaranteeing loans or advances to or subscribing to debentures of industrial concerns repayable within a period not exceeding 25 years; and extending guarantees in respect of deferred payments by importers who are able to make such arrangements with foreign manufacturers; acting as agent for the Central Government and/or with its approval, from the World Bank in respect of loans sanctioned by them to industrial concerns. Later on the scope of its operations was widened to include guaranteeing loans raised by industrial concerns from scheduled banks or state co-operative banks; deferred payments due from industrial concerns in connection with their purchase of capital goods, at home or from abroad. The IFCI was empowered to subscribe directly to the stocks or shares of an industrial concern and also to convert, at its option, the loans granted or debentures subscribed by it into stocks or shares of the concern. The general purpose of IFCI is defined as "one of making medium and long-term credit more readily available to industrial concerns in India, particularly in circumstances where normal banking accommodation is inappropriate or recourse to capital issue methods is impracticable."

Its main object is to provide "medium and long-term loans to large industrial concerns in the private sector. However, now the units from the co-operative, joint, and public sector also have been made eligible for its assistance. It provides direct rupee and foreign currency loans for setting up new industrial projects and for expansion, diversification, renovation, and modernisation of existing units. It also underwrites and directly subscribes to industrial securities, provides financial guarantees, merchant banking services, and lease finance."

Since inception, till March 31, 1997 the IFCI had sanctioned aggregate assistance of Rs. 39,682 crores for 4,983 projects and disbursed Rs. 25,107 crores.

2. Industrial Credit and Investment Corporation of India (ICICI)

It was set up on March 1, 1953 as a joint venture of the World Bank. It advances funds to both private sector and joint sector, *i.e.*, projects jointly owned by private and public sectors. One of the main objectives of ICICI is to meet the long-term needs of private industry for both domestic and foreign capital. For achieving these objectives, ICICI attempts to encourage and promote participation of private capital, both internal and external, in assisted enterprises and projects.

ICICI provides finance in the form of long-or-medium-term loans (maximum period of repayment being 15 years) or equity participation, sponsors and underwrites new issues of shares and securities, guarantees loans from other private sources, and makes funds available for re-investment by revolving investments as quickly as possible. It mainly finances the purchase of capital assets. Some types of assistance provided are : (a) underwriting of issues; (b) direct subscriptions; (c) rupee loans; (d) loans in foreign currency and (e) guarantee of repayments.

The types of assistance and scope of activities of ICICI are more or less similar to those of the IFCI. However, till a few years back, it was the only institution which was providing foreign currency loans. Even now, its foreign currency loan business is conducted on a much larger scale than that of other financial institutions. It has pioneered the development of institutional financial services in various ways. It was one of the earliest organisations to start merchant banking services in India through its merchant banking division; it has developed the field of lease finance and instalment sales: it has played an important role in setting up institutions such as Over-the-Counter Exchange, TDICI, SCICI, CRISIL, and venture capital funds, through which it provides a wide range and variety of financial services.

3. Industrial Development Bank of India (IDBI)

Like the IFCI the IDBI was set up in 1964 to provide long-term industrial funds to Indian industries. Two major components of IDBI's assistance are: direct and indirect. Direct assistance consists of :

(1) project loans.
(2) underwritings plus direct subscription to industrial enterprises.
(3) soft loans for modernisation of selected industries such as cotton textiles, jute, cement, sugar and engineering.
(4) technical development fund assistance for import of equipment and technical know-how, foreign consultancy services, drawing and designs. Indirect assistance includes :

(a) refinancing of loans granted by banks, financial institutions, including IFCI and SFCs;
(b) rediscounting of bills/promissory notes originating from sales of indigenous manufacturing industries, both in private as well as public sectors, including electricity undertakings, transport corporations and motor vehicles, trucks, jeeps and passenger buses;
(c) subscription to the shares and bonds of financial institutions, both at the Centre and in States; and
(d) seed capital assistance to new and deserving units to start new ventures.

The IDBI is now the central or apex institution in the field of industrial finance. It functions as a development financing agency in its own right, in addition to its work of co-ordinating, supplementing, and monitoring the operations of other term-lending institutions in the country. Apart from providing direct assistance of the types offered by IFCI and ICICI, it provides indirect assistance in the form of discounting/ rediscounting long-term bills/promissiory notes, refinancing of loans given by SFCs, banks and so on, and subscribing to resources of other financial institutions such as SFCs, IFCI, ICICI, and so on. It also takes us various promotional activities such as balanced regional development, entrepeneurship development, technology development and so on. The resources of the IDBI are more or less similar to those of the IFCI.

4. State Financial Corporations (SFCs)

SFCs, which are State counterpart of IFCI, also provide finance to industry. At present there are 18 such corporations in India. A State Finance Corporation can (1) guarantee loans raised by industrial concerns, which are repayable within a period not exceeding 20 years and are floated in the public market, though no such limitation is applicable if the loans are received from scheduled or state cooperative banks; (2) guarantee such deferred payments of any industrial concern as are in connection with the purchase of capital goods within India; (3) underwrite the issue of stocks, shares, bonds or debentures by industrial concerns; (4) act as an agent of the Central Government, State Government, the IFCI or any other financial institutions for grant of loans or advances, or subscription of debentures by them to an industrial concern; and (5) grant loans or advances to an industrial concern, repayable within a period not exceeding 20 years or subscribe to its debentures.

Synopsis for Learning

Q.1. What are the two components of the financial markets?

Ans. The financial market is composed of the money market and the capital market.

Q.2. What are non-banking special financial institution?

Ans. All public financial institution fall in this category. Examples are the IFCI, ICICI, IDBI, SFCs etc.

APPENDICES

A. THE FINANCE FUNCTION IN THE PUBLIC SECTOR

The problems of financial management in the public sector are quite similar to those arising in the private sector in regard to the control of expenditure, though social considerations will assume more importance. However, there is less flexibility in the ability to raise funds for capital expenditure or for increasing revenue.

The publicly owned industries, those undertakings that trade and thus come within the category of profit-making, are usually required to finance capital expenditure through raising selling prices to the consumer. Where insufficient funds can be raised in this way, particularly where the undertaking is actually suffering losses, government subsidies are usually called for, as with Indian Railways.

In the public service sector income is relatively fixed, for instance the income from local taxes and government grants for local authorities, and other avenues for raising funds are severely limited. Projects such as leisure centres, municipal theatres and so on seem rarely to be profitable, and, in truth, are not usually embarked upon with this in mind. Consequently, particularly in the service sector, the finance function is more concerned with the management of expenditure and costs and minimising the number of defaulting debtors than in the raising of revenue as such. The management of the finance function in the public sector is, in fact, a specialised study.

B. FINANCIAL MANAGEMENT IN THE 21ST CENTURY

In earlier times, the marketing manager would project sales, the engineering and production staff would determine the assets necessary to meet those demands, and the financial manager's job was simply to raise the money needed to purchase the required plant, equipment and inventories. That situation has changed much in recent years — decisions are now made in a much more coordinated manner, and financial managers generally have direct responsibility for the control process.

It is also becoming increasingly important for people in marketing, accounting, production, personnel and other areas to understand finance in order to do a good job in their own fields. Marketing people, for instance, must understand how marketing decisions affect and are affected by funds availability, by inventory levels, by excess plant capacity, and so on. Similarly, accountants must understand how accounting data are used in corporate planning and are viewed by investors. Thus, there are financial implications in virtually all business decisions. So, managers in other functional areas such as marketing, personnel and materials must know enough finance to work these implications into their own areas. Because of this, every student of business, regardless of his or her major, should be concerned with financial management. The 21st century will see continued advances in computer and communications technology. This will surely revolutionise the way financial decisions are made. Financial managers will be able to share information and to have 'face-to-face' meetings with distant colleagues. The ability to access and analyse data will also mean that quantitative analyses will assume more important in business decisions. As a result, the next generation of financial managers will need stronger computer and quantitative skills than were required in the past.

GLOSSARY

Accumulated profits Reserves and surplus.

Acquisition A business combination in which one enterprise takes over another.

Break-even chart Cost-volume-profit chart, used to analyse financial gearing as well as operating leverage.

Break-even point The point at which total revenue equals total cost.

Break-even point analysis Charting and analysing relationships, usually between sales and expenses, to determine at what size or volume point an operation breaks even between a loss and profit; it can be used in any problem area where marginal effects can be pinpointed.

Bridge finance Short-term funds provided by banks and other financial institutions to companies to enable them to cover the time gap between sales of goods to clients and realisation of sales revenue.

Budget A financial plan that specifies revenue and expenses for a given time period.

Budgetary control A process that involves comparison of actual performance with planned results and taking corrective action if there are significant unfavourable variations.

Budget (business) A quantitative expression of a plan of action that serves the functions of evaluating, co-ordinating, communicating, motivating and authorising.

Capital In business it means proprietorship interest as represented in a balance sheet by the contributed and accumulated capital equal in amount to the assets *less* the liabilities. In short, the money and technology used for operating an enterprise.

Capital asset An alternative name (used more by economists than accountants) for a fixed asset. The term 'capital assets' — unlike 'fixed assets' — covers both intangible and tangible assets.

Capital asset pricing model (CAPM) It is a model of securities market based on portfolio analysis. The capital asset pricing model (CAPM — pronounced "cap-m") is that method for estimating the cost of equity capital for an issuing firm. The model treats a stock as one potential element in an investor's portfolio. Such stock is evaluated in terms of its influence on the entire portfolio — in terms of its return and its risk.

It is assumed that the cost of equity (the return on equity required by an investor), r, equals the sum of the return on a risk-free investment, r_f, and a premium that reflects the risk of the equity, R, as:

$$r = r_f + R$$

In the CAPM, R is assumed to be estimated as a coefficient, times the difference between the overall market return, r_m and r_f as:

$$r = r_f + \beta\,(r_m - r_f)$$

where β is referred to as the beta coefficient.

Cost budget A plan of future cash receipts and payments based on specified assumptions about such items as sales growth, credit terms, issue of new capital and sales and purchases of fixed assets. The basic purpose of drawing up a cash budget is to ensure that an enterprise neither runs out of cash nor keeps cash idle when it could be profitably invested.

Capital budget A budget concerned with acquisitions of fixed assets and the related financing prepared annually to list planned capital expenditures.

Capital budgeting The process of identifying, appraising, selecting and monitoring capital investment projects. Capital budgeting is a formal process of long-term planning for relatively large, permanent acquisitions and commitments of a firm's economic resources. Long-term investment decisions relate to the following basic areas that have as their objective profit maximisation :

1. equipment acquisition and replacement required (for example, to deal with obsolescence, competition, or legal requirements);
2. cost-saving investments to promote efficiency; and
3. expansion opportunities (for example diversification, product lines, and research and development investments).

In evaluating capital bedgeting projects, management must consider two factors:

1. the cost of the investment, and
2. the potential net increase in cash inflows (or reduction in cash outflows) resulting from the proposed investment.

Four methods of capital budgeting are widely used in business :

1. the accounting (average) rate of returnmethod
2. the payback method
3. the net present value method, and
4. the internal rate of return method.

Capital gearing See Gearing Ratios.

Capitalisation The composition of a company's long-term sources of funds, *i.e.*, its capital structure, or the total market value of its issue shares (market capitalisation).

Capitalisation ratio A profitability indicator which shows the proportion of funds used by a business that come from certain sources, such as borrowed funds or permanent owners' investments. A capitalisation ratio may be calculated by dividing (1) total liabilities by the stock-holders' equity or (2) stockholders' equity by total assets.

Capital market The market for medium and long-term finance, *e.g.*, for ordinary shares, preference shares and debentures.

Capital structure The composition of an enterprise's sources of funds, especially long-term consisting of equity shares, preference shares and long-term debt.

Cash cycle The process through which cash is used to obtain inventories (stocks of goods) which are then sold on credit or for cash, and the debts are converted into cash, which are then used to buy inventories.

Commercial bank A financial institution that accepts deposits and provides a wide array (range) of financial services at a profit.

Company finance Every business needs capital. Before setting up a business there must be a pool of money to buy the physical things which will be required and to pay the bills until the business is earning income. If a business wishes to expand at a later date, it will require more money. It may be able to provide that money itself by not paying out some of its profits, but in most cases it must go outside to get the money. The capital market provides the channels by which money is collected and made available to those who want it for use in business.

Current assets Assets that the company will use or convert into cash within the year.

Debenture An unsecured bond.

Debt-asset ratio The ratio of a firm's total debt to its total assets.

Debt-equity ratio The ratio of total debt to total equity.

Degree of financial leverage The percentage change in earning per share as a result of a small, say 1%, change in earning before payment of interest and taxes.

Degree of operating leverage The percentage change in earnings before payment of interest and taxes as a result of a small (say, 1%) change in sales revenue.

Degree of total leverage The percentage change in earnings per share as a result of a small change (say, 1%) in sales revenue.

Depreciation A deduction from the value of a fixed asset to account for its gradual wearing out.

Derivatives Financial instruments that derive their value from the performance of assets, interest, currency exchange rates or indexes, a security whose value depends in some way upon the values of other more basic underlying securities, *e.g.*, futures on the long Treasury Bond and the call option on a stock.

Discount rate The interest rate that the central bank charges member banks for loans.

Dividend That part of the profits of a company which is distributed to shareholders.

Dividend payment Payment made by a company to its owners — the shareholders.

Dividend yield The ratio between a company's dividend per ordinary share and the market price per share. Dividend yields are normally calculated gross of tax.

Earnings per share (EPS) The earnings of a company attributable to the ordinary shareholders or the ratio of net income to ordinary shares outstanding.

EBIT Abbreviation for earnings before interest and taxes.

Economic life The length of time during which an asset's estimated net present value exceeds its estimated net realisable value.

Efficient market theory A market where all new information is quickly understood by market participants and becomes immediately incorporated into market prices. The theory of efficient markets holds that market prices contain all available information. It is not possible to make profits by looking at old information or at patterns of past price changes.

Equity capital A synonym for ordinary shares. Equity shares capital includes both ordinary shares and preference shares.

Equity finance Finance raised from the owners of a company (i.e., share capital and reserves) as distinct from that raised from outsiders (debt finance). In short, the sale of ownership in a firm.

Finance Monetary resources and the ways in which they are obtained and used.

Financial budget That part of the master budget of an organisation which deals with such matters as cash and capital expenditures, and proforma balance sheet and funds statements.

Financial Forecast A financial forecast for an enterprise is an estimate of the most probable financial position, results of operations and changes in financial position for one or more future periods. "Most probable" means that the forecast is based on management's judgment of the most likely set of conditions and its most likely course of action. A financial projection is an estimate of financial results based on assumptions which are not necessarily the most likely. A financial projection is sometimes used to present hypothetical courses of action for evaluation. A feasibility study is an analysis of a proposed investment or course of action. A financial forecast presents a prediction of an entity's expected financial position, results of operations, and changes in financial position. A forecast is based on assumptions about expected conditions and expected courses of action, prepared to the best of the preparer's knowledge and belief. A financial projection differs from a financial forecast in that a projection depends upon one or more hypothetical assumptions. A projection responds to the question: "What might happen if...?" Multiple projections consist of two or more projections based on a range of hypothetical assumptions.

Financial institution An organisation such as a bank or a term-lending institution whose primay activity is dealing in money or financial investments and which does not produce goods or provide non-financial services.

Financial leverage Deployment of debt capital, imposing fixed financial burden.

Financial management Management of the sources and uses of funds of an organisation, both short term and long term.

Financial manager The person responsible for developing, implementing and controlling the financial plan.

Financial planning That part of long-term planning concerned with the financial aspects of a company's objectives and strategies for meeting those objectives. It involves forecasting future capital expenditures and working capital and exploring their financial implications from operations or from new issues of shares or debentures, *i.e.*, forecasting, of several years ahead, profit and loss accounts, balance sheets and funds statements.

Financial asset investment An investment that is intended to be held for use on a continuing basis in the activities of an enterprise.

Fixed assets Assets that the company intends to keep for more than one year and use in the operation of the business. Assets that are intended for use on a continuing basis in the activities of an enterprise.

Flexible budget A budget that is adjusted for change in volume rather than over a relevant range of activity. It is usually based on linear cost-volume-profit relationships.

Forecasting Estimating or predicting future events or conditions. Forecasts may be long term or short term. Forecasting is a statistical technique that has wide applicability in business activities. Forecasting involves making judgments about future events based on an analysis of past events and factors that might affect those events in the future. The role of forecasting in business is simple. Accurate forecasts of future events can assist managers make better decisions in the present. For example, forecasting is important for marketing, production and financial matters, among others. The simplest method to forecast is to extrapolate in to the future based on information from the past.

Gearing (leverage) The relationship, measured in terms of either capital or income, between the funds provided to a company by its ordinary shareholders (equity shares) and long term sources of funds carrying a fixed interest charge or dividend (*e.g.*, unsecured loans, debentures and preference shares). A company's capital structure is said to be highly geared (leveraged) when the fixed charges claim an above-average proportion of either capital or income. The effect of gearing is to increase or decrease more than proportionately the return to the ordinary shareholders resulting from an increase or decrease in earnings before interest.

Instalment One of a series of receipts or payments made at intervals over a period of time. Instalment sale refers to a credit sale in which payments are made by instalments.

Intellectual property A general term for intangible fixed assets such as patents and copyrights.

Internal finance That part of a company's financial resources raised by the retention of profits rather than from issues of shares or debt. Also includes depreciation and other non-cash charges.

Investment bank A financial intermediary that purchases and resells bonds and stocks.

Issue by tender An issue of securities in which the public is invited to apply at or above a certain minimum price with the expectation that investors will offer to buy the securities at or just below the anticipated market price.

Issuing house An institution that advices on new issues of shares or stocks for public limited companies.

Lease A document that allows the tenant to use the owner's property for a predetermined time period in exchange for consideration.

Leverage The use of borrowed funds to increase the return on equity.

Line of credit A stated cash reserve available whenever the business wants to draw on it.

Loan capital A company's long-term sources of funds raised from creditors rather than shareholders.

Modigliani-Miller hypothesis A theory regarding the relationship between leverage and valuation. More specifically, the hypothesis suggests that the market value of the firm and its costs of capital are independent of its capital structure.

Money market That part of the financial market which deals in short-term credit instruments and provide short-term funds.

Money market mutual fund Shares in mutual funds that make short-term investments in securities of the central government and major corporations.

Mutual fund An investment company that pools contributions of investors and sells to meet the investment objectives.

Operating budget That part of the master budget of an organisation that deals with operations and may be subdivided into sales, production, selling expenses and administrative expenses.

Optimisation The use of procedures or models to produce the best possible result.

Owners' equity The owners' claim on the assets of an enterprise. That part of the finance of an enterprise provided by its owners. It is measured by the market value of the ordinary shares.

Placing The sale of — or the obtaining of — subscriptions for securities by either an issuing house or a stock-broker through the stock market and to, or by, its own clients. Placing are only allowed by the stock exchange where there is not likely to be a significant public demand for the securities. The advantage of placings is their relative cheapness.

Price-earnings ratio (P/E ratio) The multiple of last reported earnings per share that the stock market is willing to pay per ordinary share. It is the reciprocal of the earnings yield multiplied by 100. The higher the *P/E* ratio (the lower the earnings yield), the more the market thinks of the company — the cheaper the cost of equity capital to the company.

Public offering A sale by a company of bonds or shares to the public.

P/V chart A chart which measures profit on the vertical axis and volume in physical or monetary units on the horizontal. In essence, it is a simplified form of the break-even chart.

Quoted company A company listed on a stock exchange.

Refinancing The issue of new securities to repay an existing one.

Retained earnings That portion of net income of a company which is ploughed back in business.

Return on investment (CROI) The ratio of profits to assets (or net worth) of an organisational segment, company or brand.

Sales forecasting A forecast of future sales based on consideration of such factors as past sales volumes, general economic and industry conditions and various other factors. The sales forecast is the usual starting point of the budgeting process.

Seed capital Money or other assets provided to help launch a new project.

Self-financing Using retained profits as a source funds.

Short-term financing Raising funds to meet obligations that will come due within the next 12 months.

Sinking Fund - A device used to accumulate liquid funds over a specific number of years in order to meet a known need for cash at the end of that time. The cash will be required for such purpose as the redemption of a loan or the replacement of a fixed asset.

State Financial Corporations State counterparts of Industrial Finance Corporation of India, the SFCs are state level financial institutions providing funds to small and medium-sized industries. At present there are 18 such institutions in India.

Technical analysis The process of using the pattern of a stock's price over time to predict the stock's future price movement.

Term loan Long-term loan repayable in more than one year and less than ten years.

Trade credit Short-term sources of funds resulting from credit granted by the suppliers of goods or services purchased. The purchase of merchandise on an open account.

Trading on the equity Using fixed interest sources of capital to boost the rate of return on the equity.

Undercapitalisation Possessing less capital than is necessary for the scale of operation being undertaken. Undercapitalisation often arises when businesses expand too quickly, making profits but being unable to turn them into cash sufficiently fast to pay debts.

Unit Trust of India (UTI) An investment company which also aims at mobilising the savings of the public and investing them in productive enterprises.

Underwriting The acceptance, in return for a commission, of the risk that a share will be undersubscribed. The underwriter agrees to take up any shares that are not applied for by the public.

Undistributed profits Those profits which have not been withdrawn from a business undertaking by its proprietors.

Venture A new business or a new or different approach or product/service in an existing business.

Venture capital Capital provided for new and underdeveloped companies, especially those with expected above average risk and return.

Venture capital firm Financial intermediaries that specialise funding ventures with special promise.

Working capital The short term assets and liabilities of a business, *i.e.,* current assets less current liabilities.

Yield A rate of return relating cash invested to cash received. The percentage return from stock dividends, or the dividend divided by the selling price per share.

Zero-base budgeting (ZBB) An approach to the formulation of budgets in which managers have to justify their activities as though those activities were being started for the first time. It is a very time-consuming method of budgeting.

4

Personnel Management

If people of poor calibre are hired, nothing much else can be accomplished — and Gresham's law will work : the bad people will drive out the good (or cause them to deteriorate).

Robert Heller

[Syllabus

- **Meaning and importance**
- **Basic functions**
- **Nature and importance of manpower planning**
- **Recruitment, selection and placement**
- **Training : benefits of training, types of training**
- **Promotion and promotion policy**
- **Performance appraisal and job evaluation**
- **Industrial rellations and laboiur welfare**
- **Industrial discipline, code of discipline in Indian industry**
- **Workers' participation in management (significance and the position in India)**
- **Nature and importance of collective bargaining**
- **Trade unions and their functions and weaknesses**
- **Nature and scope of labour welfare activities]**

SUBJECT MATTER OF PERSONNEL MANAGEMENT

The personnel function ranks high in importance among those activites that have developed from the staff side of organisation. Among small undertakings matters appertaining to personnel are usually handled by a senior line manager with the assistance of one or two clerical workers who deal with day-to-day detail such as keeping personnel records and the like. In the larger organisations, however, there is normally a separate personnel department, headed by a personnel manager, which is responsible for all aspects of the work necessary in dealing with problems concerning employees, their conditions of work and their welfare. In the majority of cases the personnel department acts in an advisory capacity only, but so complicated and specialised have the duties of the personnel function become that in many large undertakings the personnel manager, often a director and always a senior executive, is endowed with the authority to negotiate with unions and employees' representatives, and to enter into binding arrangements on behalf of management. The personnel manager will be responsible to and report to the chief executive and will be required to give advice on and be intimately concerned with the development of an implementation of the organisation's personnel policy.

The scope of the personnel function is vast and varied and a complete expositions would require a long and extensive study. Within this chapter, therefore, only the important aspects of the functions can be touched upon in order to acquaint those interested in general management studies with the work of the personnel function.

4.1 IMPORTANCE OF MANPOWER

Personnel management refers to the practices and policies you need to carry out the people of personnel aspets of management job. These include : (i) Conducting job analyses (determining the nature of each employees' job); (ii) Planning manpower needs and recruiting job candidates; (iii) Selecting job candidates; (iii) Training new employees; (iv) Appraising performance; (v) Communicating (interviewing, counseling, discipline); and (vi) Training employees.

Manpower is perhaps the most important resource of an organisation because people are both producers and consumers. The role of human resource management in an organisation's strategic management planning is extremely important in helping firms find ways to compete effectively at home and internationally. Quality and productivity contribute the core of managing work, organisations, people and operations because they are critical to costs, sales, competitiveness and profitability. Improvements in a firm's competitive position can occur only if it is possible to make the most effective utilisation of an organisation's manpower. Moreover, an organisation cannot raise productivity but its people can.

Organisations are managed and staffed by people. Without people, organisations cannot exist. Indeed, the challenge, the opportunity, and also the frustration of creating and managing organisations frequently arise from the people-related problems that arise within them. People-related problems, in turn, frequently originate from the mistaken belief that people are all alike, that they can be treated in the same way. But this is not true. In reality, no two people are exactly alike, and everyone differs physically and psychologically from everyone else. Sitting in a sports arena, for example, will be tall people, black people, white people, elderly people, small people, fat people, thin people, young people, and so on. Even within any single organisation there will be enormous variability in psychological characteristics. Some will be outgoing, others reserved; some will be intelligent; others not so intelligent; some will prefer indoor activities, others outdoor activities. The point is that these differences demand attention so that each person can maximise his (or her) potential, so that organisations can maximise their effectiveness, and so that society as a whole can make use of its human resources.

Organisations Need People and People Need Organisations

Without people, organisations cannot function. Even in highly automated plants—such as the one designed and built by Yamazaki (a large Japanese company that makes machine tools) to run smoothly using only 12 workers — people are required to co-ordinate and control the plant's operations. Conversely, people need organisations so that they can satisfy their needs and wants, so that they can maintain their standard of living (by working in organisations), and so that modern society can continue to function.

These needs (organisations for people, people for organisations) will be ever more difficult to satisfy in the context of today's competitive business environment. And, to meet the challenges of managing, managers must understand the potential of manpower (human resources) and then secure, retain and develop these resources. This requirement is the foundation of human resource management (personnel management).

4.2 MEANING AND OBJECTIVES OF PERSONNEL MANAGEMENT

Personnel/human resource management is a staff function whose primary role is to help the organisation achieve its goals. The operation of the personnel function is dependent on the broad strategy, policies, and structure of the organisation. Small companies have different personnel problems than large companies. Organisations scattered at different places must address problems that do not create problems for centralised organisations. Manufacturing companies have somewhat different personnel concerns than service companies. A large university teaching business management courses is labour-intensive and employs hundreds of professional and non-professional personnel in various departments and areas of specialisation. On the other hand, a capital-intensive firm such as a petroleum refinery employees relatively few workers and its personnel function will be quite different from that of a university teaching management.

Whatever strategic or organisational changes occur, the personnel management department must help facilitate these changes through recruitment, selection, training, compensation, and other personnel functions.

To accomplish the organisation's goals and support its strategies, personnel objectives and strategies must also be developed. Among the more important personnel objectives are the following:

1. To establish employee recruitment and selection systems for hiring the best possible employees consistent with the organisation's needs.
2. To maximise the potential of each employee in order both to attain the organisation's goals and ensure individual career growth and personal dignity.
3. To retain employees whose performance helps the organisation realise its goals and to release those whose performance is unsatisfactory.
4. To ensure organisational compliance with state and central government laws that are applicable to the personnel management function.

The management of any organisational unit or department — marketing, finance, accounting or production — involves the accomplishment of objectives through the use of the skills and talents of people. The personnel management is considered both a line management responsibility and a staff function.

In any type of organisation — large, medium or small — human resources must be recruited, compensated, developed and motivated and performance appraisal must be finalised and implemented by managers.

The role of personnel management in an organisation's strategic management planning is of considerable importance. It helps organisations to find ways to compete effectively at home and internationally. Quality and productivity constitute the core of managing work, organisations, people and operations — because they are critical to costs, competitiveness and profitability.

Personnel management methods such as employee and motivation programmes, employees' training and education and changing the organisation's culture lead to improvement in quality and productivity in the organisations. Personnel management can be defined as the process of fulfilling organisational objectives by acquiring, retaining, terminating, developing and properly using the human resources.

4.3 IMPORTANCE OF PERSONNEL MANAGEMENT

Personnel management is important for avoiding the following consequences :"

- To hire the wrong person in the job
- To experience high turnover
- To find your people not doing their best
- To waste time with useless interviews
- To have some of one's employees think their sallaries are unfair and inequitable relative to others in the organisation.
- To allow a lack of training to undermine one's department's effectiveness.
- To commit any unfair labour practices.

The acquisition of skilled, talented and motivated employees is an important part of personnel management. The acquisition phase involves recruiting, screening, selecting and placing personnel. Retaining competent individuals is also important to an organisation. If qualified individuals regularly leave a company, it becomes necessary to continuously seek new personnel, which costs money and time. The opposite of retention is, of course, termination, an unpleasant part of any manager's job. Occasionally, some employees must be terminated for breaking rules, failing to perform adequately or job cutbacks.

Developing human resources involves training, educating, appraising and preparing personnel for present or future jobs. These activities are important for the material and psychological growth of employees. It is not possible to satisfy the need for personnel in an organisation if it does not have an active employee development programme.

For utilising the full potential of manpower, there is need to understand both individual and organisational needs. Itt is also necessary to match two things : availability of different types of manpower, over time and organisational needs for such manpower. Personnel management is normally regarded as a staff function whose role is to serve the organisation and help it achieve its objectives.

Synopsis for Learning

Q.1. What is Personnel Management ?

Ans. Personnel management is that part of the management process that specialises in the management of people in organisations.

Q.2. What are the major personnel management functions ?

Ans. Private and public sector organisations are vitally concerned with productivity and cost effectiveness in managing resources. In short, personnel/human resource management is concerned with the effective use of people in order to attain organisational goals and enhance the personal dignity, satisfaction, and well-being of employees. Personnel departments in most organisations act in a staff capacity by giving advice and performing services for supervisors and employees. In most organisations, the personnel (or human resources) department establishes policies and coordinates functions such as job analysis, personnel planning, the recruitment and selection of employees, training and development, performance appraisal, compensation and employee benefits, labour relations, employee discipline and control, health and safety at workplace.

Q.3. What is the importance of personnel management ?

Ans. Personnel management emphasises that employees are the primary source for gaining sustainable competitive advantage, that human resource activity resource specialists help organisational controllers to meet efficiency and equity objectives.

4.4 DIFFERENCE BETWEEN MODERN HUMAN RESOURCE MANAGEMENT AND TRADITIONAL PERSONNEL MANAGEMENT

The importance of personnel management has grown dramatically in the last two decades. Organisations are coming to realise that the effectiveness of their personnel function has a substantial impact on the 'bottom line' performance of the firm. For instance, poor manpower planning can result in frequent hiring followed by layoffs, which are costly in terms of unemployment compensation payments, training expenses and morale. Haphazard employees and outmoded recruitment practices can lay the firm open to expensive and embarrassing court cases.

Organisations which employ hundreds of employees usually have a personnel manager and a personnel department charged with supervising these activities. However, responsibility for personnel activities is invariably shared between the personnel department and line managers.

For instance, the personnel department may recruit and do the initial screening of the department where the new employees will work. Similarly, although the personnel department may establish performance appraisal policies and procedures, the actual evaluating and coaching of employees is done by their immediate superiors. Thus, virtually every manager is involved and needs to understand the basis of personnel management.

Personnel management refers to management of an organisation's human resources, *i.e.*, the men and women it employs. It refers to the process of bringing people into the organisation and assuring that they have the potential to be valuable resources.

While personnel management is concerned with management of existing manpower of an organisation human resource management is concerned with both human resource management and development through training and development and manpower planning. Thus, human resource management is more forward-looking.

BASIC FUNCTIONS

Personnel managers perform certain functions such as the selection, placement, training and development of appropriately qualified employees. Thus it includes two fundamentally different processes: (i) selecting people for specific organisational positions and (ii) developing the abilities and skills they will need to be effective in those and subsequent jobs or assignments.

The personnel management function does not end when an adequately trained individual is selected and placed in a position. Staffing is an ongoing process that aims at making sure that human resources are in the right place at the right time. One part of selection is bringing people into the organisation. Another is moving them within the organisation throughout their careers as needs arise and as their skills develop. One part of training and development is giving people the skills they need to make initial contribution, but another is giving them the developmental experiences throughout their careers to make them productive resources. The main functions of personnel management are the following :

1. Job Analysis and Design

Job analysis deals with the determination of specific tasks and responsibilities common to a job or class of jobs (job descriptions) as well as identifying the skills, knowledge, and abilities that a person holding the job should possess (job specifications). This information is vital in the development and validation of selection devices such as application blanks, formal interviews, and tests designed to measure an applicant's ability to perform a job. Properly designed performance appraisal systems also depend on thorough job analyses. Job analysis information is also important in the design of equitable pay structures, training programmes, and health and safety programmes. Collecting job analysis information can be a time-consuming and difficult task. Various job analysis methods are presently used.

Job design involves structuring the work so that it can be performed efficiently while providing the employee with a feeling of satisfaction or reward. Many jobs such as assembly line or clerical work can be quite monotonous because of their narrow scope and repetition. Jobs such as those performed by air traffic controllers are so complex and demanding that they create enormous stress and can cause "burnout". Still other jobs — such as those found in steam-engine driving and forestry — pose physical hazards.

2. Occupational Safety, Health, and Well-Being

Employee health, safety, and well-being have become increasingly important concerns. Thus, safety and health issues are not limited to physical injuries that occur at the workplace. Many employers are trying, through employee assistance programmes, to address a variety of employee health problems such as drug and alcohol abuse and the cumulative effects of exposure to toxic substances and psychological stressors. Additionally, employers are devoting resources to employee welfare programmes, thereby encouraging healthy lifestyles.

3. Labour-Management (Industrial) Relations and Collective Bargaining

Labour relations and collective bargaining are primarily concerned with union-management relations. Labour unions represent employees with regard to wages, hours, and working conditions. In essence, a union acts as an agent on behalf of a group of employees who have made the union their exclusive bargaining representative.

Personnel managers are concerned about unions for several reasons. Unionised (or partially unionised) employers must negotiate in good faith with the bargaining representative (union) chosen by employees. The product of union-management negotiations, the collective bargaining agreement — establishes pay scales, hours, seniority provisions — and other working conditions of employees. Once the collective bargaining agreement has been negotiated with the union, personnel managers and supervisors must deal with union representatives on an almost daily basis in implementing the agreement.

4. Manpower Planning

Manpower planning involves three essential steps: First, a supply and demand forecast for each job category is made. This step requires knowledge of both labour market conditions and the organisation's strategic position and goals. Secondly, net shortages and excesses of personnel by job category are projected for a specific time period (say, 5 years). Finally, plans are developed to eliminate the expected shortages and excesses. If a shortage of accountants is projected over the next year, then the firm can begin searching for accountants through job consultants or through recruitment on college campuses. Suppose that a manufacturer of expensive jewellery is opening a new production facility next year and will need diamond cutting experts to staff the operation. Because of the specialised nature of this business, it may not be possible to find diamond cutters whose technical background and experience are suitable. Therefore, the manufacturer may decide to train and promote current employees to fill these positions.

The careful use of a systematic manpower planning programme enables the personnel department to forecast needs, plan for employee succession, staff critical areas, and allow the organisation to meet its goals without unnecessary disruptions caused by shortages of personnel. Manpower planning can be facilitated by computer-assisted programmes and management information systems.

5. Employee Discipline and Control

A difficult and sensitive personnel management issue involves dealing with inefficient, incompetent, and troublesome employees. Examples of undesirable employee behaviours include coming to work under the influence of alcohol or drugs, theft, fighting, insubordination, and work rule violations. Personnel managers must understand the importance of industrial discipline and must have the ability to deal properly with problem employees.

6. Recruitment and Selection of Employees

Recruitment involves creating a pool of applicants from which employees may be selected. Public and private employment agencies, advertisements in newspapers and professional journals, and colleges and universities are among the sources from which organisations draw applicants. Selection deals with screening, testing and hiring the best qualified applicants from the recruitment pool. Organisations use devices such as weighted application blanks, honesty and polygraph tests, ability and interest tests, reference checks, medical examinations, and other selection predictors to determine which applicants are most likely to perform well if hired.

7. Performance Appraisal Systems

Performance appraisal systems involve the quantitative and qualitative measurement of employee performance. Ideally, a performance appraisal system should account for every task, duty, and responsibility of an employee's job, as well as the knowledge, skills, and abilities needed to perform satisfactorily — nothing more and nothing less. This means that performance appraisal systems should eliminate irrelevant factors that may bias the evaluation of an employee's performance. Factors such as personal lifestyles, political reliefs, race, sex, age, religion, and other factors outside the scope of the job should not be reflected in performance appraisals. Nearly all personnel managers should agree that such factors should not be considered, and yet these and other irrelevant factors often adversely affect the performance appraisal process.

Performance appraisal results have a number of important effects on recruitment, selection, training, and compensation.

It is, therefore, important that performance appraisal systems are based on job-relevant criteria, objectively measured, and protected from undue subjectivity and bids.

8. Employee Training and Development

Training and development programmes seek to improve the knowledge, skills, and abilities of employees. Organisations may view workers as an "investment" in human capital, and, in order to achieve an adequate "return" on this investment, corporations must be certain that employees are competent and possess up-to-date job knowledge, skills, and abilities. Some employees already possess the requisite skills when they are hired. Peter Drucker calls them 'knowledge workers'. However, many employees require periodic training and development to prevent their skills from deteriorating or becoming obsolete. Training and development programmes include skill training designed to improve employee efficiency on the job, management development programmes whose major purpose is to increase the decision-making abilities of managers, and career development programmes.

To sum up, the bottom-line measure of the personnel department's effectiveness is the degree to which it enables an organisation to attain its overall goals. Organisational outcomes such as the fulfillment of a firm's strategic choice, cost effectiveness, growth and survival, and social responsibility are all facilitated or hindered by the personnel management function.

Synopsis for Learning

Q. What are the main staffing functions?

Ans. A major function of personnel managers is making sure that the company has the staff it needs. This staffing function involves more than simply hiring personnel. Staffing has several phases: recruiting, screening, testing interviewing, conducting background checks, supervising, physical examinations, making employment decisions, and administering orientation and placement.

4.5 ORGANISATION OF THE PERSONNEL DEPARTMENT

Organisation of the personnel department function varies by size of company, emphasis on various personnel activities, and degree of centralisation of the personnel management function in large decentralised companies. Fig.4.1 shows a typical personnel management department.

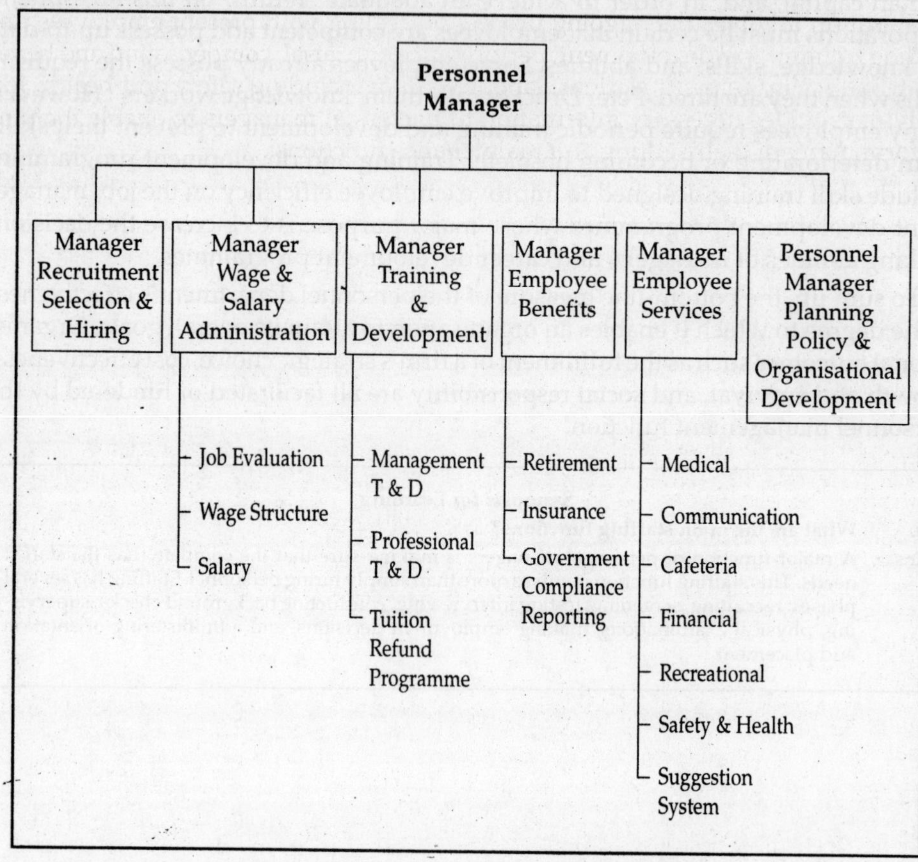

Fig. 4.1 : A Personnel Management Department

Personnel management in large organisations is performed in a staff department like the one shown in Fig.4.1. However, personnel departments in such organisations are organised according to company needs and objectives.

Human resources make a business run. Without capital resources and an entrepreneur, there would be no business. But without people to help the owners run the business, nothing would happen.

People do not automatically become productive employees. They must be recruited, hired, matched with the proper jobs, trained, appraised on their performance and paid acceptable wages. Employees' working conditions must be monitored for safety, their activities coordinated, and records maintained on their performance. If these things are done properly, most people will be satisfied with their jobs.

The upper levels of management today see the importance of a motivated and competent workforce. Managers have found it necessary to upgrade and profession their methods in managing human resources.

Human resources are absolutely critical for effective functioning of an organisation. Personnel management includes planning for the future employment needs of the organisation and taking steps to meet the needs *via* recruiting and selection, promotion, layoff, transfer, early retirement. Maintaining the human resources of an organisation involves the ongoing process of dealing with present employees including training and development, performance appraisal, compensation and benefits, labour-management relations, labour welfare including safety and health. Job analysis provides necessary information to personnel managers to enable them to perform many of their staffing and maintenance functions.

4.6 MANPOWER PLANNING

An intelligent and ultimately effective training programme depends upon effective manpower planning. Without such planning the real training needs for the future cannot be calculated. The development of manpower estimates, in turn, depends upon corporate plans and strategies :

- The first step in manpower planning must be an investigation into the existing work force at all levels from shop floor to senior management to ascertain where and how manpower is deployed, the efficiency in the way it is being used (for example, is there over-manning or under-manning) and the degree of skill attained and needed by the various employment areas.
- From this data a realistic assessment can be made of the numbers of people that may be needed over the ensuing years divided into categories of jobs and skills required. Account will be taken of probable natural wastage by retirement and by voluntary leaving — the latter estimate being based on rates and types of labour and staff turnover for preceding years. Consideration must also be given to corporate plans and how they will affect staffing requirements, and also to the likely effects on staffing that may be brought about by foreseeable changes in technology.
- While this review is going on it may also be advisable to examine the criteria laid down for various categories of jobs and perhaps to reassess them in the light of changing conditions. For instance, the qualifications as existing for a production foreman may not be adequate for future recruits to such a post in view of changing technology.
- Thus manpower planning will forecast detailed staffing needs in both the short term and the long term, and this will facilitate the introduction of effective recruitments and training procedures to ensure the employment of the right number of people of the right qualifications and experience in the right jobs.
- Those responsible for manpower planning must be alert not only to the needs and changing demands of the organisation itself but also the external factors that influence the supply of labour of all types. This may come about by changes in social behaviour, such as a reduction in certain classes of school-leavers because of the larger number entering university or college, or by legislation such as the various statutes on sex equality. Calculations must, therefore, be constantly modified to ensure the fulfillment of the organisation's manning requirement at all times.

Human resource management consist of manpower planning, recruitment, selection and hiring, training and development, performance appraisal, and rewards. The hoped-for result of the processes are high-performing satiated individuals who stay with the organisation and help it to grow.

The starting point in the personnel management process is manpower planning. The importance of manpower planning depends largely on the nature of business strategy and overall planning of the organisation.

Manpower planning parallels the plans for the business as a whole. Manpower planning focuses on questions such as: What do the proposed business strategies imply with respect to human resources? What kinds of internal and external constraints will (or do) we face? For example, restrictive work rules in a collective bargaining contract are an internal constraint, while a projected shortfall in the supply of electrical engineers (relative to the demand for them by employers) is an external constraint. What are the implications for staffing, compensation practices, training and development, and management succession? What can be done in the short run (tactically) to prepare for long-term (strategic) needs? We may consider a company example.

The ultimate objective of manpower planning is the most effective use of scarce talent in the interests of the workers and the organisation. Thus we may define manpower planning broadly as an effort to anticipate future business and environmental demands on an organisation, and to provide qualified people to fulfill that business and satisfy those demands. This general view suggests several specific, interrelated activities that together comprise an MP system. They include:

- A talent inventory to assess current human resources (skills, abilities, and potential) and to analyse how they are currently being used.
- A human resource forecast to predict future human resource requirements (the number of workers needed, the number expected to be available based on labour market characteristics, the skills mix required, internal versus external labour supply).
- Action plans to enlarge the pool of people qualified to fill the projected vacancies through such actions as recruitment, selection, training, placement, transfer, promotion, development, and compensation.
- Control and evaluation to provide feedback on the overall effectiveness of the manpower planning system by monitoring the degree of attainment of human resource objectives.

Companies use manpower planning for two main reasons:

1. to develop their business objectives and manning levels; and
2. to reduce the 'unknown factor' (*i.e.*, uncertainty regarding manpower supply and need).

Manpower planning, to be genuinely effective, must be linked with the different levels of general business planning, not as an end or goal in and of itself, but rather as a means to the end of building more competitive organisations. The overall process is directed by line managers. When line managers perceive that human resource practices help them achieve their goals, they are more likely to initiate and support MP efforts.

At the level of operational level, manpower planning is concerned with detailed forecasts of employee supply (internal and external to the organisation) and employee demand (numbers needed at some future time period). Based on the forecasts, specific action plans can be undertaken. These may involve recruitment, changes in incentives, promotions, training, or transfers. Procedures must be established to control and evaluate progress toward targeted objectives.

MEANING

Manpower Planning (MP) means :

1. *From the demand side*—analysing, reviewing and attempting to predict the numbers, by kind, of the manpower needed by the organisation to achieve its objectives;

2. *From the supply side* — attempting to predict what action is and will be necessary to ensure that the manpower needed is available when required; and finally

3. *Designing the interaction between demand and supply* — so that worker skills are utilised to the best possible advantage of the organisation and genuine needs and desires of the individual employees are taken into account.

The manpower plan represents a response of the personnel function to ensure that the necessary supply of people is forthcoming to allow the targets to be met.

Steps

The first step in the manpower planning process involves forecasting staffing needs and determining the actions needed to fulfill those needs.

Forecasting Staffing Needs

The most important step in forecasting staffing needs is a review of the organisation's objectives and strategies. This includes reviews at both the corporate enterprise level and the business unit level. If the organisation is pursuing growth objectives then there may be a need to expand the size of the firm's human resources.

Forecasting Internal Supply

Once staffing needs have been forecast, managers are in a position to forecast the internal supply of human resources. A forecast of internal supply is derived from examining the kinds of human resources internal to the organisation, the demographics of those resources (especially years until retirement), and the stability of the people presently employed.

This process may include a job analysis, which is a systematic study of what is done, when, where, how, why, and by whom in current and predicted jobs. The job analysis can be used to write job descriptions and job specifications. A job description is a written statement of job duties and responsibilities. A job description frequently includes working conditions, and the tools, materials, and equipment used to perform the job. A job specification is a list of the skills, abilities, education, experience, and other qualifications needed for the job.

The job analysis may include a human resource audit. A human resource audit is a listing of the strengths and weaknesses of current personnel. For example, such an audit may uncover weakness in the information technology skills of current employees at a time when the organisation is entering a computer system intense business.

Forecasting External Supply

Once managers have forecast internal supply, they are in a position to forecast external supply. As with forecasting internal supply, this includes a review of skills, abilities, education, experience, and other qualifications needed for the job. Especially if the organisation has always hired locally, this forecast may have implications for training to fill gaps.

Correcting Shortage or Surplus

From the forecasts and the comparisons of supplies and needs, the organisation is in a position to correct the imbalances. If there is a surplus in the organisation, management needs to decide the value of the human resources to the enterprise and if it will carry a surplus until normal turnover and retirements correct the situation. If there is a huge imbalance — and if management cannot tolerate the costs of carrying the surplus personnel — then it might resort to involuntary pay cuts, part-time work, early retirements, and terminations. Alternatively, if there is a shortage of human resources in certain areas, cross training and hiring seem to be the only alternatives.

Thus the four stages of the manpower planning process are :

1. An evaluation or appreciation of existing manpower resources.
2. An estimation of the proportion of currently employed manpower resources which are likely to be within the firm by the forecast date.
3. An assessment or forecast of labour requirements if the organisation's overall objectives are to be achieved by the forecast date.
4. Adoption of required measures to ensure that the necessary resources are available as and when required, that is, the manpower plan.

While stages 1 and 2 are linked with the supply aspect of manpower, stage 3 represents the demand aspect of manpower.

Analysing training and development needs is the final part of a manpower planning effort. Here the questions to be answered are : (a) How many people need training and development? (b) Who are the specific individuals? and (c) What kind of training is needed? These are the problems which a personnel manager has to face and solve.

Manpower planning consists of forecasting the organisation's future needs for employees, and then planning programmes to meet unfilled needs so that the organisation will have the right number and kind of employees when they are needed. Fig.4.2 shows the process.

Effective manpower planning starts with a forecast. The human resource forecast estimates the number and types of employees the organisation will need over the next one to two years. The forecast also predicts the supply of employees to fill these needs. In predicting supply, the human resource manager considers internal sources, or employees who could be promoted or shifted into the vacant positions, as well as external sources: people currently in school, working for another company, or actively seeking employment.

TECHNIQUES OF MANPOWER PLANNING

We have already noted that manpower planning involves forecasting manpower needs, assessing manpower supply and reconciling supply and demand through various personnel-related programmes. The manpower planning process is affected by the organisation's strategic management decisions and environmental uncertainities. These two factors, in turn, determine the length of the planning horizons, the type and quality of information available to manpower planners and the nature of jobs to be filled. Manpower demand forecasts and assessments of supply must be continuously monitored so that adjustments can be made in the programmes designed to reconcile the supply and demand of manpower resources. See Fig.4.2.

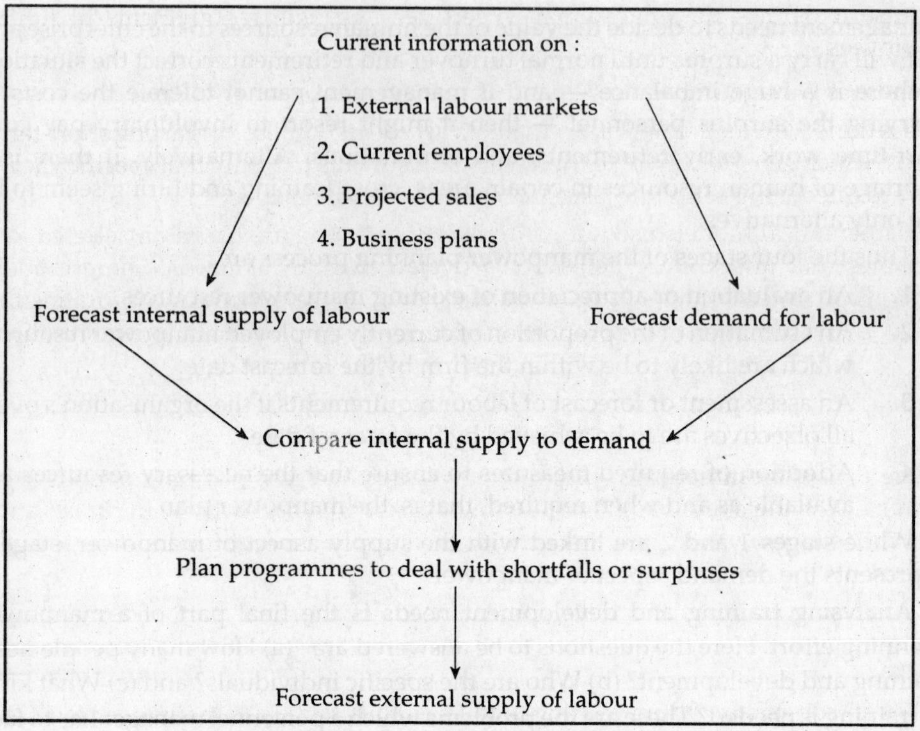

Fig. 4.2 : A Schematic Representation of Manpower Planning

Forecasting Manpower Needs (Demand)

Manpower demand refers the total human resource needs of an organisation for a given time period. The precise nature of an organisation's demand for manpower depends on various factors. Once the factors affecting the demand for manpower are identified, methods for forecasting can be designed and implemented. External factors include competition (foreign and domestic), the economic climate (such as the stock market crash of 1992), laws and regulations and changes in technology. Internal factors include budget constraints, production levels, new products and services and organisational structure.

Short-term Forecasting

Short-range forecasts usually grow out of normal budgetary processes. Manpower budgets and projections are generally based on estimates of work-loads (production schedules, passenger loads, expansions or contractions in operations). Conversion ratios that translate workload data into manpower demand estimates may be used for a short-range demand forecast. For example, as sales increase by a certain percentage, a manufacturing concern may determine by how much the number of employees in certain departments or divisions must also increase.

The use of conversion ratios provides only a rough approximation of the number of employees required and may indicate very little about the types of manpower needed. It is important for an organisation to carefully define not only the number of workers needed by the entire organisation, but also the type required at various levels, departments and locations. Job analysis information is hopeful in this respect, because it defines the educational, experience and skill requirements of future employees.

Long-term Forecasting

This is done with mathematical and statistical models. Unlike forecasting short-term needs, which generally involves necessary adjustments to assure that specific vacancies are filled, long-term forecasts are more general in nature.

Mathematical models used in manpower forecasting are based on selected key variables that affect the organisation's overall manpower needs. Some models contain both internal and external variables. For example, a model incorporating the following factors might be used to forecast overall employment in an organisation:

$$E_n = \frac{(L_{agg} + G)\frac{1}{X}}{Y}$$

where E_n is the estimated level of manpower demand in n planning periods (*e.g.*, years); L_{agg} is the overall aggregate level of current business activity in rupees and, G is the total growth in business activity anticipated through period n in today's rupees.

X is the average productivity improvement anticipated from today through planning period n (e.g., if $X = 1.80$ it means an average productivity improvement of 8%).

Y is an conversion figure relating today's overall activity to manpower required (total level of today's business activity) divided by the current number of personnel). It reflects the level of business activity per person.

The major purpose of this model is to predict E_n, the level of manpower necessary in n periods. Before putting the number into the model, estimates of G, X and Y must be made. Such estimates may be based on the previous experiences of management, as well as on future strategic choices to which the organisation's decision-makers are committed.

The application of a personnel (employment) forecasting model depends heavily on obtaining accurate estimates of total growth (G), average productivity improvement (X) and conversion ratios (Y) (*e.g.*, one employee per Rs 50,000 in sales).

Suppose we wish to estimate the number of salespersons necessary in 2000. We may use the relationship between sales and the number of salespersons we have today as a starting point. Let's assume that we currently have Rs 1,000,000 in sales today (L_{agg}). We also assume that by 2000 our sales will increase by Rs 500,000 in today's rupees (G, rupees adjusted for inflation), that there will be no increase in productivity ($X = 1.0$), and each of today's employees can support Rs 50,000 worth of sales (X). If we substitute these values into the formula we obtain

$$E_n = \frac{(L_{agg} + G)\frac{1}{X}}{Y}$$

$$E_{1999} = \frac{(\text{Rs } 1{,}000{,}000 + \text{Rs } 500{,}000)\frac{1}{1.0}}{50{,}000}$$

$$E_{1999} = \frac{(\text{Rs } 1{,}500{,}000)^8}{50{,}000} = 30 \text{ salespersons}$$

Linear Regression

Another quantitative approach, *viz.*, linear regression analysis, may also be used to estimate the manpower necessary at a future point in time, based upon such factors as sales, output or services rendered. For example, if a college is expanding, it is likely that more teachers will be needed. If there has been a satisfactory relationship in the past between the size of the faculty and the number of students enrolled, linear regression may be a useful method for estimating the number of teachers needed for expansion. The following straightline equation may be used :

$$Y = \alpha + \beta X$$

where Y = the number of faculty and X = the number of students enrolled.

If we wish to estimate the number of faculty needed in 2000, we may substitute the expected 1998 enrollment into the equation.

Another approach to determining the number of faculty members required in 2000 involves using a graph to locate the estimated number of students in 2000 on the X-axis, plot a vertical line up to the regression line and then plot a horizontal line over to the Y-axis, reading the necessary number of faculty from the Y-axis (see dotted line in Fig. 4.3). If the graph is precise, one will read the same value for the necessary faculty as one would get using the above equation. The entire process depends upon the accuracy of one's estimation of student enrollment in 2000. If the estimate of likely student enrollment in 2000 is inaccurate, then the prediction based upon it is less likely to be accurate.

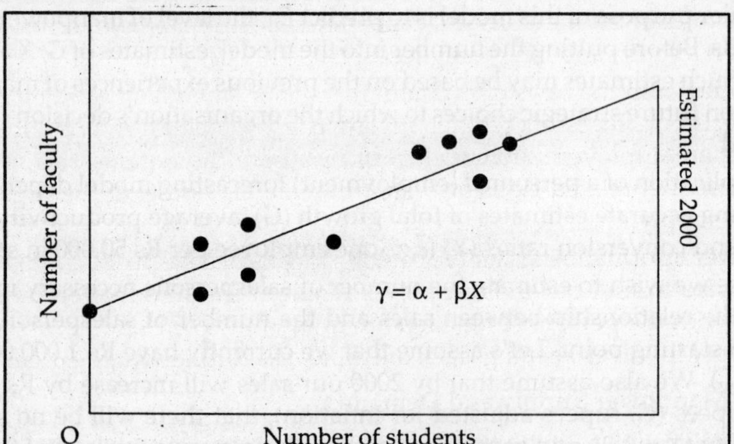

Fig. 4.3 : Linear Regression Line

The quantitative approaches presented here (conversion ratios, aggregate planning model and linear regression) represent only three methods from among many that are available. When using linear regression it is very important that the equation accurately summarises the past relationship between the two variables.

Some organisations use group estimation to obtain long-term forecasts. The complexity of organisations and the environments in which they must exist makes forecasting input from numerous.individuals — each of whom is an expert in his or her specialisation — especially useful. Although the group estimation models used may vary somewhat, most of them involve the following steps:

- Selecting a variety of specialists or experts throughout the organisation who possess knowledge or expertise relevant to the manpower forecast.
- Identifying key forecasting concerns, variables, problems and developments through scrutiny of the organisation's strategic position.
- Developing a list of specific manpower forecasting questions or issues that must be addressed by the group.
- Designing a system such as a questionnaire that will enable each specialist or expert to have input into the forecasting process.
- Once input is received and placed in an organised form, the group leader attempts to gain a general agreement on the manpower.

Forecasting Manpower Supply

Manpower planners must consider both the external supply (employees available for hire in the organisation's geographic workforce) and the internal supply (the organisation's current employees) of human resources.

It is important for personnel planners to anticipate and pinpoint changes in personnel supply. Various methods are available for doing this. A relatively straightforward method is presented in Fig. 4.3.

Although manpower planning is concerned with having an adequate number of employees to fill positions within the organisation, it is equally concerned with providing the right type of person for the job. A major function of manpower planning is to examine the skills and capabilities of current employees in light of the organisation's short- and long-term needs.

Inventories form the basis of promotion, transfer, layoff and training and development decisions. In essence, skills inventories provide an information base for monitoring an employee's potential contribution to the organisation, making informed personnel-related decisions, and, in general, assessing the organisation's manpower supply.

Manpower information systems provide a means of collecting, summarising and analysing data to find out the manpower requirement. Information requirements associated with the personnel function are numerous. For example, assessing personnel supply involves keeping track of employees throughout the organisation.

Balancing Manpower Supply and Demand

Once an organisation's manpower needs (demand) are determined and the current supply of employees is assessed, then manpower supply and demand must be balanced in order that vacancies can be filled by the right employee at the proper time. Balancing supply and demand is largely a matter of planning, timing and use of various personnel-related programmes to achieve the desired results.

Uses. The many activities included in the personnel management function start with manpower planning which refers to the process of forecasting personnel needs and developing the necessary strategies for meeting those needs. This information helps managers in several ways:

- Managers can anticipate personnel shortages or vacancies and act to create or fill jobs before problems arise.
- Managers can anticipate the types of training and development the personnel will need.
- Managers can identify the particular skills and abilities of the present employees to help develop effective career paths for them.
- Managers can evaluate the effect of human resource decisions and make any necessary changes.
- Inventories of employee skills are often maintained in computerised files. They include information about each employee's educational and training background, experience, and special skills (*e.g.*, foreign language proficiency). With the use of skill inventories, personnel managers can readily identify what skills are available in the internal labour market and what skills must be imported from the external labour market.
- Staffing changes due to retirements, sick leaves and occasional personal emergencies must also be anticipated. This involves little more than keeping track of the ages of employees and being careful to take account of absent employees and positions vacated by promotions and transfers. However, when staffing changes are due to changes in programmes or departments, manpower planning becomes more complicated. Budgetary considerations come into play. Employees associated with obsolete programmes generally will not be kept on unless they can be retrained or their skills utilised elsewhere.

More and more organisations are instituting manpower planning systems. Short-term planning (one to two years) to guide immediate recruiting needs is most common, but mid- and long-range planning (up to ten years) can also be helpful, especially for managerial jobs. When we foresee a need for many more middle managers in seven years' time, we had better begin right away to locate and develop individuals with management potential.

Synopsis for Learning

Q.1. What is manpower planning ?

Ans. Planning to match (balance) the demand for different types of people within an organisation — now and in future — with the supply of the required personnel.

Q.2. What are the three major steps of manpower planning ?

Ans. The manpower planning process involves three steps :

(i) determining the manpower requirements; how many people;
(ii) establishing the supply of manpower; and
(iii) developing policies to fill the gap between supply and demand.

This includes :

(i) A skills inventory (a listing of the abilities and skills possessed by members of the organisation)
(ii) An analysis of anticipated vacancies due to retirement, sick leaves, promotions, transfer and so on;
(iii) An analysis of anticipated expenses or curtailments in departments or programmes;
(iv) An analysis of the training and development needs suitable to planning organisational changes.

4.7 RECRUITMENT, SELECTION AND PLACEMENT

The effectiveness of an organisation at any level depends upon the skills of employees who are striving for a common purpose. The objective of the staffing process is to locate, select, acquire, and place the human resources necessary to fulfill organisational and human resource plans. The staffing process, then, may be viewed as a flow of activities that results in the placement of qualified workers in organisational positions at all levels.

In order to carry out this process, management must design the work, perform job analysis, and do manpower planning in order to determine the skills that will be necessary to meet the organisational goals. As seen in Fig. 4.1, recruitment, selection, placement, and development programmes result from these manpower plans. In a broader resources, the total staffing process encompasses the flow of human resources into, within, and out of the enterprise.

It may be noted at the outset that the two terms 'selection' and 'placement' differ in meaning. Selection is essentially a job-directed activity and placement is a person-directed activity. The selection process begins with a set of performance requirements for a particular job and ends where the person who best fits these requirements is chosen. Thus, selection is a process of matching people to existing job openings. It implies that individuals and job characteristics are relatively fixed and do not change.

In contrast, placement begins after a person has been hired and ends when he has been placed in a job most suited to him on the basis of more general characteristics.

Once the organisation has decided to hire employees to fill certain positions, managers need to attract applicants to those positions. **Recruitment** is the process of attracting individuals to apply for jobs. The recruiting process involves locating and attracting qualified applicants. Recruiting is usually done for specific open positions in the short term. Sometimes managers will recruit highly talented individuals in the long term for positions that are created later. The persons who are recruited by managers may come from inside or outside the organisation.

RECRUITMENT

The recruiting and hiring process has two separate dimensions: The organisation wants to attract candidates while the individuals are trying to select a job. The economic costs of attracting the wrong person for the job can be sustantial for the organisation. The psychological costs can also be substantial for the individual. Hiring the wrong manager — one who either quits or must be fired — is costly.

One way to deal with this problem is through realistic job previews. A realistic job preview (RJP) is a job outline that gives applicants a real picture (both positive and negative information) about the job and the organisation. RPS help individuals self-select into the job on the basis of realistic information. Since the individual's expectations for the job are based on reality, the individual's subsequent satisfaction is enhanced and the odds of turnover are less. Without RJPs the individual's expectations may be unrealistic, and subsequently unmet, resulting in dissatisfaction and turnover.

Hiring from Within. Most organisations prefer to recruit existing employees and promote them when possible. **Internal recruiting** is the process of attracting current employees to apply for higher-level jobs in the organisation. Many firms have "promote from within" policies, and union contracts may require it. Internal recruiting has the advantages of being less costly than external searches. Also internal recruiting can help retain high-performing individuals who might otherwise leave if there were no opportunities for promotion and advancement.

This policy helps motivate present employees because they relise that if they do a good job, the organisation will reward them with a promotion. Promoting from within also eliminates the cost of placing employment ads in newspapers and trade journals, sending recruits out to interview, and paying private employment agencies and executive search firms.

External recruiting is the process of attracting individuals from outside the organisation to apply for jobs. Applicants may be attracted through a variety of sources, including newspaper advertisements, employment exchanges, private employment agencies, and current employee referrals. External recruiting covers a larger pool of candidates than does internal recruiting. A firm that recruits on the outside has many potential sources of employees. Some of the most common sources include private and public employment agencies and educational institutions.

Most organisations find that certain sources of recruits are more likely than others to provide them with qualified applicants for their particular needs. For example, finance, insurance and high-tech firms find campus recruitment to be extremely effective. Most personnel managers, however, seem to prefer using newpaper ads and private employment agencies.

SELECTION

The key to a happy and efficient staff lies in proper selection, which, in turn, relies on a full understanding of what a job requires, usually embodied in a job specification. This job specification sets out the personal qualities required for the vacancy in question and will include the following, sometimes known as the ***Five-Point Plan***:

(a) **Physical requirements**. These include such attributes as age, minimum height, eyesight, manual dexterity and so on.

(b) **Intelligence**. This includes mental attributes such as thinking critically, an analytical attitude, discrimination and an inquiring mind.

(c) **Aptitudes.** Everyone has natural leanings towards certain activities. Some jobs calls for mechanical or manual aptitudes, while others require more academic aptitudes, perhaps towards mathematics or arts.

(d) **Attainments**. These can be divided into educational and training achievements, evidenced by technical or professional qualifications and practical achievements obtained through experience.

(e) **Personality and temperament**. These are easy to specify but difficult to judge in an applicant. Some jobs call for a bright and enthusing personality (some sales jobs, for example) while others demand a more placid approach. Honesty, resourcefulness, tenacity, enthusiasm and the qualities for potential leadership all come under this heading.

Once recruiting methods have been applied to a pool of applicants, the next step is to select whom to hire. The main objective of the selection process is to gather information from applicants that will predict their job success and then to hire the candidate(s) predicted to be successful.

Information about candidates can be collected in various ways, including application blanks, tests, interviews, and reference checks. The process of proving that any of these selection devices is really predictive of future job performance is called validation. All selection devices should be validated, because it is a waste of time and money to use a selection device without being certain that it helps pinpoint the best candidates.

Validation

There are two basic approaches to validation. The first is statistical or empirical validation, which involves collecting the scores of employees or applicants as the device to be validated and correlating these scores with actual job performance. A statistically significant correlation means that the selection device is a valid predictor of job performance. For instance, to the extent that GMAT scores are correlated with MBA admission grades, the GMAT would be a valid selection device for admission to a management institute.

The second major validation method is called content validation. In order to apply this method, one has to use logic and make a thorough study of the job to establish that the selection device (usually a work-sample test) measures the exact skills needed for successful job performance. For example, if a job requires a great deal of typing of tables and figures, a typing test involving this kind of material is content-valid for the job. The most critical part of content validation is a careful job analysis, showing exactly what duties are to be performed. The test is then developed to measure the applicant's ability to do those duties.

The selection process may vary from a ten-minute interview to a highly involved series of evaluations over a long period of time. In a more complete programme, the selection process is based upon careful job analysis, comprehensive manpower planning, and effective recruitment.

The steps in the actual selection process include the following six steps :

1. Preliminary screening of applicants;
2. Review of application forms;
3. Reference checks;
4. Employment interviews;
5. Physical examinations.

The sequence in which these six steps are applied may vary. Each of these steps is a tool or technique for collecting information on which to judge whether or not the applicant is qualified for a specific job.

Preliminary Screening

The selection process starts with screening, or eliminating applicants who are unlikely to succeed on the job. Screening takes place in a number of ways. One is to have job-seekers fill out an application form. The recruiter compares the information from the application with the minimum training and experience specified in the job description for the position.

Another source of information for screening is resumes. Job seekers often prefer resumes over application forms because they have more control over the format; they can arrange the information in the most useful way.

This initial screening seeks to eliminate obvious misfits in order to reduce the time and cost of actual selection. The preliminary screening is an important step in the selection process since it results in a pass-fail decision. If the requirements of the company and the qualifications and interests of the applicant appear to match the initial screening, the individual would be given a more detailed interview.

Application Blanks

Next to the interview, the application blank (or form) is the most commonly used selection tool. Typically, the application form gathers information about the education, experience and personal characteristics of the applicant. Different forms may be used for different kinds of jobs. One form may be used for hourly employees, another for managerial and professional employees, and still another for sales and clerical personnel. Some firms use a short form when an applicant applies for a job with no immediate vacancy and a long form when the applicant will be considered for a current job opening.

Application forms should be tailor-made for a specific firm, and the content of the forms should vary as necessary to cover special job requirements. For low-level jobs where the applicant is likely to have little education and cultural attainment, the form should reflect this in its overall appearance, wording, and instructions.

Employment Testing

For the applicants who pass the initial screening, the next step in the selection process is often some form of employment testing. Whereas the screening determines whether applicants have the necessary background to do the job, the testing helps determine whether they can really meet the demands of the job.

Employment tests are usually administrated after a preliminary interview has been conducted and the application blank has been examined. Tests have been developed in an effort to find more objective ways of measuring the qualifications of job applicants, as also for use in case of transfer or promotion of old employees. A properly developed and administered testing programme can provide a more objective way of judging job applicants and improve the accuracy of the selection process. Some of the more commonly used tests include performance or achievement tests, intelligence tests, aptitude tests, interest tests, personality tests, and polygraph tests.

Validity and Reliability. No matter what the purpose of an employment test, it must be both valid and reliable. A valid test measures what it is intended to measure. For example, if an applicant for the job of executive secretary is given a typing test for speed and accuracy, this would validly demonstrate typing skills. The test measures what the company wants it to measure. If the applicant takes a personality test and is turned down for the job because the results show characteristics that the firm considers inappropriate for a good secretary, the test is not valid unless the company can prove that these personality characteristics are required for the position and that the test really measures them.

Reference Checks

There is a good deal of variation among firms in the types of references requested, methods of verifying reference, and the consistency with which references and applicant data are checked. In practice, most firms have found it useful to learn how the applicant performed on previous jobs. Phoning or interviewing the applicant's past supervisors is often a useful source of information. Probing is often required since people are very cautious about what they say regarding past employees.

Employment Interviewing

After the initial screening and testing, the next step in the selection process is usually to interview the remaining applicants. The employment interview enables the interviewer to assess the applicant indirectly.

The interview may be structured or semi-structured. A structured interview is one in which the interviewer follows a prepared format that consists of a series of direct questions. In contrast, a semi-structured interview is one in which the interviewer uses prepared questions to direct the interview but allows the interviewee to develop ideas that seem important. The employment interview is still the most widely used and the most important tool in the selection process. An effective interview enables the interviewer to learn more about the job applicant's background, interests, and values; it also gives the applicant an opportunity to find out more about the job and the organisation.

Background and Reference Check

After the initial screening, tests, and interviews, the personnel staff conducts background and reference checks of candidates still under consideration. Because of the employee's rights of privacy, an increasing number of employers are unwilling to answer questions related to a former employee's education, overall character, safety record, union activity or family background.

Physical Examinations

The next step in the selection process is a physical examination. Such examinations are not highly reliable predictors of future medical problems. However, they are valuable in screening out applicants whose physical qualifications are inadequate to meet the requirements of the job they are being considered for.

A somewhat newer method used for selecting managerial talent is the assessment center. Assessment centers typically process candidates in groups of 10 to 15, exposing each group to various exercises for four to five days a week. These exercises may include such standard selection tools as interviews and tests. Meanwhile, experienced managers observe and note the behaviour of each candidate and the patterns of interpersonal relations that develop. Candidates are selected on the basis of the evaluations of these managers.

Hiring Decision

The final step in the selection process is the actual decision to hire. This final decision is usually made by the manager in the department where the individual will work. Staff in the personnel department usually take care of the preliminary steps and then recommend a candidate. The supervisor for whom the applicant will work reviews this recommendation, may conduct another interview with the candidate, and then decide to either hire the candidate or ask for another recommendation.All newly employed people become part of the in-house pool of talent that serves as a source for future internal recruiting.

Orientation and Placement

Staffing the modern organisation continues beyond selecting employees and includes orienting them and placing them in their new jobs. Orientation is the process of introducting a new employee to the job and creating a basis for the employee to cooperate with the work unit as part of a team.

Placement Decision

After the company has oriented the new employee, it places that person into the new job. This first assignment, and who the new employee works with and for, can affect this person's career and long-run contribution to the organisation.

Conclusion

However, the staffing process does not end when an adequately trained individual is selected and placed in a position. Staffing is an ongoing process that aims at making sure that human resources are in the right place at the right time. One part of selection is bringing the right people into the organisation. Another is moving them within the organisation throughout their careers as needs arise and as their skills develop. One part of employee training and development is giving people the skills they need to make an initial contribution, but another is giving them the development experiences through their careers to make them productive resources.

Training is a continuous process, due to rapid technological progress and globalisation. A company has to raise the productivity of its resources — particularly manpower — just to remain competitive. It is to be noted that a company cannot raise its productivity but people can. This is why Peter Drucker has referred to two terms in this context : knowledge workers and learning organisations.

Synopsis for Learning

Q.1. What is recruitment ?

Ans. Except under very special circumstances all recruitment of staff at all levels below that of senior executive is normally done through the personnel department. The reasons for this are that this department will have considerable experience of the labour market and sources of supply of labour, of comparative rates of pay and conditions of employment offered by competitiors, and of the organisation's personnel policy. In almost all cases all the procedures up to preparing short lists of possible employees will be carried out in the personnel department but the final list of interviewees and the ultimate selection of the final candidate will be a joint decision between the personnel officer and the line manager requiring the recruit. At operating level, for shop-floor workers and similar staff, often only the initiation of the recruiting procedure will be the responsibility of the personnel section, interviewing and selection being dealt with by the line manager or supervisor.

Thje exceptions to the rule that the personnel department should actively recruit staff include the recruitment of senior officials such as heads of departments or divisions, and staff who will evolve a close personal relationship with a senior manager or executive, such as a personal assistant or private secretary.

The first is normally a matter for the board of directors or other governing body. Selection of the latter involves the need for careful matching of personalities and so such recruitment is considered best left to the executive concerned. Nevertheless, the initial stages of recruitment are still normally the responsibility of the personnel department.

Synopsis for Learning (contd...)

Q.2. What are the sources of recruitment ?

Ans. The sources of recruitment to which the personnel department will address itself include :

(a) Present staff, particularly where the vacancy is at supervisory or middle-management level and there is a policy of internal promotion.

(b) Universities and colleges of higher and further education, where potential management material and special aptitudes are required.

(d) Local employment agencies, both government (now known as 'job centres') and private. Many private employment bureaux are specialist agencies dealing with one or two types of profession or skill only, such as those for accountants, heavy vehicle drivers and so on.

(d) The professional bodies, many of whom maintain registers of members and student members for this purpose.

(e) Advertisements in the press both at national and at a local level. Such advertisements will include particulars of the vacancy generally as set out in the job specification.

(f) Advertisements in specialist journals, particularly trade journals and the journals of the professional bodies.

Q.3. What is internal staff promotion ?

Ans. Some organisations have a policy of internal staff promotion to the exclusion of external recruitment for positions above certain supervisory or management levels. The main objective of this is to encourage staff loyalty through a clearly defined career structure and to maintain the organisation's overall and operational philosophies. In such cases, new staff will be recruited only at the lower end of the scale, and great care will be taken in the selection of newcomers.

The main weaknesses of such a policy are that it may deprive the undertaking of new ideas brought in from outside and of fresh thoughts on the organisation's effectiveness. Its great virtue is that it usually attracts recruits who want to make the organisation their career in a specific function and may use the organisation only to gain experience before moving on elsewhere. Recruitment is an expensive business and can be disruptive at certain levels. Where training is given to newcomers their leaving can mean considerable wasted expense.

Q.4. What is selection ?

Ans. Selection is the process of determining the applicant's qualifications and of choosing the best applicant for the job. The selection process includes at least three steps : 1. Application, 2. Determination of qualifications, and 3. Choice of best applicant

The process starts once the applicant indicates that he (or she) is interested in the job, extends through the phase of determining qualifications, and is completed when the choice is made of whom to hire. If the applicant rejects the employment offer, then the manager usually offers the job to the next best qualified applicant if there is more than one applicant. If there is only one, then the manager can repeat the entire process. In an increasing number of organisations, the selection process is conducted by peers on the work team.

Q.5. What is the different between recruitment and selection ?

Ans. When it is clear what jobs have to be filled and what those jobs entail, the personnel manager can begin to fill them. Staffing consists of two parts: recruiting and selecting people.

Recruiting is the process of forming a pool of qualified applicants. If the recruiting process provides only as many applicants as there are jobs, there is no selection. The company must either take what is available or leave the jobs unfilled.

Recruiting can be done through personal contacts, newspapers, magazines, TV or radio ads, and so forth. When a sufficiently large pool of applicants exists, selection can take place.

Q.6. What is validity?

Ans. In determining qualifications, the selection devices used include application forms, interviews, tests, assessment centers, reference checks, and physical examinations. When using any of these devices, the manager should examine its validity. Validity is the relationship between applicants' scores on the device and applicants' future job performance. Devices with low validity do no help the manager select the best person for the job and may be discriminatory.

Q.7. What is an application form ?

Ans. An application form is a written document to collect information on the applicant's educational background, previous work experience, and other job-related demographic data. The form should not contain questions that are irrelevant to the job, as such questions may be discriminatory. The applicant's job resume or curriculum vitae may also be attached to the application form. The application form is often used by the interviewer as a basis for discussion and further exploration.

Synopsis for Learning (contd...)

Q.8. What are interviews ?

Ans. Interviews are widely used to select applicants in nearly all organisations and for most jobs. Yet interviews are poor predictors of subsequent job performance. Nonetheless, they will probably continue to be used so that both the organisation and the individual can collect face-to-face information.

The interviewer must be careful not to ask questions in the interview that may be viewed as discriminatory. Partly for this reason and partly because there are ways to make the interview more productive, many organisations offer training for their managers on how to interview.

Q.9. What is the chief purpose of interview?

Ans. An important step in the selection process is to interview the applicant. The chief purpose of the interview is to gather additional information about the applicant and get answers to any or all questions appearing on the application form. The interviewer attempts to discover how the applicant might fit into the organisation and what his (or her) attitude would be toward the job.

Q.10. What is job analysis ?

Ans. Job analysis is the first step in the selection of workers. By making use of information obtained during the analysis, the personnel department can carry out the important task of selecting new workers and placing them in the jobs for which they are best qualified. So the next step might be called applicant analysis.

Q.11. What are job tests ?

Ans. A job test is a written or computer-generated test that measures a specific attribute, skill, or personal dimension relevant to the job. Because some tests are good predictors of subsequent job performance and some are not, validity is an especially important issue here. To help ensure validity, managers should make certain that testing conditions relating to amount of time and environment are consistent across applicants.

Q.12. What is the need for physical examination?

Ans. Many enterprises require applicants to take a physical examination. The reason is easy to find out : the firm wants to ensure whether the individual is physically able to perform the job.

Q.13. What is an assessment centre ?

Ans. An assessment center is a simulation of many of the important tasks in the job, conducted with a number of relevant exercises and situations. The experimental activities may cover a two or three-day time period. Although assessment centers are used primarily for managerial jobs, their use is spreading to other jobs.

Q.14. What are reference checks?

Ans. Reference checks are questions addressed to former employers, former co-workers, and other acquaintances concerning the experience and behaviour of the job applicant. Most of the persons listed by the job applicant as references will probably be positively biased in favour of the applicant. However, useful information can often be obtained from a reference check that could not be obtained from other sources. If the manager can find some sources in addition to the references provided by the applicant, a wealth of unbiased information may become available.

To produce the most open form of communication, reference checks are usually done verbally rather than by letter. Letters of reference have the greatest chance of being positively biased in favour of the applicant.

Q.15. What are physical examinations ?

Ans. In the job requires substantial manual effort, the employer may require a physical examination to determine physical capability to perform the job. Or if the job requires some particular physical characteristic, like keen eyesight in a pilot, the organisation may test for that characteristic with a physical examination. Additionally, a number of employers require a physical examination prior to extending health or life insurance.

Q.16. What are the usual procedure involved in selection process ?

Ans. It is usual to require applicants for posts to complete application forms, designed as far as possible to elicit information relative to the job specification. From a comparison of the completed forms received a list of possible candidates can be selected and this is usually done initially by the personnel officer. Following this, a short list of about six candidates is prepared in consultation with the manager of the department where the successful applicant will be employed. Final selection is then made by inviting all those on the short list to be interviewed, where they can be judged on a person-to-person basis.

Synopsis for Learning (contd...)

Interviewing is a skilled task and may be carried out by one interviewer, who will usually be the head of the department concerned, or by a panel (particularly for a supervisory or management post), one member of which will certainly be the personnel manager. The purpose of the interview is to gain personal knowledge of the candidates and so to assess which one is most suitable for the appointment. Basic information has been gathered from the application forms, and this information is a starting-point from which the various aspects of each applicant's knowledge, skills, personality and so on can be further assessed. The interview also provides the opportunity to give the applicants detailed information about the vacancy in question and about the organisation generally.

The amount of time and effort spent on the selection procedure will depend very largely upon the type of post involved. Where recruitment is for unskilled or semi-skilled workers it will often consist simply of a brief interview with the foreman or supervisor in whose team recruitment is necessary. Where a skilled worker is required a longer interview will be given and a senior foreman, supervisor or manager may be involved. Within the administration, selection will be more formal. Detailed application forms will have to be completed and searching interviews will be conducted with the candidates on the short list, and the more important the post the greater the care that will be taken in selection.

4.8 TRAINING OF WORKERS AND EMPLOYEES

Training and development is the process of developing knowledge, skills and behaviours in people that will enable them to better perform their current and future jobs.

There is an increased understanding that organisations must spend massive amounts of time and money on training and development to increase their competitiveness. This view is growing as more organisations come to see that human resources are their only appreciating asset. In the past training and development had stressed functional, technical and specific job-related skills. Today many organisations stress a broad range of skills, cross-functional issues, quality issues and problem-solving skills.

Decades ago a common view was that training and development was for the enrichment of the individual and did not bring any direct benefit to the organisation. Today, many see training and development as a way to ensure the consistent delivery of value to customers through highly capable employees.

Importance

Every organisation must have well-trained and experienced people to perform the activities that must be done. If current or potential job occupants can meet these requirements, training is less critical. When this is not the case, however, it becomes necessary to raise the skill levels and increase the versatility and adaptability of employees. The key focus of training is on an individual's current job. It is designed to make one more effective in one's current job. Training programmes are designed to enhance learning, so that employees are more effective and efficient on the job.

As jobs become more complex over the years, the importance of employee training increases. The rapid changes taking place in the business environment have created increased pressures for organisations to readapt the products and services produced, the manner in which products and services are produced and offered, the types of jobs required, and the types of skills necessary to complete these jobs.

Relation to Manpower Planning

There is a close link between manpower planning and the determination of training needs. There is need for training when two things are observed : inadequate job performance or a drop in productivity. The former is likely to occur in the early months on a new job. When a manager sees evidence of inadequate job performance, assuming that the individual is making a satisfactory effort, attention should be given to raising the worker's skill level. When a manager is confronted with a drop in productivity, the indication is clear that there is need for skill improvement through training.

Four Reasons

There are four reasons for the widespread popularity of training programmes :

1. Selection and placement alone usually do not provide the organisation with new employees skilful enough to be adequate performers at the beginning of their employment.
2. There is an increased need for retraining due to automation and advances in computer technology, as well as for promotion and transfer.

3. There is an increased awareness among managers that effective training programmes can result in positive gains in productivity and employee satisfaction, and reductions in both absenteeism and turnover.
4. Finally, there is the questionable practice of adopting a particular training technique simply because it is fashionable or because a competitor is using it.

Meaning

Training is the term most often applied to the acquisition of skills which generally are oriented around lower level positions in the organisation and are expected to have an immediate impact on job behaviour and possibly on labour productivity.

Manpower planning is a crucial step in determining training needs. Ideally, any such programme is consistent with both the current avaialablity of skills within the organisation and with other organisational plans that affect the organisation's use of human resources.

After an individual is chosen for hiring or promotion, the next step is often some form of training. In personnel management, the term training usually refers to teaching operational or technical employees how to do the job for which they were hired.

Training is a learning experience became it seeks a relatively permanent change in an individual that will improve his (her) ability to perform on the job. Training can involve the changing of skills, knowledge, attitudes or behaviour. It may mean changing what employees know, how they work, their attitudes toward work, or their interaction with co-workers or superiors.

Training activities include all planned organisational efforts aimed at increasing employees' abilities or modifying their behaviour. Such activities come in forms, and may be formal or informal. They may be conducted on or off the premises. Participation in them may be open or restricted, and their duration can range from several minutes to a number of years. Regardless of their specific form, the basic purpose of training is to increase the needed attributes and skills of employees. In some cases, the target is the new employee who has yet to acquire the attributes necessary to be an effective performer. In others, the target is the employee whose job has been altered by a change in technology or structure.

Basic Objectives

Ultimately, training programmes aim at altering job behaviour, but specific programmes try to accomplish this objective in several different ways. See Fig. 4.4. Some

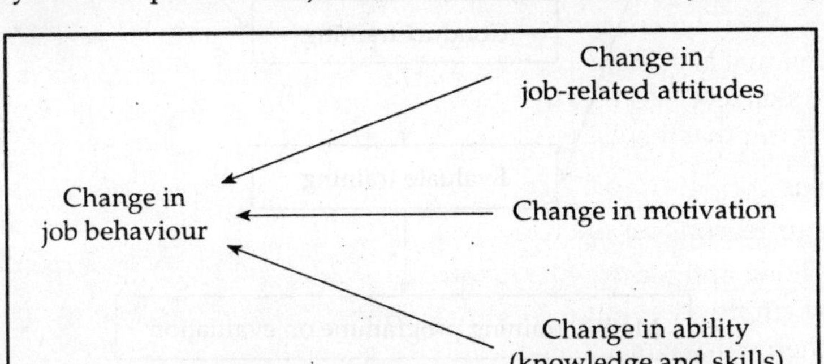

Fig. 4.4 : Different Approaches to Changing Job Behaviour Through Training

programmes attempt to affect job behaviour by alternating job-related attitudes. These include attempts to make attitudes about organisational changes more flexible and attitudes about desired behaviours more positive. For example, a training effect may be inspirational in nature and encourage commitment to organisational goals. However, the most frequent approach to changing job behaviour is to change job-related abilities. An example is any programme that gives the employee more job-related knowledge and skills, such as those regarding carpentry and house construction.

Assessment of Training Needs

It is extremely important to determine whether a need for training exists and then to plan an appropriate programme if it is needed. For instance, if people who do not

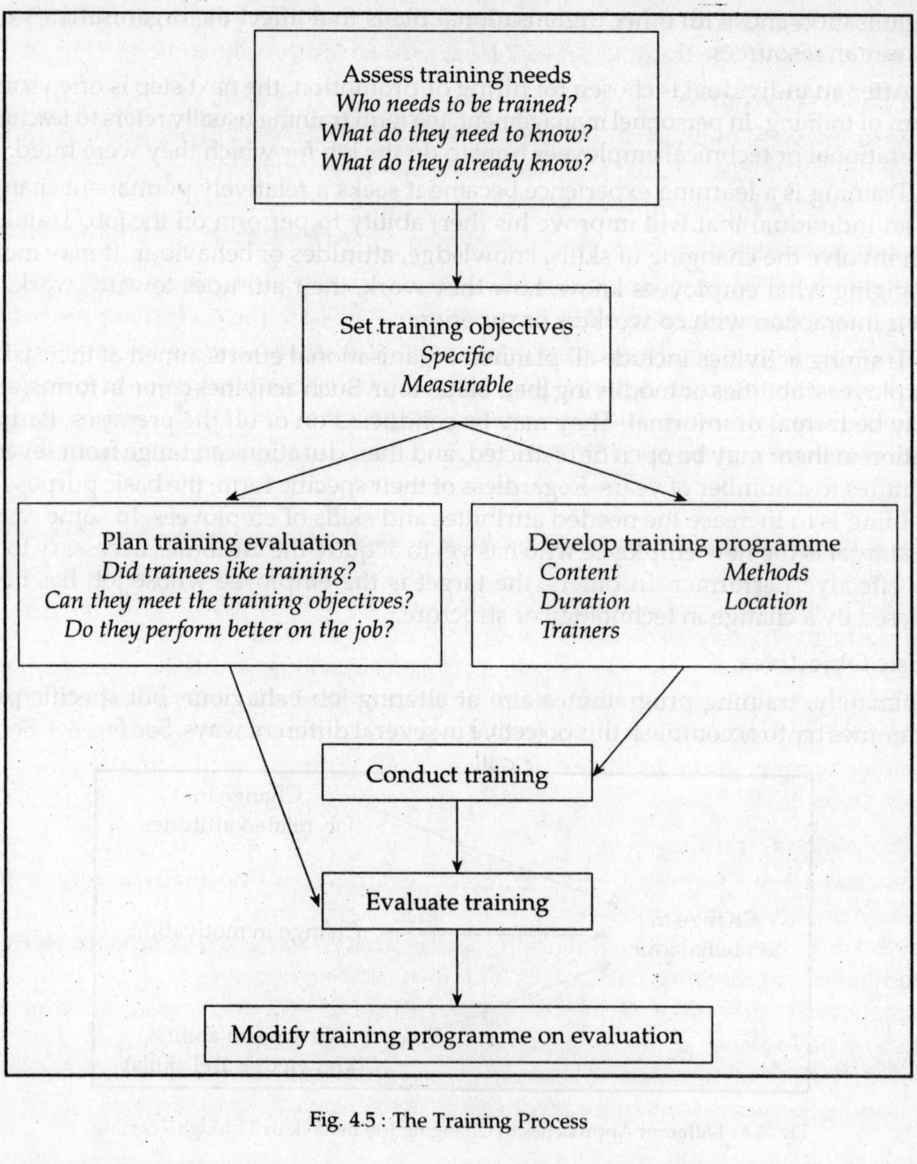

Fig. 4.5 : The Training Process

know welding are hired to be welders, the employee obviously needs a training programme on how to weld (or, the company could change its selection standards to hire only those who already have this skill). On the other hand, when a group of office workers is performing poorly, training may or may not be the (real) answer. The problem could be lack of motivation, old and obsolete equipment, poor supervision, inefficient work design, or a deficiency of skills and knowledge. Only the last could be remedied by training the office workers.

If, after thorough and careful investigation, the problem does seem to require training, one should thoroughly assess the problem level of skill and knowledge and then define the desired level of skill and knowledge in concrete, measurable form. After the training is completed trainee performance can be assessed against the objectives that were set prior to training. Training programmes should always be evaluated, because they are costly and should be modified or discontinued if they are not effective. The training process from start to finish is illustrated in Fig. 4.5.

TYPES OF TRAINING

There are several methods of training, and the type selected will depend very much upon the employee's actual job and the degree of skill required. Types of training can be broadly categorised as follows :

1. Craft training

This entails entering into an apprenticeship which results in ultimate entry into a recognised skilled trade or craft. Certain skilled jobs are the exclusive preserve of workers who have qualified by apprenticeship and others wishing to carry out this work are either prevented from doing so by the established workers or have to work at lower rates of pay. Apprenticeships have to be provided by the employer, and both employer and employee are bound by the apprenticeship indentures.

2. Operative training

This is for less skilled workers and for those trades where no formal apprenticeship schemes exist. Instruction is given on the shop floor, often supplemented by the worker's attendance at a technical college. Where the latter occurs the worker is normally given a day off each week to attend college on what is termed a 'day-release course'. Many office jobs fall under this category including shorthand-typing, typewriting, word-processing and office practice, especially where recruitment is straight from school. Many employers, however, do expect some skill to be present in other recruits and attendance at college is encouraged for the improvement of these skills.

3. Professional training

This covers both technical and commercial training and normally involves ultimately qualifying by professional or national examination. Some of the areas involved are mechanical engineering, accountancy, statistics, computer science, production engineering and so on. The new universities and colleges of higher education provide most of the training and education for such areas, either on the basis of day-release or on a 'sandwich course' basis where the worker spends a period, say a term, in college followed by a period with the employer, again followed by another period in university or college. In the latter case many of the qualifications are, in India, degrees rather than qualifications from professional bodies, such degrees being awarded by the universities or colleges under the auspices of the Council for National Academic Awards (CNAA). Such degrees rank equally in status with those awarded by the older universities. Indeed, in India, under recent legislation, polytechnics have been elevated to university status, though their courses remain, in the main, vocational rather than academic — as in the tradition of the older universities.

4. University degrees

Many of the older universities now award degrees in disciplines attractive to industry and commerce, such as degrees in accountancy, business administration, the various branches of engineering, marketing and others. Normally, however, people taking such degrees obtain them before seeking employment.

The importance of proper training is exemplified by the fact that Government of India has seen fit to encourage employers to train their employees, both by various acts of parliament and by exhortation. Various statutes are enacted from time to time and reference should be made to the latest legislation when necessary.

TRAINING METHODS

A wide variety of training methods is available. Selection of a particular method(s) depends on many considerations.

Personnel managers have a variety of choices in selecting training and development programmes. The most common training approach is on-the-job training, which is informal instruction conducted at the job site. In the actual job environment, the trainee mainly learns by doing the job, with help provided by an experienced partner.

Another traditional training approach used with operating employees is apprentice training, an approach that is similar to, but more formal than, on-the-job training. The employee learns a job by spending a relatively long time working directly with a more experienced employee, who teaches procedures, rules, and techniques.

On-the-job training

The most widely used training methods take place on the job. This is largely due to the simplicity of such methods and the impression that they are less costly to operate. On-the-job training places the employees in actual work situations and makes them appear to be immediately productive. It is learning by doing.

In short, on-the-job training is learning how to perform the job on the work site under the guidance of an experienced employee. Other training and development methods are classroom training, computer-assisted instruction, conferences, and visits to other organisations to study their process (benchmarking).

Advantage. For jobs that are difficult to simulate or can be learned quickly by watching and doing, on-the-job training makes enormous good sense.

Drawback. One major drawback of OJT is low productivity while the employees develop their skills. The second drawback can be errors — which may be dangerous for himself, his co-workers and the organisation — made by the trainees while they learn.

Conclusion. However, when the damage the trainees can do is minimal, where training facilities and personnel are limited or costly, and where it is desirable for the workers to learn the job under normal working conditions, the benefits of the on-the-job training frequently offset its drawbacks.

Apprenticeship Programmes

People seeking to enter skilled trades to become, for example, plumbers, electricians or iron-workers are often required to undergo apprenticeship training before they are accepted to expert status. The period of such training varies from job to job. During the apprenticeship period, the trainee is paid less than a fully-qualified worker.

Apprenticeship programmes put the trainee under the guidance of a master worker so that the trainee can acquire the required job knowledge and skills as early as possible. However, long apprenticeship may also create barriers to entry and help keep wages high.

Job Instruction Training

This is a systematic approach to on-the-job training. It was developed to prepare supervisors to train operatives. Job instruction training is a part of the training within industry programme.

It has four key components :

(1) Preparing the trainees by telling them about the job and overcoming their uncertainties;

(2) Presenting the instruction, giving essential information in a clear manner;

(3) Having the trainees try out the job to demonstrate that they understand; and,

(4) Placing the workers into the job, on their own, with a designated resource person to call upon if they need assistance.

Steps in Job Instruction Training

- Demonstrate to the employee how the task is to be done.
- Communicate the key component of the task to the employee.
- Do the task for the employee.
- Have the employee do a simple part of the task.
- Have the employee do the whole job while being observed.
- Let the employee do the job by himself (or herself).

Uses. Use of job instruction training can achieve impressive results. By following the above six steps, employee turnover can be reduced. Higher levels of employee morale have been witnessed as well as decreases in employee accidents by the users of the training methods.

Off-the-job Training

It covers a number of techniques — classroom lectures, films, demonstrations, case studies, and other simulation exercises, and programmed instruction. The facilities needed for each of these techniques vary from a small makeshift classroom to an elaborate development center with large lecture halls, supplemented by small conference rooms with sophisticated audio- visual equipment, two-way mirrors, and all the ultramodern gadgets and frills.

Seminars or Conferences

The seminar or conference approach is well adapted to conveying specific information — rules, procedures, or methods. The use of audio-visual or demonstrations can often make formal seminar presentations more interesting while increasing retention and possibly clarifying more difficult points.

Videos

Films can be a useful training technique. Whether purchased from standard video distributors or produced internally by the organisation, they can provide information and explicitly demonstrate skills that are not easily presented by other techniques. Videos and seminar discussions are often used in conjunction to clarify and amplify those points that the video emphasised.

Simulation Exercises

Any training activities that places the trainee in an artificial environment that closely imitates actual working conditions can be considered a simulation. Simulation activities include case exercises, experimental exercises, complex computer-based training and vestibule training.

Cases present an in-depth description of a particular problem an employee might encounter on the job. The employee attempts to find and analyse the problem, evaluate alternative courses of action, and decide what course of action would be most satisfactory.

Experimental exercise refers to short, structured learning, experiences where individuals learn by doing. Computer-based training simulates the work environment by programming a computer to imitate some of the realities of the job. Computer modelling is widely used by airlines in training pilots.

In vestibule training, employees learn their jobs on the equipment they will be using, but training is conducted away from the actual work floor. This method is, no doubt, very expensive. But it allows employees to get a full feel for doing tasks without 'real-world' business. Moreover, it minimises the problem of transferring learning to the job, since vestibule training uses the same equipment the training will use on the job.

Programmed Instruction

The programmed instruction technique can be in the form of programmed tests, manuals, or video displays, while in some organisations teaching machines are utilised. All programmed instruction approaches have a common characteristic : they condense the material to be learned into highly organised, logical sequences, which require the trainee to respond. The ideal format provides for nearly instantaneous feedback that informs the trainee if his (her) response is correct.

This method has two variants : (1) interactive videos (videos that permit the user to make changes/selections); and (2) virtual reality (a process in which the work environment is simulated by sending messages to the brain).

By using the first method employees experience greater learning in such areas as mathematics, interpersonal skills and marketing skills. The second method is a relatively new concept in corporate planning. Both the systems are promising. But they are costly. So they are used only in extremely large organisations and in very complex jobs.

A newer, less traditional approach to training is called mentoring. Specifically, a mentor is an experienced employee who coaches and counsels a less experienced employee in the latter's training and development. A new salesperson may start out by teaming up with a mentor to make calls on customers and prospects.

Assessment of Training

What are the criteria to consider in measuring the effectiveness of a training programme ? Here are some yardsticks to use :

1. ***Objectives***. Is there a clear target for each training programme, and is this target in line with a broader organisational goal ?

2. ***Cost and benefits analysis***. Is the training unit in a position to justify its programme by relating its monetary cost to expected dollar benefits to be derived from training ?

3. ***Flexibility***. Has the training group proved its ability to cope with new requirements of the organisation with reasonable despatch ?

4. ***Results***. In the various training functions, are key result areas specified and accomplishments indicated in quantitative and reasonable terms ?

5. ***Staff***. Is there an objective search procedure, including an updated manpower inventory, for staff selection and advancement ?

6. ***Audit***. Do all the various training functions undergo an independent audit periodically, not less than once a year ?

7. ***Improvements***. What feedback mechanisms are available from line operations to improve the quality, quantity and timeliness of training ?

Training and development must remain alert to trends affecting the organisation economically, socially and politically. Its leadership must be in constant touch with planned changes in the organisation's products or services and the projected manpower requirements.

Evaluation of Training

No training method is right for all situations. So trade-off must be made. For personnel management, this means choosing a training method that meets various time and cost constraints. Regardless of the methodology used, specific types of training programmes are offered frequently. Of these training programmes the most popular are video tapes, and seminars, followed by one-on-one instruction, role plays, audio tapes, simulations and case studies.

Various training methods emphasise one thing at least: the learning of routine and programmed behaviours that can immediately be applied to the job. Evaluation of these training programmes becomes easier, as the trained employee either can or cannot do the job after being trained. Whether this is measured by a test, productivity gains, or by observation of the employees' work movements we can assess whether the specific job-oriented tasks have been learned from the training programme.

Training programmes should always be evaluated. There are two basic kinds of evaluation measures: those collected when the trainee is on the job and those collected after their training. The former are easier to get but the latter are more important. Trainees may say they enjoyed the training and learned a lot, but the true test is whether their job performance is better after their training than before. As training continues to assist employees in their current jobs so too do employee development efforts to prepare them for tomorrow's work.

Conclusion

It is almost a truism that if some training and education is good, more training and education is better. However, business that puts sophisticated training efforts tailors them to each person's needs. This is done through a careful assessment of an employee's needs and potential.

One practical way to assess training needs is to compare performance on the job with the standards outlined in the job description. The manager can then pinpoint areas for continuous improvement and can develop programmes to help people improve their performance.

Continuous improvement is the constant refinement and improvement of products, services, and organisational systems to yield improved value to customers. In the spirit of continuous improvement, training and development is not a one-time event but a lifelong process.

Many organisations today recognise that due to the massive changes occurring in the business world continuous training is needed throughout employees' careers.

Synopsis for Learning

Q.1. What is the importance of employee training?

Ans. To treat the company's employees as resources, managers cannot simply hire the necessary staff and call their job finished. Rather, managers need to help employees fulfill their potential by learning new skills and developing their abilities. Managers accomplish this through employee training.

Q.2. What is training?

Ans. Training is the process of teaching employees the procedures and techniques to do their job efficiently. A great deal of training takes palce at the lower and intermediate levels of organisations. Examples include teaching employees to fill out a new cost-control report, run a simple programming on the computer, process a customer order, or operate a machine or specialised piece of equipment.

EMPLOYEE PROMOTION

As in most other human institutions, the expectations of positive contributions and a system of reward is built into business organisations. In addition to the salary or wage paid in exchange for employees' services, provision is usually made for monetary increases to reflect the increased value of services rendered in a particular job. But there are those situations in which an individual demonstrates the capacity to contribute to the organisation beyond the level of his present job and therefore can be considered a candidate for promotion. It is this subject of promotion that this section is directed.

Definition of Promotion

Promotion, in business organisations, is usually associated with the assignment of an individual to a position of more responsibility, or to one which requires the application of his particular education or experience. Were there a sufficient supply of promotional talent within all departments of a company or organisation, then the need for a systematic approach to promotion would be minimal. Unfortunately, there would also be a tendency to promote only those who had been around longest, or who had mastered the peculiarities of a particular department's practices, since new people, with different approaches or ideas applied in other departments or companies would not be introduced into the organisation.

In this context, personnel turnover can produce benefits to an organisations. However, in the process, considerable inconvenience is incurred by having to define responsibilities which change over time in almost every job context, and then having to identify those persons who may have the attributes or skills to fulfill these responsibilities.

In order to minimise the time required in identification of the factors particular to a position, and then in the selection of the individual employee most appropriate, a systematic approach to both of these processes usually evolves in large organisations where the number of such openings is frequent, or in small organisations where the turnover is volatile.

Without doubt the possibility of promotion is one of the most effective ways to encourage positive motivation and incentive in staff. There are, of course, workers who are reluctant to accept the added responsibilities that promotion brings but many do look forward to eventual promotion with the accompanying increased earnings and higher status. It is, therefore, important that an organisation has a fair and sensible promotion policy and that it is known to all relevant staff. Besides encouraging good morale it also assists the enterprise in planning the best use of its human resources. In addition, valuable members of staff who have benefitted from training programmes provided by the organisation and who have built up valuable experience are less likely to be tempted to take their expertise to a rival organisation.

- Strictly speaking, the term 'promotion' should be used for promotion within the organisation, but under this heading reference must be made to recruitment from outside — usually for the more senior posts.
- A policy of internal promotion is, generally speaking, usually accepted as the most sensible one. It encourages a sense of security in existing workers, produces continuity of staffing, and avoids breaks in the personal relationships with the enterprise which are so helpful in ensuring that procedures run smoothly. This last point is particularly important where there are relationships with external contacts such as customers and suppliers.
- Recruitment for the more senior posts from outside the organisation — while bringing in new blood and possibly new ideas — may cause resentment in existing staff, may damage morale and may lead to the most able workers— who are looking for promotion, to seek employment elsewhere. Thus, valuable staff may be lost.

Two points must be made about internal promotion :

1. **Promotion is based on past performance**. While it may be expected that like performance will continue after the promotion this may not occur. The person's attitude may change with increased authority and he may not have the temperament or personality to cope with it: or the person concerned may have been promoted beyond his level of competence. This latter occurrence is known as the 'Peter Principle — Every man rises to his highest level of incompetence !'.

2. **Problems of authority**. Sometimes, it is difficult for staff to accept the authority of someone who has been a colleague on equal terms for sometime and, equally, a promoted worker may find it difficult or embarrassing to exercise authority over these same people. It is possiblly prudent to promote employees at lower levels of management into different departments or to work with different groups.

Finally, it is important that a promotion policy be seen by all to be fair and equitable so as to avoid resentment in its implementation.

Crucial to an understanding of staffing process is the notion of an external labour market. External labour markets are made up of pools of labour with the skills needed for specific positions and groups of organisations that demand people with these skills. Organisations are on both sides of these markets. They have suppliers of labour for some positions and demand for labour for others.

Besides these external labour markets, managers must also consider internal labour markets. Supply and demand factors for individuals with specific skills exist within each organisation. This internal labour market is important to the organisation and the individual employees alike. It is important to identify this pool since it helps to determine how many employees may qualify for a promotion; which employees to transfer and when, and which skills are lacking in the organisation. The internal labour market is also important to the employees since it is likely to affect their careers. When supply is greater than demand for a specific skill within the organisation, individuals with these skills are likely not to be promoted at a very rapid rate. Furthermore, there may be some attrition as individuals with these excess skills leave the organisations and move into a broader (and perhaps more favourable) external labour market. Where there is greater demand than supply within the organisation for persons of a specific skill, such individuals may expect rapid career changes and opportunities for advancement. However, at such times the organisation may also turn to the external labour market in order to fill the available positions.

The term 'promotion' refers to the shifting of an employee to a new position in which both one's status and responsibilities are increased. Promotions are advantageous to the firm as well as the employee. Management knows that deserving employees have been taken care of, that workers are situated where they can produce the most, and that the cost of orienting and training new people has been reduced. An employee should not be given a promotion when it has not been earned or when others are better qualified or more deserving. When two employees are equally deserving as judged by their ability and performance, promotion is usually given to the person who has been with the company longer. This person is said to have seniority.

An advancement in pay that does not involve a move into a new job classification is called a ***horizontal promotion***. An advancement that moves an employee into a job with a higher rank or classification is called a ***vertical promotion***.

If management is to avoid a labour unrest and turnover, it must develop a systematic policy for promotions. Qualified employees become dissatisfied and leave if few opportunities for advancement exist or if promotions are not based on merit. In truth, an employee has hardly any incentive for self-development and hard work unless he has the opportunity to move up along the corporate ladder through promotion. An employee can improve his position either by changing organisation (or job) or by getting promotion within the same organisation. On the basis of job analysis, a company can prepare a chart illustrating job characteristics and depicting promotion trees (or lines of promotion) which are developed on the basis of certain basic job requirements such as competence, experience, educational qualification and so on. Such a chart also indicates how each job leads to another. These charts act as guidelines or road maps to employees who know in advance what is expected of them to deserve promotion to higher level jobs or to be placed in better salary scales. Such charts prepare them accordingly for planned self-advancement through self-motivation.

The term 'promotion' refers to the advancement of an employee to a better job. But in what sense? In terms of greater responsibilities, more prestige or status, greater skill, higher grade and salary and, of course, additional previleges (perks, leave travel concessions, foreign tours, etc.).

Difference between promotion and transfer

In this context it is necessary to draw a distinction between promotion and transfer. Transfer simply refers to changes in job. It may involve little, if any, changes in job responsibility, pay and status.

In fact, the term transfer refers to the shifting of an employee from one position to another without increasing his (or her) duties, responsibilities, or pay. Every business finds it necessary to transfer workers. If workers have been assigned to a job on which their work is unsatisfactory, they may be shifted to another. There are times, too, when the workload is heavier in some departments than in others, or when it is desirable to rotate workers into and out of dangerous positions. Occasionally a transfer is necessary because of personal differences among employees, or because of personality conflicts between workers and supervisors. Workers are often transferred to new communities in order to place employees where they are needed.

When a transfer must be made, management should have justifiable reasons and be certain that the employee will not suffer hardship as a result. Management should tell employees why they are being transferred, and whether their transfers are permanent or temporary.

To be able to motivate workers and make the best possible utilisation of its human resources, every company or organisation should have some type of formal, systematic and consistent policies and programmes relating to employee promotion.

A. ESSENTIALS OF A SOUND PROMOTION POLICY

There are certain essentials of a sound promotion policy.

1. Transperancy

First of all, a company should have clear-cut and explicit policies relating to employee promotion. Such policies should be based on certain criteria or objective assessment of each employee. So the policy should indicate in clear terms the ability, experience, education and other qualifications required for each job. There should not be any scope for ambiguity.

2. Internal promotion

It is also necessary to make sufficient provision for promotion from within the organisation in case of middle managers and senior managers. The first priority should be given to people belonging to the same organisation. If qualified and competent people cannot be found from the internal labour market then only the post(s) should be advertised in newspapers and professional journals so as to be able to recruit people according to the company's requirements and specifications.

If this policy is followed, employee morale will be automatically high. If employees see that there is suitable reward for appropriate effort and if there is genuine prospect or even assurance of promotion to deserving candidates then they will develop among themselves a sense of involvement and belonging. This will not only raise labour productivity by improving the industrial relations situation and by motivating the workers.

This will also make it possible to make the most effective utilisation of a company's existing manpower inasmuch as a talented and competent person will not be forced to rot or feel demoralised — and a really useful and talented worker is not forced to resign and search out better prospects elsewhere. An irrational promotion policy may cost an organisation heavily in terms of loss of some talented and competent employees.

3. Lack of external pressure

Thirdly, a sound promotion policy is one which is not influenced by pressure groups such as trade unions and political parties. It should not be such as to cause agitation among certain aggrieved workers.

4. Time-frame

The openings for immediate promotion should be notified in advance so that deserving employees may apply for promotion within a specified time period. There should not be any scope of loss of opportunity due to lack of timely information.

5. Rating

Moreover, a company should have a scientific plan for rating employees. Such a plan should be based on various job evaluation and merit rating techniques. Only by giving promotion on the basis of such ratings is it possible to ensure the two important traits of a sound promotion policy — its ***objective nature*** and its ***impartial character.***

6. Training

Deserving and competent candidates — having potential value for the organisation and selected for promotion — should be given proper and sufficient training so that they can serve the organisation better and derive the fruits of organisational growth. In today's world — characterised by rapid technological progress and information revolution and constant changes in job characteristics and job requirements — it is of considerable importance to retrain workers (as and when required) as part of the company's promotion policy. Retraining is absolutely essential for those workers who qualify for better jobs.

7. Probation

Even after a worker is promoted to a new position his (her) job should be confirmed after a year or so. This probationary period should be utilised by the worker to learn the new job as efficiently as possible. By putting the best possible effort the worker should be able to prove that he deserves confirmation.

8. Consultation

Normally, the personnel department is supposed to advice on promotion to the top management. But it is equally vital for top management or a deserving candidate's immediate superior (in the line organisation) to give due consideration and weigh-tage to the recommendations of the superior. Through such an act, line responsibility for making promotion can be suitably discharged. This will also ensure that the existing chain of command in the organisation is not upset.

9. Criteria

Various criteria of promotion may be used. The two most important criteria are merit (competence) and seniority (length of service). However, the bases for selection for promotion should be consistent and clear-cut so that there is no ambiguity in their interpretation and there is no uncertainty about a company's promotion policy. Since there is sometimes a conflict between the two criteria, it is necessary to achieve a realistic compromise between the two.

Conclusion

However, there is feeling among personnel managers that merit — as determined by job performance and by analysis of employee potential for development — should be the basis of promotion. In other words, merit should be given preference over seniority in matters relating to production inasmuch as competence is — and has always been — the fundamental determinant of an organisation's productivity and progress. The best guide to promotion by merit is provided by performance appraisal methods. Such methods give premium on merit and put discount on seniority and thus ensures the most effective utilisation of talents. The modern view is that promotion should be based on merit.

B. MERIT V. SENIORITY

Seniority refers to the length of recognised service in an organisation. Since the meaning of seniority is exact and simple, it is the objective means of promotion and it is widely accepted as a criteria of promotion. In fact, the human relations approach to management ranked seniority as the most important criterion of promotion. When promotion is made on the basis of merit a cordial industrial relations situation prevails within the organisation or enterprise, in which case there will be no scope for controversy and grievance. Another advantage of this method of promotion — promotion by seniority — is that it reduces labour turnover and training and employee development costs.

But it has certain demerits also. Promotion by seniority completely ignores merit or ability. By overvaluing experience, it gives hardly any incentive to the worker for further advancement and to perform better. Instead, it demoralises the competent worker and thus drives talent out of the organisation. Moreover, it does not conduce to higher labour productivity.

Merit alone can raise organisational productivity.

Conclusion

So the conclusion is that while formulating and evolving suitable promotion policies personnel managers should try to make a realistic compromise between seniority and merit. When two or more people are supposed to be equally competent to do a particular job, seniority (like tie breaker) should be the deciding factor in employee promotion. The most important factors to be taken into consideration in formulating a suitable promotion policy are :

(1) the length of uninterrupted service,

(2) efficiency and ability to perform a particular job or task (according to the specification of the personnel department), and

(3) physical fitness.

When the last two factors are more or less the same for competing candidates, seniority, in general, or length of continuous service, in particular, should be the governing principle (or sole criterion) of employee promotion.

Synopsis for Learning

Q.1. What is promotion?

Ans. Promotion refers to a change within the organisation to a higher position that has greater responsibilities and usually requires more advanced skills and knowledge than the previous position. Promotion normally brings greater status and an increase in pay.

Q.2. What is promotion based on open competition?

Ans. It refers to the policy of filling positions or making promotions from the most qualified people available, whether from inside or outside a given enterprise.

Q.3. What is promotion from within?

Ans. This refers to the practice of making all promotions in an enterprise from people within it if it is possible to do so.

PERFORMANCE APPRAISAL

Employee evaluation and control is perhaps the most important aspect of human resource control. It is mainly achieved through performance appraisal (PA).

Performance appraisals and their outcomes play a vital part in motivating employees. Such appraisals must convey to employees how well they have performed on mutually set goals and measures. Without proper two-way feedback about one's effort and its effect on performance, there is always the risk of decreasing an employee's initiative and drive.

Performance appraisal is an important process in organisations because it signals to members the kinds of behaviours that subsequently might be rewarded. Employee performance and reward systems are now widely used to measure the effectiveness of job performance, gauge its value, and provide appropriate reward (or punishment) — depending on performance. It is this reward for performance that reinforces the behaviour and provides the motivation for future behaviour. Thus, it is crucial that the appraisal system measure performance accurately as also the rewarding system reward it equitably. These two systems directly ensure that human resources will be motivated to achieve organisational objectives in the future. The quality of the appraisal system thus determines the productivity of human resources in the future.

"Appraisal" means to measure and evaluate against a standard of performance. "Rewarding" means to repay equitably for a service, in appropriate relationship to the quality of the service performed.

Appraising the performance of individuals and organisations is an inherent aspect of managing. Simply stated, it is impossible to make intellegent managerial decisions about individuals without measuring their performance in some manner.

The primary responsibility for performance appraisal belongs to line management. Top management must make the final policy decisions on the methods to be utilised, and managers at all levels must implement appraisal and rewarding procedures.

Appraisal is generally used for administrative purposes, such as promotions and salary increases, as well as for individual development and motivation. Other frequent uses of appraisal information are employee selection and placement, feedback to guide and reinforce training, personnel planning, and organisation planning.

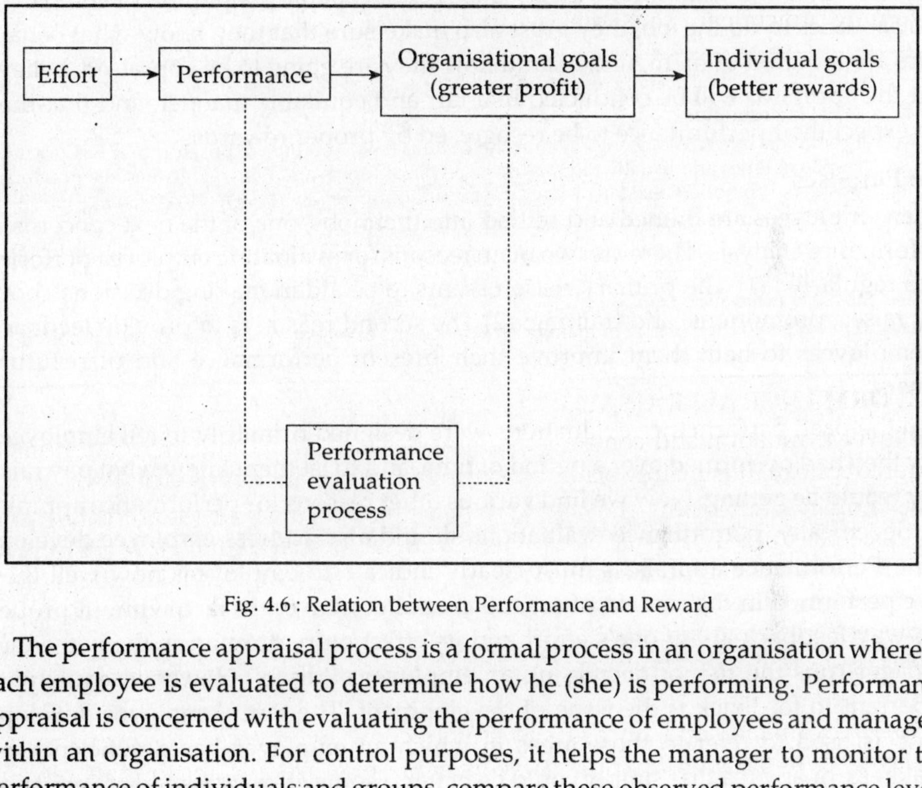

Fig. 4.6 : Relation between Performance and Reward

The performance appraisal process is a formal process in an organisation whereby each employee is evaluated to determine how he (she) is performing. Performance appraisal is concerned with evaluating the performance of employees and managers within an organisation. For control purposes, it helps the manager to monitor the performance of individuals and groups, compare these observed performance levels against some standard, and correct problems, if any. The process of performance appraisal is illustrated in Fig. 4.6, in which each step leads logically to the next, as we trace through a typical industrial job (as an example).

Importance

Performance is a vital component of employee motivation. Specifically, an employer must be concerned with the link between effort and performance, and between performance and rewards, as shown in Fig.4.6.

Employees have to know what is expected of them, and they need to know how their performance will be measured. Furthermore, they must feel confident that if they exert an effort within their capabilities, it will result in a better performance as defined by the criteria by which they are being measured. Furthermore, they must feel confident that if they perform as they are being asked, they will achieve the rewards they value.

In short, performance appraisals and their outcomes play a vital part in personnel management. If the objectives that individual employees are seeking are not clear, if the criteria for measuring that objective attainment are vague, and if employees lack confidence that their efforts will lead to a satisfactory appraisal of their performance or feel that there will be very little reward even when their performance is quite satisfactory, individuals are likely to work considerably below their potential. If personnel managers have done their job to recruit capable people and develop their basic abilities to do the job, they must also make sure that they know what behaviours are required of them, understand how they are going to be appraised, believe that the appraisal will be conducted in a fair and equitable manner, and that they can expect their performance to be recognised by proper rewards.

The Purposes

When employees are trained and settled into their jobs, one of the next concerns is performance analysis. There are two main reasons for evaluating employee performance regularly : (1) The primary reason seems to be aid in making decisions about pay raises, promotions, and training. (2) The second reason is to provide feedback to employees to help them improve their present performance and plan future careers.

In the past, performance evaluations were designed primarily to tell employees how they had performed over a period of time, and to let them know what pay raise they would be getting. Now we find various other reasons for performance appraisals. Specifically, performance evaluations should also address employee development. Performance appraisals must clearly indicate to employees how well they have performed in the context of organisational objectives. In fact, without proper two-way feedback about one's effort and its effect on performance, the personnel manager runs the risk of decreasing an employee's 'drive'. However, equally as important to feedback is the issue of development. The term 'employee development' is used to refer to those areas in which an employee has a deficiency or weakness, or an area that simply could be better if some effort was made to enhance performance.

Approaches to Appraisal

Until recently, almost all appraisal practices have been on the implicit assumption that the superior is the person in the best position to judge the performance of his (or her) subordinates. Appraisals have thus emphasised the hierarchical relationship of superior and subordinate, and have placed the superior in the position from which he can pass judgment on the subordinate.

In this emphasis on passing judgment from above, the vast majority of appraisal approaches employed some form of trait rating. Basically, the trait-rating approach requires the superior to evaluate, in some numerical or descriptive fashion, the subordinate's possession of certain personality and behaviour traits.

However, over the last 30 years, a trend away from traditional trait-oriented performance appraisal and toward a more positive motivation-oriented approach has been developing in the field of personnel management. Peter Drucker and Douglas McGregor have suggested that a participative, motivation-oriented approach to appraisal should lead to higher performance levels than does the traditional trait-oriented approach.

The Appraisal Process

As noted earlier, the basic purpose of performance appraisal is to measure the performance of individuals and/or groups at the workplace. For this to be effective and successful, it must be conducted in the following ways:

- Appraisal must be against pre-set and pre-agreed aims and objectives fully and clearly understood by all concerned. These should, additionally (where there is more than one), be given priority, and deadlines for achievement; such performance targets should be realistic and achievable in the given situation — if they are not they will be ignored; if they are too easy, they set a wider agenda for the lowering of performance standards.
- Appraisal is a process, consisting of both a series of regularised formal reviews, at which targets and objectives are to be assessed for success and failure; and a continuous relationship between appraiser and appraisee, that ensures a mutual and continuing confidence on the part of each in the other — ensuring that the organisation's strategy and purpose is being fulfilled.
- Appraisal must be a participative process between appraiser and appraisee, to ensure that the wider behavioural objective of mutual commitment to any aims and targets is achieved.
- The process must be believed in and valued, as both concept and process, by the organisation and those responsible for its direction; resources and priority must be committed to it, and it must be in-built into the manager's task, both on the continuous basis indicated above, and also to ensure that adequate time is set aside for the formal review part.
- The formal reviews should take place at least every 3-6 months; if they are more frequent than this, they tend to impose on the continuing process and relationship that should also be present; if they are less frequent, it becomes very difficult to conduct an adequate or genuine review of what has been done.
- Both appraisers and appraisees should have full understanding of this, and should be briefed and trained in it; it must be an integral part of the investment by organisations in their human resource; and the returns on appraisal should be identifiable and measurable.

Within this framework, particular organisational appraisal schemes may seek to: provide merit pay awards; identify potential; identify training and development needs; identify job-person mismatch; identify organisation development prospects; identify poor and sub-standard performance; be a vehicle for other remediable action.

1. Setting Standards

The performance appraisal process (shown in Table below) begins with the establishment of performance standards in accordance with the organisation's strategic goals.

2. Goal setting

So the second step in performance appraisal is jointly setting measurable goals. These should have evolved out of the company's strategic direction — and, more specifically, job analysis and job description. These performance standards should also be clear and objective enough to be understood and measured. The expectations a manager has in terms of work performance by his (her) employees must be clear enough in his mind so that he will be able, in near future, to communicate these expectations to his employees, mutually agree to specific job performance and measures, and appraise their performance against these established standards.

Steps in Performance Appraisal Process
1. The personnel department establishes performance standards of employees.
2. Managers and employees jointly set measurable goals.
3. Attempts are made to measure actual performance by using various methods.
4. Actual performance is compared with standards.
5. The appraisal is discussed with the employee.
6. If necessary, corrective action is taken.

Once performance standards are established, it is necessary to communicate these expectations. Communication is a two-way street: mere transference of information from the manager to the employee regarding expectations is not communication.

3. Measurement of Performance

The third step in the appraisal process is the measurement of performance. To determine what actual performance is, it is necessary to acquire information about it. The personnel manager should be concerned with how he measures and what he measures.

4. Comparison

The fourth step in the appraisal process is the comparison of actual performance with standards. At this stage the personnel manager notes deviation between standard performance and actual performance so that he can proceed to the fifth step in the process — the discussion of the appraisal with the employee.

5. Discussion

In fact, the discussion of the appraisal with the employee is the next step of any performance appraisal process. Such discussion can have negative as well as positive motivational consequence inasmuch appraising performance may touch one of the most emotionally charged activities — the assessment of another individual's contribution and ability.

6. Corrective Action

The final step in the appraisal is the initiation of corrective action where necessary. Corrective action can be of two types. One is immediate and deals predominantly with symptoms and the other is basic and seeks to find out the causes (of poor performance). Immediate corrective action is often described as 'putting out fires', whereas basic corrective action gets to the source of deviation and seeks to adjust the difference permanently (see Fig. 4.7).

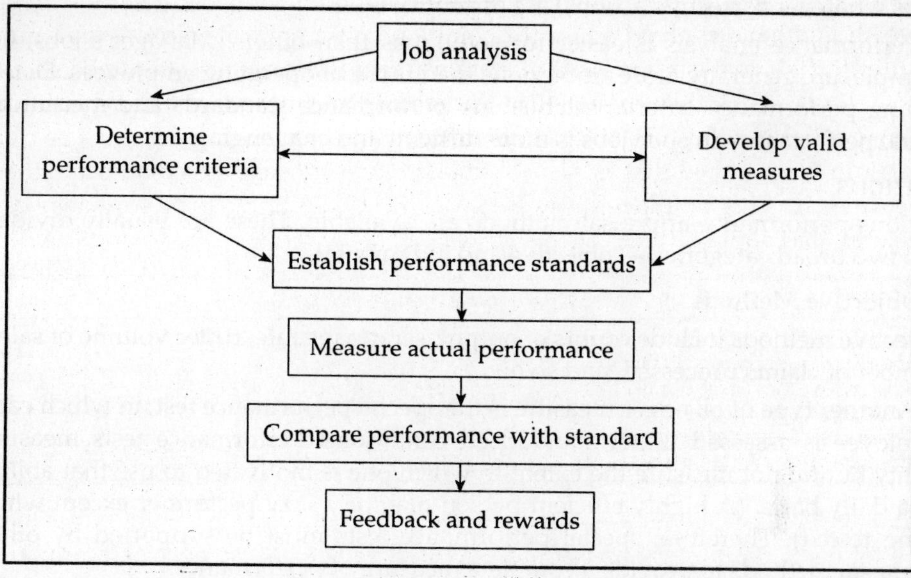

Fig. 4.7 : The Performance Appraisal Process

- Immediate action corrects something right now and gets things back on track. Basic corrective action asks how and why performance deviated. In some instances, managers may rationalise that they do not have the time to take basic corrective action and, therefore, must be content to 'perpetually' put out fires'. Good managers recognise that taking a little time to analyse the problem today may save more time tomorrow when the problem may get bigger. These steps may now be illustrated with an example.

Example. Let us assume that a manufacturer introduces a new line of machinery and, therefore, needs to establish a performance analysis framework for the machine operators.

Step 1 : Job analysis

First, a job analysis is conducted to determine the components of the job and their relative importance. For the machine operator, these components might be adjusting machine settings, making parts and inspecting them for quality. See Fig. 4.7.

Step 2 : Setting performance criteria (standards)

Performance criteria, then, would include ability to set the machine, manufacture the parts and inspect the finished products. Valid measures could include making spot checks of machine settings, counting the number of units produced, and conducting occasional follow-up inspections to verify quality.

Step 3 : Setting the desired level of actual performance

Establishing performance standards would involve setting the desired levels of actual performance. For the machine operator, these could be 98% accurate machine settings, 40 units of production per hour, and a quality acceptance rate of 93%. Actual performance is then measured and compared with the standard. Finally, the manager provides the feedback to the individual and administers whatever rewards (or takes whatever corrective actions) are appropriate.

Performance analysis is easier for some jobs than others. Manager's jobs, for example, are generally more ambiguous than those of operating employees. Determining performance criteria, establishing performance standards and measuring actual performance in such jobs is more difficult and challenging.

METHODS

Various performance appraisal methods are available. These are usually divided into two broad categories — objective and judgmental.

1. Objective Methods

Objective methods include counts of output, scrappage rate, rupee volume of sales, number of claims processed, and so on.

Another type of objective measure is the special performance test, in which each employee is assessed under standarised conditions. Performance tests measure ability but do not measure the extent to which one is motivated to use that ability on a daily basis. (A highly efficient person may be a lazy performer except when being tested). Therefore, special performance tests must be supported by other appraisal methods to provide a complete measure of performance.

2. Judgmental Methods

Some of the earliest formal appraisal plans employed open-ended essay appraisals or some form of adjective checklist. Because these approaches lacked objectivity and precision, the attention paid to psychometrics in the early 1920s led to the development of graphic rating scales.

Perhaps the most common way to measure performance is through judgmental methods, with stress on ranking and rating techniques. Ranking compares employees directly with each other and orders them from best to worst, usually on the basis of 'overall performance'.

Drawbacks: However, the ranking technique has a number of drawbacks. First it is difficult to do in large groups, because the persons in the middle of the distribution may be hard to distinguish from one another accurately. Secondly, intervals are unequal between ranks. Number one is better than number two, but by how much? This kind of information is not supplied by ranks. Third, comparison of people in different work groups is impossible. Each group has a person ranked first, but which first is the best?

The final criticism of ranking is that it is a global technique. The whole employee is being assessed at once as to overall 'goodness' or 'badness' compared with others. This is a bit simple-minded in that each employee certainly has both good and bad points. In addition, one never knows what subjective criterion each evaluator used in arriving at a global judgment. One evaluator may consider quantity of performance above everything else, whereas another may attach more importance to quality or co-operativeness. Furthermore, rankings (or ratings) do not provide useful information for feedback. To be told that one is ranked third is not nearly so helpful as to be told that the quality of one's work is outstanding, its quantity is satisfactory, one's punctuality could be improved and one's paperwork is seriously deficient.

Rating differs from ranking in that it compares each employee with a fixed standard rather than with other employees. A rating scale provides the standard.

Such scales are very common; they consist of a characteristic or performance dimension to be rated, followed by a scale on whom to make the rating. In constructing graphic rating scales, it is extremely important to select performance dimensions that are relevant to job performance. As a rule, personality traits such as 'honesty', 'loyalty', and 'creativity' should not be rated. Job behaviours and results should be the focus instead.

3. BARS

The Behaviourally Anchored Rating Scale (BARS) is a recently developed rating method. This method calls on two (or more) groups of supervisors of the job to be rated to construct the scales. They first identify relevant performance dimensions and then generate anchors : specific, observable behaviours typical of each performance level. BARS is potentially a good rating method because it requires that proper care be taken in constructing the scales. It is also costly, because a number of supervisors have to spend time constructing the scales.

BARS is designed to identify the critical areas of performance for a job, and to describe the more effective and less effective job behaviours for getting results. Performance is evaluated by asking the rater to record specific, observable job behaviours of an employee and to then compare these observations with a "BARS". As a result the supervisor is in a position to compare the employee's behaviour with behaviour that has been previously determined to be more or less effective. Such a system differentiates among behaviour, performance, and results, and, consequently, is able to provide a basis for setting developmental goals for the employee. Because it is job-specific and identifies observable and measurable behaviour, it is a more reliable and valid method for performance appraisal. The major advantage of BARS may stem from the dimensions generated rather than from any particular superiority provided by behavioural versus numerical anchors.

On the basis of above discussion, we may propose a detailed plan for implementing a **five-step** performance appraisal programme :

1. The individual discusses his job description with his superior, and they agree on the content of his job and relative importance of his major duties — the things he is paid to do and is accountable for.
2. The individual establishes performance targets for each of his responsibilities for the coming years.
3. The individual meets with the superior to discuss the individual's target programme.
4. Checkpoints are established for the evaluation of his progress; ways of measuring progress are selected.
5. The superior and subordinate meet at the end of the period to discuss the results of the subordinate's effort to meet the targets he had previously established.

Conclusion

One of the most important personnel activities consists of evaluating employees' performance. The personnel department usually helps devise the appraisal system that will be used in the firm. One's immediate supervisor is usually responsible for doing the appraisal.

It follows, therefore, that there is a necessary body of skills and knowledge required of the manager in the conduct of effective performance appraisal. Communication, articulation, target and objective setting, counselling, support, trust, dependency and assertiveness, are all clearly necessary; and they will also be required to be translated into dealings with frustrated and recalcitrant employees in particular situations.

Finally, the control of the appraisal process must always rest with the manager, and while agreement of objectives with the member of staff is desirable, this should never be at the expense of a diluted or sub-standard performance. Ideally, the manager should have the skills and abilities necessary to gain the commitment and understanding of the.employees concerned.

Synopsis for Learning

Q.1. What is performance appraisal?

Ans. Performance appraisal is a formal process whereby each employee is evaluated to determine how he (she) is performing.

Q.2. What are methods of performance appraisal?

Ans. Various performance appraisal methods are available. These are divided into two broad categories—objective and judgmental.

4.9 JOB EVALUATION

Wage structures are usually set up through a procedure called job evaluation, which is an attempt to assess the worth of each job relative to other jobs. A job evaluation compares a particular job with others to ensure that it is being fairly priced. Job evaluation can be done in different ways. But the popular way is to break a job down into identifiable components and then assign points or weights to each component. Finally, each job in the company is evaluated in terms of those components. Factors that are often assigned points are skill, responsibility, effort, and working environment.

Importance

Whenever two or more people perform different work for a third, the need exists for some kind of job evaluation. The third person, the employer, must somehow arrive at a rate of pay for each job which will not only (1) be competitive in attracting and holding employees but also (2) be seen by them as related to the relative difficulty of their jobs. If the employer establishes pay rates which fall short of either or both of these pay goals, employee dissatisfaction with pay usually will result. Loss of good employees, inability to attract employees, low moralle and low productivity are some of the business problems which often are associated with dissatisfaction about pay.

Of the two pay goals — meetings market rates and achieving satisfactory internal pay relationships — the latter has greater priority. First, the internal pay relationships are more visible to employees. If perceived by employees as being unfair, out of line, and arbitrary, pay rates within the company can be a continual source of discontent, for employees are reminded of the internal inequities every working day. Secondly, an equitable internal pay hierarchy is a prerequisite to establishing sound and workable policies concerning pay progression for employees. Finally, a thought-out and and agreed-upon set of internal relative values for jobs aids greatly in establishing an informed company posture relative to outside pay levels.

Aims and Objectives

The overall aim of job evaluation is to assess and evaluate the nature of the work to be done in a particular job; the key tasks to be carried out, and the balance, difficulty, value, frequency and importance of these. Skills, qualities, capabilities and attributes are matched up, and a market value placed on them, with particular weightings as necessary or desirable. Jobs are then placed in a ranking order matching them up against grades, job titles, salary scale(s).

The establishment of proper wage differentials for company jobs is necessary to bring forth the required caliber of labour and to encourage men to train for skilled jobs. Moreover ratings (occupation differentials expressed as labour grades or numerical point values) are necessary for the establishment of logical and practical company wage rate and salary schedules. In firms where such logical wage and salary differentials have not been established, compensation patterns are often irregular and chaotic since they will have evolved from traditional attitudes, arbitrary decisions, expediency, and favouritism. In such cases, jobs that call for greater effort, skill, and responsibility may pay less than jobs requiring fewer of these attributes; and individuals in the same or similar occupations may receive widely varying compensation. Morale is consequently low and performance poor since employees keenly fell these inequities, and management cannot explain the inconsistencies on a logical basis.

What is Job Evaluation?

Job evaluation can be defined as a systematic process designed to determine the relative worth of jobs within a single work organisation. It is the process whereby an organisation systematically establishes its compensation programme. In this process, jobs are compared in order to arrive at each job's appropriate worth.

Job evaluation is related to job analysis. Job analysis is the process of describing the duties of a job, authority relationships, skills required, conditions of work, and additional relevant information. Job analysis involves creating job descriptions and specifications. Firstly, an analysis is made of the jobs in the organisation, with particular attention given to the tasks and skills involved in performing them. This list of the specific duties of a particular job is called a job description. The personnel manager next lists the qualifications for each of these duties — the education, abilities, and experience required of the person who fills the position. This list of qualifications is called the job specification. Often, a job description and a job specification appear together on a single form and are referred to jointly as a job description.

By job evaluation we mean using the information in job analysis to systematically determine the value of each job in relation to all jobs within the organisation. In short, job evaluation seeks to rank all the jobs in the organisation and place them in a hierarchy that will reflect the relative worth of each. Importantly, this is a ranking of jobs, not people. The ranking that results is used to determine the organisation's pay structure.

Four Steps

The job evaluation process follows the following four steps : gathering the data; selecting compensable factors; evaluating a job; and assigning pay to the job. These different but related steps may now be briefly reviewed:

1. Gathering job analysis data

Firstly, information must be collected through a method of job analysis. Here validity should be a guiding principle which simply means that the job analyst must accurately capture all of the content. It is very important to capture both similarities and differences among jobs. Ambiguous, incomplete, or inaccurate job descriptions can result in some jobs being incorrectly evaluated.

2. Selecting compensable factors

Compensable factors are the factors the organisation chooses to reward through differential pay. The most typical compensable factors are skill, knowledge, responsibility, and working conditions.

3. Evaluating job using certain methods

There are four fundamental methods of job evaluation. These will be discussed in detail in the next section.

4. Assigning pay to the job

The end product of a job evaluation exercise is a hierarchy of jobs in terms of their relative value to the organisation. Assigning pay to this hierarchy of jobs is referred to as pricing the pay structure. This practice requires a policy decision on how the organisation's pay levels relate to their competitors.

Methods

Though it is obviously impossible to measure the relative value of company jobs with exact precision, it is possible to rate jobs in an objective, consistent manner on the basis of explicit criteria. Job evaluation (or job rating) is a systematic procedure for measuring the relative value and importance of occupations on the basis of their common factors (skill, training, effort) for the purpose of determining wage and salary differentials. Job evaluation deals with the occupation and not with the employee holding the position.

The four basic methods of job evaluation are (1) ranking, (2) classification, (3) point and (4) factor-comparison. Each of these methods begins with job description.

1. The Ranking Method

The ranking method is perhaps the simplest one. This method ranks the various jobs to be evaluated in relation to each other on a total basis. There is no attempt to determine the significant factors in the jobs or to evaluate the jobs in terms of their sub-elements. Rather, only a single overall judgment is made regarding the relative worth of each job in relation to the others.

Merits. This is, in fact, the most common method of job evaluation in small organisations, in which, perhaps, two secretaries, a typist, and a file clerk must be evaluated. In a small organisation in which relatively few jobs are involved and all of the people participating in the evaluation are intimately familiar with the details of all the jobs, this is perhaps a very effective method of evaluation.

Drawbacks. (1) However, this method very quickly breaks down when larger groups are involved and when there is less knowledge of each of the jobs. Since there are no written guidelines for evaluation, it is obviously important that the ranking of all the jobs be done by the same individual or group so that the subjective basis for ranking can be consistent. Even under the best of conditions, there is always the danger that the individuals doing the ranking may have imperfect knowledge of the jobs or be subject to bias. To some extent this can be overcome by the use of job descriptions; (2) Secondly, the method is subjective. There are no definite or consistent standards by which to justify the rankings; (3) Thirdly, because jobs are only ranked in terms of order, we have no knowledge of the distance between the ranks; and, (4) Perhaps the most obvious limitation of the method is its sheer unmanageability when there are a large number of jobs. It is really difficult, in practice, to rank hundreds or thousands of jobs in the organisation.

2. The Classification Method

This is by far the most common method used in civil service systems. In this method, before any jobs are examined, an *a priori* assumption is made regarding the number of pay grades to be included in the final structure. Then, following the perusal of many job descriptions, a description is written for each grade or "class" of jobs in the structure.

These descriptions cover such items as the education required, the skill required, job responsibility, and other factors that are pertinent to a particular class of jobs.

Thus, a particular job class or grade may be described as requiring a high school education, moderate finger dexterity, light physical exertion (as specifically described), and a moderately high level of judgment.

Once a description of each of the job grades has been written, the descriptions of the jobs to be evaluated are examined. Jobs are classified into the grade or level that most closely correspond to job description.

Once the classifications are established, they are ranked in an overall order of importance according to the criteria chosen, and each job is placed in its appropriate classification. The latter action is generally taken by comparing each position's job description against the classification description.

Although appearing to be somewhat less "scientific" than the point or factor-comparison methods, in many situations this method may be just as accurate. Furthermore, this method is relatively easy to understand and, therefore, appears to be straightforward and "legitimate". Thus, in many organisations, it may be easier for employees to accept this method as being honest.

Merit. The most important thing to be said in favour of this method is that it has proven itself successful and viable in classifying various kinds and levels of jobs.

Drawbacks. However, the classification method has most of the drawbacks of the ranking method, plus the difficulty of writing classification descriptions, judging which jobs go where, and dealing with jobs that appear to fall into more than one classification.

3. The Point Method

By far the most common method of job evaluation is the point method. This procedure usually examines four or more job factors common to the jobs being evaluated and rates each job on a numerical scale in relation to each factor. Thus, points are accumulated for each factor on the basis of the relative degree to which the job is seen as possessing that factor. For example, if the factor to be evaluated were "education", grade school or less might be scaled as one point; two years of high school as two points; high school graduation, three points; two years of college, four points; four years of college, five points; master's degree six points; and Ph.D., seven points. A factor such as "responsibility" might scale several different levels of financial responsibility, in terms of the value of production or the cost of errors.

The number of factors used may vary from as few as 2 to as many as 30 although several research studies have shown statistically that 4 or 5 factors seem to be about as accurate a basis for distinguishing jobs as a higher number. As can be imagined, the factors used vary widely among organisations and industries. The more common factors in use include education, responsibility for production, equipment, budget, persons, or safety, skill, experience, outside contacts, supervision, job conditions, physical effort, mental effort, and creativity. Whatever the factors in a particular system, the total points for each job are determined by summing the points assigned for each factor. Each job can then be related to other jobs on the basis of their respective total point scores.

Examples of compensable factors might include amount of formal education required, physical demands, working conditions and hazards, amount of responsibility, and degree of skill. This method breaks down jobs on the basis of various identifiable criteria (such as skill, effort, and responsibility) and then allocates points to each of these criteria. Depending on the importance of each criterion to performing the job, appropriate weights are given, points are added and jobs with similar point totals are placed in similar pay grades. Jobs requiring more education would then be assigned more points on the education factor than jobs requiring less education. Job performance under unpleasant or dangerous working conditions would be assigned more points on this factor than safe, comfortable jobs. Each job is carefully studied and evaluated on each factor and then all the points assigned to each job are added up. See Table 4.2. A job assigned 400 points should be paid more than a job assigned 300 points. Using such a system, it is easy to explain to one's employees why one job is paid more than another and thus to make the employees feel that the structures of the wages or the reward system is equitable.

Table 4.2 : Applying the Point System to Three Jobs

Compensable factors	Job					
	Office secretary		Office manager		Junior (Caretaker or Doorkeeper)	
1. Education	Moderate	60	High	80	Very Low	20
2. Responsibility	Low	40	Moderate	70	Low	40
3. Skill	High	80	Moderate	60	Low	40
4. Physical demand	Low	20	Low	20	High	45
Total points		200		230		145

N.B. The job analysis committee carefully reviews the contents of each job and decides what degree of each factor best describes the job.

The next step is setting actual wage rates on the basis of a combination of survey data and the wage structure that results from job evaluation. Often jobs with similar numbers of points are grouped together into wage grades in case of wage and salary administration. For instance, if there are 9 jobs with point totals between 375 and 400, it makes sense to group them in a single wage grade with the same pay rate[1].

Merits. Two metis of the method are :

1. The point method offers the greatest stability of the four approaches. Jobs may change over time, but the rating scales established under the point method may stay intact.
2. Additionally, the methodology underlying the approach contributes to a minimum of rating error.

Drawbacks. The main drawback of the method is that it is complex, making it costly and time-consuming to develop. The key points must be carefully and clearly identified, degrees of factors have to be agreed upon in terms that mean the same for all rates, the weight of each criterion has to be established, and point values must be assigned to degrees.

While it is expensive and time-consuming to both implement and maintain, the point method appears to be the most widely used method. However, due to its high administrative costs, one cannot justify its use in small and medium organisations.

1. A variation of the point system is the widely used Hay Plan. This method employs a standard points matrix which is applicable across organisational and national boundaries.

4. The Factor Comparison Method

The factor-comparison method is very similar to the point method, expect that it does not evaluate each of the factors on a numerical scale. While it may use the same factors as those used in the point method, the factor comparison method, rather than assigning point, ranks certain jobs in relation to each other on each factor at the outset of the process. It is important to include in this group only jobs that are widely believed to be accurately paid.

It is a sophisticated quantitative ranking method. The evaluators select key jobs in the organisation as standards. Those jobs chosen should be well-known, with established pay rates in the community, and they should consist of a representative cross-section of all jobs that are being evaluated — from the lowest to the highest paid jobs, from the most important to the least important and also cover the full range of requirements of each factor — as agreed upon by a committee representing workers and management.

Table 4.3 : Factor Comparison Method

Jobs	Hourly pay	Mental requirements	Skill requirements	Responsibility	Working conditions
1. Maintenance Electrician	Rs 26.40	Rs 4.00	Rs 2.30	Rs 3.30	Rs 1.90
2. Inventory Control Specialist	—	—	—	—	—
3. Warehouse Stocker	—	—	—	—	—
4. Secretary	—	—	—	—	—
5. Maintenance Electrician Helper	—	—	—	—	—

Jobs are compared on the basis of certain key factors or criteria such as mental requirements, skill requirements, physical requirements, responsibility, and working conditions. Once the key jobs are identified and the criteria chosen, committee members rank these jobs on the basis of such criteria.

The next step is perhaps the most important. The committee agrees upon the base rate (usually expressed on an hourly basis) for each of the key jobs and then allocates this base rate among the five criteria (as listed in Table 4.3). For example, in one organisation the job of a maintenance electrician was chosen as a key job with an hourly rate of Rs 16.40. The committee then allocated Rs 4.00 to mental effort, Rs 4.90 for skill, Rs 2.30 for physical effort, Rs 3.30 to responsibility and Rs 1.90 for working conditions. These amounts then became standards by which other jobs in the organisation could be evaluated.

The final step in factor comparison requires the committee to compare its overall judgments and resolve discrepancies, if any. The system is in place when the allocations to the key jobs are clear and understood, and high agreement has been achieved in committee members' judgment about how much responsibility each job has.

Merits. Two merits of the methods are :

(1) The factor comparison requires a unique set of standard jobs for each organisation. So it is a tailor-made approach. As such, it is automatically designed to meet the specific needs of each organisation.

(2) Secondly, jobs are compared with other jobs to determine a relative value, and since relative job values are what job evaluation seeks, the method is logical.

Drawbacks. The method has the following two drawbacks :

(1) The method is complex; it makes use of the same criteria to assess all jobs, when, in fact, jobs differ across and within organisations.

(2) It also depends on key jobs as anchor points.

The factor-comparison method is not as widely used as the point method, principally because it is much more complicated and takes more time to learn and apply. More the fact that the method is hard to understand may lead to lack of trust in its application.

Conclusion

The main organisational criterion essential to the success of any scheme of job evaluation are to do with fairness and equity of treatment for all staff, grades and occupations; clearly publicised and preset criteria for the evaluation process acceptable to and understood by all; the opportunity for representation and appeal; speed of operation; and the ability of the organisation to communicate all of the evaluation process and specific findings on individual jobs, in clear and unequivocal terms. The personnel manager should be aware that as far as job evaluation is concerned, there is no perfect system; the process involves subjective judgment. Job evaluation assumes normal performance of the job by a typical worker. So, in effect, the process ignores individual abilities or the performance of the jobholder.

In addition, it may be noted that job evaluation is concerned with the job and not the performance of the individual jobholder. Individual merit is not assessed. Neither does job evaluation eliminate collective bargaining. It determines the differential gaps between pay; it does not determine pay levels. Furthermore, job evaluation produces only a structure of pay rates. Other elements of earnings — such as incentives, pay or bonuses, etc. — are not determined by the method.

Merit Rating

In whatever way jobs are graded it is inevitable that some workers will perform better than others and deserve more pay. In order to reward the more efficient workers many organisations use a system of merit-rating.

Thus each job grade will have attached to it a band of ratings for merit, that is, an evaluation of the way the job is performed from the point of view of quality, quantity and reliability. A regular appraisal, usually annually, of job performance by each worker will be carried out objectively, preferably by the worker's immediate superior or by means of appraisal reports filled in by the supervisor or manager, and these will be held by the personnel office. The various aspects of performance will be assessed and a merit-rating applied. According to this rating within the job grade, salary enhancement and promotion prospects will be established.

Merit rating is mostly used for office workers, and the Institute of Administrative Management has devised a job grading and merit-rating scheme for this purpose which has found wide acceptance. However, merit-rating can be applied to any type of work that lends itself to individual appraisal. It will be obvious that merit-rating, unlike job grading, is concerned with people and the way they perform. In such cases appraisal interviews are usually conducted by the head of the worker's department, often with the worker's immediate supervisor in attendance.

Performance appraisal is also used to assess other aspects of a worker's performance. It assists in ascertaining a worker's potentiality for promotion, for transfer to other more demanding work and for suitability for further training. It is also used in the review of salaries and in considering the transfer from one salary scale to another. In such cases appraisal interviews are usually conducted by the head of the worker's department, often with the worker's immediate supervisor in attendance.

Synopsis for Learning

Q.1. What is job evaluation?

Ans. A major task in developing a wage structure is determining the relative worth of each job. This task of determining the relative worth of jobs is called job evaluation.

Q.2. What is the basic objective of job evaluation?

Ans. The objective of job evaluation is to ensure that internal relationships among the pay of various jobs are appropriate in light of the factors considered important by the members of the given organisation. These factors typically include the effort, training, and experience required; the difficulty, responsibility and hazards of the job; the value or contribution of the job to the organisation; and the organisation's traditions of internal job relationships. Thus, the objective of job evaluation is to ensure internal equity in the eyes of the members of the organisation, not to ensure equity in terms of some "objective" standard external to the organisation.

Q.3. What are the benefits of job evaluation?

Ans. In addition to its role in wage setting and surveys, a job evaluation programme (including job specification) clarifies the organisational lines of authority and responsibility; provides a basis for hiring, transferring, and establishing lines of job progression and channels of promotion; and serves as a basis for developing a training programme.

Q.4. What are the steps in job evaluation ?

Ans. Because of the discrepancies in pay rates both within an organisation and between different organisations (a major cause of industrial wage disputes) the process of job evaluation has been evolved.

The first step in this procedure is job analysis, the technique of obtaining detailed facts about each job and the task it involves. Two assessments can then be drawn from these facts, the job specification and the job description which states what the job entails, such as the tasks to be performed, the level of skill required, the responsibility and authority to be assumed, the type of working conditions and any particular features such as special hazards or unusual features.

The second step, following job analysis, is to determine the relative values of all jobs — one with another. From this analysis, the jobs can be evaluated and listed in order of value to the organisation, and pay scales established accordingly.

Q.5. What are the methods of job evaluation ?

Ans. The typical methods of job evaluation are :

(a) **The ranking system**. In this system, from the job analyses jobs are ranked according to the degree of difficulty and responsibility involved, all jobs of similar status being ranked equally throughout the undertaking, thus providing a basis for comparable pay scales. From the ranking job grades are established.

(b) **Job grading**. This is similar to ranking, but grades are established prior to ranking by reference to specific criteria of difficulty and responsibility within jobs, shown by the job analysis. A standard grade is thus selected and jobs are all given gradings by reference to this.

(c) **Factor points rating**. This is a method that looks at separate factors in a job and evaluates each by giving points, rather than looking at the job as a whole as is done in methods (a) and (b) Each factor — such as skill, responsibility, job conditions and mental and physical demands — is allocated a number of points according to an assessment of its difficulty or value and all the points are then added. According to the total number of points awarded each job is graded. This is considered to be a more equitable method than those in (a) and (b).

However the grading is carried out, it is essential to recognise that it is the job itself that is evaluated and not the person filling the job.

4.10 INDUSTRIAL DISCIPLINE

Industrial discipline is of considerable importance in any work situation. It is an essential factor for ensuring cohesive group action. If the people in an organisation are not properly disciplined the organisation may fail to attain its basic goal — raising total factor productivity and increasing the market value of the firm. Discipline enhances the mental strength of an individual worker and makes him more and more perfect and thus enables him to improve his performance and meet the needs of the organisation in a better way. By enforcing proper discipline on employees it is possible to avoid ineffective and inefficient performance. Lack of discipline implies inefficient performance and organisational slack (X-inefficiency). It often leads to a fall in the standard of people who are really talented, efficient and high performers.

TWO ASPECTS

Industrial discipline has two aspects — positive and negative. On one side, imposition of discipline implies creation of proper employee attitude. It also implies the creation of an organisational climate wherein the employees are willing to go by the established rules and regulations as also the procedures laid by top management. Discipline strengthens the willingness of organisational people to conform to the rules, regulations and stipulations of the organisation. Discipline gives an employee the chance to correct his (her) behaviour which violates the established norms of the organisation.

Discipline has a negative side also. Through the imposition of penalties and by giving threats to employees discipline causes people to obey the established rules of the organisation.

INGREDIENTS OF A SOUND DISCIPLINARY POLICY

1. Firstly, top management has to give due and thoughtful consideration to the need for creating a healthy work environment. This can be achieved if workers are really disciplined.
2. It is also necessary to determine at the outset what kind of discipline is desired and how to achieve the same. It is absolutely essential to have a proper code of discipline, which indicates clearly the form of discipline that can be expressed in a particular situation or to correct any anomaly in worker behaviour. This is possible if and only if the policy of discipline is formulated carefully.
3. A sound and adequate leadership is necessary for enforcing discipline.
4. Necessary and appropriate action has to be taken as and when needed with a view to improving the conduct of the workers.

IMPORTANCE

To ensure that an organisation runs smoothly there must be staff discipline. However, an autocratic management style is not acceptable today. So, this is a difficult task. No longer will workers tolerate fines or similar pecuniary penalties for what the organisation sees as departure from acceptable behaviour.

However, there must be rules of behaviour for staff which must be accepted by workers, particularly in the area of punctuality and absence. It follows, therefore, that a code of discipline must be drawn up and agreed with the workers and written into their service contracts. New recruits must be made aware of the code and the requirement for them to comply.

The surest way to achieve and maintain good staff discipline is to ensure a high morale, which is, after all, one of the marks of good management. Discipline is concerned with setting standards of performance, attitude and behaviour at work-place in the interest of ensuring that everyone knows what is expected of him and he conforms to them. If the approach taken is both positive and understood by all concerned it follows that such problems are kept to a minimum. Any organisation is allowed and expected to set its own standards, and these will be reflected both in the nature of the work itself and also in regard to the expectation of customers.

When problems occur the manager's first task is to get the individual concerned back-performing or behaving adequately and effectively. Normally, this is to be achieved by having a quiet word with the individual, pointing out to him where his behaviour or activity is falling short of the required standard, ensuring that he knows what the required standard is and concluding the discussion with an agreement that this is now the way in which matters will be conducted.

If this fails to work, various other procedures will have to be invoked. The basic objective is to remove the cause of the problem. And any and every warning issued by the manager or the organisation in the pursuit of a resolution of the problems will furnish detail — in clear terms — of the nature of it, the steps taken to try and resolve it and the levels of performance now expected of the individual. These warnings will either be orally issued, or in writing. (In either case a record will be kept by the manager concerned).

MEANING

The term discipline refers to a condition in the organisation wherein employees conduct themselves in accordance with the organisation's rules and standards of acceptable behaviour. For the most part, employees discipline themselves. This means that members conform to what is considered proper behaviour because they believe it is the right thing to do. Once they are made aware of what is expected of them, and assuming that they find these standards or rules to be reasonable, they seek to meet these expectations.

But all employees will not accept the responsibility of self-discipline. For some employees the organisation's rules and standards are not enough to elicit the accepted norms of responsible employee behaviour. These employees will require some degree of extrinsic disciplinary action frequently labelled punishment. It is this need to impose extrinsic disciplinary action that is of concern to the personnel manager.

Correcting Problems

Discipline and counseling are designed to do one thing : correct problems. Employee problems can be associated with lack of effort, poor performance and the inability to reach organisational and individual goals. If these problems are permitted to manifest to the point of termination, then both the employee and the employer lose.

In addition to the 'emotional scars' discipline or discharge may cause for the employee, the organisation is losing a once-valued employee. That individual was chosen after a careful recruiting and selection process. Getting to this point did not occur cost-free. In fact, every time an employee is terminated the organisation is, in essence, eliminating any further 'return on its investment' for the employee. The purpose of discipline and counselling, then, is to get the employee back on the right track. By helping him (or her) to perform better, organisational goals can be achieved, as well as individual goals. See Fig. 4.8 which is self-explanatory.

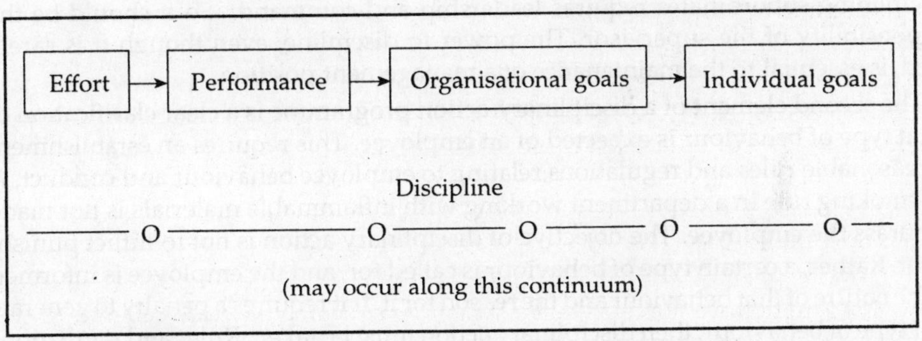

Fig. 4.8 : Linking Discipline to Motivation

In reality, most grievances arise from disciplinary actions. The labour contract usually states that management may discipline an employee 'for just cause'. However, the perception of what is 'just cause' and what is 'fair punishment' may differ between management and employees.

To avoid this kind of problem, rules should be clearly spelled out and communicated to employees. Penalties should also be made known and fit the crime. Most discipline systems use 'progressive penalties' — the more often the violation is repeated, the more serious the penalty. For instance, a first incident of go-slow practice (tardiness) might occasion only a reminder, the second a stern warning, the third a written warning in the employee's file, and the fourth a short suspension. Some violations, such as fighting, stealing from the employer, and sabotage, obviously call for a much more severe initial penalty.

Fairness

There is another aspect of discipline. The discipline process must be appropriate and fair. If discipline is handled haphazardly, or there is no apparent reason for such action to take place, this can have a detrimental effect on employee morale. And this very fact results in less effort being put. Hence organisations must make sure that they are not diminishing motivation by having a poorly operating discipline process. No doubt discipline and counselling are two necessary components of personnel management.

DISCIPLINARY ACTIONS

The term 'disciplinary action' refers to any conditioning of future behaviour by the application of either rewards or penalties. This approach would include positive motivational activities, such as praise, participation and incentive pay, as well as negative motivational techniques, such as reprimand, layoff, and fines. Both types of activities seek to condition employee behaviour in order to achieve good discipline in the organisation.

Basic Elements of the Disciplinary-Action Process

Disciplinary action usually refers to penalties that lead to a prevention of undesired behaviour. The first element of the disciplinary process is that it is a line responsibility. A staff personnel agency can and should provide advice and assistance. But disciplining subordinates requires leadership and command. So it should be the responsibility of the supervisor. The power to discipline, even though it is rarely used, is essential to the maintenance of a management position.

The second element of a disciplinary-action programme is a clear clarification of what type of behaviour is expected of an employee. This requires an establishment of reasonable rules and regulations relating to employee behaviour and conduct. A no-smoking rule in a department working with inflammable materials is not made to harass the employee. The objective of disciplinary action is not to inflict punishment. Rather, a certain type of behaviour is called for, and the employee is informed of the nature of that behaviour and the reason for it. If it requires a penalty to generate that type of behaviour, then disciplinary action must be taken. Rules and regulations are fixed in such areas as attendance, safety, theft, insubordination, intoxication, fighting, dishonesty, soliciations, smoking and housekeeping.

With reasonable authority possessed by the supervisor and the employees knowing well what is expected of them, the basis of disciplinary action has been established. When an offence takes place, it is important to establish and maintain proper records concerning the nature of the event, the participants and the work environment. Record should also be kept of any taken by the supervisor. Such written evidence is highly important, if the event forms the basis for a grievance filed by the employee. Thus, in modern management's increasingly legalistic environment, written records constitute a third basic element of a well-organised disciplinary action programme.

In taking disciplinary action, the attitude of the supervisor is very important. One should be objective in collecting facts. One should approach the problem, if possible, with a nonjudicial attitude. If a mistake is made in the handling of a grievance, then the problem will not be solved. Making a mistake in disciplining someone who does not deserve it could well mean a permanent destruction of the morale of the employee and a general loss of respect for the supervisor.

Disciplinary Action Penalties

Among the penalties available in business are :

1. Oral reprimand
2. Written reprimand
3. Loss of privileges
4. Fines

5. Layoff
6. Demotion
7. Discharge

The penalties are listed in the general order of severity, from mild to severe.

Guides to Disciplinary Action

Experience have provided *six* important guides to assist the manager in undertaking negative disciplinary action.

- Disciplinary action should be taken in private. The object is to condition behaviour, not to punish. Holding a person up to public ridicule often has the opposite, rather than the desired effect.
- An application of a penalty should always carry with it a constructive element. Disciplinary action should be applied by the immediate supervisor.
- Promptness is important in taking disciplinary action.
- An immediate supervisor should never be disciplined in the presence of his own subordinates. The concept of privacy would forbid the disciplining of anyone in the presence of others. It is very important in the case of managers, who must maintain a position of status and power in addition to the formal authority granted by the organisation.
- After the disciplinary action has been taken, the manager should attempt to develop a normal attitude toward the employee.

When management is dissatisfied with the behaviour of an employee, its goal is to effect a change more consistent with organisation requirements. Penalties or punishments constitute only one means of doing this, and should be used as a last resort. The attitude of the immediate supervisor should be one of counseling and understanding, rather than 'police and punish'.

Steps Followed

Discipline generally follows a typical sequence of four steps : verbal warning, written warning, suspension, and dismissal. Two additional steps, which would logically follow suspension — demotion and paycuts — are less popular in practice. See Fig.4.9.

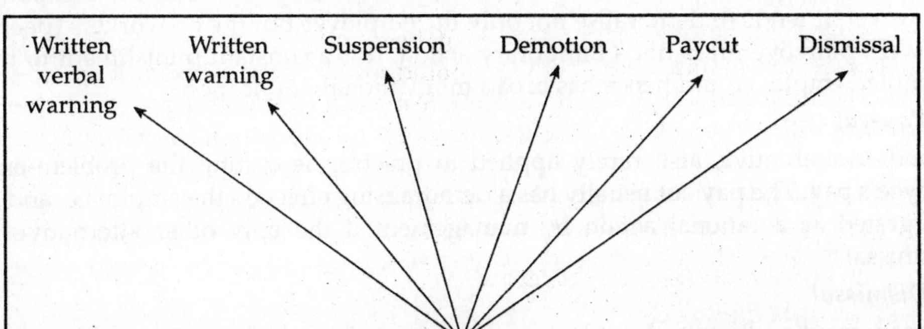

Fig. 4.9 : Disciplinary Actions

1. Written verbal warning

The mildest form of discipline is the written verbal warning. It is a temporary record of a reprimand which is then placed in the manager's file of the employee. It should state the purpose, date and outcome of the interview with the employee. This warning remains in the hands of the manager. It is not forwarded to the personnel department for inclusion in the employee's personnel file.

The written verbal reprimand is best achieved if completed in a private and informal environment. The manager should begin by clearly informing the employee of the rule that has been violated and the problem that this infraction has caused.

If the written verbal warning is effective, further disciplinary action can be avoided. If the employee fails to improve, the manager need to consider more severe action.

2. Written warning

The second step in the progressive discipline process is the written warning. In effect, it is the first formal stage of the disciplinary procedure. This is so because the written warning becomes part of the employee's official personnel file. This is achieved by not only giving the warning to the employee but sending a copy to the personnel department to be inserted in the employee's permanent record.

3. Suspension

A suspension or lay-off would be the next disciplinary step, usually taken if the prior steps have been implemented without the desired outcome. If the infraction is of a serious nature, suspension is ordered without any prior verbal or written warning.

A suspension may be for one day or several weeks; disciplinary lay-offs in excess of a month are rare. A short lay-off, without pay, is potentially a rude awakening to problem-employees. It may convince them that management is serious, and force them into accepting responsibility for following the organisation's rules.

4. Demotion

If suspension has not been effective and management wants to avoid dismissing the problem-employee, demotion may be an alternative. Demotion is a disciplinary action whereby an individual is sent back to a lower position in the company. However, it tends to demoralise not only the employee but the co-workers (peers) as well. Moreover, it is not a temporary action. It is a constant punishment to the demoted employee and hence has broad motivational implication.

5. Pay-cut

Another alternative, also rarely applied in practice, is cutting the problem-employee's pay. The pay cut usually has a demoralising effect on the employee, and is suggested as a rational action by management if the only other alternative is dismissal.

6. Dismissal

Management's ultimate disciplinary punishment is dismissing the problem employee. Dismissal should be used only for the most serious offences. Yet it may be the only feasible alternative when an employee's behaviour is so bad as to seriously interfere with a department's or the whole organisation's operation.

All organisations designate a series of offences which, for some reason or other, constitutes matters of serious or gross misconduct and for which suspension from work or dismissal may be applied. It is normally accepted that such offences constitute breaches of the law — vandalism, violence, theft and fraud. However, in certain cases, this may be extended to standards of behaviour on the part of the particular organisation — for example, failure to wear safety clothing on a building site may constitute a sufficient reason for dismissal, whereas this would not apply to other situations.

Conclusion

Dismissal should be conducted only when this appears to be the most suitable punishment for the offence (as in the case of breach of the law), or where all other means have been tried and failed and where 'not to do' would be a bad precedent. It is finally the responsibility of the manager to maintain records of all disciplinary measures conducted against staff members. Apart from the legal requirement, it enables the manager to follow up cases and to ensure that any agreed new standards of behaviour and performance are being followed.

CODE OF DISCIPLINE

The code of discipline — as spelt out in the Report of the National Commission on Labour, Ministry of Labour, Employment and Rehabilitation, Government of India — is as follows :

1. ***To maintain discipline in industry*** (both in public and private sectors) there has to be: (i) a just recognition by employees and workers of the rights and responsibilities of either party, as defined by the laws and agreements including bipartite and tripartite agreements arrived at all levels from time to time; and (ii) a proper and willing discharge by either party of its obligations consequent on such recognition.

The Central and State Governments, on their part, will arrange to examine and set right any shortcomings in the machinery they constitute for the administration of labour laws. To ensure better discipline in industry :

2. *Management and union(s) agree*

(i) that no unilateral action should be taken in connection with any industrial matter and that disputes should be settled at appropriate levels,

(ii) that the existing machinery for settlement of disputes should be utilised with the utmost expedition,

(iii) that there should be no strike or lockout without notice,

(iv) that affirming their faith in democratic principles, they bind themselves to settle all future differences, disputes and grievances by mutual negotiation, conciliation and voluntary arbitration,

(v) that neither party will have recourse to : (a) coercion; (b) intimidation; (c) victimisation, or go-slow,

(vi) they will promote constructive cooperation between their representatives at all levels and as between workers themselves and abide by the spirit of agreements mutually entered into.

(vii) that they will establish upon a mutually agreed basis, a grievance procedure which will ensure a speedy and full investigation leading to settlement.

(viii) that they will abide by various stages in the grievance procedure and take no arbitrary action which would bypass this procedure, and

(ix) that they will educate the management personnel and workers regarding their obligations to each other.

3. Management agree

(i) not to increase workloads unless agreed upon or settled otherwise,

(ii) not to support or encourage any unfair practice, such as: (a) interference with the right of employees to enrol or continue as union members; (b) discrimination, restraint or coercion against any employee because of recognised activity of trade unions; and (c) victimisation of any employee and abuse of authority in any form,

(iii) to take prompt action for: (a) settlement of grievances; and (b) implementation of settlement, awards, decisions,

(iv) to display in conspicuous places in the undertaking the provisions of this Code in local languages,

(v) to distinguish between actions justifying immediate discharge and those where discharge must be preceded by a warning, reprimand, suspension or some other form of disciplinary action and to arrange that all such disciplinary action are subjected to an appeal through normal grievance procedure,

(vi) to take appropriate disciplinary action against its officers and members in cases whose enquiries reveal that they were responsible for precipitative action by workers leading to indiscipline, and

(vii) to recognise the union in accordance with the criteria (evolved at the 16th session of the Indian Labour Conference held in May 1958).

4. Union(s) agree

(i) not to engage in any form of physical duress,

(ii) not to permit demonstrations which are not peaceful and not to permit rowdyism in demonstration,

(iii) that their members will not engage or cause other employees to engage in any union activity during working hours, unless as provided for by law, agreement or practice,

(iv) to discharge unfair labour practices, such as : (a) negligence of duty; (b) careless operation; (c) damage to property; (d) interference with or disturbance to normal work; and (e) insubordination,

(v) to take prompt action to implement awards, agreements, settlements and decisions,

(vi) to display in conspicuous places in the union offices the povisions of the Code in the local language(s), and

(vii) to express disapproval and to take appropriate action against office-bearers and members for indulging in action against the spirit of this Code.

Grievances

As with all human activity the operation of a business or other organisation is bound to produce grievances from time to time. These may be small and minor and easily settled on a personal level, or may be major resulting in strike action or threat of such action. Consequently, it is prudent to have some formal grievances procedure to settle these matters :

- Major disputes involving all or most of the work-force are normally dealt with at a senior level and may involve a trade union.
- Grievances involving one or a small number of workers are best dealt with internally and a formal procedure to deal with these should be established as it enables employers to deal with complaints quickly and fairly. An equitable grievance procedure well-known and accepted by the work-force demonstrates the employer's commitment to fair play and helps to ensure that similar problems are all dealt with on the same basis and that decisions will be consistent in like cases. It is recognised that grievances ignored or badly handled can lead to discontent which may spread beyond the staff involved.
- The exact procedures to be adopted will vary according to the size of the concern. In a small firm access by the complainant may be direct to a senior member of the company, whereas in a larger organisation there may be more than one level of management to go through if satisfaction is not forthcoming at the first level. In all cases, however, it is usual for the grievance to be taken up initially with the worker's immediate superior. Where there is a recognised union presence in an organisation it is very usual for the first step to be to the worker's shop steward. At all times, the employer must be seen to be trying to be fair.
- Unfortunately, some complaints lead to litigation and the absence of a formal grievances procedure, or the failure to adopt its provisions, may prejudice the employer's case, whereas the existence of such a procedure will demonstrate the employer's desire to be fair.

Synopsis for Learning

Q.1. What is discipline?

Ans. Discipline refers to a condition in the organisation wherein employees conduct themselves in accordance with the organisation's rules and standards of acceptable behaviour.

Q.2. What is disciplinary action?

Ans. Disciplinary action refers to any conditioning of future behaviour by the application of either rewards or penalties.

4.11 INDUSTRIAL RELATIONS

For larger industrial output, a cooperative effort between employers and workers is needed. If the relation between them are conflicting and strained, the community as a whole suffers. Hence the necessity of industrial peace. However, industrial conflict is a problem which is inherent in every industrial society. The factors which are responsible for industrial unrest and industrial conflict are diverse in nature. Industrial relations is a term used to refer to dealing with employees when they are represented by an employee association (union). Non-management employees have the legal right to organise and bargain collectively with management.

Definition

Essentially industrial relations is concerned with the relations between management and production workers and concentrates very largely upon the conditions of service, the working environment and wages. Industrial relations may be defined as the process of control over the employment relationship, the organisation of work and relations between employees and their employers.

The employment relationship is a social, economic and political relationship in which an employee provides manual and mental labour in exchange for rewards allocated by the employer. In organisations where employees are represented by a trade union the wage level is determined through the collective bargaining process. Thus, at the core of industrial relations is work, and managing the interactions between the representatives of trade unions and management is the most significant area of personnel management. Industrial relations should be seen as the system by which work place activities are regulated, the arrangement by which the owners, managers, and the staff of organisations come together to engage in productive activity. Part of this is to do with the setting of standards and promotion of consensus; it is also concerned with the management of conflict.

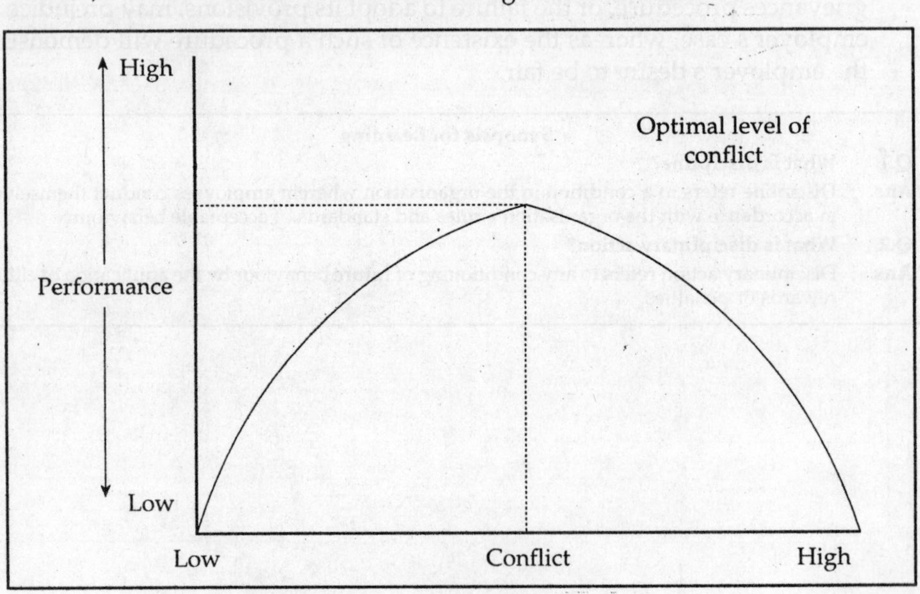

Fig. 4.10 : Organisational Conflict and Performance

Conflict

Organisational conflict might be defined as a disagreement between two or more individuals or groups. Such conflict results from disagreement between individual employees, work groups, or departments. Conflict also arises between labour and management. Conflict is bad because it connotes antagonism, hostility, unpleasantness and dissension. It is a problem which has to be avoided to improve organisational performance, as Fig. 4.10 shows.

Motivation

Employee motivation is a major concern of most managers. Motivation is an iterative process affecting the inner needs or drives that energise, channel, and maintain behaviour.

What is it that makes people do the things they do? Or, as many a manager has said after hearing about some action of a subordinate, "Now why would he do a thing like that?" The task of personnel managers is to find the secret of how to get all employees to be deeply committed to organisational goals and objectives and then pass this secret on to line managers.

Motivation is an internal driving force that results in the direction, intensity, and persistence of behaviour. It is obviously a result of the combination of a particular individual's characteristics and the situation in which the individual is placed.

The dynamic force that activates the individual is called motivation. According to Maslow's needs theory, motivation is simply the drive to reduce a tension caused by an unsatisfied need. Fig. 4.11 gives an illustration of this statement. If managers were able to satisfy all of an individual's needs, the individual would not be motivated to act. Fortunately, new needs keep on arising from time to time. The individual keeps developing higher-level and more complex needs as present needs become satisfied.

Underlying the specific on-the-job needs of people are their life-satisfaction needs. It is important to look at the totality of needs because :

1. Some workers find practically all of their life satisfactions off the job and work primarily to satisfy physical and economic needs.

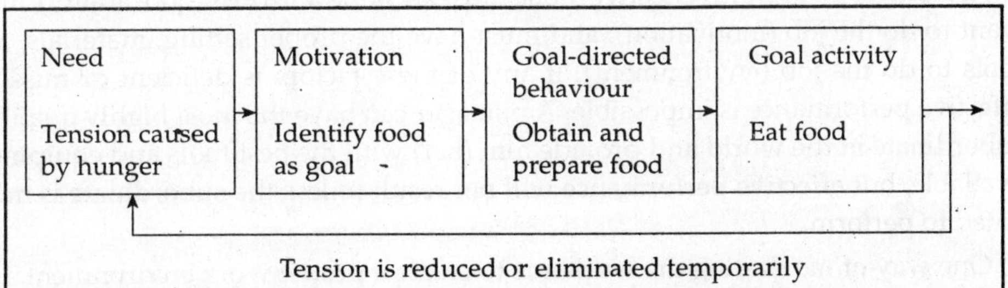

Fig. 4.11 : Motivation, according to Need Theory

2. Most workers derive part of their noneconomic life satisfactions on the job.
3. The more needs a worker has an opportunity to satisfy on the job, the more likely it is that the worker will be highly motivated to perform the job.

The motivation process begins with inner drives and needs that motivate (cause to move) the individual to work towards certain goal (see Fig.4.12) which the individual has chosen in the belief that they will satisfy inner drives and needs.

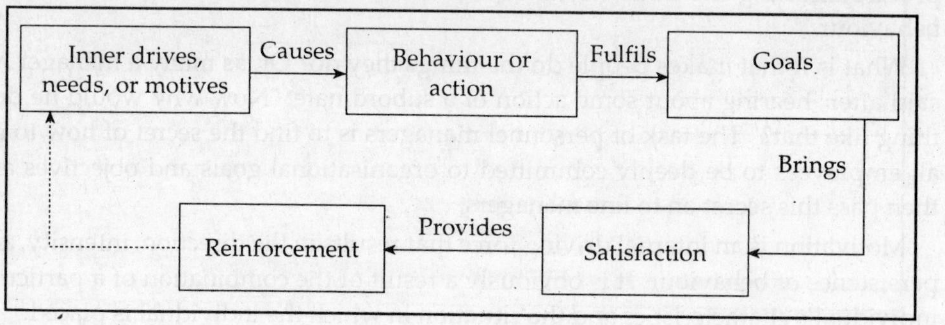

Fig. 4.12 : The Motivation Process

After attaining these needs the individual conciously or unconsciously judges whether the effort has been worthwhile. To the extent that the individual perceives the effort as rewarding, the behaviour of making the effort is reinforced and the individual will continue or repeat that kind of behaviour. Reinforcement, or what happens as a result of behaviour, affects other needs and drives as the process is repeated — hence its cyclical nature.

Employee motivation is of crucial concern to managers, mainly because of the role that such motivation plays in performance.

Basically, performance is determined by three things : ability, motivation, and environment. To perform effectively one must know how to do the job (ability), must want to do the job (motivation), and must have the proper setting, materials, and tools to do the job (environment). If any of these factors is deficient or missing, effective performance is impossible. A manager can have the most highly qualified subordinate in the world and provide him (her) with the best tools and equipment available, but effective performance will not result unless the subordinate is motivated to perform.

One way of motivating the worker is to create a proper work environment. It is possible to do this by improving the labour-management (industrial) relations. **So a sound industrial relations situation is an effective tool for personnel motivation and morale.**

The final element of the motivational process outlined in Fig. 4.13 concerns reinforcement. The main point here is that behaviour that results in rewarding consequences is likely to be repeated, whereas behaviour that results in punishing consequences is less likely to be repeated.

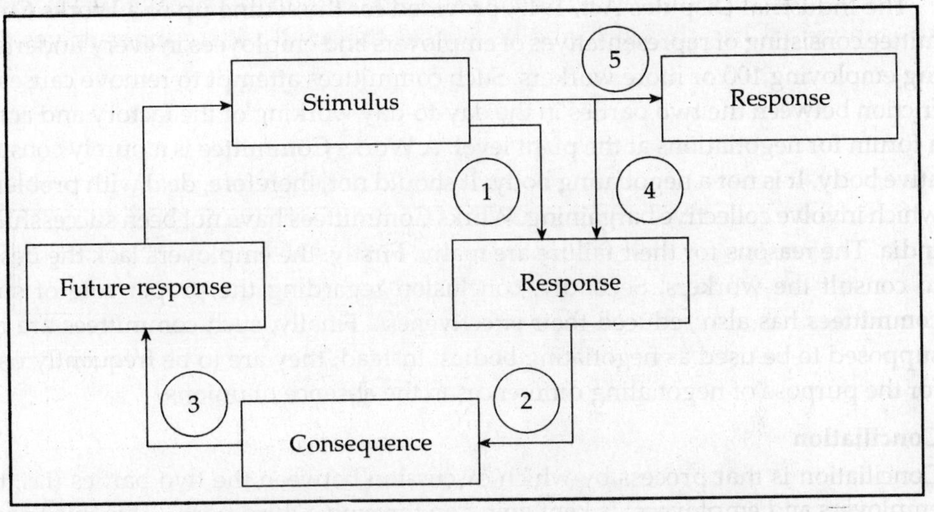

Fig. 4.13 : The Reinforcement Theory of Motivation

Fig. 4.13 shows the relation between work environment and motivation. The starting point is a stimulus (which can be thought of as the needs or motives that trigger behaviour). The individual follows path 1 to a response. As a result of this response, the individual experiences various consequences. The value of these consequences affect future responses, as shown in path 3. If the consequences were pleasant or desirable, the individual will probably choose the same response (path 4) the next time he (she) encounters the same stimulus. But if the orginal consequences were unpleasant or undersirable, a different response (path 5) is more likely.

Let us consider the case of an employee trying to get a pay rise. If he starts working harder and subsequently gets a raise, his behaviour has been reinforced. The next time he wants a raise, he is likely to try working harder again. On the other hand, if his additional effort did not result in a pay raise (due to the indifferent attitude or apathy of management), he is likely to be demoralised and try other types of behaviours (such as buttering up the boss or threatening to quit).

SETTLEMENT OF DISPUTES

There are two basic objectives of any industrial relations policy. These are: (i) prevention as well as peaceful settlement of disputes and (ii) promotion of good industrial relations via labour-management cooperation. Two types of arrangements are available in India to deal with industrial disputes. The first is the statutory arrangements and the second is voluntary arrangements. Statutory or legal arrangements are mainly covered by the Industrial Disputes Act, 1947. This type of machinery includes : (i) Works Committee, (ii) conciliation, (iii) arbitration and (iv) adjudication. We may now make a brief review of these arrangements.

Works Committee

The Industrial Disputes Act, 1947, provides a mechanism for the settlement of disputes and sets up the necessary infrastructure like Works Committee, Conciliation Officer, Conciliation Board, Court of Enquiry, Industrial Tribunal, etc.

The Industrial Disputes Act, 1947, provided for the setting up of a Works Committee consisting of representatives of employers and employees in every undertaking employing 100 or more workers. Such committees attempt to remove causes of friction between the two parties in the day-to-day working of the factory and act as a forum for negotiations at the plant level. A Works Committee is a purely consultative body. It is not a negotiating body. It should not, therefore, deal with problems which involve collective bargaining. Works Committees have not been successful in India. The reasons for their failure are many. Firstly, the employers lack the desire to consult the workers. Secondly, conclusion regarding the proper role of such committees has also reduced their effectiveness. Finally, such committees are not supposed to be used as negotiating bodies. Instead, they are to be frequently used for the purpose of negotiating differences in the absence of unions.

Conciliation

Conciliation is that process by which discussion between the two parties (*i.e.*, the employers and employees) is kept going on through a third party. This third party is known as the conciliator. Conciliation may be voluntary or compulsory.

The Industrial Disputes Act, 1947, has provided two authorities for settling disputes through conciliation : (i) Conciliation Officer and (ii) Conciliation Board. When a Works Committee fails to resolve a dispute, conciliation officers are appointed who mediate between the two parties concerned. The dispute is referred to the Conciliation Board when the Conciliation Officer's attempt to smooth out differences between the disputants fails. If a dispute still remains unsettled, the matter is referred to the Court of Enquiry. The Court is to investigate the whole dispute and submit its report to the Government.

Arbitration

Arbitration is that process in which a dispute is submitted to a third party who makes a decision and this decision is binding on both the parties. This third party is known as the arbitrator. However, this method has not found favour with the disputants.

Adjudication

The final stage in the settlement of disputes is adjudication. If attempts at conciliation and arbitration fail, the Government can refer the matter for adjudication which involves intervenetion in the dispute by a third party (*i.e.*, adjudicator) appointed by the Government. It is compulsory to refer a dispute for adjudication if the matter relates to some public utility service or if the disputants jointly or separately apply for adjudication. The Industrial Disputes Act, 1947, provides a three-tier adjudication machinery : (a) Labour Courts, (b) Industrial Tribunals and (c) National Tribunals. Labour Courts deal with minor disputes involving such issues as factory discipline, hours of work, transfer of workers, etc. The Industrial Tribunals adjudicate on more important matters like wages and bonus. National Tribunals are appointed for the most important types of disputes involving matters of nationwide importance and establishments in which several States are affected.

Voluntary Arrangements

In addition, there are voluntary arrangements for the settlement of disputes. These are Code of Discipline, Industrial Truce Resolution, Workers' Participation in Management, and so on.

A Code of Discipline was evolved at the Indian Labour Conference in 1958 and was accepted by all the central organisations of employers and employees which aimed at settling disputes on a voluntary basis. According to the Code of Discipline (i) strikes and lockouts cannot be declared without notice; (ii) no unilateral action can be taken by either party; (iii) no go-slow tactics can be followed; (iv) no resort to deliberate damange to plant or machinery or acts of violence, intimidation, coercion or instigation can be taken; and (v) the existing machinery should be utilised in case of disputes. The Code of Discipline has been accepted by all industries in the private sector. The Code is also applicable to public sector companies and corporations.

Industrial Truce Resolution

An Industrial Truce Resolution was adopted in 1962 following the national emergency proclaimed in the country in the wake of the Chinese aggression. It laid down that there should be neither interruption not slowing down of production. The Code of Discipline and the Truce Resolution, being voluntary arrangements, emphasise settlement of disputes through voluntary arbitration.

Worker's Participation in Management

The idea of workers' participation in management was first mooted during the Second Plan. The scheme was first introduced in 1975 on a selective basis at the shop-floor and the plant levels and was applied to units employing 30 or more persons. Another scheme was announced in 1977 in commercial and service organisations in the public sector employing at least 100 persons.

Synopsis for Learning

Q.1. What is meant by industrial relations?

Ans. Industrial relations may be defined as the process of control over the employer–employee relationship, the organisation of work and relations between workers and managers (supervisors).

Q.2. What is the importance of a sound industrial relations situation?

Ans. A sound industrial relation situation goes a long way in motivating the workers and raising labour productivity which reduces cost and enables a company to gain and sustain competitive advantage.

4.12 TRADE UNIONS

A trade union is an organiation of workers, acting collectively, seeking to promote and protect its mutual interests through collective bargaining. It is formed to further the social and economic interest of its members. Since more and more industries in India and other countries are gradually becoming unionised, unions have a major effect on some of the important sectors of the economy.

A trade union is an association of workers formed for the purpose of protecting the rights of the workers and improving their economic conditions. It can be defined as permanent organisation which tries to (i) improve economic conditions of labour, (ii) promote labour welfare, and (iii) protect the interest of workers by other means. Trade unions try to protect labourers' interest and promote labour welfare in various ways.

In this sense, trade unions are formed to overcome weakness of labour, viz., weak bargaining power of an individual worker, impossibility of storing labour power for obtaining better price (*i.e.*, securing higher wages), and excess supply of labour (or existence of surplus labour) which makes it possible for the employer to exploit workers with ease. Thus a trade union is a "voluntary organisation of workers formed to promote and protect their interests by collective action."

Nowadays, the terms and conditions of work of the labourers are settled by negotiation between an employer or an employer's organisation with the trade union. Such negotiation is called collective bargaining. Through collective bargaining, workers can secure higher wages and improved working conditions. In this sense, a trade union can be defined as the collective body of workers bargaining for (i) proper wages and (ii) proper work-load.

Trade unions are a collection of workers seeking to protect and promote their members' interest. Their goals basically revolve around three themes : to influence the wage and benefits offered; to influence the administration of rules; and to establish a security system for its members.

Trade unions have now spread to all places and activities. It not only concerns workers in production, also office workers, computer staff and even supervisors and managers. This is especially the case in local and central government and in the publicly owned industries.

Trade unions have both advantages and disadvantages.

Advantages

(a) Time is saved in pay negotiations when dealing with a union as compared to dealing with individuals. This is particularly relevant in respect of supervisors and managers where it helps to promote equitable schemes of remuneration and to avoid inequalities and possible consequent resentment.

(b) Where there is mutual respect — that is, where morale is good — employees can more easily be given a picture of the organisation's problems and thus obtain a better understanding of them through meetings with shop stewards and local union officials. Improved industrial relations should thus result.

(c) Workers feel the strength of association and thus are able to have, through union representatives, constructive discussions on procedures relating to working practices, disciplinary measures and the like. Where relations are good, worker dissidents are often contained by the majority of workers.

(d) Co-operation with trade unions may help an organisation to meet more easily the obligations placed on employers by government regulations and statutes.

(e) Changes in working practices and necessary redeployment of workers can be more easily effected if implemented with union co-operation. Where redundancies are inevitable union co-operation can be particularly helpful in obtaining fair compensation for those affected.

(f) Joint consultation is made possible and easy.

Disadvantages

(a) **Delay**. Managerial decisions may be delayed because of the lengthy discussions necessary at plant and local union level for these decisions to be implemented. Effective joint consultation can help minimise this.

(b) **Perspective practices**. A powerful union, particularly where there is a closed shop (where all workers are required to be union members), can perpetuate and intensify restrictive practices unnecessarily. An example would be the insistence on a qualified electrician to change the plug on a simple machine such as an electric typewriter. This puts up costs and causes delays which create further costs.

(c) **Disputes.** Where more than one union operates on a site delays and disruptions may be caused by inter-union disputes.

(d) **Unreasonable demands.** Unreasonable demands may be made on management or extra pressure created if a union is powerful, to the ultimate detriment of the organisation and even the industry.

There is no doubt that trade unions can contribute positively in all areas where they operate, provided their power is used properly and with discretion.

Role of Trade Unions in India's Socio-economic System

One of the major defects of India's trade unions is that their members are more concerned with their rights than with their duties. But rights and duties go hand in hand. As present, most trade unions confine their attention to the various demands of working class such as high wage, paid holidays, annual payment (income) in the form of bonus, and so on. There is no doubt that trade unions are formed with the primary objective of protecting and advancing the interest of its members by negotiating wage rates and conditions of employment (number of hours worked, grounds for dismissal, etc.). As such, unions exert considerable influence on the wage rates, supply of labour and costs of production in individual industries.

In India, workers do not always discharge their responsibilities fully. They do not always put the maximum effort for the benefit of the organisation and for their own benefit also. They follow "go-slow" tactics. As a result, labour cost rises, or labour productivity falls. Consequently, entrepreneurs find it profitable to substitute labour by capital. Thus, the negative attitude of union members adversely affects the prospect of employment creation in a labour surplus country like India.

At present, trade unions confine their attention to the workers demand only. Indian trade unions are more or less like strike committees. It is high time they developed among the workers a sense of discipline and responsibility to do a full day's work for a fair day's wages. The unions should make every worker understand fully his duties and responsibilities first and then his rights and privileges.

Moreover, trade unions should provide certain benefits to the workers such as compensation for accidents, medical aid, education, practical suggestions, thrift and temperance, etc.

Trends in Trade Union Movement

Unions are becoming increasingly matured, responsive and realistic in their thinking and actions. Gone are the days of cat-call strikes, bundhs, gheraos and violence.

Discussion among trade union circles nowadays relate to such issues as the productivity, total quality management, technology, competition, MNCs, exports and the like. Major unions of the telecom employees, for example are on-line with the corporatisation plans of the department. They are now more concerned about such things as gearing up for competition and inculcating a customer-friendly approach.

Unions have accepted that there is surplus labour everywhere and the fat needs to be shed. Unions are, therefore, extending co-operation to schemes like voluntary retirement and golden handshake. Thirtyfive thousand workers of National Textile Corporation alone have retired voluntarily.

Another trend witnessed these days is depolitisation of Unions. It may be noted that the federations of the unions are affilitated to one political party or the other. It may also be noted that the prominent national leaders in the post-independent India were popular trade union leaders. Being affilitated to one political party or the other, the unions were following the footsteps of their big bosses instead of protecting the workers' interests. Unions have realised the futility of such affiliations and are now separating themselves from political influence.

Unions are now formed on the basis of religion and caste. This is indicative of the socio-political realities. Workers' associations in our country are highly fragmented and the consequences has been the multiplicity of unions caused by such factors as ideological rifts, personal ambitions of leaders, craft divisions among workers, and the management's own myopia.

Multiplicity of unions weakens the bargaining strength of employees. Management's position is no better. Union leaders too are conscious about the need for single union plans. Of late, unions have presented a common front on issues like industrial sickness and the National Renewal Fund. Unions, of late, are demanding better utilisation of the fund and felt that the amount should not be used merely for financing voluntary retirement schemes.

One of the effects of trade union movement in our country has been the phenomenon of outsider leadership. Individuals who were not connected with a factory would assume leadership of the union. The clout of the central trade unions, which peaked during the post-nationalisation years, is gradually appearing. One of the reasons for this trend is the gradual realisation on the part of the workers, who are young and well-educated, that independent unions are more advantageous than being affiliated to all-India federations.

Thus, the trade unions are at cross-roads. Their membership is declining, their political support is waning, public sympathy is receding, and their relevance itself is at stake. Management is, on the other hand, on the offensive. They are able to force unions to accept terms and conditions and sign on the dotted lines.

Unions should inculcate innovative leads to regain their lost ground. One possible way is to extent unionism to non-traditional groups such as white collar and professional workers. Another way is to give up their obsession with strike and start serving the members in a better way.

Conclusion

In a mature industrial society, responsible trade unionism results from the collective action of industry, government and politics. As these groups are part of society, the change in the quality of trade unionism is a direct reflection of the prevailing social attitudes.

In the Indian context, neither trade unions nor industry have shown the willingness to play a responsible role. Since the advent of liberalisation constantly crying for an exit policy which would permit the industry to size manpower needs consistent with the market and with technology demands on the business. Governments have been talking about increasing employment and labour has been demanding a rise in wages, independent of the realities of business conditions. Given these disparate needs, how can there be responsible trade union activity ?

No doubt, trade unions in India have a bright future, provided some of the above suggestions are put into effect. It is high time the trade unions were developed on healthy lines.

It is widely believed that trade unions should develop among workers a sense of involvement and belonging so as to raise the labour productivity. It is the duty of unions to make every worker understand fully his duties and responsibilities first and his rights and privileges thereafter. By doing this, it is possible to establish a progressive nation, as has been done in Japan. There is no doubt that fair treatment to workers require the establishment of industrial democracy which calls for discipline on the one side and sincere and efficient work on the other. Industrial democracy can become a reality if there is the participation of the workers in the corporate decision-making process along with management.

If trade unions impose more discipline on workers, labour productivity will rise. So the employer will voluntarily accept the demand for higher wages. In fact, the fruits of higher productivity can be shared with the workers also.

Synopsis for Learning

Q.1. What is a trade union ?

Ans. Trade unions are the organisations of workers formed to promote and protect the interests of workers through collective action. The protection and fostering of the interests of employees in all matters relating to their employment forms the primary purpose of trade unions. Pay is the item which appears most prominently in their activities, but hours and conditions of work are also important subjects with which they deal, including safety and welfare at work and management methods of enforcing discipline.

Q.2. What are its functions?

Ans. Trade unions exist mainly to promote the interests of their members. The following points may be noted in this context : (i) *Improving pay* : Trade unions negotiate wages, piece rates, bonuses, etc.; (ii) *Improving working conditions* : Trade unions negotiate holidays and improvements in the physical environment at work; (iii) *Safeguarding jobs* : Trade unions become involved in discussions about unemployment or loss of jobs and personal grievances. Trade unions aim to achieve full employment; and (iv) *Offering monetary benefits* : Such as sickness and accident benefit, unemployment pay, strike pay and pensions. Many of these benefits have become less important with the development of the social security and state-administered welfare payments.

4.13 COLLECTIVE BARGAINING

Collective bargaining refers to negotiations between employees and employers about the establishment of procedures and rules to cover conditions of work and rates of pay. It has been formally defined as an institutional system of negotiation in which the making, interpretation and administration of rules, and the application of statutory controls affecting employer-employee relationship are decided within union-management negotiating committees. Such arrangements usually involve the joint regulation of agreed procedures.

In a broad sense, the term collective bargaining typically refers to the negotiation, administration and interpretation of a written agreement between two parties that covers a specific period of time. This agreement or contract lays out, in specific terms, the conditions of employment, that is, what is expected of employees and what limits there are in management's authority.

Collective bargaining is the process by which agreements between employers and employees, or their respective representatives, are made. Such agreements may be at national, regional, local, sectoral, or plant and unit level. This may involve very senior and highly trained personnel at sectoral or national levels, and elected representatives at the other extreme.

Two separate strands can be identified — the substantive, or what is to be negotiated; and the procedural, how it is to be done, and how procedures and other regulatory instruments are to be used.

Objective and Scope

Within this context, collective bargaining systems have three specific objectives :

1. To provide the means for agreeing the price of labour, i.e., the wage rate.
2. To provide a means of industrial government and workplace rules and regulations.
3. To provide a means for controlling the stresses and strains inherent in the work place.

The basic objective of collective bargaining is to agree upon an acceptable contract — acceptable to management, union representatives, and the union membership.

But what is covered in this contract?

The intent of collective bargaining is to write and agree on a labour contract between management and union that is satisfying to both parties. The contract contains agreements about wages, hours and other conditions of employment, including promotion, lay-off, discipline, benefits, methods of allocating overtime, vacations, rest periods, and the grievance procedure.

The union will want to have a 'union security clause' that helps ensure the union's continued existence by requiring new employees to join the union or contribute to its support or requiring present members to remain members.

Management will want to include a 'management rights clause' in the contract which says that management retains the right to make unilateral decisions in all areas except those specified in the contract. A 'no strike clause' is usually included, stating that the union will not strike during the term of the contract (usually three years). The union is still free to strike before the contract is approved or after it expires if a new one has not been agreed on.

The Basic Process

The process of collective bargaining is based on mistrust and conflict — that is, that there is a fundamental divergence of interest between employers and employees. At stake, initially, therefore, is a basis on which the two can agree to cooperate together at all. This is made more difficult or extreme where there exists a long history and tradition of workplace conflict. Collective bargaining is a strategy and structure for the management of this conflict.

Much of the process is, therefore, stylised and ritualised, and anyone who wishes to operate it effectively must understand the importance of this. The purpose must be to use the instruments and the language involved to gain workplace agreements that at least remove inherent conflicts.

The process of bargaining may go on for weeks or months, with management and representatives of the union to make proposals and counter-proposals. The resulting agreement must be ratified by the union membership. If it is not approved, the union may strike to put pressure on management, or it may choose not to strike and simply continue negotiating until a more acceptable agreement is reached.

The final agreement will reflect the problems of the particular work place and industry in which the contract is negotiated. Detailed procedures relating to control over hiring are central to collective barganining in industries with casual employment, where employees shift continually from one employer to another, as in construction. But in factory and office employment, new hiring typically is left to the decision of management.

The basic framework (optional)

There is a broad bargaining framework to as illustrated in Fig.4.14 :

Fig. 4.14 : The collective bargaining process

1. The first offer or claim is always made on the basis that it will be rejected (if for any reason it is accepted straight away, it generally causes resentment rather than instant satisfaction).
2. There then follows a process of counter-offer and counter-claim, with each party working its way gradually towards the other.
3. The content of the final agreement is usually clearly signalled before it is made; and the basis of what is genuinely acceptable to each party is signalled also.
4. Serious disputes occur either when one side is determined not to settle or when there is misunderstanding between the trade union members and the employer.
5. Settlements reached are normally stated in positive terms in relation to all concerned, to avoid the use of words such as 'loss', 'loser', 'climb-down' and 'defeat', which have negative meaning for those associated with them.

The following standpoints in the bargaining process may be usefully identified :

1. It may be necessary to settle with one group or part of the workforce, at the expense of others.
2. It may be possible to resolve problems to the satisfaction of all concerned.
3. It may not be possible to satisfy everyone.
4. It may be necessary to take a hard initial stance to try and persuade the other party to revise its expectations.

Part of the function of the process is also to structure the attitudes of each party towards the other, and to try and build impressions of honesty, trust, openness, firmness, reasonableness and fairness, as necessary. A fundamental credibility must also be established.

Four Common Issues

Irrespective of the specific issues contained in various contracts, four issues appear consistently throughout all labour contracts. Three of the four are mandatory bargaining issues which means that management must be willing to negotiate with the union. These mandatory issues are (1) wages, (2) hours, and (3) terms and conditions of employment. The fourth issue covered in almost all labour contracts is the grievance procedure, which is designed to permit the adjudication of complaints. The grievance procedure is the means by which the contract is enforced. Most of what is in a contract concerns how management will treat employees. So when employees feel that they have not been treated fairly under the contract, they file a grievance to correct the problem[1].

Resolution Methods

Despite the variety of techniques available, unions and management cannot always reach an agreement. Nevertheless, it is still in the best interests of both sides to resolve differences harmoniously. Resolution methods are approaches used to overcome

1. For instance, if the contract says that the most senior person will be given the first chance to work overtime, but a supervisor offers the overtime to a less senior employee first, the more senior employee can file a frievance.

union-management disagreements. The two most commonly used methods of resolving these disputes are mediation and arbitration.

1. Mediation

When the parties use mediation, a neutral third party helps both sides reach a settlement. A mediator has no formal authority to order either side to do anything, but instead recommends solutions in an effort to bring the parties together. Most mediators try to reduce the problems by first instructing both sides to identify their differences. Then each side is required to focus on these actual differences and make counter-proposals for dealing with the demands of the other side. Each party is encouraged to accept reasonable accommodations by the other and to compromise. This no-nonsense approach that emphasises compromise often resolves the dispute to the satisfaction of both parties.

2. Arbitration

In some cases, a neutral third party listens to both sides and then directs each side in what to do. This process is called arbitration. Under binding arbitration, both parties agree to follow the decision of the third party (the arbitrator). Under final-offer arbitration, both sides make their final offers, and the arbitrator chooses one. Arbitration has a number of benefits: (i) it may save time and money; and (ii) the parties in the dispute do not have to resort to drastic actions, and both can save face. The resolution is rendered by an impartial, qualified third party. So it is as fair as possible for both union and management.

Conclusion

The proper approach to bargaining should focus not on the relationship between the parties, but rather on the strategy of the bargaining. And one can identify the most common bargaining pattern as distributive bargaining, which assumes that management and labour have conflicting goals and are trying to get a bigger piece of a given pie. Another pattern is integrative bargaining, in which the goals of labour and management are not seen as conflicting and, as a result, both parties try to develop mutually acceptable solutions to problem areas. The intergrative approach may involve the use of special committees for joint research and fact-finding to solve difficult problems. Examples of this integrative bargaining have included changes in pensions and benefit plans, union action to control wild-cat strikes, and improvements in the grievance procedure. Both management and the union stand to gain if these issues are mutually resolved.

Synopsis for Learning

Q.1. What is collective bargaining?

Ans. Collective bargaining is a process in which management and employees, represented by the union of their choice, negotiate over the wages, bonus, and conditions of employment. Collective bargaining often involves tough negotiations between unions and management, and it often takes place when there is hostility on both sides. But there is also much more to collective bargaining. There are many basic issues that need to be resolved and many different bargaining strategies and techniques.

Q.2. What are the common approaches to bargaining?

Ans. Two major bargaining approaches are commonly used: distributive and intregative. Distributive bargaining occurs when a gain to one side is a loss to the other. Another common bargaining approach is integrative bargaining, in which both sides work together to solve a mutual problem. An example is below-industry-average productivity.

4.14 LABOUR WELFARE

Labour welfare is one of the most important aspects of industrial relations. Welfare is a convenient term to cover all those aspects of industrial life which contribute to the well-being of the worker. Concern for the human side of industry is one of the fundamentals of a sound personnel policy. In fact, it is an extra dimension of industrial relations inasmuch as it gives satisfaction to the worker that even a fair wage cannot provide (generate). This is why in advanced countries like the USA, the U.K., Japan etc. the State provides a national health service which makes medical care and attention available to all workers, irrespective of the inability to pay. National insurace schemes provide unemployment pay, sickness benefits, and supplementary benefits which are designed to see that misfortune does not deprive workers of some minimum level of income. These labour welfare services are based upon current ideas of social justice. They help to maintain the health and morale of the people, and thus make a positive contribution to the efficiency of the labour force.

Many larger farms also provide welfare services for their employees. Play-grounds, social and recreational facilities, subsidised food (through workers' can-teens) and factory medical services are some common features of the larger industrial and commercial enterprises. Such provisions conjointly contribute to-wards a happier, healthier and, hence, more efficient labour force.

Importance

With the spread of industrialisation and mechanisation, labour welfare has assumed considerable significance in recent years, not only in advanced countries, but also in emerging developing countries like our own. As Arun Manappa has rightly com-mented : "The worker, both in industry and agriculture, cannot cope with the pace of modern life with minimum sustenance amenities. He needs an added stimulus to keep body and soul together. Employees have also realised the importance of their role in providing these extra amentities." Labour welfare has proved its worth in a modern industrial society. It has contributed to efficiency in production.

In India, labour welfare has been generally accepted by employees. The role of the State is just to widen its area of applicability through selective intervention as demanded by the situation. In our socialist pattern of society labour welfare is now accepted as a social right of the average worker.

The Committee on Labour Welfare (CLW), appointed in 1969 to review the whole scheme of employee welfare in India, equated labour welfare with social security measures that contribute to improving working conditions in Indian factories. K. N. Vaid has treated it as "an expression of the assumption by industries of its respon-sibility for its employees." Such responsibilities relate to improving their conditions of work.

The International Labour Organisation (ILO) defined labour welfare as "such services, facilities and amenities as adequate canteens, rest and recreation facilities, arrangements for travel to and from work, and for the accommodation of workers employed at a distance from their houses, and such other services amenities and facilities as contribute to improve the conditions, under which workers are em-ployed."

Purposes

A labour welfare programme serves various purposes. Finally, by taking care of life's basic amenities it builds a sense of loyalty on the part of the employee towards the organisation. Secondly, by providing quicker services from the employees. Thirdly, various labour welfare measures, by welfare activities to workers an organisation gains through improved or taking care of the basic needs of life, make the worker devote his time and attention to the organisation's task." This, in its turn, enhances his efficiency and output. As Manappa has rightly commented : "As attractive package, which provides benefits throughout the course of an employee's career, serves to attract and retain the better workers and simultaneously enhance their morale." The organisation also gains financially by enjoying certain tax concessions offered for spending money on employee welfare.

Various Welfare Measures

International Labour Organisation has divided labour welfare measures in two broad categories, viz., intra-mural and extra-mural. While the former is important for providing a health, work environment, the latter is important for motivating, the worker and providing them social security. The major components of these two facts of labour welfare are listed in Table 4.4.

These facilities and benefits can be further classified into those provided by legislation and those provided voluntarily by management or as a result of bipartite settlements between management and the trade unions.

Table 4.4 : Employer Labour Welfare Amenities

Intra-mural	Extra-mural
Drinking water Toilets Creche Washing facilities Occupational safety Uniforms and protective clothing Shift allowance Canteen	Social insurance (gratuity, pension, PF, etc.) Benevolent fund Maternity benefits Health and medical facilities Family planning Education facilities Recreation facilities Leave travel facilities Workers' cooperatives Vocational training Transport to and from place of work

Classification of Labour Welfare

Labour welfare may be broadly classified into three categories : (i) Statutory, (ii) Voluntary, and (iii) Mutual. These may now be discussed in detail.

Statutory Welfare amenities

Those are to be provided irrespective of size of establishment, *e.g.*, drinking water. Again, in the case of certain amenities, there are no minimum standards laid down as in the sphere of housing, medical treatment, recreation, transport and educational facilities. This is left to the discretion of the employer.

IMPORTANCE OF LABOUR WELFARE

The importance of a comprehensive labour welfare package can hardly be over-emphasisd. Here we seek to focus on the relative importance of ten major components of the package.

1. Health and Medical Facilities

A healthy work force is of strategic importance to a modern organisation. Good health promotes efficiency; ill-health (due to malnutrition and adverse working conditions created by poor lighting, ventilation, etc.) retards it.

2. Family Planning

CLW had recommended that family planning should be made a part and parcel of labour welfare activities. This is of considerable importance for improving the living standards of workers.

3. Canteens

The importance of canteens, run on a co-operative basis, lies in the fact that these meet the nutritional requirements of workers at a subsidised rate. Canteens are also important for providing balanced diet to workers. To enable workers to make good use of this facility credit purchases are also to be allowed.

4. Creches

Under the **Factories Act** (1948), there is legal obligation of any factory employing more than 50 women workers, to provide a creche for maintaining their children under 6 years in a clean and sanitary condition. This will enable the women workers to feel safe and give more attention to their work.

5. Housing

The Government of India also realised the importance of providing housing facilities and improving housing conditions of industrial workers. The housing scheme, if implemented, will go a long way in keeping the workers healthy, and thus motivate the workers. A motivated work force will surely make a greater contribution to an organisation's output than a demoralised group of workers.

6. Recreational Facilities

It is also necessary to provide recreational facilities to workers for keeping them fit and healthy. 'Man does not live by bread alone', like most proverbs, contains a vital element of truth.

7. Transport facilities

Transport problems and hazards make workers tired and less productive. In other words, the fatigue of travel to and from work place has an adverse effect on the attendance pattern of workers. By providing transport facilities, employees can make workers more productive.

8. Allied Welfare Measures : Co-operatives and Saving Facilities

Certain allied welfare facilities may also be provided to workers in the form of cooperatives and saving facilities. While commenting on the importance of these facilities, Manappa writes : "Cooperative consumer stores are important to industrial workers because they are the only way in which workers can try and safeguard, to some extent, the real purchasing power of their money and prevent the erosion of their wages. The cooperative credit movement also helps the worker to save for unforeseen domestic crises."

For these reasons it is felt that the Government should make it compulsory for employers to introduce consumer cooperative activities in their labour welfare programmes.

9. Educational Facilities

Educational facilities for the industrial worker is also of considerable importance simply because an educated worker can cope with technological and other changes easily and quickly. The educated worker is more receptive to new processes (methods of production). An educated labour force which has the benefit of a sound technical training is more effective than one which lacks these benefits. Modern industrial techniques require highly skilled scientists, engineers, economists, accountants, managers, administrators and so on. Training can be provided by the industry itself. Moreover, educating the worker's family, especially his children, is equally important because it is essentially an investment in training the work-force of the future.

However, the sad truth is that no serious effort has been made in India to eradicate illiteracy among workers. And it is a pity that there is hardly any statutory obligation with regard to education for workers' children in any industry except the plantations. In this context one may suggest that "the provision of educational facilities either by the State or the employer, or jointly will help a great deal in improving the worker's commitment" and develop in him (or her) a sense of involvement, belonging and an urge for achievement.

10. Distress Relief and Cash Benefits

Various non-statutory welfare amenities are provided nowadays to industrial workers in India. One such benefit is an ex-gratia payment called Distress Relief and Cash Benefit paid in case of death, injury, sickness, marriage, or as a felicitation grant. It is a kind of gift made by the employer to his worker. Many industrial undertakings and establishments also provide advances at the time of festival. Distress relief is of considerable importance to workers because it helps workers to cope with sudden calamities.

Conclusion

No doubt monetary reward is more closely related to effort than anything else and can be widely used as a means of stimulating output. Thus, the Factories Act covers in detail such matters as safety, washing facilities, first aid, cleanliness, sanitation, drinking water; and in the larger units, canteens, rest rooms, and creches for children of working women. There can be no doubt of the employer's liability in these matters. Unfortunate compliance with the provisions about the Act still leaves much to be desired. Factory inspectorates are understaffed and unable to cope with their ever-expanding territory. Therefore, the first task of the personnel officer must be to see that the Act is implemented in the true sense. The approach should be not merely to comply with the law, but favourable working conditions as indicated by the law. The ultimate objective of providing monetary and non-monetary rewards to workers is to improve the quality of work life, a concept which has become very popular in the last few years.

Synopsis for Learning

Q.1. **What is labour welfare?**

Ans. The term labour welfare covers all those aspects of industrial life which contribute to the well-being of the worker.

Q.2. **What is its importance?**

Ans. It contributes considerably to efficiency in production.

4.15 QUALITY OF WORK LIFE (optional)

There are two ways of looking at what *quality of work life* means. One way equates with a set of objective organisational conditions and practices (*e.g.*, promotion-from-within policies, democratic supervision, employee involvement, safe working conditions). The other way equates Quality of Work Life with employees' perceptions that they are safe, relatively well satisfied, and able to grow and develop as human beings. This way relates Quality of Work Life to the degree to which the full range of human needs is met.

In many cases these two views merge: workers who like their organisations and the ways their jobs are structured will feel that their work fulfills them. In such cases, either way of looking at one's quality of work life will lead to a common determination of whether a good Quality of Work Life exists. In general Quality of Work Life is defined in terms of employees' perceptions of their physical and mental well-being at work.

In theory, Quality of Work Life is simple — it involves giving workers the opportunity to make decisions about their jobs, the design of their workplaces, and what they need to make products or to deliver services most effectively. It requires managers to treat workers with dignity on the job. Its focus is on employees and management operating the business together.

In practice, Quality of Work Life requires a willingness to share power, extensive training for workers and managers, and considerable patience by all involved. Workers must get to know the basics of cost, quality, profits, losses, and customer satisfaction by being exposed to more than a narrowly defined job. Managers must come to understand their new role: leaders, helpers, and information gatherers.

To make Quality of Work Life effective an essential managers have to do the following five things:

1. Managers must become leaders and coaches, not bosses and dictators.
2. Openness and trust are necessary. Quality of Work Life cannot be used as a tool to break unions or keep them out. It must remain separate from the collective bargaining contract. And it cannot be used by unions as a tool against management.
3. Information typically held by management alone must be shared, and suggestions made by non-managers must be taken seriously.
4. Quality of Work Life must change continually and go forward from initial problem solving to an actual partnership between management and workers.
5. Quality of Work Life cannot be mandated unilaterally by management.

The common denominator of Quality of Work Life experiments is joint worker-management participation for the purpose of identifying problems and opportunities in the work environment, making decisions, and implementing changes. Critics say that participation will not work over time because it requires managers to give up too much power. On the other hand, advocates argue that we are just beginning to understand what is required in order to bring about large-scale social change in organisations.

4.16 WORKERS' PARTICIPATION IN MANAGEMENT

Worker participation in the organisation — particularly in the sphere of decision-making — involves workers in the actual process of decision-making, though the latter in an advisory capacity only.

However, neither method involves workers financially, but a third proposition does, that of co-ownership. In its purest form it proposes that workers becomes actual shareholders in their companies, thus participating in the distribution of profits and having the power to vote at annual general meetings. The actual acquisition of shares by the workers poses a problem, especially as they can, if they work for a public company, purchase them through the stock market if they really desire to become co-owners.

- Two solutions have been successfully applied in practice. The first is to offer share to workers at attractive prices and the second to award shares at bonus payments. The opportunity to share in the profits of their company is considered to encourage loyalty and a co-operative attitude in the workers and to provide a positive incentive for greater productivity.
- Although it is assumed that shares will have voting rights, some managements may view this with apprehension and, in some cases, shares issued to employees have no voting rights so that control remains firmly in the hands of the existing shareholders and management. In such cases it is considered that the fact of profit-sharing is sufficient participation and incentive.

Of growing importance in the matter of industrial relations is the subject of worker participation in the organisation. Workers' participation in management is an application of the concept of democracy at the work place.

There are various methods of workers' participation in management, in terms of forms, levels and content, extending from self-management in Yugoslavia, codetermination in Germany, collective bargaining in the Anglo-American countries to joint management councils and works committees in India.

Participation is not merely to protect and further workers' interests but is also a system of checks and balances on both the groups, viz., employers and employees. And it thus requires a great sense of responsibility and educated awareness to cope with the several aspects of the participative system.

The term "participation" is a broad one, for it includes at least five types of participative methods:

1. Employee problem-solving groups
2. Union-management cooperative projects
3. Participative work design
4. Gain sharing, profit sharing, and Scanlon plans (these are methods for sharing profits with employees according to some formula)
5. Worker ownership or employee stock ownership.

Do these methods work?

In our next section we will answer this question.

Does Participation Work?

Although it is still premature to state which approaches are definitely effective and which are not, it is possible to find certain clear trends. Some of these are :

1. Worker participation programmes that are tied directly to financial incentives for employees tend to result in productivity increases for the organisation.
2. Participation programme are generally perceived positively by those who directly participate but negatively by workers who do not.
3. Participative strategies that alter the job itself tend to have a lasting impact on attitudes and productivity if the new job involves substantial increases in responsibility and autonomy. Worker participation in problem-solving that does not alter the job itself, or job rotational schemes that do not add responsibility and challenge, tend to motivate employees only over a short term.
4. Worker participation programmes die out eventually if the organisation does not change in a manager consistent with the democratic values and behaviours of the participation programmes.
   Here are some of the ways to kill worker participation:
   (i) Middle and upper management cease responding to workers' suggestions after the initial enthusiasm, if there was any, is over.
   (ii) The pay system fails to acknowledge the new activities and contributions of workers.
   (iii) Supervisors resent the increased attention to workers and undermine the programme by not cooperating with the groups.
   (iv) Participating workers develop distorted perceptions of their own promotability and value to the company, and they become disillusioned when they do not advance.
   (v) Many organisations embody a hierarchical, departmentalised structure, a set of management assumptions, and a set of norms that discourage employees from taking initiative, accepting responsibility, and cooperating with one another. The unlearning of these assumptions and norms requires a conscious attempt to alter the culture of the organisation, something that organisations are systematically setting out to do.
5. Many participative programmes underestimate the amount of training and learning necessary to support worker involvement. Workers need exposure to problem solving, group processes, and business concepts. Managers need training in the listening and feedback skills necessary to work with groups of workers who are taking responsibility for decision-making. Both workers and managers need to learn the basic interpersonal skills necessary to treat others with dignity and respect. Participation as an effort to improve Quality of Work Life requires that managers treat lower-level employees as mature individuals, for participation implies a redistribution of power within the organisation.
6. Workers sometimes reject the participation programme. Often this reaction reflects the official position of a union, which sees a threat to its long-term

strength in dealing with management. Union and non-union employees often perceive participation programmes as management manipulation in which workers are expected to contribute something for nothing. Managers frequently perceive a participation programme as something they are are doing "for" the workers. Workers detect this attitude and judge it to be patronizing at best, deceptive at worst.

7. There are interactions among different forms of participation. Thus it appears that informal participation works best when other formal mechanisms for participation already exist.
8. Performance or productivity effectiveness is associated with participation that is direct (as opposed to indirect through representatives) and long-term.

WORKERS' PARTICIPATION IN INDIA

Workers' participation in management is supposed to "usher in an era of industrial democracy" which is a pre-condition for setting up a socialist pattern of society in India. As S. C. Kuchhal has commented, industrial democracy is supposed to "yield increases in 'output per man-hour', to resolve 'inter-group tensions', to give 'work-satisfaction', and lead to 'good communication'." It makes workers feel that they have a better understanding of the industrial processes in which they take part, and gives them a sense of direct participation in industrial decision. A scheme of worker-participation is devised to ensure effective consultation with workers on points which ultimately concern them.

THE INDIAN EXPERIENCE

The idea of 'worker participation' was first popularised in India by passing The Industrial Disputes Act in 1947. The Act has empowered the Government to force any employer of any industrial establishment, employing 100 or more workers, to constitute a works committee consisting of representatives of employers and workmen engaged in that establishment. But these committees have failed in the achievement of their basic objectives.

The Second Five Year Plan (1955-56—1960-61) had envisaged a more ambitious and comprehensive programme of collaboration between the workers and management. It stated that in order to move toward a socialistic pattern of society it is necessary to make the worker feel that in his own way he is helping to build a progressive society. The creation of industrial democracy, therefore, is a prerequisite for the establishment of such a society.

Objectives

The workers' participation scheme is supposed to have the following three objectives:

Firstly, it would help raise productivity. The fruits of progress may be shared by the enterprise, the employees and the community at large.

Secondly, it would give employees "a better understanding of their role in the working of industry and of the process of production."

Finally, it would satisfy "the workers' urge for self-expression, thus leading to industrial peace, better employer-employee relations and increased co-operation".

The participation is supposed to be achieved by setting up management councils which would consist of representatives of management, technicians and workers.

The scheme of workers' participation was first introduced in India in 1974 on a selective basis, viz., in manufacturing and mining units in the public, private and co-operative sectors as well as those departmental undertakings which employ 500 or more persons. A two-tier scheme was evolved : (i) Shop Councils at the shop and/or departmental levels and (ii) Joint Councils at the enterprise level.

Shop Councils

Four salient features of the scheme of workers' participation in management are the following :

(i) In every industrial unit employing 500 or more persons, the employee is under the legal obligation to constitute a shop council for each department or shop, consisting of an equal number of representatives of employers and workers. S. C. Kuchhal has described the scheme thus : "The employers' representatives shall be nominated by the management and must consist of persons from the unit concerned. And the representatives of workers shall be from amongst the workers actually engaged in the department or the shop concerned."

(ii) Secondly, the employee has to decide in consultation with the registered trade union(s), the number of Shop Councils and departments which are to be linked up with each council of the undertaking. As a general rule, the number of members is not supposed to exceed 12.

(iii) The Shop Council has to take all decisions on the basis of consensus and not just by a voting process, provided each party refers the unanswered questions and unsettled matters to the Joint Council for consideration. It is required that each decision of Shop Council is implemented by the parties concerned within a month. Those decisions of a Shop Council which have direct or indirect effect on another shop — or the undertaking or establishment as a whole — has to be referred to the Joint Council.

(iv) Although a Shop Council is to function for a maximum period of two years, it must meet frequently as and when necessary, and, at least once a month. Moreover, "the chairman of the Shop Council shall be the nominee of the management and the worker-members of the council shall elect vice-chairperson from among themselves."

Functions

For increasing production and productivity and promoting overall efficiency of the organisation, the Council has to perform the following functions : (1) assist management in achieving the time-bound production targets; (2) help improve production, productivity and efficiency including elimination of waste; (3) ensure optimum utilisation of machinery and manpower; (4) identify areas of less productivity and adopt corrective measures at the shop level to eliminate adverse contributory factors; (5) "study absenteeism in the shop/department and recommend steps to reduce them"; (6) adopt necessary safety measures; (7) "assist in maintaining general discipline"; (8) examine physical working conditions such as lighting, ventilation, noise, dust, and reduction of fatigue; (9) look into various health and welfare measures for ensuring smooth and efficient running of the shop/department, and (10) "ensure proper flow of two-way communications between management and the workers, particularly on matters relating to production figures and schedules."

Joint Council

Only the paid employees of an unit can be members of this Council. The Chairperson of the Council and the Chief Executive will be the same person. The Vice-chairperson has to be nominated from among the worker members. The Council will have to appoint one of its members as its secretary.

The Council will function for a maximum period of two years, and has to meet at least once in three months. As in the case of a Shop Council such decision of Joint Council has to be "on the basis of consensus and not be a process of voting and shall be implemented within one month unless otherwise stated in the decision itself."

Functions

The Joint Council is supposed to deal "with matters relating to optimum production, efficiency and fixation of productivity norms of man and machine for the unit as a whole", activities of a Shop Council which have bearing on another Shop and matters arising out of Shop Councils which remain unsolved. Moreover, the Council has to deal with "matters concerning the unit or plant as a whole in respect of matters relating to work planning and achieving production targets relevant to the unit as a whole; development of skills of workmen and adequate facilities for training; preparation of schedules of working hours, rewarding workers for offering constructive suggestions; optimum use of raw materials, production of quality goods; and general health, welfare and safety measures."

Conditions for Success

There are various methods of workers' participation in management. For the sake of analysis, it can be divided into five different categories, viz., informative, consultative, associative, administrative and decisive. (i) In informative participation, there is a constant sharing of information between management and workers on such matters as production figures, the balance sheet of the company, and general economic conditions and so on. (ii) In consultative participation, workers' representatives are consulted on matters relating to provision of labour welfare facilities. Under this method, the workers' representatives just act in an advisory capacity but the final decision is taken by the management. (iii) In associative participation the management accepts the suggestions of the council for solving a current problem. The unanimous decisions regarding a problem are taken by the workers' committee. (iv) Administrative participation assumes significance only when a decision has already been taken. In this case the councils (joint bodies) enjoy the right to choose the method of implementing it. This may include such issues as administrative or welfare measures, operation of vocational training and apprenticeship schemes and preparation of work schedules. This involves higher degrees of delegation of authority and responsibility to the lower rank and file of the organisation. (v) Finally, there is decisive participation. This is the highest form of workers' participation in management. Under this method, all matters — economic, financial and administrative are brought under the scrutiny of the councils and all decisions are taken jointly.

Successful implementation of the concept of workers' participation in management demands a compulsory prelude in the form of a series of activities and initiatives that will have cultural, structural and systemic ramifications. In other words, the process begins with context setting. It is the spirit of teamwork and partnership that one should address through various measures.

1. ***Communication.*** Creation of a two-way communication forum at all levels, to share plans, achievements, development needs and business dynamics.

2. ***Shop-councils.*** In the interest of increasing the overall efficiency of the shop or department and for addressing allied issues, shop councils must be established.

3. ***Manufacturing systems re-design.*** Manufacturing systems re-designing may become a prime focus area. This exercise effectively takes care of systems implication on workmen participation in decision-making — especially on operational issues with production planning, quality and plant efficiency — thereby providing a greater sense of worth to the individual.

4. ***Workers' education.*** The Central Board of Workers' Education has an ongoing initiative for workers' representatives and the management. However, considering the current economic and labour scenario, the syllabus may require a review to accommodate contents that can provide participants with wider and a more holistic perspective.

5. ***Union development.*** An organisation should see union as an important partner in its path to progress. As such, the provision of resources and opportunities for their development, possibly as 'an organisation within an organisation' assumes critical significance.

6. ***Welfare and safety.*** Joint committees and councils for canteens, safety, industrial social work, community development, sports and recreation are active and progressive bodies and are equally important.

7. ***Training and development.*** Need-based skill and attitudinal training must become an ongoing process. The needs must be identified by the individual and his (her) superior together.

8. ***Suggestion scheme.*** Suggestions schemes have proved to be effective in calling for participations from workforce — especially in areas of quality, cost and waste control and productivity.

Scope of Concept

The scope of workers' participation is to be clearly defined after an in-depth review of the philosophy, support system and finally the activity. The last without the first two will have no meaning. Scope cannot be limited to just having a scheme for inducting workers to various levels of management. It would be too superficial. In short, legislation cannot bring about participation. It is only trust and preparedness that can.

Synopsis for Learning

Q.1. What is workers' participation in management ?

Ans. Participation of workers in the decision-making process.

Q.2. What is the importance of workers' participation in management ?

Ans. It is likely to raise labour productivity by improving the industrial relations situation and by motivating the workers.

Q.3. What are the different methods of workers' participation in management ?

Ans. Five different methods of workers' participation in management are : (i) informative, (ii) consultative, (iii) associative, (iv) administrative and (v) decisive.

4.17 MAJOR PROBLEMS OF PERSONNEL MANAGEMENT IN INDIA

Personnel management simply refers to the task of dealing with human relationships within an organisation. There are three aspects of personnel management which are relevant in the present Indian context, viz. :

1. the labour or personnel aspect concerned with recruitment, placement of employees, remuneration, promotion, incentives, discipline and productivity.
2. the welfare aspect concerned with working conditions and amenities such as canteens, creches, housing, personnel problems of the workers, schools and recreation; and
3. the industrial relations aspect concerned with trade union negotiation, settlement of disputes, joint consultation and collective bargaining.

Problems of personnel management are largely attributable to its own setting. The problems that exist in the USA and other industrially advanced countries are dissimilar to those of India. Or, for that purpose, problems in developed countries differ in their essential nature from those of less developed countries (LDCs).

Moreover, India is one of the LDCs which are endeavouring to take stride in the industrial march, but hang-over of the legacies is naturally there — largely due to its colonial heritage. The march from archaic industrial systems to the modern one is neither a very easy one nor smooth. The old set-up remains while the new set-up seeks to penetrate. Successful management demands a proper synthesis of the two — the legacies and the new elements. The problems of personnel management is to be set in the backdrop of this over-all problem.

On analysis, the problems of personnel management in India can be enumerated thus :

1. Firstly, semi-feudal outlook of the business managers set against the freedom-aspiring workers.
2. Secondly, the political democracy in which the power-aspirant and the powers that have to depend upon the workers' vote and the workers themselves constitute a very large segment fo the total vote bank.
3. Thirdly, the passage from semi-command economy to the market one is not very smooth. The workers of all types demand freedom and are more conscious of their share of the product than their own contribution to it. The needed work culture does not necessarily grow in such an environment.
4. Then there is what is called second managerial revolution — the supremacy and the dictating power of the business managers. Obviously there is a clash between owners and managers. The owners care more for their own profits in pursuance of which they try to dictate decisions which the managers very often find to be irrational.
5. There is clash of personalities among the managers themselves which, no doubt, hampers personnel management. Each department is envious of the others as a result of which it is the total organisation that suffers.
6. Moreover, despite an abundant supply of labour, the right type of labour is not too easy to find due to its migratory character (largely due to its rural

origin), lack of information about job market and different barriers to labour mobility. Moreover, high labour turnover and absenteeism constitute a perennial problem for personnel management in Indian industries. Illiteracy among workers also raises problems in recruitment and selection.

7. Unhappily, what is called the 'science of selection' is neither fully comprehended nor applied. Selections are, in a large number of cases, made on the basis of recommendations and often through political influence.
8. Politics within organisations as is reflected in the multiplicity of trade unions is also a hindrance to establishing a healthy industrial relations situation. The feeling of unity of outlook and purpose is, no doubt, hampered.

Remedies

The remedies suggest themselves :

1. The outlook of all — the owners, the managers and all other workers — has to be changed. Each group will have to be inspired with the common purpose — success of the whole organisation.
2. The owners will have to be trained so that they can act as mentors. If they are not, they should refrain from dictating terms and endeavour to act as moderators — when there is clash among different managers. The spirit that each one will shine in the light of the organisation will have to be created.
3. The science of selection will have to be followed and, as far as practicable, the old and obsolete 'hire and fire system' will have to be disallowed as a rule.
4. There is also the need of enlightened trade unionism, for which proper education should be spread. While at the job level attempt should be made at human resources development, workers should be made to feel that they can have high wages if the volume of total product is higher. Most workers in India are poor. They find it difficult to make the two ends meet. A poor worker cannot be expected to work hard and contribute substantially to an organisation's output. There is lack of motivation and morale among industrial workers. Good morale cannot be achieved by methods and machines, but must be founded on mutual trust and confidence.
5. Fifthly, industrial democracy will have to be cultivated. Even the workers should be made to feel that they have a role in decision-making. If the atmosphere of 'what touches all is largely decided by all' comes to prevail, the problem of personnel management is largely solved. Thus military discipline and willing participation in the industrial process will have to be combined for achieving the needed result in industrial enterprises.
6. In fact, the personnel function is concerned with the whole social group. There will be occasions when group and individual interests conflict and compete for priority. The personnel manager has to take account of both interests and to recommend in particular instances where they can be reconciled and, if not, which should prevail. It seems clear, therefore, that the personnel function should not be limited solely to concern for the individual; it has also concern for the group.

The problem of high labour turnover can be solved by formulating and adopting a properly planned recruitment policy. This will minimise the disruption of work by constantly changing personnel. Illiteracy among the working population should be taken care of through proper worker education.

It is also of considerable importance to have a systematic and planned recruitment programme, as proper selection and placement go a long way toward building up a stable working force, reducing labour turnover and eventually reducing labour costs.

There is need for joint consultation in matters relating to industrial disputes. No doubt the Industrial Disputes Act, 1947, requires the setting up of works committees for the purpose. The duty of such committees are : (1) to promote measures for securing and prescribing amity and good relations between the employers and the workers and to that end (2) to comment upon matters of their common interest or concern and endeavour to remove any material differences of opinion in respect of such matters.

In India management, with a few exceptions, has been sceptical of the value of joint consultation; the trade unions have been suspicious. The latter treated Works Committees as a subtle move by 'capitalists', through the ruling party, to undermine the power of organised labour.

Creating confidence among the employees in the decisions of Works Committees is one of the most difficult tasks and it is management that must make the greatest effort to instil this confidence. It is only when this confidence has been established that the Works Committees can effectively contribute towards sound relationships between management and employees.

It has to be borne in mind that personnel management is essentially the task of dealing with human relationships within an organisation. A factory, a business, or a work place consists of people working together. One may even suggest that the job of personnel management is neither managing men nor work but administering a social system. However impressive the vast machinery of modern industry may be, there is no getting away from the oft-forgotten fact that **the machinery is useless without human beings to design and run it**. Even the automated factory of the future will still require the human brain apart from the electronic computer and the army of men who make and maintain the wonderful machine. To get the work done in any organisation the people engaged in it require two things if they are to work happily and efficiently together : (i) the human satisfaction of a reasonable livelihood; and (ii) the social satisfaction of doing a job well. It is time personnel managers in India took note of these realities. After all, personnel management essentially deals with people at work and with relationships within an enterprise.

Personnel management in India should aim to achieve both efficiency and justice, neither of which can be secured successfully without the other. It should seek to bring together and develop into an effective organisation the men and women who make up an enterprise, enabling each to make his own best contribution to its success, both as an individual and as a member of a working group. It should seek to provide fair terms and conditions of employment and satisfying work for those employed. The objectives should be:

(1) to maintain good relationships within an organisation;

(2) to enable each person to make his maximum personal contribution to the organisation as a member of a working group; and

(3) to achieve these things through respect for human personality and the well-being of the individual.

Exit Options

One final point may be noted in this context. No doubt there is a need for a rapid increase in foreign direct investment in manufacturing, services and infrastructure. But international investors demand the right to hire and fire as an essential prerogative. The moot point is that having the right to fire does not necessarily result in the indiscriminate firing of employees. On the contrary, most management invest heavily in creating business-related skills at large costs and over an extended duration. Therefore, the decision to reduce the workforce is never taken lightly. One has also to contend with the possibility of skilled people going over to the competitor.

The right to exercise exit options only enforces a greater sense of discipline among all concerned, and leads to a responsible social environment. In India, the ease with which managers hire people through permanent and contract employment is unbelievable. A time has come to find out how to create employment without burdening an institution with poor productivity. Legislation can certainly improve discipline but not create employment.

It will be impossible to find a single solution that could be applied across industries and throughout the various socio-economic regions. It would be desirable to develop solutions for specific industry sectors in different regions by constituting groups of persons representing the industry, political and government agencies. Above all, a massive communication process needs to be put in place, involving management, labour and trade unions, on fairness in mutual relationships, and on the expectations and responsibilities in developing a sustainable competitive advantage for India.

Synopsis for Learning

Q.1. What is the essence of personnel management in developing countries like India?

Ans. In the Indian context, personnel management is neither managing men nor work but administering a social system. It basic objective should be to achieve efficiency and justice.

Q.2. What are the problems of personnel management in India?

Ans. The major problems relating to personnel management in the context of industrial organisations in India are the following :

(a) Lack of worker motivation and morale; (b) lack of discipline; (c) frequent strikes and lock-outs; (d) lack of management support for workers' participation schemes; and, (e) multiplicity of trade unions and their lack of responsibility and undue political interference.

GLOSSARY

Arbitration The hearing and resolution of a labour dispute, usually performed by a neutral third party.

Assessment center A facility where performance simulation tests are administered. These are made up of a series of exercises and are used for selection, development and performance appraisals.

Attribution theory A theory of performance evaluation based on the perception of who is in control of an employee's performance.

Attrition A process whereby the jobs of incumbents who leave for any reason will not be filled.

Burnout Chronic and long-term stress at the workplace.

Checklist appraisal A performance appraisal type in which a rater checks off those attributes of an employee that apply.

Closed shop A union security arrangement whereby workers could not be hired by an employer unless they were already members of the union.

Co-determination stage A labour-management relationship characterised as separate but equal.

Coaching A development activity in which a manager takes an active role in guiding another manager.

Collaboration stage A labour-management relationship characterised as working together for a common cause.

Collective bargaining The negotiation, administration and interpretation of a written agreement between two parties, at least one of which represents a group that is acting collectively, that covers a specific period of time.

Comparable worth Equal pay for similar jobs, jobs similar in skills, responsibility, working conditions, and effort.

Contract negotiation The process whereby management and labour agree on the details of their contract.

Co-operative stage A labour-management relationship characterised as working together on a few specific issues.

Delegation A management function through which activities are assigned to individuals at lower levels in the organisation.

Demotion A disciplinary action whereby an individual is sent back to a lower position in the company.

Discipline A condition in the organisation when employees conduct themselves in accordance with the organisation's rules and standards of accepted behaviour.

Dismissal A disciplinary action that results in the termination of an employee.

Downsizing An activity in an organisation aimed at creating greater efficiency by eliminating certain superfluous jobs.

Employee counselling A process whereby employees are guided in overcoming performance problems.

Empowerment Affording employees more delegation, participative management, work teams, goal setting, and training.

Factor comparison method A method of job analysis in which job factors are compared to determine the worth of the job.

Graphic rating scales A performance appraisal method that lists a number of traits and a range of performance for each.

Grievance arbitration Specialised steps followed for handling contractual disputes arising from a collective bargaining.

Human resource inventory Describes the skills that are available within the organisation.

Human resource management A process consisting of the inception, development, motivation, and maintenance of human resources. The process of planning personnel needs; staffing the organisation, and training, developing, appraising and maintaining an organisation's personnel.

Human resource planning (a) The process by which an organisation ensures that it has the right number and kinds of people, at the right places, at the right time, capable of effectively and efficiently completing those tasks that will enable the organisation in achieving its overall objective. (b) The process of forecasting personnel needs and developing the necessary strategies for meeting those needs.

Impression management Influencing performance evaluations by portraying an image that is desired by the appraiser.

Individual ranking Ranking employee's performance from highest to lowest.

Initial screening The first step in the selection process whereby enquiries about a job are screened.

Internal search A 'promotion from within' concept.

Interviews A selection method that involves a face-to-face meeting with the candidate.

Job analysis Provides information about job currently being done and the knowledge, skills and abilities that individuals need to perform the jobs adequately.

Job evaluation Specifies the relative value of each job in the organisation.

Mediation A resolution method in which a neutral third party with no formal authority helps both sides reach a settlement.

Mediator A person who uses persuasion to help two parties resolve their differences.

Motivation The willingness to do something, conditioned by the action's ability to satisfy some need.

On-the-job-training Informal instruction conducted at the job site.

Participative management A management concept giving employees more control over the day-to-day activities on their job. Also known as worker participation in management.

Peer rating A performance appraisal in which all the workers rate each other.

Performance appraisal process A formal process in an organisation whereby each employee is evaluated to determine how he (she) is performing.

Point method Breaking down jobs based on identifiable criteria and the degree to which these criteria exist on the job.

Positive discipline A disciplinary process whereby the punitive nature of discipline is removed.

Promotion A change within the organisation to a higher position that has greater responsibilities and usually requires more advanced skills and knowledge than the previous position. Promotion normally brings greater status and an increase in pay and perks.

Ranking method Rating employees from highest to lowest.

Social security . Retirement, disability, and survivor benefits paid by the government to aged, former members of the labour force, the disabled, or their survivors. A legally required benefit that provides disability payments, old-age benefits, and survivors' benefits.

Staffing Filling, and keeping, the positions in the organisation structure with competent people. This is done through (i) identifying workforce requirements, (2) inventorying the people available, (3) recruiting, (4) selecting candidates for positions, (5) placing candidates and (6) promoting, (7) appraising, (8) planning the career of workers, (9) compensating, and (10) training or otherwise developing people.

Strike A collective refusal to work until a dispute is resolved.

Structured interviews An interview in which there are fixed questions that are presented to every applicant. Such an interview follows a personal format that consists of a series of direct questions.

Supervisory appraisal A performance appraisal in which the immediate supervisor evaluates the performance of a subordinate.

Subordinate rating A performance appraisal in which the workers evaluate their superiors.

Suspension A period of time off from work as a result of a disciplinary process.

Training A learning experience that seeks a relatively permanent change in an individual that will improve his (her) ability to perform on the job or the process of teaching employees the procedures and techniques to efficiently do their jobs.

Union Organisation of workers, acting collectively, seeking to protect and promote their mutual interests through collective bargaining. An organisation of workers who have joined forces to achieve common goals — such as higher wages and improved working conditions.

Verbal warning The first step in the disciplinary process.

White-collar jobs Jobs that involve clerical, office or managerial work.

Work sampling A selection device requiring the job applicant to actually perform a small part of the job.

Work sharing A work concept whereby two or more individuals share one full-time job with the remaining time spent on individual pursuits.

Workmen's compensation Payment to workers or their heirs for death or permanent or total disability that resulted from job-related activities.

Written reminder A more formalised step in positive discipline.

Written tests An organisational selection tool designed to indicate whether an applicant will be successful on the job, if hired.

Written warning The first formal step in the disciplinary process.

Yellow-dog contract An agreement whereby employees state that they are not now — nor will they be in the future — union members.

5

Materials Management

Materials management has the "total control and thus combines those managerial acts connected with control of goods at all stages in a firm's operations".

Dean S. Ammer

[Syllabus

- **Introduction** : Concept and objectives of materials management, relationship of materials management with other areas of management functions
- **Purchasing Management** : Objectives and functions of industrial purchasing
- **Purchase Policies and Procedures**
- **Principles of Purchasing, Purchasing Cycle, Sources Selection and Vendor Development, Commercial Terms and Conditions of Purchase**
- **Pricing and Discounts**
- **Negotiations in Purchasing**
- **Imports and Customs Clearance**
- **Stores Functions** : Receipt, inspection and issue of materials (excluding problems), stock verification, reconciliation and adjustment.
- **Disposal of surplus, scrap and obsolete materials.**
- **Inventory Control** : Types of inventory, need for inventory control, selective inventory control : VED, SDE, FSN classification of inventories — just-in-time inventory. **]**

SUBJECT MATTER OF MATERIALS MANAGEMENT

The wealth of a country is measured by its gross national product — the output of goods and services produced by the nation in a given time.

Goods are physical objects, something we can touch, feel, or see. Services are the performance of some useful functions such as banking, medical care, restaurants, clothing stores, or social services.

No doubt we may have rich natural resources in our economy such as mineral deposits, farm land, and forests. But these are only potential sources of wealth.

A production function is needed to transform our resources into useful goods. Production takes place in all forms of transformation — extracting minerals from the earth, farming, lumbering, fishing and using these resources to manufacture useful products.

There are many stages between the extraction of resource material and the final consumer product. At each stage in the development of the final product value is added, thus creating more wealth.

If ore is extracted from the earth and sold, wealth is gained from our efforts, but those who continue to transform the raw material will gain more and usually far greater wealth. Japan is a prime example of this.

It has very few natural resources and buys most of the raw materials it needs. .

However, the Japanese have developed one of the wealthiest economies in the world by transforming the raw materials they purchase and adding value to them through manufacturing.

5.1 INTRODUCTION : CONCEPTS AND OBJECTIVES OF MATERIALS MANAGEMENT

Manufacturing companies are in the business of converting raw materials to a form that is of far more value and use to the customer than the original raw materials. Logs are converted into tables and chairs, iron ore into steel and steel into cars and refrigerators. This conversion process, called manufacturing or production, makes a society wealthier and creates a better standard of living.

To get the most value out of our resources, we must design production processes that make products most efficiently. Once the processes exist, we need to manage their operation so that they can produce goods most economically. Managing the operation means planning for and controlling the resources used in the process : labour, capital and material. All are important, but the major way in which management plans and controls is through the flow of materials. The flow of materials controls the performance of the process. If the right materials in the right quantities are not available at the right time, the process cannot produce what it should. Labour and machinery will be poorly utilised. The profitability and even the existence of the company will be at stake.

Materials management is a balancing act. The objective is to be able to deliver what customers want, when and where they want it, and do so at minimum cost. To achieve this objective, materials management must make trade-offs between the level of customer service and the cost of providing that service. As a rule, costs rise as the service level increases, and materials management must find that combination of inputs to maximise service and minimise cost. For example, customer service can be improved by establishing warehouses in major markets. However, that means extra cost in operating the warehouse and in the extra inventory carried. To some extent, these costs will be offset by potential savings in transportation costs if lower cost transportation can be used.

By grouping all those activities involved in the movement and storage of goods into one department, the firm is in a better position to provide maximum service at minimum cost and increase profit. The overall concern of materials management is the balance between priority and capacity. The marketplace sets demand. Materials management must plan the firm's priorities (what goods to make and when) to meet that demand. Capacity is the ability of the system to produce or deliver goods. Priority and capacity must be planned and controlled to meet customer demand at minimum cost. Materials management is responsible for doing this.

Materials management concerns itself not merely with the cost of materials but pays equal attention to the cost we incur on materials which, in most cases, are usually hidden. Even a rupee saved on these costs add to the profits made by a manufacturing unit.

Materials management is a coordinating function responsible for planning and controlling materials flow. Its objectives are :

- Maximise the use of the firm's resources.
- Provide the required level of customer service.

Manufacturing creates wealth by adding value to goods. To improve productivity and wealth, a company must first design efficient and effective systems for manufacturing. It must then manage these systems to make the best use of labour, capital and material. One of the most effective ways of doing this is through the planning and control of the flow of materials into, through, and out of manufacturing. There are three elements to a material flow system : supply, manufacturing planning and control and physical distribution. They are connected — what happens in one system affects the others.

Traditionally, there are conflicts in the objectives of a company and in the objectives of marketing, finance and production. The role of materials management is to balance these conflicting objectives by coordinating the flow of materials, so customer servcice is maintained and the resources of the company are properly used.

Materials management is a body of knowledge which helps the production/operations manager to improve the productivity of capital by reducing the materials cost. About two-thirds of any company's sales turnover are spent to purchase materials. It is, therefore, of considerable importance to reduce this materials bill as much as possible, since any such reduction will result in greater profit.

Materials management refers to management of materials. It broadly covers purchases of materials purchased or acquired from outside sources, transporting the materials to its place to use, keeping the materials in stock, maintaining an optimum level of inventory of materials, issuing the materials as and when required and, finally, keeping an overall account of the materials — whether in process or in stores. Purchasing, store-keeping, inventory control, transportation, etc. are different aspects of materials management.

FUNCTIONS

All activities concerned form the materials part of the materials management function. These functions are :

1. Purchasing

Purchasing is one of the basic functions of materials management. The objectives of industrial purchasing are the following :

(a) To maintain continuity of production.

(b) To buy for the best ultimate value, not necessarily always at the lowest price.

(c) To increase profits.

Effective functioning of the purchasing function is vital to the smooth operation of many other departments.

2. Inventory Control

The word 'inventory' is defined as the 'materials lying in storage or idle materials'.

Inventory control is the technique of maintaining all classes of inventory at optimum levels, with the minimum investment of capital. In other words, inventory control means balancing the two opposite forces, *i.e.*, overstocking with all financial hazards and understocking leading to operational bottlenecks.

3. Stores Management

Proper receipts, inspection, storage and preservations, safety and issue of materials with efficient documentation assist in good house-keeping of materials in a warehouse. This avoids shortage and surplus during annual or continuous stock taking and prevents loss or deterioration of materials in hand.

4. Disposal of Surplus/Scrap/Obsolete Materials

Another important area where materials management can play an effective role is in the disposal of surplus/obsolete materials. Over a period of time manufacturing units accumulate large amounts of obsolete and surplus materials. Since the materials department is in constant touch with the market, the disposal of such materials is always to the advantage of the materials department. Not only is the materials departments in touch with the market, it is also aware of the consumption of materials in the various divisions of the company and also in similar units in the industry. By virtue of this knowledge, the materials department is in a position to sell the surplus materials to advantage or dispose it off as per the company's policy.

OBJECTIVES

The objectives of materials management department are :

A. Primary Objectives

1. Low price.
2. High inventory turnover ($Inventory\ turnover = \frac{Sale}{Average\ Inventory}$).
3. Low cost of acquisition and possession.
4. Continuity of supply.
5. Consistency of quality.
6. Low payroll (wage) cost.
7. Favourable supplier relations.
8. Development of personnel.
9. Maintenance of regular records.

These objectives may now be briefly described.

Low price

This is one of the most important objectives of materials management. It means that the materials or services as received by the company should be purchased at the lowest possible cost.

High inventory turnover

This means that the average inventory locked up is low compared to the sales volume. Inventory means idle money and, therefore, the lower it is, the higher will be the profit. Storage and carrying cost of inventory will, therefore, also be lower if the volume is small.

Low cost acquisition and possession

This means that the materials are acquired and kept in stores at a low cost.

Continuity of supplies

One of the main objectives of proper (scientific) materials management is to ensure that there is no disruption in supply which might hamper the smooth flow of production. Continuity of supply is necessary to ensure uninterrupted production.

Consistency of quality

Materials of the right quality have to be bought. Otherwise the quality of the end-product may suffer. Hence, the quality will have to be good and consistent.

Low payroll cost

Like any other department, the materials department should be run at the lowest possible cost.

Favourable supplier relations

As the name signifies, in order to ensure continuity of supply and consistency of quality, it is necessary to have a favourable supplier/buyer relation.

Development of personnel

Regular developments are taking place in the materials management field. It is necessary that the persons dealing with materials management are appraised of the latest ideas and trends. Hence, the development and training of personnel engaged in materials functions is absolutely essential.

Maintenance of regular records

For any efficiently run department it is necessary to have good, updated and easily accessible records.

B. Secondary Objectives

1. Favourable reciprocal relations.
2. New materials and products.
3. Make or buy decision.
4. Standardisation.
5. Product improvement.
6. Inter-departmental harmony.
7. Forecast.

Favourable reciprocal relations

It sometimes pays to buy materials from the companies to whom the end products are sold. This is called reciprocal relationship. A good materials management department should encourage such reciprocal relationships with other companies.

New materials and products

The materials manager is always in touch with the outside world. He acts as an information centre for the management and informs the management, not only about the materials and products which his company requires, but also about the development of new products produced by its competitors.

Make or buy decision

The decision as to whether an item should be made from within the company, *i.e.*, with its own resources, or purchased from outside (external) sources is a very important one.

The materials department, alongwith the help of the engineering department, by taking the pros and cons of making or buying, should buy from outside sources only if it is economical to do so.

Standardisation

Materials required by the company and bought from outside should be standardised so as to have a fewer number of materials. This will reduce total inventory.

Product improvement

The materials department should also help the company in improving the quality of the end product by suggesting various alternative methods.

Inter-departmental harmony

The materials department should have a good relationship with the other departments inside the company.

Forecast

The materials department has to prepare the materials budget and forecast of payments. The department will also forecast the prices of materials to be purchased.

Conclusion

The above objectives vary in relative importance from company to company, depending upon the requirements. For example, in an aerospace industry, the 'quality' objective will perhaps gain maximum importance as sacrificing quality in an aerospace industry would result in serious accident and eventual death of persons. For some other industries, where there is a stiff competition, the price objective may assume primary importance. It is, therefore, necessary to balance these diverse (and often conflicting) objectives in order to achieve the overall objective or goal of the company.

RELATIONSHIP OF MATERIALS MANAGEMENT WITH OTHER AREAS OF MANAGEMENT FUNCTIONS

The materials management development does not operate in isolation. It works with other departments within an organisation. It has relations with almost all the departments of a company. This point may now be briefly discussed.

Relationship between the Purchase and the Stores Department

The stores function is, in essence, a complementary function to the purchase department. Its job includes the requisitioning of all stores materials needed for the company's operations, physical handling of the supplies received, issuing of such materials, and inventory control relating to these materials. A close relationship between purchase and stores is necessary to ensure that materials are ordered strictly in terms of actual requirements and in the overall interest of economy (*i.e.*, cost saving).

The relationship between purchase and stores must be such that neither tends to be dominated by the objective of the other. The materials department, due to the very nature of its functions, will have to maintain continuing and close relationships with several other departments in the company as well as with the suppliers. The relationship of the purchase department with other departments involves not only the direct cost of materials but also several other indirect costs which together contribute to the overall corporate expenditure and has implications for efficiency and profits. The relationship of materials departments with the production, sales and stores are given below.

Relation with Production Department

The production department is the chief customer of purchase and materials department. The principal function of the purchase department is to procure materials needed for production. The production department must, in its turn, be able to rely upon such services. If the purchase department has failed to obtain the materials in time in spite of timely information and sufficient notice given by the production department, then production will suffer. They might have to switch over to some other product (for which raw materials are readily available).

Otherwise, production may stop altogether. Both of these are uneconomical and will minimise the profits of the company. Several things may happen if the materials do not arrive on time. Another area in which both production and purchasing can jointly lead to cost reduction is in regard to specifications. It is usually the production department that specifies quantity and quality of materials as also the required delivery dates. With regard to costs the production manager's performance depends largely on the purchase manager's ability to obtain maximum value for the money spent.

Relationship with Sales Department

There is a close relationship between purchase and sales. The function of the sales department is to market the product and the success of this function is very closely dependent upon the product, its price, its quality and the reliability of delivery. For all these the sales department has to depend upon both the purchase department and the production department, among others. The final price of the product will depend largely upon the price which the purchase department has paid for the materials and, in many cases, the sale price is quoted on the basis of calculations made on estimated purchase price. To that extent, the purchase department has a great responsibility to ensure that the prices paid by them contribute to overall economy, *i.e.*, cost saving.

To a very great extent the delivery dates of sales will depend upon the delivery schedule indicated by purchasing department with its suppliers. This is especially so in regard to components, parts, sub-contracted castings or forgings and so on. A failure on the part of the sales to fulfill its delivery obligations or maintain delivery schedules can have adverse effects on company sales. The quality of the products sold has a close relation with the quality of the raw materials and components procured by the purchase department. The purchase department may also help the sales department by having reciprocal business relations.

Relationship with Planning Department

The planning department is responsible for the preparation of long and short range plans for the company. Such plans have to take account of the business environment in which the company operates.

The purchase department, being in touch with the market, can to a very great extent help the planning department to draw up plans, by keeping a proper track on market developments. It can also give prompt advice on changes which are likely to influence the schedule and plans of the company.

It can help the planning department through proper forecast of materials supplies and markets, especially with regard to new products and new sources of supply.

Relationship with the Maintenance Department

The maintenance department carries out a service function whose objective is to keep all the equipment, machinery and other facilities in good working condition all the time. For carrying out this function properly and smoothly it requires repair and maintenance materials. It is in the rightness of things to ensure that production is continuous without either a slowdown or shutdown that may arise due to delay in procurement of maintenance spares and supplies. The relationship, therefore, between maintenance and purchasing is almost parallel to that between production and purchasing.

Relationship with the Accounts Department

Since the purchase department spends the major portion of company sales income its interaction with accounts departments takes place practically on a day-to-day basis. The accounts department has to arrange for finance to meet the suppliers' bills. For this, it is necessary for the purchase department to give advance notice to the accounts department regarding such money requirements. The purchasing people spend almost 45% to 60% of the company's sales turnover. The accounts department has also to ensure that the company's rules and regulations relating to monetary transactions are properly followed. It should also ensure that all receipts of materials and payment is released to the supplier. Prompt payment according to the terms of the purchase order is very important for maintaining good relations between the buyer and the supplier.

Organisation of Materials Department

There are three possible types of organisations of materials department:

1. Organisation by Function

This generally means that the organisation is based on specialisation. Such an organisation chart is shown below :

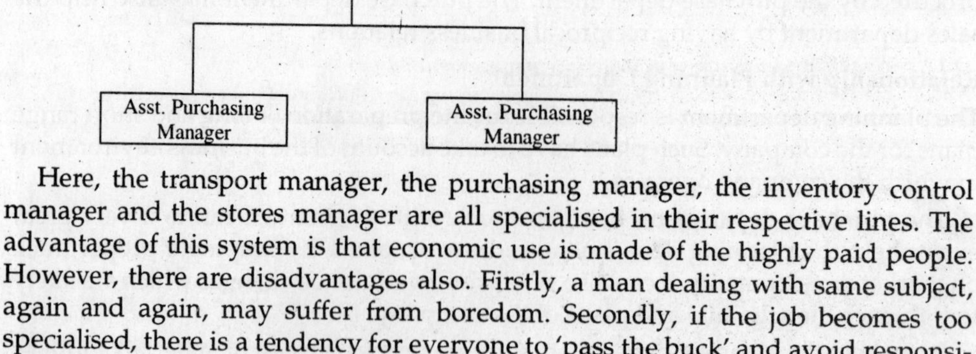

Here, the transport manager, the purchasing manager, the inventory control manager and the stores manager are all specialised in their respective lines. The advantage of this system is that economic use is made of the highly paid people. However, there are disadvantages also. Firstly, a man dealing with same subject, again and again, may suffer from boredom. Secondly, if the job becomes too specialised, there is a tendency for everyone to 'pass the buck' and avoid responsibility somehow for solving a problem that is not part of one's routine job.

2. *Organisation by Location*

This is applicable to companies having plants located at various places. The organisation chart is shown below:

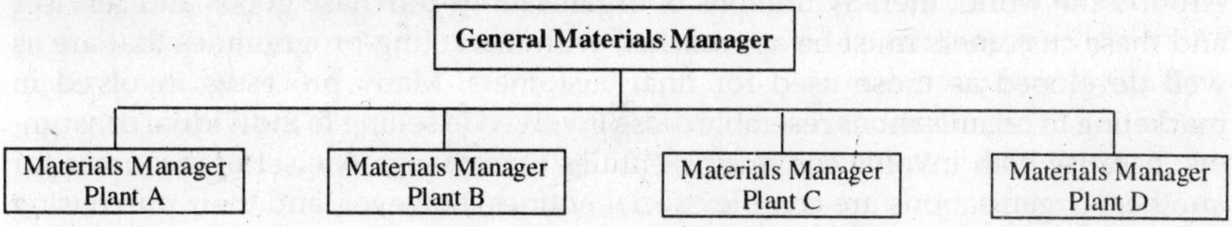

The advantage of such organisation is that things will move quickly and there will be continuity of supply. However, one disadvantage is that prices of items may not be the same in different plants at the same time.

3. *Organisation by Product*

This type of organisation is found in companies dealing with a larger number of end products and where specialised knowledge in various types of raw materials required for these products is necessary. The organisation chart is shown below :

(i) **Flat Organisation**

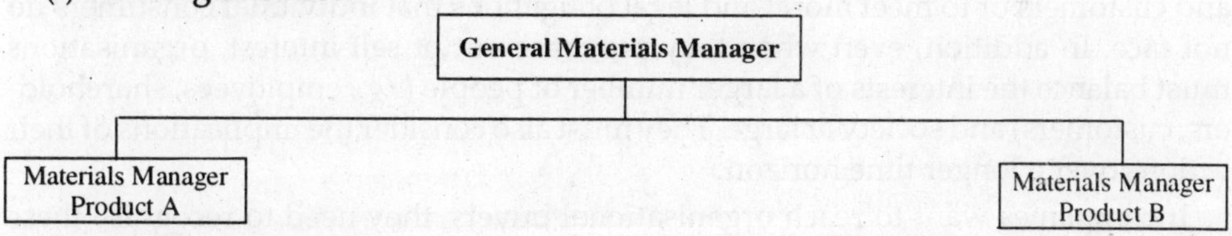

(ii) **Deep Organisation**

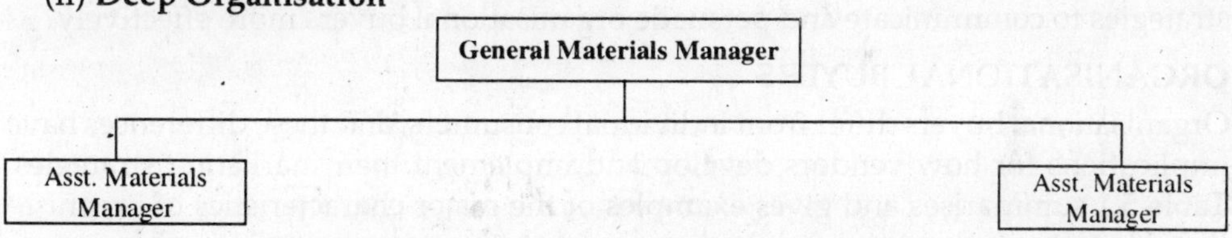

Normally, the materials management department's organisation chart is a combination of all these various organisation charts. Since such a chart is complicated one, it is not presented here.

Synopsis for Learning

Q.1. What is the importance of materials management ?

Ans. Effective management of materials and purchasing can contribute significantly to the success of most modern organisations. The acquisition of materials, supplies, services and equipment — of the right qualities, in the right quantities, at the right prices, at the right time, and on a continuing basis — long has occupied the attention of many managers in both the public and private sectors. The rapidly changing supply scene, with cycles of abundance and shortages, varying prices, lead times and availabilities, provides a continuing challenge to those organisations wishing to obtain a maximum contribution from this area.

Q.2. What are the functions of materials management ?

Ans. Materials management includes three major activities : (i) Anticipating material requirements, (ii) Sourcing; and (iii) obtaining materials. The specific functions which might be included under the materials manager are inventory control, receiving, stores and scrap and surplus disposal.

5.2 PURCHASING MANAGEMENT : OBJECTIVES AND FUNCTIONS OF INDUSTRIAL PURCHASING

Around the world, literally millions of organisations purchase goods and services and these customers must be approached with marketing programmes that are as well developed as those used for final customers. Many processes involved in marketing to organisations resemble those involved in selling to individual consumers, because both involve convincing entities to exchange one set of resources for another. Organisations are complex social entities, however, and their purchasing decision processes can differ substantially and in important ways from those of individual consumers.

It may be noted at the beginning that individual consumers and organisational buyers purchase goods and services for different reasons. Some organisational purchases are directly aimed at improving company welfare. In this respect, organisational buyers are motivated by self-interest similar to those individual consumers show.

Organisations purchase other goods and services, however, to benefit employees and customers or to meet moral and legal obligations that individual consumers do not face. In addition, even when they purchase out of self-interest, organisations must balance the interests of a larger number of people (*e.g.*, employees, shareholders, customers) and society at large. They must also consider the implications of their actions over a longer time horizon.

If companies want to reach organisational buyers, they need to recognise these differences in purchase objectives and time horizons and to design marketing strategies to communicate and persuade organisational buyers more effectively.

ORGANISATIONAL BUYERS

Organisational buyers differ from individual consumers, and these differences have implications for how vendors develop and implement their marketing strategies. Table 5.1 summarises and gives examples of the major characteristics of organisational buyers.

Table 5.1 : Characteristics of Organisational Buyers

Characteristic	Example
Organisational buyers are usually larger than individual consumers in terms of resources and the amount of their purchases.	Apparel retailers such as Nu York purchase hundreds of the same shirt for blouse, whereas individual consumers purchase only one.
Organisational buyers are fewer in number than individual consumers.	The output from most steel mills in the United States is sold directly to less than 50 Fortune 500 firms.
Organisational buyers in different industries tend to be geographically concentrated.	Most automobile manufacturing in the United States takes place in Michigan, Ohio and California.
Relationships between organisational buyers and their suppliers tend to be close in terms of shared tasks and mutual influence.	Multilayer buy-sell agreements are the norm between Japanese manufacturers and their suppliers.
Organisational buying decisions are often managed by purchasing professionals and involve decision groups composed of representatives from different areas.	The purchase of engineering workstations involves personnel from finance, information systems, engineering, manufacturing, materials management, plant engineering and senior management.

SIZE AND CONCENTRATION

Two obvious differences between individual consumers and organisational buyers are their size and number. Organisational buyers usually represent a relatively small number of large entities that have substantial resources and influence on their markets compared to those of the millions of individual customers for consumer products. Vendors can seldom afford to ignore even a single customer. In contrast, companies marketing to individual consumers often ignore single individuals — and sometimes even large groups of customers — without losing much of their business. In addition, because organisational customers represent a small, demanding and highly competitive group, vendors must adjust to each customer's competitors who buy similar equipment.

No doubt, having a small number of large customers makes it easier for vendors to serve each customer individually and cater to their needs more accurately. However, the disadvantage is that customers expect a higher level of attention because of their greater purchase volume. Expectations for more attention often surface as demands for customised delivery schedules, discounts and changes to the product design, among other things.

One additional factor related to the small number of buyers is that they tend to be more geographically concentrated than individual consumers. Geographic concentration is an advantage because it reduces direct distribution costs.

MULTIPLE DECISION MAKERS AND COMPLEX DECISIONS

Organisational buyers also differ from individual customers in that the former often involve many decision makers from different areas of the organisation acting together. The size of the decision unit depends on the type of purchase. In marketing, decision-making units are traditionally called buying centres — individuals and groups who participate in purchase decision processes and share common goals and risks arising from the decision. In organisations in which members function more autonomously and share many job responsibilities, decision-making units have also been called buying networks. Regardless of which term is used, decision units in organisations are unique in that their members often apply different criteria to the same buying decisions.

Many organisational buyers also follow formal policies and procedures in making purchases, buyers and they tend to exhibit less loyalty to any one supplier.

Another set of differences between organisational and individual customers arises from the greater complexity of organisational decision processes relative to those of individual consumers. Although the fundamentals of adoption and diffusion are the same for all consumers — individuals as well as organisations — the actual processes by which organisations make decisions and what they demand of sellers may differ substantially from that of individuals. It follows, therefore, that buying decisions in organisations typically take longer and require more attention and greater detail than individual purchases.

CLOSE AND INTRICATE RELATIONSHIPS

Relationships between buyers and sellers in organisational markets tend to be closer and more intricate than relationships between consumer-products companies and their individual customers. This is partly due to the fact that only a small number of large customers are involved. Such relationships also arise from the complex nature of the products and services purchases. Quite often, vendors adapt their products and services to the needs of buyers in terms of technology, lot sizes, delivery schedules and other factors. The object is to satisfy concerns from different areas of the buyer's business. Adaptation requires that buyers and sellers cooperate extensively throughout the transaction process and seek to build trust. Personnel at multiple levels of both buyer and seller organisations form extended networks during the development process, through which they try to understand one another, and commit to one another's success beyond what is seen in all buyer-seller deals at the individual consumer level.

Industrial buying decisions may also involve other organisations, such as labour unions affected by the proposed changes, other suppliers, or government officials who must approve changes to a manufacturing facility. Even citizen groups concerned with tax implications or the environmental impact of a proposed product or service may get involved in such decisions. Some organisational purchases require consultation between the vendor and each affected party and it may take months or even years for a final decision.

In recent years, we have seen an important trend in buyer-seller relationships : the emergence of partner relationships. In these arrangements, buyers and sellers display genuine interest in each other's welfare. They share detailed information about products, costs and manufacturing operations and they look for ways to integrate their efforts to everyone's benefit. Vendors benefit from partner relationships because they lower the costs of selling and administration below those typical of transaction-based relationships.

Professional Buyers

The relationship that sellers have with organisational buyers also differs from that with consumers because organisations often have professional buyers who manage the buying process. In small buying organisations, the owner often handles purchasing and makes primary decisions. In medium-sized and large organisations, however, professional buyers often supervise and coordinate the actual buying processes. They also negotiate the best prices and terms from vendors. Vendors must work closely with professional buyers and gain access to all functional areas that can influence the buying decision.

Categories of Organisational Buyers

Although at some level of detail every organisation is uniquely different from every other organisation, organisational buyers can be grouped on the basis of their primary objectives. Table 2 summarises three objective-based categories of organisational customers : industrial buyers, resellers and institutional buyers.

Industrial Buyers

Industrial buyers are the largest group of organisational buyers in terms of rupee sales and they buy various (and numerous) products and services. Industrial buyers produce goods and services for resale. They buy goods and services as components of their products or to make producing such goods easier and more efficient.

Industrial buyers are normally independent. For maximising profits they always try to ensure that the value that purchased products add to their output exceeds the cost of the purchases.

Table 5.2 : Categories of Organisational Buyers and their Distinguishing Characteristics			
Characteristics	**Industrial Buyers**	**Resellers**	**Institutional Buyers**
Primary Motivation	Profitability	Profitability	Serving constituencies
Primary Use of Purchased Goods	Inclusion or consumption in the production of goods and services	Reselling to individual consumers and/or other organisations	Inclusion or consumption in the production of goods and services
Primary Concerns	Cost, delivery schedules, quality, reliability, adequate supplies	Cost, promotional discounts, depth of assortment	Quality, performance that meets specification
Typical Decision-making Unit	Group representing all affected functional areas	Single buyer responsible for the product category	Group representing all affected areas
Most Commonly Purchased Goods	Raw materials, components, manufacturing facilities and machinery	Finished goods and supplies, retail space and fixtures	Finished goods and supplies, capital goods and installations
Biggest Challenges to Markets	Technological innovations that maintain differentiation	Private sourcing and low loyalty to suppliers	Shifting priorities with changing political administrators
Examples	Kellogg purchasing new equipment for making cereal	Major grocery store choosing which types of cereals to keep in stock	The Pentagon purchasing cereals for its overseas troops

Industrial buyers also make purchases that help them differentiate their products. Most industrial buyers compete with other companies that produce similar goods and they are interested in technological aspects of products that help to differentiate their own products and services from those of competitors. Industrial buyers will frequently pay a premium for goods and services that help differentiate their products in most consumer markets.

Resellers

Although they do not buy as much in terms of volume as industrial buyers, resellers represent the largest market in terms of the number of companies involved. As the name implies, resellers purchase products and services for resale. They also purchase products and services such as advertising, packaging and supplies that help them in the resale of other goods. Most often, resellers purchase finished products ready for distribution. Like industrial buyers, resellers are concerned with profits and are sensitive to costs.

Resellers vary in the types of products and services they sell and consequently in the variety of products they purchase. Resellers are most loyal to suppliers who offer unique products or beneficial services.

Institutional Buyers

Institutional buyers — organisations that provide services to society at large — include central, state and local governments; charitable health-care organisations; colleges and universities; and other non-profit organisations.

Institutional buyers differ from industrial buyers and resellers in that they seldom work toward profit, even though they can be sensitive to costs. Institutional buyers purchase a wide range of products and services. Some buyers buy highly sophisticated goods and place great emphasis on technological advances and confidentiality. Most other institutional buyers, however, purchase standard-grade goods that meet rigid performance specifications and pay fair prices for them. The prospect of fair profits for quality products makes institutional buyers attractive to many vendors.

Industrial Buying

Purchasing is the "process of buying". Many assume purchasing is solely the responsibility of the purchasing department. However, the function is much broader and, if it is carried out effectively, all departments in the company are involved. Obtaining the right material, in the right quantities, with the right delivery (time and place), from the right source, and at the right price are all purchasing functions.

Choosing the right material requires input from the marketing, engineering, manufacturing and purchasing departments. Quantities and delivery of finished goods are established by the needs of the marketplace. However, manufacturing planning and control (MPC) must decide when to order which raw materials so that marketplace demands can be satisfied. Purchasing is then responsible for placing the orders and for ensuring that the goods arrive on time.

The purchasing department has the major responibility for locating suitable sources of supply and for negotiating prices. Input from other departments is required in finding and evaluating sources of supply and to help the purchasing department in price negotiation. Purchasing, in its broad sense, is everyone's business.

Organisational Buying Activities

Organisational buying activities centre on the level of experience and information that firms have in purchasing certain products and services. In making a routine purchase, buyers have little need for information because of their past experience with the purchasing situation. When a purchasing situation is entirely new, information needs may be extensive due to the firm's lack of experience with the product, service or suppliers. In the purchase of a new computer system, for example, buyers will be very concerned with identifying computer characteristics (*e.g.*, programmes and peripheral equipment) that will satisfy their needs, services provided to maintain the system and the supplier's capability to provide those services.

Buying activities also consists of various phases of decision-making. Depending on the type of buying situation, whether it is routine or new, these phases will vary in their degree of importance. Effective industrial marketing strategy, then, requires that marketers focus their attention on the type of buying situation a firm is facing, where it is in its decision-making process (which phase), and what criteria various influencers will emphasise in the purchasing decision.

Purchasing and Profit Leverage

On the average, manufacturing firms spend about 50% of their sales revenue in the purchase of raw materials, components and supplies. This gives the purchasing function a strong chance to increase company profits. As a simple example, suppose a firm spends 50% of its revenue on purchased goods and shows a net profit before taxes of 10%. For every Rs 100 of sales, they receive Rs 10 of profit and spend Rs 50 on purchases. Other expenses are Rs 40. For the moment, assume that all costs vary with sales. These figures are shown in the following as a simplified income statement:

INCOME STATEMENT

Sales		Rs 100
Cost of goods sold	Rs	
Purchases	50	
Other expenses	40	90
Profit before tax		10

To increase profits by Re 1, a 10% increase in profits, sales must be increased to Rs 110. Purchases and other expenses increase to Rs 55 and Rs 44. The following modified income statement shows these figures :

INCOME STATEMENT (SALES INCREASE)

Sales		Rs 110
Cost of goods sold	Rs	
Purchases	55	
Other expenses	44	99
Profit before tax		11

However, if the firm can reduce the cost of purchases from Rs 50 and Rs 49, a 2% reduction, it would gain the same 10% increase in profits. In this particular example, a 2% reduction in purchase cost has the same impact on profit as a 10% increase in sales.

INCOME STATEMENT (REDUCED PURCHASE COST)

Sales		Rs 100
Cost of goods sold	Rs	
Purchases Rs	49	
Other expenses	40	89
Profit before tax		11

PURCHASING OBJECTIVES

Purchasing is responsible for establishing the flow of materials into the firm, following-up with the supplier and expediting delivery. Missed deliveries can create havoc for manufacturing and sales, but purchasing can reduce problems for both areas, further adding to the profit.

The objectives of purchasing can be divided into four categories :

1. Obtaining goods and services of the required quantity and quality.
2. Obtaining goods and services at the lowest cost.
3. Ensuring the best possible service and prompt delivery by the supplier.
4. Developing and maintaining good supplier relations and developing potential suppliers.

To satisfy these objectives, four basic functions must be performed :

(i) Determining purchasing specifications : right quality, right quantity and right delivery (time and place).

(ii) Selecting supplier (right source).

(iii) Negotiating terms and conditions of purchase (right price).

(iv) Issuing and administration of purchase orders.

TWO SETS OF OBJECTIVES

Before vendors can respond effectively to customer information needs, they must understand the various criteria that customers use in evaluating potential suppliers. Different groups of individuals will view the supplier's offering from their unique perspectives. While industrial buying tends to reflect organisational goals, organisation members are influenced by both task and non-task objectives.

Task-oriented objectives involve a few important considerations such as price, quality, service and return on investment. Non-task objectives centre on personal factors such as the desire for job security, recognition, promotion and salary increases. When supplier's offerings are similar in such factors as product attributes, price and delivery, buyers have little basis for task-oriented choices. Since they can effectively satisfy organisational goals through several suppliers, buyers often tend to be more influenced by personal factors, or non-task objectives. However, when wide differences exist in product/service factors, industrial buyers are more accountable for their choices and tend to place more emphasis on cost and price.

Generalisations of organisational buying objectives across industrial buying decisions cannot be made. In fact, research indicates that buying centre members often employ different criteria in evaluating suppliers. Purchasing agents, for example, may value price and delivery factors; their importance placed on such criteria varies with the type of purchase being considered. The challenge, then, is to examine the purchasing decision from the buying firm's point of view, determine the roles of buying centre members and find out the task and non-task objectives that influence and motivate the buyers.

Task-oriented Objectives

Organisations that are in business to make a profit are largely interested in purchasing at the lowest possible price. But they do not want to compromise on such factors as technical service, product quality and certainty of delivery. Non-profit organisations, however, are concerned with budgetary constraints. For them, buying at the lowest possible price may be necessary to operate within predetermined budgets. Therefore, task-oriented objectives that achieve the organisational goals are of much importance to the purchase department.

Price. Buyers are concerned with the 'evaluated price' of a product. Customers do not buy products; they buy value (satisfaction). Therefore, in evaluating price, buyers consider various factors that generate or minimise costs, such as : "What amount of scrap or waste will result from the use of the material?" "What will the cost of processing the material be?" and "How much power will the machine consume?" Such measures as return on investment are also used when purchasing capital equipment. The proposed purchase of a new machine, for example, may be supported by expected increases in productivity or reduced labour costs.

Price, however, cannot be considered in isolation. A supplier who has a reputation for high-quality products and dependable delivery may be given a contract even though his prices are higher. The costs of shutting down manufacturing due to faulty equipment or missed deliveries may far exceed the higher price. One should not, therefore, overestimate the importance of price; one should also note that low bidders often fail to meet other important criteria of buyers.

Services. Multiple services are required by industrial buyers to achieve organisational goals. Such services include technical assistance, availability of spare parts, repair capability and training information.

Technical contributions of suppliers are highly valued wherever equipment, materials or parts are in use. Many firms tend to favour suppliers with reputations for being technical leaders in their fields. The availability of replacement parts is often vital to manufacturers who prefer to make their own repairs. Complex manufacturing and office equipment requires user training to ensure maximum productivity. The marketer who can offer sound technical advice, adequate training and a ready supply of replacement parts very often has a differential advantage over less capable competitors.

Quality. Organisational customers try to find out quantity levels that are consistent with specifications and the intended use of the product. They are reluctant to pay for extra quality and are unwilling to compromise specifications for a reduced price. The crucial factor is uniformity or consistency in product quality that will guarantee uniformity in end products, reduce costly inspections and testing of incoming shipments, and ensure an easy (or a smooth) mixing with the production process. When consistency or uniformity requirements are not met, costly problems are created for the buying firm.

Assurance of Supply. Interruptions in the flow of parts and materials can cause a shutdown of the production process, resulting in costly delays and lost sales. Physical distribution services rank second to product quality in influencing the purchasing decision. To guard against interruptions in supply, which can be caused by a number of factors (*e.g.*, strikes, accidents, fires or natural catastrophes), purchasing agents are reluctant to rely on a single source of supply. Instead, they often choose to spread their buying over two more suppliers whenever possible. When buyers divide their purchases between(among) suppliers, one of them, the preferred supplier, often gets the major portion of the order quantities.

Reciprocity. Giving consideration to selecting suppliers because of their value as customers is known as 'reciprocity'. The objective of reciprocity is for the buyer and seller to reach an agreement on an exchange of business that is mutually beneficial and has become an important part of the responsibility of purchasing and materials management. Large-volume purchasing and the need for speciality suppliers (brought about by intensified national and foreign competition and increased product differentiation) leads to close relationships at the executive level that foster awareness of mutual dependence for achieving increased profits. Because of the increasing shortages in raw materials and the rising costs of raw materials and other inputs, purchasing managers may initiate reciprocal arrangements to meet their firms' basic purchasing needs.

Non-task Objectives

The major factors that influence the purchasing decision are social considerations, such as friendship, reputation and mutually beneficial interactions. Organisations work best when people accomplish personal and organisational objectives simultaneously. A buyer can take pride, a personal objective, in making a correct buying decision that also accomplishes an organisational objective. In this case, a single action accomplishes two different objectives. At the same time, caution must be exercised to avoid overemphasising the buyer's personal goals at the expense of the organisation's objectives.

RELATION BETWEEN PURCHASING ACTIVITIES AND BUYER BEHAVIOUR

Organisational buying behaviour is ultimately influenced by forces within the organisation as well as environmental forces. The status and operating procedures of purchasing, the degree of involvement and interaction of various groups and group members and their different perceptions — all have a significant impact on purchasing decisions. Our purpose here is to discuss :

1. How purchasing activities within the organisational structure influence buying behaviour.
2. The factors influencing the size and interaction of buying centres.
3. How groups and individuals differ in their approach to buying.
4. How organisational buyers choose and evaluate suppliers.

Seldom does an organisational buyer make a decision in isolation. Purchasing decisions are influenced by organisational, group and individual forces, as well as forces within the external environment. The position of purchasing and its status within the organisation has a significant influence on industrial buying behaviour. Purchases are also affected by a complex set of decisions made by the several individuals in buying centres — individuals with different levels of information and expertise and different backgrounds, who interact at different stages of the purchasing decision process.

PURCHASING INFLUENCE ON BUYER BEHAVIOUR

International material shortages, rising costs of materials and energy, fluctuating nationalistic moods, conflicting social goals, profit squeezes and greater government regulation of business during the mid-1970s together increased the importance of the purchasing function considerably. To all these must be added the realisation that efficient and effective purchasing, through the use of material requirements planning and just-in-time inventory control systems, is a key factor in maintaining profits and solving cash flow problems. The average industrial firm spends approximately 60% of its sales revenue on materials, services and capital equipment. Purchasing is now being looked at as "asset-management through asset-utilisation and inventory control". Today, purchasing manager regularly attends meetings with other major functional departments of the firm. A typical asset management team includes procurement specialists, cost/price analysts and engineers.

MATERIAL REQUIREMENTS PLANNING

One major change in the purchasing function is the use of *material requirements planning* (*MRP*). Under *MRP* a firm estimates its future sales, schedules production accordingly, and then orders parts and materials to coordinate with production schedules so that inventories will not become too large or too small. MRP is conceptually simple, but, in practice, it can require various considerations. An input part, for example, may be used at more than one stage in a production process that takes place over a period of time. Thus, multiple deliveries may be necessary to minimise inventory costs and existing inventories continuously monitored to accomodate for inaccuracies in sales forecasts and subsequent production.

To utilise MRP, number of firms are combining the functions of purchasing, transportation, inventory control, receiving and, in some cases, production control under one functional area referred to as *materials management*.

To keep track of orders and the various supply sources available, many organisations have also begun using computers, some of which are directly linked to suppliers. Since irregular deliveries and defective parts delivered by suppliers can require various adjustments in a producer's MRP scheduling, these computerised systems are used to find and eliminate weak suppliers.

In general, the effectiveness of MRP depends on the buyer notifying the supplier of material needs in advance of production schedules. Suppliers who sell to organisations using MRP must work closely with customer firms to ensure that MRP systems are effective. The resultant benefits of MRP to both the supplier and customer, however, are controlled inventory levels, better management of production costs, timely deliveries, and an overall increase in efficiency and effectiveness of operations.

JUST-IN-TIME (JIT) PURCHASING

During the last decade, a new form of exchange has developed between suppliers of component parts and materials. Rather than using multiple sourcing, many companies are using just-in-time. Just-in-time is an inventory control system which enables a manufacturer to maintain minimum inventory levels by relying on only one supplier to deliver frequent shipments (sometimes daily) just-in-time for assembly into final products.

One objective of JIT is to develop long-term, one-supplier relationships to reduce the risk of interrupted material flows. An advantage of such a relationship is the resultant improved quality of items supplied, referred to as "zero-defect quality levels". The use of JIT necessitates that the supplier deliver the ordered product at the precise time in the precise quality. It also requires the integration of the buyer-seller's materials management, engineering, purchasing, production and marketing systems to promote the efficient flow of parts and materials. Under JIT, then, cost factors are less important and material specifications are more flexible. This does not imply a lack of concern for costs or quality. Rather, it creates an atmosphere in which both buyer and seller contribute towards optimal cost/benefit trade-offs, with both cost and performance receiving due consideration.

CENTRALISED PURCHASING

In addition to MRP and JIT, there is a growing tendency towards centralisation of purchasing. Important differences in buying behaviour occur between centralised and decentralised purchasing functions. When purchasing is centralised, purchasing specialists concentrate their attention on selected items, developing extensive knowledge of supply and demand conditions. Thus, they are more familiar with cost factors that affect the supplying industry and understand well how vendors within the industry operate. This specialised knowledge, when combined with the volume buying that centralised purchasing controls, increases the firm's buying strength and its supplier options.

Centralised purchasers also tend to place different priorities on selected buying criteria. In comparison to local units where the emphasis is more on short-term cost efficiency and profit considerations, centralised units place more emphasis on long-term supply availability and supplier relationships. Further influencers outside the purchasing unit appear to have more influence on purchasing decisions at the local level. Engineers and other technical personnel are inclined to be overly specific in their preferences regarding materials, component parts and sources of supply. Less specialised, non-technical local purchasing agents often lack the expertise and self-perceived status to challenge these preferences.

Buyer Technology

The advent of computers has significantly improved the function of purchasing. Typical computer applications in purchasing include calculating economic order quantities, determining optimal lead times, tracking critical delivery schedules and monitoring supplier performance indices. In fact, computers have been the primary factor in the implementation of MRP.

Computer systems are now employed in highly repetitive buying due to their ability to handle such tasks faster, cheaper and more accurately than buyers. Although totally computerised handling of new task buying situations is unlikely in the near future, computerised data analysis allows purchasing managers more time to evaluate and negotiate with potential suppliers.

Marketing Implications

MRP, JIT and centralised purchasing have a definite impact on performance. This is so due to the growing professionalism of purchasing manager who are more technical and financially oriented in their approach to buying. Buyers are not only becoming more professional, but, in many cases, the scope of their responsibility becomes wider and wider. Sales people must possess the tools necessary to respond properly to their needs and be able to provide information on a broad range of functions and buying criteria.

THREE TYPES OF PURCHASES

Purchase decisions in industrial and business markets are of the following three types :

(i) ***Straight re-buy decisions.*** These are standard, routine and repetitive. They would include orders for routine raw materials such as steel stock; screws, nuts and bolts, lubricants and fuel oil. Such purchases are often made under long term contracts. In case of such purchases stock control is necessary when current stock levels reach a minimum safety level.

(ii) ***Modified re-buy decisions.*** This relates to purchase situations in which some kind of review is necessary. Whatever the reason for the review, the purchase manager must examine alternative sources of supply, or alternative products capable of meeting an existing need. The need for a review of the existing supply arrangements might be necessary due to growing dissastifaction with current suppliers, or increasing prices of materials. Alternatively, 'value analysis' may have shown that the specific requirement can be met in a different way, either cheaply or obtaining better value for money.

(iii) *New task purchasing*. It relates to new types of goods or services never purchased before. In such cases there is the need for maximum search, analysis, evaluation and selection by purchasing people, particularly where the item to be purchased is complex. Since in case of new task purchasing there is no previous experience of the product to be purchased, there is maximum risk for the organisation. It may, therefore, be necessary to make a thorough search or investigation of relevant aspects of purchase.

Synopsis for Learning

Q.1. What is purchasing ?

Ans. The term 'purchasing' describes the process of buying: learning of the need, locating and selecting a supplier, negotiating price and other pertinent terms and following up to ensure delivery. Procurement is a somewhat broader term and includes purchasing, stores, traffic, receiving, incoming inspection and salvage.

Q.2. What is the importance purchasing ?

Ans. The procurement of supplies for any type of enterprise is often not given the importance which the job demands. In many cases, over 50% of money spent is on materials purchased and this may exceed payments for salaries and wages.

Materials may be purchased at too high a price, or the wrong quality, or too great a quantity, which may lead to obsolescence and loss of interest on capital. Too little purchase means production delays. So incorrect buying can have a strong effect upon profits.

5.3 THE PURCHASING FUNCTION : A BROAD OVERVIEW

The purchasing function used to be part of the production function and enjoyed very little status in the organisation. Over the past few decades, however, the purchasing activity has grown in stature through recognition of the contribution it makes to the success of any enterprise and it is now recognised as a separate function in its own right.

- It is interesting to consider the enormous impact efficient purchasing (or procurement as it is often called) has on the costs of an organisation. By rational buying the purchasing department can generate profit immediately. The huge responsibility falling on those concerned with purchasing, therefore, is clearly visible. This has come about because of the increasing size of organisations, the increasing complexity of materials and components and the extreme competition met in the modern market.
- The purchasing function differs from most others in that those carrying out this work are to a large extent tied to their own industry. However, there are many activites within the purchasing function that are common to many industries and other types of enterprise.

Common Purchasing Activities

Activities common to most industries are:

(a) All buyers will need to have a wide knowledge of the markets from which they have to make their purchases, whether these are raw materials, manufactured components or — as in wholesale and retail trading — finished goods. The knowledge will extend to how the suppliers perform in regard to reliability and delivery performance.

(b) In most manufacturing industries buyers will have to interact closely with the production department to ascertain their precise requirements. In retail selling the buyer has a key role in the success of the enterprise in that he (or she) must closely watch consumer behaviour and attitude — their taste and demand.

(c) Though inventory control may or may not be the direct responsibility of the purchasing officer, he is primarily responsible for ensuring that sufficent supplies of materials or components are available to maintain continuity of production or sales. The buyer may do this by contracts with suppliers for regular deliveries or by building up stocks to be used as and when required. The former keeps a minimum of capital tied up in store but there is always the risk of suppliers not keeping to delivery undertakings. The suppliers in their turn try to ensure that materials or components are readily available.

(d) In most organisations the purchasing department is responsible for negotiating purchase prices and terms of credit.

(e) Purchasing is also generally responsible for ensuring that the goods ordered and invoiced are actually received and that the price charged are those quoted. To mimimise risk, necessary checks are to be carried out by people not directly involved in placing the orders.

(f) Purchasing will constantly monitor expected deliveries to ensure that suppliers fulfil their commitments regarding quality and delivery dates.

(g) Purchasing will constantly investigate the market
(i) to seek better products, prices, terms or deliveries;
(ii) to find out alternative suppliers to ensure continuity of deliveries in case the main source suddenly fails for any reason.

PURCHASING'S RELATIONS WITH OTHER FUNCTIONS

- The purchasing department probably has direct relations with more functional departments throughout the organisation than any other single department.
- Its primary relationship in manufacturing and similar industrial enterprises is with the three aspects of production — production engineering, production planning and production control. It serves production engineering by advising on the availability and costs of both equipment and materials. The buying department, by its constant investigations into all the appropriate sources of supply, has a wide knowledge and experience with which to advice on these important matters. A similar service is provided for production planning where information concering availability and continuity of supplies is vital if production is to be planned effectively. Equally, production control benefits from the activities of the purchasing department since this department is concerned with monitoring delivery performance of suppliers and finding out alternative sources of supply if delays or breakdowns in the main sources of supply occur or are likely to occur in near future.
- The purchasing department also has a direct relationship with the marketing function. It is because customers' remarks and complaints, especially in respect of material quality, have a direct bearing on what is purchased and, sometimes, where.
- Purchasing is also very much to do with finance: the buying department is a major spender in any organisation. Its link with the accounts department is, therefore, obvious. Credit terms in regard to payment times and cash discounts are as important as the actual purchase prices. Again, proper timing of purchases can have a positive effect on working capital. If, for example, credit terms are for remittance at the end of the month following delivery, then orders for delivery in the first week of a month allow for two months' credit before payment is due. Many such devices are also used by the purchasing department to benefit the financial aspect of the organisation, very often, for example the buyer may be able to strike a good bargain for the organisation, and an efficient purchasing officer is one who is always alert and is able to make use of such favourable offers. On the other hand, prudence must always prevail in this connection as the costs of storage can easily absorb may savings made by favourable prices.

PURCHASING POLICY

As with other functions, there must be a clear policy on purchasing laid down. This is, of course, ultimately the responsibility of top management, but the purchasing officer will have a great deal of advice to give on this matter :

- Perhaps the first item of purchasing policy to be considered will be the level of stocks to be carried. The normal pattern of deliveries by suppliers may determine this. If supplies are generally constant then reliance can be placed on a continuing receipt of goods ordered, but if they are erratic it may be more prudent to establish a stock to ensure regular input to production. Costs of holding stores, quantity discounts, the possible financial implications of production stoppages, and vulnerability to deterioration and to theft will all play a part in making this decision.
- Secondly, certain raw materials are subject to wide price fluctuations. So it may be both rational and profitable to purchase large quantities when they become available at low prices. There are two advantages in doing this. First, the production department gains the benefit of low-priced inputs which will lead to lower selling prices. This will give the final products a competitive price edge. Alternatively, the lower cost may give an opportunity to make higher profits if there is a market for the company's product. Second, when raw-materials prices rise the organisation may be able to dispose of its surplus stocks at a profit and, thus, make a gain just by holding the stocks.
- Thirdly, is entering into short- or long-term contracts for the purchase of materials to be part of the purchasing policy or is it to be the policy to go to the market as and when materials are actually required? When prices generally are rising, or when supplies are difficult or uncertain, such a practice is attractive. On the other hand, being committed to one supplier at fixed prices may be damaging if prices fall suddenly or supplies from the contractor fail for some reason.

Synopsis for Learning

Q.1. What are the broad objectives of purchasing ?

Ans. The main objectives of purchasing are the following :
buying materials at the lowest cost consistent with the service and quality required;
avoiding any waste or duplication, while maintaining the lowest possible outlay on stock consistent with making the material needed for production available as and when required.

Q.2. What is the essence of purchasing ?

Ans. Purchasing is the activity responsible for getting the right materials to the right place, at the right time, in the right quantity and at the right price.

Q.3. What are the functions of the purchasing department ?

Ans. The purchasing department is responsible for :
(i) material and equipment purchases while adhering to the company's purchasing policy;
(ii) studying all markets for prices, trends and delivery times and maintaining accurate records of sources of materials, etc.

OBJECTIVES OF EFFICIENT PURCHASING

The objectives of efficent purchasing can be set out in the "seven rights" which may be expressed to buy:

the **RIGHT** goods
at the **RIGHT** price
in the **RIGHT** quantity
of the **RIGHT** quality
at the **RIGHT** time
delivered to the **RIGHT** place
on the **RIGHT** terms

These — the seven aspects of efficent purchasing — are self-explanatory and enter into all buying operations.

STOCK CONTROL

- The question of whether stocks of materials and components should be the responsibility of the purchasing function has no universal answer. Some undertakings have such stocks under the control of production on the basis that the physical availability of these items is part of the manufacturing function. Others say that as the purchasing department is responsible for procurement then it is this department's responsibility to control and account for stocks. Many others believe that storage and stock control should be a department separate from either, particularly as the financial value of stocks held is usually very considerable.
- These three point of view are really relevant only where operations are conducted on one site or on a very small number of nearby sites, and relate largely to manufacturing activities. Other industries and activities such as building construction — where operations are carried out on sites — have the question answered for them. Every building site and every civil engineering site, for example, must of necessity have materials and components at hand under the direct control of the site manager (by whatever name he is known).
- The main objectives of stockholding and stock control are to ensure an adequate flow of materials and components required for the organisation's operations, to keep minimum stocks commensurate with operational requirements to ensure the good physical condition and safety of the stocks held and to reduce the possibilities of fraud and theft as much as possible. The procedures required to carry out these objectives will vary according to the types of stores held, their physical disposition and the rates of usage.
- Finally, there seems to be no common usage of the words stock(s) and stores and they are used in the same sense most of the time.

Synopsis for Learning

Q.1. **What are the objectives of efficient purchasing ?**

Ans. There are seven aspects of efficient purchasing. These enter into all buying decisions.

Q.2. **Is stock control a responsibility of the purchasing function?**

Ans. There is difference of opinion regarding whether stock control is a function of the purchasing department. There are three different opinions on this issue.

Q.3. **What are the main objectives of stock holding and stock control?**

Ans. The main objectives of stockholding and stock control is to ensure an adequate flow of materials and components required for an organisation's operations, to keep minimum stocks necessary to meet organisational requirements to ensure good physical condition and safety of stocks held and to reduce the possibility of theft and fraud as much as possible.

5.4 NEGOTIATION IN PURCHASING

Price negotiation is typical in industrial marketing, particularly in complex buying situations where buyers and sellers make a number of proposals and counterproposals before a price is agreed upon. In this sense, negotiation and open bidding are virtually synonymous. Most major purchases by institutions, government agencies, and commercial business are negotiated. Not only price, but service, delivery, technical assistance, product characteristics, and quality are commonly negotiated.

The process of negotation may begin with a quotation or a bid that is later modified to reflect the specific requirements of the buying company and the special strengths of the seller. In the case of open bidding, negotiations are often carried on simultaneously with a number of suppliers until enough information has been exchanged to allow for a competitive bid.

Negotiation is almost always employed in the selling and purchase of a new product due to the uncertainties involved. With little or no experience in manufacturing or estimating costs of such products, sellers often prefer to negotiate rather than volunteer a fixed price.

Many industrial buyers also prefer to negotiate price, believing that negotiated prices are closer to the "right" price than orginal quotations. Buyers generally have specific goals in mind when negotiating with prospective suppliers. These goals, while subject to some flexibility, are based on a careful examination of the buying firm's needs and alternatives[1].

The successful negotiation of a contract requires skill, experience, and preparation on the buyer's part. The purchaser must analyse the supplier's strengths and weaknesses compared to potential competitors.

Negotiation between buyer and seller involves some from of bargaining strategy that is influenced by the relative strengths of the two parties. In general, there are four types of negotiating strategies: (1) *a negotiated strategy* in which buyer and seller

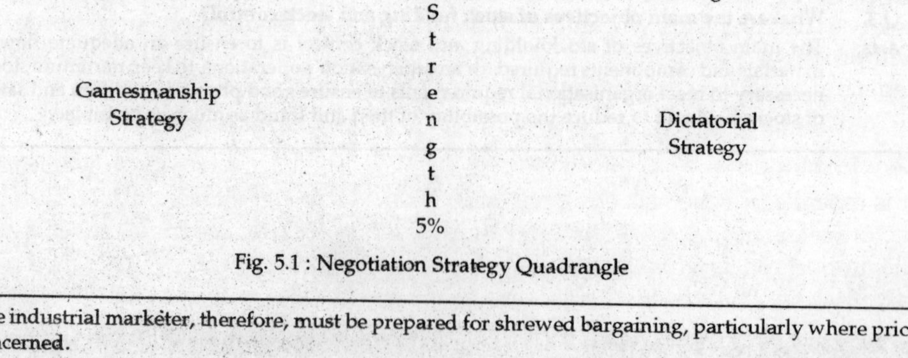

Fig. 5.1 : Negotiation Strategy Quadrangle

1. The industrial marketer, therefore, must be prepared for shrewed bargaining, particularly where price is concerned.

have a close match of strengths and will negotiate a price that would be fair to both parties, (2) *a dictatorial strategy* in which buyer is weak relative to the seller and the seller will attempt to set a price that is most favourable to his (or her) firm, (3) *a defensive strategy* in which seller is weak relative to the buyer, and (4) *a gamesmanship strategy* in which both parties are weak and will play "hide and seek" to arrive at price. Fig. 5.1 illustrates the relationship among these four strategies.

Measuring Buyer and Seller Strength

To determine the type of negotiating strategy to be employed, the strength of the seller's bargaining power relative to that of the buyer must be measured. It is possible to determine this power by a number of criteria. For instance, a buyer's bargaining power depends on such factors as the size of the organization, the amount of past purchases, future buying power, length of time in business, and the firm's need for the product. The strength of a seller can be measured by criteria such as company image, product quality and uniqueness, delivery capability, technical assistance, and after-sale services. The strengths of both the buyer and the seller are a function of these various criteria and must be measured in relative terms (that is, the buyer's strength relative to seller's). Therefore, once strength have been evaluated for both the buyer and the seller, an overall measure of strength/weakness must be derived.

Evaluating Buyer and Seller Product Need

Once negotiation strategies become dear, tractical measures must be taken. While the buyer and seller will attempt to negotiate price, the tactics to be employed in the negotiation process will depend on the buyer's need for the product with respect to the seller's need for the sale.

A buyer's product need can be classified as acute, moderate, or marginal. If the proposed purchase is an immediate replacement of a defective machine critical to the manufacturing process, the buyer is not likely to be price sensitive. In such a case, the buyer's need is acute. Any seller taking undue advantage of this situation through price hike, however, may face retaliation in future negotiations. A moderate need would exist if the buyer had some time, even though limited, to enagage in a supplier search before finalising the order. When a firm is searching for office supplies to replenish stocks three months later, the need would be classified as marginal because the buyer has ample time to locate and obtain a satisfactory price from an acceptable supplier.

The seller's need to make the sale must also be compared to the buyer's need for the product. An acute product sale need occur when a company is operating well below capacity, needs working capital, or desires to secure a prototype order that will probably lead to repeat business. On the other hand, if production is near full capacity, or a buyer is not likely to place repeat orders, the product sale would be classified as marginal.

Determining Key Negotiable Factors

It is essential for the seller to determine where the buyer stands with respect to all factors relevant to the negotiation. Some factors will be totally irrelevant (for example, import tariffs when buyer and seller are in the same country). Other factors will fall into one of two categories: non-negotiable factors and nonvalue factors. For example, a buyer may require delivery of component parts in six weeks to support a planned production schedule that cannot be delayed, but the seller is unable to supply the component as per specifications in that time span. In this case, the delivery date is definitely not a negotiable item. However, a discussion with the buyer's engineers shows that a product is already in the seller's inventory and differing from the standard component in only non-critical details. This should be acceptable to the buyer, particularly when it is offered at a lower price. The coupling of specification revision and price reduction becomes a major trade-off item, *i.e.*, in order to get one benefit (lower price), the other benefit (timely delivery of the original item) has to be sacrificed. Neither buyer nor seller care that the substitute component is painted green instead of blue.

This simple example illustrates that most industrial negotiations are clearly aimed at a win-win result, not a win-lose outcome. Experienced negotiators on both sides of the desk realise that any worhtwhile transaction must yield something of value to both buyer and seller. The key lies in open-mined and flexible investigation of alternatives when the intial desires of either party can show the most creativity and intitiative.

Price Negotiation

Price can be negotiated if the buyer has the knowledge and the capacity to do so. A small retailer probably has little bargaining power, but a large buyer may have much. Through negotiation, the buyer and seller try to resolve conditions of purchase to mutual benefit of both parties. Skill and careful planning are required for the negotiation to be successful. It also takes a great deal of time and effort, so the potential profit must justify the expense.

One important factor in the apporach to negotiation is the type of product. There are four categories:

1. **Commodities.** Commodities are materials such as copper, coal, wheat, meat, and metals. Price is set by market supply and demand and can fluctuate widely. Negotiation is concerned with contracts for future prices.

2. **Standard products.** These items are provided by many suppliers. Since the items are standard and the choice of suppliers large, prices are determined on the basis of listed catalogue prices. There is not much room for negotiation except for large purchases.

3. **Items of small value.** These are items such as maintenance or cleaning supplies and represent purchases of such small value that price negotiation is of little purpose. The prime objective should be to keep the cost of ordering low. Firms will negotiate a contract with a supplier that can supply many items and set up a simple ordering system that reduces the cost of ordering.

4. **Made-to-order items.** This category includes items made to specification or on which quotations from several sources are received. These can generally be negotiated.

Synopsis for Learning

Q.1. Why their is need for negotiation in purchasing ?

Ans. There is always need for negotiation in purchasing due to the uncertainties involved.

Q.2. What are the essentials of successful negotiation?

Ans. Successful negotiation requires skill, experience, and preparation on the buyer's part. The purchaser must analyse the supplier's strengths and weaknesses compared to potential competitors.

5.5 THE PURCHASING CYCLE

The purchasing cycle consists of the following steps:

1. Receiving and analysing purchasing requisitions.
2. Selecting suppliers. Finding potential suppliers, issuing requests for quotations, receiving and analysing quotations, and selecting the right supplier.
3. Determining the right price.
4. Issuing purchase orders.
5. Following-up to ensure that delivery dates are met.
6. Receiving and accepting goods.
7. Approving supplier's invoice for payment.

Receiving and analysing purchasing requisition

Purchase requisitions start with the department or person who will be the ultimate user. In the material requirements planning environnment, the planner releases a planned order authorising the purchasing department to go ahead and process a purchase order. The purchase requisition contains, at least, the following information:

- Identity of originator, signed approval, and account to which cost is assigned.
- Material specification.
- Quantity and unit of measure.
- Required delivery date and place.
- Any other supplementary information required.

Selecting suppliers

Identifying and selecting suppliers are important responsibilitiess of the purchasing department. For routine items or those that have not been purchased in the past, a list of apporved suppliers is kept. If the item has not been purchased before or there is no acceptable supplier on file, a search must be made. If the order is of small value or for standard items, a supplier can probably be found in a catalogue, trade journal, or directory.

Requesting quotations

For major items, it is usually desirable to issue a request for quotation. This is a written inquiry that is sent to many suppliers to ensure that competitive and reliable quotations are received. It is not a sales order. After the suppliers have completed the quotations and returned it to the buyer, the quotations are analysed for price, compliance to specification, terms and conditions of sale, delivery, and payment terms. For items where specifications can be accurately written, the choice is probably made on price, delivery, and terms of sale. For items where specifications cannot be accurately written, the items quoted will vary. The quotations must be evaluated for technical factors and price. Usually both the issuing and purchasing departments are involved in the decision.

Determining the right price

This is the responsibility of the purchasing department and is closely tied to the selection of suppliers. The purchasing department is also responsible for price negotiation and will try to obtain the best price from the supplier.

Issuing a purchasing order

A purchase order is a legal offer to purchase. Once accepted by the supplier, it becomes legal contract for delivery of the goods according to the terms and conditions specified in the purchase agreement. The purchase order is prepared from the purchase requisition or the quotations and from any other additional information needed. A copy is sent to the supplier; copies are retained by purchasing and are also sent to other departments such as accounting, the originating department, and receiving.

Following-up and delivery

The supplier is responsible for delivering the items ordered on time. The purchasing department is responsible for ensuring that suppliers do deliver on time. If there is doubt that delivery dates can be met, purchasing must find out the problem in time and take corrective action. This might involve expediting transportation, alternate sources of supply, working with the supplier to solve its problems, or rescheduling production.

The purchasing department is also responsible for working with the supplier on any changes in delivery requirements. Demand for items changes with time, and it may be necessary to expedite certain items or push delivery back on some others. The buyer must keep the supplier informed of the true requirements so that the supplier is able to provide what is wanted and when.

Receiving and accepting goods

When the goods are received, the receiving department inspects the goods to ensure that correct ones have been sent, are in the right quantity, and the bill of lading supplied by the carrier. The receiving department then accepts the goods and writes up a receiving report noting any variance. If further inspection is required, such as by quality control, the goods are sent to quality control or held there for inspection. If the goods are received damaged, the receiving department will advise the purchasing department and hold the goods for further action. Provided the goods are in order and require no further inspection, they will be sent to the originating department or to inventory.

A copy of the receiving report is then sent to the purchasing department noting any variance or discrepancy from the purchase order. If the order is considered complete in all respects, the receiving department closes out its copy of the purchase order and advises the purchasing department accordingly. If it is not, the purchase order is held open awaiting completion. If the goods have also been inspected by the quality control department, they, too, will advise the purchasing department whether the goods have been accepted or not.

Approving supplier's invoice for payment

When the supplier's invoice is received, there are three pieces of information that should agree: the purchase order, the receiving report, and the invoice. The items and the quantities should be the same on all; the prices, and extensions to prices, should be the same on the purchase order and the invoice. All discounts and terms of the original purchase order must be checked against the invoice. It is the job of the purchasing department to verify these and to resolve any difference. Once approved, the invoice is sent to accounts payble for payment.

5.6 DIFFERENT ASPECTS OF PURCHASING

Purchasing has different aspects. The first concern of purchasing — what to buy — is not necessarily a simple decision. For example, someone deciding to buy a car considers how the car will be used, how often, how much one is willing to pay, and so on. Only then can an individual specify the type of car needed to make the "best buy." There are certain problems that organisations face when developing specifications of products and the type of specifications that may be used. These problems may now be briefly discussed.

In purchasing an item or a service from a supplier, several factors are included in the package bought. These must be considered when specification are being developed and can be divided into three broad categories:

- Quantity requirements
- Price requirements
- Functional requirements.

Quantity Requirements

Market demand first determines the quantities needed. The quantity is important because it will be a factor in the way the product is designed to be made at minimum cost, or a suitable standard item would be selected. However, if the demand were for several thousand, the item would be designed to take advantage of economies of scale, thus satisfying the functional needs at a better price.

Price Requirements

The price specification represents the economic value that the buyer puts on the item — the amount the individual is willing to pay. If the item is to be sold at a low price, the manufacturer will not want to pay a high price for a component part. The economic value placed on the item must relate to the use of the item and its expected selling price.

Functional Requirements

Functional specifications are concerned with the end use of the item and what the item is expected to do. By their nature, functional specifications are perhaps the most important.

In a sence, functional specifications are the most difficult to define. To be successful, they must satisfy the real need or purpose of an item. In many cases, the real need has both practical and other elements to it.

Functional specifications and quality. Functional specifications are intimately tied to the quality of a product of service.

There are many definitions of quality, but they all center on the idea of user satisfaction. An item has the required quality if it satisfies the needs of the user.

It is the responsibility of the purchasing people to make sure the supplier can provide the required quality level. For purchasing and manufacturing, quality means conforming to specifications or requirements.

To the final user, quality is related to his (or her) expectation of how the product should perform. Customers do not care why product or service is defective. They want satisfaction. If the product is what the customer wants, well designed, well made and well serviced, the quality is treated as satisfactory.

Functional specifications should define the quality level needed. They should described all those characteristics of a product determined by its final use.

Function, quantity, service, and price are interrelated. It is difficult to specify one without consideration of the others. Indeed, the final specification is a compromise of them all, and the successful specification is the best combination of the lot. However, functional specifications, ultimately, are the ones that drive the others. If the product does not perform adequately for the price, it will not sell.

Functional Specification Description

Functional specification can be described in the following ways or by a combination of them:

1. By brand.
2. By specification of physical and chemical characteristics, material and method of manufacture, and performance.
3. By engineering drawings.
4. Miscellaneous.

Description by Brand

Description by brand is most often used in wholesale or retail businesses but is also used extensively in manufacturing. This is particularly true under the following circumstances:

- Items are patented, or the process is secret.
- The supplier has special expertise that the buyer lacks.
- The quantity bought is so small that it is not worth the buyer's effort to develop specifications.
- The supplier, through advertising or direct sales effort, has created a preference on the part of the buyer's customers or staff.

When buying by brand, the customer is relying on the reputation and integrity of the supplier. The assumption is that the supplier wishes to maintain the brand's reputation and will maintain and guarantee the quility of the product so that repeat purchases gives the buyer the same satisfaction.

Most of the objections to purchasing by brand center on cost. Branded items, as a group, usually have price levels that are higher than nonbranded items. It may be less costly to develop specifications for generic products than to rely on brands. The other major disadvantage of specifying by brand is that it restricts the number of potential suppliers and reduces competition. Consequently, the usual practice, when specifying by brand, is to ask for the item by brand name or equivalent. In theory, this allows for competition.

Description by Specification

There are various ways of describing a product, but they usually include one or more of the following. Whatever method is used, description by specification depends on the buyer describing in detail exactly what is needed:

- **Physical and chemical characteristics.** The buyer must define the physical and chemical properties of the materials wanted. Petroleum products, pharmaceuticals, and paints are often specified in this way.
- **Material and method of manufacture.** Sometimes the method of manufacture determines the performance and use of a product. For example, hot and cold-rolled steels are made differently and have different characteristics.
- **Performance.** This method is used where the buyer is primarily concerned with what the item is required to do and is prepared to have the supplier decide how necessary performance is to be attained. For example, a water pump might be specified as having to deliver so many gallons / litres per minute. Performance specifications are relatively easy to prepare and take advantage of the supplier's specialised knowledge.

Whatever the method of specification, there are several characteristics to description by specification:

- To be useful, specifications must be carefully designed. If they are too loosely drawn, they may not provide a satisfactory product. If they are too detailed and elaborate, they are costly to develop, are difficult to inspect, and may discourage possible suppliers.
- Specifications must allow for multiple sources and for competitive bidding.
- If performance specifications are used, the buyer is assured that if the product does not give the desired results, the seller is responsible. They provide a standard for measuring and checking the materials supplied.
- Not all items lend themselves to specification. For example, it may not be easy to specify colour schemes or the appearance of an item.
- An item described by specification may be no more suitable, and a lot more expensive, than a supplier's standard brand.
- If the specifications are set by the buyer, they may be expensive to develop. They will be used only where there is sufficient volume of purchase to warrant the cost or where it is not possible to describe what is wanted in any other way.

Sources of Specification

There are two major sources of specification:

1. Buyer specifications.
2. Standard specifications.

Buyer specifications. Buyer-developed spacifications are usually expensive and time-consuming to develop. Companies usually do not use this method unless there is no suitable standard specification available or unless the volume of work makes it less costly to do so.

Standard specifications. Standard specifications are developed through much study and effort by governmental and nongovernment agencies. They usually apply to raw or semifinished goods, component parts, or the composition of material. In most cases, they have become accepted standards used by industrial buyers.

There are various advantages to using standard specifications. Firstly, they are widely known and accepted, manufacured, and sold, they are lower in price than nonstandard items. Finally, because they have been developed with inputs from a larger number of producers and suppliers, they are usually set by the government.

Engineering Drawings

Engineering drawings describe in detail the exact configuration of the parts and the assembly. They also give information on such things as finishes, tolerance, and material to be used. These drawings are a major method of specifying what is wanted and are widely used because often there is no other way to describe the configuration of parts or the way they are to fit together. They are produced by the engineering design department and are expensive to produce, but give an exact description of the part required.

Miscellaneous

There are a variety of other methods of specification. At times, samples are used, for example, where colours or patterns are to be specified. Often a variety of methods can be used, and the buyer must select the best one.

The method of description is communication with the supplier. How well it is done will affect the success of the purchase and sometimes the price paid.

Selection of Sources

The objective of purchasing is to get all the right things together — quality, quantity, delivery, and price. Once the decision is made about what to buy, the selection of the right supplier is the next most important purchasing decision. A good supplier is one that has the technology to make the product to the required quality, has the capacity to make the quantities needed, and can run the business well enough to make a profit and still sell a product at a competitive price.

Sourcing

There are three types of sourcing: sole, multiple, and single.

1. *Sole sourcing* implies that only one supplier is available because of patents, technical specifications, raw material, location, and so forth.
2. *Multiple sourcing* is the use of more than one supplier for an item. The potential advantages of multiple sourcing are that competition will result in lower price and better service and that there will be a continuity of supply. In practice there is a tendency towards a strained relation between supplier and customer.
3. *Single sourcing* is a planned decision by the organisation to select one supplier for an item when several sources are available. It is intended to produce a long-term partnership.

Factors in Selecting Suppliers

In fact, function, quantity, service, and price specifications are what the supplier is expected to provide and are the basis for selection and evaluation. If we give due importance to all these factors, then we have to take into account the following factors in selecting a supplier:

Technical ability. Does the supplier have the technical ability to make or supply the product? Does the supplier have a programme of product development and improvement? Can the supplier assist in improving the product?

These questions are important since, often, the buyer will depend upon the supplier to provide product improvements that will increase or reduce the cost of the buyer's products. Sometimems the supplier can suggest changes in product specification that will improve the quality of product and reduce cost.

Manufacturing capability. Manufacturing must be able to meet the specifications for the product consistently while producing as few defects as possible. This means that the supplier's manufacturing facilities must be able to supply the quality and quantity of the products wanted. The supplier must have a good quality control programme, competent and capable manufacturing personnel, and good manufacturing planning and control systems to ensure timely delivery. These are important in ensuring that the supplier can supply the quality and quantity wanted.

Reliability. In selecting a supplier, it is desirable to pick one that is reputable, stable, and financially strong. If a long-term workable relationship is to be established there must be mutual trust and assurance that the supplier is financially strong enough to stay in business.

After-sales service. If the product is of a technical nature or likely to need replacement parts or technical support, the supplier must have a good after-sales service. This should include a good service organisation and inventory of service parts.

Supplier location. Sometimes it is desirable that the supplier be located near the buyer, or at least maintain an inventory locally. A close location helps reduce delivery times. It also means materials can be delivered quickly in times of shortage or emergency.

Other considerations. Sometimes other factors such as credit terms, reciprocal business, and willingness of the supplier to hold inventory for the buyer are to be taken into consideration.

Price. The supplier should be able to provide competitive prices. This does not necessarily mean the lowest price. It is one that considers the ability of the supplier to provide the necessary materials in the quantity and quality wanted, at the time wanted, as well as any other services needed.

In today's business world, the type of relationship between the supplier and the buyer is important to both. Ideally, the relationship will be on-going with a mutual interdependence.

The supplier can rely on future business, and the buyer will have an assured supply of quality product, technical support, and product improvement. Communications between buyer and supplier must be open and full so that both parties understand the problems of the other and can work together to solve the same to their mutual advantage. Thus, supplier selection and supplier relations are very important.

Identifying Suppliers

One major responsibility of the purchasing department is to continue to research all possible sources of supply. Some aids for identifying available sources of supply are:

- Salespersons of the supplier company.

- Catalogues.
- Trade magazines.
- Information obtained by the salespeople of the buyer firm.

Final Selection of Supplier

Some factors in evaluating potential suppliers are quantitative, and a rupee value can be put on them. Price is the obvious example. Other factors are qualitative and require some judgement to determine them. These are usually described in detail. The supplier's technical competence is an example.

The challenge is finding some method of combining these two major factors that will enable a buyer to choose the best supplier. One method is the ranking method, described also.

1. Select those factors that must be considered in evaluating potential suppliers.
2. **Assign a weight to each factor.** This weight determines the importance of the factor in relation to the others. As a general rule, a scale of one to ten is used. If one factor is given a weight of five and another a weight of ten, the second one is considered twice as important as the first.
3. **Rate the suppliers for each factor.** This rating is not associated with the weight. Rather, suppliers are rated on their ability to meet the requirements of each factor. Again, usually a scale of one to ten is used.
4. **Rank the suppliers.** For each supplier, the weight of each factor is multiplied by the supplier rating for that factor. For example, if a factor had weight of 8 and a supplier was rated 3 for that factor, the ranking value for that factor would be 24. The supplier rankings are then added to produce a total ranking. The suppliers can then be listed by total ranking and the supplier with the highest ranking chosen.

Table 1 : Supplier Ranking

Factor	Weight	Rating of Suppliers				Ranking of Suppliers			
Suppliers		A	B	C	D	A	B	C	D
Function	10	8	10	6	6	80	100	60	60
Cost	8	3	5	9	10	24	40	72	80
Service	8	9	4	5	7	72	32	40	56
Technical Assistance	5	7	9	4	2	35	45	20	10
Credit Terms	2	4	3	6	8	8	6	12	16
Total (rank of suppliers)						219	223	204	222

Table 1 illustrates this method of selecting suppliers. In this example, supplier B, with the biggest total of 223, will be selected.

The ranking method is an attempt to quantify those things that are not quantified by nature. It attempts to put figures on subjective judgement. It is not a perfect method, but it forces the buying company to consider the relative importance of the various factors.

5.7 PURCHASING POLICIES AND PROCEDURES

In a modern industrial system, purchasing function has a very vital role to play and it becomes more and more important as the complexity of business and industry increases. Purchasing is an activity directed toward securing materials, equipment, etc. required for the proper and efficient functioning of the business . It is a function that goes beyond simple buying and includes planning, policy-making and other commercial and managerial aspects. The main objective of the whole purchasing function is to bring profits for the organisation — better returns for the money invested.

Five main areas relating to purchasing management are:

1. Objectives and functions of purchasing
2. Purchase policy and procedure
3. Principles of purchasing which involve
   (a) Purchasing cycle
   (b) Sources selection and vendor
   (c) Commercial terms and conditions of purchase
   (d) Pricing and discounts
4. Negotiation in purchasing
5. Imports and customs clearance.

Objectives of purchasing

In the last chapter we have discussed in detail the objectives and functions of industrial purchasing. Four broad areas or specific objectives of purchase department are :

(a) Economic purchase operation

Purchasing is an economic function that contributes to the profits of an organisation and thus is vital to its existence. To perform this function properly the purchasers should have sufficient knowledge in many fields apart from buying, such as the macroeconomic environment, engineering basics, mode of transport, import procedures, government laws and regulations and so on.

(b) Consistent market survey

Secondly, it is necessary to make necessary forecasts where prices of materials fluctuate widely. Such forecast is an important aspect of market survey which helps in locating and developing new sources of supply. Through market survey it is possible to gather information about materials — their prices, qualities and sources. Analysis of data gathered and evaluation of information obtained enable the purchaser to take the correct decision.

(c) Proper control over financial commitments

Since the materials bill and services provided constitute 50-60% of a company's turnover there is huge financial commitment. Hence proper controls right from the negotiation stage are essential all the time.

(d) To provide information and assistance to top management and other concerned departments

Forecast of price trends, market situation — such as possible scarcity of materials, future investment commitments vs. working capital — are some of the areas where management must be kept informed from time to time. A company's purchase strategy and policy should be formulated on the basis of such information.

POLICIES

A policy is a general guideline for decision-making. An objective is the end; policy is the means to that end. An objective involves a target; a policy involves the procedure to be followed to reach the target. A policy is essentially a statement relating to those principles or procedure by which a company seeks to realise its objectives. Procedure is a series of step-by-step actions needed for the implementation of a policy decision.

There is hardly any standard purchasing policy and procedure which can be applied to all industries. These policies may vary from company to company — depending on the size and type of business, products and services produced and various other factors.

An organisation may have several policies regarding purchasing. The most important aspects of purchasing policy are :

(i) Centralisation or decentralisation.

(ii) Method of purchase of materials (a) volume of purchase — large or small, (b) seasonal purchase or annual rate contract, (c) sub-contracting or ancillarisation and so on.

(iii) The delegation of power relating to purchase — whether the purchase department alone should undertake the responsibilities for all types of purchases or some purchases can be also done by the user department or not.

(iv) Policies in regard to procurement of materials through foreign collaborators from government undertakings, etc.

(v) Communication — all communication with suppliers should necessarily be done by the purchasing department. The user department may send feed back to the purchase department as and when required.

(vi) Authorisation of the purchase deparatment to seek clarification about requirement, specification, delivery schedule, brandname, trademark etc. in the best interest of the organisation.

(vii) Responsibilities and accountability of purchase personnel.

(viii) Purchase ethics — code of conduct.

(ix) Public relations.

PROCEDURES

Purchasing procedures should be standardised in its scope and flexible enough to accommodate any changes that occur in the business environment and commercial climate. The procedure of indent — *i.e.*, when to indent, how to indent and what are the responsibilities and authorities in regard to scrutiny of any indent — should clearly be indicated. It is also necessary to maintain purchase files, records, vendors files containing information on various range of products produced and sold by the vendors. There are various legal implications of purchasing like offer and acceptance, mode of despatch — FOB, CF, CIF, FOR prices, guarantee and warranty, arbitration, force majeure, cancellation of orders, etc. The detailed procedures relating to all these legal aspects of purchasing should clearly be explained to the purchase personnel as guiding principles. The procedures regarding the functional relationship between the purchase department and other departments should also be clearly stated or defined.

The procedure regarding materials requisition, vendors enlistment, enquiries, conditions of purchase order, follow-up, inspection, delivery, guarantee and warranty, invoicing, bill passing, maintenance of records and performance appraisal of vendors — all should clearly be expressed and circulated.

Source Selection

By procuring and providing right qualilty of required materials of the right quantity and at the right price, the purchase department has the maximum scope to contribute toward corporate profitability. So competent suppliers capable of providing quality inputs are to be selected. This is no doubt a very difficult task, but at the same time the most important one. If a right supplier is selected there may be hardly any problem regarding quality, price and delivery.

A wrong choice of supplier will create regular problems such as supply of inferior quality of materials, failure to meet the supply schedule according to buyer's need, claim of higher price on flimsy ground and even stoppage of supply for bargaining, thereby putting the buyer in a difficult situation. The ultimate objective of purchasing function is defeated if there is any interruption in production schedule due to stock-out of certain items.

So the right selection of source of inputs is very important. In any type of industrial purchasing if the right source or the proper supplier is selected (after evaluation of his capability), there may not be any major problem in fulfilling the ultimate objective of purchasing.

But if proper selection cannot be made with proper evaluation then at every stage the purchaser may face problems with the supplier and cannot perform his alloted task properly.

Two things are important in this context. Firstly, to ensure proper quality it is also necessary to ascertain the right quality. Secondly, it is also necessary to properly evaluate the supplier to ensure his competence to meet the requirement of buyer in respect of quantity and quality of materials.

Developing good and reliable alternative sources of supply is one of the most important responsibilities of a purchasing manager . If the right supplier is selected, then all the benefits of good purchasing — such as competitive pricing, reliable quality, timely delivery and good technical service — can be assured and enjoyed. After a competent supplier is selected, he must be motivated, assisted and periodically evaluated so that a satisfactory service can be obtained in the short run.

Industrial buyers must take three important supplier-oriented actions:

(a) Reward and motivate satisfactory suppliers.

(b) Eliminate unsatisfactory suppliers.

(c) Develop new suppliers.

Vendor Development

In many cases a buyer finds no established supplier for a particular item. The item might currently be imported or it might be an altogether new item. In such cases it would be necessary to develop vendors. The first line of approach is to locate a manufacturer who produces an item almost similar to the one required. He may be encouraged to take up the new line of production.

To facilitate procurement of materials needed all organisations need to develop sources of supply for the required materials. Vendor development helps to locate sources of new materials and enlarges/increases sources of other materials. This is why many organisations have accepted source selection as a corporate policy. Right selection of vendors helps in bringing about a fair competition among the suppliers. This ensures fair prices and satisfactory quality of products. It also ensures that supply failures are kept at a minimum. A well-planned vendor development programme should also improve the buyer's relation with the vendor.

Of late, materials management has been accepted as a strategic business function. This is why appropriate source selection is so important. This is because this function has impact on the activities such as inventory mangement, production planning and control, cash flow requirements and maintaining product quality. For properly performing this function, it is essential, first to understand what is expected of the vendors so that they can meet the organisational needs. The different aspects of buying can be used for proper evaluation of vendors and ascertaining exactly what is expected of the vendors.

For development of new source(s) of supply a very close co-operation and good relationship between the buyer and the seller are necessary. No doubt, suppliers can make or mar the future of a business organisation depending on the extent to which they are motivated. The purchaser's primary interest lies in getting for his company the best value from his suppliers.

The relationship between a buyer and a vendor is reciprocal. One needs the other for mutual benefits of their respective organisations. A buyer has to take the help of a vendor to a great extent. Without such help the smooth and timely functioning of an organisation is bound to be seriously affected, if not totally stopped.

Development of new sources is necessary for one of the following reasons :

(a) Establishment of indigenous sources of supply to substitute imported materials.

(b) To achieve functional improvement, *i.e.*, improve the functioning of the production/operations department.

(c) To reduce the overall cost of a product.

(d) In the case of monopoly situation the price of the goods are frequently changed without showing any reason. Even commercial terms and conditions of purchase of different items such as payment schedule, cash loss, performance guarantee, etc. are not accepted by all of the monopoly vendors. If few more alternative sources can be located, then lower price, improved delivery, better quality etc. may be obtained.

(e) Due to delay in delivery of the materials by the existing vendors, stock-out situation arises. This leads to stoppage of production.

(f) It is often observed that after securing purchase order the vendor does not send his acceptance within the stipulated time or is not at all interested in replying to various correspondences of buyer when follow-up action is taken. Such situation causes concern to the buyer and increases the cost of purchasing materials.

(g) Proximity of vendors which is necessary for saving time, transportation costs, etc.

(h) Corporate diversification (*i.e.*, development of new products or processes) which makes the need for vendor development more urgent and pressing.

(i) When performance of the existing vendor is excellent but his capacity is limited, *i.e.*, when he cannot meet the requirement of bulk purchase.

(j) To ensure availability of materials from more than one source.

Furthermore, to keep pace with the changes and developments taking place very rapidly throughout the world, regular development of vendor for more and more new and sophisticated items is necessary to ensure survival and growth in a high competitive business environment.

Vendor development is not a new thing. All organisations have to perform this function properly in their own interest. If the vendor is not capable of supplying materials or the vendor is not up to the mark then the development of vendors should be given prime importance.

First of all, it is necessary to find out what is the problem with the existing vendor. After finding the problem one has to see whether the problem is genuine or not. If it is found that the problem is genuine then the buyer has to sit with the vendor for solving the problem. If the problem is of a technological nature it has to be solved immediately. A vendor may be good in all respects but may not have any technical knowhow for that particular product or is not having any R&D facilities. In this case, the buyer has to provide technical assistance.

This is very important in case of import-substitute items. The buyer may even provide R&D facilities in the vendor's premises to enable the latter to carry out different types of tests and research for development of new products, new materials or for import-substitute items. This R&D facility not only assures product quality but results in cost saving as well infrastructure the need for quality control at the buyer's end. The transfer of R&D instructions to the vendor will reduce the additional overhead cost of the buyer.

If the problem is financial then the purchasing company should go ahead from a different point. Every manufacturing unit can undertake total manufacture of its products, but this would enhance the overhead cost and lead to shortage of production capacity of the manufacturing unit.

For all these reasons every manufacturer should develop vendors. A potential vendor may be financially weak but should be developed even by providing financial assistance. This will surely be beneficial to the buyer in the long run.

A vendor may be good in all respects but may not have any managerial capability or competence. In such a situation, the buyer may even provide managerial assistance to the vendor. Many large buyers even sort out industrial relation problems of their vendors by providing their managerial skills which ultimately ensure smooth flow of materials supplies. Development of managerial quality in vendors helps to derive extra benefits from the purchase function way.

Indian Examples

In India, the vendors were developed in such industries as textiles, cement, paper, steel, engineering, electronics and power. The Government of India had to import 90% of the equipment required for power generating immediately after independence. But, the present situation is completely different. Now, only 10% of the equipment required by the power plants is imported. This has become possible due to the constant effort of Bharat Heavy Electrical Limited. BHEL has developed right sources for developing major items of power generating equipment. For example, it has developed REMCO for supplying meters, Jyoti for pumps, Jayashree for insulator, Bharat Bijlee for transformers and Incorporated Engineers for fuel oil system. HMT has developed 2,000 MT press for BHEL, Trichy. These are all examples of vendor development which has greatly contributed to import substitution in India's core industries.

Two Phases

Vendor development in the micro level can be divided into two phases. The first phase of ancillary development process covers selection of source, approval of samples and bulk supplies and, ultimately, recognition of the vendor as a regular source. The second phase of ancillary development process relies on a new concept called 'self-certification'. Under this scheme only those suppliers who are in a position to assure quality to meet purchaser's requirements fully are considered.

Under this scheme, the entire amount supplied by the vendor will not be subjected to lot by lot inspection but will go to stores straightaway. The vendor must meet the norms evolved for the system and should continue to show consistency through good performance. This system will not only cut down the inspection cost but also give due recognition to those suppliers who are able to ensure and maintain quality of materials. For joining this scheme, the vendor should have commitment to quality exhibited by sound inspection system in his workshop with adequate process controls. Moreover, his incoming performance at the purchaser's work place should be consistent, *i.e.*, it should conform to the quality needed by the purchaser over a period of time.

Vendor Analysis

A periodical vendor analysis is a must for building up an efficient source of supply. Such a analysis seeks to evaluate each vendor on the basis of his past performance and overall worth to the buying company. The performance of each vendor would be ascertained by referring to the vendor performance evaluation sheet which would show the vendor's delivery schedules, rejection rates, backings, follow-ups, etc. Record of each vendor will be kept in a register.

Other factors which would need consideration would be amendment of orders, response to queries, special consideration reported and so on. These may be recorded as and when the events take place. This sheet tabulates certain key factors which, in turn, assist in the evaluation of future tenders. The sheet also gives a rating scale to be applied to each factor. By giving appropriate rating for each factor, a total number of points across all the factors could be obtained.

Vendors are generally evaluated on the basis of the following attributes: (a) Delivery as per schedule; (b) Reliable quality; (c) Quick replacement of rejections; (d) Supplies without asking for amendments; (e) Supplies without asking for financial consideration; and (f) Answering queries readily.

Synopsis for Learning

Q.1. What are the steps involved in the purchasing cycle?

Ans. The steps are : (1) receiving and analysing purchasing requisition, (2) selecting suppliers and requesting for quotations, (3) determining the right price, (4) issuing a purchase order, (5) following up and delivery, (6) receiving and accepting goods and (7) appraising the suppliers invoice for payment.

Q.2. What are the different aspects of purchasing?

Ans. Three important aspects of purchasing are : (1) quantities requirements, (2) price requirements and (3) functional requirements.

Q.3. What should be the proper purchasing policy for a company?

Ans. A policy is a general guideline for decision-making. An organisation may have several policies regarding purchasing.

Q.4. What should be the purchasing procedures for modern organisations?

Ans. Purchasing procedures should be standarised in its scope and flexible enough to accommodate any changes that occur in the business environment and commercial climate.

Q.5. What are the two most important aspects of purchasing?

Ans. Two most important aspects of purchasing are : (1) source selection and (2) vendor development.

5.8 PRINCIPLES OF PURCHASING

Purchasing, or procurement, as it is normally known in Business Management, is buying certain specific items at the correct price with a view to carrying out certain specific functions for the overall benefit of the company. The whole process consists of converting raw materials into various forms that have higher value to consumers. The primary responsibility of the purchasing department is to procure required materials for maintaining steady supply. The object is to ensure uninterrupted production/operation and save money which will serve the overall interest of the company. The main objectives of industrial purchasing are :

1. to maintain continuity of supply of materials for ensuring production.
2. to contribute to the competitiveness of the end product.
3. to contribute towards higher productivity.
4. to get the maximum value for money, not necessarily at the lowest initial price.
5. to reduce the cost of end (finished) products.
6. to improve the quality of end products.
7. to eliminate extra material cost.
8. to contribute towards standardisation (variety reduction) and value analysis programmes, and
9. to increase profit.

The main objective and principle of purchasing is to buy the materials and services of the right quality in the right quantity at the right price, from the right source, and with delivery at the right time and place to support company's operations with a continuous flow of materials and services.

Six Principles

These are the six main principles of purchasing :

(i) Right Quality

Quality has been defined as the capability of doing a certain thing or the power to satisfy a particular need. In other words quality means the useful value of a specific thing for a specific purpose to fulfil. The starting point for determining the quality of the materials needed in an organisation is the end use, *i.e.*, what is intended to be done or accomplished. We then have to establish a specification and this is what quality is all about. A full and complete quality specification is an essential part of a purchase contract.

The quality of a material has a direct relationship with its end use. In other words, an inappropriate quality would mean that the end product is either too good or too bad for a particular purpose. Both these have a direct effect on costs and competitiveness of the end product. In one case, some extra cost has to make the quality more than is necessary and, in other case, the quality of the incurred product would suffer. We can express quality in various ways, *i.e.*, dimensions, weights, and measures, chemical properties, physical properties, strength, power, limit and tolerance, hardness, finish, colour, capacity, durability, performance characteristics, appearance, design, etc.

The quality requirement should be determined first and then correctly specified. Ambiguity in defining quality is one of the major problems in purchasing. This can be avoided by ensuring that the supplier really understands exactly what is required by the purchaser. If the supplier does not understand the quality requirements correctly, certain wrong types of materials would be supplied. This, in its turn, may lead to various problems like production stoppages, rejection of finished product(s) by quality control people, and the emergence of a high quantity (percentage) scrap, at the end of the production process. All these amount to waste.

Right quality means that the quality should be just right, neither too high nor too low. A production process would always like to have the best quality available in order to make sure that the end product is of best quality available in case of spares and components. It is necessary to ensure that the machine does not go out of control due to poor quality of such materials. It is important for the purchaser to know the exact purpose for which the materials are required and he must try to convince the production people to accept the materials which would serve the purpose. At the same time he must not take any undue risk in buying inferior materials which might be more expensive in the long run. In case of doubt, he must discuss the matter with the production person and gather knowledge from him regarding the usage. The purchaser should also have knowledge of the materials of various brands as also qualities available in the market.

(ii) Right Quantity

The purchaser must buy the materials in the right quantity to ensure that there is no stoppage of production or no extra stock piling. Normally, the inventory control wing of purchase (stores) department, fixes up the economic order quantity (EOQ), *i.e.*, the quantity which should be purchased at a time to get the maximum benefit at minimum total cost. This requirement is mentioned in the purchase order and it is necessary to see that the materials are delivered.

(iii) Right Price

It is not easy to determine the right price of material. However, through cost and value analyses one can guess what an item should cost. Thereafter, the purchaser's negotiation skill, his relations with the supplier and the nature of competition in the market will together determine the actual purchase price.

This function is of prime importance because this is where the purchaser can be really of much help to the company. But to perform this function properly, the purchaser must have a thorough idea about the market prices, especially the current prices of raw materials, their likely future trends, and environmental conditions which affect prices. The purchaser should not be forced by the seller to accept any price quoted by the supplier. There are various ways of determining the right price.

The supplier may be asked to give a break-up of prices showing the cost of raw materials, overhead, profit, etc., and the buyer should check up the various cost items by comparing them with the available data. He may also take the help of production department. In some situations tendering to a large number of suppliers may also help in obtaining the correct price. However, the purchaser must use his own judgement because often the suppliers form a cartel or an association (a ring) and they quote high prices. This would really pose a very serious problem. The purchaser can either break the ring or call all the bidders to reduce their prices on a rational basis. For purchasing of engineering items one should have the basic technical knowledge to deal with the suppliers.

One should have an idea about the right price of the materials and current prices should be compared with the past prices to find out how much the prices have gone up over a certain period of time.

(iv) Right Source

Right source means the source which is reliable in all respect such as quality, delivery, after sales service, etc. It is obvious that when all the other things have been done right (*i.e.*, selection of right quality, quantity and prices), the source of supply from where the materials have been obtained should be automatically right.

However, there are cases where anomaly occurs and it is, therefore, necessary to get the materials from the right source. A right supplier must fulfil the following basic conditions :

(a) He must be fully equipped to manufacture and supply the items ordered.

(b) He must look into the interest of the company and assist the buyer whenever there is any scope of cost reduction by way of supplying alternative materials suited for the purpose.

(c) He must also assist the buyer in market research.

(d) He must be polite.

(e) He must be in a position to assist the buyer in improving on delivery negotiations whenever necessary.

(f) He must be a man of integrity.

For source selection or to develop the right source of supply initial information about the name and address of the suppliers can be had with the help of the following:

(1) Suppliers' catalogue
(2) Trade requisition and directories
(3) Trade journals
(4) Yellow pages of telephone directory
(5) Vendors files
(6) Buyers' guides
(7) Salespersons
(8) Trade exhibits — industrial trade fairs
(9) Company personnel
(10) Buyer-seller meet
(11) Purchasing departments of similar organisations.

There are various ways of ascertaining the right suppliers. Typical vendor registration forms are given to the supplier by the purchase department. Such forms should give all the necessary information as required by the buyer.

On receipt of the complete form, a representative of the buyer should call at the vendor's premises and submit his report (containing all his findings).

He should ascertain the following factors during his visit and inspection at the supplier's plant :

(i) Technical know-how of the supplier for manufacturing items.
(ii) Financial capability of the supplier to undertake the job.
(iii) Organisational set-up and manpower of the supplier.
(iv) Records of past performance of the supplier in delivering materials at the right time and in right quality and quantity.
(v) Ability to deliver materials promptly and in required quantity.
(vi) Own manufacturing unit.
(vii) Quality control system of the firm.
(viii) Staff and line capability of the firm.
(ix) Service level.
(x) History of labour relations in the firm.

If this report meets the need of that particular company, the vendor may be registered on the approved suppliers' list and be given a trial order. Performances of the vendor should be only judged after satisfactory and timely execution of orders.

A right supplier today might become a wrong supplier next year. As safeguard against this possibility, the purchase department should also keep some record of the performance of different suppliers. There are some typical ways of evaluating a supplier's performance. Moreover, various norms or criteria could be used to compare one supplier with another.

(v) Right Time

Just as one has to buy the materials in the right quantity, he must also obtain them exactly when required. The delivery timings are again fixed by the indentor or the stock control department. It is the primary duty of the purchase department to follow up the orders and to ensure that the flow of materials remains unchanged. It should also be seen that the materials are delivered exactly on time. This function is very important in India as the suppliers often fail to maintain the delivery schedule.

(vi) Right Place (of Delivery)

The function of purchase department is not over until the materials are delivered at the right place. Therefore, this also becomes a primary function of the purchase department. Suppose the godown of the purchase department is in Calcutta's Taratala area and the material is booked to Howrah railway station. It must be ensured that the materials are cleared from Howrah and delivered to the godown.

Synopsis for Learning

Q.1. What are the two main principles of purchasing ?

Ans. The two main principles of purchasing are : (i) buying materials at the lowest cost consistent with the service and quality required; and (ii) avoiding any waste or duplication, while maintaining the lowest possible outlay on stock consistent with making the material needed for production available when required.

Q.2. What is the main concern of the purchasing department ?

Ans. The purchasing department is mainly concerned with the availability of alternative materials and the possibility of obtaining the quality required at an acceptable price.

5.9 PRICING AND DISCOUNTS

A. Pricing

Price of any material is related to its quality and is expressed in terms of money. In industry, business and trade there are basically two methods of pricing the products:

1. ***Published Price List.*** The established manufacturing organisation fixes up the price of its product(s) on the basis of an analysis of its cost of production and after adding a percentage of profit. So the price of the product = cost of production + profit. Such established organisations periodically publish the price lists of the various items produced by them. The price list so published indicates the prices for items of different sizes or quantities. The published price list and catalogues of various suppliers can be compared and decision on purchase can be taken. If so required, negotiations can also be made to finalise the price volume discount as also terms of payment.

2. ***Competitive Bidding.*** Purchase enquiries in the form of tender are usually sent to approved and enlisted suppliers (in case of a specific tender) and published in the newspapers, journals, etc. (in case of open tender). Requests for bids ask vendors to quote the price at which they will supply the materials. Competitive bidding is considered on five criteria : (i) volume and value of purchase, (ii) quality of and specification of materials, (iii) market condition of demand and supply position, (iii) the relative bargaining power of the seller and buyer, and (vi) availability of time for finalisation of purchase contract and physical delivery.

Normally, in pricing a product cost analysis and assessment of total cost — which includes materials cost, overhead cost, labour and processing cost — are to be made. So the price of a product is fixed by adding cost of production (including quality control and packing) and profit. The percentage of profit to be added to cost depends on market conditions and marketing strategy.

(i) ***Fixed and firm price.*** In fixed and firm price there will be no change in price quoted by seller and accepted by buyer during the period of contract and will remain valid even if there is a change in the market conditions.

(ii) ***Going rate (market) price.*** In some cases the price does not remain same but is changed from time to time in the light of market conditions. Materials controlled and regulated by Government for selling and distribution come under this system. Coal, oil and petroleum, gas, steel, cement, gold, etc. are few examples. Prices of these items fluctuate almost regularly and the ruling market price is to be paid on the day of taking delivery.

(iii) ***Cost-plus Pricing.*** In case of long-term contract with ancillary industries, sub-contractors and for construction, erection and service contract, price is determined by adding up all cost of production/construction. To this total some percentage of profit is added.

(a) ***Fixed price with escalation clause.*** In quoting fixed and firm price the seller always tries to foresee any price hike in future and so adds a margin just to be on the safe side. Of course, price cannot be raised on an *ad hoc* basis. Rather, price can be negotiated in anticipation of any changes in the cost of labour, material and transport charges. Such negotiation can be made up for expected price changes —

both upward and downward. The buyer should set a limit on the upward escalation and tie such escalation with some published price index, fuel cost, labour cost, transport charges, etc. An escalation clause seeks to protect both the seller and buyer against any risk associated with price change.

(b) ***Price decline protection clause***. Price can also be negotiated when it starts falling. This is just opposite of the escalation clause and it is intended to protect the buyer when prices of materials fall.

(iv) ***Minimum Price***. In cost-plus pricing contract, if it is not possible for the buyer to keep watch on the procedures of calculation of seller or sub-contractor's costing and pricing system, maximum guaranteed price may be fixed on the basis of cost analysis, keeping in view the maximum possible cost-plus price. In this case, the final price on cost-plus basis will never be allowed to exceed the maximum guaranteed price.

B. Discounts

(i) ***Price discounts***. A price discount is normally offered by the sellers on volume of sales, *i.e.*, quantity and on payment terms for two main reasons : (1) to derive the benefit of more volume of sale and (ii) quick realisation of sales, revenue or turnover. Various types of discounts are offered in buying and selling :

(a) *Trade discounts* : Trade discounts are allowed to wholesaler and distributors. The objective is to encourage and help them to perform certain vital marketing functions on behalf of the manufacturer with a view to promoting sales. These discounts amount to reduced price. They pay less than the list price, *i.e.*, price paid by customers. The margin between the list price and the reduced price is the profit of the dealer/wholesaler. Trade discounts can also be finalised by the manufacturer with the dealers as percentage of the sale price. It is also called dealers' commission and is expressed as a percentage of list price, *i.e.*, price which is officially quoted.

(b) *Quantity discounts*. Discounts on price are also given to a buyer on the basis of quantity purchased. In this system, discounts on listed price are given when the volume of purchase exceeds a certain minimum level (number). A simple example is given below :

Quantity	Rate per Unit	Discount
Upto 1000 units	Rs. 2.50 per unit	Nil
1,001 to 2,000 units	—	5%
2,001 to 5,000 units	—	10%
5,001 to 10,000 units	—	15%
Above 10,000	—	20%

In this case, price discount goes up with an increase in the volume purchased. It is a system of graded incentives.

(c) *Cumulative discount*. In this case, quantity may not be fixed as per the contract. The buyer is given a discount on the basis of actual quantity purchased. The total discount is given at an appropriate rate on the total quantity purchased. But in case of cumulative discount, the rate of price reduction which is allowed continues to increase as the (total) volume of purchase increases.

(ii) ***Payment discounts*** : Discounts are also offered by many sellers on terms of payment, particularly on prompt payment of bills. Such discounts are offered as percentage of the net invoice price and are of the following two types :

(a) *Discount on advance payment* : If payment of the bill is made in advance on proforma invoice, price reduction may be considered by seller. For example, 5% discount may be given if payment is made 15 days in advance. Indian Railways allowd waiver of 15% surcharge on freight charges in case of pre-payment of freight at the time of booking of materials at the originating booking station. Similar principles are followed by many original equipment manufacturers or dealers who allow discounts (on list price) to the buyers in case of pre-payment of bills.

(b) *Cash discounts*. In case of immediate payment on delivery of materials discounts are also considered on the list price. Such discount may be slightly less than that in case of advance payment. If 5% discount is offered in advance payment, additional 2% discount may also be allowed if payment is made on delivery. Discounts on payment terms need be negotiated and finalised very carefully with proper cost analysis, keeping in view the comparative rate of interest on capital vis-a-vis discounts offered by the seller.

Synopsis for Learning

Q.1. What are the methods of pricing industrial products?

Ans. Two methods of pricing industrial products are : (1) published price list and (2) competitive bidding. Published list price is based on cost and has a number of varients.

Q.2. What are the types of discounts offered in purchasing?

Ans. Two main types of discounts offered in purchasing are : (1) price discounts and (2) payment discounts. Each has several varients.

5.10 IMPORTS AND CUSTOMS CLEARANCE

Importing is one of the most important functions of materials management. Normally, the purchasing function is limited to receiving materials from local, regional and national sources, as importing of materials from foreign countries is not always desirable and is also subject to certain conditions, such as availability of foreign exchange as also the import restrictions imposed by the Government. These conditions are not static and may change from time to time.

In spite of various restrictive conditions, the importing function cannot be completely eliminated. The following points may be noted in this context.

1. In order to import materials from foreign countries, a buyer needs foreign exchange. As such, government policy for imports is determined by the availability of foreign exchange.
2. Furthermore, import of certain categories of materials is restricted or banned — for giving protection to domestic industry from foreign competition. However, in India, the position has changed considerably after the introduction of various liberalisation policies since July 1991.
3. However, to rationalise its import policy, the Government of India reviews from time to time its import trade control policies and procedures, taking into consideration all aspects of national and international importance. As a result, sometimes import policies are liberalised for higher utilisation of domestic production capacity. Thus, importing is not only a purchasing function but an essential economic function of a country for achieving self-sufficiency in commerce and industry.

Procedures

The following steps are followed for importing :

1. Sanction at foreign exchange

The first step of import function is to ascertain whether the materials to be imported are banned, restricted, canalised or free items. In case, these are banned items on the ground of availability from domestic manufacturers, action is to be taken to find out these items from indigenous sources. If, however, these are not available domestically, certificates of non-availability are to be obtained from domestic manufacturers and presented to the Government in order to get clearance for imports as well as for allocation of required foreign exchange. In case of restricted items, application is to be made to the Government by giving proper justifications for import, so that the Government may review the import policies and issue clearance for imports under special circumstnaces. In case of canalised items, the Government normally directs the users to get their requirements from the canalised agencies of the Government— such as, MMTC, STC, SAIL — which import raw materials as centralised organisations, with a view to distributing the materials needed by different indigenous industries. For import of free items, import clearance is given by the Government to various industries in order to meet their normal requirements for a particular period. Industries also can get import entitlements on their exports as a measure of incentive for more and more exports.

2. Selecting foreign suppliers

In case of proprietary items, the names and addresses of the foreign suppliers/manufacturers are readily available with the importers. But if the items are to be newly imported, the details of the suppliers/manufacturers are to be collected through the foreign consulates/embassies, foreign journals and Indian consulates in foreign countries and also through global tenders. Correspondence is then initiated with the foreign suppliers and finally suppliers are chosen on the basis of price and quality/specification of the items, delivery schedule, terms of payment and other conditions involved in the transaction.

3. Placing letter of intent and formal purchase order

At this stage, the importer is to firmly decide the foreign source of supply and place letter of intent on the suppliers in case all formalities are not yet completed. This is sometimes required to get advantage of the offered price which is valid for a certain period only. When all formalities are over, a firm order is placed with the supplier(s). In the order all the required clauses are to be clearly mentioned such as name and address of the suppliers, reference number of their offer, detailed quantity, quality/specification, testing, unit price (F.O.B., F.A.S., Ex-works, C&F, CIF) as also total price of the items to be imported, delivery period, mode of shipment, terms and mode of payment, packing and marking specification, transit insurance, documents required for clearance, particulars of foreign exchange sanction (such as the import licence/foreign exchange release order) and guarantee and acceptance of the purchase order. Unless the clauses are clearly stated in the purchase order and properly followed by the foreign suppliers, there may be various complications afterwards leading to long delay in clearance of the imported goods. Various other inconveniences, detrimental to the interests of the importing organisation as well as the importing country, may also be caused in the process.

4. Payment for release of the shipping documents for clearance

On receipt of the acceptance of the supplier, the importer arranges to open letter of credit in a local bank in favour of the foreign supplier. The latter will receive payment from its bank on timely shipment of ordered goods to the importer and on submission of the specified shipping documents within a specified period to the bank (strictly as per terms and conditions of the purchase order as laid down in the letter of credit). The foreign bank then forwards the shipping documents to the local bank, which releases the same to the importer on getting payment as per terms of the letter of credit. Payment can also be made to the foreign suppliers against "sight draft".

5. Transportation of the materials to the importer or end-user

At all the stages the importers will be involved with the shipping company, forwarding agents, insurance company, customs, port and inland transportation, agencies for making the imported items available to the end-user's sites. In case of canalised items, the canalising agencies are involved at this stage for customs and port clearance and the actual users take delivery of their required materials by their own management either from the port or from the agents' godowns. In case of imports of canalised items through "High seas sale" all these activities are to be performed by the actual users on receipt of shipping documents from the canalised agencies after shipment of the goods.

5.11 STORES FUNCTIONS

The organisation of the stores control division should be such as to handle and control efficiently its large investment in stores. The preservation of stores from deterioration and their protection against hazards like fire and burglary are essential. Therefore, accuracy in the maintenance of records and preparation of documents are very important. Some of these documents, particularly those relating to receipt and issues, have to be sent to other sections of the materials management department, such as inventory control, purchase and stores accounts for necessary action. The purpose and responsibility of stores function should, therefore, be regarded as an important function by the management. So, it should be headed by a responsible and competent officer who can maintain close contact with other sections of the department and give prompt service to the using department.

Stores Organisation

The specialisation of production and the ever-increasing complexity of modern industries require a high standard of performance in stores work. To achieve the required efficiency the organisations should be well-balanced with definitiness, flexibility and coordination.

Principles of Organisation

Four different types of stores commonly in operations are :

(i) Central store; (ii) Regional store; (iii) Divisional store; (iv) Sub-store.

Based on the functions, the stores organisation can be broadly divided into two divisions : 1. Transit Stores and 2. Holding Stores.

The primary function of holding store is to accept the materials passed by inspection cell to preserve them, to issue on demand and to keep account of all the transactions.

The proximity of materials to operational sites is normally the guiding factor in deciding the size and location of various store units. This has however to be so balanced with the financial viability that the store set-up is not only operationally effective but is most economical as well. For a large undertaking or organisation spread over a wider area the central store is really useful.

Attempts at Centralisation

The main advantage of centralisation of stores in a very big organisation is that it saves time of the employees in getting the required stores. Moreover, a subsidiary store may be maintained, at each of the shops, of items specially needed by it. Through a central store the daily (or weekly) requirement of routine store and any special requirement(s) are met from time to time. This saves the time of the departmental employees since they have to go to the central store only on rare occasions — when they need special items unexpectedly needed by them.

Two Main functions

The stores function is important for many organisations and industrial concerns. The function of stores can be divided into two main parts, namely :

1. In modern store-keeping, queueing theory is often adopted for issue of materials from stores.

(a) Primary functions

(b) Secondary functions.

Primary Functions

The main objective of the store is to provide necessary inputs to the production/operations departments at a minimum cost. To ensure this the following activities are to be performed :

(i) To make available a balanced flow of raw materials, components, tools, equipment and other stores required for operation.

(ii) To provide maintenance materials, spare parts and general stores as required.

(iii) To receive and issue materials after physical inspection and proper identification.

(iv) To store and preserve materials.

(v) To ensure safety and security of materials.

(vi) To arrange for collection, acceptance of scrap and other discarded materials for disposal.

Secondary Functions

The secondary activities related to the stores functions are :

1. Collection, inspection and acceptance
2. Stores accounting
3. Stock control
4. Feedback information to materials control section
5. Help in standardisation and variety reduction
6. Service information such as :
   (a) Demand for materials and parts giving specification, quantities and deliveries required
   (b) Notification when stocks are running low
   (c) Details of deliveries rejected on inspection
   (d) Certification of invoices for quantity and quality
   (e) Particulars of anticipated changes in consumption
   (f) Procurement of items urgently required in case of breakdowns
   (g) Listing of obsolete, surplus and scrap materials for disposal.

RECEIPTS AND INSPECTION

One of the functions of stores department is to receive goods from all sources and to make necessary arrangements for collection, inspection and acceptance. Since firms make payments against suppliers' invoices, suitable documents are to be prepared for the materials accepted. In order to do this efficiently, a proper (systematic) procedure has to be followed.

RECEIPTS

Receipts are of four types :

1. From outside agencies like the railways, road transport agencies and suppliers' own transport.
2. Collection from firm's premises

3. Transfer of goods from one sub-store to another.
4. Return of stores from production and other departments.

TIME OF DELIVERY

It is essential that all the firms who send the goods — particularly through road transport — clearly notify the time, duration and the day when the stores are open for acceptance. This can be done by mentioning the same in the purchase order.

COPY OF THE ORDER

All the copies of the purchase orders together with subsequent amendments and copy of the correspondence of the concerned order must be endorsed by the receipts section which knows what has exactly been ordered. Advance intimation will help them to know the size and type of consignment and to take necessary advance action for clearance of the goods (especially heavy/bulky ones) on arrival.

ADVICE NOTE

Certain organisations advise the buyers with an advance copy of despatch-advice note. This gives sufficient information to the storekeeper so that necessary action can be taken for speedy clearance of materials.

RAILWAY RECEIPT/LORRY RECEIPT

It is most important that the receipt section gets a copy of the above note because it is an essential document for clearance of goods in-transit. Timely clearance avoids demurrage/wharfage.

IDENTIFICATION OF STORES

The normal way of identification of stores is by simple description. But this by itself is totally unsatisfactory simply because an item can be described in various ways. For example, the same materials can be described by different names. There should be some logical basis for identification of stores. Alphabetical letters or code numbers can be used reducing proper identification of stores.

STANDARDISATION AND CODIFICATION

Standardisation simply refers to variety reduction. In the context of materials management it refers to the standard specification and the work of reducing sizes and numbers (types) to the minimum. Four types of standards are generally used in manufacturing industries — International Standard, National Standard, Industry Standard and Company Standard. Certain industries have developed commonly accepted specifications which have come to be known as industry standards. There are also international and national standards, *e.g.*, the standards set by ISI/BIS, ASTM (American Society of Testing and Materials), ASME (American Society of Mechanical Engineers) and BSI (British Standards Institutes), ISO (International Standard Organisation) and so on.

ISSUE OF MATERIALS

Since one of the primary functions of the stores is to provide service to the operation departments, the efficiency of the stores organisation is judged by the standard of service it provides. It is important that the procedure for issue of materials is well drawn out and well-organised.

BASIC REQUIREMENT

Since large sums of money remain blocked in materials, it is essential for the custodian of materials to ensure that the issue of materials are made only under proper authorisation. In fact, authorisation of stores is very vital. Moreover, for efficient operation, the following points to be considered:

(a) Authorisation of issues
(b) Identification of requirements
(c) Timing of issues.

(a) AUTHORISATION OF ISSUES

Since materials represents money, for the issue of materials there must be some authorisation by responsible officers nominated by the management. Such authorisation should be given clearly in the form of a directive circular. The object is to avoid misunderstanding and unpleasantness that may arise due to the refusal by the storekeeper to issue materials. In many industries, the designation of the person authorised to draw materials along with their specimen signature are sent to the stores for verification.

The request for issue of materials is invariably made in written form or documents for proper authorisation. It is the primary responsibility of the storekeeper to verify all such documents for proper authorisation before the materials are issued.

Even though certain persons are authorised to draw goods from the stores, management normally imposes a few restrictions for drawal of the goods beyond a certain level of consumption. In all such cases, a clear directive must be given to the stores department.

(b) IDENTIFICATION OF REQUIREMENT

Largely due to ignorance, in several cases the correct description of the items are not given by the user department. Often the code number given may not tally with the description of the goods, and *vice versa*. Hence an experienced store-keeper should use his intelligence to identify the mistake and suggest to the indentor the correct item. Details about materials requirements such as part number, code number, etc. ensure that it is supplied without delay and unnecessary correspondence.

(c) TIMING OF ISSUE

The stores manager should ensure that the indenting departments are fully aware of the timing of issues. However, there may be sudden rush during the peak hours. This may put undue pressure on the stores department and may lead to sudden stoppage of production, in case of undue delay.

So our intelligent store-keeper should study carefully the requirements of various departments and stagger (spread) the timings in such a way that each department can draw their requirements without loss of time[1].

METHODS OF ISSUING MATERIALS

Issues from stores must be efficiently organised so that the requirements of the production/operations department can be met.

1. Issue on request

This is the most orthodox way of issue wherein the indenting department normally sends a man and collect the materials from stores.

2. Issue per schedule

In a batch production unit sometime, the requisition for issue of stores is sent well ahead indicating when, *i.e.*, the time and date it is required. The stores department will collect all the materials and keep them ready. Then it will intimate the indenting department about this. Depending on the prevailing practice of the industry either they are collected from stores or delivered at the shop floor. This is desirable in order to prevent any loss of man-hour caused by sudden absenteeism of a worker in the production department.

3. Imprest issues

In this system a list of certain items — especially for tools and components and in specified quantities — is approved. The list is then held in a sub-store or tool kit near the shop floor.

4. Replacement issue

In most engineering industries a large number of workshop machines are used. So there will be considerable requirements of tools and gauges. When a fresh issue has to be made the machine shop operator may be asked to return the old ones to the stores and obtain new one for replacement. This is done without issue notes and the storekeeper has to maintain proper records of such replacement.

5. Loan issues

The issue of stores on loan should, as far as possible, be discouraged. Situations often arise where some amount of spares, electrical fitting, etc. are required on emergency basis due to some breakdowns. In such cases the materials are to be issued on a loan basis. However, the storekeeper is to maintain a separate record and ensure that they are returned before year-ending when annual stock-taking begins.

6. Stock records

In a store-house where thousands of transactions take place some amount of records are to maintained. This makes it possible for the storekeeper to make an entry of all transactions.

Synopsis for Learning

Q.1. What are three stores functions ?

Ans. Three stores functions are receipt, inspection and issue of materials.

Q.2. What are the duties of the storekeeper ?

Ans. Six duties of the store keeper are :

1. Supervise and guide staff in their duties.
2. See records are up-to-date and all departments are given an efficient service.
3. Co-operate with planning, purchasing and inspection department.
4. Receive goods from outside, check number and arrange for inspection and reporting variances from order to purchasing section.
5. Check stock physically at least once a year and ensure that it is stored neatly and safely.

Q.3. What is the importance of the stores function ?

Ans. The stores function is a very important part of materials management. A good stores system serves a number of purposes, such as preparation of accurate stock level reports, detection of discrepancies on time, prompt clearance of goods, reduction in demurrages and losses in claims. For all these reasons, many organisations appoint a stores manager.

Q.4. What are the limits to inspection ?

Ans. Since, all kinds of inspection, even counting the items, cost money inspection of each and every item in the lot may not always be possible. In short 100% inspection is always not practicable due to various considerations such as cost, time, destructability and fatigue.

STOCK VERIFICATION AND RECONCILIATION

The process of verifying the physical (quantity) balance of the entire range of stores, and comparing the same with the balance of ledger is known as stock verification. Some discrepancies are often observed in the process. Where the physical quantity is in excess of the ledger balance, there is surplus and, in the converse case, there is shortage.

PURPOSE

Physical stock verification which involves actual counting, measuring, weighing of all items in stock is necessary for the following four reasons:

(a) To support the value of stock shown in the balance sheet through physical verification;

(b) To verify the accuracy of stock records;

(c) To disclose the possibility of fraud, theft or loss, or deterioration; and

(d) To reveal the weakness of the system, if any (i.e., whether the stock is in safe custody).

METHODS

There are three methods of stock verification. These are :

(i) Periodic stock verification

(ii) Perpetual stock verification

(iii) Blind stock taking.

PERIODIC VERIFICATION : Under this method the whole of the stock is covered at the same time at the end of a financial year. This can be done only in a small organisation. But this method does not suit big industrial organisations, since complete stoppage of work for several days is not possible just for the purpose of stock taking.

PERPETUAL VERIFICATION: Under this method physical stock verification is spread throughout the year according to a predetermined programme. And each item is physically examined at least once a year.

ADVANTAGES

Four main advantages of perpetual verification are :

(i) During physical verification neither the stores nor the works are to be closed.

(ii) The normal stores transaction and posting can continue without interruptions.

(iii) Surpluses and shortages arising from time to time can be written-off after proper investigation.

(iv) The job of stock verification can be done on time.

BLIND VERIFICATION: Under this system the stock verifiers are given the location, but not details about code numbers, description and stock record balances. The underlying logic here is that the verifier will not have his own idea about the stock position and he may just mention the same figures in record without actual verification of stock.

This method is not very popular. It virtually serves no purpose when the entire operation of stores has to be well-planned. The modern trend is toward the application of the ABC technique for stock verification.

WHO SHOULD DO THE STOCK TAKING

In some of the organisations, store-keepers are required to take stock of their own stores. This is not a correct procedure. It not only induces them to conceal genuine discrepancies to avoid punishment but leads to deliberate pilferage or fraud where surpluses are found.

It is in the rightness of things to employ full-time stock verifier or internal auditors for doing this job. However, they can take the help of store-keepers and even engineering staff for proper identification.

TREATMENT OF DISCREPANCIES (RECONCILIATION)

Often the amounts of stock found by physical examination do not agree with stock records. So certain discrepancies exist. Where physical stock is more, there is surplus and where it is less than the stock records there is shortage.

SURPLUSES

Surpluses arises for the following three reasons:

(a) Where materials are not issued from the bins, but the entry of issues is posted.

(b) Where the amount of materials issued is less than the quantity for which entry (issue) is made.

(c) Where no issues are made but only issue entry is made in the stock record.

SHORTAGES

Shortage may occur for the following *six* reasons:

(a) Excess physical issue than the actual issue entries posted.

(b) Issues made but corresponding entries not made in issue column.

(c) Excess quantity issued than the quantity for which entries are made in the issue column.

(d) Issue of materials without requisition.

(e) Misappropriation.

(f) Defective instruments.

INVESTIGATION OF DISCREPANCIES

Where the discrepancies are minor no further investigation is made. Only necessary action is taken for adjustment of such marginal discrepancies. But where the discrepancies are substantial an investigation has to be made.

The various steps involved in investigation are :

(a) Examining the stock records to verify whether there is any error from the date of last verification.

(b) Checking the units of issue.

(c) Checking the adjacent bins to verify whether the items have been wrongly placed.

(d) Checking all the receipts and issue documents for the said items.

(e) Checking whether any adjustments were made to reconcile the previous discrepancies into the last verification.

Only after a thorough examination and investigation by the storekeeper, declaration of surpluses and shortages should be made.

RECONCILIATION AND ADJUSTMENT

Once discrepancies are found, the next action is to make necessary adjustments. This is done by preparing necessary adjustment documents and after obtaining proper "write off" sanction, in case of shortages, from the competent authorities. The inventory lists are then corrected accordingly.

Reasons for Reconciliation

Five main reason for reconciliation are :

(a) The Stores A/c are inaccurate and give a wrong view of the actual position.

(b) Cost A/c are also wrong and require correction.

(c) Unscrupulous storekeeper can, if he so desire, rectify surpluses either by pilfering or by deliberate issue of materials.

(d) The storekeeper can also set right shortages by manipulating weights and measures.

(e) For balance sheet purposes the correct picture of stores held in stock should be prepared and presented.

It is also necessary to identify the causes of the excesses and/or shortages, as are found through investigation. If any error in posting entries in the stores ledger and bin card is found necessary, corrective actions are to be taken for such discrepancy. If, however, no reason is found, miscellaneous receipt vouchers are to be issued on suspense account for adjustment of any excess stock. Similarly, for adjustment of any shortages in physical stock, a write-off proposal is to be placed. This will give necessary details (such as the relevant facts and figures) so that it can be approved. Once the approval is obtained, miscellaneous voucher is to be issued for two reasons:

(1) to avoid carry out of wrong position of stock, and,

(2) to have the correct figure for all operational purposes.

Synopsis for Learning

Q.1. What is stock verification?

Ans. Stock verification refers to the process of verifying the physical (quantity) balance of the entire range of stores and comparing the same with the balance of ledgers.

Q.2. What is the essence of reconciliation?

Ans. Once discrepencies are found the next action is to make necessary adjustments. This is done by preparing necessary adjustmental documents. The inventory lists are then corrected properly.

5.12 DISPOSAL OF SURPLUS, SCRAP AND OBSOLETE MATERIALS

SURPLUS

Surplus stock are those materials which are procured and stocked in excess of an organisation's production/operational requirements. Surplus stock arises due to four different reasons, *viz.*, (i) unplanned purchase, (ii) lack of coordination between production, maintenance and materials departments, (iii) wasteful processes in production and (iv) unscientific inventory management.

In fact, all materials purchases by a firm for its operation are always not fully consumed. So a residue is left at the end. Surplus also occurs from obsolete or damaged stocks. Of late, due to rapid technological progress, product and materials often get changed. This results in the accumulation of surplus stock due to obsolescence. Obsolete products and their parts and components constitute a continuing source of surplus materials.

Production planning is usually finalised well in advance in accordance with sales forecast. Any subsequent change in products, process or technology can completely alter the schedule of materials required for any particular production system. Another reason of surplus store is forward buying. In some special circumstances forward buying may, no doubt, be economical. However, it creates the problems of surplus stock. This problem arises due to obsolescence, deterioration or excess carrying costs.

SCRAP

Scraps are generated through production waste or as by-product of operations in the shop floor or the production systems. It is important that scraps are sorted according to the type of metal, alloy, grade, size, greasiness, cleanliness, weight etc. One problem — of size — often arises. So it is necessary to specify the minimum material for the specific final item of material utilisation. However, in most manufacturing systems, due to non-availability of the correct size of sheet plates and rods, bigger sizes are often procured and used, leaving the remaining off-cuts as waste. So it is necessary to specify the minimum material for the specific final item of material utilisation. And, to ensure this, control of off-ends is also important.

OBSOLETE MATERIALS

Due to technological changes and advancement every organisation may have to adopt the latest operational practice or production method. Therefore any materials, part, component assembly, sub-assembly required to be kept in the store to meet the demand for consumption for previous product, process and technology may not have any usage in the latest systems and procedures. The unusable old stock items in the new systems of latest product are considered to be obsolete materials. No doubt such items are useful to other organisations still following the previous method. Disposal of surplus, scrap, obsolete, damaged and non-moving items are to be taken care of by the stores manager. Firstly it is necessary to review, at least once a year, all stocks held from time to time. The object is to identify items which are obsolete and surplus. This has to be supported by the normal stock-taking exercises or done separately and independently at periodic intervals, or on a continuous basis. Disposal can be made through the following routes:

(1) Feedback: Circulation within the company to its various units at various locations and to different departments to get necessary feedback of the requirement of surplus or obsolete stock of one unit to another unit.

(2) Return to the supplier: If there is no requirement from within the company units/departments, then materials should be returned to its original supplier at original cost after deducting a small amount as a restocking charge. Good suppliers do take back such unused materials in order to develop better business relationship. Nowadays, the industrial buyers insist on incorporating buy-back clause during finalisation of purchase contract.

(3) Direct sale to another company: Surplus and obsolete materials of one company may serve a useful purpose in another company having the same product line and an identical production system. In such cases, attempts should be made to sell surplus and obsolete materials to those firms. Sometimes scrap of some company becomes the raw materials of another. These categories of scrap cover steel scrap, machine shop turnings, plate scrap, punching scrap, copper bearings scrap, brass scrap, old scrap zinc, tin scrap, scrap lead, nickel chrome, stainless steel, old packing materials, used paper, and so on.

(4) Sale to dealer or broker: Sale to a dealer or broker may be done by auction, with notification on 'as is where is' basis. It may be open auction or tender. Yearly rate contract system can also be followed where the dealers are to collect the scrap from the particular area of production shop. The contract procedure and legal formalities adopted in buying are applicable in sales of surplus, obsolete materials, scrap and waste.

(5) Sale to employees: Some organisations follow the practice of selling the surplus, obsolete and non-moving items to their employees at a very low price. This sometimes satisfy the employees who make some gain by re-selling the materials or by using the same in their houses.

(6) Donation to Educational/Research Institutions: Various schools, colleges, polytechnics, engineering and technology institutes, universities, research centers, medical colleges and scientific laboratories require various tools and equipment for research. This is why many organisations follow the practice of disposing off unwanted materials to the academic institutions as a good gesture and also to enjoy some tax benefit.

In fine, disposal of surplus, scrap and redundant materials is to be made in a planned way to get maximum revenue or derive other benefits to the organisation. Efficient managers are those who can covert "waste into wealth".

Synopsis for Learning

Q.1. What are surplus, scrap and obsolate materials?

Ans. Surplus stocks are those which are procured and stocked in excess of an organisation's requirements. Scrap are generated through production waste or as by-product of operations. The unusable old stock of items in the new systems of production are called obsolete materials.

5.13 SELECTIVE INVENTORY CONTROL

A key factor in managing production/operations is inventory control. In its broadest sense, inventory control implies securing and maintaining the optimal quantities and types of physical resources required by the organisation's strategic plan. The importance of inventory in production/operations management is underscored when we visualise a manufacturing process as a flow of materials through a process that changes the form of those materials into finished goods. Thus, inventory control is at the heart of production control.

Inventory Management as a Strategic Factor

An effective inventory control system has four essential features :

1. A sound materials plan controls quantities ordered, order dates and reorder dates in coordination with changes in specifications due to product or production changes. This materials plan is the foundation of the entire system; the other three elements build on it.
2. A commitment to executing the plan requires adherence to the specified order dates and lead times. Through adherence to the discipline of the plan, a company avoids the unnecessary inventory costs associated with administrative mistakes.
3. Constant evaluation of ways to reduce inventory levels commits managers to continuous review of the inventory system. Through the commitment to continuous review, the company instills the attitude that proaction to potential problems is preference to reaction to actual problems.
4. Insistence on maintaining accurate records of inventory levels and characteristics reflects a company's understanding that a major challenge in any inventory control system is keeping accurate records. The different inventory items indicate the importance of this part of the plan. The following methods are used for inventory planning and control, *viz.*, economic order quantity, material requirements planning, the advanced version of MRP — manufacturing resource planning (MRP II), and just-in-time purchasing (JIT).

Type of Inventories

The particular inventories that must be managed depend on the nature of the particular business. The following inventory types are generally found in all businesses. Raw materials are the ingredients that go into the final product. Raw materials are the adhesive, gauze and paper required to make sanitary bandages; the grains, sweeteners, preservatives, paper and adhesive required to make and box breakfast cereals; the paper, ink and binding required to make books. The exact form of the raw material depends on the manufacturing process.

Some manufacturers take nature's own resources and convert them to a product. Steel-making firms must have iron ore and coal to produce steel, which is then sold to auto manufacturers. For them, steel becomes a raw material. Other manufacturers assembly component parts into a final product. Their raw materials inventory consists of many different components supplied by other manufacturers.

Every business requires materials that do not become part of the final product. These materials, termed MRO (maintenance, repair and operating) items, are usually small in number and expense, compared with other inventories. Nevertheless, they are essential to the operation of the plant. Examples of MRO items include stationery and other office-related materials, repair tools and parts, lubricants and cleaning supplies.

Work-in-process

Raw materials moving through the stages of production are termed *work in process*. Depending on the length and complexity of the production process, work-in-process inventory can be relatively large or small. Controlling work-in-process inventory is an important element of scheduling goods through the various stages of production as rapidly as possible and in order of priority.

Finished goods

Finished goods inventory consists of final, unsold products. Finished goods are stored at the manufacturing facilities or at some point in the distribution channel — at warehouses or retailers, for example. Job order manufacturers carry little, if any, finished goods inventory, since their products are made to customer specifications. Process and assembly manufacturers typically carry large finished goods inventory. Automobile manufacturers, for example, must produce large quantities in anticipation of — rather than in response to — customer demand.

The relative size of the inventory depends on the relative certainty of customer demand. Firms in the fortunate position of having unmet demand have no finished goods inventory except that being transported to customers.

Inventory is costly. The organisation must store it, move it from place to place, and safeguard it. The organisation also incurs the opportunity cost of having funds that are tied up in inventory and, therefore, unavailable for other, profit-making, investments.

Inventory is costly, and organisations would prefer to do other things with their funds. In most instances, firms consider inventory to be a major source of cost. Managers in these firms seek approaches to controlling inventory cost. One of the most widely used approaches is the economic order quantity (EOQ) model.

Inventories are materials and supplies that a business or institution carries either for sale or to provide inputs or supplies to the production process. All businesses and institutions require inventories. Often they are a major part of total assets.

Inventory means stock of goods. To the finance manager inventory means the value of raw materials, consumables, spares, work-in-progress, finished goods and scrap in which the company's funds have been invested.

The classic definition of inventory is that it is an idle resource of any kind having an economic value. From this it follows that inventory control is essentially the planning and designing procedure for maintenance of an optimum level of idle resources.

Inventories are very important to manufacturing firms because they represent 20% to 60% of total assets. As inventories are used, their value is converted into cash, which improves cash flow and return on investment. There is a cost for carrying inventories, which increases operating costs and decreases profit. So good inventory management is very important for any manufacturing company.

Inventory management is responsible for planning and controlling inventory from the raw material stage to the customer. Since inventory either results from production or supports it, the two cannot be managed separately and, therefore, must be coordinated.

Aggregate Inventory Management

Aggregate inventory management deals with managing inventories according to their classification (raw material, work-in-process and finished goods) and the functions they perform. It is concerned with the costs and benefits of carrying the different classifications of inventories. As such, aggregate inventory management involves the following :

(i) Flow and kinds of inventory needed.
(ii) Supply and demand patterns.
(iii) Functions that inventories perform.
(iv) Objectives of inventory management.
(v) Costs associated with inventories.

Item Inventory Management

Inventory is management both at the aggregate level and at the item level. Management must fix decision rules about inventory items so that the staff responsible for inventory control can do their job well. These rules include :

(i) Which individual inventory items are most important.
(ii) How individual items are to be controlled.
(iii) How much to order at one time.
(iv) When to place an order.

Some factors influencing inventory management decisions include :

(i) Types of inventory based on the flow of material.
(ii) Supply and demand patterns.
(iii) Functions performed by inventory.
(iv) Objectives of inventory management.
(v) Inventory costs.

Supply and Demand Patterns

If supply was exactly matched by demand, there would be little need for inventory. Goods could be made at the same rate as demand and no inventory would build up. For this situation to exist, demand must be predictable, stable and relatively constant for a long period of time.

If this is so, manufacturing can produce goods on a line-flow basis, matching production to demand. Using this system, raw materials are fed to production as required and work flow from one workstation to another is balanced. So little work-in-process inventory is required and goods are delivered to the customer at the rate desired by him.

However, demand for most products is neither sufficient nor constant enough to setting up of a complete production plant in one area. Rather these products are made in lots or batches. Workstations are organised by function, for example, all machine tools in one area, all welding in another and assembly in another. Work moves in lots from one workstation to another as required by technology and production conditions. Depending on the nature of the system, three types of inventories are built up — raw materials, work-in-process and finished goods.

Functions of Inventories

The basic purpose of inventories is to balance supply and demand. Inventory serves as a link between :

- Supply and demand
- Customer demand and finished goods
- Finished goods and component availability.
- Requirements for an operation and the output from the preceding operation.
- Parts and materials to begin production and the suppliers of materials.

Based on this, inventories can be classified according to the function they perform.

Anticipation Inventory

These inventories are built-up in anticipation of future demand. For example, they are created ahead of a peak selling season, a promotion programme, a major vacation or a festival season, or possibly the chance of a strike. They are built up to help level production and to reduce the cost of changing production rates.

Fluctuation Inventory (Safety Sock)

Inventory is held to cover random or unpredictable fluctuations in supply and demand or lead time. If demand or lead time is greater than forecast, a stockout will occur. Safety stock is carried to protect against this possibility. Its purpose is to prevent disruptions in manufacturing or deliveries to customers. Safety stock is also called buffer stock or reserve stock.

Lot-Size Inventory

Items purchased or manufactured in quantities greater than needed immediately create lot-size inventories. This is to take advantage of quantity discounts, to reduce shipping time and cost, clerical and setup costs and in cases where it is impossible to make or purchase items at the same rate they will be used or sold. Lot-size inventory is sometimes called cycle stock. It is the portion of inventory which gradually gets exhausted as customers' orders are received.

Maintenance, Repair and Operating Supplies

Maintenance, repair and operating supplies are items used to support general operations and maintenance but which do not become directly part of a product. They include maintenance supplies, spare parts and consumables such as cleaning compounds, lubricants, pencils and erasers.

Objectives of Inventory Management

A firm wishing to maximise profit will have at least the following objectives :

- Maximum customer service.

- Low-cost plant operation.
- Minimum inventory investment.

Customer Service

Inventories help to maximise customer service by protecting against uncertainty. If the inventory manager could forecast exactly what customers want and when, he could plan to meet demand with no uncertainty. However, demand and the lead time to get an item are often uncertain, possibly resulting in stockouts and customer dissatisfaction. For these reasons, it may be necessary to carry extra inventory to protect against uncertainty. This inventory is called safety stock.

Operating Efficiency

Inventories help make a manufacturing operation more efficient. As a result productivity increases in four ways:

1. Inventories allow operations with different rates of production to operate separately and more economically. If two or more operations in sequence have different rates of output and are to be operated efficiently, inventories must build up between them.
2. In case of seasonal products like coke, or ice-cream or woollen garments demand is not uniform throughout the year. By producing at the same (uniform) rate per period, manufacturing can continually produce an amount equal to the average demand. By following this strategy the costs of changing production levels can be avoided.
3. Inventories allow manufacturing to run longer production runs, which result in (i) lower setup costs per item; and (ii) an increase in production capacity (since production resources are used most of the time for processing as opposed to set-up).
4. Inventories allow manufacturing to purchase in larger quantities. This results in lower ordering costs per unit and volume discounts.

If inventory is carried, there has to be a benefit that exceeds the costs of carrying it. Perhaps the main reason for carrying inventory beyond current needs is that it costs less to carry it than not. The costs associated with carrying inventory are of the different types, as shown below.

Inventory Costs

The following costs are to be incurred in inventory management decisions :

- Item cost
- Carrying cost
- Ordering costs
- Stockout costs
- Capacity-related costs.

Item Cost

The price paid for a purcahsed item consists of the cost of the item and any other direct costs associated in getting the item into the plant. For an item manufactured in-house, the cost includes direct material, direct labour and factory overhead.

Carrying Costs

These costs include all expenses incurred by the firm due to the volume of inventory carried. As inventory increases, so do these costs.

Ordering Costs

Ordering costs are those associated with placing an order either with the factory or a supplier. The cost of placing an order does not depend upon the quantity ordered. Whether a lot of 10 or 100 is ordered, the costs associated with placing the order are essentially the same. However, the annual cost of ordering depends upon the number of orders placed per annum. This can be reduced by ordering more at one time, resulting in the placing of fewer orders. However, this drives up the inventory level and the annual cost of carrying inventory.

Stockout Costs

If demand during the lead time exceeds its expected level, we can expect a stockout. A stockout can potentially be expensive because of back-order costs, lost sales and possibly lost customers. Stockouts can be reduced by carrying extra inventory to protect against those times when the demand during lead time is greater than forecast.

Capacity-associated Costs

When output levels must be changed, there may be costs for overtime, hiring, training, extra shifts and layoffs. These costs can be avoided by adjusting production properly, that is, by producing items in slack periods for sale in peak periods. However, this leads to inventory build-up in the slack periods.

Financial Aspects of Inventory

When inventory is purcahsed as raw material, it is recorded as an asset. When it enters production, it is recorded as work-in-process inventory (WIP). As it is processed, its value increases by the amount of direct labour applied to it and the overhead (fixed cost) involved in its processing.

From a financial point of view, inventory is an asset and represents money that is tied up and cannot be used for other purposes. But inventory has a carrying cost — interest cost, storage and risk. Finance wants as little inventory as possible and needs some measure of the level of inventory. Total inventory investment is one measure, but in itself does not relate to sales. Two measures that do relate to sales are the inventory turns ratio and days of supply.

Inventory turns. A convenient measure of how effectively inventories are being used is the inventory turnover :

$$\text{Inventory turnover} = \frac{\text{Annual cost of goods sold}}{\text{Average value of inventory in rupees}}$$

For example, if the annual cost of goods sold is Rs 1 million and the average inventory is Rs 500,000 then

$$\text{Inventory turnover} = \frac{\text{Rs } 1{,}000{,}000}{\text{Rs } 500{,}000} = 2$$

What does this mean? It simply means that with Rs 500,000 of inventory a company is able to generate Rs 1 million in sales. If, through better materials management, the firm is able to increase its turnover to 10, the same sales are generated with only Rs 100,000 of average inventory. If the annual cost of carrying inventory is 25% of the inventory value, the reduction of Rs 400,000 in inventory results in a cost reduction (and profit increase) of Rs 80,000. In short, if material costs are reduced by a certain amount (say Rs 50,000), income increases by the same amount (Rs 50,000). So materials management can have a direct effect on a company's net revenue (or profit).

Days of supply. This is a measure of the equivalent number of days of inventory on hand, based on usage. The equation to calculate the days of supply is

$$\text{Days of supply} = \frac{\text{Inventory on hand}}{\text{Average daily usage}}$$

Concept of Inventory Control

Since inventory is a form of business investment, control of inventory is a must for any type of business. A good control system provides for self-control and only requires attention only in an exception situation. An organisation may also have one or more control system for managing its inventory. Since there are usually thousands of different items in inventory, the control mechanism should achieve its basic purpose at the lowest possible cost.

Effective inventory control system

An inventory control system is a co-ordinated set of rules for routinely answering the question of when to order and how much to order and how routine and non-routine situations are to be treated through predetermined rules and procedures.

An effective system has the following objectives:

(1) To ensure the availability of sufficient goods and materials.

(2) To identify excess and fast moving and slow moving items.

(3) To provide accurate, concise and timely reports to management.

Importance of Inventory Control

The inventory turnover has to be managed scientifically in any organisation. Since inventories are money, management of investment is to yield the best result.

A good inventory control system has the following advantages:

(i) Firstly, it minimises possibility of delays in production and ensures adequate supply of items to the customer.

(ii) Secondly, it makes use of available capital in a most effective way and avoids unnecessary expenditure on high inventories.

(iii) Thirdly, it takes advantages of quantity discounts on bulk purchase.

(iv) Fourthly, it eliminates the possibility of duplicate ordering.

(v) Finally, it helps in minimising the loss due to deterioration, damage and pilferage.

Types of Inventory

Inventory may be divided into two broad categories:

1. **Direct inventories :** Those items which play a direct role in the manufacturing and become an integral part of finished goods. Direct inventories may be classified into four groups :

   (a) ***Raw materials inventories:*** This type of inventories provide for :

   (i) Economical bulk purchasing.

   (ii) To enable production rate changes.

   (iii) To provide production buffer against delays in transportation.

   (iv) For seasonal fluctuation.

   (b) ***WIP inventories:*** Such inventories are needed :

   (i) To enable economical lot production.

   (ii) To cater to the variety of products.

   (iii) To provide replacement for wastages.

   (iv) To maintain uniform production even though sales may vary.

   (c) ***Finished Goods:*** Such inventories are required :

   (i) For providing "off-shelf" delivery.

   (ii) For stabilising the level of production.

   (iii) For promoting sales.

   (d) ***Spare Parts***: These are needed for replacement purposes in case of machine breakdowns, *i.e.*, for breakdown maintenance or to replace a machine which has lost its economic life and may go out of use soon (*i.e.*, productive maintenance).

2. **Indirect inventories:** These include those item which are necessary for manufacturing but do not become parts of the finished product, such as lubricants, grease oil, petrol, office materials, maintenance materials, etc.

Need for Inventory Control

Inventory is an asset, an investment. And, like all investments, it may be too high or too low. It may be well managed or poorly managed. The ultimate objective of inventory control is to obtain better returns on investment.

Funds locked up in excessive inventories could have been better utilised in some other internal investment opportunities of the firm which might have resulted in better returns, *i.e.*, greater profits.

On the other hand, inadequate investment in inventories can raise costs of of operations, as well as costs of stock-outs. This may lead to production stoppages and lowering the return on total investment.

Four immediate objectives of inventory control are :

(i) Maintaining liquidity of stocks;

(ii) Avoiding stock-outs;

(iii) Avoiding obsolescence and spoilage

(iv) Minimising the costs of holding inventories.

SELECTIVE INVENTORY CONTROL

Inventory in a company of medium size comprise thousands of items. The control of all these items in stock creates a serious problem for management. It becomes difficult to keep track of each and every item and exercise the same type of control on each. As a general rule over-stocking or stock-outs do not affect all the items in store. It is quite common to come across some items which move so fast that it is difficult to keep them replenished. At the same time, in the next bin there are other items that have been gathering dust or rust for weeks or even months and tying up quite a good amount of capital. Therefore, in order to exercise proper inventory control it is necessary to take a selective approach and each item treated differently according to its importance. This is essential for deriving maximum benefit with minimum effort.

In order to segregate the items in order of importance on the basis of selective approach, different methods have been developed. These methods give practical solution to the problem of controlling inventory. Each method is based on a particular criterion and a specific purpose. The most important of all such methods is the ABC analysis. The others are FSN analysis, VED analysis and SDE analysis. Each one of these methods is described below.

Management must, therefore, monitor the delivery, performance, quality and price of inputs from suppliers. Purchasing control seeks to ensure availability, acceptable quality, continued reliable sources and at the same time, reduce costs.

What can managers do to facilitate control of inputs? They need to gather information on the dates that supplies arrive and their condition on arrival. They need to gather data about the quality of suppliers and their compatability with operations processes. Finally, they need to obtain data on supplier price performance. Are the prices of the delivered goods the same as those quoted when the order was placed ?

This information can be used to rate suppliers, identify problem suppliers and guide management in choosing future suppliers. Trends can be detected. Suppliers can be evaluated, for instance, on responsiveness, service, reliability and competitiveness.

Building Close Links with Suppliers

A rapidly growing trend in manufacturing is turning suppliers into partners. Instead of using ten or twelve vendors it is better to use only two or three vendors and working closely with them to improve efficiency and quality.

Motorola, for instance, sends its design-and-manufacturing engineers to suppliers to help with any problem. Other firms now routinely send inspection teams to rate suppliers' operations. They are assessing these suppliers' manufacturing and delivery techniques, and process control systems that identify causes of defects. Companies have to develop long-term relationships with suppliers. As collaborators and partners, rather than adversaries, firms are finding that they can achieve better quality of inputs, fewer defects and lower costs. Furthermore, when problems arise with suppliers, open communication channels facilitate quick resolutions.

Economic Order Quantity Model

One of the best-known techniques for mathematically deriving the optimum quantity for a purchase order is the economic order quantity model (EOQ). The EOQ model seeks to balance four costs involved in ordering and carrying inventory : the purchase costs (purchase price plus delivery charge less discounts); the ordering

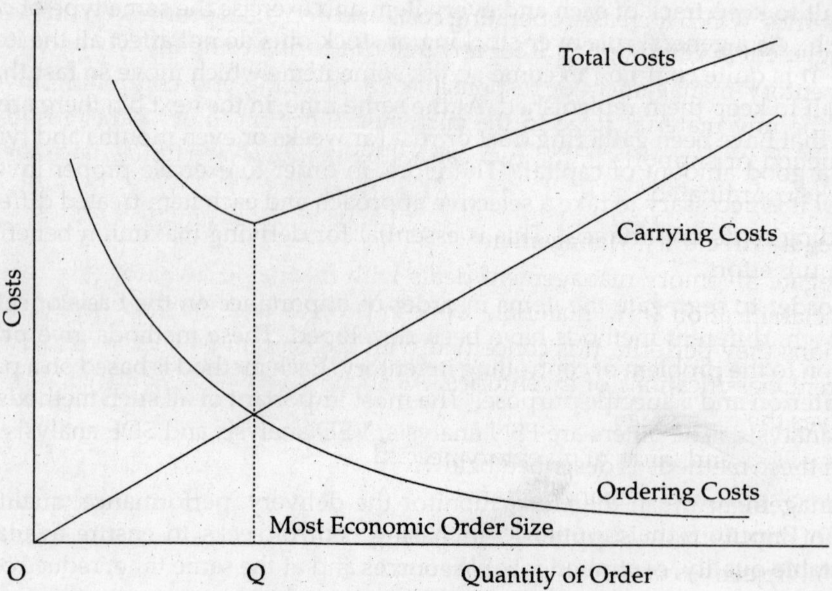

Fig. 5.2 : Determining the *EOQ*

costs (paperwork, follow-up, inspection when the item arrives, and other processing costs), carrying costs (money tied up in inventory, storage, insurance, taxes and so forth), and stockout costs (profits foregone from orders lost, the cost of reestablishing goodwill, and additional expenses incurred to expedite delivery of materials).

The objective of the EOQ model, as shown in Fig. 5.2 is to minimise the total costs of two of these four costs — carrying costs and ordering costs. As the amount ordered gets larger and larger, average inventory increases and so do carrying costs. But placing larger orders means fewer orders and, thus, lowers ordering costs. For example, if annual demand for an inventory item is 26,000 units and we order 500 each time, we will place 52 (26,000/500) orders per year. This gives us an average inventory of 250 (500/2) units. However, if the order quantity is increased to 2,000 units, there will be fewer orders placed, 13 (26,000/2,000), but the average inventory on hand will increase to 1,000 (2,000/2) units. Thus, as holding costs go up, ordering costs go down, and vice versa. As shown in Fig. 2, the lowest total cost — and thus the most economic order quantity — is reached at the lowest point on the total cost curve. That is the point at which ordering cost equals carrying cost. It is called the *economic order quantity*.

To calculate this optimal order quantity, we need the following information : forecasted demand for the item during the period (*D*), the cost of placing each order (*OC*), the value or purchase price of the item (*V*), and the carrying cost of maintaining the total inventory, expressed as a percentage (CC). We can now present the standard *EOQ* formula and show its use :

$$EOQ = \sqrt{\frac{2 \times 4{,}000 \times 75}{V \times CC}} = \sqrt{6{,}000} = 77.46 \text{ units} = 78 \text{ units.}$$

The inventory model suggests to management that it is most economic to order in quantities or lots of approximately 78 units; in other words, they should order about 52 (4,000/78) times a year.

What would happen if the supplier of the video devices offered Playback a 5 % discount on purchases if Playback buys in minimum quantities of 120 units? Should Playback's management now purchase in quantities of 78 or 120? Without the discount and, therefore, ordering 78 each time, Playback's annual costs for this video player would be as follows :

$$EOQ = \sqrt{\frac{2 \times D \times OC}{V \times CC}}$$

As an example, Playback Electronics, a retailer of high-quality sound and video equipment, is trying to ascertain its economic order quantities. The item in question is a Century videotape recorder. The company forecasts sales of 4,000 units a year. Purchasing believes that the cost of each recorder will be Rs 500. The accountants estimate the cost of placing an order for video players at Rs 75 per order and annual insurance, taxes and other carrying costs at 20% of the recorder's worth. Using the *EOQ* formula and the information above, we find

Purchase cost : Rs 500 x 4,000	20,00,000
Carrying cost : $\frac{78}{2}$ x Rs 500 x 0.20	3,900
(average inventory units) x (value of item) x (percentage)	Rs
Ordering cost = (number of orders) x (Cost to place order) : 52 x 75	3,900
Total cost	20,07,800

With the 5% discount for ordering 120 units, the item cost would be Rs 475. The annual inventory costs would be as follows :

	Rs
Purchase cost : Rs 475 x 4,000	19,00,000
Carrying cost $\frac{120}{2}$ x 475 x 0.20	5,700
Ordering cost $\frac{4,000}{120}$ × 75	2,500
Total cost	19,08,200

These calculations suggest to management that it should take the 5% discount. Even though it has to stock larger quantities, the savings are almost Rs 1,00,000 a year.

Limitations of the model

The EOQ model assumes that demand and lead time are known and constant. If these conditions cannot be met, the model should not be used. For example, it generally should not be used for manufactured component inventory, since the components are taken out of stock all at once or in lumps or in lots, rather than at a constant rate. However, this means that the EOQ model is useless when demand is variable. The model can still be of some use in trade-offs in costs and the need to control lot sizes.

Inventory Ordering Systems

In many chequebooks, after you use up about 95% of the cheques, you find a reorder form included among the cheques; it reminds you that it's time to reorder. This is an example of a fixed-point reordering system. At some preestablished point in the operations process, the system is designed to "flag" the fact that the inventory needs to be replenished. It is triggered when the inventory reaches a certain point or level.

The goal of a fixed-point reordering system is to minimise inventory carrying costs and to ensure a reasonable level of customer service (limiting the probability of an item running out — a *stockout*). Therefore, the reorder point should be established to equate the time remaining before a stockout and the lead time to receive delivery of the reordered quantity. In such cases, the newly ordered items would arrive at the same time as the last item in inventory was used up. More realistically, management does not usually allow the inventory to fall below some safety stock level (See Fig. 5.2). By using certain statistical methods, it is possible to set a reorder point at a level that gives an organisation enough inventory to get through the lead time period and some reasonable insurance against a stockout. This buffer, or safety, stock gives protection against greater usage than expected during the lead time or an unexpected delay in receiving the item.

As a simple example, in determining a cheque reorder point, let's assume that the lead time averages three weeks and we write about twenty cheques a week. We would need sixty cheques to get us through a 'normal' reordering lead time. If we feel, on the basis of past experience, that a one-week safety stock would be sufficient to get us through most lead time periods, the order should be placed when there are 80 (60 + 20) cheques left. This is the reorder point. It may also be noted that the more safety stock, the less the risk of stockout. But the additional inventory will add to the carrying costs. Thus we again have a cost-benefit calculation before taking a decision. At times it may be in the rightness of things (cost-wise) to run out of stock.

One very effective use of the fixed-point reordering system is to keep the item — for example, pens and duplicating paper in an office or boxes of shoes in a retail shoe store — in two separate containers. Inventory is drawn from one until it is empty. At that point, a reorder is placed and items are drawn from the second container. If demand for an item has been estimated properly, the replacement order to replenish the stock should arrive before the second container is used up.

Computer Control

Another, more recent, version of the fixed point reorder system relies on computer control. Sales are automatically recorded by a central computer that has been programmed to initiate a purchase order for an item when its inventory reaches some critical fixed point. A number of retail stores have such systems. The cash registers are actually computers, and each sale automatically adjusts the store's inventory record. When the inventory of an item touches the critical point, the computer tells management to reorder or, in some systems, actually prints out the purchase order requisition.

Fixed Inventory Re-ordering System

Another common inventory system is the fixed interval reordering system. The fixed interval system uses time as the determining factor for inventory control. At a predetermined time — say, once a week or every ninety days — the inventory is counted, and an order is placed for the number of items necessary to bring the inventory back to the desired level. The desired level is established so that if demand and ordering lead time are average, consumption will draw the inventory down to zero (or some safety lead time can be added) just as the next order arrives. This system may have some transportation economies and quantity discount economies over the fixed-point system. For example, it may allow us to consolidate orders from one supplier if we review all the items we purchase from this source at the same time. This is not possible in the other system.

ABC INVENTORY CONTROL

Control of inventory is exercised by controlling individual items called stock-keeping units. In controlling inventory, four questions are to be answered :

- What is the importance of the inventory item ?
- How are they to be controlled ?
- How much should be ordered at one time ?
- When should an order be placed ?

The ABC inventory classification system answers the first two questions by determining the importance of items and, thus, allowing different levels of control based on the relative importance of items.

Most companies carry a large number of items in stock. To have better control at a reasonable cost, it is useful to classify the items according to their relative importance. Usually, this is based on annual rupee usage, but other criteria may be used.

Many companies have thousands of items in inventory. However, evidence indicates that roughly 10% of the items in most organisations' inventory account for 50% of the annual rupee inventory value. Another 20% of the items account for 30% of the value. The remaining 70% of the items appear to account for only 20% of the value. These have been labelled as A, B and C categories, respectively. Thus, we have the name ABC system (See Fig.5.3).

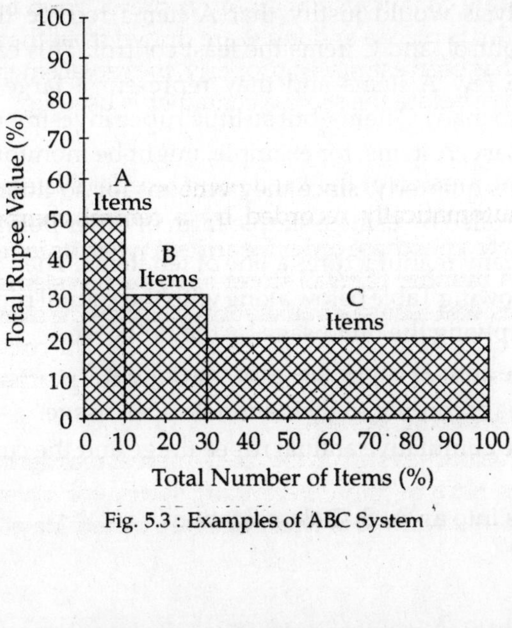

Fig. 5.3 : Examples of ABC System

The ABC principle is based on the observation that a small number of items often dominate the results achieved in any situation. Thus, as noted above, the relationship between the percentage of items and the percentage of annual rupee usage follows a pattern in which :

A — About 20% of the items account for about 80% of the rupee usage.

B — About 30% of the items account for about 15% of the rupee usage.

C — About 50% of the items account for about 5% of the rupee usage.

The percentages are approximate and should not be taken as a rough and ready measure. This type of distribution can be used to help control inventory.

Steps in Making an ABC Analysis

1. Establish the item characteristics that influence the results of inventory management. This is usually annual rupee usage but there may be other criteria, such as scarcity of material.
2. Classify items into groups based on the established criteria.
3. Apply a degree of control in proportion to the importance of the group.

The factors affecting the importance of an item include annual rupee usage, unit cost and scarcity of material. For simplicity, only annual rupee usage. The procedure for classifying by annual rupee usage is as follows :

1. Determine the annual usage for each item.
2. Multiply the annual usage of each item by its cost to get its total annual rupee usage.
3. List the items according to their annual rupee usage.
4. Calculate the cumulative annual rupee usage and the cumulative percentage of items.
5. Examine the annual usage distribution and group the items into A, B and C groups based on percentage of annual usage.

Cost-benefit analysis would justify that A items receive the tightest control, B items moderate control, and C items the least control. This can be accomplished because ther are so few A items and they represent a large rupee investment. Similarly, there are so many C items, but so little rupee investment, that tight control would not be necessary. A items, for example, might be monitored weekly, B items monthly and C items quarterly, since they account for so little rupee value. Or C items might be controlled by using a simple form of order point.

Example. A company manufactures a line of ten items. Their usage and unit cost are shown in the following Table below along with the annual rupee usage. The latter is obtained by multiplying the unit usage by the unit cost.

(a) Calculate the annual rupee usage for each item.

(b) List the items according to their annual rupee usage.

(c) Calculate the cumulative annual rupee usage and the cumulative percent of items.

(d) Group items into an A, B, C classification.

Answer. (a) Calculate the annual rupee usage for each item.

Part Number	Unit Usage	Unit Cost (Rs)	Annual Rupee Usage
1	1,100	2	2,200
2	600	40	24,000
3	100	4	400
4	1,300	1	1,300
5	100	60	6,000
6	10	25	250
7	100	2	200
8	1,500	2	3,000
9	200	2	400
10	500	1	500
Total	**5,510**	—	**38,250**

Answer. b, c and d

Part Number	Annual Rupees Usage	Cumulative Rupees Usage	Cumulative % of Rupee Usage	Cumulative % of Items	Class
2	24,000	24,000	62.75	10	A
5	6,000	30,000	78.43	20	A
8	3,000	33,000	86.27	30	B
1	2,200	35,200	92.03	40	B
4	1,300	36,500	95.42	50	B
10	500	37,000	96.73	60	C
9	400	37,400	97.78	70	C
3	400	37,800	98.82	80	C
6	250	38,050	99.48	90	C
7	200	38,250	100.00	100	C

The percentage of value and the percentage of items can be shown as in Fig. 5.4 (see next page).

Control Based on ABC Classification

Using the ABC approach, there are two general rules to follow :

1. ***Have a large number of low-value items.*** C items represent about 50% of the items but account for only about 5% of the total inventory value. Carrying extra stock of C items adds little to the total value of the inventory. C items are really only important if there is a shortage of one of them — when they become extremely important — so a supply should always be on hand. For example, order a year's supply at a time and carry plenty of safety stock. That way there is only once a year when a stockout is even possible.

2. ***Use the money and control effort saved to reduce the inventory of high-value items.*** A items represent about 20% of the items and account for about 80% of the value. They are extremely important. So they need the maximum control and the most frequent review.

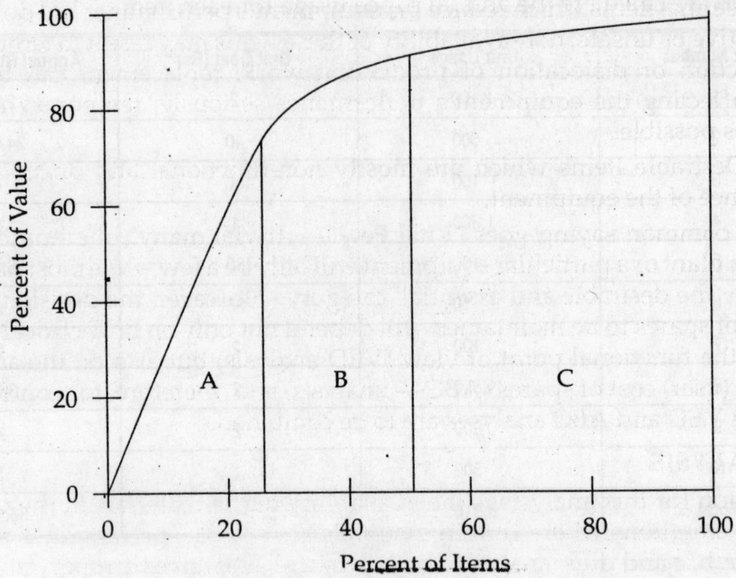

Fig. 5.4 : ABC Curve : percentage of value versus percentage of items

Different controls used with different classifications might be the following :

A Items : highest priority — Tight control including complete accurate records, regular and frequent review by management, frequent review of demand forecasts and close follow-up and expenditing to reduce lead time.

B Items : medium priority — Normal controls with good records, regular attention and normal processing.

C items : lowest priority — Simplest possible controls — make sure there are plenty. Simple or no records, perhaps use a two-bin system or periodic review system. Order large quantities and carry safety stock.

VED ANALYSIS

VED stands for vital, essential and desirable. This analysis relates to the classification of maintenance spare parts and denotes the essentiality of stocking spares. The spares are split into three categories in order of importance. From the view-points of functional utility, the effects of non-availability at the time of requirement or the operation, process, production, plant or equipment and the urgency of replacement in case of breakdown. Some spares are so important that their non-availability renders the equipment or a number of equipment in a process line completely inoperative, or even causes extreme damage to plant, equipment or human life. On the other hand some spares are non-functional, serving relatively unimportant purposes, and their replacement can be postponed or alternative methods of repair found. All these factors will have direct effects on the stocks of spares to be maintained. Therefore, it is necessary to classify the spares in the following categories:

V — Vital items which render the equipment or the whole line operation in a process totally and immediately inoperative or unsafe; and if these items go out of stock or are not readily available, there is loss of production for the whole period.

E — Essential items which reduce the equipment's performance but do not render it inoperative or unsafe; non-availability of these items may result in temporary loss of production or dislocation of production work; replacement can be delayed without affecting the equipment's performance seriously; temporary repairs are sometimes possible.

D — Desirable items which are mostly non-functional and do not affect the performance of the equipment.

As the common saying goes "Vital Few — trivial many", the number of vital spares in a plant or a particular equipment will only be a few while most of the spares will fall in 'the desirable and essential' category. However, the decision regarding the stock of spares to be maintained will depend not only on how critical the spares are from the functional point of view (VED analysis) but also on the annual consumption (user) cost of spares (ABC — analysis) and, therefore, for control of spare parts both VED and ABC analyses are to be combined.

SDE ANALYSIS

The criterion for this analysis is the availability of the materials in the market. In industrial situations where certain materials are scarce (specially in a developing country like India) this analysis is very useful and gives proper guideline for deciding the inventory policies.

The characteristics of the three categories - SD and E - are :

S — Refers to scarce items, items which are in short supply. Usually these are raw materials, spare parts and imported items.

D — Stands for difficult items, items which are not readily available in local markets and have to be procured from far away places, or items for which there are a limited number of suppliers; or items for which quality suppliers are difficult to get.

E — Refer to items which are easily available in the local markets.

FSN ANALYSIS

Here the items are classified into fast-moving (F), slow-moving (S) and Non-moving (N) items on the basis of quantity and rate of consumption. The non-moving items (usually, not consumed over a period of two years) are of great importance. It is found that many companies maintain huge stocks of non-moving items blocking quite a lot of capital. Moreover, there are thousands of such items. Scrutiny of these items is made to determine whether they could be used or to be disposed off. The classification of fast and slow moving items helps in arrangement of stocks in stores and their distribution and handling methods.

Conclusion

It may be noted that all the items in store are not of same importance. Moreover, if the company follows a uniform policy of ordering and keeping records of all these items, the work involved will be huge. At the same time no useful purpose will be served as most of the attention will be diverted to less important items, the number of which is quite high. Therefore, in order to achieve the best result with minimum effort, it is necessary to concentrate on important items and put maximum efforts on them. The principle followed in this sort of selective control is "Thick on the best and thin on the rest". It is normally advantageous to put best efforts on A, H, V and S items for selective inventory control.

Synopsis for Learning

Q.1. What is the importance of material control ?

Ans. Production planning and control require material control. Material control is responsible for ensuring that the right quantity and quality of material is available when and where required. At the same time capital must not be tied up unduly, nor must there be undue loss from deterioration and obsolescence.

Q.2. What is inventory control all about ?

Ans. The problem of holding the minimum amount of inventory necessary to satisfy production requirements and yet not be too high is a typical problem. Inventory control is concerned with the relationship between :
(i) cost of holding stock, *i.e.*, capital tied up, deterioration and obsolescence and cost of warehouse space;
(ii) loss of profit in being unable to meet demand through storage of materials;
(iii) amount and variability of demand;
(iv) cost of placing order;
(v) discounts obtainable by ordering large quantities.

Q.3. How do you classify inventories ?

Ans. There are many ways to classify inventories. The main types are the following :
(i) *Raw materials*. These are purchased items received which have not entered the production process, *viz.*, purchased materials, component parts and subassemblies.
(ii) *Work-in-process (WIP)* : Raw materials that have entered the manufacturing process and are being worked on or waiting to be worked on.
(iii) *Finished goods* : The finished goods of the production process that are ready to be sold as completed items. They may be held at a factory or central warehouse or at various points in the distribution system.
(iv) *Distribution inventories* : Finished goods located in the distribution system.
(v) *Maintenance, repair and operational supplies* : Items used in production that do not become part of the product. These include hand tools, spare parts, lubricants and cleaning supplies.

Q.4. What are the benefits and costs of holding inventories ?

Ans. There are benefits as well as costs to having inventory. The problem is to balance the cost of carrying inventory with the following :
Customer service : The lower the inventory level, the higher the likelihood of a stockout and the potential cost of back orders, lost sales and lost customers. The higher the inventory level, the higher the level of customer service.
Operating efficiency. Inventories decouple one operation from another and allow manufacturing to operate more efficiently. They allow levelling production and avoid the costs of changing production levels. Carrying inventory allows longer production runs and reduces the number of setups. Finally, inventories let manufacturing purchase in larger quantities. The ABC inventory classification system prioritises individual items so that inventory and costs can be better controlled.
Cost of placing orders. Inventory can be reduced by ordering less each time an order is placed. However, this increases the annual cost of ordering.
Transportation and handling costs. The more often goods have to be moved and the smaller the quantities moved, the greater the transportation and material handling costs.

Q.5. Which factors influence inventory management ?

Ans. Inventory management is influenced by several factors :
(i) The classification of the inventory, whether raw material, work-in-process, or finished goods.
(ii) The functions that inventory serves: anticipation, fluctuation, lot size or transportation.
(iii) Supply and demand patterns.
(iv) The costs associated with carrying (or not carrying) inventory.

Q.6. What do you mean by item-wise management of inventory ?

Ans. Besides managing inventory at the aggregate level, it must also be managed at the item level. Management needs to establish decision rules about inventory items so that inventory control personnel can do their job effectively.

Q.7. What are the modern methods of inventory control ?

Ans. Statistical methods can be used to evaluate the level of stock needed, while providing an acceptable level of protection. If the delivery period for replacement is short, the percentage of possible out-of-stock items may be calculated and a decision to risk being out of stock may be made, if there is a low probability of the events occurring.

REDUCING INVENTORIES

A major portion of many companies' assets is tied up in inventories. Firms that can significantly cut their inventories of raw materials and of in-process and finished goods can reduce costs and improve their efficiency.

JUST-IN-TIME CLASSIFICATION OF INVENTORIES

The concept of just-in-time is considered to be a Japanese origin and a creation of Toyota Corporation. Toyota developed the system in order to reduce inventory in the production systems, reduce costs and increase quality. JIT has attracted a great deal of interest and enthusiasm in contemporary American industries and management literature. American manufacturing concerns noticed Japanese manufacturing firms' use of JIT when the Japanese began making their products faster, at a lower cost and with better quality than their American counterparts.

JIT is the terminology attributed to concepts and management philosophy used in controlling inventories in a production process. A narrow application of JIT refers to the timing of supplies delivered to the production process. In this process raw materials arrive when and where they are needed and in the exact quantities needed. This concept has broadened to include all aspects of the manufacturing processes.

JIT has the goals of reducing inventory almost to the point of zero. By reducing lead times from suppliers, through operations and to customers, total costs are reduced. Using JIT along with total quality control and the aggressive use of flexible manufacturing technologies, the Japanese have consistently out-performed the U.S. in cost, quality and on-time delivery.

In Japan, JIT systems are called *kanban*. The derivation of the word gets to the essence of the just-in-one concept. Kanban is Japanese for 'card' or 'sign'. Japanese suppliers ship parts to manufacturers in containers, each of which has a card, or kanban, slipped into a side pocket. When a production worker opens a container, he (or she) takes out the card and sends it back to the supplier. That leads to the shipping of a second container of parts that, ideally, reaches the production worker just as the last part is being used up in the first container. The ultimate goal of a JIT inventory system is to eliminate raw material inventories by precisely coordinating production and supply deliveries. When the system works as designed, it results in a number of positive benefits for a manufacturer : reduced inventories, reduced setup time, better work flow, shorter manufacturing time, less space consumption and even higher quality. Of course, suppliers must be found who can be depended on to deliver quality materials on time. Since there are no inventories, there is no slack in the system to absorb defective materials or delays in shipment.

JIT stands for Just-in-Time. This is the extreme end of what is known as JIC (Just-in-Case) inventory system practised in most organisations in India. The term 'zero inventories' does not mean literally nil inventories. Small amount of inventories are maintained that is required to sustain the production activity and this amount is equal to the irreducible minimum. JIT seeks elimination of all waste, *i.e.*, anything not essential to meet the product demand such as scrap, rework, excessive inventories, low labour utilisation and others. Production of part, component or sub-assembly must occur just in time, neither earlier or not later. This is accomplished by a "Pull" system instead of a "Push" system used in traditional production system. In the rational production inventory system the final product is explored to determine the quantities required of sub-assembly and components for undertaking the manufacturing in order to meet the product demand on pre-determined schedule. As the components are pushed from stage to stage, the various operations are to be completed in order to make the final product. Since delay can occur at any one of the stages, safety stocks are created to ensure continuous supply of parts. In JIT inventory system, the advance stage of production just draws the right amount of inventory from the preceding stage to keep the production activity going. Furthermore, production activity is carried out on the basis of actual demand. Essentially, JIT purchasing means providing materials to the production facility just as they are required for use. The objective of zero inventory requires a new approach to suppliers. The most important is the abandonment of the concept that suppliers are adversaries. Instead, in a JIT system, suppliers are regarded as partners. There will still be tough negotiation sessions, arguments and disagreements. But the essence is that both the buyer and supplier will work together towards mutually beneficial goals. A JIT manufacturing facility will focus on fast cycle time manufacturing and small lot production. Cycle time is the time gap between the start of a job in the production process and its completion. Table 5.3 shows the difference between the JIT purchasing and traditional buying :

Table 5.3 : Difference Between the JIT Purchasing and Traditional Buying

Category	Traditional Buying	JIT Purchasing
Suppliers/buyer relationship	Adversarial	Partnership
Contract Period	Short or Long Term	Long Term
Quantity	Large	Small
Transportation	Full truck load of a single item	Full truck load of many items
Quality	Inspection	No inspection
Communication	Purchase Order	Verbal or electronic
No. of Suppliers	Many — the more the better	Few or single
Design Process	Make the print, then ask for quote	Ask for supplier ideas, then print

In the JIT environment, a well performing vendor can be exempted from normal inspection. Thus four major components of ordering costs can be eliminated, and the negotating and transportation cost components can be reduced considerably. So total order cost falls drastically under this method.

(a) ***Ordering cost using conventional purchasing practices*** :
Total ordering cost = Negotiation + Open order status paper + expediting + receiving + receiving inspection + transportation.

(b) ***Ordering cost using JIT Purchasing*** :
Total ordering cost = Negotiation + transportation

(c) ***Replenishment lead time using conventional practices :***
Total replenishment lead time = Paper work lead time + manufacturing time for vendor + transportation lead time + receiving and inspection.

(d) ***Replenishment lead time using JIT Purchasing :***
Total replenishment lead time = Paper work lead time + manufacturing time for vendor + transportation lead time.

Just in time is just a common sense way of doing business and a journey towards improvement and perfection. Only in Japan it has been practised as a total system.

In India, JIT has endless opportunities, more so due to the numerous problems associated with purchasing — transportation costs and bottlenecks, and power cuts. Even if partially implemented, a JIT attempt would surely improve the purchasing effectiveness and make an impact on other functions. JIT is based on three norms : (i) few suppliers, (ii) small deliveries and (iii) quality at source.

For JIT to work, the supplier has to be a part of the company. The refinement of JIT is "*Kanban*". "*Kanban*" is the Japanese word for a tag or cord which is attached to a standard container of inventory or to a group of sub-assemblies.

The concept of JIT is central to Japanese production management and in productivity improvement. JIT means produce and delivery goods just in time to be sold, sub-assemblies just in time to be reassembled into finished goods and parts just in time to be transformed into fabricated items.

To achieve the objective of JIT system, the Japanese have tried to reduce drastically the machine set up times so that it is economical to carry on production operations in small batches. The idea is to make one piece available just in time to ensure that the next operation can proceed smoothly.

Conclusion

JIT would be impractical without its emphasis on quality. The elimination of defective parts and quality inspections by employees are means by which quality is ensured. As a primary goal JIT produces just what is demanded by the market. Traditionally, production was geared towards increasing inventory. By reducing inventories, the firm is forced to reduce the weaknesses in its operation. Inventory levels are not optimised as defined by the economic order quantity (EOQ) model. Historically, inventory turnover measures have been of secondary concern in American firms. The classical model of cost accounting has inventory valuation as its primary driver of financial information. A change in cost accounting is needed to accommodate JIT. Inventory valuation will then become a secondary concern. Under the JIT system the levels of inventory on hand are lowered since the company is now demand-driven instead of building products and waiting for orders to occur.

A JIT system is not for every manufacturer. It requires that suppliers be located in close proximity to the manufacturer's production facility and that suppliers be capable of providing consistently defect-free materials. Such a system also requires reliable transportation links between suppliers and manufacturers; efficient receiving, handling and distribution of materials, and scientific production planning. When these conditions are met, JIT can help management to reduce inventory costs.

Under the traditional EOQ model high levels of inventory tie up a significant amount of capital that could be invested in more productive assets. If inventory levels are minimised, less time is involved in the handling and transaction costs of pulling goods out of raw materials, work-in-process and finished goods. Consequently, these unnecessary costs aren't passed on to the consumer. With today's technology changing so rapidly, products that are put into inventory for several months in anticipation of future sales might become obsolete or need to be reworked in order to satisfy customer needs.

Today's consumers are demanding better quality products. In order to obtain better quality in the manufacturing environment several factors must be considered: (1) suppliers of parts must be able to deliver parts on the time when needed and achieve an almost zero defect rate; (2) employees will need to be trained on how to properly operate the machines and tools that are necessary to perform their jobs; and (3) ability to produce the product correctly the first time. This will lead to reduced repair and retest costs, less scrap and a reduction in manual inspection time.

Since the beginning of the 1990s, an increasing number of American firms have been developing JIT production systems. JIT production systems can be operative within one to two years, but it takes five to ten years to achieve optimal results.

Synopsis for Learning

Q.1. What is just-in-time ?

Ans. The just-in-time philosophy and techniques that seek the elimination of waste and continuous improvements were developed for repetitive manufacturing and are perhaps most applicable there. However, many basic concepts are appropriate to any form of manufacturing organisation.

Q.2. How does just-in-time system reduce inventory ?

Ans. Today, the concepts of Just-in-Time (JIT) manufacturing stress the need to supply customers with what they want when they want it and to keep inventories at a minimum. These objectives put further stress on the relationship among production, marketing and finance. An important way to resolving these conflicting objectives is to provide close coordination of the supply, production and distribution functions. The problem is to balance conflicting objectives to minimise the total of all the costs involved and maximise customer service consistent with the goals of the organisation. This requires some type of integrated materials management that is responsible for supply, production and distribution. Rather than having the planning and control of these functions spread among marketing, production, and distribution, they should occur in a single area of responsibility. Because the JIT system reduces the inventory in the system, in some respects this should make inventory management easier.

Q.3. What are the benefits of just-in-time ?

Ans. Five main benefits of just-in-time are :

(i) Greater productivity, smaller inventory
(ii) Better quality / less waste
(iii) Better motivated employees
(iv) Fewer stockrooms, less materials handling
(v) Less inventory control staff.

GLOSSARY

Economic order quantity The quantity of goods which minimises the total of storage costs and ordering costs. A formula is used to find the optimum ordering quantity, which gives the lowest ordering costs (by buying large amounts) and lowest storage costs (by keeping goods for a short period).

Inventory turnover A measure of the number of times the average inventory of merchandise is sold, or turned over, during a year. It is computed by dividing the cost of goods sold (or total sales) by the average inventory levell in one year.

Just-in-time This refers to an inventory control system that is designed to minimise inventory in production operations. It seeks to eliminate waste by supplying required parts to the production line at the 'last minute'.

Perpetual inventory The continuous recording of stock movements enabling the stock position to be available at any time.

Reorder level The quantity of a stock item which indicates that an order for replenishment is required to be placed.

Total Quality Management This is a cost effective system for integrating the continuous quality improvement efforts of people at all levels in an organisation to deliver products and services which ensure customer satisfaction.

APPENDICES
Advanced Treatment of Some Important Topics

MARKETING MANAGEMENT

1. MARKETING STRATEGIES

When one considers marketing decisions and how they can affect demand for a firm's product, those actions that change prices, modify advertising campaigns, or establish special promotions come immediately to mind. Such actions are called marketing programme.

Often, several different marketing programmes are used jointly. In other situations, managers may need to choose among marketing programmes due to budget constraints. To make the best choice among marketing programmes in such situations and to ensure that the decisions will fulfill management's expectation for the product, marketing managers should first establish a clear marketing strategy.

Meaning. Marketing strategies are plans that specify the impact a firm hopes to achieve on the demand for a product or product line in a given target market. Firms sometimes feel that the best marketing opportunity comes from expanding primary demand, whereas the best growth opportunity may come from expanding selective demand. The basic options in developing marketing strategies are listed in Table A.1. For example, if Fast Foods designs a new marketing campaign promoting consumption of soup for dinner (a primary-demand strategy), the Fast-Foods brand is likely to benefit from the campaign (thus stimulating selective demand).

Table A.1 : Basic Elements of a Marketing Strategy

Target market selection	All buyers in the relevant market Buyers in one or more segments
Type of demand to be stimulated	**Primary demand** Among new users Amount current users **Selective demand** In new served markets Among competitors' customers In current customer base

In short, a marketing strategy is the link between the corporate strategy and the situation analysis on the one hand and the action-oriented marketing programmes on the other. Marketing programmes should flow from, and be consistent with, the marketing strategy. In turn, the selection of a marketing strategy should be based on the result of the earlier steps in the planning process.

PRIMARY-DEMAND STRATEGIES

Primary-demand strategies seek to increase the level of demand for a product form or class. Firms that are pioneers in marketing new product forms (such as Procter & Gamble in disposable diapers or Texas Instruments in pocket calculators) will, by necessity, pursue primary-demand strategies. In addition, firms with large shares in established markets (such as Microsoft in personal computer software) often devote at least part of their marketing effort to the expansion of primary demand because, as market leaders, they have the most to gain from expanding the market.

Basically, there are two sources of new demand for a product form or class: nonusers and users who might expand their rate of usage. Primary-demand strategies can, therefore, be categorised in terms of how the strategy is directed.

Strategies for Attracting Nonusers

To increase the number of users, the firm must increase customers' willingness or ability to buy the product.

INCREASING THE WILLINGNESS TO BUY

The willingness to buy may be stimulated by one of the three approaches:

1. Clearly demonstrating the benefits already offered by a product form
2. Developing new product with benefits that will be more appealing to certain segments (*i.e.*, parts of the market).
3. Sharing or promoting new benefits from exisiting products.

A focus on sharing the basic product-form benefits is often necessary when a new product form is being marketed.When new product make much additions to the benefits offered by existing products, the needs of potential customers will be met. Often, trade associations undertake primary-demand strategies on behalf of the producers in a market to highlight benefits that may not be much known to potential customers.

The importance of this considerable type of is considerable when a new product or class is introduced, because new products seldom sell themselves. Furthermore, this strategy may not be important in advanced countries if a product is well-established, but can be critical in bringing a product to a new market in a different culture, *e.g.*, a third world country.

INCREASING THE ABILITY TO BUY

The ability to buy can be improved by offering lower prices or credit, or by providing greater availability (through more distributors, more frequent delivery, or fewer stockouts). For example, reduced prices brought rapid sales increase to the cellular phone market in the early 1980s. Similarly, innovative financing plans can often help to increase primary demand.

Strategies for Increasing the Purchasing Rate among Users

When managers are concerned with gaining more rapid growth in a sluggish but mature market, the marketing strategy may be geared toward increasing the willingness to buy more often or in more volume, using one of the following approaches.

BROADENING USAGE

Buyers may use the same product more widely if the variety of use occasions can be expanded. In recent years, a number of advertising campaigns have been conducted to suggest broadened applications for products or services.

INCREASING PRODUCT CONSUMPTION LEVELS

Lower prices or special-volume packaging may lead to higher average volumes and, possibly, to more rapid consumption for products such as soft drinks and snacks. Or, consumption levels may be increased if buyers' feelings of the benefits of a product or service change.

ENCOURAGING REPLACEMENT

Product redesign may be taken as a selective-demand strategy. It is, however, largely a primary-demand strategy in the fashion industry and in other durable-goods industries. Although a refrigerator may well last 20 years, many replacement sales will be made earlier if product convenience, space utilisation, and operating costs can be improved.

In short, primary-demand strategies may be implemented in a number of ways, as shown in Table A.2. Although these strategies are generally less widely used than selective-demand strategies, they can be very useful if market measurements show large gaps between market potential and industry sales. Moreover, the analysis of the buying process may identify the factors limiting the ability or willingness to buy or to adopt a product class or form. If so, managers should have some insights into the kinds of programmes that can be used to stimulate primary demand.

Table A.2 : Primary-Demand Marketing Strategies

How Demand is Impacted	Basic Strategies for Influencing Demand
1. Attract nonusers	Increase willingness to buy Increase ability to buy
2. Increase rate of purchase among users	Broaden usage occasions Increase rate of consumption Increase rate of replacement

SELECTIVE-DEMAND STRATEGIES

As shown in Table A.3, selective demand can influence the market in three distinct ways: (1) by expanding the served market, (2) by taking away competitors' customers, and (3) by retaining and expanding sales within the firm's current customer base.

Table A.3 : Selective-Demand Marketing Strategies

How Demand is Impacted	Basic Strategies for Influencing Demand
1. Expand served market	Broaden distribution Product-line extension
2. Acquire competitors' customers	Head-to-head competition Superior quality price-cost leadership Differentiation Benefit/attribute positioning Customer-based positioning
3. Retain/expand demand within current customer base	Maintain satisfaction Relationship marketing Complementary products

Strategies for Expanding the Served Market

Firms define their relevant market in terms of the product forms or class in which they compete. The served market is that portion of the relevant market that a firm chooses to serve, as reflected by the scope of its product and distribution offerings.

When the opportunities for building market share within already served markets become more limited, firms often pursue sales expansion by broadening the scope of their distribution or by expanding the product line. These marketing strategies are virtually dictated if the corporate strategy emphasizes market development or product development.

BROADENING DISTRIBUTION

A firm's sales and distribution programmes are designed to make product available to the target market and often to gain effective delivery, display, or promotional support. As firms grow, the increase in their capital may allow them to move into new market areas. In other cases, firms may have to move the new channels of distribution in order to serve all portions of a market.

PRODUCT-LINE EXTENSION

A firm can expand the line of products it offers within a market through new-product development programmes. To be specific, a firm can choose from two main routes when using new product development to serve new markets.

A *vertical product-line extension* involves adding a new product at a different price(s). A *horizontal product-line extension* occurs when a firm adds a new product with different features at more or less the same price(s).

Strategies for Acquring Competitors' Customers

A firm's most direct competitors are those it competes with within the same served market. When buyers make choice within a given served market, those who view the choice process as nonroutine will compare the alternatives in terms of the various attributes. Because choices will largely be based on these customer acquisition strategies it will depend on how the product is positioned in the market. This means that a product's position shows how it is treated relative to its competitor(s). From a managerial perspective, a firm has two basic strategic options : head-to-head positioning or differentiated positioning .

HEAD-TO-HEAD POSITIONING

With this strategy a firm offers basically the same benefits as the competing products, but tries to beat the competitors somehow. One approach to head-to-head competition is to make a superior marketing effort (in terms of quality, selection, availability, or brand name recognition).

Alternatively, firms may compete on a price-cost leadership basis by offering comparable quality at a lower price. If an industry is characterised by intensive competition (as is the case in the airline industry and long-distance phone service), direct price competition is likely soon. Although leading firms often enjoy cost advantages, small firms can, at times, also succeed on price leadership.

A limitation of head-to-head competition is that, if the similarity among competitors marketing strategies is very strong, various common marketing problems can arise. Firstly, if several brands offer the same price and the same nonprice benefits, they are collectively more affected by strong new rivals who offer a unque nonprice benefit. Secondly, these commonly positioned brands will have a more difficult time standing out in the minds of consumers or distributors. Thus, to gain a competitive advantage, they may have to spend more on marketing communications (advertising, promotion, or personal selling).

DIFFERENTIATED POSITIONING

In differentiated positioning, a firm is trying to distinguish itself either by offering distinctive attributes (or benefits) or by meetings the needs of a specific customer. In *benefit/attribute* positioning, firms emphasise unique attributes, unique packaging advantages or unique benefits.

In *customer-oriented positioning* (also known as niching), a firm tries to separate itself from major competitors by serving one or a limited number of special customer groups in a market. Often, niches are defined in terms of particular usage situations or buyer characteristics.

POSITIONING AND BRAND EQUITY

Products that are successful in implementing a positioning strategy usually develop a high level of brand equity. ***Brand equity*** is the added value that knowledge about a brand bring to a product offering over and above its basic functional qualities. The foundations of brand equity are (1) extensive brand awareness and (2) strong, unique, and favourable brand associations. Such associations may offer benefits. These associations can often be developed if the product gives performance supported by extensive promotional efforts.

Brand equity may give various benefits to the firm. Specifically, with strong brand equity, a firm can more easily obtain strong promotional support from wholeselers or retailers. Also, a strong brand equity reinforces customer loyalty to a product. When a strong existing brand is used on new products, the cost of creating market awareness and trial for the new product will be very low. Finally, brand equity often allows a firm to establish a price premium, as in the case of certain personal computers.

Strategies for Retaining / Expanding Demand within the Current Customer Base

Of late, managers have started realising that it usually costs more to attract new customers than to retain the loyalty of existing ones. So money spent on customer retention is more productive than expenditure is made to acquire new customers. Consequently, more emphasis is now given on strategies which seek to miximise future sales opportunities from existing customers. Three such strategic options are:

1. Maintain a high level of customer satisfaction.
2. Build a strong economic or interpersonal relationship with the customers.
3. Develop complementary products that will appeal to current customers.

MAINTAIN STATISFACTION

Loyalty occurs if a customer continues to purchase goods or services from the same source over time. Customer satisfaction is the main cause of loyalty. In addition, satisfaction and loyalty are increased by a strong brand equity. Brands like Coca-Cola (in soft drinks), Campbell's (in soups), Gillette (in razors), and Kellogg's (in cereals) have maintained their leading market shares for a long time largely because of their brand image. This equity can be maintained and enhanced as long as such firms continue to maintain a high level of product quality.

However, even in the best quality-oriented organisations, poor quality of goods or services will occasionally occur. Usually, this results in dissatisfied customers who may or may not complain. One way to maintain satisfaction in those situations is to design a complaint management system. In such systems, managers usually classify customer complaints to determine whether the problem is a product brakedown or can be explained by incorrect usage, inflated expectations, or simple misunderstandiings. Whereas complaint management for product brakdowns can usually be handled under warranty policies, a major challenge lies in deciding what policy should govern company response to the other types of complaints. Emerging evidence seems to suggest that firms should liberally accept complaints as valid and should compensate complainants. The arguments for this point of view are:

1. Dissatisfied customers who are persuaded to stay are likely to be more loyal and profitable than before.
2. Generous complaint management encourages more complaints from unhappy customers who otherwise would simply not repurchase in the future.
3. Consumer complaints can include useful feedback for the design of products and services that better meet the needs of existing customers

RELATIONSHIP MARKETING

A relationship marketing strategy is designed to enhance the chances of repeat business through development of formal interpersonal ties with the buyer. Long-term relationships are often established through contractual or membership arrangements with customers or distributors. Typically, these arrangements are only successful because of some discount or an economic incentive associated with the cost of purchasing. In industrial marketing, for example, simplification programmes such as long-term protection against price increases or inventory management assistance are frequently so desirable to buyers or to distributors that they will commit themselves to use one supplier as their sole source of supply for a period of time. Another recent development involves the placement of computer terminals (and often, associated software) in customers' offices. These terminals are then hooked into the sellers' terminals, enabling customers to order products instantly (and thus better manage their inventories), check on the progress of deliveries and other technical assistance.

A particular from of relationship marketing that has become increasingly popular is *frequency marketing*, a strategy designed to encourage increased purchases from a firm's best customers. Such marketing requires the establishment of customer databases that permit the targeting of messages and incentives directly to key customers.

COMPLEMENTARY PRODUCTS

An increase in the sales of one product could lead to increased sales for related complementary products. Complementary products can often be designed and marketed in a way that helps retain customers. Expanding the number of realtionships between a seller and a buyer makes switching to an alternative supplier more expensive for the customer. Many financial instituations try to get chequeing-account customers to use the institution as a source for their credit cards, loans, and savings accounts. As consumers concentrate their business in one financial institu-ation, they will be less likely to switch their business for any one product because it would reduce the convenience of banking at one place.

In other case, the primary strategic value of complementary products is to apply leverage to the business relationships with current customers in order to sell additional products. Two popular ways of implementing this strategy are *bunding* and *systems selling*. Bundling involves the development of a specific combination of products sold together (such as personal computers, printers, and software) at a special price. This can be especially effective if some of the products in the bundle are more popular than others; in such cases, some buyers wil purchase the full bundle — including the less desirable elements — in order to save money.

Conclusion

Although marketing strategies indicate general approaches that can be employed to achieve product objectives, the implementation of these strategies through marketing programmes is the most time-consuming part of marketing management.

Marketing programmes (such as product-development programmes, advertising programmes, direct marketing and sales promotion programming and sales and distribution programmes) show the specific activities that will be necessary to implement a strategy. For instance, if a strategy requires that the firm achieve distributor cooperation, the details of how the sales force will achieve cooperation must be worked out in the sales and distribution programme. No matter how appropriate a strategy might appear, it will fail if it is not properly implemented. Consequently, clear statements regarding target markets and marketing strategies are necessary to ensure that the correct programmes will be developed.

In short, a marketing strategy serves as the major link between corporate marketing planning and situation analysis on the one hand and development of specific programme on the other. Figure A.1 shows this relationship.

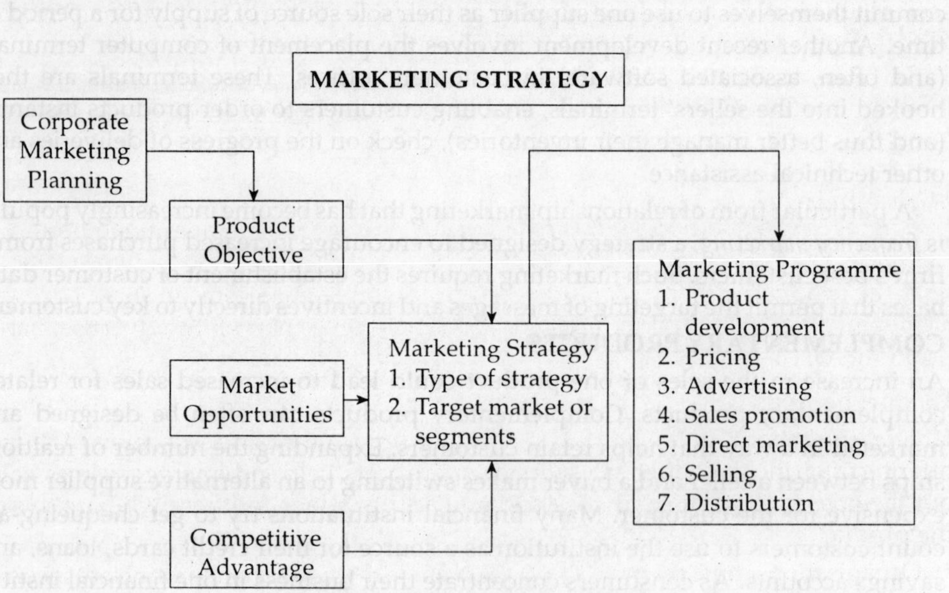

Fig. A.1 : Relationship of marketing strategy to corporate marketing planning and programmes

Perhaps the most important aspect of this relationship is the fact that marketing strategy should be viewed from a dynamic perspective: As the corporate strategy or the situation analysis changes over time, the marketing strategy should also change.

2. MARKETING MIX

The marketing mix takes congnisance of the way in which each of these elements is combined and interacts with the others in the marketing of goods and services — 'the offerings'. Consumers of these offerings will normally hold one of the elements more important than the others. In turn, the forces and pressures of the markets in which the offerings are made also reflect their relative importance.

Product

The first of these elements to be considered is the product (or service or offering) in question; 'product' in this context is the term habitually used to describe anything that is offered to a market sector for consumption. The product mix is the range of products offered by an organisation; this is dertermined by the matching of the organisation's capabilities and capacities with the markets and niches to be serviced and by the scope and scale of its operations — it is a complex process. People buy the benefits that they expect to accrue from a product rather than its features; organisations, therefore, sell those benefits. To the consumer, the items are not merely food and drink but part of a way of life with which they wish to be associated.

Quality and durability

Product quality and durability must be considered. The two are not mutually exclusive (a disposable syringe is only to be used once but it has to work that once). There is also no point in offereing a highly durable product to the stated market sector if that is not what the sector wants (fashionable shoes and clothes, for example, are offered to some sectors on the basis that they are today's style).

Branding gives credence and confidence, especially where the brand is well known. The consumer is content with what is offered and comfortable with the appearance of a name on the product.

Packaging

Packaging is used both to present the product to its best advantage and to protect it up to the point of consumption. It is instrumental in reinforcing the identity of and with the product — many soap powders, for example, now come in small boxes as a consideration to the environment — and this becomes part of the advertising and promotional campaign.

Product benefits

Finally, the benefits of the products should be seen in their widest context. The full offering often includes after-sales service, spare parts, help and emergency lines, call-out facilities and product advice and familiarity sessions for those who are to sell the product.

Organisations must set price levels that enable them to generate sufficient income to keep shareholders and any other stakeholders happy and contented. They must further set prices to ensure that sufficient income is generated to ensure continuity of operations and to provide sufficient general cash flow to meet the needs of the organisation: above all, it must be profitable.

The price of an item must reflect both the willingness and capability of the customer to pay. If one is offering in niches where the customers and consumers are always paid by cash (as distinct from cheque or credit or debit cards or finance plans) then prices must reflect the volume of cash carried and must be sensitive to the competing demands on it.

Price reflects the range and complexity of offerings made, the relationship with the consumer and the degree of choice that the consumer has. Price also impinges upon the areas relating to the desired market share for the product on the part of the organisation: prices being offered by the competition; and the prices of substitute goods. There may also be particular revenue targets required by the organisation. However, large and complex organisations generally have a measure of flexibility in this area; for example, they can offset possible losses on one product through great gains on another. In such cases, price will be seen as a component only of a wider marketing strategy.

Organisations need a measure of flexibility in the determination of price that will enable them to respond to any competitive moves elsewhere in the market. The activities of competitors — both offensive and defensive — therefore, have an important bearing on pricing decisions — this may be instrumental in allowing or restricting one's abilities to move one's prices as one desires.

Finally, it is necessary to consider what is actually included in the price of an item or commodity. For example, when a car is bought the consumer achieves personal transport and mobility. However, the price paid may also include the concept of the 'lifetime of the car', including regular servicing, after-sales arrangements, emergency cover, insurance policies, finance plans that cover the purchase of the car as well as the other accessories that may go with it.

From a marketing point of view, therefore, there is a context in which the arriving at and arrangement of the price of a commodity has to be seen. There are financial cost and contribution elements that must be considered.

Promotion

This is the combination of methods used to generate public awareness, identity, confidence, desire and conviction in a product and ultimately its adoption and usage by the general public. The methods used in the pursuit of this are: advertising in all mass media including newspapers, television and radio; sponsorship of events, other products and activities; sales calling by organisational representatives to generate new business and general awareness and to maintain and service business; brochures designed to generate the image required of the product and to demonstrate the features and benefits that its consumers are perceived to require; product placement, by which producers of films, brochures, magazines, novels, stories and television serials are persuaded to adopt distinctive brands of product — such as cars and clothing to be used and worn by their heroes and heroines — thus assisting in the generation of positive images and high level identity; other publicity features such as general awareness-raising articles, news items and general interest stories, featuring particular products and services; and price, which may also be integrated into the promotional campaign adopted.

Place

The fourth element of the marketing strategy is place, that is, getting the products and services to the customers and clients. This means knowing who they are, where they are, how they want the products and services delivered, what the nature and level of their expectations are, and how these may best be satisfied. Part of the creative process involved in marketing is concerned with both meeting this requirement on the part of the customer and also generating an expectation that if they do go to a particular place then this particular need will be satisfied.

The concept of place derives much from the segmentation process (see above). The other main feature here that must be considered is that of location. This reflects the nature of distribution networks, especially those concerned with getting the product or service to the point at which consumers buy it or take delivery of it.

The question of location also relates to the production and operation philosophies that are concerned with the traditional view that an organisation would locate near the sources of raw materials if the items that it produced lost weight during the production and manufacturing processes; and that, conversely, they would locate near the market if their processes resulted in the products gaining weight. Location also reflects any sectoral or regional demands or desires or constraints.

The other matters that concern the 'place' element of the marketing strategy are principally to do with the nature and style of distribution adopted. The product or service in question may go straight from the organisation to its customers; conversely, it may go through a highly sophisticated channel of distribution. The key requirements on the part of the customer of flexibility, responsiveness, ease of access and general convenience remain the key to conducting continuing and effective business.

Varying the marketing strategy

The precise nature of individual marketing will depend upon the product and the ways in which it is to be offered in the particular sectors; and the rationale for this depends upon the key marketing strategies and standpoints adopted by the organisation. Organisations may seek to vary their marketing strategies in the interests of generating or regenerating new business initiatives; for example, organisations will bring down the price of commodities that are nevertheless sold on a quality rather than a price-sensitive basis if by doing so they consider that an advantage can be gained; conversely a manufacturing organisation may release its products for sale in a supermarket, thus trading off the exclusivity of its product in return for the ability to generate a much wider accessibility and acceptance.

Customer assessments will also be conducted in order to gain a general understanding of their motives, desires, preferred images and identity with the particular product or range of products that is to be offered. Finally, modelling activities will need to be commissioned or conducted by the organisation with a view to assessing the extent of the profitability or effectiveness of the range of activities in question. Marketing research and development is thus an integral part of and critical to the success of wider strategic aspects, and critical to the determination of the organisation's future direction and instrumental in the determination of its success.

3. PRICING POLICY AND STRATEGY

Pricing is an indispensable part of industrial marketing strategy. It must be carefully interrelated to the firm's product, distribution, and communication strategies. From a marketing perspective, price represents the value customers place on a product at some point in time. The marketing manager has the challenging responsibility of blending the various elements of the marketing mix to ensure that the total offering is not only responsive to the needs of the market, but also provides a return consistent with the firm's profit objectives. This is no doubt a difficult and challenging task.

Pricing strategies must be related to overall business objectives and marketing strategy. The success of any business depends on a blend of long-run profit, growth, and survival objectives. Price, because of its influence on unit sales volume and profit margins, affects long-run profit objectives. By contributing to a positive cash flow, price helps to finance growth objectives. And maintaining profitability through sound pricing practices is necessary to ensure the firm's survival over time. It should be recognised, however, that a diversified firm with multiple product lines can operate several pricing strategies at a time. They must be consistent with one another as well as with overall marketing strategy.

Pricing Objectives

The pricing policy pursued would have a close connection with the objectives of the firm. Even if these are clearly defined, however, empirical investigation shows that not all pricing is in harmony with general company objectives. Four important pricing objectives of large firms are :

1. **Target return on investment**. This is one of the most common pricing objectives. The aim of a business must be to earn what is considered to be a satisfactory rate of return on the capital which it employs. This, in all probability, will be regarded as a long-term rather than a short-term objective.

2. **Price and margin stabilisation**. A second important aim in company pricing policy may be that of securing long-term stability of the price of products. This policy for most businesses has had to remain an aspiration rather than an achievement. Even in an inflationary situation, however, a firm may seek to hold prices at a given level for as long a period as possible.

A company following such a policy will seek to set a price in the first place which is based on the 'full cost' principle, earning a conventional margin of profit. If such a price can be established, it will be regarded by the management as 'fair' and an attempt will be made to maintain it unaltered despite short-term fluctuations of cost which may be either favourablle or adverse to the firm. In this way, it is sought to retain the goodwill of customers.

3. **Market share**. For those companies in an oligopoly situation where a significant share of the market has been obtained, market share usually becomes an extremely important policy objective.

4. **Meeting competition**. When a firm enters an established market or seeks to enter such a market, it may have to accept the price already ruling there. There may be available to the firm some discretion in setting prices. When a firm, particularly a large firm, claims that its prices must be set to meet competition in the market, it may be found that it possesses a higher degree of control that it is prepared to admit.

In some cases, however, the policy of meeting competition' really means forestalling potential competition. Pricing policy is used to try to deter new firms from entering the industry.

New Product Introduction

Generally, two broad strategies are available in pricing a new product: (1) market skimming — setting an artificially high price that the market will not be able to sustain in the long run and (2) market penetration — setting price at or near the level it would eventually reach after competition developed.

Market Skimming Strategy

A market skimming strategy — charging an artifically high price and then gradually reducing it over time — has the advantage of generating greater profits per unit earlier than would be possible with a lower price. If development and marketing costs can be recovered before competitors enter, surplus earnings can be used for product improvement and expansion into large-volume markets, thus reducing per unit cost. Unless late-arriving competitors achieve a real breakthrough in product design or processing, they will high cost producers and, thus, cannot survive for long.

The greatest disadvantage to market skimming is that the high margins attract competition. A firm that has a successful price skimming strategy can expect competitors to introduce similar products. Therefore, skimming is more effective when the product has strong patent protection, or other barriers to market entry exist, such as complex technology or high capital requirements. Other conditions that favour price skimming are shown in Table A.2.

Table A.2 : Conditions Favouring Price Skimming

1.	Product has a strong patent protection or other barriers to market entry.
2.	Genuine product innovation that is likely to represent substantial value to potential users.
3.	Buyers who are willing to pay a premium to enjoy the product's benefits.
4.	A relatively short life span, so that a quick recovery of investment is essential.
5.	Potential competitors are relatively weak or unlikely to arrive, and so on.
6.	Uncertainty concerning the market's price sensitivity. If the initial price proves to be wrong, the firm can always lower price, whereas a low price may be difficult to raise.

Market Penetration Strategy

Penetration pricing is based on the assumption that demand for the product is highly elastic. By setting a relatively low price, the firm hopes to stimulate market growth and capture a large share of it. The advantage is that penetration pricing tends to discourage competition, because there is less opportunity to reap an unusually high return on investment. Penetration pricing may also be used to achieve economies of scale. By seeking a dominant market share, a firm may increase both its scale and efficiency of operation, realising lower production costs than competitors and, thus, greater potential profits.

There are, however, two primary disadvantages to penetration pricing. Firstly, a larger volume must be sold before start-up costs are recovered. Thus, short-run profits are sacrificed to gain market share and long-run profits. Secondly, although the absolute magnitude of profits could be higher than that realised with a skimming strategy, the profit ratios (the return on assets or investment, or the profit on sales) could be lower. Firms that judge their success on these ratios will be reluctant to use a penetration strategy. Conditions favourable to penetration pricing are outlined in Table A.3.

Skimming and penetration pricing strategies are only guides and cannot be applied in all situations. Some situations will require that an intermediate price be set — somewhere between a high or low initial price. The choice of an appropriate pricing strategy for new products is dependent upon the firm's objectives, the relevant customer segments, the impact of price on the actions of present and future competition, cost considerations, and appropriate distribution strategies.

Table A.3 : Conditions Favourable to Penetration Pricing

1.	The market appears to be highly price-sensitive.
2.	Unit cost of production and distribution fall with an increase in the rate of output.
3.	Strong potential competitors exist who are seeking new profitable ventures.
4.	The firm's primary goal is significant market share rather than maximized short-term profits.
5.	The product has hidden or subtle benefits that will become obvious only after use.
6.	The sale of complementary products will also increase.

Product Life-Cycle Considerations

During the course of a product's life cycle, the competitive situation and market demand level will vary greatly. The product itself, along with promotion and distribution, must change accordingly. In like manner, for price to remain an effective marketing tool, it must be constantly monitored and adjusted when appropriate.

Growth. During the product growth stage, when more customers develop a use for the product and competitors are able to offer subsitutes, price will take on more importance in the purchasing decision. However, in an expanding market, suppliers tend to emphasise nonprice factors as their primary selling points. The exceptions are those firms that are experimenting with low price in the initial stage and desirous of achieving a dominant market share in the long run. In general, the price in this stage falls below the introductory level.

Maturity. By the time a product enters the maturity stage, the level of competition has peaked, and product differentiation is minimal. Consequently, although buyers will still insist on product quality and service dependability, price considerations will heavily influence their buying decisions. And since a supplier can increase volume in a flat market only by cutting into the market share of competitors, price wars become very common.

Decline. Since many competitors will have already left the market, particularly those with heavy emphasis on growth strategies, the decline stage can be a fairly profitable one for the remaining suppliers. Assuming a firm has developed a very positive image by providing a quality product, competitively priced, dependably shipped, and consistently serviced, there is no reason why profits should fall to zero in the decline stage. Industrial firms, both sellers and buyers, realise the necessary relationship between production volumes and incurred costs. Within reason, the well-accepted firm can increase prices during the decline stage and maintain an acceptable profit level, as long as some segments of the market continue to feel a need for the product and will adjust their value perceptions to match the required selling price.

Flexible Pricing Strategy

In the past, the pricing structure of most large industrial firms has been rather rigid. Price was established by adding a traditional markup to costs, by following the industrial leader, or by aiming for some predetermined return on investment.

The need to adapt to such a dynamic environment has brought about flexibility in pricing and a willingness to cut prices aggressively to hold market share. Smaller firms are not consistently willing to play "follow the price leader." On the contrary, many smaller companies have successfully undercut the price leader.

Flexible pricing strategy — that is, the willingness to adjust prices or profit margins on specific products when market conditions change — is now very common in any type of marketing. However, price flexibility does not always mean a change in list prices. Fixed prices, even during mild inflation, quantity discounts to encourage more and more people to buy the good, and emphasis on nonprice factors can each contribute to strategic flexiblity.

Pricing for Profits

The goal of most business organisations is to maximise long-term profits. If a firm aims at maximising short-term profit then the firm's managers will try to get the highest possible profits now by charging high product prices in price-inelastic markets. Such a policy will induce entry by competitors and will reduce profits in future time periods. Alternatively, if it aims at maximising long-term profit it will follow a policy of greater market penetration and lower prices. This strategy will not maximise current-period profits, but can increase the size of the future profit stream and discourage potential competitors. Which strategy the firm chooses will depend upon the management's beliefs regarding the magnitude and regularity of future profits as well as upon the firm's marketing policy.

Pricing decisions, then, are influenced by both short-term conditions and possible long-term consequences. For instance, if the price of a new product is set at a level high enough to attract competitors into the market, potential profits over the long run could be considerably less than if the price has been set lower to accelerate growth and discourage competition. On the other hand, pricing decisions are often influenced by the need to achieve an early recovery of the firm's product development costs, and this short-term goal is given greater priority over any longer-term considerations. This is particularly true when the product's lifetime is uncertain or of estimated short duration.

Conclusion

Pricing decisions, however, cannot just be based on demand and cost relationships, product line considerations, or long-term profit goals alone. They must also support the firm's marketing objectives and correlate with any unique market situations that may exist (for example, price leadership patterns, reciprocity from major customers, and the bargaining power of strong and powerful buyers).

Clearly, it is not always possible to analyse all the variables affecting the pricing decision. It is essential, therefore, to determine which variables are most important to the particular decision at hand and then analyse and respond to these.

While specific, quantitative solutions should be sought, the price setter is often "forced to rely heavily on rough data, broad impressions, and logic rather than on numerical computations." The risks involved, however, in pricing without carefully studying the interrelation of demand, costs, and competition can be really damaging, particularly in the pricing of new products. Thus, while the price of a particular product or service, given the competitive situation, cannot exceed the value of its benefit to the buyer, neither can it fall below the cost to the seller.

Price setting in today's environment calls for a proactive approach to pricing. Marketing managers must base pricing decisions on current market information, monitor competitor and customer responses, and carefully analyse their pricing decisions.

Profitable pricing decisions, however, rest on a clear understanding of two important variables, cost and demand. Cost is a function of demand, and that demand is a function of how the customers value the product. Thus, in setting price, the firm cannot ignore costs and profits, but the market-oriented firm will have a target price driving costs rather than costs driving price. This is true not only when establishing price for the first time, but throughout the life of the product. In addition, costs will change over the product life cycle, as will customer demand and competitive pressures. Hence, marketers must anticipate the changing role and importance of price.

While price is a prime determinant of the manufacturer's profit, it also affects the profit margins and commissions of middlemen. Manufacturers cannot ignore the functions performed on their behalf by middlemen or fail to compensate for them adquately.

Because the success of any business depends on the attainment of long-run profit objectives, which are directly influenced by price, pricing strategies must be viewed as more than just part of the marketing mix. They are the financial framework for the firm's overall business objective.

4. RESALE PRICE MAINTENANCE

Resale price and retail price are not the same thing. Resale price maintenance refers to "the practice of policy adopted by a manufacturer whereby he fixes a price of his product to be sold to customers by retailers". It refers to a contractual arrangement made between the supplier (the manufacturer) and the resellers (wholesalers and retailers). Such an arrangement imposes the condition that the reseller will have to sell the product at a price fixed by the supplier. In case the dealer does not sell the product at a price fixed by the manufacturer, the latter may stop supplying the product to the former. As N.R. Nair and S.R. Nair comment : "Normally, strict enforcement of the suggested price is possible only when a manufacturer uses a selective or exclusive distribution system". In their view, a second condition has to be fulfilled to make this arrangement possible. The particular brand should have achieved a high degree of consumer acceptance and must have gained popularity. It is also necessary to know the difference between direct price maintenance and resale price maintenance. Under the former arrangement, manufacturers use their cash retail outlets, such as chain stores.

REP in India

In India, resale price maintenance has been held in check by the MRTP Act. The Act explains and elaborates the term 'RPM' thus :

Resale price in relation to the sale of goods of any description means that any price notified to the dealer or otherwise published by or on behalf of the supplier of the goods in question (whether lawfully or not) as the price or minimum price which is to be charged on, or is recommended as appropriate for, a sale of that description or any prescribed (or purporting to be prescribed for that purpose) by any contract or agreement between the wholesaler or retailer and any such supplier.

Three Methods

In India resale price is fixed in three ways :

1. A minimum price below which a product cannot be sold.
2. A maximum price above which a product cannot be sold.
3. A stipulated price at which a product has to be sold (no change is allowed).

Restrictive Trade Practice

According to the MRTP Act the first and the third methods are treated as restrictive trade practices and thus are unlawful. But the second is not because it normally allows a flexibility for the retailer to fix the final price (*i.e.*, the price paid by the ultimate consumer).

Under Section 33(f), "the practice of stipulating sale of goods on prices not exceeding the specified price is not considered a restrictive practice. But any agreement entered into by a seller and a distributor having a clause relating to RPM requires the registration of such an agreement with the Registrar of Restrictive Trade Practices".[1]

1. Nair and Nair in *Marketing* (S. Chand & Co., New Delhi, 1994), p. 264. It may, however, be noted that many sections of the MRTP Act have lost their relevance due to the liberalisation of economic policies in India since July 1991.

Objectives

The basic idea behind resale price maintenance was to avoid cutthroat competition among retailers. But this pricing practice enabled manufacturers to earn extra profits through exclusive or selective distribution system. Through this type of distribution system it would be possible for some companies to develop some sort of **brand monopoly** and thus exploit the consumers by charging a high price. In fact, this practice would cause much hardship not only to manufacturers but also to small-scale units which would be forced to close their business. Keeping these points in view the **Monopoly Inquiry Commission** opined that the agreement relating to RPM was against public interest and had to be stopped. The Commission also felt that this destroyed competition among actual distributors of the article and often kept the price which the ultimate consumer had to pay higher than what it would otherwise have been.

Benefits and Burden

However, resale price maintenance is not a totally bad thing. It has a positive side also. As Nair and Nair put it, "it enables small traders and shopkeepers to withstand the competition of the big merchants and powerful chain stores". At the same time, we have to take into account the loss of welfare (or injury to public interest) due to lessened competition in efficient salesmanship. Since the consumer is forced to pay a stipulated price and cannot bargain with the selllers for a low price, once the prices have been fixed, both consumer sovereignty and consumer protection against unfair trade practice lose their relevance. This is why in order to protect the interest of the consumers the MRTP Act has imposed two important regulations :

1. Firstly, the manufacturers and wholesalers are prevented from fixing a minimum price to the retailer.
2. No retailer should be forced to sell goods at the retail price fixed by the manufacturers (original suppliers).

5. SELLING AND MARKETING

Introduction

In an age when advancing technology has dramatically increased the speed at which goods and services can be produced and distributed and has facilitated the ease with which organisations can communicate, it is still the level of human performance that is the most variable factor in the efficient functioning of a firm with its customers. Sales operation represent this link, between a firm and its customers, at its most direct point of contact. Sales operations are where the action in business takes place and represent a vital revenue-generating function. Today, sales operation represent not only personal selling but also a range of customer contact positions including telephone sales, customer or service technial advisers as well as traditional salespeople. Leading companies fully realise that sales operation, linking the firm with its customers, is an area that needs to be carefully monitored and exceptionally well-managed if the enterprise is to succeed.

Selling and Marketing Concept

The role of selling as part of the marketing mix is, no doubt, very important. The salesperson's primary role is to contribute to the achievement of the sales, marketing and corporate goals set by the enterprise.

The difference between marketing and selling is that **selling focuses on the needs of the seller, marketing on the needs of the buyer**. Selling is preoccupied with the seller's need to convert his product into cash; marketing with the idea of satisfying the needs of the customer by means of the product and the whole range of things associated with creating, delivering, and, finally, consuming it.

An outdated view of the selling holds that marketing and selling are opposites rather than complementary functions. However, the truth is that successful enterprises have moved from a sales to a marketing orientation. Selling has not been replaced by marketing, but changed by it.

Marketing is seen as giving the customers what they want while selling is seen as disposing off or getting rid of something somehow. Most salespeople operate where repeat business is the norm and continuing relationships are important, such as in selling to retailers, industrial users and many others.

In any type of business the marketing management approach is to identify the needs and wants of potential customers, observe trends in the relevant market, make decisions on the information available about product and services and implement actions as effectively as possible.

Selling reflects the same approach at the individual customer level and is a vital part of successful marketing plans. There are no doubt differences between marketing and selling, but differences lie in scale rather than in philosophy and method. Like many business situations, the selling effort and the salesperson may make the difference of whether or not a sale is made. An important difference from many commercial transactions is that repeat purchases are not important to either buyer or seller.

Traditionally, the function of the salesforce was to sell a firm's output to a large number of retail outlets or direct customers or users. In modern markets, supply usually exceeds demand, the effect of which is a need to adopt a marketing philosophy — 'make what we can sell, not sell what we make'. Changes in the methods and channels of distribution and an increasingly competitive environment have also changed the role of selling, strongly placing it as an essential part of marketing effort. One effort of this has been some neglect of the operational importance of selling in marketing plans, while another effect has been some spectacular successes using traditional hard-selling techniques. Selling is not a thing of the past. So effective marketing management will have to carefully integrate personal selling with other promotional tools, in relation to other functions within the organisation and in relation to environmental factors affecting their operations.

Personal Selling

Personal selling is the final link in the exchange process between buyer and seller. A suitable definition of personal selling is the personal contact with one or more purchasers for the purpose of making a sale. Part of this contact involves salesmanship, which has been defined as 'seller-initiated effort that provides prospective buyers with information, and other benefits, motivating or persuading them to make buying decisions in favour of the seller's product or service. Sales management can be defined as the process of planning, organising, directing, staffing and controlling the sales operation to achieve the firm's objectives through subordinates.

The modern role of personal selling is as one aspect of the promotional mix, promotion being one part of the marketing mix. This point will be discussed in detail later in this appendix.

Role of Salespeople

Co-ordinating promotional activity will make the selling job easier and reduce the need for a hard-sell approach or excessive promotional expenditure. The essential nature of selling in a marketing-oriented, competitive enterprise has several indispensable functions — providing information persuasion, and creating, building and sustaining relationships.

1. Supplying Information

The first of these — the information role — is perhaps the most obvious. Where market opportunities and customer needs have been correctly identified and interpreted and the product/service package offered at a suitable price in the desired location, information needs to be provided to existing and potential customers via some means of communication. At various stages in the buying process, this communication is most effectively achieved by face-to-face personal contact. This information role is a two-way communication process from sales-people to customers and with the needs of prospective and satisfied customers being conveyed via salespeople back to management responsible for the marketing decisions. This is increasingly combined with a customer support or service role to look after customers and protect their ongoing relationship. This is the information task of sales people.

2. Persuasion

A second role that salespeople must perform is that of persuasion. In a competitive economy, most commercial enterprises appeal to prospective customers faced with lots of choice. As a result, the adoption of marketing-oriented activites is no guarantee of a long-term competitive advantage. Potential customers will have to be convinced that their needs have been correctly identified by the product and company represented to their benefit over any competing alternative.

3. Creating

Today, the salesperson's most vital role is creating, building and sustaining profitable relationships. Relationship marketing is based on an intimacy between the firm and its customers.The field salesforce of a company has traditionally been a vital link between the firm and its customers and a prime platform for communicating the firm's marketing message to its customers and the voice of the customer to the firm. However, salespeople and sales managers have in the past been oriented towards "closing the sale " as the main driving force behind the sales management efforts of the firm. Relationship marketing has shifted attention from "closing ' the singular sale to creating the necessary conditions for a long-term relationship between the firm and its customers that in the long run results in successful sales through repeat orders.

The role of the salesperson is continuing to move away from the traditional aggressive and persuasive selling towards a new role of 'relationship manager'. This change in title is designed to facilitate the transition of the salesforce's task from selling to advising and counselling, from talking to listening and from pushing to helping. The new reality of relationship marketing directs salespeople and sales managers to develop long-term relationship with their customers based on mutual trust and commitment. Each selling occasion is an opportunity to strengthen the relationship between them and their customer, and increase the loyalty of the customer to the firm.

Personal selling is an essential element in marketing. It is the promotional means involving face-to-face contact with buyers and must be performed by salespeople who are customer-oriented and who seek solutions to customers' problems in the long-term interests of their company and their customers. It would be wrong to claim that personal selling is the key element in the marketing mix since the combination and integration of elements of the marketing mix is more important than any one element. Table A.4 demonstrates the relative importance of these elements.

Table A.4 : The relative importance of elements of marketing communications

Type of marketing activity	Industrial goods	Consumer durables	Consumer non-durables
Sales management and personal selling	Very high	High	High
Media advertising	Very low	Moderate	High
Special promotions	Low	Moderate	Moderate
Pack, brand, other	Low	Low	Moderate

Personal selling should operate within and as part of integrated marketing effort.

Role of the Modern Salesperson

The most significant difference between selling and other elements in the marketing effort is personal contact. The need for personal contact varies depending on a variety of factors such as the type of customer, the frequency of purchase, the newness of the product and so on. In some situations, the information provision role can be achieved by impersonal means such as advertising. A fresh comparison of these media is shown in Table A.5.

Table A.5 : Advertising and Personal Selling Compared

Advertising	Personal selling
Directed at a mass audience	Directed at the individual
Impersonal, indirect contact	Personal, direct contact
Less directly adaptable	High level of adaptability
Working in breadth (that is, large numbers/limited message)	Working in depth (few contacts, more detailed communication)
One-way	Two-way
Organised feedback (via marketing research)	Direct feedback
Relatively cheap per contact	Expensive per contact
Pull effect (customer or prospect contacting the seller)	Push effect (active sales leads are pursued)

Every sales situation is in some way unique and sales management must be concerned with understanding buyer-seller interaction, yet also realise that control over sales situations is not possible. The extent and desirability of personal selling varies with the stage in the buying process and between different categories of goods. The formal process of personal selling usually includes distinct identifiable stages such as:

- making contact
- arousing interest
- creating preferences
- making specific proposals
- closing the sale
- retaining business.

These stages relate to various marketing methods of communication. Effective selling must also take account of customers' needs, which may be very specific. Such needs also keep on changing as situations change.

Sales management must also take account of the role that salespeople can be expected to perform and the specific tasks to be achieved. Possible sales tasks including taking orders, display of product, advice to distributors and users, after-sales service, collecting payment, stock checks, training others and completing deliveries. The type of selling is crucial to the tasks to be performed and the way in which salespeople are to be managed. It is unrealistic, and a sign of weak management, to expect salespeople to undertake the complete sales process and a comprehensive series of sales tasks. Clear role definition and task clarity are the cornerstones of sound sales management practice. This means that the role of the salespersons must be stated very clearly and his tasks should be properly classified.

The mass concern or sales management is value for money from the salesforce. This is a continuing problem.

TYPES OF SELLING

Introduction

The fundamental purpose for which salespeople are employed is to retain existing business and win new customers. This purpose involves more than mere order-taking and salespeople can be described and classified under a variety of job titles, for example technical adviser, sales engineer, marketing representative and consultant. Today, the trend in closer relationships between buyer and seller organisations in industrial, consumer and service firms relies — to a greater extent than in the past— on the knowledge, skills and abilities of the salesperson to create and sustain these relationships. Therefore, the way in which the selling jobs is conducted vary greatly. In other words, variations do exist between types of selling. Moreover, there are many forms of communication between a firm and its customers.

Basic Differences in Selling Situations

In the modern world, selling is the outcome of a marketing process. The salesperson is, by necessity, a marketing manager dealing at the individual customer level rather than with groups of customers or market segments. It can increasingly be observed that companies can no longer afford to separate marketing, as a strategic and planning activity, from the operational implications of customer account management. The implication is that salespeople will require marketing knowledge and skill and marketing positions will increasingly require knowledge and ability in interpersonal relations and negotiations. In many companies, a re-emergence of a marketing/sales management position can be expected. This similarity between marketing and sales is shown in Table A.6.

The sales process ahould be seen in the context of customer problem-solving rather than as merly selling available product. Any new salesperson or new sales situation is best approached by an intial assessment of the nature of the customer's problem, just as marketing research should be a prerequisite for evaluating a new market or a new product. This is particularly true of larger-value sales, where continutity of business in the future is important. With some low-value and low-risk purchases, traditional salesmanship and a classic 'hard sales' approach may work for the company and improve its profitability. However, in most organisational buying, a failure adequately to assess customers need will be a cause of failure. Selling techniques must be made on the basis of an insight response rather than a conditioned response which may be effective in direc selling situations.

Table A.6 : Comparison of Sales and Marketing Activity

Stage	Salesperson	Marketing manager
Marketing research / assessment	Uses personal experience, customers' records and questions	Uses formal market research, target markets and defines segments
Strategy/planning	Emphasises relevant features which match company with customer	Establishes product/price/service position in the market
Marketing mix / implementation	Use of discounts, terms and credit	Price policy
Distribution	Use of back-up and collaboration when required	Sales policy
Promotion	Use of print, samples, factory visits and entertaining	Advertising and sales promotion

The conditioned response is where salespeople have been trained in advance to deal with problems and objection preventing a successful close. Examples of this are normally found in direct selling of life insurance, vacuum cleaners and encyclopaedia. Such sales through representatives are often very effective.

Sales technique and presentation are more commonly based on an insight response in which salespeople must identify buyer's problems and objections as they arise and react with appropriate benefits. Success will ultimately depend on the ability of salespeople to search out individual buyer's needs, assess the problem and react accordingly. The salesperson's skill lies in satisfying customer needs.

6. THE EFFECTIVENESS OF ADVERTISING AND PACKAGING

Managers must consider when each tool of communication such as advertising, promotion, and publicity of communication is appropriate and what combination of tools is most desirable in any overall marketing programme. Furthermore, communication or promotion-mix decision represent only one area under the control of management; product, price and distribution programmes must be intergrated with communication options in any overall marketing effort.

Purpose

No doubt advertising is one of the most pervasive and least costly modes of communication available to a manager.

In general, advertising and other elements of the communication mix try to increase sales in one or more of five ways:

1. Recruit new users who have never tried the product class.
2. Encourage former users to renew purchases.
3. Encourage users of competing brands to switch.
4. Recruit switchers who are not loyal to any brand.
5. Increase consumption by current users.

Any one of these methods willl increase sales, but the objectives and effects of advertising are actually more complex than the five ways noted above.Advertising may lack any particular objectives relative to a target audience, instead aiming merely to build a positive company image in employees and the public at large or, occasionally, to serve simply as an advertiser's expression of pride with no particular utlitarian goal in mind.

The purpose of advertising is to influence either consumers' psychological states or their behaviour. Psychological variables include, among others, brand awareness, knowledge of product attributes, beliefs about the consequences of product use, emotional reactions towards a brand (*e.g.*, interest, liking), and intentions to purchase. Behavioural variables include among others, trial purchase, brand loyalty, increased usage, brand change (switching to another brand) and overall sales.

EFFECTIVENESS

Does it really pay to advertise? Organisations certainly believe so, or they would not pay so much money to do it. But does advertising really help organisations reach their goals?

Most executives maintain that the ultimate objective of advertising is to influence sales, either immediately or in the long run. No doubt there is a positive relationship between advertising and sales, but the relationship does not always show cause and effect. Sales are very complex phenomena influenced by a variety of factors, which can vary from situation to situation and from period to period. For example, sales are influenced by the prices of competing products, the prices of complements, and the prices of the firm's own brand. Then, too, sales are affected by product quality, packaging, distribution practices, promotion and deals, changing customer tastes, and economic and social conditions. Advertising probably determines sales to a certain extent as well, but to separate the relative impact of each force is difficult, if not impossible . Nevertheless, a company's monetary commitment to advertising each year suggests that it plays a important role.

Managers must decide how much to spend on advertising, which media to use, what messages to transmit, how to present the messages, and so forth as part of the overall promotion mix. Although managers may not be able to directly link these controllable factors to actual market sales responses, they can examine the influence of particular ads on consumer psychology and behaviour to see how effective the ads will be. In effect, managers judge ad efficacy by measuring ad impact on intervening variables (consumer psychological responses) between seeing or hearing ads and finally buying the product.

Most often, advertisers measure ad influence through people's brand-name awareness, knowledge, recall, recognition, beliefs about product attributes, interests, attitudes, or intentions as a function of exposure to ads. Most tests of ad effectiveness are performed on television as a function of exposure to ads, although magazine and radio ads undergo considerable testing as well. Typically, sponsors hire independent research services to conduct such tests. The term 'copy testing' describes most tests that measure how effectively particular ads influence consumers' psychological ad responses.

Recall and recognition tests are the most commonly applied procedures in ad effectiveness testing. Recall and recognition, however, entail somewhat different mental processes. In recall tests, respondents are given minimal cues and asked to generate the target information from memory. In recognition tests, respondents are presented with the target ad and asked whether they have seen it before. Recall is thus more difficult than recognition. But both measure aspects of memory. Recognition scorce may also carry considerable amounts of measurement error, which researchers remedy by deriving "proven recognition" scores; differences in recognition scores between respondents previously exposed to an ad and those not exposed.

Masked recognition procedures can sometimes produce more accurate scores. Reseachers cover or remove the name of the brand from an ad and ask readers to identify the brand in the ad they have seen before.This task lies between the recall and pure recognition tasks .

RELATION BETWEEN ADVERTISING AND PACKAGING

Like advertising, packing is now taken as a technique of sales promotion. It is called 'a silent salesperson' since it has advertising appeal, identifying power and intrinsic value. Packaging may simultaneously affect production, distribution, advertising or sales promotion.

Packaging performs a two-dimensional function. Firstly, it protects the product. Secondly, it plays a promotional role. This role has become more important in recent years (particularly in case of consumer goods). The reason is easy to find out. No doubt, brand name now plays a very important role in marketing and brand names are made popular through advertisement. But this is not whole truth. As Nair and Nair put it, "the reminding of brand names and making a brand acceptable to consumers is achieved through proper packaging. Packaging must, therefore, support and reinforce the brand identity the company is trying to build". So under modern marketing management, companies should base their entire advertising campaign on the merits of their packaging rather than that of their products.

FINANCIAL MANAGEMENT

1. PROFIT MAXIMISATION

One measure of a firm's success is the difference between the revenue it receives for its product and the cost of producing that product. This is called the firm's profit. More specifically, profit (Π) equals the difference between total revenue (TR) and total cost (TC) :

$$\Pi = TR - TC$$

Total revenue is merely the firm's total receipts from the sale of its goods, and services. To an economist, total cost is the opportunity cost of using all the resources involved in producing the firm's goods and services. An input's opportunity cost is its value in an alternative use. This means that total cost includes the replacement cost of purchased inputs, the opportunity cost of time spent by the owner(s) running the firm, and the rental value of any capital that is owned by the firm.

Most firms are profit-seeking enterprises. The present value of profits equals the value today of all current and future profits and can be written as follows:

$$PV(\Pi) = \Pi_0 + \frac{\Pi_1}{1 + r} + \frac{\Pi_2}{(1 + r)^2} + \cdots$$

where Π denotes profit and r is the discount rate. The concept of present value helps us to find out today's value of profits that will be made in the future. For example, Re 1 two years in the future is only worth Re $1 / (1 + r)^2$ today because the firm can invest Re $1 / (1 + r)^2$ today in a bank account that pays an interest rate r and end up with Re 1 in two years. Accordingly, the value today of Π_2, profit in two years equals $\Pi_2/(1 + r)^2$.

There are a number of reasons for assuming that firms maximise the present value of profits. Firstly, this maximises the owners command over resources. Moreover, competition from other, profit-maximising firms may force firms that do not maximise profits out of business. Accordingly, there is ample reason to suppose that the owner-manufacturer will tend to maximise profit. There are some theories which suggest that most firms do not make any attempt to maximise profits. Instead firms 'satisfice' or set targets below what could be achieved. Some firms sacrifice short-term profit deliberately for making more profits in the long run. For these and other criticisms, it is felt that firms can do better by maximising wealth rather than profit. Wealth maximisation refers to maximisation of the market value of the firm.

2. WEALTH MAXIMISATION

A business is an asset. There is, however, one very important difference between a single asset and a business : this is that a single asset usually represents only a small proportion of the owner's wealth. It is unlikely that this will be so in the case of a business and, hence, its valuation will depend in part on the other assets owned by the person or group on whose behalf the valuation is being made. In other words, the value of a business could be said to be given by : the value of the owner's total stock of assets on the assumption that the business is owned *minus* the value of the owner's total stock of assets without the business.

The bases of valuation of a business will be dependent on the circumstances in which the valuation is being made. When a company requires new capital and proposes to raise this by the issue of new shares it will be necessary to value the company in order that an appropriate and equitable price will be derived for the new issue. Often, when a company is faced with a takeover bid, it will be advantageous to obtain a valuation in order that the bid may either be defended or a fair price agreed for the company's shares.

In addition, there is also a need for the shareholders of the company to have some indication of the current value of the company by referring to the rate of return which they obtain on their investment. Indeed, it is argued that this knowledge should be in the possession of all investors on the ground that the most efficient use of the nation's resources will be achieved if investment is made in those companies which give the maximum return.

A valuation model based on earnings

The standard valuation model for any asset is based on the cash flows that will be generated by the use of the asset — the 'present value model', *i.e.*,

$$V_0 = \sum_{j=0}^{\infty} \frac{Y_j - X_j}{(1 + K)^j} \qquad \ldots (1)$$

where V_n is the value of the asset at time t_0, K is the discount rate, Y_1 is the cash receipt generated by the asset in the year j, X_j is the cash expense associated with the asset in year j. In practice, however, the models employed in the valuation of businesses are often based on the net profits of the business as disclosed by the accounts of the enterprise rather than on the cash flows generated by the business.

Such earnings-based models are not as conceptually sound as cash flow models and are, with the increasing use of discounted cash flow techniques in business, of less importance nowadays than in the past. They are, however, still used and do have the advantage of simplicity as fewer adjustments have to be made to the figures reported in a company's accounts than is the case when cash flow models are employed. It, therefore, seems appropriate to consider the circumstances under which the differences between the two approaches may not be significant.

Now if C_j is the expense of the business in year j on an accrual basis and R_j is the revenue of the business in year j on an accrual basis, than the profit of the business in year j is given by

$$P_j = R_j - C_j$$

Over the life of the business the cash receipt from sales must be the same as the revenue accrued (if bad debts and discounts are ignored), *i.e.*,

$$\sum_{j=0}^{\infty} Y_j = \sum_{j=0}^{\infty} R_j$$

and the cash payments must be the same as the expenses calculated on an accruals basis (again ignoring bad debts and discounts), *i.e.*,

$$\sum_{j=0}^{\infty} X_j = \sum_{j=0}^{\infty} C_j$$

If the net expenditure on fixed assets per year is approximately the same as the annual depreciation charge, and if the business investment in net current assets is approximately constant, then it follows that

$$Y_j \approx R_j \text{ and } X_j \approx C_j$$

The valuation model, equation (1), can then be restated as follows :

$$V_o = \sum_{j=0}^{\infty} \frac{Y_j - X_j}{(1+K)^j} \quad \ldots (2)$$

and thus

$$V_o = \sum_{j=0}^{\infty} \frac{Y_j - C_j}{(1+K)^j} = \sum_{j=0}^{\infty} \frac{P_j}{(1+K)^j}$$

Therefore, the value of the firm can be stated in terms of the discounted value of the expected profits to be earned over the firm's lifetime.

The nature of the discounting process is such that the latter terms in the series have less impact on the overall valuation V_0 than the earlier terms. In other words, for a given P_j and K, $P_j / (1 + K)^j$ becomes smaller as j becomes larger. Thus the importance of the assumptions referred to above relating to the purchase of fixed assets and investments in working capital is reduced as the years pass.

It might be argued that this formulation overstates the value of the business because not all the profit is paid to the proprietor, but some is reinvested in the business. Thus the cash flow to the proprietor is less than the profit flow to the business. This is generally true, but the recognition of this point lead us to modify but not abandon our approach. A rational proprietor with a discount rate K would only reinvest the profits of the business where the expected rate of return on that investment was greater than K. Consider, for example, the reinvestment of I from the profits in year 1. Then the profit paid to the proprietor falls from P_1 to $P_1 - I$. However, this investment must earn at least rate K, so the profits in year 2 must be increased from P_2 to at least $P_2 + I(1 + K)$ if this was a 1-year investment.

Thus, in place of the valuation

$$V_o = P_o + \frac{P_1}{1+K} + \frac{P_2}{(1+K)^2} + \cdots + \frac{P_n}{(1+K)^n} + \cdots$$

we have, if it is assumed that the amount invested earns a return of K [*i.e.*, that profits of year 2 are $P_2 + I(1 + K)$] a value V'_0, which is given by

$$V'_o = P_o + \frac{P_1 + I}{1 + K} + \frac{P_2 + I(1 + K)}{(1 + K)^2} + \cdots + \frac{P_n}{(1 + K)^n} + \cdots$$

$$= P_o + \frac{P_1}{1 + K} + \frac{P_2}{(1 + K)^2} + \cdots + \frac{P_n}{(1 + K)^n} + \cdots$$

$$= V_o$$

The same analysis can be applied to investments made in later years.

If it is assumed that the amounts invested will earn a greater return than K then the value V_0 can be regarded as providing a lower limit of the range of values of the business.

We have thus established a theoretical model for the valuation of a business as a going concern, based upon the discounted value of the future earnings of the business.

Valuation of a business as a going concern

Initially, in formulating a solution to the valuation problem, we will confine the discussion to the case of a business which is being valued as a going concern and whose management and assets will be unchanged as a result of the circumstances leading to the requirement for a valuation.

Asset valuation approach

The simplest approach to the problem of valuation will be an asset valuation approach. It can be argued that if a business is acquiring or retaining an asset, then the value of that asset to the business must — in the case of acquisition of the asset, be greater than the cost of the asset and — in the case of retention of the asset — be greater than the net realisable value of the asset. If, therefore, all the assets of the business are valued at their net realisable values, then the sum of those values will clearly be less than their value to the business.

Super-profits method

It is sometimes suggeted that the earnings stream of a business can be divided into two elements — the first is the expected return on the value of the tangible assets employed in the business while the second is an additional amount, known as the *super-profit*. The super-profit is, therefore, the difference between the maintainable profit and the expected return on the tangible assets employed. The essence of the super-profit method is that the additional profits are regarded as riskier than the expected return and that the super-profit should, therefore, be capitalised at a lower multiple (or higher capitalisation rate) than the expected return.

MATERIALS MANAGEMENT

1. STORES FUNCTIONS : RECEIPT, INSPECTION AND ISSUE OF MATERIALS

The stores function can be divided into three parts, *viz.*, receipt, inspection and issue of materials. It has to be noted that the whole process of production/operations management starts with the stores function. This is why proper performance of the stores function ensures timely flow of necessary information for decision-making. We may now refer to the three aspects of stores functions separately.

RECEIPT

Materials may be received either from internal divisions or from external suppliers. Normally, materials are received some time before they are sent to the production department for use. A copy of any purchase order is normally sent to the stores. This enables the stores manager to verify whether the materials, as they arrive, are of the right quantity as also whether the materials have reached on time. Sometimes suppliers send a packaging slip which gives detailed information about the contents of the package. If delivery schedules are not maintained by the supplier, then

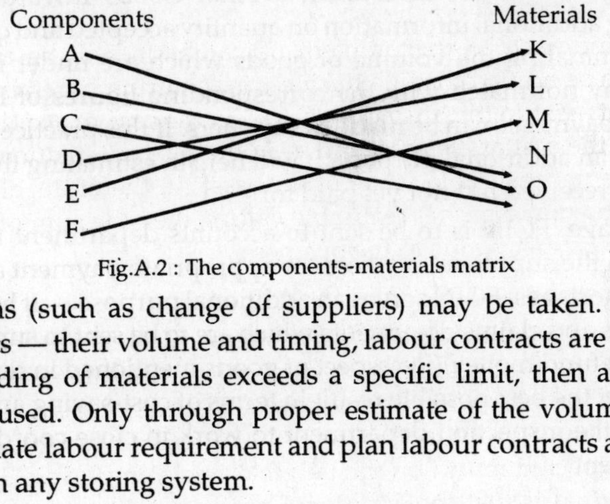

Fig.A.2 : The components-materials matrix

corrective actions (such as change of suppliers) may be taken. On the basis of materials receipts — their volume and timing, labour contracts are to be given. If, at any time, unloading of materials exceeds a specific limit, then additional labour hours are to be used. Only through proper estimate of the volume of receipt it is possible to estimate labour requirement and plan labour contracts accordingly. This is the first step in any storing system.

The second step in the stores function consists of receipt of advice note by stores from suppliers. Such a note gives necessary information about at least four things : despatch, carrier details (mode of transportation), description of the consignment and value. This note has to be sent in advance to ensure quick and easy clearance of materials.

In the third step, the transport organisation (like the railways, or road transport companies) send consignment notes to the stores concerned a few days in advance. This enables the stores department to acquire the materials as and when they arrive.

These three documents, *viz.*, purchase order, suppliers' advice and consignment note, enable the stores manager to plan and ensure timely clearance of materials at the lowest possible cost (by minimising demurrages).

INSPECTION

If there is not much difference between the actual amount the amount shown in the three documents, the consignment is sent for inspection. There is need for additional procedures only in case of shortages. Shortage claims are to be made within a time limit. Otherwise, they will not be entertained. So, it is in the rightness of things to prepare documents and keep them in an index form which gives detailed, datewise information on both the quantum of shortage and the loss of value. As a safeguard against, shortages the store personnel can take open delivery in the presence of the representatives of the transport agency and get a written document (indicating shortage) endorsed.

Immediately after the consignment stage, the inspection stage follows. As soon as the materials are cleared from the receiving section and sent for inspection, a Provisional Goods Inwards Note (PGIN) is prepared. This note gives information on various things such as materials code, quantity received, rate, date of receipt, mode of transport (or carrier details), supplier details, location code and description of the material. This document has to be endorsed by the receiving section of the stores. Immediately after the completion of inspection, the inspection department is left with two options : (1) either to endorse the PGIN indicating quantity accepted and rejected, or (2) to send an inspection report to the stores. On the basis of any of actions taken by the stores department a Final Goods Inward Note (FGIN) is prepared, giving additional information on quantity accepted and quantity received. This helps in estimating the volume of goods which are under inspection as per FGIN. These may not match with the corresponding figures of PGIN. Only after receiving FGIN payments can be made to suppliers. If this practice is followed, then the FGIN serves an additional purpose. It will help in estimating the requirement of funds for goods received but not yet paid for.

In the next stage, FGIN is to be sent to accounts department for checking and verification with the suppliers' invoices for appropriate payment and recoveries of dues in case of shortages. FGIN serves an additional purpose — it helps in preparing shortages reports and claims documents which are to be sent to suppliers on time to enable them to refund money (in respect of goods mentioned in documents but not delivered). To get the best possible result in terms of cost-saving and time-saving, it is necessary for the inspection department to work in close coordination with the stores management.

Internal Supplies

So far we have discussed systems for receipt from outside suppliers. But materials are often received from internal divisions in which case transfer notes are used. Alternatively if materials are returned from user departments, return to stores documents are to be used.

In case the scrap is also handed over to the Stores Department, scrap cards, indicating the nature and weight of the scrap, are to be prepared.

Organisational Aspects

For reducing paper work, ensuring as less materials movement as possible and quick and timely clearance of documents many organisations have integrated inspection department with materials management. Such integration also leads to prompt payment of bills and timely recovery of claims. However, this arrangement has one major drawback. There is often a conflict of interests between quality and service to the user department.

In some organisations inspection is integrated with the respective user departments. This also creates a problem. If a high level of output is to be produced in a short period (or if production targets are very high), quality cannot be maintained. This very fact is likely to due considerable damage to the image of the company.

It appears that maintaining quality standards is to some extent the responsibility of the, inspection department. If this is true then inspection is to be treated as an independent activity. This means that the manager in charge of quality control enjoys sufficient freedom. He is responsible to only of the General Manager. However, this arrangement is free true from defects. Too much emphasis on quality may lead to wastage of money. If a company spends Rs 2 more per unit to improve the quality of a product, which sells a slightly higher price (say Re 1 more), then the company is going to lose. The more the company is able to sell the greater the loss.

ISSUES

The third and final stage of the stores function consists of issues, which are of two types, *viz.*, (1) issues to the consuming departments and (2) issues to outside suppliers for processing and conversion. There are certain common requirements in both the cases :

(1) The Control of Issues

Issues of materials are based on production programmes. On the basis of issues and bills of materials, work orders are printed. These are very useful and valuable documents. A work order lists the quantity of each materials issued against each component which requires that material. See Fig.A.3. Here components *A*, *B* and *C* require material *O*, component *D*, material *L* and component *E*, material *O* and component *F* requires material *M*. Thus, consumption of materials is automatically controlled. It is because the work order gives details of the quantity of materials to be issued as also the corresponding quantities of the components to be manufactured. Due to production constraints the requirement of materials should not exceed a certain limit. This very fact ensures consumption control. In fact, any materials requirement over and above the quantity indicated in the work order means huge wastage and scrapping. Normally junior personnel in the stores department do not have the authority to issue materials beyond the quantity indicated in the work order. This leads to automatic control. It is because every time extra material is required, there is need to draw the attention of the top management and obtain its permission. If, however, materials are issued on commercial basis it is necessary to ensure proper control through stores registers.

2. Delegation of Authority

The second important aspect of issue is delegation of authority. Usually consumption of direct materials such as fuel, oil, electricity, oxygen and tools is controlled through work orders, on the basis of two things : (a) past experience and (b) suitable delegation. For example, the stores assistant may have the necessary authority to issue materials upto Rs 2,000 and the stores officer's limit may be Rs 5,000 and so on. Through such delegation it is possible to ensure automatic control of consumption.

Additionally, ad hoc material requisitions are also made at times. For this it is necessary to prepare consolidated statements of such items on a periodic basis. In some companies, serial controls are maintained and issues, as also receipts are posted in kardex formulating stock balances from time to time. Such updating is very important because the stores record is the first step of inventory management in all types of organisations.

When issues are made to outside suppliers stricter or more controls are to be imposed and maintained. Adequate controls are necessary to take care of payments and claims.

Finally, we may refer to subcontracting. This involves sub-contracting supply of materials by the sub-contracting organisation(s). Here, controls are to be exercised through despatch notes, consignment notes and purchase orders.

CONCLUSION

In short, stores function is a very important part of materials management. A good stores system serves a number of purposes such as preparation of accurate stock status reports, detection of discrepancies on time, prompt clearance of goods in order to expedite bill payment, reduction in demurrages and losses in claims. For all these reasons, many organisations set up a separate a stores management department. Furthermore for streamlining systems and procedures, it is necessary to carry out Organisation and Management (O&M) studies on a regular basis.

Since all kinds of inspection, even counting the items cost money, inspection of each and every item in the lot may not always be possible. In short, cent percentage inspection is not always practicable due to various considerations such as cost, time, destructibility and fatigue.

2. PURCHASING CYCLE

The following steps constitute the typical purchasing cycle :

1. Recognising, defining and describing the need;
2. Transmitting the need;
3. Investigating and selecting the supplier;
4. Preparing and issuing the purchase order;
5. Following up the order;
6. Receiving and inspecting the materials;
7. Auditing the invoice; and
8. Closing the order.

The actual process of purchasing cycle starts with the receipt of ident by the purchase department from the production (operations) department.

There are basically four categories of items : (a) stock item, (b) non-stock item, (c) capital item and (d) other (misc.) items.

Indent should carefully specify :

(i) Full description of the items giving detaills of specification and drawings, etc.

(ii) Quantity required to be procured.

(iii) Date at which the items are required.

Besides the above, there are other details which an indent for a particular category must contain, *e.g.*,

(iv) ***Stock Items*** : Details regarding last purchase — quantity, price, date of ordering, last suppliers etc. Details regarding consumption and stock.

(v) ***Non-stock items*** : Specific purpose for which the items are required.

(vi) ***Capital items*** : Details of scheme/purchase for which the items are required with sanction of the top management.

There are various forms of indenting. These should suit the requirements of the company.

Scrutiny of Indent

On receipt of the indent the purchase department has to scrutinise it carefully to ensure that it gives all the necessary details required for issuing tenders. In case the indent is incomplete it should be referred back to the originator/indentor.

Tendering

The next step is to make enquiries or call tenders. Basically, there are four types of tenders: (i) limited; (ii) open; (iii) single; and (iv) verbal.

Limited Tendering

This involves issuing tender to a few selected tenderers only.

Open Tendering

Under this system the tender is open to any supplier who can quote for the materials as per requirements. This is usually done by publishing the tender in the newspaper, trade journals and other bulletins.

Single tendering

This refers to sending the tender to one particular party. Normally, it is either for an item where there is only one supplier or for an item where the purchaser has developed confidence in one supplier only and would just like to verify the current price, delivery, etc. Single tenders are also sent for items of proprietary nature.

Verbal Tendering

Where there is no time to wait for the supplier to quote, verbal tendering becomes necessary. This could either be done by telephoning the supplier or across the table.

Receiving / Opening / Scrutiny of Tender

The offers received against tenders are scrutinised on the basis of price, conformity to specification, reliability of the supplier, lead time, after-sales service and other such considerations and accepted accordingly.

Negotiation. In case of any confusion and/or ambiguity negotiation can be made with the supplier for clarification before finalising terms and conditions.

Ordering. The next step is to prepare and issue the purchase order. A purchase order is the commitment by a buyer to oblige the supplier. It is submitted in acceptance of a formal quotation or offer. It becomes a legal contract only when it is accepted by the seller.

Acknowledgement. After placement of purchase order formal acknowledgement regarding its acceptance must be obtained from the supplier.

Follow-up of Order

Orders are to be followed-up for ensuring correct delivery either by :

(i) telephonic message/writing letter; or

(ii) making visits to the supplier's office/factory.

Orders should be regularly followed-up. Moreover, various modern methods must be used. Follow-up actions can also be taken for expediting the order(s). In case the supplier is unable to maintain delivery schedule, precautionary steps like warning the supplier/developing alternative sources must be taken immediately.

Cancellation of Order. In case the supplier fails to deliver the goods in right quality or in right time the purchaser reserves the right to cancel the order and obtain his requirement from elsewhere.

Receiving, inspection of materials. The materials, when delivered, are received by the storekeeper and sent for inspection. Materials approved are stored and subsequently issued to the actual user. Materials rejected are sent back to supplier for rectification/replacement.

After receipt, inspection and approval, the auditing of invoice is done and part/full payment is made. At this stage, the purchasing cycle is complete.

3. NEGOTIATIONS IN PURCHASING

Negotiation means conferring, discussing and bargaining to reach an agreement on business transactions. There are five objectives of negotiations :

1. to obtain a fair and reasonable price for the quality specified.
2. to get the supplier to fulfil the contract in time.
3. to exert some control over the manner in which the contract is performed.
4. to persuade the supplier to extend maximum possible cooperation to the organisational buyer.
5. to develop a sound and continuing relationship with the competent supplier.

Negotiation in purchasing becomes necessary in the following situations:

(i) if competitive bidding is missing;
(ii) if there are many variable factors affecting quality and service;
(iii) if sellers are manufacturing a product as per buyer's design engineering — buyer's objective is to influence not only the supplier's production capability but also to exercise control over the supplier.
(iv) business risk or the risk of transaction cannot be accurately estimated or measured.
(v) tooling and set-up costs represent a large percentage of total cost.
(vi) long period of time is required to supply (or delivery) the items purchased.
(vii) production is frequently interrupted due to numerous change in order since different production processes are involved.
(viii) thorough analysis is required to solve difficult 'make or buy' decision.
(ix) products of a specific supplier (and others) are desired are not considered.

Negotiation is an art, success of which depends upon the relative bargaining power of two parties. The seller's bargaining strength is based on three things : (i) how badly the seller wants the contract; (ii) how certain he feels of getting it and (iii) how much time is available to reach agreement on suitable terms.

On the other hand, buyer's bargaining strength is based on three other factors, *viz.*, (i) the extent of competition present amongst the potential suppliers, (ii) the adequacy of cost or price analysis, and (iii) the thoroughness with which he has prepared for negotiation.

Negotiation is done on the basis of source selection, vendor's production efficiency, the vendor's managerial competence, pricing and all other important considerations that are involved in any type of competitive bidding. When adequate price competition does not exist a fair price should be determined first by analysing cost, profit and price through homework and then through negotiation. Negotiation is particularly useful where the seller is the single source of supply or controls multiple sources. A good negotiator should possess all the information through market research, market analysis, value analysis and cost analysis. He should also take the view of trade union leaders about the activities of the supplier. To be able to negotiate with vendors the buyer has to be aware of the past performance of the vendors. Negotiation is, no doubt, as an art. It is a skill that can be adopted in situations involving purchase of materials and a person cannot be successful purchase executive without being a good negotiator. The purchase executive should have the capacity to use the information gathered from various sources to the advantage of his company.

The negotiation process provides a means for the buyer and seller, through give and takes to eliminate unjustified or unnecessary expenses or wastes. It should not be taken as a means for depriving the vendor of a reasonable amount of profit or as an opportunity for obtaining unreasonable concessions. In reality the most successful negotiations are those which produce results that give benefit to both sides and which provide the framework for a long-term, mutually beneficial relationship.

Basic Areas of Consideration in Price Negotiation/Evaluation

Two basic areas for consideration in any price negotiation are :

(i) ***Quality***. Once the need has been established and transformed into a request to purchase, the quality requirement becomes the most important and difficult aspect of the broad function called price evaluation. Quality assumes importance at various phases of this function.

(ii) ***Quantity***. Bulk purchase of materials generally represents a saving. There are various factors to consider before obtaining price discounts by purchasing in large quantities. These are the following :

1. General economic conditions
2. Consideration of buyer's or seller's market
3. Seasonal factors
4. Cost of money
5. Terms of payment
6. Escalation clause — as during inflation and deflation :
   (i) Such a clause should provide for adjustment of price — both upward and downward.
   (ii) Price should be documented and tied with actual costs of production and new price(s) should be published to make it officially known to actual and intending buyers.
   (iii) A maximum percentage of escalation or a ceiling should be fixed in order to protect the buyers.
7. ***Buying policies***. Buying policies should reflect basic corporate policy as to how a particular company carries on its business.
8. ***Government action***. There is a great deal of government legislation regarding price fixation. No well-managed company would tolerate its agent accepting illegal price from a vendor.
9. Freight costs
10. Packaging and material handling
11. Value analysis
12. Taxes
13. Insurance
14. Duties.

4. SOURCES OF WASTE IN MANUFACTURING

Anything in the product life cycle that does not add value of the product is waste. In the context of materials management, we refer to the following two types of waste:

A. Waste Caused by Poor Product Specification and Design

Waste making starts with the policies set by management in responding to the needs of the marketplace. Management is responsible for establishing policies for the market segments the company wishes to serve and for deciding how broad or specialised the product line is to be. These policies affect the costs of manufacturing. For example, if the range and variety of product are large, production runs will be short, and machines must be changed over frequently. There will be little opportunity to use specialised machinery and fixtures. On the other hand, a company with a limited product range can probably produce goods on an assembly-line basis and take advantage of special-purpose machinery. In addition, the greater the diversity of products, the more complex the manufacturing process becomes, and the more difficult it is to plan and control.

Component standardisation. Companies can specialise in the products they make and still offer customers a wide range of options. If companies standardise on the component parts used in the different models they make, they can supply the customer with a variety of models and options made from standard components. Parts standardisation has many advantages in manufacturing. It creates larger quantities of specific components that allow longer production runs. This, in its turn, makes it more economical to use more specialised machinery, fixtures and assembly methods. Standardisation reduces the planning and control effort needed, the number of items required and the inventory that has to be carried.

The "ideal" product is one that meets or exceeds customer expectations, makes the best use of material and can be manufactured with a minimum of waste (at least cost). As well as satisfying the customer, the product's design determines both the basic manufacturing processes that have to be used and the cost and quality of the product. The product should be so designed that it can be made by the most efficient productive process with the smallest number of operations, motions and parts and includes all of the features that are important to the customer.

B. Waste Caused in Manufacturing

Manufacturing takes the design and specifications of the product and, using the manufacturing resources, converts them into useful products. Firstly, however, production engineering must design a system capable of making the product. They do so by selecting the manufacturing steps, machinery and equipment and by designing the plant layout and work methods. Manufacturing must then plan and control the operation to produce the goods. This involves manufacturing planning and control, quality management, maintenance and industrial relations.

Seven sources of waste : Toyota has identified seven important sources of waste in manufacturing. The first four relate to the design of the manufacturing system and the last three to the operation and management of the system:

1. ***The process***. The best process is one that has the capability to consistently make the product with an absolute minimum of scrap, in the quanties needed, and with

the least cost added. Waste, or cost, is added to the process if the wrong type or size of machines are used, if the process is not being operated correctly, or if the wrong tools and fixtures are used.

2. ***Methods***. Waste is added if the methods of performing tasks by the operators cause wasted movement, time, or effort. Activities that do not add value to the product should be eliminated. Searching for tools, unnecessary walking or motions are all examples of waste.

3. ***Movement***. Moving and storing components adds cost but not value. For example, goods received may be stored and then issued to production. This requires labour to put away, find and deliver to production. Records must be kept and a storage system maintained. Poorly planned layouts may make it necessary to move products over long distances, thus increasing the movement cost and possibly storage and record-keeping costs.

4. ***Product defects***. Defects interrupt the smooth flow of work. If the scrap is not identified, the next workstation receiving it will waste time trying to use the defective parts of waiting for good material. Schedules must be adjusted. If the next step is the customer, then the cost will be even higher. Sorting out or reworking defects are also waste.

5. ***Waiting time***. There are two kinds of waiting time: that of the operator and that of material. If the operator has no productive work to do or there are delays in getting material or instructions, there will be waste. Ideally, material passes from one work center to the next and is processed without waiting in queue.

6. ***Overproduction***. Overproduction is producing products beyond those needed for immediate use. When this occurs, raw materials and labour are consumed for parts not needed, resulting in unnece sary inventories. Considering the costs of carrying inventory, this can be very expensive. Overpro duction causes extra handling of material, extra planning and control effort and quality problems. Because of the extra inventory and work-in-process, overproduction adds confusion, tends to bury problems in inventory and often leads to producing components that are not needed instead of those that are. Overproduction is not necessary as long as market demand is met. Machines and operators do not always need to be fully utilised.

7. ***Inventory***. Inventory costs money to carry and excess inventory adds extra cost to the product. However, there are other costs in carrying excess inventory.

To remain competitive, a manufacturing organisation must produce better products at lower cost while responding quickly to the marketplace.

5. DISPOSAL OF SCRAP SURPLUS OR OBSOLETE MATERIALS

Managers are concerned with the effective, efficient, and profitable disposal of scrap, surplus, obsolete, and waste materials generated within the firm. In recent years, disposal problems have become more complex, as well as more important, as companies have become larger, more diversified in product lines, and more decentralised in management. More recently, a new dimension has been added to the overall disposal problem: the need to develop and use new methods to avoid the generation of solid waste products and better means of disposing of other wastes which are discharged into the air and waterways, causing pollution. So the purchasing executive must always remain conscious of the implications of new technology which seeks to avoid and eliminate causes of pollution.

Not only does the proper sale of scrap, surplus, and waste result in additional income for the seller, it also prevents pollution and serves to conserve raw materials, resources and energy.

The disposal of all kinds of scrap and surplus materials should always be handled to minimise the net loss or, if possible, achieve the highest potential gain. The first tasks of the manager, therefore, should be to balance against each other the net returns obtained from each one of several methods of disposal. Thus, excess materials can frequently be transferred from one plant of a company to another of the same company. Such a procedure involves little outlay except for packing, handling, and shipping. At other times, by reprocessing or reconditioning, the materials can be salvaged for use within the plant. Such cases clearly involve a much larger expense, and there may be some question as to whether — once the materials have beem so treated — its value — either for the purpose originally intended or for some substitute use — is great enough to justify the expense. Since the decision whether to undertake the reclamation of any particular lot of materials is essentially one of production costs and of the resultant quality, it should be — and commonly is — made by the production or engineering department instead of by the scrap department. The most the purchasing manager can do is to suggest that this treatment be considered before the materials are disposed of in other ways.

Categories of Materials for Disposal

No matter how well a company may be managed, some excess, waste, scrap, surplus, ans obsolete materials are bound to develop. Every organisation tries, of course, to keep such materials at a minimum. But try as it may, this never will be wholly successful. The existence of this class of materials is the result of various causes, among which are overoptimism in the sales forecast; changes in design and specifications; errors in estimating factory usage; inevitable losses in processing; careless use of materials by factory personnel; and overbuying resulting from attempts to avoid the threat of rising prices or to secure quantity discounts on large purchases.

In this context, we have distinguished among the following categories of materials for disposal:

1. Excess or Surplus Materials

Excess (or surplus) materials is that stock which is in excess of a reasonable requirement of the organisation. It arises because of errors in the amount bought or because anticipated production did not materialise. Such materials may be handled in various ways. In some cases it may be desirable merely to store it until required, particularly if the material is slightly durable, if storage costs are not very high, and if there is a reasonable expectation that the materials will be required in the future. Occasionally it may be substituted for more active material. Or, if the company operates a number of plants, it may be possible to transfer the excess to another plant. There are times, however, when these conditions do not exist and when fairly prompt sale is desirable. The chances for change in the style or design may be so great as to diminish considerably the probability that this particular material may be required. Or, it maybe perishable. Factory requirements may be such as to postpone the demand for large amounts of this material so far into the future that the most economical action is to dispose of it and repurchase it in future.

Many companies set some rough rule of thumb by which to determine when a stock item is to be treated as surplus. This rule suggests that all materials should be grouped into rough classifications, and normal requirement and supply periods established for each. Mere classification in itself is not enough. As with all classes of material, systematic, physical stock-taking, continuous review of inventory records, and occasional cleanup activities are also necessary.

Another source of excess material usually appears on the completion of a construction project. Provision is also made for the proper or counting of using material created or resulting from demolition work carried on in conjunction with construction projects.

2. Obsolete Materials or Equipment

Obsolete materials differ from excess stock. Whereas the latter presumably could be consumed at some future date, the former is unlikely ever to be used inside the organisation which purchased it. Materials becomes obsolete as a result of a change in the production process or when some better material is substituted for that originally used. Once materials have been declared obsolete, it is wise to dispose of them at the best price that can be obtained.

3. Rejected End Products

Because of the uncertainties of the production process, or because of complex end-product quality specifications, a certain percentage of completed products may be rejected by outgoing quality control as unsatisfactory. In some instances these finished products can be repaired or reworked to bring them up to standard, but, in other instances, it is not economic to do so. As an alternative the firm may find it necessary to destroy the rejected items (as is done in the pharmaceutical industry); or remove the distinguishing mark or identification; or melt the product down to recover any valuable metal content.

4. Scrap Materials

Scrap materials differ from excess or obsolete stock since they cannot properly be classified as new or unused. **Scrap** is a term which may be applied to materials or equipment which is no longer serviceable and has been discarded. It includes such items as worn machinery and old tools. In such cases, scrap arises because the company is replacing old machines with others which are more modern and more productive . A concern buying new machines, tools, and other equipment normally maintains a depreciation charge intended to cover the original cost of such items, so that the value of a machine has been written off by the time it is finally discarded. Such a depreciation charge normally covers an obsolesence factor as well as ordinary wear and tear. Actually, however, a discarded or scrapped machine may still have a value for some other manufacturer in the same type of business or in some other industry. It, consequently, may go disposed of at a price which will show a profit in many instances. This replacement of old or obsolete machines by others capable of larger production at the same or lower cost provides a real profit-making opportunity.

Another form of scrap is represented by the many by-products of the production process. Start-up adjustment scrap is frequently significant and one major reason for a significant price increase for small custom orders. The faster and the more automated the equipment, the higher the start-up scrap will be as a percentage of the total materials used in small orders. Commonly, items of this class, which are a normal part of the production process, are considered a form of scrap — such materials may frequently be salvaged.

Various specifications are used primarily by industrial scrap merchants when they describe lots for sale to the industrial buyer. They also could be used by the purchasing department in the sale of scrap generated in the firm, but if there are impurities (not allowed for by the specificationm) in the lot, then there is a risk that the sale might be voided.

5. Waste

Waste is defined as materials or supplies which are changed during the production process and which — through carelessness, faulty production methods, poor handling, or other causes — have been spoiled, broken, or otherwise rendered unfit for further use or reclamation. In some instances, waste can be defined simply as the residue of materials which results from the normal manufacturing process and which has no economic (resale) value. An example is the smoke produced by burning fuel or in the smelting process, or the lubricating oil which has become so badly contaminated as a result of the normal manufacturing process that it cannot be reclaimed. However, what is waste today and has no current economic value may change tomorrow.

Theoretically, waste should not exist. However, there will never be a time when some waste will not exist in every plant as 'mechanical advantage' (output ÷ input) will always be less thgan 1, *i.e.*, efficiency of a machine can never be 100%. Every effort should be made to reduce the waste factor to the lowest possible point. Its reduction can be brought about in many ways, such as the installation of new precesses and by improved production layout. The objective is to realise as large a return as possible from disposal of these items.

RESPONSIBILITY FOR MATERIALS DISPOSAL

The question of the responsibility for the management of materials disposal in an organisation is rather difficult to answer. In large companies where substantial amounts of scrap, obsolete, surplus, and waste materials are generated, a separate department may be set up. The manager of such a department may report to the general manager or the production manager.

Some very legitimate reasons for assigning disposal of materials to the purchasing/materials management function include: (1) knowledge of probable price trends, (2) contact with salespeople is a good source of information as to possible users of the materials, (3) familiarity with the materials within the organisation, and unless a specific department is established within the firm to handle this function, purchasing is probably the only logical choice.

In large, diversified and decentralised types of organisation salvage materials generated in any part of the company are considered for use in all parts of the company before being offered for sale outside the company.

The conclusion is that, except in the cases of companies with separate salvage department, management has found the purchasing department — because of its knowledge of materials, markets, prices, and possible uses — in a better position than other departments of the company to salvage what can be used and to dispose off what cannot.

Keys to Profitable Disposal

Every effort should be made through good planning and taking advantage of modern technology to minimise the quantity of materials generated.

If scrap results as a normal, unavoidable part of the operation, it is essential that it be segregated by type, alloy, grade, size, and weight. This should be done at the point where scrap is generated.

Also, every effort should be made to obtain *maximum competition* from sources available to buy scrap or surplus materials. Purchasing should actively attempt to find new buyers and encourage them to compete in terms of price paid and service provided.

Disposal Channels

There are several possible means of materials disposal. In general, the options are, in order of maximum return to the selling company, the following:

Use Elsewhere within the Firm on an "As Is" Basis. An attempt should be made to use the materials "as is," or with economical modification, for a purpose other than that for which it was purchased. In the case of a multidivision operation, periodically each division should circulate to all other divisions a list of scrap/surplus/obsolete materials and equipment— arrangements then may be made for interplant transfer of some of the items.

Reclaim for Use within the Plant. For example, can the materials be reclaimed or modified for use by welding? Welding has become a very important factor in disposing of materials to advantage. In addition to economic advantages, this may provide a partial solution to some of today's environmental problems.

Sell to Another Firm for Use on an "As Is" Basis. Can any other manufacaturer use the materials either "as is ", or with economical modifications? Sales can often be made direct to other users who may be able to use a disposal item in lieu of a raw material they currently are buying. Or, one firm's surplus or obsolete equipment may solve another firm's equipment requirements aptly. Some companies permit employees to buy, as part of their industrial relations programme, used equipment or surplus materials at a preset price. If this is done, adequate controls should be established to assure that the return to the firm is at a reasonable level.

Return to the Vendor. A large quantity of steel scrap is sold by large quantity purchasers directly to the mills or plants, who use it as a raw material in the steel production process. Normally, the firm using this disposal avenue must be a large consumer. In the case of surplus (new) inventory items, the original vendor may be willing to allow full credit on returned items.

Sale through a Broker. Brokers exist for the sale of both scrap and also for used equipment. Their role is to bring buyer and seller together, for which they take a commission. A great deal of metal scrap is disposed off through this channel.

Sale to a local Scrap or Surplus Dealer. All communities of any size will have one or more scrap-dealers. The return from sale through this channel is likely to be low, for four reasons: (1) there may be only one dealer, a noncompetitive, sole buying source; (2) the dealer assumes the risk of investment, holding, and attempting to find a buyer. The profit margin for assuming this risk may be quite high; (3) extra movement and handling, which is costly, is involved; and (4) the seller usually does not become an expert in the scrap market, due to the relatively small volumes involved; the scrap or surplus dealer is an expert. However, the industrial scrap merchant may provide several valuable services, for example, recommendations on handling, sorting, and processing methods; supply collection containers; and provide pick up of materials.

Discard, Destroy, or Donate the Materials or Item. If no buyer or user can be found for the item, the firm may have to destroy or bury the item. This can be quite costly and caution should be taken to protect the environment and to assure that disposal methods for dangerous materials do not create a safety hazard to the public.

Disposal Procedures

When scrap is sold, careful attention should be given to the selection of a buyer and to the procedure for handling the sale. The telephone directory (especially the yellow pages) provides lists of dealers who buy scrap and waste products.

In connection with the selling and delivery of materials, a system should be set up which will be consistently followed and will afford the company protection against all possible loss through slipshod methods, dishonest employees, and irregular practice on the part of the purchaser. All sales should be approved by a department head and cash sales should be handled through the cashier and never by the individual whose duty it is to negotiate the sale. All delivery of by-products sold should be effected through the issuing of an order form and sufficient number of copies made to provide a complete record for all departments involved in the transaction. The shiping department should determine the weight, count, and so on, and this figure should go to the billing department without going through the hands of those who negotiate the sale.

Any department responsible for the performance of this function should maintain a list of reputable dealers in the particular line of materials or equipment to be disposed off and should periodically review this list. At frequent intervals, the proper plant official should be instructed to clean up the stock and report on the weights and quantities of the different items or classes of items ready for disposal.

A common procedure is to send out invitations to four or five dealers to call and inspect the lots at the factory and quote their prices F.O.B. factory-yard. Such transactions usually are subject to the accepted bidder check of weights and quantities and are paid for in cash before removal. Not infrequently, acceptable and dependable purchasers with whom satisfactory connections have already been established are relied on as desirable purchasers and no bids are called for from others.

If a firm generates large amounts of scrap materials consistently, the bidders may be asked to bid on the purchase of this scrap over a six-month or one-year time period. However, it is advisable to rebid or renegotiate such contracts at least annually, to encourage competition, and, naturally, higher return.

The contract for sale of scrap items should include price and how determined, quantities involved (all or a percentage), time of delivery. F.O.B. point, cancellation privileges, how weights are determined, and payment terms.

6. PRICING AND DISCOUNTS

Price is not the only factor in making purchasing decisions. However, all other things being the same, it is the most important. In the average manufacturing company, purchases account for about 50% of the cost of goods sold, and any savings made in purchase cost has a direct influence on profits.

However, remember that "you only get what you pay for." The trick is to know what you want and not pay more than necessary. When a purchase is made, the buyer receives a package of function, quantity, service, and price characteristics that are suited to the individual's needs. The idea of "best buy" is the mixture that serves the purpose best.

Basis for Pricing

The term "fair price" is sometimes used to described what should be paid for an item. But what is a fair price? No doubt, it is the lowest price at which the item can be bought. However, there are other considerations, especialy for repeat purchases where the buyer and seller want to establish a good working relationship. In truth, a fair price is one that is competitive, gives the seller a profit, and enables the buyer, ultimately, to sell at a profit. Sellers who charge too little to cover their costs will be forced to go out of business. In order to survive, they may attempt to cut costs by reducing quality and service. In the end, both the buyer and seller must be satisfied.

Since an industrial buyer wants to pay a fair price and no more, it is necessary to develop some basis for establishing such a price. Price has an upper and a lower limit. The market decides the upper limit. What buyers are willing to pay is based on their demand, supply, and needs. The seller sets the lower limit. It is determined by the costs of production and selling the product and profit margin. If buyers are to arrive at a fair price, they must develop an understanding of market demand and supply, competitive prices, and the methods of arriving at a cost.

Industrial buying decisions are typically more realistic and "fact-oriented" than decisions made by consumers. However, industrial products have a direct impact on the profits of both buyer and seller. Price, thus, becomes a critical factor, with each party considering various factors to determine the relative importance of price in a specific negotiation.

Net Price

Because industrial products are sold to different types of customers who buy in different quantities and are located in different areas or regions, pricing polices involve adjustments to the base price to account for these differences. The most important price to industrial buyers is the net price. Net price refers to the list price less allowances for various cost-related concessions made by the buyer, such as volume purchases. List price is the published figure distributed to all customers, regardless of their type or classification. List pricing is used by manufacturs for two primary reasons. Firstly, the various products that are described in a catalogue preclude the printing of a new catalogue each time the price of one or more items is changed. Secondly, list pricing provides a common base from which various types of discounts can be subtracted.

Discount Pricing

Consumers will sometimes refrain from making a purchase because they may consider the price to be too high for the quality of the product offered and/or for what they think they can afford. This common resistance to buying can be overcome sometimes through the judicious use of two price changing tactics: (1) the use of "sales" or "specials" and (2) discount pricing.

Discount pricing involves a deduction from the published price list to (1) account for the cost and benefits of dealing with different classifications of customers, (2) encourage customers to buy in large volumes, and (3) encourage rapid payment by customers.

For industrial buying, discounts are offered as a matter of course. Typically, discounts are given for three reasons. One is to serve as inducements for purchase, much the same as in consumer buying during sales. A second is to meet the competition. The third is that buyers expect the discount and failure to meet this expectation risks including an imbalance in the *quid pro quo* (*i.e.*, exchange of favour) inherent in such exchanges. In general, there are three types of discounts offered in the industrial purchase : trade, cash and quantity discounts. Each is briefly described below:

1. **Trade Discounts**. Trade discounts are used by manufacturers to account for benefits derived from dealing with various groups of customers or middlemen. Discounts offered to distributors should cover the operating costs they incur in putting sales effort and associated services (local inventory, customer credit, and technical support) and allow them a reasonable profit margin.

2. **Cash Discounts**. To encourage rapid payment and allow for better cash flow cash discounts are typically granted in the industrial market. A discount is a price reduction offered to the buyer under the condition that the discounted price be paid within a certain period of time; otherwise the full price must be paid. The most common terms are 2/10, net 30. This means that a 2% discount is provided if the bill is paid within 10 days, but if the option is not taken, then the full price is due within 30 days. For example, assume that a buyer agreed on a purchase price of Rs 6,000 and was offered 2/10, net 30. Then, if the bill were paid within 10 days, Rs 5,880 would be due; otherwise, the full Rs 6,000 would be payable within 30 days. Other cash discounts are, of course, offered, such as 3/10, net 30, for instance.

From a buyer's standpoint, cash discounts represent a cost savings and in this way function as incentives. From the seller's viewpoint, cash discounts are believed to encourage prompt payment and to build goodwill.

3. **Quantity Discounts**. Price reductions based on how much a buyer purchases are termed quantity discounts. To encourage volume purchasing and maintain buyer loyalty, quantity discounts are given for the volume of goods purchased either on individual orders or a series of orders over a longer period of time, usually one year. These discounts are termed as non-cumulative and cumulative, respectively. Cumulative discounts have the effect of "locking in" a customer's purchases for a long period, thus reducing both marketing cost and competitive pressure, while providing a smoother, more cost-effective production flow. Noncumulative discounts tend to encourage larger individual orders, which reduce costs of storage,

order processing, and delivery for the seller. A cumulative quantity discount is based on the total amount purchased over a period of time. A noncumulative quantity discount is based on the amount purchased at a single point in time. A quantity discount might be set on the criterion of units bought (*e.g.*, Rs 2.00 per unit for 1 to 99 units, Rs 1.95 per unit for 100 to 499 units and Rs 1.90 per unit for 500 or more units) or the rupee value of the purchase (*e.g.*, a 5% discount for orders from Rs3,000 up to and including Rs 10,000, and an 8 % discount for orders of more than Rs10,000). Due to legal constraints (*e.g.*, the MRTP Act), quantity discounts must reflect cost savings due, for example, to savings in billing or shipping.

What are the effects of quantity discounts? Aside from the obvious financial motivations on the part of buyers and demand stimulation motives on the part of sellers, there is the possibility that quantity purchases could alter the balance of power between buyer and seller. To the extent that quantity discounts induce large purchases and result in buyers concentrating their orders from one or a few sellers, the vulnerability of either party can be affected, depending on the importance and magnitude of the sale for the parties and the alternatives available to each. Switching costs will be incurred as a function of the substitutability of one seller to another for the buyer, the cirtical nature of the resources to both buyer and seller, and the level of the resources exchanged.

Geographical Pricing

Geographical factors are an important concern in pricing decisions because shipping costs may impact the ultimate price to be paid by buyers and the ability of the selling firm to remain competitive in discount markets. Thus, decisions must be made on how these costs will be included in prices of material.

Basically, the selling firm has three options in handling shipping costs. When the seller concentrates on local markets or sells products wherein shipping charges are minimal compared to product value (precious metals and microprocessors), these costs are a minor issue. However, unlike consumers buying at various local retailers, industrial buyers are often involved with multiple suppliers located at various distances from the delivery point. Moreover, many products (basic metals, unsophisticated capital equipment, etc.) have a high weight-to-value ratio. In such cases, shipping charges are a large part of total (production plus transportation) cost.

The seller must weight the importance of covering costs, by passing them on to the customer, against the need to be competitive in distant target markets. If there is a signification product differentiation, the seller may gamble that buyers will ignore a difference in shipping charges. However, this may not be true in the case of basic commodities with little or no difference from those of competitors.

EXAMINATION TECHNIQUE

B.Com. (H) students should tackle their 'best' questions first and leave the others until later rather than feel under any obligation to adhere to the numerical order specified in the question paper.

It is vital to allocate sufficient time for all questions: rare is the entrant who can secure a pass mark (40%) from the totals for, say, two to three questions out of the four requested.

There is no rule which restricts the length of answers (other than the need to write on all four question adequately), and the deliberate compression of material merely makes the candidate's work look unappealing.

Those entrants who really wish to gurantee a pass for themselves must make an effort to familiarise themselves with management problems and the operation of policies within their own organisations, so that they can quote specific illustrations in their answers.

Candidates must pay more attention to the effectiveness with which they express themselves. A competent adminiistrator must be able to communicate in writting through letters, reports, memoranda, etc. His credibility, and thus his ability to get things done is substantially undermined if he appears not to be able to spell simple words, or if he cannot correctly distinguish among recruitment, selection and promotion, between job evaluation and merit ranging between financial planning and financial control. Spelling mistakes are especially penalised when the words appear in the examination paper itself.

Candidates should write coherent answers in a logical and convincing way, with checklist points numbered in sequence, liberal use of underlined headings so that scripts are easier and more pleasant to read, and references to some up-to-date and well- informed sources in the subject area.

No doubt the citation of actual examples is one of the best ways in which the more meritorious candidates demonstrate their excellence.

Candidates must answer the question asked, and not some other question derived from their own imagination. If they see some key phrase like 'manpower planning' or 'promotion policy', they should not expect to earn high marks for simply writing down all they know about the subject in question. Where students are being evaluated, it is not only on their knowledge, but also on their ability to organise and marshal their thoughts, and even on their capacity for thinking spontaneously and creatively about the implications of some issue.

UNIVERSITY OF CALCUTTA

B. COM. (PART I) HONS. EXAMINATION

1999

BUSINESS MANAGEMENT—Honours

Fourth Paper

Full Marks — 100

Candidates are required to give their answers in their own words as far as practicable

The figures in the margin indicate full marks

Answer **ONE** question from Each Group

Group—A

1. Briefly explain the significance of management. 6
2. Why is F.W.Taylor called the Father of Scientific Management ? 6

Group—B

3. (a) Discuss the importance of packaging in Marketing Management. 16

   (b) "Packaging is an aid to advertising". Discuss. 6
4. (a) What is Sales Management ? 6

   (b) Discuss the importance of Sales Management in the context of modern marketing. 16

Group—C

5. (a) Discuss, in brief, the concept of 'profit maximisation' and 'wealth maximisation'. 8

   (b) Discuss the features of financial planning. 16
6. (a) Distinguish between fixed capital and working capital. 8

   (b) Discuss the factors that determine the quantum of fixed capital and working capital of an industrial organisation. 16

Group—D

7. (a) What do you mean by 'training' ? Discuss the importance of training. 8

   (b) Discuss the 'On-the-job' & 'Off-the-job' training methods. 16
8. (a) Discuss the need for promotion in organisation. 8

   (b) State the advantages and disadvantages of promotion on the basis of 'merit' and on the basis of 'seniority'. 16

Group—E

9. (a) Explain the concept of 'separate entity' of company. 8

   (b) Discuss the essential features of a joint-stock company. 16
10. (a) Briefly discuss the essential features of Company Management. 8

    (b) Discuss the major problems of Company Management. 16

QUESTION BANK ON MANAGEMENT

PAPER—III

1993-2000

1. MARKETING MANAGEMENT

1. (a) Describe briefly the importance of marketing. (b) Discuss the salient features of marketing management. [1993]

2. (a) Explain the importance of packaging. (b) Discuss the nature and importance of Public Distribution System. [1993]

3. (a) Show the different phases of product life cycle with the help of a diagram. (b) What is meant by modern marketing concept? In the context of the present-day market economy, discuss the need for applying and implementing the said concept in business in India. [1994]

4. (a) Advertising and salesmanship play a complementary role. Discuss.

(b) What is sales promotion? Discuss the principal techniques of sales promotion that can be used for stimulating sales of a new brand of consumer product. [1994]

5. (a) Distinguish between marketing and selling. (b) Explain the significance of branding of products. What is its importance in marketing? [1995]

6. (a) Give an outline of the structure of sales organisation with the help of a diagram. (b) Describe the principal functions of the sales manager of a business firm. [1995]

7. (a) Explain the significance of marketing management. (b) What are the salient features of marketing in India? Discuss. [1996]

8. (a) What are the main elements of marketing mix? (b) Discuss the essential promotional strategies in marketing. [1996]

9. (a) Distinguish between marketing and selling. (b) Explain the significance of branding of products. What is its importance in marketing? [1997]

10. (a) What do you mean by product-life-cycle? (b) Prescribe an effective marketing strategy for a firm engaged in the production of conumber goods. [1997]

11. (a) Distinguish between Market Research and Marketing Research.

(b) What is meant by marketing mix? Analyse in this connection the various elements of marketing mix. [1998]

12. (a) Explain the concept of 'Resale Price Maintenance'.

(b) State the significance of pricing in marketing management. Briefly discuss the various pricing methods adopted in pricing of a product. [1998]

13. (a) Discuss the importance of packaging in Marketing Management.

(b) "Packaging is an aid to advertising."—Discuss. [1999]

14. (a) What is Sales Management?

(b) Discuss the importance of Sales Management in the context of modern marketing. [1999]

15. Write in brief, about the benefits of storing and warehousing. [2000]

16. State the importance of Marketing Research. [2000]

17. Distinguish between Skimming Pricing and Penetration Pricing. [2000]

18. (a) Advertising expenditure is a wasteful one. Discuss. [2000]

(b) What are the factors to be considered for selecting a distribution channel? [2000]

19. 'The knowledge about Product Life Cycle influences marketing mix'. Discuss. [2000]

2. FINANCIAL MANAGEMENT

1. (a) What is meant by financial management? (b) Describe the main features of a sound capital structure of a business enterprise. What factors should be taken into consideration in case of capital gearing? [1993]

2. (a) Discuss the importance and nature of financial control. (b) Examine the different methods of providing loans and advances to business undertakings by commercial banks. [1993]

3. (a) Discuss the objective of Financial Management. (b) What are the features of a sound capital plan of a company? How do you determine the Fixed Capital and Working Capital requirements of a company? [1994]

4. (a) What is meant by Retined Earnings? Why do companies retain a part of their earnings? (b) Discuss the role of non-banking special financial institutions in providing long-term finance to the corporate business sector. [1994]

5. (a) What do you mean by "Trading on Equity"? Explain with an illustration. (b) What are the methods of determining the required capital of a company?—Discuss. Distinguish between over-capitalisation and under-capitalisation. [1995]

6. (a) Discuss the nature and purpose of financial planning. (b) What are the internal and external sources from which a large public limited company can procure its finance? Discuss the basic features of each of the aforesaid sources. [1995]

7. (a) Discuss the principal objectives of financial management. (b) Discuss the various (i) Financial and (ii) Legal aspects for determining the dividend policy of a public limited company. [1996]

8. (a) Show, with the help of a diagram, the organisation structure of the finance department of a big business firm. (b) Analyse the nature of financial control of a business firm, and mention any four of the methods of the aforesaid control. [1996]

9. (a) What are the objectives of Financial Management? (b) What are the features of a sound capital structure of a Company? How do you determine the fixed capital and working capital requirements of a company? [1997]

10. (a) Why is Financial Planning important? (b) What are the different sources from which a large public limited company can procure its finance? Compare and contrast the merits and demerits of each of these sources. [1997]

11. (a) Explain the example the concept of 'Trading on equity'.

(b) What is over capitalisation and under Capitalisation? Explain their causes, evils and remedies. [1998]

12. (a) Explain the need for financial control in business management.

(b) What are the factors to be considered for determining a sound dividend policy? [1998]

13. (a) Discuss, in brief, the concepts of 'profit maximisation' and 'wealth maximisation'.

(b) Discuss the features of financial planning. [1999]

14. (a) Distinguish between fixed capital and working capital.

(b) Discuss the factors that determing the quantum of fixed capital and working capital of an industrial organisation. [1999]

15. What do you mean by overcapitalisation and undercapitalisation? [2000]

16. What is 'Trading on Equity'? [2000]

17. Distinguish between Preference Shares and Debentures. [2000]

18. (a) State the internal and external sources of finance to meet long-term, medium-term and short-term requirements of a business organisation.

(b) Discuss, in brief, the need for foreign capital in a developing country like India. [2000]

19. (a) Discuss the concept of 'Return on Investment' as a tool for financial control.

(b) What are the features of a sound financial plan? [2000]

3. PERSONNEL MANAGEMENT

1. (a) What is the importance of training of workers and employees? (b) What factors would you take into account for the purpose of job-evaluation of a large industrial undertaking and why? Discuss any two methods of job-evaluation. [1993]

2. (a) Briefly discuss the need for industrial discipline. (b) Examine the pros and cons of participation of workers' representatives in the management of business firm. [1993]

3. (a) Discuss the importance of personnel management. (b) What is meant by manpower planning? Describe its objectives and techniques. [1994]

4. (a) A sound industrial relations is an effective tool for personnel motivation and morale. Discuss. (b) What do you understand by labour welfare? Discuss the importance of labour welfare measures in the context of industries in India. [1994]

5. (a) Expalin the meaning of personnel management and mention its basic functions. (b) What are the major problems relating to personnel management in the context of industrial organisation in India? How could those problems be solved? [1995]

6. (a) Explain the need for discipline in industry. (b) Discuss the importance and the various methods of workers' participation in management. [1995]

7. (a) "Manpower is the most valuable resource of a business."—Examine the statement. (b) Discuss the principles and methods relating to selection of personnel of large-scale industrial enterprise. [1996]

8. (a) State the importance of performance of appraisal of employees. (b) What should be the role of trade unions in the present-day socio-economic of India? Disucss. [1996]

9. (a) Industrial discipline is the key to industrial prosperity—Comment. (b) The idea of worker's participation in management is a mere sop to pacify angry workers without disturbing the status quo.—Do you agree with or oppose the statement? Give reasons in support of your answer. [1997]

10. (a) How does Human Resource Management (HRM) differ from traditional personnel management? (b) "Training is a continuum." Explain the statement in the context of Human Resource Development (HRD). [1997]

11. (a) Explain the significance of manpower planning.

(b) Discuss the importance of performance appraisal. What are the methods adopted in performance appraisal? [1998]

12. (a) Distinguish between job-analysis and job-evaluation.

(b) What is Collective Bargaining? State the considerations involved in making the process of collective bargaining effective. [1998]

13. (a) What do you mean by 'training'? Discuss the importance of training.

(b) Discuss the 'On-the-job' and 'of-the-job' training methods. [1999]

14. (a) Discuss the need for promotion in organisation.

(b) State the advantages and disadvantages of promotion on the basis of 'merit' and on the basis of 'seniority'. [1999]

15. State the importance of manpower planning. [2000]

16. Mention the benefits of training. [2000]

17. Distinguish between 'Job Analysis' and 'Job Evaluation'. [2000]

18. (a) What do you mean by 'morale'? [2000]

(b) How is morale related to productivity? [2000]

(c) What are the factors that influence the morale of workers? [2000]

19. (a) What are the objectives of Performance Appraisal?

(b) Explain the concept of Workers' Participation in Management. [2000]

4. MATERIALS MANAGEMENT

1. State the advantages of decentralised purchase. [2000]

2. Write a short note on Forward Buying. [2000]

3. What do you mean by ABC Analysis? [2000]

4. (a) Discuss the need for and importance of Inventory Control. [2000]

(b) What do you mean by 'Perpetual Stock Verification System'? [2000]

5. (a) What do you mean by Surplus, Scrap and Obsolete materials? [2000]

(b) Distinguish between Inventory Carrying Cost and Ordering Cost. [2000]